CRYPTOGRAPHY and NETWORK SECURITY

OTHER POPULAR TITLES BY THE SAME AUTHOR

- 9789386173126 Multimedia and Animation
- 9789386173669 Machine Learning
- 9789382609131 Big Data and Hadoop
- 9789386173676 Data Science & Analytics

CRYPTOGRAPHY
and
NETWORK SECURITY

V. K. JAIN

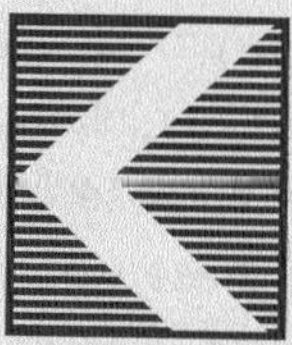

KHANNA BOOK PUBLISHING CO. (P) LTD.

Publisher of Engineering and Computer Books

4C/4344, Ansari Road, Darya Ganj, New Delhi-110002

Phone : 011-23244447-48 **Mobile:** +91-9910909320

E-mail : contact@khannabooks.com

Website : www.khannabooks.com

Dear Readers,

To prevent the piracy, this book is secured with HIGH SECURITY HOLOGRAM on the front title cover. In case you don't find the hologram on the front cover title, please write us to at contact@khannabooks.com or whatsapp us at +91-99109 09320 and avail special gift voucher for yourself.

Specimen of Hologram on front Cover title:

Moreover, there is a SPECIAL DISCOUNT COUPON for you with EVERY HOLOGRAM.

How to avail this SPECIAL DISCOUNT:

Step 1: Scratch the hologram
Step 2: Under the scratch area, your "coupon code" is available
Step 3: Logon to www.khannabooks.com
Step 4: Use your "coupon code" in the shopping cart and get your copy at a special discount
Step 5: Enjoy your reading!

Thanks,
Khanna Publishing House

Price: ₹ 625.00

CRYPTOGRAPHY AND NETWORK SECURITY
by **V. K. JAIN**

ISBN: 978-93-80016-80-1

Reprint Edition: 2026

To view complete list of books, please scan the QR Code:

Published by:
Khanna Book Publishing Co. (P) Ltd.
CIN: U22110DL1998PTC095547

Visit us at: www.khannabooks.com
Write us at: contact@khannabooks.com

Printed in Bharat.

FROM THE AUTHOR'S DESK

Cryptography is a discipline that embodies principles, means, and methods for the transformation of data in order to hide its information content, establish its authenticity, prevent its undetected modification, prevent its repudiation, and/or prevent its unauthorised use. It is one of the technological means to provide security for data on information and communications systems. Cryptography can be used to protect the confidentiality of data, such as financial or personal data, whether that data is in storage or in transit. Cryptography can also be used to verify the integrity of data by revealing whether data has been altered and identifying the person or device that sent it. These techniques are critical to the development and use of national and global information and communications networks and technologies, as well as the development of electronic commerce.

In the past decade, cryptography has done more to damage the security of digital systems than it has to enhance it. For the most part, cryptography has done little more than give Internet users a false sense of security by promising security but not delivering it. And that's not good for anyone except the attackers.

The reasons for this have less to do with cryptography as a mathematical science, and much more to do with cryptography as an engineering discipline. The fundamentals of cryptography are important, but far more important is how those fundamentals are implemented and used.

The book has been written as per syllabus of DOEACC CE4-R3 "Network Security and Cryptography " but not limited to the requirement of that syllabus. The author has collected information from several Indian Universities and optimized the contents of the book accordingly.

These students are the book's primary audience. Cryptographic concepts are explained using diagrams to illustrate component relationships and data flows. At every step aim is to examine the relationship between the security measures and the vulnerabilities they address. This will guide readers in safely applying cryptographic techniques.

This book is also intended for people who know very little about cryptography but need to make technical decisions about cryptographic security. Many people face this situation when they need to transmit business data safely over the Internet. This often includes people responsible for the data, like business analysts and managers, as well as those who must install and maintain the protections, like information systems administrators and managers. This book requires no prior knowledge of cryptography or related mathematics. Descriptions of low-level crypto mechanisms focus on presenting the concepts instead of the details.

This book is intended as a reference book for professional cryptographers, presenting the techniques and algorithms of greatest interest to the current practitioner, along with the supporting motivation and background material. It also provides a comprehensive source from which to learn cryptography, serving both students and instructors. In addition, the rigorous treatment, breadth, and extensive bibliographic material should make it an important reference for research professionals.

While composing this book my intention was not to introduce a collection of new techniques and protocols, but rather to selectively present techniques from those currently available in the public domain.

Computer science has the greatest drawback of its ,in non- standardization of the stuff not only of its software but in courseware also. A vast amount of curriculum exists at different levels. Department of electronics and Computer Society of India

together has done a great service to nation by way of accrediting the courses and thus prescribing the syllabi for different levels.

The various facades of computer science are changing its attributes with such a fast speed that its very difficult to keep track of latest development and its a great task to get aware with the latest happenings in the field. Therefore in presenting the state-of-the art text ware, immense help had been sought by the author from various literature forms who in turn expresses his gratitude to the authors of the works from where information has been derived.

I am to acknowledge with great sense of gratitude to Mrs.Heera Jain and Naveena Bajaj M.Sc., Anurag Jain Director NICT (Vikas Marg Branch) and Jyotsna Agarwal for the great help provided in Manu scripting and in preparation of the figures etc.

ER. V.K. JAIN

B.E., M.Tech, FIE, FIETE

MISHRAE (Life Member)

New Delhi

Chartered Engineer and retired Supt. Engineer (Elect) CPWD

e-mail vkbajaj1944@hotmail.com

CONTENTS

1

Introduction to Network Security and Cryptography

1.1 NETWORKS

Networking is the practice of linking two or more computing devices together for the purpose of sharing data. Networks are built with a mix of computer hardware and computer software. The following are the broad concepts in networking:

- Area Networks
- Internet
- Intranet
- Virtual Private networks

1.1.1 Network Design

Computer networks also differ in their design. The two types of high-level network design are called *client-server* and *peer-to-peer*. Client-server networks feature centralized server computers that store email, Web pages, files and or applications. On a peer-to-peer network, conversely, all computers tend to support the same functions. Client-server networks are much more common in business and peer-to-peer networks much more common in homes.

A network topology represents its layout or structure from the point of view of data flow. In so-called bus networks, for example, all of the computers share and communicate across one common conduit, whereas in a star network, all data flows through one centralized device. Common types of network topologies include bus, star, ring and mesh.

Devices can be connected together in a number of different network topologies.The most common network is the peer to peer network. Once a network has grown larger than a few devices, it is often necessary to introduce a client/server architecture. The introduction of a server often makes managing information easier as all important data can be protected on a single machine.Networks can grow very large, encompassing millions of devices & spanning the whole world.Modern networks are intended to be resilient in the event of one or more nodes failing.

1.1.2 Network Protocols

In networking, the communication language used by computer devices is called the protocol. Yet another way to classify computer networks is by the set of protocols they support. Networks often implement multiple protocols to support specific applications. Popular protocols include TCP/IP, the most common protocol found on the Internet and in home networks.

Most networks use the TCP/IP protocol. TCP/IP was designed during the cold war in order to ensure that US military networks kept working in the event of a nuclear strike.The most widely used version of TCP/IP is IPv4. A new, improved version of TCP/IP has been invented called IPv6.IPv6 is slowly gaining acceptance worldwide. It is being implemented most quickly in the Far East, where IPv4 use is most troublesome due to a lack of available IP addresses.

1.1.3 Wired vs Wireless Networking

Many of the same network protocols, like TCP/IP, work in both wired and wireless networks. Networks with Ethernet cables predominated in businesses, schools, and homes for several decades. Recently, however, wireless networking alternatives have emerged as the premier technology for building new computer networks.

1.1.4 Area Networks

Area Networks can be categorized in several different ways. One approach defines the type of network according to the geographic area it spans. Local area networks (LANs), for example, typically reach across a single home, whereas wide area networks (WANs), reach across cities, states, or even across the world. The Internet is the world's largest public WAN.

One way to categorize the different types of computer network designs is by their scope or scale. For historical reasons, the networking industry refers to nearly every type of design as some kind of area network. Common examples of area network types are:

- LAN - Local Area Network
- WLAN - Wireless Local Area Network
- WAN - Wide Area Network
- MAN - Metropolitan Area Network
- SAN - Storage Area Network, System Area Network, Server Area Network, or sometimes Small Area Network

- CAN - Campus Area Network, Controller Area Network, or sometimes Cluster Area Network
- PAN - Personal Area Network
- DAN - Desk Area Network

LAN and WAN were the original categories of area networks, while the others have gradually emerged over many years of technology evolution.

✍ Note that these network types are a separate concept from network topologies such as bus, ring and star.

---

(1) LAN - Local Area Network

A LAN connects network devices over a relatively short distance. A networked office building, school, or home usually contains a single LAN, though sometimes one building will contain a few small LANs (perhaps one per room), and occasionally a LAN will span a group of nearby buildings. In TCP/IP networking, a LAN is often but not always implemented as a single IP subnet.

In addition to operating in a limited space, LANs are also typically owned, controlled, and managed by a single person or organization. They also tend to use certain connectivity technologies, primarily Ethernet and Token Ring.

(2) WAN - Wide Area Network

As the term implies, a WAN spans a large physical distance. The Internet is the largest WAN, spanning the Earth.

A WAN is a geographically-dispersed collection of LANs. A network device called a router connects LANs to a WAN. In IP networking, the router maintains both a LAN address and a WAN address.

A WAN differs from a LAN in several important ways. Most WANs (like the Internet) are not owned by any one organization but rather exist under collective or distributed ownership and management. WANs tend to use technology like ATM, Frame Relay and X.25 for connectivity over the longer distances.

(3) LAN, WAN and Home Networking

Residences typically employ one LAN and connect to the Internet WAN via an Internet Service Provider (ISP) using a broadband modem. The ISP provides a WAN IP address to the modem, and all of the computers on the home network use LAN (so-called private) IP addresses. All computers on the home LAN can communicate directly with each other but must go through a central gateway, typically a broadband router, to reach the ISP.

(4) Other Types of Area Networks

While LAN and WAN are by far the most popular network types mentioned, you may also commonly see references to these others:

- Wireless Local Area Network - a LAN based on WiFi wireless network technology
- Metropolitan Area Network - a network spanning a physical area larger than a LAN but smaller than a WAN, such as a city. A MAN is typically owned an operated by a single entity such as a government body or large corporation.
- Campus Area Network - a network spanning multiple LANs but smaller than a MAN, such as on a university or local business campus.
- Storage Area Network - connects servers to data storage devices through a technology like Fibre Channel.
- System Area Network - links high-performance computers with high-speed connections in a cluster configuration. Also known as Cluster Area Network.

(5) Internet Service

The technologies used to connect to the Internet are different than those used for connecting devices on local area network. DSL, cable modem and fiber provide fixed broadband Internet service, while WiMax and LTE additionally support mobile connectivity. In geographic areas where these high-speed options are unavailable, subscribers are forced to use older cellular services, satellite or even dial-up Internet instead.

WiMax is the industry term for a long-range wireless networking standard. WiMax technology has the potential to deliver high-speed Internet access to rural areas and other locations not serviced by cable or DSL technology. WiMax also offers an alternative to satellite Internet services.

WiMax technology is based on the IEEE 802.16 WAN communications standard. WiMax signals can function over a distance of several miles / kilometers. Data rates for WiMax can reach up to 75 megabits per second (Mb/s). A number of wireless signaling options exist ranging anywhere from the 2 GHz range up to 66 GHz.

(6) Internetworking

As per Wikipedia, the free internet based encyclopedia, Internetworking involves connecting two or more computer networks via gateways using a common routing technology. The result is called an internetwork (often shortened to internet). The most notable example of internetworking is the Internet (capitalized), a network of networks based on many underlying hardware technologies, but unified by an internetworking protocol standard, the Internet Protocol Suite (TCP/IP).

The network elements used to connect individual networks are known as routers, but were originally called gateways, a term that was deprecated in this context, due to confusion with functionally different devices using the same name.

The interconnection of networks with bridges (link layer devices) is sometimes incorrectly termed "internetworking", but the resulting system is simply a larger, single subnetwork, and no internetworking protocol (such as IP) is required to traverse it. However, a single computer network may be converted into an internetwork by dividing the network into segments and then adding routers between the segments.

The original term for an internetwork was catenet. Internetworking started as a way to connect disparate types of networking technology, but it became widespread through the developing need to connect two or more local area networks via some sort of wide area network. The definition now includes the connection of other types of computer networks such as personal area networks.

The Internet Protocol is designed to provide an unreliable (i.e., not guaranteed) packet service across the network. The architecture avoids intermediate network elements maintaining any state of the network. Instead, this function is assigned to the endpoints of each communication session. To transfer data reliably, applications must utilize an appropriate Transport Layer protocol, such as Transmission Control Protocol (TCP), which provides a reliable stream. Some applications use a simpler, connection-less transport protocol, User Datagram Protocol (UDP), for tasks which do not require reliable delivery of data or that require real-time service, such as video streaming.

1.2 OPEN SYSTEMS INTERCONNECT (OSI) MODEEL OF NETWORKING

The OSI model, was created by the ISO (International Standards Organization). OSI Model follows what happens to the user's file as it passes through the different OSI Model layers starting at the Application Layer and working down the Physical Layer. These are the 7 Layers of the OSI model (listed from top to bottom):

1. Physical Layer (Bottom Layer)
2. Data Link Layer
3. Network Layer
4. Transport Layer
5. Session Layer
6. Presentation Layer
7. Application Layer (Layer)

1.2.1 The Application Layer

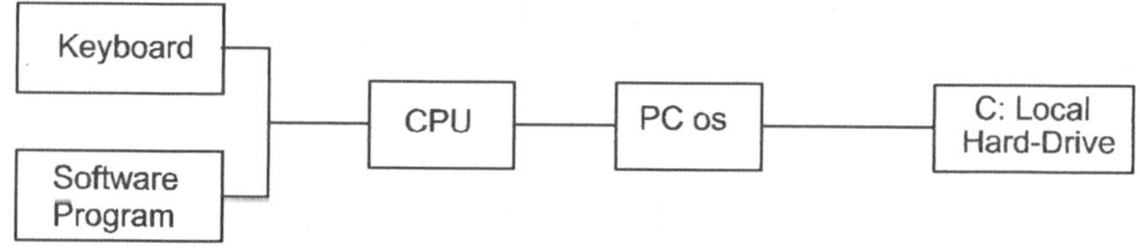

Figure 1.1 Basic PC Logical Flowchart

The Application Layer provides network services to application programs. Provides network service to application for application programs such as file transfers and electronic mails. The flowchart shown in Fig. 1.1 illustrates a basic PC logic flowchart. The Keyboard & Application are shown as inputs to the CPU (requesting access to the hard disk). The Keyboard requests accesses through user inquiries (such as "DIR" commands) and the Application seeks access through "File Openings" and "Saves". The CPU, through the Disk Operating System, sends and receives data from the local hard disk ("C:" in this example).

A PC (workstation) connected to a network has a software "Network Redirector", the name depends on the network, Terminate and Stay Resident (TSR) between the CPU and PC operating system (OS) (as in Fig 1.2.) which presents the network hard disk as another local hard disk to the CPU e.g. "G:", "F:", "E:" etc. All requests by the CPU are intercepted by this software and checks to see if either a local or a network drive is requested. If a local drive is requested, the request is passed on to PC OS. However, if a network drive is requested, the request is then passed on to the network operating system (NOS).

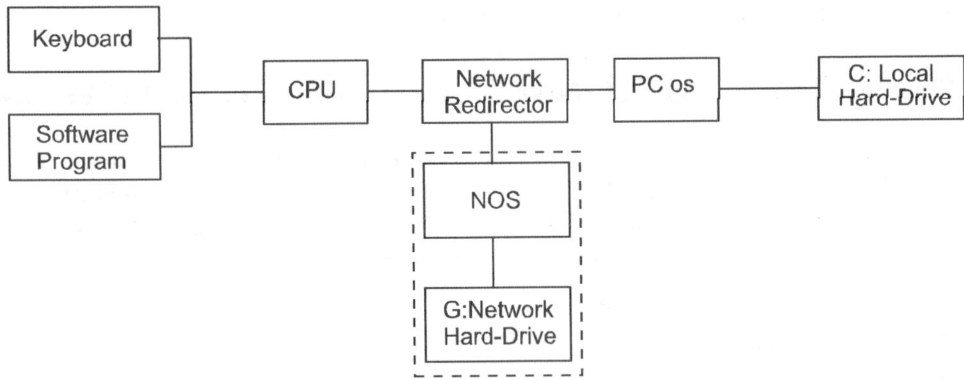

Figure 1.2 Simple Network Redirection

The Application layer of the OSI Model, is shown in Fig. 1.3.

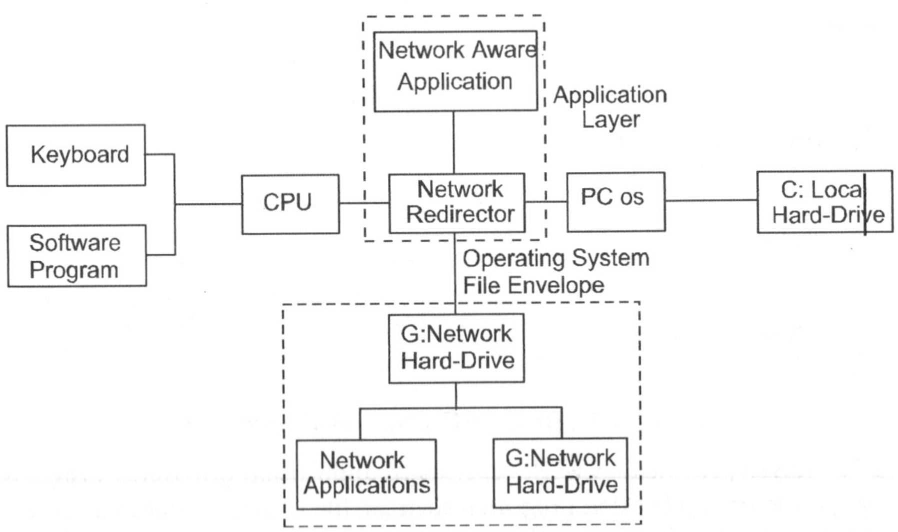

Figure 1.3 PC Workstation with Network Aware Software

The application layer contains a variety of protocols that are needed network communication.

1.2.2 The Presentation Layer

The Presentation Layer facilitates data representation and interpretation. This layer uses a set form of translations that allows the data to be interpreted properly. Presentation layer can add data encryption for security reasons.

The presentation layer is concerned with the syntax and semantics of the information transmitted. When the Network Redirector sends CPU operating system native code to the network operating system: the coding and format of the data is not recognizable by the network operating system. The data consists of file transfers and network calls by network aware programs. These items are represented as character strings, integers, floating point numbers, and data structures composed of several simpler items. Different computers have different codes for representing character strings, integers and so on. In order to make it possible for computers with different representation to communicate, the data structures to be exchanged can be defined in an abstract way, along with a standard encoding to be used "on the wire". The job of managing these abstract data structures and converting from the representation used inside the computer to the network standard representation is handled by the presentation layer. The Presentation layer presents data to and from the terminal using special control characters to control the screen display.

The Presentation Layer also controls security at the file level: this provides both file locking and user security.

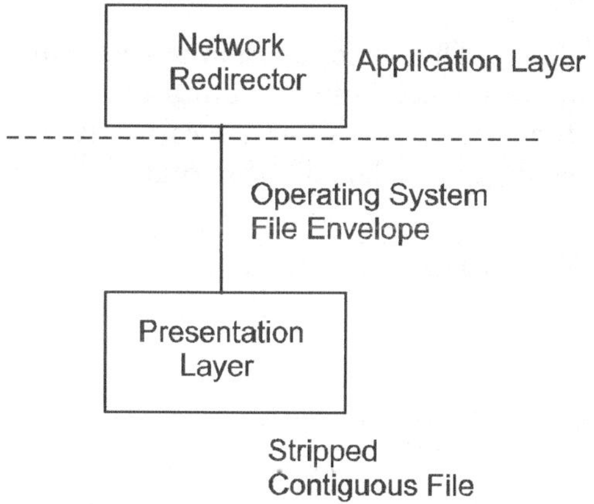

Figure 1.4 Presentation Layer

Data compression can also be used here to reduce the number of bits that have to be transmitted and cryptography is frequently required for privacy and authentication.

1.2.3 The Session Layer

The Session Layer is the inter-host communication: This layer allows users on different machines to establish sessions between them that is it manages the communications between the workstation and the network by directing the information to the correct destination, and identifying the source to the destination, the type of information as data or control, manages the initial start-up of a session, and the orderly closing of a session and manages Log on procedures and Password recognition an in Fig.1.5.

Like the transport layer a session allows ordinary data transport, but it also provides some enhanced services useful in a some applications, such as allowing a user to log into a remote time-sharing system or to transfer a file between two machines, manage dialogue control.

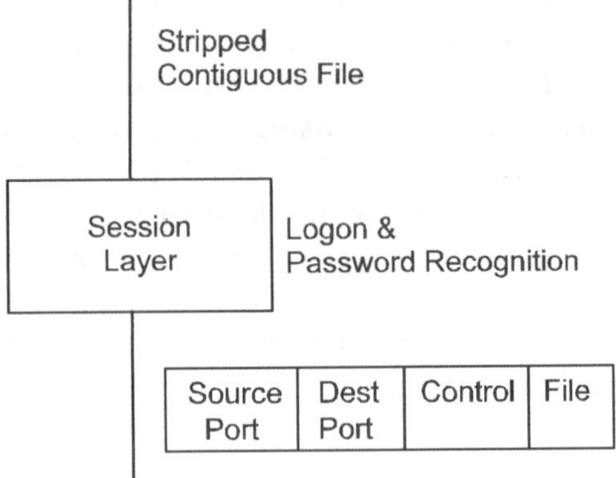

Figure 1.5 Session Layer

1.2.4 The Transport Layer

End-to-end connection reliability. The basic function of the transport layer, is to accept data from the session layer, split it up into smaller units of data segments pass these to the network layer, and ensure that the pieces all arrive correctly at the other end and combines incoming segments into a contiguous file. All this must be done efficiently.

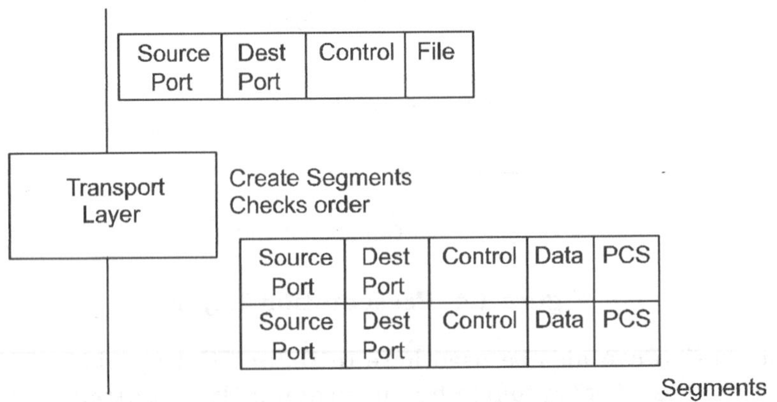

Figure 1.6 Transport Layer

TCP establishes connections between two hosts on the network through 'sockets' which are determined by the IP address and port number. TCP keeps track of the packet delivery order and the packets that must be resent. Maintaining this information for each connection makes TCP a stateful protocol. UDP on the other hand provides a low overhead transmission service, but with less error checking. NFS is built on of UDP because of its speed and statelessness. Statelessness simplifies the crash recovery.

1.2.5 The Network Layer

The Network Layer searches and links address and helps determining the best path. The Network layer is concerned with the path through the network (controlling the operation of the subnet). This includes routing of packets to destination, switching, and controlling the flow of information between hosts. Routes could be based on static tables or dynamic determined anew for each packet, to reflect the current network load. The Network layer converts the segments into smaller datagrams the network can handle: network hardware source and destination addresses are also added. The Network layer does not guarantee that the datagram will reach its destination. The transport layer also controls the traffic density.

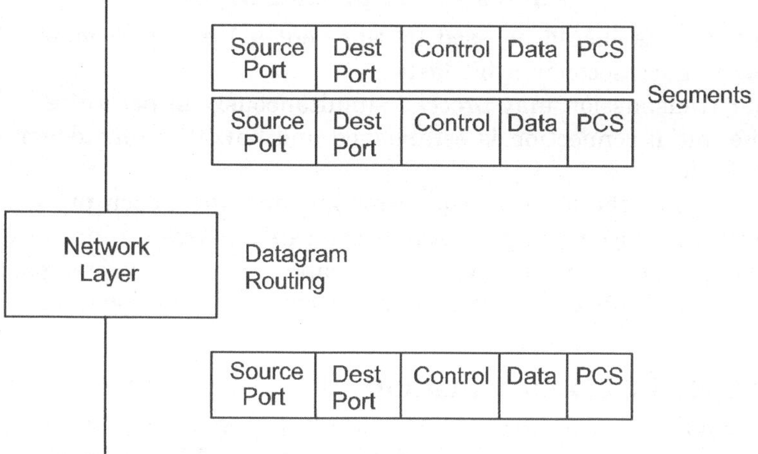

Figure 1.7 Network Layer

1.2.6 The Data Link Layer

The Data Link layer is primarily concerned with bit sequences for Media access. The Data Link layer is a firmware layer of the network interface card by taking a raw transmission facility and transform it into a line that appears free of transmission errors in the network layer and it works at the bit level, and adds start/ s flags and bit error checking (CRC or parity), error checking is at the bit level only and packets with errors are discarded and a request for re-transmission is sent out, to the packet frame as it puts the datagrams into packets (frames of bits: 1s & 0s) for transmission, and assembles received packets into datagrams.

Transmission of data is accomplished by having the sender break the input data up into data frames of a few hundred bytes, transmit the frames sequentially, and process the acknowledgment frames sent back by the receiver and creates and recognize frame boundaries by attaching special bit patterns to the beginning and end of the frame carefully to avoid confusion.

1.2.7 The Physical Layer

The Physical Layer manages transmission of binary data. The Physical layer is concerned with the transmission of raw bits over a communication channel. When transmitting data over the network it has to be ensured that when one side sends a 1 bit, it is received by the other side as a 1 bit, not as a 0 bit depending on:

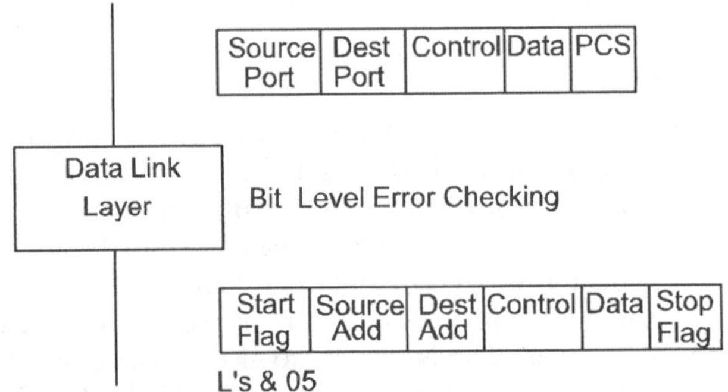

Figure 1.8 Data Link Layer

- How many volts should be used to represent a 1 and how many for a 0.
- How many microseconds a bit lasts.
- Whether transmission may proceed simultaneously in both directions.
- How the initial connection is established and how it is torn down when both sides are finished.
- How many pins the network connector has and what each pin is used for.

The physical layer also manages the network card's hardware interface to the network.

The hardware interface involves the type of cabling (coax or twisted pair etc.), frequency of operation (1 mbps, 10 mbps etc.), voltage levels, cable terminations, topography (star, bus, ring etc.).

1.2.8 Layer-Specific Communication

Normally each layer adds a Header (which contain information that specifically addresses layer-to-layer communication) and a Trailer to its Data, which consists of the next higher layer's Header, Trailer and Data as it moves through the layers. As illustrated Figure 1.9 the

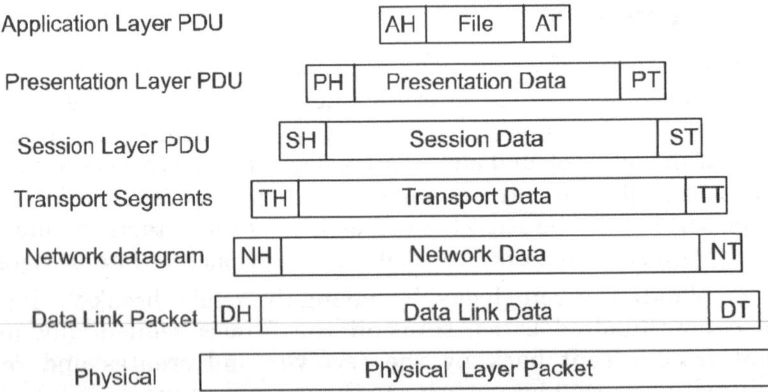

Figure 1.9 Physical Layer

Transport Header (TH) contains information that only the Transport layer sees. All other layers below the Transport layer pass the Transport Header as part of their Data.

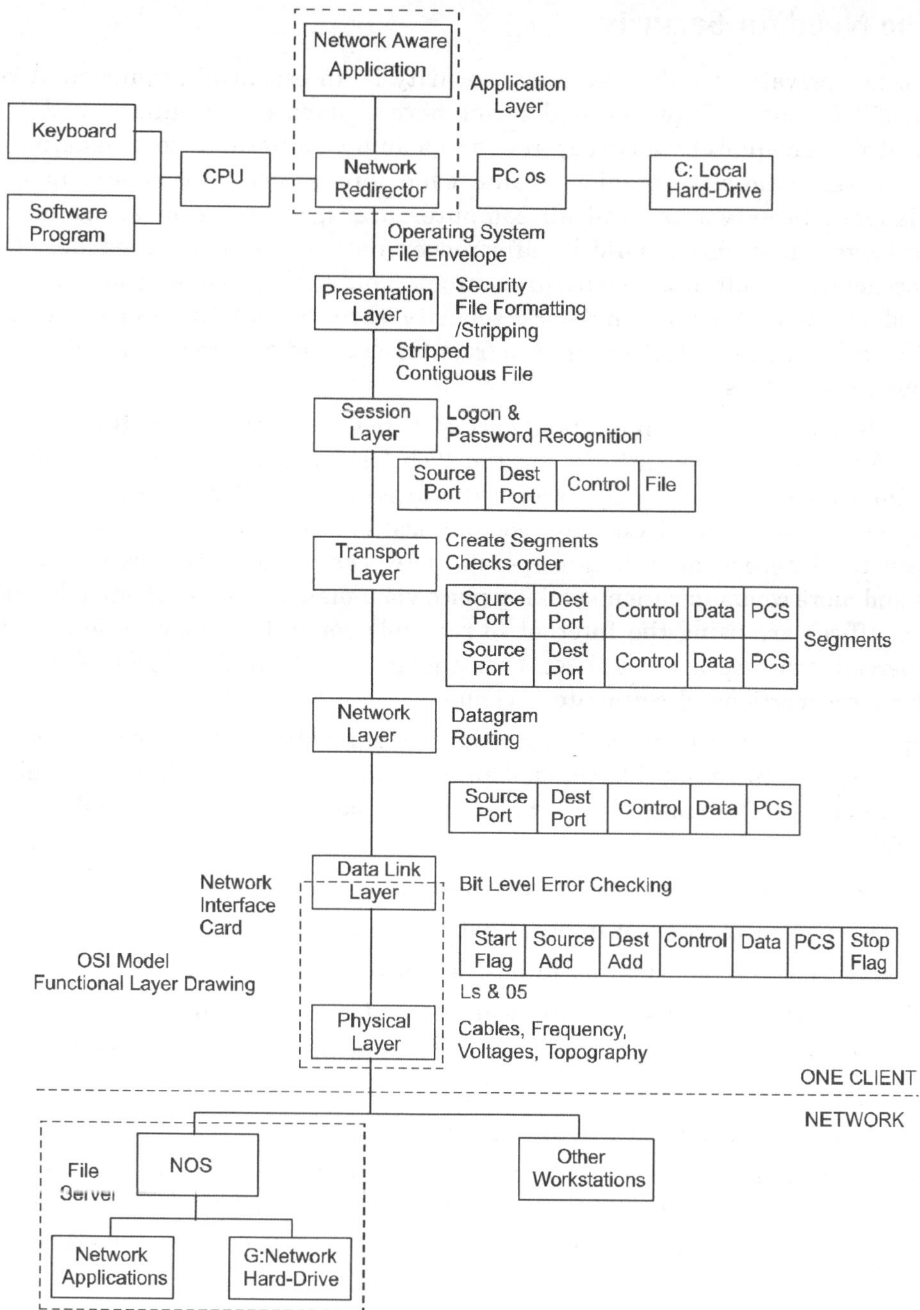

Figure 1.10 OSI Model Functional Drawing

PDU - Protocol Data Unit (a fancy name for Layer Frame)

1.3 IMPORTANCE OF SECURITY IN NETWORKS

1.3.1 The Need for Security

Like any other private or public systems, security is an essential requirement.With the explosion of the public Internet and e-commerce, private computers, and computer networks, if not adequately secured, are increasingly vulnerable to damaging attacks. Hackers, viruses, vindictive employees and even human error all represent clear and present dangers to networks. And all computer users, from the most casual Internet surfers to large enterprises, could be affected by network security breaches. However, security breaches can often be easily prevented. This book provides you with a general overview of the most common network security threats and the steps you and your organization can take to protect yourselves from threats and ensure that the data traveling across your networks is safe.

The Web has become an important part of home and work life.Malware authors are leveraging this fact to deliver attacks via the Web for financial gain rather than personal fame.The Internet has undoubtedly become the largest public data network, enabling and facilitating both personal and business communications worldwide. The volume of traffic moving over the Internet, as well as corporate networks, is expanding exponentially every day. More and more communication is taking place via e-mail; mobile workers, telecommuters, and branch offices are using the Internet to remotely connect to their corporate networks; and commercial transactions completed over the Internet, via the World Wide Web, now account for large portions of corporate revenue.

Computer security is required because most organizations can be damaged by hostile software or intruders. Increased reliance on data communications results in greater vulnerability of data and systems. There may be several forms of damage which are obviously interrelated. These include:

- Damage or destruction of computer systems.
- Damage or destruction of internal data.
- Loss of sensitive information to hostile parties.
- Use of sensitive information to steal items of monitary value.
- Use of sensitive information against the organization's customers which may result in legal action by customers against the organization and loss of customers.
- Damage to the reputation of an organization.
- Monitary damage due to loss of sensitive information, destruction of data, hostile use of sensitie data, or damage to the organization's reputation. Losses associated with computerized fraud and thefts are much larger than non-computerized fraud and theft.

The methods used to accomplish these unscrupulous objectives are many and varied depending on the circumstances. This chapter will help administrators understand some of these methods and explain some countermeasures.

1.3.2 Why do people perform Network Security Attacks

According to OPENXTRA There are as many reasons for performing network security attacks as there are network security attacks. But, there are a number of common themes, in no particular order.OPENXTRA is a small, friendly company set up to provide Network and IT Managers and Network/Cable Installation Engineers with network monitoring and management tools that have been selected for quality, reliability and ease of use.

- **Terrorism** - It would be surprising if the likes of al-Qa'ida didn't consider attacking the Internet. Arab countries are full of under employed, bright, educated young men some of whom are likely to fall under the spell of radical Islamic groups like al-Qa'ida.
- **Industrial Espionage** - If you're a company that has fallen behind in the R&D stakes maybe you might be tempted to cheat a little by hiring a cracker to try to discover some secrets from your competitors. Saves all of the hard work of actually having to do the work yourself.
- **Kudos** - One way to impress your buddies down at your local hacking collective is to crack loads of computer systems, the harder they are to crack the better.
- **Vandalism** - Most email viruses released have no real intent save for pure vandalism. The perpetrator doesn't get paid, there is no commercial pay-off. Indeed, there isn't usually much skill involved either to impress your buddies with. Most viruses are created using one of a number of virus toolkits. So why do it? Because they can, there are few bad consequences for the purportrator. It gives some people a kick to think that they have inconvenienced a whole load of people.
- **Accidents** - Many people find themselves performing network security attacks completely by accident. Either they are unaware that they have a trojan on their system or they activate an attachment received via email.
- **Money** - If you are selective about what you crack there can be a financial payoff. Financial institutions take considerable efforts to reduce their risk from network security attacks, and with good reason. If a perpetrator can crack a bank they stand to make a ton of money.

1.3.3 Security Audit

A security audit is a specified process designed to assess the security risks facing a business and the controls or countermeasures adopted by the business to mitigate those risks. It is typically a human process, managed by a team of "auditors" with technical and business knowledge of the company's information technology assets and business processes. As part of any audit, these teams will interview key personnel, conduct vulnerability assessments, catalog existing security policies and controls, and examine IT assets covered by the scope of the audit. In most cases, they rely heavily on technology tools to perform the audit.

Often, security audits are best understood by focusing on the specific questions they are designed to answer. For example:

- How difficult are passwords to crack?
- Do network assets have access control lists?
- Do access logs exist that record who accesses what data?
- Are personal computers regularly scanned for adware or malware?
- Who has access to backed-up media in the organization?

These are just a small sample of the questions that any security audit should attempt to answer.

1.3.4 Security Limitations and Applications

In many ways, computer security is almost a statistical game. You can reduce but not eliminate the chance that you may be penetrated by an intruder or virus. This is mainly for one reason. No one can ever know *all the software vulnerabilities of all software* used on a system.

This is why even those who consider themselves hackers will say that the number one computer security threat is the lack of quality in the applications and operating systems. At this point, one could talk about the various corporate entities that write software and why software lacks the quality that many of us believe that it should possess, but that subject is not only way beyond the scope of this document, but also way beyond the scope of this project.

The bottom line here is that unless you can remove all the application and operating system problems that allow viruses and intruders to penetrate networks, you can never secure your network. Additionally the users on your network are potentially a greater security risk than any programs. Obviously removing all vulnerabilities is impossible and will not secure your network against user errors. Considering the possibility that an operating system without a network interface can be completely secure, but even this cannot be guaranteed. Unknown viruses or trojan programs can creep in with applications on CDs or floppies. This has been known to happen. Although an attacker may not be able to get data from the system, they can damage or destroy data.

(1) Layered Security

The fact that complete security is impossible is the reason security experts recommend "layered security". The idea is to have multiple ways of preventing an intrusion to decrease the chance that intrusions will be successful. For example, you should have virus protection on your client computers. To help layer this security you should also filter viruses at your email server. To help even more, you should block the most dangerous types of email attachments to prevent unrecognized viruses and other hostile software from entering your network. Another good defense layer would also include educating your users about viruses, how they spread, and how to avoid them.

(2) Hackers

There are many documents that attempt to define the term hacker. The term hacker is a connotative term. This means that it is more defined by people's beliefs rather than by a dictionary. Some believe that a hacker is a very skilled computer person. Others believe that hackers are those that perform unauthorized break ins to computer systems. The media and many sources have caused many uninformed people to believe that a hacker is a threat to computer and network security while this is not the case. A hacker is no more likely to break the law than anyone else. I use the more accurate descriptive term, "intruder" to describe those who intrude into networks or systems without authorization.

(3) Physical Security

Be sure the your organization properly secures locations and consider the following:

- Servers - Contain your data and information about how to access that data.
- Workstations - Man contain some sensitive data and can be used to attack other computers.
- Routers, switches, bridges, hubs and any other network equipment may be used as an access point to your network.
- Network wiring and media and where they pass through may be used to access your network or place a wireless access point to your network.
- External media which may be used between organizational sites or to other sites the organization does business with.
- Locations of staff who may have information that a hostile party can use.
- Some employees may take data home or may take laptops home or use laptops on the internet from home then bring them to work. Any information on these laptops should be considered to be at risk and these laptops should be secure according to proper policy when connected externally on the network.

1.4 ENEMIES OF NETWORK SECURITY

To plan and implement a good security strategy, first be aware of some of the issues which determined, motivated attackers exploit to compromise systems. But before detailing these issues, the terminology used when identifying an attacker must be defined.

Within the community of individuals who find and exploit vulnerabilities in systems and networks are several distinct groups. These groups are often described by the shade of hat that they "wear" when performing their security investigations and this shade is indicative of their intent.

Who Perpetrates Network Security Attacks?

There is no simple answer to who perpetrates network security attacks. But, the perpetrators can be categorised into two main groups:

- Hackers (in non-computer speak) or more correctly, crackers
- Users

1.4.1 Hackers

Information Theft by Hacking

Information theft is big business today. Malevolent hackers break into business networks to steal credit card or social security numbers for profit. Small and medium-sized businesses are at risk because they are seen as an easier mark than large corporations. Protecting the perimeter of the network is a good start, but it isn't enough, since many information thefts have help from a trusted insider, such as an employee or contractor.

Information theft can be costly to small and medium-sized businesses, since they rely on satisfied customers and a good reputation to help grow their business. Businesses that don't adequately protect their information could face negative publicity, government fines, or even lawsuits. For example, new consumer laws enacted in California require any business that suspects customer information has been viewed by unauthorized people must notify all their customers. Any security strategy must prevent theft of sensitive electronic information from both inside and outside the business.

Sometimes the term "hacker attacks" is used to indicate hacker attacks that are not automated by programs such as viruses, worms, or trojan horse programs. There are various forms that exploit weakneses in security. Many of these may cause loss of service or system crashes.

This generic and often over-romanticized term applies to computer enthusiasts who take pleasure in gaining access to other people's computers or networks. Many hackers are content with simply breaking in and leaving their "footprints," which are joke applications or messages on computer desktops. Other hackers, often referred to as "crackers," are more malicious, crashing entire computer systems, stealing or damaging confidential data, defacing Web pages, and ultimately disrupting business. Some amateur hackers merely locate hacking tools online and deploy them without much understanding of how they work or their effects.

The modern meaning of the term hacker has origins dating back to the 1960s and the Massachusetts Institute of Technology (MIT) Tech Model Railroad Club, which designed train sets of large scale and intricate detail. Hacker was a name used for club members who discovered a clever trick or workaround for a problem.

The term 'hacker' can be used to describe enthusiasm for a game or sport, or, more recently, one's computer proficiency. More commonly, however, the term is used to describe a skilled computer user who uses this knowledge to gain an advantage over people who are less familiar with computing technology. Often times, a hacker's efforts are used to facilitate or perpetrate cyber crime.

The term hacker has since come to describe everything from computer buffs to gifted programmers. A common trait among most hackers is a willingness to explore in detail how computer systems and networks function with little or no outside motivation. Open source software developers often consider themselves and their colleagues to be hackers, and use the word as a term of respect.

The white hat hacker is one who tests networks and systems to examine their performance and determine how vulnerable they are to intrusion. Usually, white hat hackers crack their own systems or the systems of a client who has specifically employed them for the purposes of security auditing. Academic researchers and professional security consultants are two examples of white hat hackers.

A black hat hacker is synonymous with a cracker. In general, crackers are less focused on programming and the academic side of breaking into systems. They often rely on available cracking programs and exploit well known vulnerabilities in systems to uncover sensitive information for personal gain or to inflict damage on the target system or network.

The grey hat hacker, on the other hand, has the skills and intent of a white hat hacker in most situations but uses his knowledge for less than noble purposes on occasion. A grey hat hacker can be thought of as a white hat hacker who wears a black hat at times to accomplish his own agenda.

Grey hat hackers typically subscribe to another form of the hacker ethic, which says it is acceptable to break into systems as long as the hacker does not commit theft or breach confidentiality. Some would argue, however, that the act of breaking into a system is in itself unethical.

Regardless of the intent of the intruder, it is important to know the weaknesses a cracker may likely attempt to exploit. The remainder of the chapter focuses on these issues.

(1) "Hacking" into a machine.

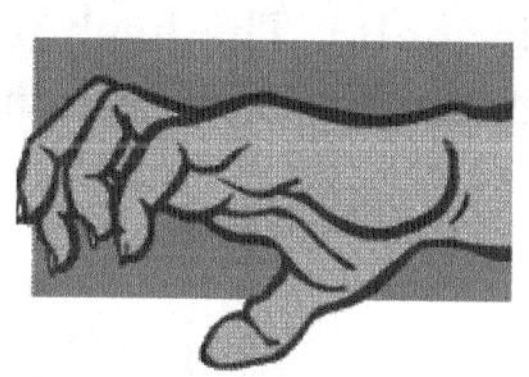

Hacking generally involves gaining unauthorized access to a computer and altering the system in such a way as to permit continued access, along with changing the configuration, purpose, or operation of the target machine, all without the knowledge or approval of the system owners. It also refers to the development of tools to perform all the above.

It can be as simple as guessing the password of an active account, or creating an exploit to take advantage of a software vulnerability.

(2) Cracking" codes, licenses, etc.

'Cracking' and 'Crackers' refer to persons who breach information security measures. Often the two sets of terms, hackers and crackers, are used interchangeably. However, computer enthusiasts, benign hackers, understandably take exception to this.

(3) Password Guessing:

Password guessing is just what the name suggests. It requires a valid user ID. Either manually or automatically, you start submitting what is most likely the password of a particular user. For example, if the user's account name is Kris, you, or your software, might try Kringle. You keep trying until you hit paydirt, or are locked out. In any case, complex passwords provide protection against this type of attack.

(4) Password Cracking

Passwords are the most common method of authentication used to control access to digital resources. They are also the easiest way to gain unauthorized access to these resources. Armed with password cracking software, an intruder can discover a dictionary word password, or simple variation, in a matter of seconds. When you consider how much information is protected solely by passwords, it quickly becomes clear that good passwords are vital to preserving confidentiality.

Passwords are the most common method of authentication used to control access to digital resources. They are also the easiest way to gain unauthorized access to these resources. Armed with password cracking software, an intruder can discover a dictionary word password, or simple variation, in a matter of seconds. When you consider how much information is protected solely by passwords, it quickly becomes clear that good passwords are vital to preserving confidentiality.

Passwords must be protected against unauthorized disclosure, modification, & removal.

There are three different types of attacks against passwords: guessing, cracking, and disclosure via social engineering.

Password cracking is done using a copy of the system file that stores account passwords, presumably in encrypted form. All current operating systems store passwords in an encrypted form by running the passwords through a one way hash (encryption formula). The hash is then stored, not the clear text password. Unfortunately, encryption is no guarantee of protection as we will see. Hashes can be cracked.

Hacker Attacks

(1) **Spoofing** - An attacker may fake their IP address so the receiver thinks it is sent from a location that it is not actually from. There are various forms and results to this attack. The attack may be directed to a specific computer addressed as though it is from that same computer. This may make the computer think that it is talking to itself. This may cause some operating systems such as Windows to crash or lock up.

(2) **Gaining access through source routing.** Hackers may be able to break through other friendly but less secure networks and get access to your network using this method.

(3) **Session hijacking** - An attacker may watch a session open on a network. Once authentication is complete, they may attack the client computer to disable it, and use IP spoofing to claim to be the client who was just authenticated and steal the session. This attack can be prevented if the two legitimate systems share a secret which is checked periodically during the session.

(4) **Server spoofing** - A C2MYAZZ utility can be run on Windows 95 stations to request LANMAN (in the clear) authentication from the client. The attacker will run this utility while acting like the server while the user attempts to login. If the client is tricked into sending LANMAN authentication, the attacker can read their usernameand password from the network packets sent.

(5) **DNS poisoning** - This is an attack where DNS information is falsified. This attack can succeed under the right conditions, but may not be real practical as an attack form. The attacker will sendincorrect DNS information which can cause traffic to be diverted. The DNS information can be falsified since name servers do not verify the source of a DNS reply. When a DNS request is sent, an attacker can send a false DNS reply with additional bogus information which the requesting DNS server may cache. This attack can be used to divert users from a correct webserver such as a bank and capture information from customers when they attempt to logon.

(6) **Teardrop** - a normal packet is sent. A second packet is sent which has a fragmentation offset claiming to be inside the first fragment. This second fragment is too small to even extend outside the first fragment. This may cause an unexpected error condition to occur on the victim host which can cause a buffer overflow and possible system crash on many operating systems.

(7) **Ping broadcast** - A ping request packet is sent to a broadcast network address where there are many hosts. The source address is shown in the packet to be the IP address of the computer to be attacked. If the router to the network passes the ping broadcast, all computers on the network will respond with a ping reply to the sttacked system. The attacked system will be flooded with ping responses which will cause it to be unable to operate on the network for some time, and may even cause it to lock up. The attacked computer may be on someone else's network. One countermeasure to this attack is to block incoming traffic that is sent to a broadcast address.

(8) **Ping of death** - An oversized ICMP datagram can crash IP devices that were made before 1996.

(9) **Smurf** - An attack where a ping request is sent to a broadcast network address with the sending address spoofed so many ping replies will come back to the victim and overload the ability of the victim to process the replies.

(10) **Browser Hijacker** - Browser hijackers, or hijackware, alter web browser settings to redirect you to a different homepage, typically to questionable websites (adult, gaming, celebrity). Those programs which redirect surfers to adult sites will sometimes

leave telltale bookmarks, which have been known to cost people their jobs.Some hijackware redirects you to a page that has an ad telling you that your computer is infected and that you should purchase and run their virus checker. Other browser hijackers are written purely for increasing pageviews to a particular website in order to get more advertising revenue.

Browser hijackers are often accidentally downloaded from freeware or email attachments. For prevention, read freeware user agreements carefully, as hijackware will sometimes reveal itself in the fine print. For example, one of the first browser hijackers was CWS (Cool Web Search), which was relatively harmless, though famously annoying.

1.4.2 CRACKERS

When crackers are mentioned most people think of spotty teenagers sitting in their bedrooms. It is a realistic view, after all yesterday's teenage hacker is tomorrows adult hacker.

Crackers vary in sophistication from the so called 'script kiddies' who are, perhaps the least technically sophisticated (though not necessarily the least damaging) to uber cognisant and experienced crackers. They do have one thing in common. They are trying to crack your network. They sit down and systematicaly attempt to break your network. This means that you must sit down and systematicaly ensure that they don't crack your network. It's kinda like a burglar. If you make your house nice and secure then the burglar is going to find somewhere easier to ply their trade.

The one good thing about your typical cracker is that at least they exist outside of your network. This gives you a great advantage. You construct the boundary that the cracker must penetrate in order to gain access to your network. So, at least you have a defendable border where you can deploy a range of tools to defend yourself.

Typically, hackers follow a form of the hacker ethic which dictates that the quest for information and expertise is essential, and that sharing this knowledge is the hackers duty to the community. During this quest for knowledge, some hackers enjoy the academic challenges of circumventing security controls on computer systems. For this reason, the press often uses the term hacker to describe those who illicitly access systems and networks with unscrupulous, malicious, or criminal intent. The more accurate term for this type of computer hacker is cracker — a term created by hackers in the mid-1980s to differentiate the two communities.

1.4.3 Users

Perhaps the most underestimated group of attackers is your own users. They may not have the level of sophistication of your average cracker, but they do have *one* big advantage. They wander into your office every day straight past all of your security defenses. They are plugged into the very heart of your network, behind your carefully constructed defenses.

For the vast majority of the time, your users are pretty benign. Users pose their most serious risk when combined with a cleverly worded trojan email. Some trojan emails are particularly clever in their psychology. We received one ourselves about a month ago purporting to be from administrator@openxtra.co.uk telling us that we needed to run the included attachment in order to cure a security problem on our machines. It made me look twice and I AM the administrator! In larger organisations where users are disconnected from their IT personel, some users may be tempted to do exactly what the email suggests.

Whilst your users are benign most of the time, they do sometimes perpetrate attacks completely by accident. Many companies grow in an ad-hoc manner, adding systems as and when necessary. Consequently, some things that really are essential are left undone. I recently saw a classical example of a system ripe to be attacked by a careless user. The router, through which all Internet traffic flowed, was hanging down against a wall with only a power cable supporting it. Of course, the router was just in an open piece of the office, where anybody could brush past it at any time. Another classic is placing servers under somebody's desk. A sure fire recipe for some unplanned downtime and possible data loss.

(a) Unaware Staff

As employees focus on their specific job duties, they often overlook standard network security rules. For example, they might choose passwords that are very simple to remember so that they can log on to their networks easily. However, such passwords might be easy to guess or crack by hackers using simple common sense or a widely available password cracking software utility. Employees can unconsciously cause other security breaches including the accidental contraction and spreading of computer viruses. One of the most common ways to pick up a virus is from a floppy disk or by downloading files from the Internet. Employees who transport data via floppy disks can unwittingly infect their corporate networks with viruses they picked up from computers in copy centers or libraries. They might not even know if viruses are resident on their PCs. Corporations also face the risk of infection when employees download files, such as PowerPoint presentations, from the Internet. Surprisingly, companies must also be wary of human error. Employees, whether they are computer novices or computer savvy, can make such mistakes as erroneously installing virus protection software or accidentally overlooking warnings regarding security threats.

As per Annual Computer Security Institute and FB (US) Survey, 2001 "Ninety-one percent of respondents detected employee abuse of Internet access privileges."

(b) Disgruntled Staff

Far more unsettling than the prospect of employee error causing harm to a network is the potential for an angry or vengeful staff member to inflict damage. Angry employees, often those who have been reprimanded, fired, or laid off, might vindictively infect their corporate networks with viruses or intentionally delete crucial files. This group is especially dangerous because it is usually far more aware of the network, the value of the information within it, where high-priority information is located, and the safeguards protecting it.

(c) Snoops

Whether content or disgruntled, some employees might also be curious or mischievous. Employees known as "snoops" partake in corporate espionage, gaining unauthorized access to confidential data in order to provide competitors with otherwise inaccessible information. Others are simply satisfying their personal curiosities by accessing private information, such as financial data, a romantic e-mail correspondence between coworkers, or the salary of a colleague. Some of these activities might be relatively harmless, but others, such as previewing private financial, patient, or human resources data, are far more serious, can be damaging to reputations, and can cause financial liability for a company.

1.4.4 Internet Dialer

There are legitimate Internet dialers, but the malware variety does sinister things including making phone calls to 1-900 numbers secretly through your modem. The result is been monster phone bills and lots of family feuds. Internet dialers only work on dialup connections (modem-based). Since not everyone has a broadband connection yet, dialers are still a serious threat and can cost victims a fortune in long distance calls.

Although dialer use is regulated in many countries, malware dialers obviously do not heed the law. Given this, a simple way to avoid malware dialer's altogether is by switching to non-dialup Internet service such as cable, DSL, or satellite.

1.4.5 Malware :Malacious Programs z

Malware is a generic term used to refer to any computer program (software) that runs without the full knowledge and consent of the system owner. There are many different types of malware. Common examples include bots, back doors, rootkits, and spyware. Malware often causes computers to operate more slowly, and may damage files.

Five years ago, the term "malware", if used at all, simply referred to viruses. Over the last few years, however, hackers and spammers have developed all sorts of new ways to invade your computer. Today, Malware, or malicious software, simply means any unwanted code or program that embeds itself on a computer without the user's knowledge.

This quick summary is a brief reminder of current Malware trends and new threats which are expected to grow in 2007:

- Mobile attacks using SMS (SMiShing), whereby malware such as MSIL/Xrove infects smartphones via ActiveSync.
- Media malware using MPEG video files or CODECs for MP3 audio players. Thanks to the popularity of video sharing sites like YouTube, this mode of attack is expected to grow.
- Increase in zombie computers and botnets.
- Return of parasitic malware, which operate by modifying files already existent on your hard drive.
- Increased silent and targed attacks on transactions instead of computers.

- Suicidal malware that uses polymorphic techniques to evade detection.

The US government and other nations are trying to do something about malware, including becoming party to the Council of Europe Convention on Cybercrime, which takes effect Jan 1, 2007. But, it is an uphill battle for lawmakers, and one that is unlikely to have a significant effect in the next few years. As a consequence, individuals and corporations must continue to educate themselves about the development of new malware threats in order to stay one step ahead of attackers.

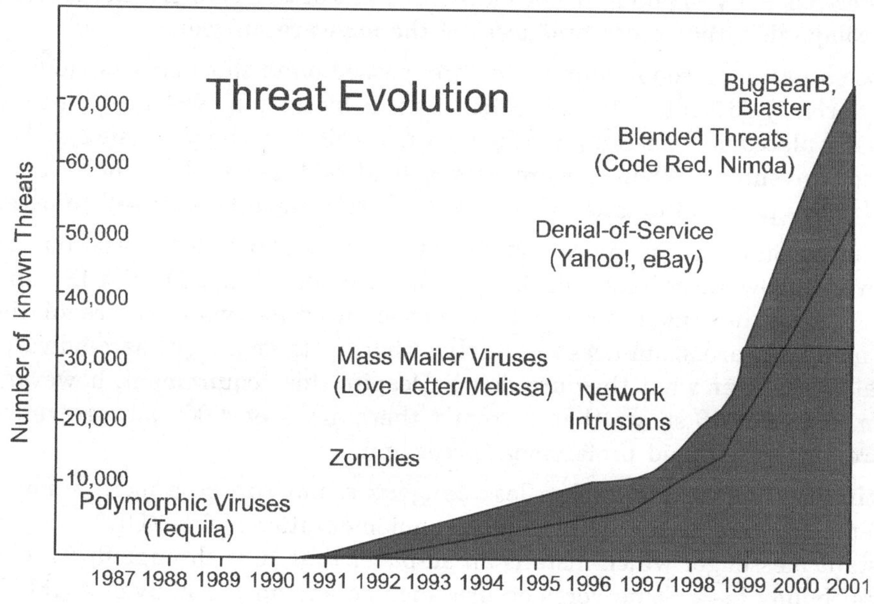

Figure 1.11 Threat Evolution

Malware is growing quickly. McAfee Avert Labs expected in 2006 to have recorded their 225,000th unique computer/ network threat, finding 50,000 threats between Jan and Nov of 2006 alone. The motive for creating malware has been profit or spying in most cases, and as profits from creating malware have grown, paid professionals have begun to make new and ever more dangerous forms. The return on creating malware has been high in large part because so many victims do not know what to look out for; individuals often still think of malware in the same simplistic forms of five years ago. This guide covers some of the newest trends in malware, and it will give you a better understanding of what sorts of threats you and your computer face.

Following programs are Malware programs:

(1) Adware

(2) Spyware

(3) Ransomware

(4) Worm

(5) Trojan Horse

(6) Virus

(7) Vandals

(1) Adware

The most common form of malware is adware. It's a type of spyware that secretly imbeds itself on your computer and analyzes your web browsing habits and then related banner advertising occasionally in popup windows. While most of the advertisements you see are for legitimate companies, the actual producers of the spyware are not.

Because a user's personal details are often passed on to third parties, adware has been criticized by privacy advocates. Adware usually works by tracking web browser cookies, which were originally placed on your computer by legitimate sites for purposes such as keeping your shopping cart inventory. When adware gets a hold of these cookies, however, they often contain too many personal details, which the adware companies can sell to others.

The United States government now has strict rules about cookie use, but ironically, it does not even follow these rules itself; See indictments of the DEA, CIA, and NSA for instance). So given that the government has not followed its own cookie regulations, do not expect too many adware spammers to comply either. In theory, legitimate adware programs must reveal to the user what they are doing. Despite this requirement, however, a McAfee report from August 2006 shows that currently there are over 4,000 adware variants, many of which are written by paid professional programmers.

Legitimate - Adware is a often less dangerous, but can be a more annoying form of malware. Like spyware, there are legitimate implementations with EULAs. A good example is AOL Instant messenger which installs an ad-payer that runs through different ads on the messenger's "buddy list". Some versions also include ads on the individual IM Window.

Illegitimate - Adware can still be dangerous, however. The more obnoxious versions redirect your browser, preventing you from visiting certain web pages, and even changing your home page. More often than not, the sites you are sent to are pornographic in nature. Adware can install unwanted "toolbars" or other items on your web- browser.

(2) Spyware

Spyware and adware are both forms of malware. While not normally a risk to your computer files or programs, they pose a great threat to your privacy. Also, unlike most forms of malware, spyware and adware are sometimes created by legitimate corporations and used legally, albeit without knowledgeable consent on the part of the user.

Spyware and adware are both forms of malware. While not normally a risk to your computer files or programs, they pose a great threat to your privacy. Also, unlike most forms of malware, spyware and adware are sometimes created by legitimate corporations and used legally, albeit without knowledgeable consent on the part of the user.

Legitimate - "Legal" spyware normally consists of monitoring programs that are installed when you install another program. The purpose of the spyware, in this case, is usually to track what webpages you go to, and report the findings to the company. The information collected is used to improve marketing.

Illegitimate - Illegitimate spyware is one of the largest threats to personal information security. This type of malware does not come with a EULA, or if it does, it is so obtuse and confusing that even a careful reading will not reveal the software's full operation and purpose. The worst forms of spyware compromise the confidentiality and integrity of your entire computer. That's because spyware begets more spyware. Spyware slowly, over time, increments on your PC, adding more and more elements in dribs and drabs via the network. Spyware vendors support the installation of each other's products on the target computer. This makes good business sense. If I install your spyware product after I install my product on a machine I've targeted, you will do the same for me. This increases our distribution network. As a business model, this is a win-win for spyware vendors. It's a big loss for the computer owner. Over time, a system will become so bogged down with spyware that owners will just abandon their machines and buy a new one. Consumer Reports stated in the September 2006 issue that nearly a million U.S. housholds did just that. Total damage from spyware is estimated at $2.6 billion.

Spyware is a favorite money maker for Bot Masters. They are paid on a per placement basis. If they can install spyware on your unprotected machine, they can earn money from the spyware developers. The developers don't care how their software gets installed on your computer. Their value lies in volume. The more machines their software is installed on, the more data they collect.

Spyware & Stalking

The most insidious form of spyware is a keylogger. This tool, readily available in many forms on the Internet, is designed to record every keystroke typed by a user. That includes passwords, social security numbers, credit card numbers, web sites visited, instant messages, and the contents of emails. Keyloggers can be combined with other software that sends this information to a remote host where the data can be analyzed and exploited. It's not only criminals who are intersted in this information. Keyloggers are being marketed to domestic partners and spouses as a way of tracking their activities on line. In a recent case that resulted in indictments of both the perpetrators and software developers, a product called LoverSpy was installed on the victim's machine via an electronic greeting card. LoverSpy then sent all the information it collected back to the stalker.

(3) Ransomware

Ransomware is the most recent and another clear indication that security of networks and network resources needs to be taken more seriously.In this type of attack, the hacker (and that has become a really dirty word) installs a code on server or a PC, locking out certain files. Then a ransom demand is made, to deliver the unlocking codes. Very few of these attacks have been reported so far, and the one that has been accepted publicly had the files unencrypted without paying the ransom of $200. Although this attempt seems childish, it reminds of the extortion threats that organizations had received in the previous years for paying up or be subjected to DoS or DDoS attacks.

It is suspected that many more organizations would have received such ransom demands, but not many are acknowledging them. However, what is sure is that such attacks would get more refined, cracking the codes will be more difficult, and modes of payment will be more refined. A bank account is surely not a safe means of receiving ransom money.

(4) Worm

Worms are a self-propagating (they multiply on their own) form of malware. Worms hunt for security flaws in other computers on the same network as an infected computer and copy themselves onto the new computer through that loophole. This way of multiplying makes worms particularly dangerous, because they can result in huge network traffic floods or outages, as well as mass infection over a short time.

While worms are not a new malware threat, recent developments in the ways that worms spread have made them much more deadly. A worm discovered in November of 2006 named W32/Realor, for instance, can launch websites on its own. Another new worm is VBS/ Eliles, which is a mass-mailer that can send SMS messages to mobile phones. One Windows worm called 'The Mobler', supposedly transports itself via Symbian cell phones. For 2007, it is expected that worms which spread through mobile technologies will continue to spread.

(5) Trojan Horse

Trojan horses are masters of disguise. Trojan horse programs, or trojans, are delivery vehicles for destructive code. Trojans appear to be harmless or useful software programs, such as computer games, but they are actually enemies in disguise. Trojans can delete data, mail copies of themselves to e-mail address lists, and open up computers to additional attacks. Trojans can be contracted only by copying the trojan horse program to a system, via a disk, downloading from the Internet, or opening an e-mail attachment. Neither trojans nor viruses can be spread through an e-mail message itself—they are spread only through e-mail attachments.This form of malware pretends to be innocuous plugins, add-ons, or even CODECs (Encoder/ Decoder) for multimedia audio or video players such as WinAmp, and other harmless software. The creators of trojan horses often use an e-mail or a web page written to trick you into installing the Trojan. Trojan horses may live on websites with music or video downloads or even some of the new batch of web2.0 alpha- or beta-mode application sites.

Once installed, Trojans then download malicious code and programs such as keyloggers, screenscapers, or worms from remote servers, often through non-standard ports on your computer.

A recent example of a dangerous trojan horse is the J2ME/ Redbrowser Trojan, which runs on Java-enabled smartphones/ PDAs by pretending to access WAP pages but sending SMS messages to an unauthorized number at your expense [2]. Another example of a growing threat is the Skype Trojan, discovered in December 2006, which operates on the Skype VoIP soft client.

(6) Virus

The term "virus" has been used fairly generically in the history of computing, but technically speaking, it refers to software that inserts malicious code into existing documents or even other code [1], and which is then spread by various means. Some early viruses were pranks, others were propagated via MS-Word documents attached in emails.

Viruses are the most widely known security threats, because they often garner extensive press coverage. Viruses are computer programs that are written by devious programmers and are designed to replicate themselves and infect computers when triggered by a specific event. For example, viruses called macro viruses attach themselves to files that contain macro instructions (routines that can be repeated automatically, such as mail merges) and are then activated every time the macro runs. The effects of some viruses are relatively benign and cause annoying interruptions such as displaying a comical message when striking a certain letter on the keyboard. Other viruses are more destructive and cause such problems as deleting files from a hard drive or slowing down a system.

A network can be infected by a virus only if the virus enters the network through an outside source—most often through an infected floppy disk or a file downloaded from the Internet. When one computer on the network becomes infected, the other computers on the network are highly susceptible to contracting the virus.As per Annual Computer Security Institute and FBI Survey, 2001 "85 percent of respondents detected computer security breaches within the last 12 months, up 42% from 1996."

Today, E-mail is still responsible for about 90% of all viruses spread according to ICSA Labs, but now they are often hidden in password-protected ZIP attachments, making them harder to detect. Viruses have also started showing up in many different forms (macro, file, boot sector, network, email, etc.) and are used for many purposes, including infecting computers to acts as zombies in botnets. These botnets are then used to send spam e-mail or sometimes for fraudulent ad clicking, in order to generate revenue. Other viruses are designed not to generate revenue, but to take down Microsoft. A recent example is a Windows virus shipped with Apple video iPod devices.

According to CISCO, Computer worms and viruses remain the most common security threat, with 75 percent of small and medium businesses affected by at least one virus in the last year [Maritz Research, 2005]. Worms and viruses can have a devastating effect on business continuity and the bottom line. Smarter, more destructive strains are spreading faster than ever, infecting an entire office in seconds. Cleaning the infected computers takes much longer. The catastrophic results are lost orders, corrupted databases, and angry customers. As businesses struggle to update their computers with the latest operating system patches and antivirus software, new viruses can penetrate their defenses any day of the week. Meanwhile, employees spread viruses and spyware by unwittingly accessing malicious Websites, downloading untrustworthy material, or opening malicious e-mail attachments. These attacks are unintentionally invited into the organization, but still cause significant financial losses. Security systems must detect and repel worms, viruses, and spyware at all points in the network.

(7) Vandals

Web sites have come alive through the development of such software applications as ActiveX and Java Applets. These devices enable animation and other special effects to run, making Web sites more attractive and interactive. However, the ease with which these applications can be downloaded and run has provided a new vehicle for inflicting damage. A vandal is a software application or applet that causes destruction of varying degrees. A vandal can destroy just a single file or a major portion of a computer system.

(8) Drive-By Download (DBD)

In general, the term "drive-by download" (DBD) refers to any malware installed without user consent or knowledge. This malware can download spyware, a virus, etc., and this can happen while viewing a website or popup window, or from an email message.

The reason "drive-by downloads" are so dangerous, is that it requires no action by a surfer to get infected. A hyperlink does not even have to be clicked for the install to occur, as some DBDs exploit browser flaws - the target has often been Internet Explorer.

One of the more well-known incidents involved the legitimate website Kingsofchaos.com and their visitors. A browser flaw allowed a "drive-by download" to replace legitimate popup ads and install malware on the site's visitors. Today, however, "drive-by downloads" occur almost entirely at questionable sites.

(9) Piggyback

Piggyback malware refers to embedded malicious code within an otherwise harmless executable file. According to a recent study, 4% of websites and 5% of available downloads were infected with any of 89 types of malware [1]. This means that even trusted sites might cause your computer to be infected, thus rendering IP/ site blacklists less effective. Typically suspect piggyback sites are those having downloads for games, music, and wallpapers, as well as celebrity and adult sites.

A more recent trend in malware, to is to piggyback off of open source code. Another new trend is piggybacking malware when file sharing via VoIP or VoIM clients. Again, one of the aspects of piggybacking that makes it so dangerous, is that the person sending the malware often does not know it himself.

(10) Keylogger

In the past, keyloggers have been legitimate software used by law enforcement. The FBI used [1] a Trojan to download a keylogger called Magic Lantern, which helped indict Nicodemo Scarfo, Jr., for running an illegal gambling organization. Keyloggers are also used by companies to monitor employees, and by parents to monitor children online.

Unfortunately, however, keyloggers can also be a highly malicious form of spyware that monitors every keystroke a computer user makes, as well as system events. Using a keylogger, thieves can quickly steal passwords, email addresses, IM (Instant Messenger) usernames, bank account numbers, and other sensitive details.

In the corporate world, keyloggers are often used to glean company secrets as well as data that government regulations say should be protected by various laws (HIPAA, SOX, etc.) In their most malicious form, keylogger attacks are usually combined with other malware that can disable firewalls and install mini FTP servers for uploading keylogs.

A new technique for installing keyloggers surfaced in Fall 2006: e-greeting cards. Fake emails were sent out containing a dangerous link which would redirect the browser to an "exploit server". This server would check for web browser patches to find vulnerabilities, then download a rootkit and keylogger, when possible. To look legit, the final redirect was to a real Yahoo greeting card, but without any sender details listed on the ecard.

(11) Rootkit

Rootkits are amongst the most sinister of all types of malware, going to the operating system and disabling security features such as firewalls and anti-virus programs, thus rendering themselves invisible. They also install other malicious code, change DNS settings and system configurations, access private files, and generally affect security and system performance.A rootkit is a way to disguise the presence of malware on a computer. It gives false information about the state of the system. Rootkits accomplish this by substituting a corrupt version of a legitimate piece of software. For example, one version of a rootkit lies about who is logged into the machine. On Unix computers, typing "who" lists everyone currently logged into the system. A rootkit version of this utility would lie, hiding the fact that an unauthorized user had access to the system.

Rootkits are difficult to detect and remove

Rootkits have been used by law enforcement and were not always considered malware. That all changed with the infamous Sony BMG rootkit that was first declared malware by the state of California. Sony, in their zeal to protect the copyrights on s ome of their CDs and DVDs, introduced DRM (Digital Rights Management) onto each CD. The discs, when played, would install a rootkit on a user's computer, disabling certain system features. Unfortunately, this also opened up these computers to attacks by Trojans and other malware.

There are several types of rootkits: *persistent, memory-based, user-mode*, and *kernel-mode*. In 2007 it is widely expected that there will be an increase in rootkits aimed at 32-bit platforms, and a reduction in kernel-mode rootkits because of Microsoft's Vista PatchGuard. It's not easy to detect a rootkit, as some can preserve direct deletion and reinstall themselves, and a new type of invisible rootkit make rootkits an even more malicious threat in the future.

(12) Bots (AIM Bot, IRC Bot, etc.):

'Bot' is the common term used to describe a computer that can be remotely accessed and controlled in conjunction with thousands of other computers that have been compromised in the same fashion. Bots are created with malware that allows an individual unauthorized, remote access to a networked computer. This type of malware is known as a backdoor. A bot-type infection is one that enables someone to access and control your computer remotely in conjunction with thousands of additional computers that have an identical piece of malware installed.

A backdoor does more than permit someone to remotely log into your machine. It usually allows the intruder to log in with the highest level of privileges available to a user (admin or root). This gives the intruder the ability to install additional software on your computer (spyware, more malware) and instruct it to perform certain tasks such as send out spam, host and distribute copyrighted materials, serve as a counterfeit web site in a phishing scam, or participate in a Distributed Denial of Service (DDoS) attack.

How does a system become a bot? Either the machine is not properly patched which permits an intruder to exploit a vulnerability, or the owner of the machine is tricked into installing the malware that gives the intruder access. This can be done by sending an email or IM with a malicious attachment or link that takes the unsuspecting user to a web site that installs the malware. One of the most common vulnerabilities exploited by Bot Masters is weak or non-existent passwords on the computer's local accounts, particularly the admin account.

A bot is of no value to a Bot Master if it is discovered so hackers try to design this software to be as unobtrusive and surreptitious as possible. Ideally, the victim never realizes that their machine has been "botted."

Bot Master(s)

The Bot Master or Bot Herder is the person who creates and controls one or more Botnets. For an excellent discussion on the activities and methods of a bot master, please see this article that was published in the Washington Post on 2/19/06: Invasion of the Computer Snatchers. Bot Masters can make good money at what they do. Some estimates run as high as six figures annually. That's more than enough motivation to hack into your machine.

BotNets

Bots operate in herds or nets. How big can a herd get? In January 2006, when Jeanson James Ancheta of California was arrested on computer felony charges, he was controlling a botnet of over 400,000 machines. Security giant McAfee detected 28,000 distinct bot networks active in 2005, more than triple the amount in 2004. The world wide infection rate is estimated at 7%, or 47 million of the 681 million PCs connected to the Internet. Bots and botnets are the single most important tool used today by cyber criminals.

The value of a botnet lies in its size, distribution, and the relative ease with which it can be controlled despite the large number of machines involved and their disparate locations. They are rented out to individuals for specific tasks. One common use of botnets is a Distributed Denial of Service attack followed by an extortion demand. A botnet is engaged to generate huge volumes of network traffic that is directed at a target site. The criminals who hired the botnet demand payment from the victim in exchange for calling off the attack. The traffic flow is so large that the target is threatened with being shut down leading to a loss of business or intersite operations. Many victims have no other recourse and quietly agree to the payment demands.

All in all, botnets are responsible for the majority of annoying, malicious, and criminal activity seen on the Internet. That is why it is so important to keep your computer from running with a herd!

(13) Back Door

A back door is software that listens on the network for a remote connection. Connecting to the back door provides surreptitious access to the computer. Access is usually extensive in that it allows an intruder to poke around your hard drive and see just about anything there is to see. Some back doors listen passively, waiting for the connection to be made; others announce their presence, attempting to make contact with a command and control system on the Internet. More active back doors are often used in combination with bots.

(14) Data Interception

Data transmitted via any type of network can be subject to interception by unauthorized parties. The perpetrators might eavesdrop on communications or even alter the data packets being transmitted. Perpetrators can use various methods to intercept the data. IP spoofing, for example, entails posing as an authorized party in the data transmission by using the Internet Protocol (IP) address of one of the data recipients.

(15) Social Engineering

Social engineering is the increasingly prevalent act of obtaining confidential network security information through non-technical means. For example, a social engineer might pose as a technical support representative and make calls to employees to gather password information. Other examples of social engineering include bribing a coworker to gain access to a server or searching a colleague's office to find a password that has been written in a hidden spot.

(16) Spam

Spam is the commonly used term for unsolicited electronic mail or the action of broadcasting unsolicited advertising messages via e-mail. Spam is usually harmless, but it can be a nuisance, taking up the recipient's time and storage space.

1.4.6 Unauthorized Access

The ultimate aim of any network security attack is to either deprive you of use of your system or more commonly to give at least partial control of your system to the cracker.

Most systems rely on a very simple mechanism to keep intruders at bay. The good old username & password are used very widely. The main problem with passwords is that we're only human. We like nice, easy to understand passwords we won't forget. As the number of passwords we are expected to remember rises, the human desire to have memorable passwords becomes even more imperative. That's all well and good except for the fact that what is easy to remember for us is also easy to crack.

There are loads of programs that have been produced to crack passwords using the 'brute force' method. A bad password on a Microsoft Windows system can be cracked in less than a second. Worse still, some systems send passwords over the network as clear text.

There are plenty of tools available to collect those too.Once a user name & password have been obtained the system treats the cracker just like an authorized user would be.

(1) Unauthorized Access

"Unauthorized access" is a very high-level term that can refer to a number of different sorts of attacks. The goal of these attacks is to access some resource that your machine should not provide the attacker. For example, a host might be a web server, and should provide anyone with requested web pages. However, that host should not provide command shell access without being sure that the person making such a request is someone who should get it, such as a local administrator.

(2) Executing Commands Illicitly

It's obviously undesirable for an unknown and untrusted person to be able to execute commands on your server machines. There are two main classifications of the severity of this problem: normal user access, and administrator access. A normal user can do a number of things on a system (such as read files, mail them to other people, etc.) that an attacker should not be able to do. This might, then, be all the access that an attacker needs. On the other hand, an attacker might wish to make configuration changes to a host (perhaps changing its IP address, putting a start-up script in place to cause the machine to shut down every time it's started, or something similar). In this case, the attacker will need to gain administrator privileges on the host.

(3) Confidentiality Breaches

We need to examine the threat model: what is it that you're trying to protect yourself against? There is certain information that could be quite damaging if it fell into the hands of a competitor, an enemy, or the public. In these cases, it's possible that compromise of a normal user's account on the machine can be enough to cause damage (perhaps in the form of PR, or obtaining information that can be used against the company, etc.)

While many of the perpetrators of these sorts of break-ins are merely thrill-seekers interested in nothing more than to see a shell prompt for your computer on their screen, there are those who are more malicious, as we'll consider next. (Additionally, keep in mind that it's possible that someone who is normally interested in nothing more than the thrill could be persuaded to do more: perhaps an unscrupulous competitor is willing to hire such a person to hurt you.)

(4) Destructive Behavior

Among the destructive sorts of break-ins and attacks, there are two major categories.

(a) Data Diddling

The data diddler is likely the worst sort, since the fact of a break-in might not be immediately obvious. Perhaps he's toying with the numbers in your spreadsheets, or changing the dates in your projections and plans. Maybe he's changing the account numbers for the auto-deposit of certain paychecks. In any case, rare is the case when you'll come in to work one day, and simply know that something is wrong. An accounting procedure might turn up a discrepancy in the books three or four months after the fact. Trying to track the problem down will certainly be difficult, and once that problem is discovered, how can any of your numbers from that time period be trusted? How far back do you have to go before you think that your data is safe?

(b) Data Destruction.

Some of those perpetrate attacks are simply twisted jerks who like to delete things. In these cases, the impact on your computing capability — and consequently your business — can be nothing less than if a fire or other disaster caused your computing equipment to be completely destroyed.

1.4.7 Denial of Service (DoS) : Business Non-availability

Computer worms and viruses can drastically affect the reliability of network resources, which in turn affects businesses' ability to respond quickly to their customers; but worms and viruses are not the only threat to business availability. With networks so critical to day-to-day business operations, cyber-terrorists have begun targeting businesses for blackmail, threatening to bring down Websites and e-commerce operations unless their demands are met. These denial-of-service (DoS) attacks send large volumes of traffic to a critical network element, either causing it to fail or to be unable to process legitimate traffic. Once again, the results are disastrous: data and orders are lost and customer requests are not answered. If these attacks become public, a company's credibility is damaged. While most of the publicity surrounding DoS outages has focused on major banks and global 500 companies, small and medium-sized businesses are not immune. They are viewed as less prepared for attacks than large corporations.

There are many other less dramatic but more likely attacks that threaten small and medium business availability and therefore profitability and customer satisfaction. For example, a resource theft attack breaches business computers and networks, using them for illegal file sharing of music, movies, or software. Often, businesses are unaware that a security breach is underway. Meanwhile, their computers and networks are slow to respond to customers, and their unwitting participation in illegal file sharing leaves them vulnerable to lawsuits.

DoS type attacks, like the one currently underway against SCO, have a number of different forms and targets.

Any system out in the wilds of the Internet is exposed to DoS attacks. The intent of a DoS attack is to render your systems inoperative for the duration of the attack. Attacks range in sophistication from a single disgruntled person to a massive, worldwide, cooperative attempt to disrupt a large corporation.

In the old days, all that was necessary to bring down a whole corporation's email was to send them a large file as an email attachment. The speed of the Internet links were sufficiently slow so as to saturate the link for an extended period. Things have moved on from this. Even the smallest companies can afford to have their systems hosted on infrastructure supplied by Tier-1 backbone providers. Consequently, it takes more than a single large file to take most systems down.

Unfortunately the world of DoS attacks have moved on too. Now, the power of the Internet can be used to power todays network security attacks. There are tens of millions of machines now connected to the Internet. Many of them are managed by people who are not as concerned about network security attacks as you are. Indeed many are completely ignorant of the dangers. This problem has been exacerbated by the wide adoption of always on broadband. When people connected to the Internet via dialup, their ignorance only gave a very narrow pipe to the DoS attacker. Now, much greater damage can be wreaked on the Internet by a poorly defended broadband PC.

1.4.8 Phishing

Phishing (pronounced "Fishing") is a method used to gather personal or financial information for the purpose of commiting fraud. These email requests simulate legitimate businesses such as EBay, PayPal, and various financial institutions. They can be very deceptive. The authors go to great lengths to make their fraudulent requests look as legitimate as possible. There is usually a matter of some urgency that requires you to respond within a short time frame, and if you have an account with the business or institution that is replicated, you may be convinced that the request is real. Phishing is typically carried out by email or instant messaging where recipients are instructed to click on a link that takes them to a counterfeit web site that requests their personal information.

Phishing is a social engineering technique used to collect personal information such as bank account or credit card numbers, account names and passwords, or social security numbers. The primary method involves posing as a legitimate source requesting this information such as a bank or credit union, Internet financial service providers such as Ebay and PayPal, and even government agencies like the IRS.

Phishing is typically carried out by email or instant messaging where recipients are instructed to click on a link that takes them to a counterfeit web site that requests their personal information.

Some variations include "Spear Phishing" which targets members or employees of specific organizations. "Whaling" describes phishing attempts directed at high level, executive employees. "Vishing" combines email messages with instructions to call a toll-free number rather than click on a web link.

What to do?

In all cases, the best course of action is to ignore and delete the fraudulent message. If there's any doubt about its legitimacy, please contact the University's Help Desk at 442-3700. You can also send samples to the Information Security Officer to be included on this page.

The Russian Business Network uses topical greeting card messages to distribute its malware package called "Stormworm."

......Original Message......

From: Hallmark Cards [malto: postbode @ hallmark [dot]be]

Sent: Wednesday, February 06, 2008 4:28 AM

Subject: You have a card send from a friend!

The Hallmark logo is being pulled from ecards.msn.co..uk.

Hello,

A friend has sent you a Hallmark Ecard

It would be nice to know which friend. But then, you could check with them to see if they really sent you the card.

Click here to view your Ecard

Here's where the stinger lies. The link above points to an executable that will install the Stormworm code. The full link is http://maui.dnsdc3.com/~admin/postcard.gif.exe

Figure 1.12(a)

Confirmm--Or Lose--Your Email Account

This message is very typical of phishing attempts to trick college and University members into revealing their account passwords.

From: ADMIN HELPDESK [mailto:adminhelpdesk10@gmall.com]

Check out the address that will receive your reply. As you can see, it has nothing to do with any University. It's hosted by gmail. But, in some cases you will see a From address that looks real as in the following example.

From: Online Services <onlineservices@albany.edu>

In this case, taken from a separate phish, the From: address looks like areal albany.edu account. In fact, if you tried to reply to this message,a sepaate, totally different address would appear in the To: field of your response. That's because the From address is not necessarily the address that will receive your reply. The real reply-to address can be hidden until you actually try to reply. But after deciding to respond, most people don't check to see if the addresses are, indeed the same.

Sent: Friday, April 18, 2008 9:22 AM

Subject: VERIFY YOUR ALBANY, EDU EMAIL ACCOUNT NOW.

Figure 1.12(b)

You are usually instructed to click on a link to provide the requested personal information. The link takes you to a counterfeit web site run by thieves. The web site is designed to convince you that you are dealing with a legitimate business or financial services provider, going so far as to load many of its visual elements (e.g., company logos) from the real site.

All of these requests are fraudulent. No legitimate business will ask you for personal or account information via an email solicitation. If you receive such a request, you can safely ignore it, or report it to the Anti-Phishing Working Group at http://www.antiphishing.org where you can find additional information and samples of phishing scams.

1.4.9 Human Error

It is understood that an individual with no understanding of networks can easily set up a flawed and vulnerable network. However, some executives need to be aware that even their system administrators could be lacking in their understanding of wireless network implementations. With the broad number of floating, corporate hotspots being found everyday it has be to be assumed that some of those hotspots were put into place by knowledgeable IT staff within those corporations. However, some of those techs missed something. Maybe a manager gave some of his development staff permission to install a wireless router while providing no oversight to the installation. Though developers may know something about software architecture and design, they may or may not know anything about network security. Perhaps the local system admin doesn't thoroughly understand networking principles. Maybe s/he lacks the tools necessary to carefully monitor network traffic and detect anomalies that could indicate the presence of a rogue access point. Worst case, s/he might not even care. This can be extremely problematic in that network assets may be compromised, unbeknownst anyone in the organization. Your company should make sure that system administrators are well trained with a strong background in computer and network security.

In any system, the human components are the weakest link. Wireless networking is certainly no exception. Your organization should define strict policies and procedures related to wireless networking within a well-publicized company document. It is especially important with regard to wireless networking that employees are made aware of these rules. As you saw in the opening vignette, an unwitting employee with good intentions compromised company data without even knowing she had done so. Because wireless hardware is cheap and relatively easy to use, the risk of your network containing rogue access points is great. You should be sure to set standards for any wireless hardware configurations within the company network and perform routine network audits to ensure that there are no open doors. We will discuss more specifics of wireless networking policies and procedures in our discussions on defense methods.

1.4.10 Rogue Access Points

It is easy for even a novice to acquire equipment and set up a wireless network. If this is done from within another network, it creates what is known as a subnet, which can create back doors to its parent. There are many easily overlooked mistakes that can be made in configuring a wireless network, many of which novice users will overlook. Individuals who wish to intrude upon a network can also plant rogue access points themselves. Network administrators must make sure to implement strict polices regarding the deployment of wireless hardware, and audit their networks often with reliable tools to ensure that these rogue access points do not exist.

1.4.11 Warchalking

Another point of interest before moving on is something, which is possibly more of a compelling idea than a physical reality called warchalking. It is a modern version of the hobo sign language used to alert one another to places providing shelter, food, and potential trouble. Using a fairly universal hobo sign language, individuals mark structures that have hotspots associated with them. In many cases these symbols incorporate much information about each node and the type of security currently being implemented. According to John Hiler, a New Yorker who writes about blog culture on his microcontent news site http://www.microcontentnew.com, warchalking is a "perfect storm" of three major tech themes. "It's got Wi-Fi. It's got the tie-in to hobo language, which is really cool from a linguistics point of view. And it ties into the spirit of democracy, which was the original intention of the Web," he said. "It's the subversive idea of giving the finger to the local land-line monopoly."

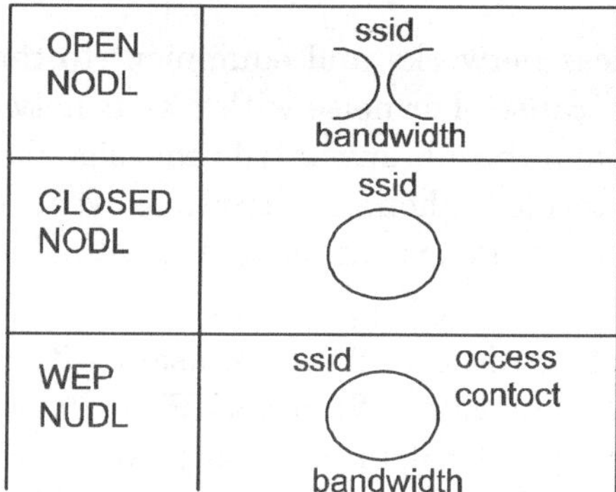

Figure 1.13 Common Warchalking Symbols and Terminology

1.4.12 MAC Address Spoofing

Media Access Control (MAC) addresses [4] act as personal identification numbers for verifying the identity of authorized clients on wireless networks. However, existing encryption standards are not foolproof. A hacker can pick off authorized MAC addresses and steal bandwidth, corrupt or download files, and wreak havoc on an entire network. While securing your wireless LAN by using an authorized list of MAC addresses for authentication will provide some security, they were never intended to be used in this way.

There are a few legitimate reasons and examples of why you would want to spoof your MAC address:

(1) A firewall could be set up to only accept traffic from a certain MAC address at a certain time. An administrator could generate a list of MAC addresses that would change every certain number of days, hours, or even minutes. The user would have to set their MAC address within the time window to send packets to the firewall.

(2) Some ISP's keep track of the MAC address that a subscriber is using. They only allow registered addresses to connect to the Internet, and charge more money for additional IP clients. It might become inconvenient to be limited to a particular MAC address if a user needs to change the gateway or change cards in the gateway temporarily and would have to re-register a new MAC address just to move some equipment around for a few days.

Even if you are using encryption or virtual private networks (VPNs), MAC addresses are always in the air. With software such as Kismet or Ethereal, a hacker can capture the MAC address of an authorized user. They can then change their MAC address to the valid user's MAC address using any number of spoofing or cloning utilities, or even manually changing the Windows registry entry. Now the hacker can connect to the wireless LAN and bypass any MAC address filtering. Netstumbler can also be used with a MAC spoofing utility or MAC address modifying utility such as SMAC to achieve the same results.

1.4.13 Noisy Neighbors

The proximity of other wireless networks and equipment to that of your own is of utmost importance, for these can be a cause of or noise within your network. Because we are dealing with radio waves passing through the air, unwanted radio signals can wander into our domain from outside sources such as cordless phones, microwave ovens, or the neighboring business' 802.11 router. This noise, or interference can have a drastic effect on network performance and reliability.

Aside from the noise related issues, network users within an earshot of your access point could be consuming your bandwidth. Windows XP's built-in Wireless Zero Configuration utility, for example, is set up by default to join the wireless network with the best signal. Once it has successfully connected, it stores the network SSID as a "preferred network" and will connect to it each time it comes within range. Though this is convenient in most circumstances for the network client, it can lead to unwanted network users. Even with WEP enabled, which can keep unwanted clients from joining your network; would-be clients knocking on the door, requesting connections, can consume significant bandwidth. Auditing and scanning your network, methods of which we will discuss later, can minimize noise from and overlapping of neighbor networks.

Interference of this type was recently experienced at a conference in Las Vegas, Nevada. Attendees were invited to connect to the conference's wireless network at a designated hotspot within the venue. One attendee in particular attempted to connect to the advertised access point for ten minutes before giving up and venturing to a nearby Starbucks coffee house where he paid $9.95 for a day's access to T-Mobile. The problem at the conference center was due to two problems. First, there were some 35 active access points in the large display room, all using the same 802.11b/g frequencies and, thus, causing both interference and using overall bandwidth. Secondly, the little bandwidth that was left was being shared by dozens of users of these public access points.

1.4.14 Improper Design

Improper or unknown boundary definitions constitute another possibility for network design error. Wireless network interface cards (NIC) and routers come with a variety of antennas. Some antennas broadcast in a single direction, and while they are not very accommodating to the surrounding area, they definitely help narrow the boundaries. The real danger comes in omni-directional antennas that broadcast in all directions, providing easy-access to the wireless network. Below is an illustration giving an example of improper boundary definition for a wireless network.

Caveat: *Both of these antenna installations are omni-directional. The one on the left is confined to a single floor and does not broadcast beyond the walls. The one the right, however, does both.*

Notice how the second example in the illustration shows the access boundary of the wireless network extending outside the corporate structure in which the network has been implemented.

Insecure-by-default hardware, unqualified system administrators and coverage boundaries that are out of control make up the key characteristics of faulty wireless network design.

1.4.15 Man-In-The-Middle Attacks

Hailing from the early days of cryptography, man-in-the-middle attacks are an old strategy applied to a new technology. The key concept behind a MITM attack is exactly as it sounds, one entity with malicious intent intercepts a message between two communicating entities. The hijacker can then send the message onto the receiver as if it had never been delayed, and even alter the message's content. Used in war, this could be a valuable tool for intercepting and altering the enemy's message to suit the opposing side's purposes. In World War II, if the Axis forces needed to send information to deployed troops, they would send it with a decryption key. This key would be the primary tool for decoding the message and properly deciphering it. If the Allies could intercept this message and break the code, then they would be executing a MITM attack. Upon successful completion of the attack, they'd have three options as to how they'd like to exploit the position.

- The message could be intercepted, altered and sent onto the recipient with fraudulent information.
- The message could be blocked and prevented from proceeding any further.
- The message could simply be read and sent on its way without the recipient's knowledge.
- The concept for MITM attacks on wireless networks is the same.

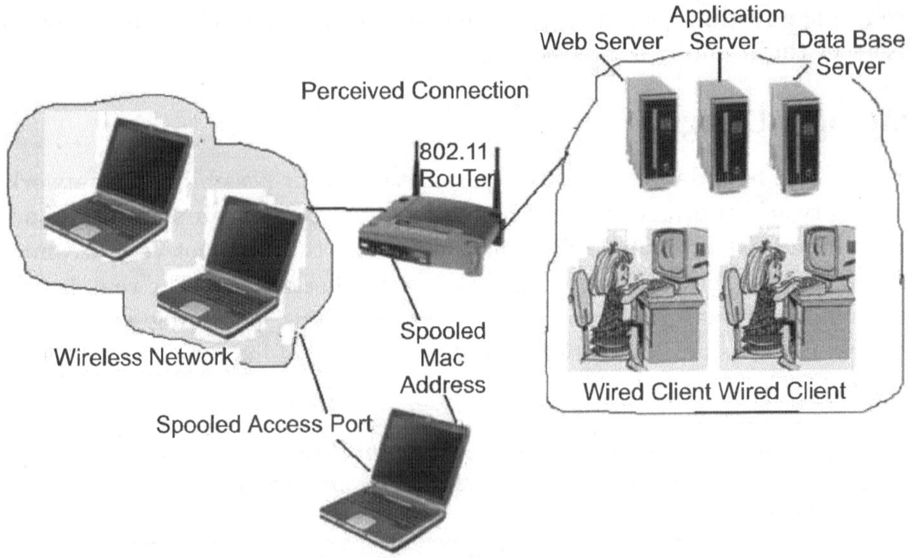

Figure 1.14 A Diagram Depicting the Anatomy of a Man-In-The-Middle Attack

The method of attack is simple in application, provided you have the right kind of software. Fortunately for a hacker (unfortunate for a director in charge of security), there are several applications available as freeware that perform the tasks necessary to execute a proper MITM attack.

The first task associated with an MITM attack comes into play after the initial tasks for hacking a wireless network have been performed. That is to say, we are assuming that a target network has been located, and that the attacker is within acceptable range of a target access point. Once these tasks have been performed the MITM process can begin.

After having captured information about the target access point, a "soft AP" can be set up by placing a WLAN card on the attacker's machine into host mode with the same, or similar, properties as the legitimate access point. This soft AP can then attract clients who think they are connecting to a familiar network. At such a time, the attacker can use another WLAN card to forward the traffic to the real access point, all the while capturing any information that moves across its path.

In some access controlled networks, all hosts on a network store a list of acceptable MAC addresses for their respective network. Using the ARP method, those systems can validate IP addresses that request access to their network by resolving them against a known table of valid IP/MAC addresses. MITM can thwart this defense by piggybacking on another attack method called ARP Spoofing. Many systems easily accept ARP commands and freely allow their MAC lists to be updated. Using software like ARPoison[6], an attacker can add their own MAC address to the list or trick the system into sending that table to the hijacker's system. ARPoison uses the ARP Spoofing to trick the network into sending all of their ARP requests to the hijacker's system instead of a valid host. Once the request comes in, the hijacker can reroute the information to a valid host, but only after they have had extensive access to the transaction. Once the attacker has established themselves as valid members of the network they can

- Execute a denial of service(DoS)[8] by sending all host requests to invalid host addresses, thus causing bounce backs.
- Monitor all transactions between the hosts (hence "Man-In-The-Middle").
- Join the network by adding the attacker's MAC address to the acceptable list.

There are many other types of software applications that can perform these ARP poisoning methods, as well as execute other hacking techniques such as port sniffing. By utilizing Level two layer vulnerabilities through ARP Spoofing, MITM techniques are easy to execute, and expensive to detect.

1.4.16 Social Engineering Attacks

Most of us will surrender our passwords under certain circumstances. For example, someone posing as a Help Desk employee could request your password ostensibly to correct a problem with your account. Phishing email is designed to harvest valid user account names and passwords. Many times friends will ask you for a password so they can use your computer. Don't give it to them. Instead, log in for them, or, if you do provide it, change your password immediately afterwords. It's good practice to periodically change passwords, as well as use multiple passwords for different accounts. And, of course, your passwords should always be at least 8 characters and contain a mix of numbers, special characters, and upper & lower case.

(1) Social Engineering

In the spring of 2006, an information security company in Europe conducted a survey just outside Victoria Station in London, asking people about their Easter candy giving habits. They stopped people at random and lured them into participating in the survey with the promise of winning up to 60 pounds of chocolate. Eighty-one percent of commuters they spoke with were willing to part with all the personal information needed to steal their identity for the chance to win the imaginary sweets.

Social networking web sites encourage people to create profiles about themselves and then communicate with others and form online networks of friends.

People can participate in a range of activities once members. These can include chatting with each other, sharing photos & videos and posting comments in online forums, blogs or discussion groups. Profiles may contain personal information such as real life photos and descriptive comments about the member.

Social networking web sites are like online diaries and are usually free to join. Some websites have millions of members.

In the spring of 2006, an information security company in Europe conducted a survey just outside Victoria Station in London, asking people about their Easter candy giving habits. They stopped people at random and lured them into participating in the survey with the promise of winning up to 60 pounds of chocolate. Eighty-one percent of commuters they spoke with were willing to part with all the personal information needed to steal their identity for the chance to win the imaginary sweets.

In June of 2006, a consultant service was asked to test the security of a credit union. The consultant was told that the employees were aware that something was up and would be on the look out for attempts to get past their security measures. The individual in charge of the test gathered together all the leftover USB pen give-aways lying around his office. He had one of his staff write a simple Trojan horse that collected passwords and emailed them back to the consultant company, and loaded it onto the USB pens. He then went to the office of the credit union at 6:00 am and scattered the pens all around the grounds: parking lots, picnic areas, entry ways, etc. Later that morning he watched while the employees arrived for work. Sure enough, they started picking up the pens when they found them and put them in their pockets. Back at the consultant's offices, the staff there began receiving emails containing passwords and other confidential information that was being transmitted by the Trojan. Curiosity had gotten the better of the credit union employees. They had loaded the USB drives on to the company's computers and opened a hole in the company's security measures. Confidential information was leaking from their systems...and they didn't even know it.

These are two classic examples of social engineering, manipulating human behavior to put people and information at risk. In this section, we'll examine different social engineering techniques and tactics.

(2) Social Engineering Techniques

- **Impersonation & Pulling Rank**

Impersonation involves an attacker assuming the role of an individual who pretends to have some legitimate need for the information being sought. The assumed role could be that of an actual employee, or someone outside the organization who purports to have a relationship with the company, or is simply doing some work on the company premises (e.g. phone repair).

This can easily evolve into a slightly different tack where the attacker assumes the role of someone in a position of authority, i.e., pulling rank. It doesn't require a precise impersonation of the company officer, just an assumption of that position's authority. Who among us doesn't want to please the boss, or the boss's administrative assistant? By adopting a high status attitude, an attacker can get what she is looking for.

A particularly effective variation of this technique is to impersonate someone with authority coupled with an urgent situation that pressures an employee for an immediate response.

- **Conformity**

Conformity is another powerful social force. If an attacker can convince an employee that everyone else has already performed the actions requested, such as confirming account names and passwords, it becomes very difficult for an individual to resist.

A variation on this theme is diffusion of responsibility. If an attacker can convince his victim that the victim's supervisor has already approved the action, and if the assignment of duties among staff is not clearly delineated, it is possible to fool the employee into revealing the sought-after information.

- **Helplessness**

A combination of friendliness and helplessness can trigger an outpouring of information, particularly from help desk staff. Help Desk employees are especially vulnerable to individuals who show an appreciation for their assistance. A natural response is to provide even more information when the customer is so eager for, as well as impressed by, your knowledge. By playing dumb and carefully asking leading questions (baiting), prompted by the real time responses of the help desk agent, an attacker can come away from the encounter with a wealth of information about a company's IT organization.

- **Surveys**

As demonstrated by the Easter candy example cited above, surveys are an information gathering instrument tailor made for attackers. They require no special relationship between the attacker and the victim, and are by their very nature designed to elicit information in a question and answer format. Through careful coordination, a team of attackers might be able to prepare employees ahead of time for the survey process and even provide them with permission to disclose sensitive information!

- **Shoulder Surfing & Eavesdropping**

Shoulder surfing and eavesdropping can be very effective in gathering useful information about a company's personnel and operations. The term shoulder surfing refers to any direct observation of sensitive information such as individuals keying in passwords or PINs, the display of information on computer monitors, or simply personnel forms with SSNs left exposed on someone's desk.

Eavesdropping is defined as listening in on conversations among individuals associated with the target organization. In the context of Information Security it extends to remote listening and recording devices, including the interception of telephone calls, fax transmissions, e-mails, and data transmissions, particularly on unsecured wireless networks.

(3) Social Engineering Tactics

When browsing a webpage, it is common to run across many different hyperlinks that can bring you to other pages or files. However, a common method of infecting a computer is to mislabel a link. It's important to know that a hyperlink can be called anything! KaptainKangaroo.org could really point to sleazyporn.com. This is a common tactic used to fool people into visiting sites they normally would avoid. By mislabeling the link, cyber criminals hope to force you to visit a counterfeit site (phishing) or sites that will install malware on your PC.

Sending poison links via AIM has proven to be particularly effective in deceiving people. Since the message came from your buddy, it must be legit, right? Wrong! AIM viruses can generate their own IMs and send them out to everyone on your buddy list. Using AIM to infect computers with malware has proven to be very popular with cyber thieves because they can take advantage of the implicit trust built into the relationship between you and your buddies.

What are the Dangers of Social Networking Web Sites

Each social networking web site has its own rules and restrictions on the types of members who can join. Some websites have age restrictions, country restrictions or restrictions based on the level of interest in a particular topic.

With any social networking web site however, there are a number of dangers that exist.

- **Paedophiles and Child Abuse:** Adults seeking children for their own sexual gratification may be lurking in social networking web sites, pretending to be other children. Online relationship may be formed which could lead to real life meetings.
- **Personal Information:** Children may be able to post identifiable personal information in profiles
- **Time Wasting / Internet Addiction:** Children and teenagers may spend hours online modifying their profiles and communicating with others. Tasks, such as homework, may suffer as a result.
- **No Age Verification:** Many social networking web sites do not have age verification technologies in place, so people of all ages could be members, even if it is against the terms and conditions of joining.
- **Cyber Bullying and Flaming:** Many web sites let you rate another member's profile. This opens the opportunity up for cyber bullying and nasty comments to be made. Negative comments can also appear in discussion groups and blogs.

Identity Theft

Identity theft occurs when a thief uses another person's SSN and other identifying information to fraudulently open new accounts and obtain financial gain at the expense of the victim. It is one of the fastest growing crimes in America. Everyone is a potential target. As of 2005, an estimated 41M Americans were affected at a cost of $5b annually. Phishing and spyware accounted for approximately 9% of these incidents. It is the primary reason why it is so important to properly protect personally identifiable information (name, SSN, driver's license number, etc.)

Preventative Measures You Can Take

With all theses threats everyone needs to be careful not to disclose information to the wrong people. With this in mind, here are a few steps that can help keep your identity safe.

(1) Call your bank using the number printed on your statements, or listed in a phone book. Do not use a number listed in a email. Some phishing scams have been known to ask you to call the "bank's" toll-free phone number where accomplices or an automated system will ask for your account number.

(2) Use separate passwords for diferent financial sites. That way, if one is stolen, all your accounts won't be compromised.

(3) Never fill out a form or survey from an untrusted source.

(4) Watch for misleading URLs. You can sometimes reveal discrepancies between the text and the real URL by rolling over the link with your mouse and looking at what is displayed at the bottom of your browser window.

(5) Look for character replacements in URLs, like 1 for L , 7 for T, etc.

(6) Never click on links in emails or IMs, open attachments, or accept files unless you verify their legitimacy with the sender.

1.4.17 Cookies

A cookie is a small file which stores information related to your Internet (web browsing) activity and then reports this back to the website that created the cookie.Amongst other uses, cookies enable websites to be customised for individual users.Cookies can however, cause potential security problems as information such as credit card details might be collected via a cookie.Cookies will only store information that you provide and can be easily removed off your computer.In Australia the Privacy Act Amendment (Cth 2000) ensures that cookies do not infringe on the privacy of Australians.

As with any type of crime, the threats to the privacy and integrity of data come from a very small minority of vandals. However, while one car thief can steal only one car at a time, a single hacker working from a basic computer can generate damage to a large number of computer networks that wreaks havoc around the world. Perhaps even more worrisome is the fact that the threats can come from people we know. In fact, most network security experts claim that the majority of network attacks are initiated by employees who work inside the corporations where breaches have occurred. Employees, through mischief, mAnita, or mistake, often manage to damage their own companies' networks and destroy data. Furthermore, with the recent pervasiveness of remote connectivity technologies, businesses are expanding to include larger numbers of telecommuters, branch offices, and business partners. These remote employees and partners pose the same threats as internal employees, as well as the risk of security breaches if their remote networking assets are not properly secured and monitored. Whether you want to secure a car, a home, a nation, or a computer network, a general knowledge of who the potential enemies are and how they work is essential.

1.4.18 Forcing Security Legislation

Aside from these malicious security threats, new laws and regulations require that small and medium-sized businesses protect the privacy and integrity of the information entrusted to them. The European Union and many individual countries have legislation governing the protection of personal data in the hands of organizations. Countries have also drafted additional laws governing specific information, such as healthcare information. For example, in the United States, the Health Insurance Portability and Accountability Act (HIPAA) requires health care organizations, including every doctor's office, to put safeguards in place to ensure the privacy of health information and prevent unauthorized access. The onus is on businesses to comply with laws and regulations that apply to their business in their markets. Unfortunately, many smaller businesses find their resources only stretch so far. Yet customers want assurance that the information they entrust to businesses is kept private.

Let us introduce Anita and Bunty, two people who want to communicate "securely." This being a networking text, we should remark that Anita and Bunty may be two routers that want to securely exchange routing tables, two hosts that want to establish a secure transport connection, or two email applications that want to exchange secure e-mail - all case studies that we will consider later in this chapter. Anita and Bunty are well-known fixtures in the security community, perhaps because their names are more fun than a generic entity named "A" that wants to securely communicate with a generic entity named "B." Illicit love affairs, wartime communication, and business transactions are the commonly cited human needs for secure communications; preferring the first to the latter two, we're happy to use Anita and Bunty as our sender and receiver, and imagine them in this first scenario.

1.5 VULNERABILITY OF REQUIREMENT OF SECURITY FOR TRAFFIC OVER INTERNET

In 2001 the SANS Institute and the National Infrastructure Protection Center (NIPC) at the FBI released a document summarizing the Ten Most Critical Internet Security Vulnerabilities. Thousands of organizations relied on that list, and on the expanded Top-20 lists that followed in succeeding years, to prioritize their efforts so they could close the most dangerous holes first.

The threat landscape is very dynamic, which in turn makes it necessary to adopt newer security measures. Just over the last year, the kinds of vulnerabilities that are being exploited are very different from the ones being exploited in the past. The SANS Top 2007 list is not "cumulative."

(1) Client-side Vulnerabilities in:

1. Web Browsers
2. Office Software
3. Email Clients
4. Media Players

(2) Server-side Vulnerabilities in:

1. Web Applications
2. Windows Services
3. Unix and Mac OS Services
4. Backup Software

5. Anti-virus Software
6. Management Servers
7. Database Software

(3) Security Policy and Personnel:

1. Excessive User Rights and Unauthorized Devices
2. Phishing/Spear Phishing
3. Unencrypted Laptops and Removable Media

(4) Application Abuse:

1. Instant Messaging
2. Peer-to-Peer Programs

(5) Network Devices:

1. VoIP Servers and Phones

(6) Zero Day Attacks:

1. Zero Day Attacks

1.5.1 Client-side Vulnerabilities in:

(1) Web Browsers

Vulnerabilities are bugs (flaws) in applications.

Microsoft Internet Explorer is the world's most popular web browser and is installed by default on every Microsoft Windows system. Unpatched or older versions of Internet Explorer contain multiple vulnerabilities that can lead to memory corruption, spoofing and execution of arbitrary scripts or code. The most critical issues are the ones that lead to remote code execution without any user interaction when a user visits a malicious web page or reads a malicious email. Exploit code for many of these critical Internet Explorer flaws is publicly available. In addition, Internet Explorer has been leveraged to exploit vulnerabilities in other core Windows components such as HTML Help and the Graphics Rendering Engine. During the past year, hundreds of vulnerabilities in ActiveX controls installed by Microsoft and other software vendors have been discovered. These are also being exploited via Internet Explorer.

Mozilla Firefox is the second most popular web browser after Internet Explorer. It also has a fair share of vulnerabilities. In 2007, it has released several updates to address publicly disclosed vulnerabilities. Similarly to Internet Explorer, unpatched or older versions of Firefox contain multiple vulnerabilities that can lead to memory corruption, spoofing and execution of arbitrary scripts or code. The web sites exploiting the browser vulnerabilities typically host a several exploits, and even launch the appropriate exploit(s) based on which browser the potential victim is using.

With the explosion of rich content in web sites, a parallel increase has been seen in the number of Browser Helper Object and third-party plug-ins used to access various MIME file types such as multimedia and documents. These plug-ins often support client-side web scripting languages such as Macromedia Flash or Shockwave. Many of these plug-ins are installed (semi-)transparently by a website. Users may thus not be aware that an at-risk helper object or plug-in is installed on his/her system. These additional plug-ins introduce more avenues for hackers to exploit to compromise computers of users visiting malicious web sites.

(2) Office Software

Software Vulnerabilities

Vulnerabilities are bugs (flaws) in applications (e.g., Web servers and Web browsers) that, if exploited, may cause the application to do things it should not. Such behaviors let an attacker compromise the system on which the software is installed and may include such things as:

- Running arbitrary instructions of the attacker's choosing
- Downloading files from the Internet
- Running a local file
- Crashing the application

Symantec tracks all major software vulnerabilities on its Security Focus Web site (www.securityfocus.com)

Beginning in 2003, underlying vulnerabilities in the Windows operating system (in MS-RPC DCOM and LSASS components) allowed worms such as Blaster and Sasser to self replicate and spread. Subsequent releases of Microsoft Windows XP SP2 and SP3 have eliminated many of these operating system vulnerabilities. However, a recent outbreak of the Downadup/Conficker worm using a known MS-RPC vulnerability (MS08-067) illustrates the need for continued vigilance in monitoring all published vulnerabilities that affect the operating system.

More recently, attacks have shifted to the Web browser, ActiveX controls, browser plug-ins, multimedia, document viewers and other third party applications. A single vulnerability in one of these may render a user's system defenseless and open to attack, simply by virtue of a user visiting a compromised Web page..

Although the base operating systems encourage users to automatically download and install published updates in response to known vulnerabilities, published data1 shows that end-users have a poor track record of applying patches to their systems to address known published vulnerabilities. A recent article2 stated that 600 million browsers were insecure without even taking into account the impact of vulnerable third party plug-ins, ActiveX controls and multimedia plug-ins.

We continue to see a wide variety of vulnerabilities exploited on a daily basis. This includes unknown or recently announced vulnerabilities without patches but also those recently patched. Additional vulnerabilities we have observed being exploited in 2008, include various

Web Browser, ActiveX controls, browser plug-ins, document readers and other third party applications.

This section includes vulnerabilities for office productivity suites that include e-mail clients, word processors, spreadsheet applications, document viewers and presentation applications. Vulnerabilities in office products are typically exploited via the following attack vectors:

An attacker sends a specially crafted office document in an email. When the attachment is opened, the malformed contents in the document exploit vulnerabilities in the office software. An attacker hosts a malicious document on a web server or shared folder, and entices a user to browse to the web page or the shared folder. Note that, in most situations, Internet Explorer automatically opens Microsoft Office documents. Hence, browsing the malicious web page or folder is sufficient for vulnerability exploitation in many cases. An attacker runs an NNTP (news) server or hijacks an RSS feed that sends malicious documents to news and RSS clients. In all these scenarios, viruses, trojans, spyware, ad-ware, rootkits, keyboard loggers, or any other program of the attacker's choice, can be installed on victim's computer.

Microsoft Office is the most widely used email and productivity suite worldwide. It includes Outlook, Word, PowerPoint, Excel, Visio, FrontPage and Access.

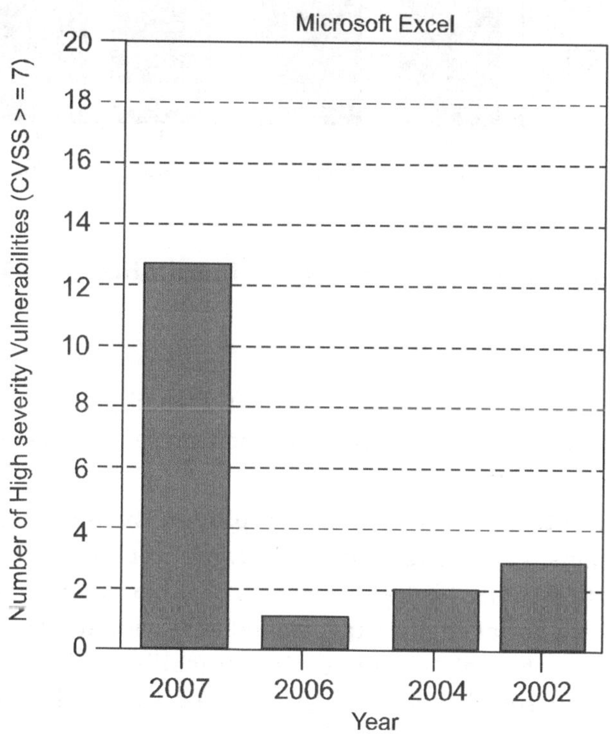

Figure 1.15 Number of High Severity Vulnerabilities in Microsoft Excel Software

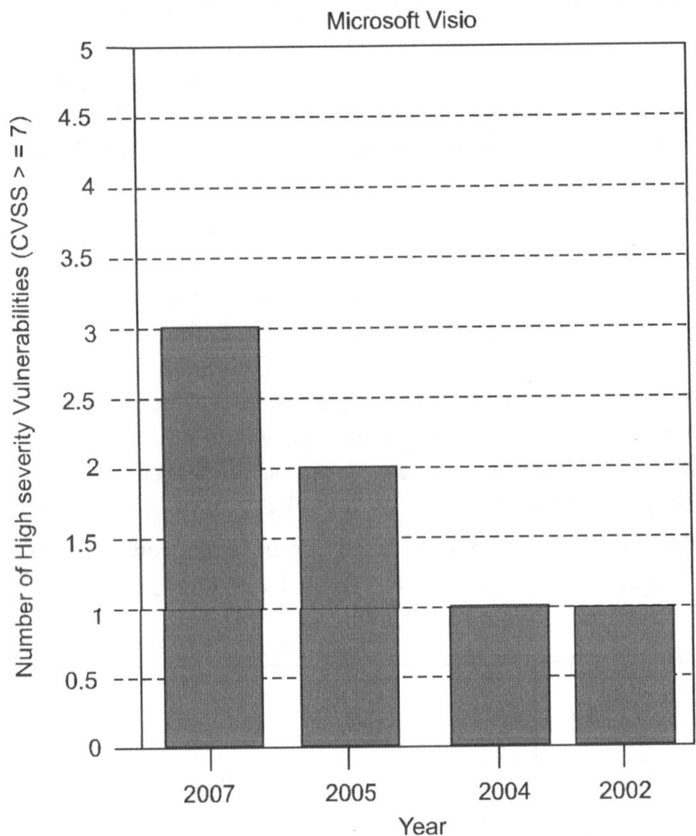

Figure 1.16 Number of High Severity Vulnerabilities for Microsoft Visio

(3) Email Clients

E-mail is one of the vital applications of the Internet. E-mail provides tremendous savings it terms of time, money and efficiency. Given its omnipresence, e-mail provides a common vector for multiple vulnerabilities.

Multiple avenues of attack that can be employed through email: Distribution of malware (viruses, Trojans, keyloggers, spyware, adware, rootkits etc); **Phishing** - Attempts to lure email user into revealing his/her passwords or other confidential information; Spam - unsolicited (junk) email; Social engineering; Denial of service attacks - sending high volume of email messages to a potential "victim" server or mailbox; These attacks can result in: damage to applications, data, or operating system; disclosure of confidential information; propagation of malware; use of affected systems as "bots" (infected machines under the control of persons other than the intended users, used as proxies for attacks on other systems or for storage and distribution of pirated content and pornography); lack of availability of systems and services; waste of time, money and labor. Virtually all contemporary operating systems can be used as platforms for e-mail client applications.

The most popular e-mail applications currently are: Microsoft Outlook (Microsoft Windows only) and Outlook Express (Microsoft Windows only; old versions were available for Apple Macintosh); Mozilla Thunderbird (Microsoft Windows, Linux, Mac OS X); Mail.app (Macintosh only) There are other popular email clients (Opera mail, Pegasus, Mozilla SeaMonkey, The Bat!, Eudora etc), but their usage share is relatively low.

(4) Media Players

To play or display any multimedia content (music, video, pictures, drawings, etc.), regardless of origin, your computer needs an application called a media player. Music and videos are commonly downloaded from the Internet, usually for entertainment, news, education, and/or business content.

Most modern operating systems are automatically configured with at least one *standard media player* software package. Third party applications are also available that play formats not normally supported by the standard application set. Such support is usually required for proprietary formats that vendors must license in order to add compatibility to their media player application. These additional applications are usually installed on an as-needed basis - at times even automatically - in order to provide support for the requested multimedia content. Once these applications are installed they may be easily forgotten and overlooked by IT administrators who are responsible for patch management and support, usually because they are not aware of their existence on each deployed system.

Over the past year vulnerabilities have been released for most popular media players available today. While the severity of the vulnerabilities varies, these vulnerabilities can often be used to install malware such as viruses, bot-net applications, root kits, spy-ware, and ad-ware.

While this list does provide a detailed overview of popular media players and their associated vulnerabilities, it does not attempt to be an exhaustive list of all media players and their associated vulnerabilities. Many of these vulnerabilities do have publicly available exploit code and are being actively exploited in the wild.

The media players for the major platforms are: Windows: Windows Media Player, RealPlayer, Apple Quicktime, Adobe Flash Player, Apple iTunes Mac OS: RealPlayer, Apple Quicktime, Apple iTunes, Adobe Flash Player Linux/Unix: RealPlayer, Adobe Flash

1.5.2 Server-side Vulnerabilities in:

(1) Web Applications

Web-based applications such as Content Management Systems (CMS), Wikis, Portals, Bulletin Boards, and Discussion Forums are used by small and large organizations. A large number of organizations also develop and maintain custom-built web applications for their businesses (indeed, in many cases, such applications are the business). Every week hundreds of vulnerabilities are reported in commercially available and open source web applications, and are actively exploited. Please note that the custom-built web applications are also attacked and exploited even though the vulnerabilities in these applications are not reported and tracked by public vulnerability databases such as @RISK, CVE or BugTraq. The number of attempted attacks for some of the large web hosting farms range from hundreds of thousands to even millions every day.

All web frameworks (PHP, .NET, J2EE, Ruby on Rails, ColdFusion, etc.) and all types of web applications are at risk from web application security defects, ranging from insufficient validation through to application logic errors. The most exploited types of vulnerabilities are:

PHP Remote File Include: PHP is the most common web application language and framework in use today. By default, PHP allows file functions to access resources on the Internet using a feature called "allow_url_fopen". When PHP scripts allow user input to influence file names, remote file inclusion can be the result. This attack allows (but is not limited to): Remote code execution Remote root kit installation On Windows, complete system compromise may be possible through the use of PHP's SMB file wrappers SQL Injection: Injections, particularly SQL injections, are common in web applications. Injections are possible due to intermingling of user supplied data within dynamic queries or within poorly constructed stored procedures. SQL injections allow attackers: To create, read, update, or delete any arbitrary data available to the application In the worst case scenario, to completely compromise the database system and systems around it Cross-Site Scripting (XSS): Cross site scripting, better known as XSS, is the most pernicious and easily found web application security issue. XSS allows attackers to deface web sites, insert hostile content, conduct phishing attacks, take over the user's browser using JavaScript malware, and force users to conduct commands not of their own choosing - an attack known as cross-site request forgeries, better known as CSRF. Cross-site request forgeries (CSRF): CSRF forces legitimate users to execute commands without their consent. This type of attack is extremely hard to prevent unless the application is free of cross-site scripting vectors, including DOM injections. With the rise of Ajax techniques, and better knowledge of how to properly exploit XSS attacks, CSRF attacks are becoming extremely sophisticated, both as an active individual attack and as automated worms, such as the Samy MySpace Worm. S1.2 How to Determine If You Are at Risk

Web scanning tools can help find these vulnerabilities, particularly if they are known bugs. However, to find all potential vulnerabilities requires a source code review as well as an application penetration test. These should be done by the developers prior to release of any important web application.

(2) Windows Services

The family of Windows Operating systems supports a wide variety of services, networking methods and technologies. Many of these components are implemented as Service Control Programs (SCP) under the control of Service Control Manager (SCM), which runs as "services.exe". Vulnerabilities in the services that implement these operating system functions are some of the most common avenues for exploitation. When you first install Microsoft Windows Server 2003, Microsoft Windows XP, or Windows Vista some services are installed and configured to run by default whenever the computer is restarted. On Windows Server 2003 the specific services enabled with correspond to the role that is assigned to each server. You may not need all of the default services in your environment, and you should disable any unneeded services to enhance security. A service must log on to access resources and objects in the operating system, and most services are not designed to have their default logon account changed. If you change the default account password, the service will probably fail. If you select an account that does not have permission to log on as a service, the Microsoft Management Console (MMC) Services snap-in automatically grants that account the ability to log on as a service on the computer. However, this automatic configuration does not guarantee that the service will start. Windows Operating Systems include three built-in local accounts that are used as the logon accounts for various system services:

- **Local System account:** The Local System account is a powerful account that has full access to the computer and acts as the computer on the network. If a service uses the Local System account to log on to a domain controller, that service has access to the entire domain. Some services are configured by default to use the Local System account, and this should not be changed. The Local System account does not have a user-accessible password.
- **Local Service accountL:** The Local Service account is a special, built-in account that is similar to an authenticated user account. It has the same level of access to resources and objects as members of the Users group. This limited access helps safeguard your computer if individual services or processes are compromised. Services that use the Local Service account access network resources as a null session with anonymous credentials. The name of this account is NT AUTHORITY\Local Service, and it does not have a user-accessible password.
- **Network Service account:** The Network Service account is also a special, built-in account that is similar to an authenticated user account. Like the Local Service account, it has the same level of access to resources and objects as members of the Users group, which helps safeguard your computer. Services that use the Network Service account access network resources with the credentials of the computer account. The name of the account is NT AUTHORITY\Network Service, and it does not have a user-accessible password.
- **Graphical user interface (GUI):** based tools can help you edit services. However, versions of these tools that were included with earlier versions of the Windows operating system (before Windows Server 2003) automatically apply permissions to each service when you configure any of the properties of a service. Tools such as the Group Policy Object Editor and the MMC Security Templates snap-in use the Security Configuration Editor DLL to apply these permissions. For example, when you use the MMC Security Templates snap-in to configure the startup state of a service in Windows XP, the following dialog box will display:

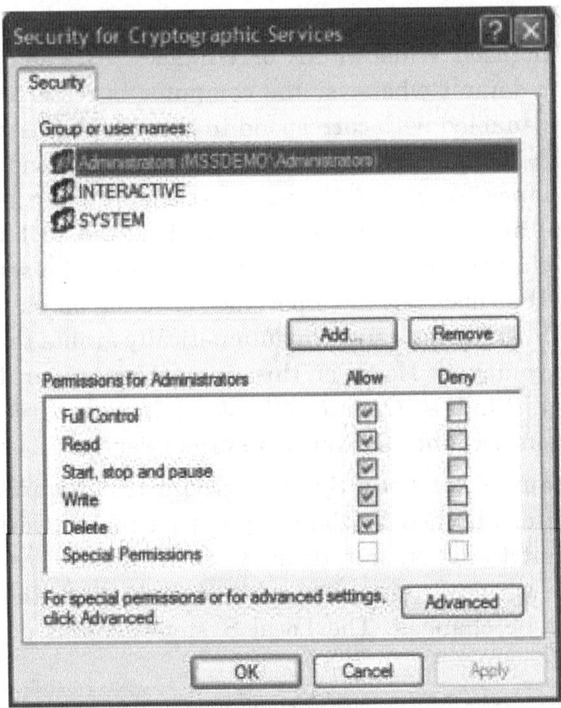

Figure 1.17 Services Security Dialog Box

Regardless of whether you click OK or Cancel, the permissions will be applied to the service that is being configured. Unfortunately, the permissions that this dialog box proposes do not match the default permissions for most services that are included with Windows. In fact, the permissions will cause a variety of problems for many services.

(3) UNIX/Mac OS Services

Most Unix/Linux systems include multiple standard services in their default installation. Mac OS X often suffers from the same vulnerabilities as Unix systems, since it is based on Unix. Unnecessary services should be disabled, and all servers facing open networks should be protected by a firewall.

For services which provide remote login and/or remote service, traffic cannot be simply blocked by firewalls. Buffer overflow vulnerabilities and flaws in authentication functions can often allow a vector for arbitrary code execution, sometimes with administrative privileges, so gathering vulnerability information and patching rapidly are very important. Every year, buffer overflow vulnerabilities in Unix/Linux services are found.

These services, even if fully patched, can be the cause of unintended compromises. Brute-force attacks against remote services such as SSH, FTP, and telnet are still the most common form of attack to compromise servers facing the Internet. Over the last couple of years a concerted effort has been made by attackers to recover passwords used by these applications via brute-force attacks. Increasingly worms and bots have brute-force password engines built into them. Systems with weak passwords for user accounts are actively and routinely compromised; often privilege escalations are used to gain further privileges, and rootkits installed to hide the compromise. It is important to remember that brute forcing passwords can be a used as a technique to compromise even a fully patched system.

Security-conscious administrators should use SSH or another encrypted protocol as their method of interactive remote access. If the version of SSH is current and it is fully patched, the service is generally assumed to be safe. However, regardless of whether it is up to date and patched SSH can still be compromised via brute-force password-guessing attacks. Use public key authentication mechanism for SSH to thwart such attacks. For the other interactive services, audit passwords to ensure they are of sufficient complexity to resist a brute-force attack.

Minimizing the number of running services on a host will also make it more secure. Many services have been used to further exploits and some combinations of services (such as web servers and FTP servers that share published directories) are particularly prone to exploits.

(4) Backup Software

Backup software is an extremely valuable asset for any organization. Backup software typically runs on many systems throughout an enterprise. In recent years, the trend has been to consolidate backup functions onto few servers, or even a single server. The hosts requiring backup services communicate with the backup server via the network. Interaction with the server generally conforms to a push approach, where the client sends data to the server to be backed up, or a pull approach, where the server polls for new data to be backed up from the client, or a combination of these two approaches. During 2007 many critical backup software vulnerabilities were discovered. Since the backup software generally runs with high privileges to read all files on a system, vulnerabilities in backup software have led to severe security vulnerabilities. Some of these vulnerabilities were exploited to completely compromise systems running backup servers and/or backup clients. Attackers leveraged these flaws for enterprise-wide compromise and obtained access to the sensitive backed-up data. Exploits have been publicly posted for many of these flaws, and these vulnerabilities are often exploited in the wild.

The following popular backup software packages have had critical vulnerabilities:

- Computer Associates (CA) BrightStor ARCServe has had dozens of easy-to-exploit vulnerabilities with exploit code widely available.
- Symantec Veritas NetBackup/Backup Exec has had a few recently reported vulnerabilities.
- EMC Legato Networker also has had one publicly reported vulnerability.

Backup data often contains all of, or at least large portions of, the data on a given system. Generally the backup data is stored in a centralized location and is often unencrypted. Physical security of backup media is of the utmost importance, as theft or analysis of backup media can provide complete access to critical data with little or no additional effort. If at all possible, backed up data should be encrypted with strong encryption, and the methods for decryption should be available only to trusted individuals.

(5) Anti-virus Software

Anti-virus software is seen as a required basic tool within the "defense-in-depth" toolbox to protect systems today. Anti-virus software is now installed on almost all desktops, servers and gateways to combat virus outbreaks. During 2007, attackers have shifted their focus to exploit security products used by a large number of end users. This includes anti-virus and personal firewall software. The discovery of vulnerabilities in anti-virus software is not limited to desktop and server platforms: gateway solutions are also affected, and compromising a gateway could cause a much larger impact since the gateway is the outer layer of protection and the only protection against some threats in many small organizations.

Multiple remote code execution vulnerabilities have been discovered in the anti-virus software provided by various vendors including Symantec, F-Secure, Trend Micro, McAfee, Computer Associates, ClamAV and Sophos. These vulnerabilities can be used to take a complete control of the user's system with limited or no user interaction.

Anti-virus software has also been found to be vulnerable to "evasion" attacks. By specially crafting a malicious file (for instance, an HTML file with an executable header) it may be possible to bypass anti-virus scanning. These evasion attacks can be exploited to create a vector for malware propagation, or bypass systems that would otherwise limit malware propagation.

(6) Management Servers

Applications such as on-server virus and spam filters, directory servers, and management and monitoring systems pose a unique security challenge; in addition to opportunities for compromising the system hosting them, they provide opportunities to attack other systems.

These applications can be divided into multiple categories:

- **Directory Servers:** Used to maintain user and system information. Compromising these applications can give access to large amounts of information, including usernames and (possibly encrypted) passwords. * Monitoring Systems - Used to monitor various other systems. These applications often have user accounts on monitored clients, allowing an attacker easy access to client systems.
- **Configuration and Patch Systems:** These systems are used to maintain client configurations and patches. Compromising these systems provides an easy path to further distribute malware.
- **Spam and Virus Scanners:** Vulnerabilities in these systems can often be exploited with little or no user interaction, by simply sending a specially-crafted email message. Once compromised, attackers can more easily send spam and virus-containing emails. Additionally, these systems often contain vital information, such as users' mailboxes. These applications run on a variety of operating systems, including Microsoft Windows, Solaris, HP-UX, Novell Netware, and others.

(7) Database Software

Databases provide the ability to store, search and manipulate large amounts of data. They are key elements of many systems, even though their presence may not be directly visible to users. They are found in many common applications including financial, banking, customer relationship management and system monitoring software.

Due to the valuable information they often store, such as personal and financial details, databases are often a target of attack and are of particular interest to identity thieves. Database systems are often very complex, combining the core database with a collection of applications. Some of these applications are supplied by the database vendor, others (such as web applications) are written by users in house. A flaw in any of these components can compromise the stored data. It is not sufficient to protect the database alone, all the associated applications need to be secured. The most common vulnerabilities in database systems are:

(1) Use of default configurations with default user names and passwords: SQL Injection via the database's own tools, third part applications or web front-ends added by users. Huge numbers of vulnerabilities in this class are announced every year. Use of weak passwords for privileged accounts. Buffer overflows in processes that listen on well known ports. Many different database systems are available. Some of the most common are Microsoft SQL Server (proprietary, runs on Windows), Oracle (proprietary, runs on many platforms), IBM DB2 and IBM Informix (both proprietary, run on multiple platforms), Sybase (proprietary, runs on many platforms), MySQL and PostgreSQL (both open source and available on many platforms).

All modern databases can be accessed over networks, which means that anyone with network access and readily available query tools can attempt to connect directly to the database. The commonly used default connections are: Microsoft SQL via TCP port 1433 and UDP port 1434, Oracle via TCP port 1521, IBM DB2 via ports 523 and 50000 up, IBM Informix via TCP ports 9088 and 9099, Sybase via TCP 4100 or 2025, MySQL via TCP port 3306, and PostgreSQL via TCP port 5432.

Due to the network connections they provide, databases may suffer from worms; there have been examples of worms attacking Microsoft SQL and Oracle.In addition to addressing the specific vulnerabilities mentioned here, administrators concerned with database security should consider:

The impact of standards such as the Payment Card Industry Data Security Standard that may require encryption of some information such as credit card numbers or prohibit the storage of some types of information. The risks of transferring entire databases or large quantities of data onto mobile devices: there have been numerous reports of personal data being lost through the theft of laptops.

1.5.3 Security Policy aand Personnel Vulnerabilities

(1) Excessive User Rights and Unauthorized Devices

Some attacks cannot be effectively prevented by technical controls alone. Unwary users can be enticed to do unsafe things. Clever users can find unsafe ways to get things done, unintentionally exposing their employers to multiple threats. To prevent such threats from exploiting these weaknesses, administrative controls are needed to supplement technical and physical controls.

In time, technical controls may be able to enforce policies that proscribe user behavior; but until this is achieved, periodic reviews are essential in order to ensure that administrative controls are effective. It is also essential to establish a process that will detect these violations and ensure that any non-compliant system is brought back to a state of compliance in an efficient manner.

(*a*) Unauthorized and/or infected devices on network

The best efforts to secure an information system are futile if users connect unauthorized devices to the network or to a computer system. A rogue wireless access point can be an open door to any malicious individual wanting to gain access to the network. A personal laptop connected to a corporate network can introduce whatever malware infecting it onto the network. Unsecured corporate laptops that have been connected to an unsafe public networks will eventually bring back all the malware they have collected to be shared with the entire organization. Thousands of computers have been compromised by attacks where the laptop's owner is specifically targeted in order to infect the laptop with a Trojan horse that "calls home" once it has been connected to the corporate network. This allows an outsider full access into a previously secure network. The same goes for an outsider able to connect an unknown device onto the corporate network, this could simply be a laptop or a higher risk issue like a wireless access point.

Policies must address such issues as rogue devices and infected systems in order to ensure adequate protection of the corporate computing infrastructure, but without verification policies are usually ineffective. Network access control has become an important tool to address such issues. Continuous monitoring of data flows and network connections can immediately identify unauthorized devices. In addition, network access control systems can detect malware as well as ensure that patches and malware signatures are up to date. They can then segregate systems which do not meet the policy and place them in quarantine until they have met corporate standards defined in the policy.

(*b*) Excessive User Rights and Unauthorized software

Unmanaged software introduces multiple risks for the corporation. That software may contain security vulnerabilities, and users may not be sufficiently informed or motivated to apply patches regularly. Furthermore users (or people using their computer without corporate approval like children or spouses) can install software which, without the users' knowledge, contains malware which could lead to a network or data compromise. Users may also install software providing functionality (e.g. peer-to-peer file sharing) that invites new vulnerabilities into the network environment. Those responsible for information security should consider implementing policies, and associated detective and corrective controls, to mitigate such vulnerabilities.

Organizations are vulnerable if users are granted sufficient rights which allow them to install software themselves in an uncontrolled fashion. It can also lead to pirated software being installed on corporate systems which opens another range of issues from a legal perspective. In order to address this, it is essential to enforce a policy of limiting user rights to the least privilege required to perform job related duties. This will in fact eliminate issues relating to malware, potentially unwanted programs and pirated software being installed by the user himself.

(2) Phishing/Spear Phishing

Phishing is a social engineering technique that targets users. While various application add-ons can provide some defense against phishing techniques, all operating systems can be considered equally affected because the attack target is the end user. There is a natural human instinct to trust; phishing attacks attempt to exploit this. While they leverage flaws in browsers, email systems, and DNS, they do so only to enhance the appearance of legitimacy: ultimately it is the end user that is tricked into providing information to the phishers.

(*a*) Online Identity Theft

Identity Theft is the phrase used to describe an action where a person uses the identity of another to fraudulently obtain credit, goods, services, or to commit crimes. Examples of these crimes are bank and credit card fraud, wire fraud, mail fraud, money laundering, bankruptcy fraud and computer crimes. With the advance of the Internet, the traditional fraud schemes became magnified, in particular with Online identity theft crimes.

The word "phishing" was first used around 1996 when hackers began stealing America On-Line accounts by sending email to AOL users, that appeared to come from AOL. Phishing attacks now target users of online banking, payment services such as PayPal, online e-commerce sites, and web-based e-mail sites. Phishing attacks are growing quickly in number and sophistication. In fact, most major banks in the USA, the UK and Australia have been hit with phishing attacks.

(*b*) Spear Phishing

Spear phishing is a highly targeted phishing attack. Spear phishers send e-mails that include information about staff or current organizational issues that make it appear genuine to employees or members within a certain company, government agency, organization, or group. The message may look like it comes from your employer or from a colleague who might send an e-mail message to everyone in the company, such as the head of human resources or the person who manages the computer systems, and could include requests for user names or passwords or tell recipients to download malicious attachments from an infected web site. Spear phishing has become one of the most damaging forms of attacks on military organizations in the US and other developed countries. Attackers gain user name and password information and then break in to ex filtrate sensitive military information.

(*c*) Voice Phishing

A newer form of phishing replaces a web site with a telephone number. In this form of phishing, an email tells you to call a specific number where an audio response unit, at the end of a compromised voice phone line, waits to take your account number, personal identification number, password, or other valuable personal data. The person/audio unit on the other end of the voice phone line might claim that your account will be closed or other problems could occur if you don't respond.

(3) Unencrypted Laptops and Removable Media

Loss of laptops and removable media has become a major liability for corporations and government agencies as well as for general consumers. All too frequently, a major loss of personal or identifying information is traced back to the loss of a single laptop or piece of removable media.

In the past, personal data was stored in paper records or on centralized systems. With growth in computer storage, it is possible to store large amounts of personal information on laptops, desktops, or portable media. This portability places data at a greater risk of loss or compromise, both from mAnita and simple human forgetfulness. Since removable storage devices are designed specifically for portability, they also tend to be easy to lose or misplace.

Since portable storage devices are often shared between machines, they provide a potent vector for malware propagation. Users often share media between enterprise and personal systems, providing an obvious opportunity for viruses and other malware to spread between networks and physical locations. Table 1.1 details the identities exposed by recent laptop loses.

Table 1.1: Identities exposed by recent laptop losses

	Company	IDs exposed by loss of unencrypted device
1	Gap Inc.(San Francisco, CA)	800,000
2	New York City Financial Information Services Agency (New York, NY)	
3	Connecticut Department of Revenue Services (Hartford, CT)	106,000
4	TSA (Arlington, VA)	100,000
5	Yuba County Health and Human Services (Yuba County, CA)	70,000
6	Home Depot (Boston, MA)	10,000
7	Transportation Security Administration (Arlington, VA)	3,930

Every company has some data that must be protected: trade secrets, personally identifying information about employees, human resources and payroll data, sales data, price sheets, contacts, customer databases, and so on. In the absence of active controls that ensure all portable devices and removable media are encrypted and accounted for, some risk of loss is present. Here are questions that can help determine the level of risk:

- What policy is in place regarding moving sensitive data onto removable media or portable computers?
- What encryption is installed and used on laptops, portable computers, and removable storage?
- What controls are in place to track access to sensitive data in order to determine inappropriate data transfer has taken place?
- What controls are in place to make sure all storage devices are shredded (or wiped) so the data is no longer accessible or recoverable when disposed of?

1.5.4 Application Abuse Vulnerabilities

(1) Instant Messaging

Instant messaging (IM) is increasingly being accepted as a legitimate method of communication for both personal and business use. IM applications are available on diverse platforms, ranging from traditional PC-based IM to Mobile IM on Personal Digital Assistants (PDAs) and Cell Phones. This widespread use of instant messaging, while convenient for users, can significantly increase the security risks for both organizations and individual users. Attacks include variants of e-mail worms spread through the use of instant messaging, new variations in the establishment and spread of botnets, and the use of compromised instant messaging accounts to lure users into revealing sensitive information.

The general risk areas related to instant messaging are:

- **Malware** — Worms, viruses, and Trojans transferred through instant messaging. Many bots are controlled via IRC (instant message) channels.
- **Information confidentiality** — Information transferred via instant messaging can be subject to disclosure at several points during the communication. The messages generally pass through networks and servers not under your control. Also, most IM programs now offer file sharing services. The process of file sharing may leave duplicates of confidential documents in shared folders of all participants after the IM session has been terminated.
- **Network** — Denial of service attacks; excessive network capacity utilization, even through legitimate use.
- **Application vulnerabilities** — Instant messaging applications may contain vulnerabilities that can be exploited to compromise affected systems. In addition to the IM application, possible vulnerabilities include errors in supporting software and improper interfaces with modules of supporting software. Some of the IM application functionality may rely on modules from other programs and the underlying operating system, inheriting vulnerabilities present in these programs. In addition, since only specific modules may be called, the security processes built into higher levels of the called support application may be bypassed, creating new attack vectors.

Mobile IM can present significant security risks beyond those associated with PC-based IM. Devices such as cell phones with IM capability often do not have password protection or encryption of locally stored data. The result is that masquerade attacks against e-mail and IM contacts are trivial to implement from lost Mobile IM devices. The wireless nature of mobile devices further complicates implementing proper mobile device security during IM sessions.

Popular instant message applications include: AOL Instant Messenger (AIM), Gaim, ICQ, Jabber Messenger, Lotus Sametime, Skype, QQ, Windows Live Messenger (WLM), Google Talk, Trillian and Yahoo! Messenger. Instant messaging protocols include: IRC, MSNP, OSCAR, SIMPLE, XMPP and YMSG.

(2) Peer to Peer (P2P) File Sharing Applications

Peer to Peer networks consist of collections of computers or "nodes" that simultaneously function as both "clients" and "servers" to achieve a common purpose. The nodes may exchange data, share resources, provide directory services, support communications and provide real time collaboration tools.

Several control and communication architectures are utilized. Centralized index servers can provide directory services for data and service availability. In fully distributed networks each node helps with the indexing and directory services and is fully equivalent. Hybrid architectures combine the features of both to different degrees and groups of nodes may "elect/promote" certain nodes to act as regional index/directory servers.

Many legitimate applications use P2P. Software tool vendors, including Microsoft and Sun, provide a variety of tools and encourage development of P2P applications. However, like any data transfer tool, P2P applications can be misused or exploited to illegally share copyrighted material; obtain confidential data; expose users to unwanted pornography, violence or propaganda; distribute and execute malware (viruses, spyware, bots, etc.); overload the network; mine usage and behavior patterns; and control bots, all of which can create a legal liability. The liability and legal prosecution may not be limited to the perpetrator and may be extended to the network sponsor, supporters or members.

The P2P networks themselves may be attacked by modifying legitimate files with malware, seeding malware files into shared directories, exploiting vulnerabilities in the protocol or errors in coding, blocking (filtering) the protocol, denial of service by making the network function slowly, spamming and identity attacks that identify network users and harass them. Legal action has been successfully used to shut down some popular networks that were culprits of copyright infringement.

The Storm Worm uses eDonkey/Overnet Peer to Peer protocol to communicate with infected hosts. It is estimated to run on as many as 1,000,000 to 50,000,000 infected and compromised computer systems as of September 2007.

P2P concepts and techniques are evolving and can be found in:

- **File sharing networks:** Whose main goal is to share resources such as storage and bandwidth. These operate through a distributed network of clients, sharing directories of files or entire hard drives of data. Clients participate by downloading files from other users, making their data available to others and coordinating file searches for other users.
- **Cloud Computing:** (Also called distributed processing, grid computing, mesh networks) where hundreds or thousands of computers are deployed to provide a virtual computing environment to accomplish a given task by distributing processing load and data. Cloud computing brings servers on-line as needed, and the end user does not know where the data resides or executes at any point. In some cases, the application runs on a combination of servers and on the user's PC. Server clouds can reside physically in large facilities controlled by one organization or they can also reside all over the Internet. Because resizable computing capacity is based on virtual servers the data owner does not really know where his programs and data reside physically. Most of the P2P programs use a set of default ports but they can automatically or manually be set to use different ports if necessary to circumvent detection, firewalls, or egress filters. The trend seems to be moving towards the use of http wrappers and encryption to easily bypass corporate restrictions.

1.5.5 Network Devices: Threats to Network Security

Bad practices when configuring the following aspects of a network can increase the risk of attack.

(1) Insecure Architectures

A misconfigured network is a primary entry point for unauthorized users. Leaving a trust-based, open local network vulnerable to the highly-insecure Internet is much like leaving a door ajar in a crime-ridden neighborhood — nothing may happen for an arbitrary amount of time, but eventually someone exploits the opportunity.

(2) Broadcast Networks

System administrators often fail to realize the importance of networking hardware in their security schemes. Simple hardware such as hubs and routers rely on the broadcast or non-switched principle; that is, whenever a node transmits data across the network to a recipient node, the hub or router sends a broadcast of the data packets until the recipient node receives and processes the data. This method is the most vulnerable to address resolution protocol (arp) or media access control (MAC) address spoofing by both outside intruders and unauthorized users on local hosts.

(3) Centralized Servers

Another potential networking pitfall is the use of centralized computing. A common cost-cutting measure for many businesses is to consolidate all services to a single powerful machine. This can be convenient as it is easier to manage and costs considerably less than multiple-server configurations. However, a centralized server introduces a single point of failure on the network. If the central server is compromised, it may render the network completely useless or worse, prone to data manipulation or theft. In these situations, a central server becomes an open door which allows access to the entire network.

(4) VoIP Servers and Phones

Use of VoIP technologies has continued to expand during the past year. Rapid adoption to garner the economic advantages of VoIP has led many to overlook, or even set aside, security concerns. Vulnerabilities can exist throughout a VoIP network, from mismanaged and unpatched call proxy and media servers to the VoIP phones themselves. Vulnerabilities have been found in products such as Cisco Unified Call Manager and Asterisk, along with VoIP phones from multiple vendors. By leveraging those vulnerabilities, attackers can carry out VoIP phishing scams, eavesdropping, toll fraud, or denial-of-service attacks. Poorly designed implementations can provide inroads to data networks and researchers are continuing to uncover additional areas for potential attack, such as cross site scripting through VoIP clients.

As many VoIP servers — especially the ones at VoIP service providers — are an interface between SS7 (traditional phone signaling) and IP networks, an attacker capable of compromising a vulnerable VoIP server could potentially manipulate the SS7 signaling interconnection to disrupt services on the Public Switched Telephone Network (PSTN).

1.5.6 Zero Day Vulnerabilities

Zero Day Attacks

A zero day vulnerability occurs when a flaw in software code has been discovered and exploits of the flaw appear before a fix or patch is available. Once a working exploit of the vulnerability is released into the wild, users of the affected software will be compromised until a software patch is available or some form of mitigation is taken by the user. Several zero day attacks were recorded in 2007 although that number has dropped from the previous year.

Here are some observations on vunerabilities:

Operating systems have fewer vulnerabilities that can lead to massive Internet worms. For instance, during 2002-2005, Microsoft Windows worms like Blaster, Nachi, Sasser and Zotob infected a large number of systems on the Internet. There have not been any new large-scale worms targeting Windows services since 2005. On the other hand, vulnerabilities found anti-virus, backup or other application software, can result in worms. Most notable was the worm exploiting the Symantec anti-virus buffer overflow flaw last year. We have seen significant growth in the number of client-side vulnerabilities, including vulnerabilities in browsers, in office software, in media players and in other desktop applications. These vulnerabilities are being discovered on multiple operating systems and are being massively exploited in the wild, often to drive recruitment for botnets. Users who are allowed by their employers to browse the Internet have become a source of major security risk for their organizations.

A few years back securing servers and services was seen as the primary task for securing an organization. Today it is equally important, perhaps even more important, to prevent users having their computers compromised via malicious web pages or other client-targeting attacks. Web application vulnerabilities in open-source as well as custom-built applications account for almost half the total number of vulnerabilities being discovered in the past year. These vulnerabilities are being exploited widely to convert trusted web sites into malicious servers serving client-side exploits and phishing scams. The default configurations for many operating systems and services continue to be weak and continue to include default passwords. As a result, many systems have been compromised via dictionary and brute-force password guessing attacks in 2007! Attackers are finding more creative ways to obtain sensitive data from organizations. Therefore, it is now critical to check the nature of any data leaving an organization's boundary.

1.6 SHARE OF DIFFERENT INFORMATION TYPES ON INTERNETWORK

While the Internet has transformed and greatly improved the way we do business, this vast network and its associated technologies have opened the door to an increasing number of security threats from which corporations must protect themselves. Although network attacks are presumably more serious when they are inflicted upon businesses that store sensitive data, such as personal medical or financial records, the consequences of attacks on any entity range from mildly inconvenient to completely debilitating—important data can be lost, privacy can be violated, and several hours, or even days, of network downtime can ensue.

The information flow was Approximately 5,175 petabits per day in 2007, according to IDC.The amount of information transmitted globally over the Internet will continue to double each year over the next five years, according to IDC.

ipoque has analyzed the Internet traffic in five regions of the world between August and September 2007. Comprehensive statistics about user behavior provide a unique overview of the Internet's current state. The major share of information flow is on :

- Peer-to-Peer (P2P) file sharing,
- Internet telephony (VoIP),
- Skype,
- Video streaming,
- Instant Messaging (IM),
- File hosting and Encrypted P2P protocols.

Three petabytes of anonymous data flows (representing over one million users) in Australia, Eastern Europe, Germany, the Middle East and Southern Europe alone. BitTorrent and eDonkey are the most popular P2P networks. Following types of application share the major portion of information flow on internet:

- Video: Movie, Music, Anime, Porn, TV
- Audio: Music, Audio book (aBook)
- Software: Application, Game
- eBook: eBook
- Picture: Porn, Other

P2P is still producing more traffic in the Internet then all other applications combined. Its average proportion during the measurement period regionally varies between 49% in the Middle East and 83% in Eastern Europe.

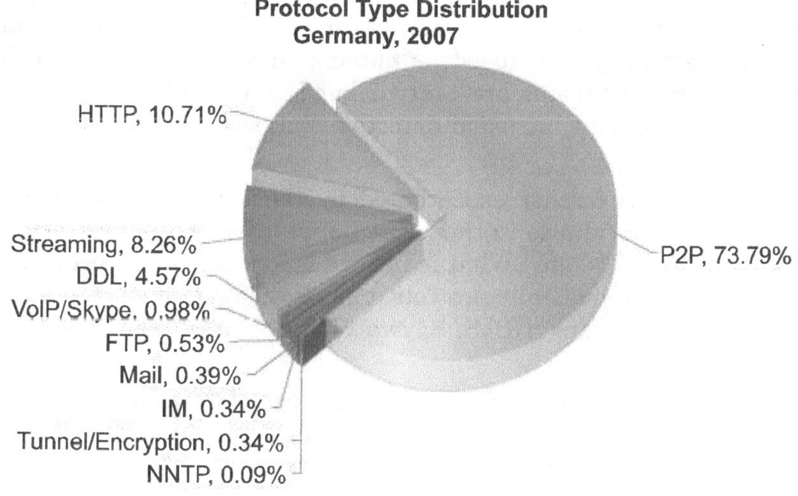

Figure 1.18 Protocol Type Distribution in Internet Traffic

1.6.1 Security Breaches and Threats on Public/Private Networks and Inter-Networks

Despite the costly risks of potential security breaches, the Internet can be one of the safest means by which to conduct business. For example, giving credit card information to a telemarketer over the phone or a waiter in a restaurant can be more risky than submitting the information via a Web site, because electronic commerce transactions are usually protected by security technology.

Waiters and telemarketers are not always monitored or trustworthy. Yet the fear of security problems can be just as harmful to businesses as actual security breaches. General fear and suspicion of computers still exists and with that comes a distrust of the Internet. This distrust can limit the business opportunities for companies, especially those that are completely Web based. Thus, companies must enact security policies and instate safeguards that not only are effective, but are also perceived as effective. Organizations must be able to adequately communicate how they plan to protect their customers.

Small and medium-sized businesses use the Internet and networked applications to reach new customers and serve their existing ones more effectively. At the same time, new security threats and legislation puts increased pressure on business networks to be reliable and secure.

In addition to protecting their customers, corporations must protect their employees and partners from security breaches. The Internet, intranets, and extranets enable fast and effective communication between employees and partners. However, such communication and efficiency can of course be impeded by the effects of a network attack. An attack may directly cause several hours of downtime for employees, and networks must be taken down in order for damage to be repaired or data to be restored. Clearly, loss of precious time and data can greatly impact employee efficiency and morale.

Today's cyber-threat environment is increasingly severe, compounded by the growing number of vulnerabilities that are discovered weekly, the emergence of new types of attacks (e.g., blended threats and Spyware), the shrinking time between vulnerability discovery and exploit development, the propagation speeds of automated worm attacks, and the dissolving network perimeter. IT security teams are overwhelmed and traditional point solutions like firewalls, antivirus software, and intrusion detection systems are inadequate protection by themselves.

The threat landscape is further exacerbated by the challenges involved in applying patches in a timely manner, and also in the case of organizations that cannot enforce patch management (Universities, ISPs, etc.).What is needed is a new type of security element that pervades the network and automatically protects organizations from a broad variety of attack types (e.g., worms, viruses, Trojans, DDoS, Spyware) and from all potential points of attack –inside or out.

Ultimately, security will be embedded within the network fabric, where traffic of all types (e.g., data, voice, video, graphics, fax) is not just routed from source to destination, but delivered with the necessary quality of service, and delivered securely.

Though many companies now use antivirus software, intrusion-detection systems, and firewalls, hackers and worms still infiltrate business-technology systems and cause serious damage. Attacks such as Blaster, MyDoom, and Witty cost businesses more than $10 billion annually.

Legislation is another force that drives the need for network security. Governments recognize both the importance of the Internet and the fact that substantial portions of the world's economic output are dependent on it. However, they also recognize that opening up the world's economic infrastructure to abuse by criminals could cause major economic damage. National governments are therefore developing laws intended to regulate the vast flow of electronic information.

Furthermore, to accommodate the regulations enacted by governments, the computer industry has developed a portfolio of security standards to help to secure data and to prove that it is secure. Businesses that do not have demonstrable security policies to protect their data will be in breach of these standards and penalized accordingly.

It is found that inadequate network security is usually caused by a failure to implement security policies and make use of security tools that are readily available. It's vital that companies complete professional risk assessments and develop comprehensive security plans and infrastructures that are publicly supported by upper management.

According to recent studies, security is the biggest challenge facing small and medium-sized businesses. Ever-changing security threats from both inside and outside the business network can wreak havoc on business operations, affecting profitability and customer satisfaction. Small and medium-sized businesses must also comply with new regulations and laws created to protect consumer privacy and secure electronic information.

1.6.2 Trends affecting information security

In a keynote speech CTO of U.S. managed security services provider Counterpane Internet Security, identified 10 trends affecting information security today.

(1) Information is more valuable than ever. For example, Amazon.com relies on information to make purchasing of books easier through its one-click purchasing system.Information also has value for controlling access, such as single sign-on and authentication for users, and law enforcement, which uses information to help track criminals and gather evidence.

(2) Networks are critical infrastructure. The Internet was not designed to serve as critical infrastructure but noting that hasn't stopped more critical systems from migrating to the Internet.

The Internet helps companies run more efficiently and eases communication between people, but there are real economic risks involved. "If the Net goes down, or part of the Net goes down, it really affects the economy.

(3) Users do not necessarily control information about themselves. For example, ISPs have control over records the Web sites that users visit and e-mail messages they send and receive. Also, some mobile operators keep a copy of users' phone books on their servers. There's a lot of value in information about you, but you have no control over the security of that information, even though it may be highly personal.Managed Security Providers are increase the coverage they give to customers

and their business will grow. Why? Because it's a cost effective way to get security, and because not all organizations will have expertise in-house to deal with the variety of threats and issues.

(4) Hacking is increasingly a criminal profession. Hacking is no longer for hobbyists. More and more, attacks are organized and led by criminals who are driven by a profit motive. The nature of the attacks is changing because the adversary is changing. Extortion related to denial-of-service attacks and phishing attacks are two examples of criminal attacks. In addition, there is a black market for exploits that allow attackers to penetrate corporate IT systems.

(5) Complexity is net user's enemy. As systems get more complex they get less secure. The Internet is the most complex machine ever built. Advances in security technology simply have not kept pace with the Internet's growth.Security is getting better, but complexity is getting worse faster.

(6) Attacks are faster than patches. New vulnerabilities and exploits are being discovered faster than vendors can patch them. In other cases, vulnerabilities in some embedded systems, such as Cisco routers, cannot be patched, leaving companies vulnerable.

(7) Worms are more sophisticated than ever. They already contain vulnerability assessment tools, and are scanning corporate defenses for weaknesses and using Google for intelligence gathering. This trend is a result of more worms being criminal.

(8) The endpoint is the weakest link. It doesn't matter how good your authentication schemes are if the remote computer isn't trustworthy. In many cases, computers outside user's security are the weakest link. These computers are often infected with worms and spyware, presenting an opportunity for attackers.

(9) End users are seen as threats. It's also useful to test the security of your network from the inside.There are a wide range of statistics available that indicate a high proportion of network attacks come from employees. This can be achieved by giving penetration testers a realistic amount of inside knowledge and network access, and then discovering what kind of trouble they can get into.Companies are increasingly developing software that is intended to defend against the end user forexample digital rights management (DRM) software as an example. More and more we're seeing security that doesn't protect the user, but protects against the user.In at least one case, involving DRM software installed by Sony without users' permission, the software caused damage to the end user's computer. "Rules and regulation around this is going to be a big battleground.Schneier said, predicting that a battle will be fought between PC software that is protecting the user and software that is designed to protect against the user.

(10) Regulations will drive security audits. There's no shortage of regulations that detail how companies should handle data. Regulations such as the Sarbanes-Oxley Act will be the driving force behind corporate security audits.

In 2008, the majority of malicious code attacks targeted applications, not operating systems. This fact combined with growing focus on cybersecurity will force software companies to embrace secure software development efforts such as the Open Web Application Security Project (OWASP) or the SANS Software Security Institute. Ironically, Microsoft and its Pro

Network partners like Security Innovation are best positioned to bring secure software development best practices to the masses.

1.7 TYPES OF ATTACKS

1.7.1 Broad Categories Security Threats

General security threats fall into four broad categories:

- Loss of use.
- Loss of performance.
- Disclosure of information.
- Loss of integrity.

(1) **Loss of Use :** This type of loss can affect both equipment and data. It can result from such causes as theft, vandalism, fire, and natural catastrophes, such as earthquakes and floods. Data on magnetic media is particularly susceptible to accidental or deliberate corruption or erasure by magnetic fields, and data on disk can be lost due to head crashes. Regardless of cause, this type of loss is characterized by the inability to use the property. This is usually accompanied by the need to spend funds to replace it.

(2) **Loss of Performance :** This type of loss can result from such causes as simple wear and tear, incorrect usage, and sabotage. The loss is characterized by a decrease in operating efficiency, and may go on for some time before being discovered.

(3) **Disclosure of Information :** This type of loss may result from accident, theft or simple mistakes. The types of information involved can range from business records to scientific and military data. The loss is generally characterized by a loss of some economic, scientific, or military advantage.

(4) **Loss of Integrity :** Integrity constitutes a loss of quality or trust in data resulting from incorrect or malicious modification.

Often, they are used in combination. Behavioral threats, more commonly known as social engineering, are designed to get you to install malicious software (malware), or to reveal personal information. Malware generally provides unauthorized access to and use of your computer. Revealing personal information such as account numbers or your social security number can lead to fraud and identity theft. Listed below are brief descriptions of common social engineering techniques and different types of malware.

1.7.2 Classification by Environment

There are essentially two types of threats:

- Behavioral and
- Software.

1.7.3 Classification by Action type

- Passive Attacks

- Active Attacks
- Deliberate Attacks on Network

(1) Passive Attacks

Passive Attack is an attempt to steal information stored in a system by electronic eavesdropping (wiretapping) or similar means. Although, in contrast to active attack, passive attack does not attempt to interfere with the stored data, it may still constitute a criminal offense.

- Primarily listening to traffic
- Auth. Users can eavesdrop on line
- Tap into patch panels
- Intercept microwave transmissions
- Tap lines to phone co.
- Capture electromagnetic emissions
- Fiber optic prevents most opportunities

(2) Active Attacks

Active attack is an act of persistent attempt to introduce invalid data into a system, and/or to damage or destroy data already stored in it. In many countries, it is a criminal offense to attempt any such action. See also denial of service attack and passive attack.

- Read stored data
- Modify data in storage or during transmission
- Disrupt service

Difference between Active attacks and Passive attacks

An attack can take place on any of the communications link. For an active attack, the attacker needs to gain physical control of a portion of the link and be able to insert and capture transmissions (medium could be telephone twisted pair, coaxial cable, or optical fiber). For a passive attack, the attacker merely needs to be able to observe transmissions (may be inductive taps).

(3) Deliberate Attacks on Network

These are discussed in detail in section 1.9 below.

1.7.4 Information Cracking Attacks

There are three types of crack attacks:

- Dictionary attacks
- Brute force attacks
- Hybrid attacks

(a) Dictionary Attacks

If dictionary words are allowed as passwords, they can be readily broken, even when encrypted. That's because software has been created that gives the intruder the ability to take an entire dictionary's worth of words, run it through various encryption algorithms, and compare the results with the encrypted password file. If a match is found to the password hash, the cracker works backswords to discover what the password is. Simply put, dictionary words offer no protection at all as passwords. If you are thinking of using foreign words, forget it. Even Klingon dictionaries have been hashed for use with password crackers running dictionary attacks.

A dictionary attack consists of trying "every word in the dictionary" as a possible password for an encrypted message.A dictionary attack is generally more efficient than a brute force attack, because users typically choose poor passwords.Dictionary attacks are generally far less successful against systems that use passphrases instead of passwords.

Improving Dictionary Attacks

There are two methods of improving the success of a dictionary attack:

- The first method of improving the success of a dictionary attack is to use a larger dictionary, or more dictionaries. Technical dictionaries and foreign language dictionaries will increase the overall chance of discovering the correct password.
- The second method of improving the success of a dictionary attack is to perform string manipulation on the dictionary. For example, the dictionary may have the word "password" in it. Common string manipulation techniques will try the word backwards (drowssap), with common number-letter replacements (p4ssw0rd), or with different capitalization (Password).

Of course, very small dictionaries may lead to the fastest success, if one or more of the targets is encrypted with a very weak password. A short list of girls names can yield amazing results. A dictionary of potential passwords is more accurately known as a **wordlist**.

If the dictionary attack fails...If an extensive dictionary attack fails, it may be worthwhile to resort to a brute force attack. A brute force attack is more certain to achieve results eventually than a dictionary attack.

(b) Brute-force Attacks

A brute force attack tries every possible combination of letter, number, and punctuation value and format. A brute force attack will always succeed in cracking a password hash. However, depending on the strength of the password, the hashing formula, and the speed of the computer, it could take many years to crack some passwords. Most criminals want quick results.A brute force attack consists of trying every possible code, combination, or password until you find the right one.

Determining the Difficulty of a Brute Force Attack

The difficulty of a brute force attack depends on several factors, such as:

- How long can the key be?
- How many possible values can each component of the key have?
- How long will it take to attempt each key? Is there a mechanism which will lock the attacker out after a number of failed attempts?

As an example, imagine a system which only allows 4 digit PIN codes. This means that there are a maximum of 10,000 possible PIN combinations. Increasing Security Against a Brute Force AttackFrom the example above, PIN security could be increased by:

- Increasing the length of the PIN Allowing the PIN to contain characters other than numbers, such as * or # Imposing a 30 second delay between failed authentication attempts
- Locking the account after 5 failed authentication attempts A brute force attack will always succeed, eventually. However, brute force attacks against systems with sufficiently long key sizes may require billions of years to complete

Brute Force Attacks vs. Dictionary Attacks

In most cases, a dictionary attack will work more quickly than a brute force attack. A brute force attack is, however, more certain to achieve results eventually than a dictionary attack.

(c) Hybrid Attacks

Hybrid attacks build on dictionary attacks by adding or substituting other characters or numbers for certain letters in dictionary words. Many people perform a simple substitution, or prepend or append a character to a dictionary word to create a password (e.g., J0hn23). These passwords can be cracked fairly quickly with software designed to make the same types of substitutions.

In 1999 a distinct trend was seen in the hybridisation of viruses.The term has been widened to include attacks where there's the ability of a particular attack tool to insert malicious code into a server and make that server in turn attack clients. It's equivalent to what hackers may have had five years ago as a personal skill set, and it's transferred into software-automated attack tools.

Hybrid threats are also known by other terms, for example security vendor Symantec refers to them as blended threats. According to information provided by Symantec, these threats are characterised by the fact they're multi-faceted in their operating methods and effects.

Blended threats require comprehensive security solutions that provide multiple layers of defence and response, with triggers to pre-determined responses when threats are encountered.Comprehensive security solutions include the ability to secure all levels within the IT infrastructure (gateway, server and client) as well as the ability to apply complementary security functions in a synergistic fashion.

Symantec sees one of the most dangerous characteristics of a blended threat being that it exploits vulnerabilities, for example unauthorised administrative access to servers such as opening up the information stored on the server at the root level. Exploiting known vulnerabilities such as buffer overflows, http input validation vulnerabilities and known default passwords are other threats the vendor cites.

Examples of ways automated attacks could be set up are by trying to bypass a firewall, exploiting open services on a Web server, or weaknesses in the way mail protocols are set up. The bigger picture enterprises have to look at includes worst case scenarios—what the impact would be if their business was hit by a hybrid attack. There could be a financial impact if systems are taken offline, for example if the company is an e-commerce operator. There also may be the PR issue of having to explain what happened to partners and users.

1.7.5 Classification Based on Services

Innumerable types of network attacks have been documented, and they are commonly classified in three general categories:

- Reconnaissance attacks,
- Access attacks
- Denial of Service (DoS) attacks.

Reconnaissance attacks are essentially information gathering activities by which hackers collect data that is used to later compromise networks. Usually, software tools, such as sniffers and scanners, are used to map out network resources and exploit potential weaknesses in the targeted networks, hosts, and applications. For example, software exists that is specifically designed to crack passwords. Such software was created for network administrators to assist employees who have forgotten their passwords or to determine the passwords of employees who have left the company without telling anyone what their passwords were. Placed in the wrong hands, however, this software can become a very dangerous weapon.

Access attacks are conducted to exploit vulnerabilities in such network areas as authentication services and File Transfer Protocol (FTP) functionality in order to gain entry to e-mail accounts, databases, and other confidential information.

DOS attacks prevent access to part or all of a computer system. They are usually achieved by sending large amounts of jumbled or otherwise unmanageable data to a machine that is connected to a corporate network or the Internet, blocking legitimate traffic from getting through. Even more malicious is a Distributed Denial of Service attack (DDoS) in which the attacker compromises multiple machines or hosts.

1.7.6 Email Based Network Security Attacks

The fact that email is used as a means to access the very heart of a network explains why it is so popular as a means for network security attacks.Email has been broken pretty much from the beginning of the commercial Internet. That we have gone for more than a decade with such a broken system at the core of the Internet I find quite baffling. But, whatever the whys and wherefores, it is a fact.As a network manager you've got to deal with the world as it exists now, not how it should be. Of all the network security attacks I deal with, email is by far the biggest time waster. I suspect that I am far from alone.

The main network security attack that can be perpetrated via email is to use email as a vehicle by which worms can be carried into the very heart of your network. How else can a cracker have their software executed on, potentially, thousands of machines behind all of the perimeter defences erected by a company?

1.7.7 Wireless Specific Network Security Attacks

Wireless networks differ from fixed networks in many ways. From a security perspective the biggest difference is that a fixed network has a well defined boundary. If you mount a good defence on the boundary of your network, the chances are you are going to be OK.A wireless network doesn't provide such an easily defined boundary. The boundary of your wireless network could be miles away from where you think it is. There are techniques for reducing the size of your boundary,but it will be time consuming and expensive to guarantee that the boundary stays within your office.

So, for most installations, it is a given that the boundary of your network is not inside your building. It is the external boundary problem that makes wireless security more problematic than wired security.

With modern directional aerials it is possible to pick up wireless networks from as far away as four miles.The recent (20.02.09) attacks perpetrated against SCO over the past month or two hasn't happened in isolation. In order for such a huge denial of service (DoS) attack to take place, literally thousands of networks worldwide must have been compromised. The people who perpetrate such attacks don't use their own bandwidth. Using your own network would mean that they'd be caught pretty quickly. It doesn't take long to tie an IP address to a name and address.

1.7.8 Unknown Security Attacks

With every new advance in computing and communications, some malicious hacker finds new ways to exploit that technology for gain or mischief.

New hardware or software releases present a new opportunity. Peer-to-peer networking and Internet Messaging (IM) were still relatively new applications when their users were attacked by malicious code written specifically for them. Mobile phones are now targets of viruses. No one knows what's coming next, but the best defense is one that will be able to easily adapt to future threats without breaking the bank.

1.7.9 Web Based Attacks

1.7.9.1 Anatomy of a Web attack

We begin by looking at the overall anatomy of a typical Web based attack. The diagram illustrates the three distinct phases of activity which together make up a typical Web based attack.

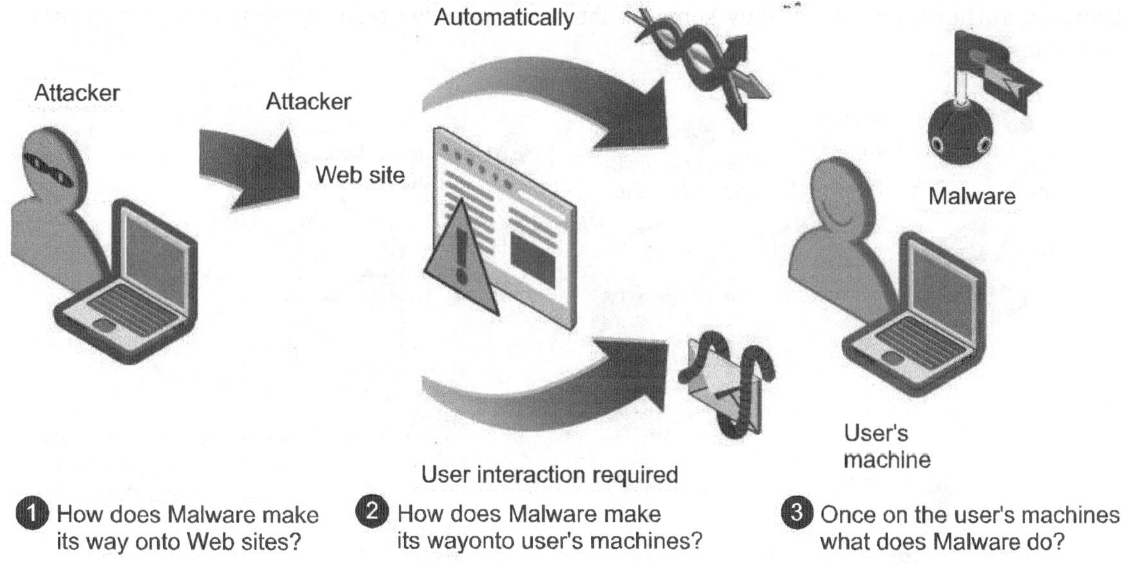

Figure 1.19 Anatomy of a web Attack

Many different flavors of Web based attacks were observed but in general each followed the same basic sequence of events leading from attacker to victim:

1. Attacker breaks into a legitimate Web site and posts malware

Malware is no longer exclusive to malicious Web sites. Today it is common place for legitimate mainstream Web sites to act as parasitic hosts that serve up malware to their unsuspecting visitors. Sections 1.7.9.4 and 1.7.9.5 examine the complexity of modern Web sites and the common techniques by which they are compromised.

2. Attacking enduser machines

Malware on a Web site makes its way down on to a user's machine when that user visits the host Web site. Section 3 details some of the techniques which enable this to happen automatically with no user interaction required – often called a 'drive-by-download'.

3. Leveraging end user machines for malicious activity

The most malicious activities begin once new malware has established a presence on a user's machine.

1.7.9.2 How Do Web Sites get infected?

Throughout 2008, Symantec observed a high number of legitimate Web sites being compromised and inconspicuously repurposed to serve Web attacks to their unknowing Web site visitors. In this section, we examine why legitimate sites have become targets for malware authors, and we review some of the more popular techniques used to compromise such sites.

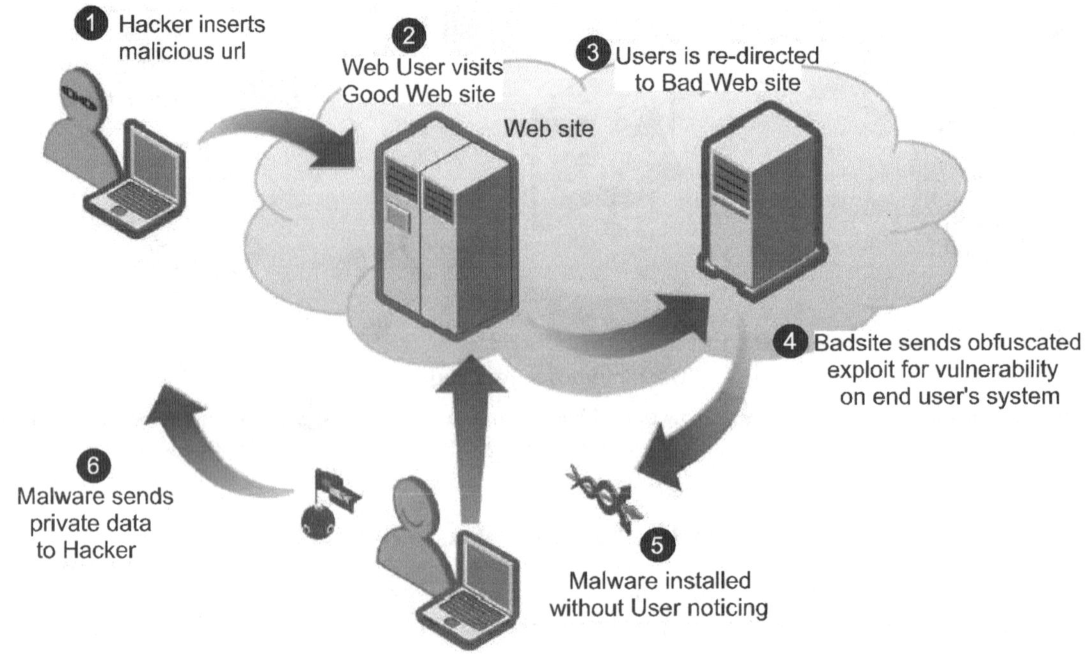

Figure 1.20 Web Site getting attacked

1.7.9.3 Why target mainstream Web Sites?

It used to be that attempts to install malware on a user's computer via the Web typically came from the darker corners of the Internet. By targeting Web sites that promote illicit activity such as adult material or pirated software, malware authors knew they could find a plentiful supply of users more focused on their short term needs than on cautiously evaluating what they were downloading to their computer.

Today, malware authors are looking for wider targets. Few Web sites are immune from being compromised and used as a host to deliver malware to their unsuspecting visitors. Mainstream Web sites provide a large base of users for malware authors to target.

Perhaps more significantly, they provide a set of users who are less likely to be concerned about being the victim of a malware attack because they hold the belief that if they only surf to mainstream Web Sites, they will be safe.

In 2008, Symantec observed Web attacks from 808,000 unique domains, many of which are mainstream Web sites, including: news, travel, online retail, games, real estate, government and many others. Unfortunately, the notion of being safe if one only visits good sites no longer holds true.

1.7.9.4 The Complexity of Modern Web sites

It seems that each new year brings with it a new media type to be served up to users via the Web. This, along with the ever increasing complexity of computing functions that now happen on the Web, means that today's Web servers have evolved into very complex pieces of code. When you visit a Web site, you are not going to a single static page, but a combination of many different Web content sources, dynamically constructed using many different scripting technologies, plug-in components, and databases.

These pieces must all communicate with each other, typically over a network which potentially exposes weaknesses that can be probed and attacked. Furthermore, some of the content for a site may come from an entirely different site under a third-parties' control. Consider how advertisements are displayed on most Web sites. Such advertisements are sourced or displayed from third party hosting sites where the Web site administrator has little, if any, control over which ads get displayed on their Web site. It is not uncommon for a Web site to have ten (10) or twenty (20) different domains from which Web site content is pulled to make up one single Web page that a user views!

The task of keeping such Web servers secure has not kept up with the growth and the complexity of building out a Web site. As a result, more and more Web sites are vulnerable to attack.

1.7.9.5 How are legitimate Web sites compromised?

There are many different attack vectors through which good sites may find themselves exposed. Over the course of 2008, we observed numerous instances of the following attack techniques:

1. SQL Injection Attacks
2. Malicious Advertisements
3. Search Engine Result Redirection
4. Attacks on the backend virtual hosting companies
5. Vulnerabilities in the Web server or forum hosting software
6. C ross-site scripting (XSS) attacks

The following sections examine a couple of the more popular techniques we continue to observe in everyday use today.

(1) SQL Injection Attacks

Today many Web sites, particularly larger, high-traffic Web sites, serve up content that is dynamically constructed from information held in databases. As users interact with such sites, information is read from and written to the database. As a result of this, the task of securing the Web site must extend to the databases themselves, as well as the data that is stored within them.

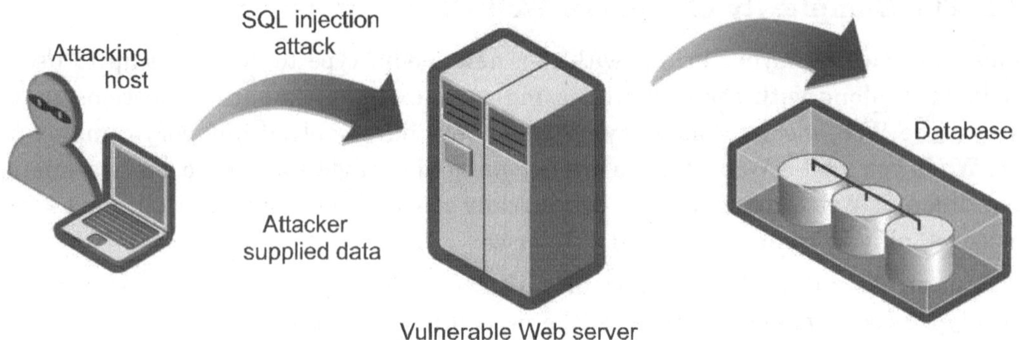

Figure 1.21 SQL Injection Attack

One popular type of attack involves compromising the database using a technique known as SQL injection. This technique works by finding flaws in Web sites that have databases running behind them. In many cases a poorly validated input field in a Web input form (e.g. a login form or an account query form) will allow an attacker to insert (or inject) additional SQL instructions which may then be passed directly into the backend database. With some trial and error probing, this technique provides attackers with the layout of the database, and given this data, they can add their own malicious content to be later served up to unsuspecting users of the compromised site. Typically, this added content contains hidden links to a malicious Web site that has already been set up to serve malware attacks to the unsuspecting user's computer using a variety of browser based exploits.

One very popular piece of malware we have observed, called Trojan.Asprox, automates this type of attack lifecycle. The first component of Trojan.Asprox uses popular search engines to find potentially vulnerable Web pages. It then attacks these sites using the SQL injection technique.

The automated attack continually tests successive Web sites until it finds one with a vulnerable input field and then inserts malicious HTML code directly into the database. Typically, this malicious HTML code is in the form of HTML tags like IFRAMES which point to malicious script code or malicious pages. IFRAMES are HTML tags which makes it possible to embed an HTML page inside another HTML page. The following illustrates what an inserted hidden IFRAME might look like.

```
<html>
<head>
        <title>This is my home page</title>
</head>
<body>
        <p>This is my home page</p>
<if rame src='                    ' width='1'height='1' style='visibility: hidden:'>
</if rame>
</body>

</html>
```

When this page is requested by an unsuspecting victim, the Web server fetches data from the compromised database in the process of constructing the Web page and serves this malicious code (in red above) to the victim. If the browser or its plug-ins are vulnerable, the victim's browser starts executing malicious code referred by the malicious IFRAME.

(2) Malicious advertisements (Malvertisements)

Symantec has observed an increase in the use of malicious advertisements as an effective method for attacking users of legitimate Web sites by delivering the attack through one of the many ad content providers supplying content to the legitimate Web site –not directly from the Web site itself. Many Web sites today display advertisements hosted by third-party advertising sites. Reputable advertising companies validate the ads they serve in order to check for attacks. However, due to both the sheer volume of online ads published every day and the automated nature of the publishing mechanisms, it is inevitable that some malicious ad content slips through and is inadvertently hosted on entirely legitimate Web sites. Compounding the problem is the fact that a single malicious advertisement may only appear once every 1,000 page views or only to viewers from a certain geographic region, thus making it more challenging to detect and eradicate.

Many of these ads are authored using a scripting language called JavaScript. Functions in this scripting language can easily be misused to silently redirect the user to a malicious page. As a result, although the hosting Web site is itself clean, the ad on the Web site may redirect the user to a malicious page hosting Web attacks. In the past year, we have observed such malicious ads on many legitimate Web sites of reputable brands.

In one example we found, visitors to a popular real estate Web site reported occasional protection alerts from their endpoint security software. Users who were not running endpoint security software noted pop-ups and system slow-downs. Clearly there was something amiss. When administrators of the Web site investigated the problem, they were unable to find any security issues. However, when security researchers took a closer look, they found the Web site contained occasional malicious advertisements that would automatically infect the user. The Web site included hundreds of different ads that rotated based on the search parameters and/or the end-user's geography; this made the attack initially difficult to detect.

(3) Getting onto a user's computer (Part 1 – Automatically)

In this section we look at techniques used to automatically deliver malware content from Web sites on to a user's computer.

The drive-by download

One of the most insidious forms of malware infection today is known as a "drive-by download." Just by browsing to a Web site allows executable content to be automatically downloaded onto a user's computer without their knowledge or permission. No user interaction is required.

The figure 1.22 illustrates the typical sequence of events that take place in a successful drive-by download. We see many examples like this every day.

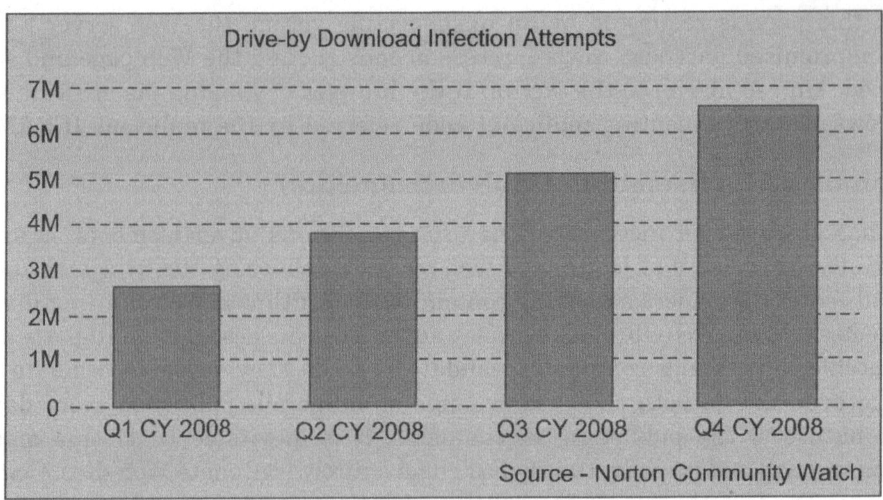

Figure 1.22 Drive-by Download Infection Attempts

(1) Attacker compromises a legitimate 'good' Web site

The attack begins with an attacker who has found a way into a 'good' Web site. In the previous section we outlined some of the common techniques by which this happens, such as a SQL injection attack. The attacker is able to insert a hidden IFRAME into one or more of the pages on the legitimate Web site. This link points to a separate malicious Web site where the actual malicious code will be served up to the unsuspecting user.

(2) User visits the 'good' Web site

The user, who keeps their computer updated with Windows Update (to ensure the base operating system and browser on their machine have all the latest software patches) visits the compromised 'good' site. Unfortunately, the multimedia plug-ins and document viewers running on their system (on which listen to music and view documents) is out of date, and unbeknownst to them, have vulnerabilities that can be remotely compromised.

(3) User is silently redirected to the 'bad' Web site

The hidden IFRAME from the page on the 'good' site causes the user's browser to silently pull content from the 'bad' Web site.

As it does so, the 'bad' site is able to determine what operating system, Web browser and vulnerable plug-ins are running on the user's computer. From this, the bad site determines that the user is running a vulnerable multimedia plug-in attached to their browser.

(4) Malicious code is downloaded to the user

The bad Web site sends specially crafted multimedia data that contains an attack to the victim's computer; once this content has been played by the multimedia player, the attacker has gained control of the computer.

(5) Malicious code is installed on the user's computer

Leveraging the vulnerability present in the user's multimedia player, one or more malware files are installed on the user's computer.

(6) Malicious software takes advantage of the user's system

The malicious code now steals personal information (e.g., online banking information, email, gaming passwords) and sends it back to the attacker. The entire attack is usually invisible to the victim and leaves no apparent clues to indicate that the computer has been compromised.

1.8 SECURE COMMUNICATION

Suppose Anita and Bunty are two friends who want to communicate securely. This needs to be a networking text and these two may be taken as routers that want to securely exchange routing tables, two hosts that want to establish a secured transport connection, or two email applications that want to exchange secure e-mail: Anita (or Alice) and Bunty (or Bob) are the example fixtures. Illicit love affairs, wartime communications and business transactions are the common society needs for secure communications. Anita and Bunty are *sender* and *receiver* in all of such examples through out in this text, although most of other authors use the name Alice and Bob.

We said that Anita and Bunty want to communicate "securely," but what precisely does this mean? Certainly, Anita wants only Bunty to be able to understand a message that she has sent, even though they are communicating over an "insecure" medium where an intruder (Trudy, the intruder) may intercept, read, and perform computations on whatever is transmitted from Anita to Bunty. Bunty also wants to be sure that the message that he receives from Anita was indeed sent by Anita, and Anita wants to make sure that the person with whom she is communicating is indeed Bunty. Anita and Bunty also want to make sure that the contents of Anita's message have not been altered in transit. Given these considerations, we can identify the following desirable properties of secure communication:

- **Secrecy.** Only the sender and intended receiver should be able to understand the contents of the transmitted message. Because eavesdroppers may intercept the message, this necessarily requires that the message be somehow encrypted (disguise data) so that an intercepted message can not be decrypted (understood) by an interceptor. This aspect of secrecy is probably the most commonly perceived meaning of the term "secure communication." Note, however, that this is not only a restricted definition of secure communication (we list additional aspects of secure communication below), but a rather restricted definition of secrecy as well. For example, Anita might also want the mere fact that she is communicating with Bunty (or the timing or frequency of her communications) to be a secret! We will study cryptographic techniques for encrypting and decrypting data in next lesson.
- **Authentication.** Both the sender and receiver need to confirm the identity of other party involved in the communication - to confirm that the other party is indeed who or what they claim to be. Face-to-face human communication solves this problem easily by visual recognition. When communicating entities exchange messages over a medium where they can not "see" the other party, authentication is not so simple. Why, for instance, should

you believe that a received email containing a text string saying that the email came from a friend of yours indeed came from that friend?

- **Message Integrity.** Even if the sender and receiver are able to authenticate each other, they also want to insure that the content of their communication is not altered, either malicously or by accident, in transmission. Extensions to the checksumming techniques that we encountered in reliable transport and data link protocols will also be studied in section 6.5; these techniques also rely on cryptographic concepts in section 5.1.

Having established what we mean by secure communication, let us next consider exactly what is meant by an "insecure channel." What information does an intruder have access to, and what actions can be taken on the transmitted data? Figure 1.23 illustrates the scenario.

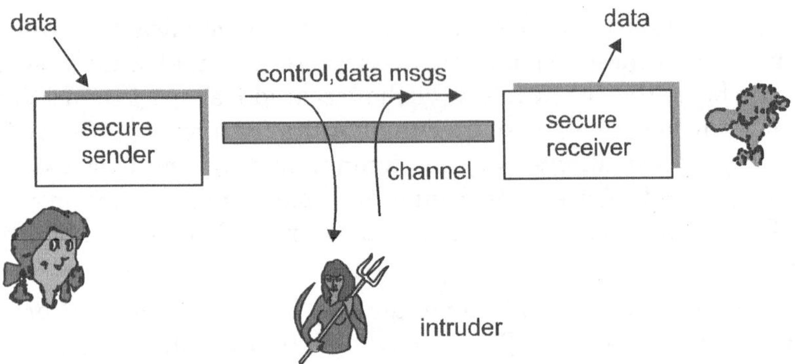

Figure 1.23 Sender, Receiver and Intruder (Anita, Bunty, and Trudy)

Anita, the sender, wants to send data to Bunty, the receiver. In order to securely exchange data, while meeting the requirements of secrecy, authentication, and message integrity, Anita and Bunty will exchange both control message and data messages (in much the same way that TCP senders and receivers exchange both control segments and data segments). All, or some of these message will typically be encrypted. A passive intruder can listen to and record the control and data messages on the channel; an active intruder can remove messages from the channel and/or itself add messages into the channel.

1.9 NETWORK SECURITY CONSIDERATIONS IN THE INTERNET

Before delving into the technical aspects of network security in the following sections, let's conclude our introduction by relating our fictitious characters - Anita, Bunty, and Trudy - to "real world" scenarios in today's Internet.

Let's begin with Trudy, the network intruder. Can a "real world" network intruder really listen to and record network messages? Is it easy to do so? Can an intruder actively inject or remove messages from the network? The answer to all of these questions is an emphatic "YES." A packet sniffer is a program running in a network attached device that passively receives all data-link-layer frames passing by the device's network interface. In a broadcast environment such as an Ethernet LAN, this means that the packet sniffer receives all frames being transmitted from or to all hosts on the local area network. Any host with an Ethernet card can easily serve as a packet sniffer, as the Ethernet interface card needs only be set to "promiscuous mode" to receive all passing Ethernet frames. These frames can then be passed on to application programs that extract application-level data. For example, in the telnet scenario shown in Figure 1.24, the login password prompt sent from A to B, as well as the password entered at B are "sniffed" at host C. Packet sniffing is a double-edged sword - it can be invaluable to a network administrator for network monitoring and management but also used by the unethical hacker. Packet-sniffing software is freely available at various WWW sites, and as commercial products. Professors teaching a networking course have been known to assign lab exercises that involve writing a packet-sniffing and application-level-data-reconstruction program.

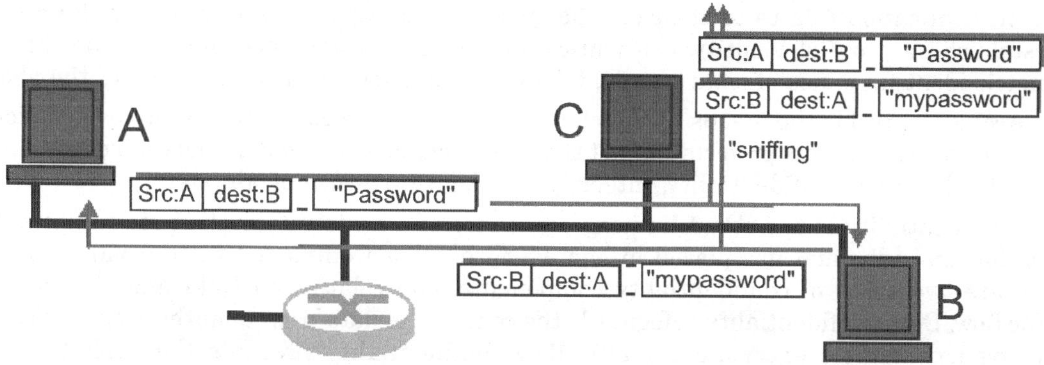

Figure 1.24 Telnet Scenario Example

Any Internet-connected device (e.g., a host) necessarily sends IP datagrams into the network. These datagrams carry the sender's IP address, as well as application-layer data. A user with complete control over that device's software (in particular its operating system) can easily modify the device's protocols to place an arbitrary IP address into a datagram's source address field. This is known as IP spoofing. A user can thus craft an IP packet containing any payload (application-level) data it desires and make it appear as if that data was sent from an arbitrary IP host. Packet sniffing and IP spoofing are just two of the more common forms of security "attacks" on the Internet.

Having established that there are indeed real bogeymen (a.k.a. "Trudy") loose in the Internet, what are the Internet equivalents of Anita and Bunty, our two friends who need to communicate securely? Certainly, "Bunty" and "Anita" might be human user at two end systems, e.g., a real Anita and a real Bunty who really do want to exchange secure email. (e.g., a user wanting to enter a credit card in a WWW form for an electronic purchase). They might also be participants in an electronic commerce transaction, e.g., a real Anita might want to securely transfer her credit card number to a WWW server to purchase an item on-line. Similarly, a real Anita might want to interact with her back on-line. As noted in [RFC 1636], however, the parties needing secure communication might also themselves be part of the network infrastructure. Recall that the domain name system, or routing daemons that exchange routing tables require secure communication between two parties. The same is true for network management applications, a topic we examine in the following chapter. An intruder that could actively interfere with, control, or corrupt DNS lookups and updates, routing computations, or network management functions could wreak havoc in the Internet.

1.10 SECURITY SERVICES

Security over the Internet is mainly concerned with securing communications in and out of a particular site. There have been many frameworks used to describe the security aspects of systems, the following is one used by ISO 7498-2. There are five main security services:

(1) Authentication
(2) Access Control
(3) Confidentiality
(4) Integrity, and
(5) Non-repudiation.

Authentication relates to ensuring that users and computers are who they claim to be by establishing proof of identity. Authentication can be accomplished for example through biometric identifiers, use of smart cards, tokens, or password or a combination of the above.

Access Control is the means by which the ability to use a computer resource is explicitly enabled or restricted. This protects against the unauthorised use and manipulation of resources. This should protect confidentiality, integrity and legitimate use of a system.

Confidentiality is the act of limiting disclosure of private information maintaining the trust that an individual has placed in one which has been entrusted with private matters. There are two types of confidentiality components, one relating to Data and the other to Traffic flow. Data confidentiality safeguards the contents of data from unauthorised disclosure, by using for example encryption. Traffic flow confidentiality prevents the exploitation of information relating to traffic flow, by again using encryption or traffic padding.

Integrity is the property that information is changed only in specified and authorised manner. There are several components to integrity, these are data integrity, program integrity, system integrity, and network integrity. Data integrity refers to the accuracy, consistency and completeness of data. Program integrity refers to the quality of the software design and protection against changes. System integrity is the capability of an automated system to perform its intended function in an unimpaired manner, free from deliberate or inadvertent unauthorised manipulation. Network integrity extends system integrity to networks.

Non-repudiation assures that information and/or actions that purport to be from (or purport not to be from) a user or system are as claimed. In other words, it provides evidence to prevent a person from unilaterally modifying or terminating obligations arising out of a transaction effected by computer-based means.

Having identified the relevant security threats to a system, the system operator can apply various security services and mechanisms to confront these threats and implement a desired security policy. In this section a general description of such services and techniques is provided. The science behind these methods is researched and developed as part of the broad discipline of Cryptography. Cryptography embodies the mathematical principles, means, and methods for the transformation of data in order to hide its information content, prevent its undetected modification, and/or prevent its unauthorized use. Cryptographic functions may be used as part of encipherment, decipherment, data integrity, authentication exchanges, password storage and checking, etc. to help achieve confidentiality, integrity, and/or authentication.

The following subsections summarize some key security services and mechanisms.

1.10.1 Encipherment and Data Confidentiality

Encipherment is a security mechanism that involves the transformation of data into some unreadable form. Its purpose is to ensure privacy by keeping the information hidden from anyone for whom it is not intended, even those who can see enciphered data. Decipherment is the reverse of encipherment. That is, it is the transformation of encrypted data back into some intelligible form. Encipherment which is performed on cleartext (intelligible data) to produce ciphertext (encrypted data whose semantic content is not available). The result of decipherment is either cleartext, or ciphertext under some cover.

Encipherment can provide confidentiality of either data or traffic flow information and can play a part in, or complement other security mechanisms.

Encipherment and Decipherment require the use of some secret information, usually referred to as a key, which directs specific transformations. This is one of two cryptovariables used: The other is the initialization variable, which is sometimes required to preserve the apparent randomness of ciphertext.

Encipherment techniques can be symmetric or secret key, where knowledge of the encipherment key implies knowledge of the private decipherment key and vice versa, or asymmetric. In asymmetric algorithms, generally one key is called public (because it is publicly available), while the other is called private (because it is kept secret). Once a private key has been compromised, the system (or at least the use of that private key) is no longer secure. Both encipherment techniques are used to provide the data confidentiality service.

Modern cryptographic systems also provides mechanisms for authentication, for instance through digital signatures that bind a document to the possessor of a specific key, or digital timestamps which bind a document to its creation at a given time. In general the existence of an encipherment mechanism implies the use of a key management mechanism.

1.10.2 Public Key Cryptography

Figure 1.25 illustrates a simple public key cryptographic system that provides data confidentiality. When Anita wishes to send a secret message to Bunty, she looks up Bunty's public key in a directory, uses it to encrypt the message, and sends it off. Bunty then uses his private key to decrypt the message and read it. No one listening in can decrypt the message. Anyone can send Bunty an encrypted message but only Bunty can read it. Clearly one requirement is that no one can figure out the private key from the corresponding public key.

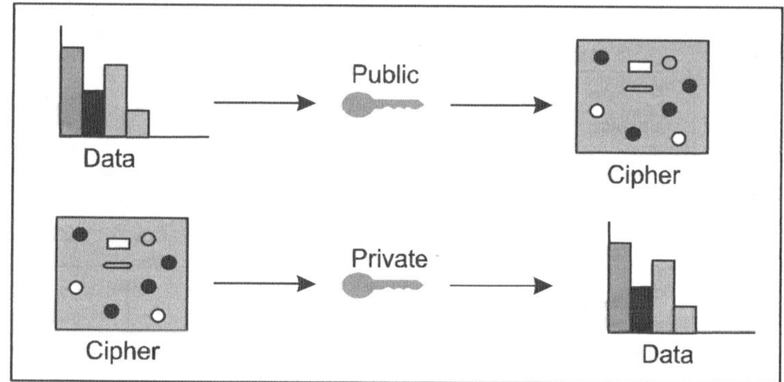

Figure 1.25 A Public Key Cryptographic System (PKCS)

1.10.3 Digital Signatures

Digital signature is the process of binding some information (e.g., a document) to its originator (e.g., the signer).

The essential characteristic of a digital signature is that the signed data unit cannot be created without using the private key. This means that:

(1) The signed data unit cannot be created by any individual except the holder of the private key.

(2) The recipient cannot create the signed data unit.

(3) The sender cannot deny sending the signed data unit.

Therefore, using only publicly available information-the public key-it is possible to identify the signer of a data unit as the possessor of the private key. It is also possible to prove the identity of the signer of the data unit to a reliable third party in case of later conflict.

Thus, a digital signature attests to the contents of a message, as well as to the identity of the signer. As long as a secure hash function (a function that is easy to compute in one direction than the opposite direction) is used, one cannot take away a person's signature from one document and transpose it on another one, or alter a signed message in any way. The slightest change in a digitally signed document will cause the digital signature verification process to fail. However, if a signature verification fails, it is in general difficult to determine whether there was an attempted forgery or simply a transmission error.

In short, a digital signature mechanism involves the two procedures of signing a data unit, and verifying the signed data unit. The former process uses information which is private (i.e. unique and confidential) to the signer. The second process uses procedures and information which are publicly available but from which the signer's private information cannot be deduced.

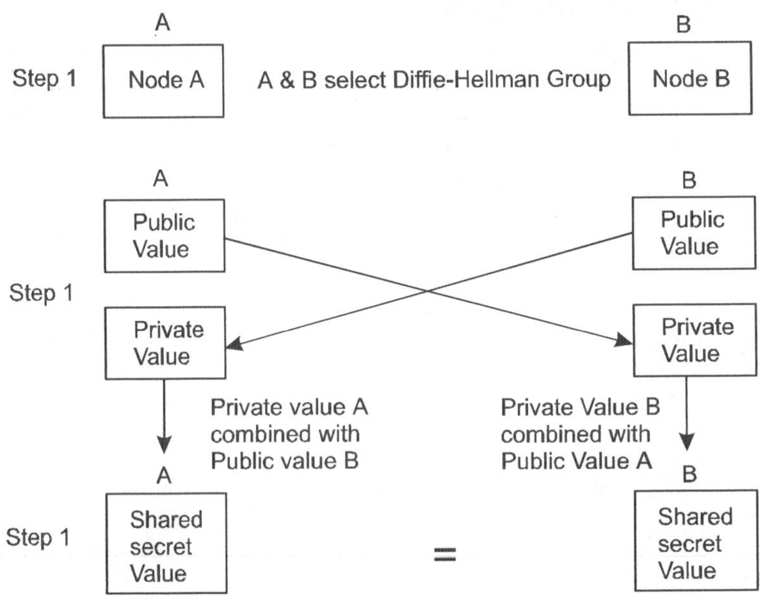

Figure 1.26 A Digital Signature Mechanism 1#1

Figure 1.26 illustrates a digital signature mechanism. To sign a message, Anita appends the information she wishes to send to an enciphered summary of the information. The summary is produced by means of a one-way hash function (h), while the enciphering is carried out using Anita's secret key (E). Thus the message sent to Bunty is of the form:

```
X{info} = info + Xs[h(info)]
```

The encipherment using the secret key ensures that the signature cannot be forged. The one-way nature of the hash function ensures that false information, generated so as to have the same hash result (and thus signature), cannot be substituted.

In his turn, upon receipt of Anita's message, Bunty verifies the signature by applying the one-way hash function to the information, and comparing the result with that obtained by deciphering the signature using the public key of Anita. If these two are the same, it is verified that Anita is the "true" sender of the message. It should be clear and imperative that for the authentication to be performed correctly, both Anita and Bunty must be using the same hash function.

1.11 SECURITY MECHANISMS

In order to address the security services there are a number of mechanisms used. The main security mechanisms used are, Encryption, Digital signatures, Access Control, Data integrity checks, Authentication Exchange, Traffic Padding, Routing Control and Notarisation.

(1) *Encryption* is the process of converting data to a form that appears to bear no relation to the original data. In a multi-user setting, encryption allows secure communication over an insecure channel such as the Internet. There are two types of encryption systems. The first known as *symmetric* (also traditional or secret key) uses the same key to code and decode the data. The second known as *asymmetric* (or public-key) use a pair of keys, one public and the other private. The public and private keys differ in such a way that it is computationally infeasible to determine the private key from the public key. This allows the public key to be revealed without endangering the private key. This methods supports security services such as authentication, confidentiality, data integrity and non-repudiation. In practice however, public key systems such as RSA are combined with a secret key cryptosystem such as DES to encrypt a message by means of an RSA digital envelope.

(2) *Digital signatures* are a means to guarantee the authenticity of a set of input data in the same way as a written signature verifies the authenticity of a paper document. That is, digital signatures provide a means by which a message can be authenticated as having been sent by a particular originator. This mechanism uses encryption to achieve a unique electronic signature for each user. Digital signatures address the issues of authentication and non-repudiation.

(3) *Access Control* is a process that ensures that a person or system has the permission to use a particular computer resource. Such controls may be built into the operating system, they could be incorporated into application programs or major utilities (such as communication systems and DBMS) or may be implemented through add on security packages. Access Control can be applied at either end of the communication path and at the intermediate points. A method of access control is the use of firewalls.

(4) *Data Integrity Checks* include mechanisms such as parity checks and the use of automatically generated block checksums. This requires that both the originator and the receiver compare check sequences to verify that the data has not been modified.

(5) *Authentication Exchange* is a dialogue between a claimant and a verifier, to assure the verifier of the claimant's identity. This may operate between the sender and the receiver in the case of mutual authentication and between the sender, the receiver and a third party in the case of third party authentication.

(6) *Traffic Padding* is a mechanism that disguises data characteristics to provide protection against traffic analysis. This mechanism can include the padding of messages and the generation of dummy messages in order to disguise traffic.

(7) *Routing Control* enables messages to flow through different routes over a network hence making the complete message difficult to trace and identify.

(8) *Notarisation* is the use of a third party that is trusted by the communication entities. The notary can arbitrate between the communicating entities. One example of the use of such a mechanism is in the third party validation of digital signatures.

1.12 SECURITY SERVICES

The following are considered to be the security services which can be provided optionally within the framework of the OSI Reference Model. The authentication services require authentication information comprising locally stored information and data that is transferred (credentials) to facilitate the authentication.

1.12.1 Authentication

These services provide for the authentication of a communicating peer entity and the source of data as described below.

1.12.1.1 Peer Entity Authentication

This service, when provided by the (N)-layer, provides corroboration to the **(N + 1)**-entity that the peer entity is the claimed **(N + 1)**-entity.This service is provided for use at the establishment of, or at times during, the data transfer phase of a connection to confirm the identities of one or more of the entities connected to one or more of the other entities. This service provides confidence, at the time of usage only, that an entity is not attempting a masquerade or an unauthorized replay of a previous connection. One-way and mutual peer entity authentication schemes, with or without a liveness check, are possible and can provide varying degrees of protection.

1.12.1.2 Data Origin Authentication

This service, when provided by the (N)-layer, provides corroboration to an (N + 1)-entity that the source of the data is the claimed peer (N + 1)-entity.

The data origin authentication service provides the corroboration of the source of a data unit. The service does not provide protection against duplication or modification of data units.

1.12.2 Access Control

This service provides protection against unauthorized use of resources accessible via OSI. These may be OSI or non-OSI resources accessed via OSI protocols. This protection service may be applied to various types of access to a resource (e.g., the use of a communications resource; the reading, the writing, or the deletion of an information resource; the execution of a processing resource) or to all accesses to a resource. The control of access will be in accordance with various security policies.

1.12.3 Data Confidentiality

These services provide for the protection of data from unauthorized disclosure as described below.

Recommendation X.800 9

1.12.3.1 Connection confidentiality

This service provides for the confidentiality of all (N)-user-data on an (N)-connection.

✍ **Note** – Depending on use and layer, it may not be appropriate to protect all data, e.g. expedited data or data in a connection request.

1.12.3.2 Connectionless confidentiality

This service provides for the confidentiality of all (N)-user-data in a single connectionless (N)-SDU.

1.12.3.3 Selective field confidentiality

This service provides for the confidentiality of selected fields within the (N)-user-data on an (N)-connection or in a single connectionless (N)-SDU.

1.12.3.4 Traffic flow confidentiality

This service provides for the protection of the information which might be derived from observation of traffic flows.

1.12.4 Data integrity

These services counter active threats and may take one of the forms described below.

✍ **Note** – On a connection, the use of the peer entity authentication service at the start of the connection and the data integrity service during the life of the connection can jointly provide for the corroboration of the source of all data units transfered on the connection, the integrity of those data units, and may additionally provide for the detection of duplication of data units, e.g. by the use of sequence numbers.

1.12.4.1 Connection integrity with recovery

This service provides for the integrity of all (N)-user-data on an (N)-connection and detects any modification, insertion, deletion or replay of any data within an entire SDU sequence (with recovery attempted).

Contd....

1.12.4.2

Connection integrity without recovery As for § 1.12.4.1 but with no recovery attempted.

1.12.4.3 Selective field connection integrity

This service provides for the integrity of selected fields within the (N)-user data of an (N)-SDU transferred over a connection and takes the form of determination of whether the selected fields have been modified, inserted, deleted or replayed.

1.12.4.4 Connectionless integrityx

This service, when provided by the (N)-layer, provides integrity assurance to the requesting (N + 1)-entity. This service provides for the integrity of a single connectionless SDU and may take the form of determination of whether a received SDU has been modified. Additionally, a limited form of detection of replay may be provided.

1.12.4.5 Selective field connectionless integrity

This service provides for the integrity of selected fields within a single connectionless SDU and takes the form of determination of whether the selected fields have been modified.

1.12.5 Non-repudiation

This service may take one or both of two forms.

1.12.1.121 Non-repudiation with proof of origin

The recipient of data is provided with proof of the origin of data. This will protect against any attempt by the sender to falsely deny sending the data or its contents.

1.12.1.12 Non-repudiation with proof of delivery

The sender of data is provided with proof of delivery of data. This will protect against any subsequent attempt by the recipient to falsely deny receiving the data or its contents.

1.13 SPECIFIC SECURITY MECHANISMS

The following mechanisms may be incorporated into the appropriate (N)-layer in order to provide some of the services described in § 1.12.

1.13.1 Encipherment

1.13.1.1 Encipherment can provide confidentiality of either data or traffic flow information and can play a part in or complement a number of other security mechanisms as described in the following sections.

Contd....

1.13.1.2 Encipherment algorithms may be reversible or irreversible. There are two general classifications of reversible encipherment algorithm:

(a) symmetric (i.e. secret key) encipherment, in which knowledge of the encipherment key implies knowledge of the decipherment key and vice versa; and

(b) asymmetric (e.g. public key) encipherment, in which knowledge of the encipherment key does not imply knowledge of the decipherment key, or vice versa. The two keys of such a system are sometimes referred to as the "public key" and the "private key".

Irreversible encipherment algorithms may or may not use a key. When they use a key, this key may be public or secret.

1.13.1.3 The existence of an encipherment mechanism implies the use of a key management mechanism except in the case of some irreversible encipherment algorithms.

1.13.2 Digital signature mechanisms

These mechanisms define two procedures:

(a) signing a data unit, and

(b) verifying a signed data unit.

The first process uses information which is private (i.e. unique and confidential) to the signer. The second process uses procedures and information which are publicly available but from which the signer's private information cannot be deduced.

1.13.2.1 The signing process involves either an encipherment of the data unit or the production of a cryptographic checkvalue of the data unit, using the signer's private information as a private key.

1.13.2.2 The verification process involves using the public procedures and information to determine whether the signature was produced with the signer's private information.

1.13.2.3 The essential characteristic of the signature mechanism is that the signature can only be produced using the signer's private information. Thus when the signature is verified, it can subsequently be proven to a third party (e.g. a judge or arbitrator) at any time that only the unique holder of the private information could have produced the signature.

Recommendation X.800 11

1.13.3 Access Control Mechanisms

1.13.3.1 Access control mechanisms are those mechanisms which are used to enforce a policy of limiting access to a resource to only those users who are authorized. Techniques include the use of access control lists or matrices (which usually contain the identities of controlled items and authorized users e.g. people or processes), passwords, and capabilities, labels or tokens, the possession of which may be used to indicate access rights. Where capabilities are used, they should be unforceable and should be conveyed in a trusted manner.

Contd....

These mechanisms may use the authenticated identity of an entity or information about the entity (such as membership in a known set of entities) or capabilities of the entity, in order to determine and enforce the access rights of the entity. If the entity attempts to use an unauthorized resource, or an authorized resource with an improper type of access, then the access control function will reject the attempt and may additionally report the incident for the purposes of generating an alarm and/or recording it as part of a security audit trail. Any notification to the sender of a denial of access for a connectionless data transmission can be provided only as a result of access controls imposed at the origin.

1.13.3.2 Access Control Mechanisms

Access control mechanisms may, for example, be based on use of one or more of the following:

(a) Acess control information bases, where the access rights of peer entities are maintained. This information may be maintained by authorization centres or by the entity being accessed, and may be in the form of an access control list or matrix of hierarchical or distributed structure. This presupposes that peer entity authentication has been assured.

(b) Authentication information such as passwords, possession and subsequent presentation of which is evidence of the accessing entity's authorization;

(c) Capabilities, possession and subsequent presentation of which is evidence of the right to access the entity or resource defined by the capability.

Note – A capability should be unforceable and should be conveyed in a trusted manner.

(d) Security labels, which when associated with an entity may be used to grant or deny access, usually according to a security policy.

(e) Time of attempted access.

(f) Route of attempted access, and

(g) Duration of access.

1.13.3.3 Access control mechanisms may be applied at either end of a communications association and/or at any intermediate point.

Access controls involved at the origin or any intermediate point are used to determine whether the sender is authorized to communicate with the recipient and/or to use the required communications resources.

The requirements of the peer level access control mechanisms at the destination end of a connectionless data transmission must be known a priori at the origin, and must be recorded in the security management information base

1.13.4 Data Integrity Mechanisms

1.13.4.1 Two aspects of data integrity are: the integrity of a single data unit or field; and the integrity of a stream of data units or fields. In general, different mechanisms are used to

Contd....

provide these two types of integrity service, although provision of the second without the first is not practical.

1.13.4.2 Determining the integrity of a single data unit involves two processes, one at the sending entity and one at the receiving entity. The sending entity appends to a data unit a quantity which is a function of the data itself. This quantity may be supplementary information such as a block check code or a cryptographic checkvalue and may itself be enciphered. The receiving entity generates a corresponding quantity and compares it with the received quantity to determine whether the data has been modified in transit. This mechanism alone will not protect against the replay of a single data unit. In appropriate layers of the architecture, detection of manipulation may lead to recovery action (for example, via retransmissions or error correction) at that or a higher layer.

1.13.4.3 For connection-mode data transfer, protecting the integrity of a sequence of data units (i.e. protecting against misordering, losing, replaying and inserting or modifying data) requires additionally some form of explicit ordering such as sequence numbering, time stamping, or cryptographic chaining.

1.13.4.4 For connectionless data transmission, time stamping may be used to provide a limited form of protection against replay of individual data units.

1.13.5 Authentication exchange mechanism

1.13.5.1

Some of the techniques which may be applied to authentication exchanges are:

(a) use of authentication information, such as passwords supplied by a sending entity and checked by the receiving entity;

(b) cryptographic techniques; and

(c) use of characteristics and/or possessions of the entity.

1.13.5.1.2 The mechanisms may be incorporated into the (N)-layer in order to provide peer entity authentication. If the mechanism does not succeed in authenticating the entity, this will result in rejection or termination of the connection and may also cause an entry in the security audit trail and/or a report to a security management centre.

1.13.5.1.3 When cryptographic techniques are used, they may be combined with "handshaking" protocols to protect against replay (i.e. to ensure liveness).

1.13.5.1.4 The choices of authentication exchange techniques will depend upon the circumstances in which they will need to be used with:

(a) time stamping and synchronized clocks;

(b) two and three way handshakes (for unilateral and mutual authentication respectively); and

(c) non-repudiation services achieved by digital signature and/or notarization mechanisms.

Contd....

1.13.6 Traffic padding mechanism

Traffic padding mechanisms can be used to provide various levels of protection against traffic analysis. This mechanism can be effective only if the traffic padding is protected by a confidentiality service.

1.13.7 Routing Control mechanism

1.13.7.1 Routes can be chosen either dynamically or by prearrangement so as to use only physically secure subnetworks, relays or links.

1.13.7.2 End-systems may, on detection of persistent manipulation attacks, wish to instruct the network service provider to establish a connection via a different route.

1.13.7.3 Data carrying certain security labels may be forbidden by the security policy to pass through certain subnetworks, relays or links. Also the initiator of a connection (or the sender of a connectionless data unit) may specify routing caveats which request that specific sub-networks, links or relays be avoided.

1.13.8 Notarization mechanism

1.13.8.1 Properties about the data communicated between two or more entities, such as its integrity, origin, time and destination, can be assured by the provision of a notarization mechanism. The assurance is provided by a third party notary, which is trusted by the communicating entities, and which holds the necessary information to provide the required assurance in a testifiable manner. Each instance of communication may use digital signature, encipherment, and integrity mechanisms as appropriate to the service being provided by the notary. When such a notarization mechanism is invoked, the data is communicated between the communicating entities via the protected instances of communication and the notary.

1.14 PERVASIVE SECURITY MECHANISMS

This subsection describes a number of mechanisms which are not specific to any particular service. Thus, in § 7, they are not explicitly described as being in any particular layer. Some of these pervasive security mechanisms can be regarded as aspects of security management. The importance of these mechanisms is, in general, directly related to the level of security required.

1.14.1 Trusted functionality

1.14.1.1 Trusted functionality may be used to extend the scope, or to establish the effectiveness, of other security mechanisms. Any functionality which directly provides, or provides access to, security mechanisms, should be trustworthy.

1.14.1.2 The procedures used to ensure that trust may be placed in such hardware and software are outside the scope of this Recommendation and, in any case, vary with the level of perceived threat and value of information to be protected.

Contd....

1.14.1.3 These procedures are, in general, costly and difficult to implement. The problems can be minimized by choosing an architecture which permits implementation of security functions in modules which can be made separate from, and provided from, non-security-related functions.

1.14.1.4 Any protection of associations above the layer at which the protection is applied must be provided by other means, e.g. by appropriate trusted functionality.

1.14.2 Security labels

1.14.2.1 Resources including data items, may have security labels associated with them, e.g. to indicate a sensitivity level. It is often necessary to convey the appropriate security label with data in transit. A security label may be additional data associated with the data transferred or may be implicit, e.g. implied by the use of a specific key to encipher data or implied by the context of the data such as the source or route. Explicit security labels must be clearly identifiable in order that they can be appropriately checked. In addition they must be securely bound to the data with which they are associated.

1.14.3 Event detection

1.14.3.1 Security-relevant event detection includes the detection of apparent violations of security and may also include detection of "normal" events, such as a successful access (or log on). Security-relevant events may be detected by entities within OSI including security mechanisms. The specification of what constitutes an event is maintained by event handling management (see § 8.3.1). Detection of various security-relevant events may, for example, cause one or more of the following actions:

(a) Aces

(a) local reporting of the event;

(b) remote reporting of the event;

(c) logging the event (see § 1.14.3); and

(d) recovery action (see § 1.14.4)

Examples of such security-relevant events are:

(a) a specific security violation;

(b) a specific selected event; and

(c) an overflow on a count of a number of occurrences.

1.14.3.2 Standardization in this field will take into consideration the transmission of relevant information for event reporting and event logging, and the syntactic and semantic definition to be used for the transmission of event reporting and event logging.

1.14.4 Security audit trail

1.14.4.1 Security audit trails provide a valuable security mechanism as potentially they permit detection and investigation of breaches of security by permitting a subsequent security audit. A security audit is an independent review and examination of system records and

Contd....

activities in order to test for adequacy of system controls, to ensure compliance with established policy and operational procedures, to aid in damage assessment, and to recommend any indicated changes in controls, policy and procedures. A security audit requires the recording of security-relevant information in a security audit trail, and the analysis and reporting of information from the security audit trail. The logging or recording is considered to be a security mechanism and is described in this section. The analysis and report generation is considered a security management function (see § 8.3.2).

1.14.4.2 Collection of security audit trail information may be adapted to various requirements by specifying the kind(s) of security-relevant events to be recorded (e.g. apparent security violations or completion of successful operations). The known existence of a security audit trail may serve as a deterrent to some potential sources of security attacks.

1.14.4.3 OSI security audit trail considerations will take into account what information shall optionally be logged, under what conditions that information shall be logged, and the syntactic and semantic definition to be used for the interchange of the security audit trail information.

1.14.5 Security recovery

1.14.5.1 Security recovery deals with requests from mechanisms such as event handling and management functions, and takes recovery actions as the result of applying a set of rules. These recovery actions may be of three kinds:

(a) immediate;

(b) temporary; and

(c) long term.

For example:

(*a*) Immediate actions may create an immediate abort of operations, like disconnection.

(*b*) Temporary actions may produce temporary invalidation of an entity.

(*c*) Long term actions may be an introduction of an entity into a "black list" or the changing of a key.

1.14.5.2 Subjects for standardization include protocols for recovery actions and for security recovery management.

1.15 ILLUSTRATION OF RELATIONSHIP OF SECURITY SERVICES AND MECHANISMS

Table 1.1 illustrates which mechanisms, alone or in combination with others, are considered to be sometimes appropriate for the provision of each service. This table presents an overview of these relationships and is not definitive. The services and mechanisms referred to in this table are described in §§ 1.12 and 1.13.

Table 1.2 : Illustration of relationship of security services and mechanisms

Mechanism / Service	Encipherment	Digital signature	Access control	Data integrity	Authenn-cation exchange	Traffic padding	Routing control	Notari-zation
Peer entry authentication	Y	Y	.	.	Y	.	.	.
Data ongm authentication	Y	Y	.	.	.	.	.	.
Access control service	.	.	Y	.	.	.	.	.
Connection confidentiality	Y	.	.	.	.	.	Y	.
Connectionless confidentiality	Y	.	.	.	.	.	Y	.
Selective field confidentiality	Y	.	.	.	.	.	.	.
Traffic flow confidentiality	Y	.	.	.	.	Y	Y	.
Connection Integrity with recovery	Y	.	.	Y	.	.	.	.
Connection integrity without recovery	Y	.	.	Y	.	.	.	.
Selective field connection integrity	Y	.	.	Y	.	.	.	.
Connectionless integrity	Y	Y	.	Y	.	.	.	.
Selective field connectionless integrity	Y	Y	.	Y	.	.	.	.
Non-repudration. Origin	.	Y	.	Y	.	.	.	.
Non-repudiation. Delivery	.	Y	.	Y	.	.	.	.

Y Yes: the mechanism is considered to be appropiate, either on its own or in combination with other mechanisms.

The mechanism is considered not to be appropriate.

Note – In some instances, the mechanism provides more than is necessary for the relevant service but could nevertheless be used.

1.16 THE RELATIONSHIP OF SERVICES, MECHANISMS AND LAYERS

1.16.1 Security Layering Principles

1.16.1.1

The following principles were used in order to determine the allocation of security services to layers and the consequent placement of security mechanisms in the layers:

(a) the number of alternative ways of achieving a service should be minimized;

(b) it is acceptable to build secure systems by providing security services in more than one layer;

(c) additional functionality required for security should not unnecessarily duplicate the existing OSI functions;

(d) violation of layer independence should be avoided;

REFERENCES

1. Boscia and Shaw, "NASA Advanced Supercomputing Division: Wireless Firewall Gateway White Paper", http://www.nas.nasa.gov/Groups/Networks/Projects/Wireless/, September 3, 2004.
2. Cisco Systems, Inc. "A Comprehensive Review of 802.11 Wireless LAN Security and the Cisco Wireless Security Suite", http://www.cisco.com/warp/public/cc/pd/witc/ao1200ap/prodlit/wswpf_wp.pdf, 2002.
3. The Honeynet Project, "Know Your Enemy: Sebek", http://www.securitydocs.com/library/2769, December 10, 2004.
4. Karygiannis and Owens, "Wireless Network Security 802.11, Bluetooth and Handheld Devices", http://csrc.nist.gov/publications/nistpubs/800-48/NIST_SP_800-48.pdf.
5. Vladimirov, Gavrilenko, Mikhailovsky. Wi-Foo: The Secrets of Wireless Hacking. Boston: Addison-Wesley, 2004
6. WarDriving, http://www.worldwidewardrive.org
7. Webopedia, http://www.webopedia.com
8. "Wireless Security Recommendations for Rutgers",http://techdir.rutgers.edu/wireless.html, November 3, 2003.
9. Rec. X.200 – Reference Model of open systems interconnection for CCITT applications.
10. ISO 7498 – Information processing systems – Open systems interconnection – Basic Reference Model (1984).
11. ISO 7498-4 – Information processing systems – Open systems interconnection – Basic Reference Model –Part 4 : Management framework (1989).
12. ISO 7498/AD1 – Information processing systems – Open systems interconnection – Basic Reference Model –Addendum 1: Connectionless-mode transmission (1987).
13. ISO 8648 – Information processing systems – Open systems interconnection – Internal organization of the network layer (1988).
14. Teare, Diane (July 1999). 'Designing Cisco Networks'. Indianapolis: Cisco Press. http://www.cisco.com/en/US/tech/tk1330/tsd_technology_support_technical_reference_chapter09186a0080759781.html.
15. M. Blaze, W. Diffie, R. Rivest, B. Schneier, T. Shimomura, E. Thompson, and M. Weiner, "Minimal Key Lengths for Symmetric Ciphers to Provide Adequate Commercial Security," http://www.counterpane.com/keylength.html.

16. W. Diffie and S. Landau, Privacy on the Line, The Politics of Wiretapping and Encryption, MIT Press, 1998.
17. [EFF 1999] Electronic Frontier Foundation, "Cracking DES," http://www.eff.org/DEScracker.
18. [FIPS-46-1] US National Bureau of Standards, "Data Encryption Standard", Federal Information Processing Standard (FIPS) Publication 46-1, January 1988.
19. D. Kahn, The Codebreakers, the Story of Secret Writing, The Macmillan Company, 1967.
20. C. Kaufman, R. Perlman, M. Speciner, Network Security, Private Communication in a Public World, Prentice Hall, 1995.
21. G. Kessler, "An Overview of Cryptography," Hill Associates Inc, http://www.hill.com/library/crypto.html.
22. [NIST 1993] National Institute of Standards and Technology, Federal Information. Data Encryption Standard, Processing Standards Publication 46-2, 1993.
23. [NIST 1999] National Institute of Standards and Technology, "Dat Encryption Standard Fact Sheet," http://csrc.nist.gov/cryptval/des/des.txt.
24. [NIST 1999b] National Institute of Standards and Technology, "Draft Federal Information Processing Standard (FIPS) 46-3, Data Encryption Standard (DES), and Request for Comments," [RFC 1321] R. Rivest, "The MD5 Message-Digest Algorithm," RFC 1321, April 1992.
25. [RFC 2437] B. Kaliski, J. Staddon, "PKCS #1: RSA Cryptography Specifications, Version 2," RFC 2437, October 1998.
26. [RFC 2420] H. Kummert, "The PPP Triple-DES Encryption Protocol (3DESE)," RFC 2420, Sept. 1998.
27. [RSA 1978] R.L. Rivest, A. Shamir, and L.M. Adleman, "A method for obtaining digital signatures and public-key cryptosystems," Communications of the ACM, 21(2): 120-126, February 1978.
28. [RSA 1997] RSA Data Security Inc, "DES RSA Challege Cracked: Government encryption standard DES takes a fall," http://www.rsa.com/des.
29. [RSA 1999] RSA Laboratories, "How large a key should be used in RSA?" http://www.rsa.com/rsalabs/faq/html/3-1-5.html.
30. [RSA 1999b] RSA Laboratories, "How fast is RSA," http://www.rsa.com/rsalabs/faq/html/3-1-2.html.
31. [RSA 1999c] RSA Laboratories, "RSA Labs FAQ," http://www.rsa.com/rsalabs/faq/index.html.
32. B. Schneier, Applied Cryptography: Protocols, Algorithms, and Source Code in C, John Wiley and Sons, 1995.
33. S. Singh, "The Code Book : The Evolution of Secrecy from Mary, Queen of Scots to Quantum Cryptography," Doubleday Press, 1999.

□□□

2

Basic Concepts in Data Encryption

2.1 INTRODUCTION TO CRYPTOGRAPHY

Greek for "hidden writing", Cryptography is art and science of transforming information into an intermediate form which secures that information while in storage or in transit. A part of cryptology, further divided into secret codes and ciphers. As opposed to *steganography*, which seeks to hide the existence of any message, cryptography seeks to render a message unintelligible even when the message is completely exposed.

When Julius Caesar sent messages to his generals, he didn't trust his messengers. So he replaced every A in his messages with a D, every B with an E, and so on through the alphabet. Only someone who knew the "shift by 3" rule could decipher his messages.

Cryptography is the science of using mathematics to encrypt and decrypt data. Cryptography enables you to store sensitive information or transmit it across insecure networks (like the Internet) so that it cannot be read by anyone except the intended recipient.While cryptography is the science of securing data, cryptanalysis is the science of analyzing and breaking secure communication. Classical cryptanalysis involves an interesting combination of analytical reasoning, application of mathematical tools, pattern finding, patience, determination, and luck. Cryptanalysts are also called attackers. Cryptology embraces both cryptography and cryptanalysis. Encryption technologies can be used to assure your data is confidential.

Cryptography, to most people, is concerned with keeping communications private. Indeed, the protection of sensitive communications has been the emphasis of cryptography throughout much of its history. As we will see, however, this is only one part of today's cryptography.Encryption is the transformation of data into some unreadable form. Its purpose is to ensure privacy by keeping the information hidden from anyone for whom it is not intended, even those who can see the encrypted data. Decryption is the reverse of encryption ; it is the transformation of encrypted data back into some intelligible form. Encryption and decryption require the use of some secret information, usually referred to as a key. Depending on the encryption mechanism used, the same key might be used for both encryption and decryption, while for other mechanisms, the keys used for encryption and decryption might be different.

But today's cryptography is more than secret writing, more than encryption and decryption. Authentication is as fundamental a part of our lives as privacy. We use authentication though out our everyday life, when we sign our name to some document for instance, and as we move to a world where our decisions and agreements are communicated electronically, we need to replicate these procedures. Cryptography provides mechanisms for such procedures. A digital signature binds a document to the possessor of a particular key, while a digital timestamp binds a document to its creation at a particular time. These cryptographic mechanisms can be used to control access to a shared disk drive, a high security installation or to a pay-per-view TV channel.

But the field of cryptography contains even more when we include some of the things cryptography enables us to do. With just a few basic tools it is possible to build elaborate schemes and protocols which allow us to pay using electronic money , to prove we know certain information without revealing the information itself, and to share a secret quantity in such a way that no fewer than three from a pool of five people (for instance) can reconstruct the secret.

While modern cryptography is growing increasingly diverse, cryptography is fundamentally based on problems that are difficult to solve. A problem may be difficult because its solution requires some secret knowledge, such as decrypting an encrypted message or signing some digital document, or the problem may be hard because it is intrinsically difficult to complete, such as finding a message which produces a given hash value.

So as the field of cryptography has advanced, the dividing lines for what is and what is not cryptography have become blurred. Cryptography today might be summed up as the study of techniques and applications that depend on the existence of difficult problems.

Cryptography includes at least

- secrecy (confidentiality, or privacy, or information security) and
- message authentication (integrity).

Cryptography may also include

- nonrepudiation (the inability to deny sending a message),
- access control (user or source authentication), and
- availability (keeping security services available).

Modern cryptography generally depends upon translating a message into one of an astronomical number of different intermediate representations, or ciphertexts, as selected by a key. If all possible intermediate representations have similar appearance, it may be necessary to try all possible keys to find the one which deciphers the message. By creating mechanisms with an astronomical number of keys, we can make this approach impractical.

What Cryptography Can Do

Potentially, cryptography can hide information while it is in transit or storage. In general, cryptography can:

- Provide secrecy.
- Authenticate that a message has not changed in transit.
- Implicitly authenticate the sender.
- Cryptography hides words: At most, it can only hide talking about contraband or illegal actions. But in a country with "freedom of speech," we normally expect crimes to be more than just "talk."
- Cryptography can kill in the sense that boots can kill; that is, as a part of some other process, but that does not make cryptography like a rifle or a tank.
- Cryptography is defensive, and can protect ordinary commerce and ordinary people. Cryptography may be to our private information as our home is to our private property, and our home is our "castle.
- Potentially, cryptography can hide secrets, either from others, or during communication. There are many good and non-criminal reasons to have secrets: Certainly, those engaged in commercial research and development (R&D) have "secrets" they must keep. Professors and writers may want to keep their work private, until an appropriate time. Negotiations for new jobs are generally secret, and romance often is as well, or at least we might prefer that detailed discussions not be exposed.
- One possible application for cryptography is to secure on-line communications between work and home, perhaps leading to a society-wide reduction in driving,something we could all appreciate.

What Cryptography Can Not Do

- Cryptography can only hide information after it is encrypted and while it remains encrypted. But secret information generally does not start out encrypted, so there is normally an original period during which the secret is not protected. And secret information generally is not used in encrypted form, so it is again outside the cryptographic envelope every time the secret is used.

Secrets are often related to public information, and subsequent activities based on the secret can indicate what that secret is. And while cryptography can hide words, it cannot hide:

- Physical contraband,
- Cash,
- Physical meetings and training,
- Movement to and from a central location,
- An extravagant lifestyle with no visible means of support, or
- Actions.

And cryptography simply cannot protect against:

- Informants,

- Undercover spying,
- Bugs,
- Photographic evidence, or
- Testimony.

It is a joke to imagine that cryptography alone could protect most information against Government investigation. Cryptography is only a small part of the protection needed for "absolute" secrecy.

Cryptography with Keys.Usually, we arrange to select among a huge number of possible intermediate forms by using some sort of "pass phrase" or key. Normally, this is some moderately-long language phrase which we can remember, instead of something we have to write down (which someone else could then find).

Those who have one of the original keys can expose the information hidden in the message. This reduces the problem of protecting information to:

(1) Performing transformations, and

(2) Protecting the keys.

This is similar to locking our possessions in our house and keeping the keys in our pocket.

Problems with Keys

The physical key model reminds us of various things that can go wrong with keys:

- We can lose our keys.
- We can forget which key is which.
- We can give a key to the wrong person.
- Somebody can steal a key.
- Somebody can pick the lock.
- Somebody can go through a window.
- Somebody can break down the door.
- Somebody can ask for entry, and unwisely be let in.
- Somebody can get a warrant, then legally do whatever is required.
- Somebody can burn down the house, thus making everything irrelevant.

Even absolutely perfect keys cannot solve all problems, nor can they guarantee privacy. Indeed, when cryptography is used for communications, generally at least two people know what is being communicated. So either party could reveal a secret:

- By accident.
- To someone else.
- Through third-party eavesdropping.
- As revenge, for actions real or imagined.
- For payment.
- Under duress.
- In testimony.

When it is substantially less costly to acquire the secret by means other then a technical attack on the cipher, cryptography has pretty much succeeded in doing what it can do.

2.1.2 Coding and Cryptography

Transmitting messages across noisy channels is an important practical problem. Coding theory provides explicit ways of ensuring that messages remain legible even in the presence of errors. Cryptography on the other hand, makes sure that messages remain unreadable | except to the intended recipient. These complementary techniques turn out to have much in common mathematically.

According to "Recommendation.x.800 on " Security Architecture for Open Systems Interconnection for CCITT Applications " Cryptography is a discipline which embodies principles, means, and methods for the transformation of data in order to hide its information content, prevent its undetected modification and/or prevent its unauthorized use.

Note – Cryptography determines the methods used in encipherment and decipherment. An attack on a cryptographic principle, means, or method is cryptanalysis.

2.1.3 Dimensions of Cryptographic Systems

Cryptographic systems are generically classified along three independent dimensions:

(a) The type of operation used for transforming plaintext to ciphertext. All encryption algorithms are based on two general principles: substitution, in which each element in the plaintext is mapped into another element, and transposition, in which elements in plaintext are rearranged. The fundamental requirement is that no information be lost, this means that all operations are reversible. Most systems, referred to as product systems, involved multiple stages of substitutions and transpositions.

(b) The number of keys used. If both sender and receiver use the same key, the system is referred to as symmetric, single-key, or conventional encryption. If the sender and receiver each uses a different key, the system is referred as asymmetric, two keys, or public key encryption.

(c) The way in which the plain text is processed. A block cipher processes the input one block of elements at a time, producing an output block for each input block A stream cipher processes the input elements continuously, producing output as it goes along.

2.2 CONVENTIONAL ENCRYPTION

Conventional encryption, also referred to as symmetric encryption or single-key encryption, was the only type of encryption in use prior to the development of public key encryption. It remains by far the more widely used of the two types of encryption.

By itself, ciphertext is literally meaningless, in the sense of having no one clear interpretation. In so-called perfect ciphers, any ciphertext (of appropriate size) can be interpreted as any message, just by selecting an appropriate key. In fact, any number of different messages can produce exactly the same ciphertext, by using the appropriate keys. In other ciphers, this may not always be possible, but it must always be considered. To attack and break a cipher, it is necessary to somehow confirm that the message we generate from ciphertext is the exact particular message which was sent.

2.2.1 A Concrete Example

Most of us have encountered a simple form of ciphering in grade school, and it usually goes something like this:

A Simple Cipher

On a piece of lined paper, write the alphabet in order, one character per line:

```
A
B
C
...
```

Then, on each line, we write another character to the right. In this second column, we also want to use each alphabetic character exactly once, but we want to place them in some different order.

```
A F
B W
C A
.....
```

When we have done this, we can take any message and encipher it letter-by-letter.

(1) Enciphering

To encipher a letter, we find that letter in the left column, then use the associated letter from the right column and write that down. Each letter in the right column thus becomes a substitute for the associated letter in the left column.

(2) Deciphering

Deciphering is similar, except that we find the ciphertext letter in the right column, then use the associated plaintext letter from the left column. This is a little harder, because the letters in the right column are not in order. But if we wanted to, we could make a list where the ciphertext letters were in order; this would be the inverse of the enciphering transformation. And if we have both lists, enciphering and deciphering are both easy.

(3) Ciphering

Ciphering entails the use of a cipher. The general term which includes both enciphering and deciphering

2.2.2 Encryption and Decryption

Data that can be read and understood without any special measures is called plaintext or cleartext. The method of disguising plaintext in such a way as to hide its substance is called encryption. Encrypting plaintext results in unreadable gibberish called ciphertext. You use encryption to ensure that information is hidden from anyone for whom it is not intended, even those who can see the encrypted data. The process of reverting ciphertext to its original plaintext is called decryption. Figure 2.1 illustrates this process.

encryption decryption

plaintext ciphertext plaintext

Figure 2.1 Encryption and Decryption

Many times when data is exchanged electronically the privacy of the data is a requirement. The use of encryption restricts unintended recipients from viewing the data, which are deemed confidential and potentially dangerous if made known to irresponsible parties. Today, encryption is the procedure of transforming plaintext, data that can be read by anyone, to ciphertext, data that can only be read by someone with a secret decryption key.

A message before being changed in any way is called plaintext. Plaintext messages are converted to ciphertext via some encryption method. A particular such method is called a *cryptosystem*.

In conventional encryption, the original intelligible message, referred to as plaintext is converted into apparently random nonsense, referred to as ciphertext. The encryption process consists of an algorithm and a key. The key is a value, independent of the plaintext, that controls the algorithm. The algorithm will produce different output depending on the specific key being used at the time. Changing the key changes the output of the algorithm.

Figure 2.2 shows the operation on the conventional encryption. Once the ciphertext is produced, it is transmitted. Upon reception, the ciphertext can be transformed back to the original plaintext by using a decryption algorithm and the same key that was used for encryption.

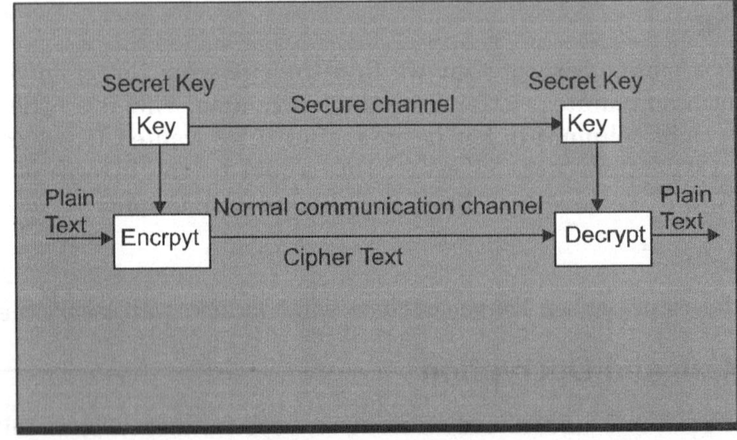

Figure 2.2 Conventional (Symmetric) Key Systems

The encryption algorithm must be powerful enough so that is it impractical to decrypt the message on the basis of ciphertext alone. Beyond that, the security of conventional encryption depends on the secrecy of the key, not the secrecy of the algorithm. That is, it is assumed that it is impractical to decrypt the message on the basis of the ciphertext plus knowledge of the encryption/decryption algorithm. In other word, we don't need to keep the algorithm secret; we need to keep only the key secret.

This feature of conventional encryption is what makes it feasible for widespread use. The fact that the algorithm need to be kept secret means that manufacturers can and have developed low-cost chip implementations of data encryption algorithms. These chips are widely available and incorporated into a number of products. With the use of conventional encryption, the principal security problem is maintaining the secrecy of the key.

2.2.3 Properties of a Good Cipher

A cryptographic algorithm, or cipher, is a mathematical function used in the encryption and decryption process. A cryptographic algorithm works in combination with a key—a word, number, or phrase—to encrypt the plaintext. The same plaintext encrypts to different ciphertext with different keys. The security of encrypted data is entirely dependent on two things: the strength of the cryptographic algorithm and the secrecy of the key. A cryptographic algorithm, plus all possible keys and all the protocols that make it work comprise a cryptosystem. Pretty Good Privacy (PGP as discussed in chapter 8) is a cryptosystem.

Cipher is in general, a method of key-selected secret transformation between plaintext and ciphertext Specifically, a secrecy mechanism or process which operates on individual characters or bits independent of semantic content. As opposed to a secret code, which generally operates on words, phrases or sentences, each of which may carry some amount of complete meaning.

A good cipher can transform secret information into a multitude of different intermediate forms, each of which represents the original information. Any of these intermediate forms or ciphertexts can be produced by ciphering the information under a particular key value. The intent is that the original information only be exposed by one of the many possible keyed interpretations of that ciphertext. Yet the correct interpretation is available merely by deciphering under the appropriate key.

A cipher appears to reduce the protection of secret information to enciphering under some key, and then keeping that key secret. This is a great reduction of effort and potential exposure, and is much like keeping your valuables in your house, and then locking the door when you leave. But there are also similar limitations and potential problems.

With a good cipher, the resulting ciphertext can be stored or transmitted otherwise exposed without also exposing the secret information hidden inside. This means that ciphertext can be stored in, or transmitted through, systems which have no secrecy protection. For transmitted information, this also means that the cipher itself must be distributed in multiple places, so in general the cipher cannot be assumed to be secret. With a good cipher, only the deciphering key need be kept secret.

• Ciphertext

Ciphertext is the text that has been encrypted to make it unintelligible to anyone who lacks essential information about the encryption scheme.The required information is generally a specific value, known as the encryption (or decryption) key. Conventional-, public-,or private-key encryption strategies may be used to create ciphertext. Ciphertext is the result of enciphering. Ciphertext will contain the same information as the original plaintext, but hide the original information, typically under the control of a key. Without the key it should be impractical to recover the original information from the ciphertext.

• Ciphertext Expansion

When the ciphertext is larger than the original plaintext Ciphertext Expansion is needed.Ciphertext expansion is the general situation: Stream ciphers need a message key, and block ciphers with a small block need some form of plaintext randomization, which generally needs an IV to protect the first block. Only block ciphers with a large size block generally can avoid ciphertext expansion, and then only if each block can be expected to hold sufficient uniqueness or "entropy" to prevent a codebook attack.

It is certainly true that in most situations of new construction a few extra bytes are not going to be a problem. However, in some situations, and especially when a cipher is to be installed into an existing system, the ability to encipher data without requiring additional storage can be a big advantage. Ciphering data without expansion supports the ciphering of data structures which have been defined and fixed by the rest of the system, provided only that one can place the cipher at the interface "between" two parts of the system. This is also especially efficient, as it avoids the process of acquiring a different, larger, amount of store for each ciphering. Such an installation also can apply to the entire system, and not require the re-engineering of all applications to support cryptography in each one.

2.2.4 Key distribution

For conventional encryption to work, the two parties to an exchange must have the same key, and that key must be protected from access by others Furthermore, frequent key changes are usually desirable to limit the amount of data compromised if an attacker learn the key. Therefore, the strength of any cryptographic system rests with the key distribution technique, a term that refer to the means of delivering a key to the two parties who wish to exchange data without allowing other users to see the key. For two parties A and B. key distribution can be achieved in a number of ways, as follows:

- A key can be selected by A and physically delivered to B.
- A third party can select the key and physically deliver it to A and B
- If A and B have previously and recently used a key, one party can transmit the new key to the other, encrypted by using the old key.
- If A and B each has an encrypted connection to a third party C, C can deliver the key on the encrypted links to A and B.

The scale of the problem depends on the number of communicating pairs that must be supported. If we used one key for each pair of hosts on the network, Thus, if there are N hosts then the number of required keys is $N * (N - 1)/2$. Then the total number of keys required for the network will be very high, which makes it difficult to handle all these keys.

2.2.5 Session Key's Lifetime

The more frequently session keys are exchanged, the more secure they are, since the opponent has less ciphertext to work with for any given session key. On the other hand, the distribution of session keys delays the start of any exchange and places a burden on network utilization. A security manager must try to balance these competing consideration in determining the lifetime of a particular session key.

For connection-oriented protocol, one obvious choice is to use the same session key for the length of time that the connection is open, using a new session key for each new session. If a logical connection has a very long lifetime, then it would be prudent to change the session key periodically.

For a connectionless protocol, such as transaction-oriented protocol, there is no explicit connection initiation or termination. Thus, it is not obvious how often one needs to change the session key. The most secure approach is to use a new session key for each exchange. However, this negates one of the principal benefits of connectionless protocols, which is minimum overhead and minimum delay of each transaction. A better strategy is to use a given session key for a certain fixed period only or for a certain number of transactions.

2.3 TYPES OF CIPHERS (TAXONOMY)

For the analysis of cipher operation it is useful to collect ciphers into groups based on their functioning (or intended functioning). The goal is to group ciphers which are essentially similar, so that as we gain an understanding of one cipher, we can apply that understanding to others in the same group. We thus classify not by the components which make up the cipher, but instead on the "black-box" operation of the cipher itself.

We seek to hide distinctions of size, because operation is independent of size, and because size effects are usually straightforward. We thus classify serious block ciphers as keyed simple substitution, just like newspaper amusement ciphers, despite their obvious differences in strength and construction. This allows us to compare the results from an ideal tiny cipher to those from a large cipher construction; the grouping thus can provide benchmark characteristics for measuring large cipher constructions.

We could of course treat each cipher as an entity unto itself, or relate ciphers by their dates of discovery, the tree of developments which produced them, or by known strength. But each of these criteria is more or less limited to telling us "this cipher is what it is." We already know that. What we want to know is what other ciphers function in a similar way, and then whatever is known about those ciphers. In this way, every cipher need not be an island unto itself, but instead can be judged and compared in a related community of similar techniques.

Our primary distinction is between ciphers which handle all the data at once (block ciphers), and those which handle some, then some more, then some more (stream ciphers). We thus see the usual repeated use of a block cipher as a stream meta-cipher which has the block cipher as a component. It is also possible for a stream cipher to be re-keyed or re-originate frequently, and so appear to operate on "blocks." Such a cipher, however, would not have the overall diffusion we normally associate with a block cipher, and so might usefully be regarded as a stream meta-cipherwith a stream cipher component.

The goal is not to give each cipher a label, but instead to seek insight. Each cipher in a particular general class carries with it the consequences of that class. And because these groupings ignore.

2.3.1 Stream Cipher

A stream cipher is a symmetric encryption algorithm. Stream ciphers can be designed to be exceptionally fast, much faster in fact than any block cipher. While block ciphers operate on large blocks of data, stream ciphers typically operate on smaller units of plaintext, usually bits. The encryption of any particular plaintext with a block cipher will result in the same ciphertext when the same key is used. With a stream cipher, the transformation of these smaller plaintext units will vary, depending on when they are encountered during the encryption process.

A stream cipher generates what is called a keystream and encryption is provided by combining the keystream with the plaintext, usually with the bitwise exclusive-or operation. The generation of the keystream can be independent of the plaintext and ciphertext (yielding what is termed a synchronous stream cipher) or it can depend on the data and its encryption (in which case the stream cipher is said to be self-synchronizing). Most stream cipher designs are for synchronous stream ciphers.

Current interest in stream ciphers is most commonly attributed to the appealing theoretical properties of the one-time pad , but there have been, as yet, no attempts to standardize on any particular stream cipher proposal as has been the case with block ciphers. Interestingly, certain modes of operation of a block cipher effectively transform it into a keystream generator and in this way, any block cipher can be used as a stream cipher. However A stream cipher does not need to accumulate some amount of data or multiple data elements for ciphering to complete. (Since we define only two main "types" of cipher, a stream cipher is the opposite of a block cipher and vise versa. It is extremely important that the definitions for block and stream ciphering enclose the universe of all possible ciphers.)

- A stream cipher has the ability to transform individual elements one-by-one. The actual transformation usually is a block transformation, and may be repeated with the same or different keying.

- In a stream cipher, data diffusion may or may not occur, but if it does, it is necessarily one-way (from earlier to later elements).
- Since elements are ciphered one-by-one, changing part of the plaintext can affect that part and possibly later parts of the ciphertext; this is a stream cipher signature.
- The simple re-use of a block transformation to cover more data than a single block is a stream operation.

A cipher which directly handles messages of arbitrary size, by ciphering individual elements, such as bits or bytes. This avoids the need to accumulate data into a block before ciphering, as is necessary in a conventional block cipher. But note that a stream cipher can be seen as an operating mode, a "streaming" of a tiny block transformation. Stream ciphers can be called "combiner-style" ciphers.

Stream Cipher Diffusion

In a conventional stream cipher, each element (for example, each byte) of the message is ciphered independently, and does not affect any other element.

In a few stream cipher designs, the value of one message byte may change the enciphering of subsequent message bytes; this is forward data diffusion. But a stream cipher cannot change the enciphering of previous message bytes. In contrast, changing even the last bit in a block cipher block will generally change about half of the earlier bits within that same block. Changing a bit in one block may even affect later blocks if we have some sort of stream meta-cipher composed of block cipher transformations, like CBC.

Note – That a stream cipher generally does not need data diffusion for strength, as does a block cipher. In a block cipher, it may be possible to separate individual components of the cipher if their separate effects are not hidden by diffusion. But a stream cipher generally re-uses the same transformation, and has no multiple data components to hide.

2.3.2 Block Cipher

A block cipher requires the accumulation of some amount of data or multiple data elements for ciphering to complete. (Sometimes stream ciphers accumulate data for convenience, as incylinder ciphers, which nevertheless logically cipher each character independently.)

Note – That this definition is somewhat broader than the now common understanding of a huge, and thus emulated, Simple Substitution. But there are ciphers which require blocked plaintext and which do not emulate Simple Substitution, and calling these something other than "block" ciphers negates the advantage of a taxonomy.

A conventional block cipher is built from small components with a design intended to simulate a substitution table of a size vastly larger than anything which could be practically realized.

If a block cipher is a huge simple substitution, a stream cipher can be a small substitution which is in some way altered for each bit or byte enciphered. Clearly, repeatedly using a small unchanging substitution (or even a linear transformation) is not going to be secure in a situation where The Opponent will have a substantial quantity of known plaintext. One way to use a small transformation securely is to use a simple additive combiner to mix data with a really random confusion sequence; done properly, this is an "unbreakable" one-time pad. logically, a stream cipher can be seen as the general concept of repeatedly using a block transformation to handle more than one block of data. Even the simple repeated use of a block cipher in ECB mode would be "streaming" the cipher. And use in more complex chaining modes like CBC are even more clearly stream meta-ciphers which use block transformations.

One common idea that comes up again and again with novice cryptographers is to take a textual key phrase, and then add (or exclusive-OR) the key with the data, byte-by-byte, starting the key over each time it is exhausted. This is a very simple and weak stream cipher, with a short and repeatedly-used running key and an additive combiner. I suppose that part of the problem in seeing this weakness is in distinguishing between different types of stream cipher "key": In a real stream cipher, even a single bit change in a key phrase would be expected to produce a different running key sequence, a sequence which would not repeat across a message of any practical size. In the weak version, a single bit change in the short running key would affect only one bit each time it was used, and would do so repeatedly, as the keying sequence was re-used over and over again. In any additive stream cipher, the re-use of a keying sequence is absolutely deadly. And a real stream cipher would almost certainly use a random message key as the key which actually protects data.

There are a whole range of things which can distinguish one cipher from another. But perhaps the easiest and most useful distinction is that between stream ciphers and block ciphers. Logically, a block cipher is just simple substitution: A block of plaintext data is collected and then substituted into an arbitrary ciphertext value. So a toy version of a block cipher is just a table look-up, much like the amusement ciphers in newspapers. Of course, a realistic block cipher has a block width which is far too large to hold the transformation in any physical table. Because of the large block size, the invertible transformation must be simulated, in some way dynamically constructed for each block enciphered.

In a block cipher, any possible permutation of "table" values is a potential key. So if we have a 64-bit block, there would theoretically be 264 factorial possible keys, which is a huge, huge value. But the well-known 64-bit block cipher DES has "only" 256 keys, which is as nothing in comparison. In part, this is because any real mechanism can only emulate the theoretical ideal of a huge simple substitution. But mostly, 56-bit keys have in the past been thought to be "large enough." Now we expect at least 128 bits, or perhaps somewhat more.

2.3.2.1 Public Key Ciphers

Public key ciphers are generally block ciphers, with the unusual property that one key is used to encipher, and a different, apparently unrelated key is used to decipher a message. So if we keep one of the keys private, we can release the other key (the "public" key), and anyone can use that to encipher a message to us. Then we use our private key to decipher any such messages. It is interesting that someone who enciphers a message to us cannot decipher their own message even if they want to.

The prototypical public key cipher is RSA, which uses the arithmetic of huge numeric values. These values may contain 1,000 bits or more (over 400 decimal digits), in which each and every bit is significant. The keyspace is much smaller, however, because there are very severe constraints on the keys; not just any random value will do. So a 1,000-bit public key may have a brute-force strength similar to a 128-bit secret key cipher.

Because public key ciphers operate on huge values, they are very slow, and so are normally used just to encipher a random message key. The message key is then used by a conventional secret key cipher which actually enciphers the data.

At first glance, public key ciphers apparently solve the key distribution problem. But in fact they also open up the new possibility of a man-in-the-middle attack. To avoid this, it is necessary to assure that one is using exactly the correct key for the desired user. This requires authentication (validation or certification) via some sort of secure channel, and that can take as much effort as a secure secret key exchange. A man-in-the-middle attack is extremely worrisome, because it does not involve breaking any cipher, which means that all the effort spent in cipher design and analysis and mathematical proofs and public review would be completely irrelevant.

2.3.3 Substitution Cipher

- A "codebook" or "simple substitution."
- Each code value becomes a distinguishable element. Thus, substitution generally converts a collection of independent elements to a single related unit.
- Keying constitutes a permutation or re-arrangement of the fixed set of possible code values.
- Avalanche or data diffusion is a natural consequence of an arbitrary selection among all possible code values.
- The usual complete binary substitution distributes bit-changes between code values binomially, and this effect can be sampled and examined statistically.
- Avalanche is two-way diffusion in the sense that "later" plaintext can change "earlier" ciphertext.

2.3.4 Transposition Cipher

- Clearly, it is necessary for all message elements which will be transposed to be collected before operations begin; this is the block cipher signature.
- Any possible transposition is necessarily a subset of an arbitrary substitution; thus, transposition can be seen as a particular keying subset of substitution.

Notice, however, that the usual avalanche signature of substitution is not present, and of course the actual data values are not changed at all by transposition, just moved about.Also notice that we are close to using the idea of permutation in two very different ways: first as a particular n-bit to n-bit substitution, and second as a particular re-arrangement of characters in the block. These have wildly different ciphering effects.

2.3.5 Cylinder

- A cipher which has or simulates the use of a number of different alphabet disks on a common rod.
- Primary keying is the arrangement of the alphabet around each disk, and the selection and arrangement of disks.
- By entering the plaintext on one row, any of `n-1` other rows can be sent as ciphertext; this selection is an IV.

If the plaintext data are redundant, it is possible to avoid sending the IV by selecting the one of `n-1` possible decipherings which shows redundancy. But this is not generally possible when ciphering arbitrary binary data.

- If an IV is selected first, each character ciphering in that "chunk" is independent of each other ciphering. There is no data diffusion.
- In general, each disk is used at fixed periodic intervals through the text, which is weak.
- The ciphertext selection is homophonic, in the sense that different ciphertext rows each represent exactly the same plaintext.

Cylinder operation is not polyphonic in the usual sense: While a single ciphertext can imply any other row is plaintext, generally only one row has a reasonable plaintext meaning.

CONFUSION SEQUENCE

- With a truly random sequence, used once, we have a one time pad.
- With a pseudorandom confusion sequence and a simple additive combiner, we have a Vernam cipher.

A simple additive transformation becomes weak upon the second character ciphered, or immediately, under known plaintext, making strength dependent on the confusion sequence.

- More complex transformations imply the need for correspondingly less strong confusion sequences.

Autokey

- Normally the use of ciphertext, but also perhaps plaintext, as the cipher key.
- Can create a random-like confusion stream which will re-synchronize after ciphertext data loss.

Under known-plaintext, the common "ciphertext feedback" version exposes both the confusion sequence and the input which creates that sequence. This is a lot of pressure on a single transformation.

2.3.6 Monoaiphabetic (e.g., Des CBC) Ciphering

- The repeated use of a single fixed substitution.
- A conventional block cipher simulates a large substitution.
- A substitution becomes weak when its code values are re-used.

Code value re-use can be minimized by randomizing the plaintext block (e.g., CBC). This distributes the plaintext evenly across the possible block values, but at some point the transformation itself must change or be exposed.

Another alternative is to use a very large block so that code value re-use is made exceedingly unlikely. A large block also has room for a dynamic keying field which would make code value re-use even more unlikely.

2.3.7 Poiyaiphabetic Ciphering

The use of multiple fixed substitutions.

- By itself, the use of multiple alphabets in a regular sequence is inherently not much stronger than just a single alphabet.

It is of course possible to select an alphabet or transformation at pseudo-random, for example by re-keying DES after every block ciphered. This brings back sequence strength as an issue, and opens up the sequence generator starting state as an IV.

- A related possibility is the use of a latin square combiner which effectively selects among a balanced set of different fixed substitution alphabets.

2.3.8 Dynamic Ciphering

- The use of one (monoalphabetic) or multiple (polyalphabetic) substitutions which change during ciphering.

2.3.9 Iterative Ciphering

- The iterative re-use of a stream cipher with a new random IV on each iteration so as to eventually achieve the effect of a message key.
- Each iteration seemingly must expand the ciphertext by the size of the IV, although this is probably about the same expansion we would have with a message key.
- Unfortunately, each iteration will take some time.

It is possible to transform or encipher a message or plaintext into "an intermediate form" or ciphertext in which the information is present but hidden. Then we can release the transformed message (the ciphertext) without exposing the information it represents.

By using different transformations, we can create many different ciphertexts for the exact same message. So if we select a particular transformation "at random," we can hope that anyone wishing to expose the message ("break" the cipher) can do no better than simply trying all available transformations (or on average, half) one-by-one. This is a brute force attack.

(1) The Single Transformation

The grade school cipher is a simple substitution cipher, a streaming or repeated letter-by-letter application of the same transformation. That "transformation" is the particular arrangement of letters in the second column, a permutation of the alphabet. There can be many such arrangements. But in this case the key is that particular arrangement. We can copy it and give it to someone and then send secret messages to them. But if that sheet is acquired — or even copied — by someone else, the enciphered messages would be exposed. This means that we have to keep the transformation secret.

(2) Many Transformations

Now suppose we have a full notebook of lined pages, each of which contains a different arrangement in the second column. Suppose each page is numbered. Now we just pick a number and encipher our message using that particular page. That number thus becomes our key, which is now a sort of numeric shorthand for the full transformation. So even if the notebook is exposed, someone who wishes to expose our message must try about half of the transformations in the book before finding the right one. Since exposing the notebook does not immediately expose our messages, maybe we can leave the notebook unprotected. We also can use the same notebook for messages to different people, and each of them can use the exact same notebook for their own messages to each other. Different people can use the same notebook and yet still cipher messages which are difficult to expose without knowing the right key.

Note that there is some potential for confusion in first calling the transformation a key, and then calling the number which selects that transformation also a key. But both of these act to select a particular ciphertext construction from among many, and they are only two of the various kinds of "key" in cryptography.

(3) Weak and Strong Transformations

The simple substitution used in our grade school cipher is very weak, because it "leaks" information: The more often a particular plaintext letter is used, the more often the associated ciphertext letter appears. And since language uses some letters more than others, simply by counting the number of times each ciphertext letter occurs we can make a good guess about which plaintext letter it represents. Then we can try our guess and see if it produces something we can understand. It usually does not take too long before we can break the cipher, even without having the key. In fact, we develop the ultimate key (the enciphering transformation) to break the cipher.

A "real" cipher will have a far more complex transformation. For example, the usual 64-bit block cipher will encipher 8 plaintext letters at the same time, and a change in any one of those letters will change all 8 letters of the resulting ciphertext. This is still simple substitution, but with a huge alphabet. Instead of using 26 letters, a 64-bit block cipher views each of 264 different block values as a separate letter, which is something like 18,000,000,000,000,000,000 "letters."

The difference between intermediate forms is the interpretation of the ciphertext data. Different ciphers and different keys will produce different interpretations (different plaintexts) for the exact same ciphertext. The uncertainty of how to interpret any particular ciphertext is how information is "hidden."

Naturally, the intended recipient needs to know how to transform or decipher the intermediate form back into the original message, and this is the key distribution problem.

2.4 ENCRYPTION TECHNOLOGY

On a daily basis your information, sometimes sensitive information, is being disclosed to persons whom you do not wish. This is normally completely unintentional. Consider now what is happening throughout your enterprise. Employees are exchanging PC held data by a variety of means are used, including:

- placing data on shared LAN servers for the other party to access
- copying data to floppy and sending it or handing it to the other person
- transmitting data across a network

These are all common 'business as usual' or 'how we work' scenarios. In all these cases and more, however, the data is in clear, ready to be read when intercepted (by accident or design) by a third party.Often, the third party will stumble across the data unintentionally. Usually, this will not matter, but sometimes it might! In most cases, the impact of unwanted disclosure upon your enterprise will be negligible.... but again, not always. The risk of serious disclosure (an individual serious event or multiple less serious events) is always there.

Passwords, locks, access privileges, and *even biometric devices* do not always deter the determined intruder. A common tool like a protocol analyzer can be hooked up to the network and the intruder can watch all data, including passwords, pass by. Data encryption is the answer.

With encryption, data is scrambled before transmission, making it unreadable as it passes over the wire, even if it is intercepted. To scramble or encrypt this data, its bits must be transformed according to an algorithm. The data is transmitted, and at the receiving end, a system of keys is used to decode the bits into intelligible information. Keys are necessary for encoding and decoding. Encryption usually requires extra hardware because of the processing power required. Hardware-based encryption schemes are more difficult to crack than software-based methods.

Consider all the types of data that you own: personnel information, financial details, customer details, future plans... the list is endless. You do have data therefore which is important and which you definitely do not wish to be disclosed to other parties (either internal or external). But how do you encourage your sub-ordinate to ensure that the report/ data is sent to other party which is truely concerned with you in a manner not susceptible to disclosure? The answer is a lot simpler than you may think! DES Encryption!

A common data encryption standard specified by the U.S. government is Data Encryption Standard (DES). Another standard used by the government, called CCEP, is more recently developed than DES and will someday supplant the older standard. DES defines how the data should be encrypted and the specifications for an electronic key. It uses one 64-bit key for encryption and decryption. This can cause problems because the key must be in the hands of the sender and receiver. The only way to get it from place to place is to transmit it. Transmitting the key introduces a security threat. The Public Key System, with matched public and private keys, is a solution.

Encryption may be done before data is stored or transmitted. Some networks only encrypt data when it is sent, which makes wire tapping more difficult but does not keep intruders from taking data from a disk. Other networks also encrypt data on the hard disk.

Data is encrypted as it is written and decrypted as it is read from the disk. Having encryption working in both places keeps network data much more secure. Encrypting passwords, as NetWare 386 does, is sometimes sufficient to deter the casual data thief. To further enhance encryption's effectiveness, keys should be changed at random intervals. This prevents intruders from discovering either the key or the time the key is changed. Alternative keys should be available, too, in case the original set is compromised. The best network encryption schemes hide much of the encryption hassle from end users by taking care of key management and encryption automatically.

2.4.1 Use of Data Encryption in Today's Context: E-Commerce

Web-commerce has grown into one of the fastest-growing sector of industry in the past two years. Billions of dollars have passed hands in the process and each entrepreneur wants a slice of the dough. To make this possible, data encryption plays a very central role in ensuring customers that paying for anything online is secure.

In order to enable secure online transaction, data encryption plays four important functions:

- Digital authentication allows both the customers and the merchant to be sure that they are dealing with whom the other party claims to be. This is absolutely necessary before sending credit card details to the merchant and also allow merchants to verify that the customer is the real owner of the credit card being used.
- Integrity ensures that the messages received re not changed during transmission by any third party.
- Non-repudiation prevents customers or merchants denying they ever received or sent a particular message or order.
- In the event that information is intercepted, encryption ensures privacy that prevents third parties from reading and or using the information to their own advantage.
- What kind of encryption does e-commerce use?

There are two methods of encryption employed:

- Private-key encryption (secret-key or symmetric encryption) in which users share a common key.
- Public-key encryption (also known as asymmetric encryption) where different keys are used for encryption and decryption.

These systems have their advantages and disadvantages and so secure transaction protocols such as Netscape's Secure Sockets layer and Secure Electronic Transaction use a combination of both.

2.4.2 Deciphering Encrypted Data

Strategies for Deciphering

Usually, amateur cryptanalysts began by compiling a list of known classic codes and cipher methodologies that can be used to encrypt secret messages. However, today powerful computers are used to analyse the ciphertext and look out for certain keys used to encrypt (possibly several times) the message.

None of these methods are guaranteed to work on the first try. Trial and errors are common, but with experience, seasoned cryptographers could recognise certain patterns that could provide some clue to the first step that should be taken.

Probable Word

When important messages are relayed, often unimaginative choice of words could give away the encryption, as specialists in the field of cryptography have amassed a set of most probable words as the nature of the message exhibits. For instance, in decoding love letters, frequency ordering looks for words such as 'love, heart, fire, miss, life, light' which are most frequently used. Hence it is important to rephrase messages before they are encrypted and transmitted.

Event-triggered Messages

Nothing can emphasize the importance of encrypting a message well. The slightest carelessness may well reveal subsequent messages. However, not having code books does not mean a message should be transmitted as plaintext. On the other hand, encrypted messages containing obvious news, such as weather report on certain phenomenon that is most obvious to the enemy, could prove to be a fatal leak.

Sometimes, the use of common phrase to describe a sudden, unforeseen event may give away the encryption. This is exploited by the British in the World War II, when they deliberately sank a lighted buoy in order to trigger certain predicted sequence in German encrypted message, to assist decrypting.

2.4.3 Encryption Errors

As mentioned in Security, often the job of the cryptanalyst to decrypt certain data is made much easier whenever error that occurred is not handled properly and results in a 'leak'. Error in Encryption leads to Compromises.

When message-handling operator makes error in encrypting data. Compromises may occur during requested re-transmission in these cases:

(1) This message can be encrypted using a different key. In any case, it is possible for interceptors to compare the two ciphertext and work out the encryption.

(2) Sometimes, two identical messages encrypted with two keys, one old key known to the interceptor and one new, may also be fatal.

(3) When a request for re-transmission results in transmission of plaintext, instead of a repeat of the ciphertext.

2.4.3.1 Human Operator Errors

Most of encryption method that has been broken, was solved as a result of a tiny error on the part of the cipher officer. Since the nature of the profession is such that a crypto clerk needs to be deliver a flawless service to an organisation of considerable importance to the state, in war times, this group of people received pressure of time and demand for ultimate secrecy. Hence certain errors occurred as a result. Most of encryption method that has been broken, was solved as a result of a tiny error on the part of the cipher officer. As with Germany's ENIGMA encryption, Stuart Milner-Barry wrote that if not for human errors, "[it] was intrinsically a perfectly secure machine.

These errors include:

- Frequent use of words naturally occurring in certain type of activity may give a big clue to any cryptanalyst. Hence messages should have been paraphrased in such manner that the use of these words is as minimal as possible.
- The use of immutable words for certain sudden occurrence or perhaps events that may have been triggered on purpose by the interceptor. The sequence of these words is looked out for by potential cryptanalysts.
- The use of less likely occurring characters to represent null spacings.

When message-handling operator makes error in encrypting data. Compromises may occur during requested re-transmission in these cases:

This message can be encrypted using a different key. In any case, it is possible for interceptors to compare the two ciphertext and work out the encryption. Sometimes, two different messages encrypted with the same key may also be fatal. When a request for re-transmission results in transmission of plaintext, instead of a repeat of the ciphertext.The gravity of this blunder is apparent when one considers how anyone could intercept the plaintext message and compare this with the previously encrypted message, and therefore figure out the encryption method and possibly, selection of key.

Probable Word

When important messages are relayed, often unimaginative choice of words could give away the encryption, as specialists in the field of cryptography have amassed a set of most probable words as the nature of the message exhibits. For instance, in decoding love letters, frequency ordering looks for words such as 'love, heart, fire, miss, life, light' which are most frequently used. Hence it is important to rephrase messages before they are encrypted and transmitted.

Special Characters

The use of certain clear symbols (or even nulls) for spacing or punctuation has been proven disastrous for those who committed this sin. The double appearance of certain important words could also give away the encryption.

Event-triggered Messages

Nothing can emphasize the importance of encrypting a message well. The slightest carelessness may well reveal subsequent messages. However, not having code books does not mean a message should be transmitted as plaintext. On the other hand, encrypted messages containing obvious news, such as weather report on certain phenomenon that is most obvious to the enemy, could prove to be a fatal leak.

Sometimes, the use of common phrase to describe a sudden, unforeseen event may give away the encryption. This is exploited by the British in the World War II, when they deliberately sank a lighted buoy in order to trigger certain predicted sequence in German encrypted message, to assist decrypting.

Poor Choice of Passwords

The use of commonly used, easily memorable phrases as passwords is highly inadvisable, especially if these bear strong association with the encryptor.

Physical Copy of Crypt Documents

The presence of a physical copy of transmitted data must be destroyed at all cost, since the most obvious, frequently practised method of interception is by physically seizing the crypt documents.

Captured Cryptographic Device

In military operations, whenever a particular installation falls into the captivity of the enemy, the most important step to do would be to secure or destroy any device or code books that are used to encrypt message. Historically, failure to do this had brought about serious setbacks as enemies eavesdropped easily to subsequent communications. During WW II, in many instances, captured submarines or vessels left their encrypting devices intact, to the enemy's advantage.

Illusion of Security Using 'Complicated' Cryptosystem

Altering existing methods by introducing suitable superficial complications may well be a double-edged sword, as it lulls cryptographer into a false sense of security.

2.5 PRINCIPLES OF CRYPTOGRAPHY

Although cryptography has a long history dating back to Julius Caesar (we will look at the so-called Caesar cipher shortly), modern cryptographic techniques, including many of those used in today's Internet, are based on advances made in past twenty years. The books Kahn 1967, Singh 1999 provide a fascinating look at this long history. A detailed (but entertaining and readable) technical discussion of cryptography, particularly from a network standpoint, is. Diffie in 1998 provided a compelling and up-to-date examination of the political and social (e.g., privacy) issues that are now inextricably intertwined with cryptography. A complete discussion of cryptography itself requires a complete book and so below we only touch on the essential aspects of cryptography, particularly as they are practiced in today's Internet.

Cryptographic techniques allow a sender to disguise data so that an intruder can gain no information from the intercepted data. The receiver, of course must be able to recover the original data from the disguised data. Figure 2.3 illustrates some of the important terminology:

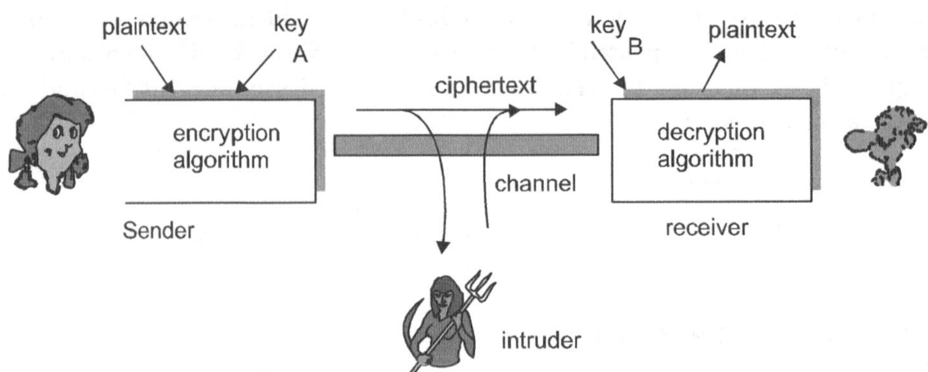

Figure 2.3 Cryptographic Components

Suppose now that Anita wants to send a message to Bunty. Anita's message in its original form (e.g., "Bunty, I love you. Anita") is known as plaintext, or cleartext. Anita encrypts her plaintext message using an encryption algorithm so that the encrypted message, known as ciphertext, looks unintelligible to any intruder. Interestingly, in many modern cryptographic systems, including those used in the Internet, the encryption technique itself is known - published, standardized, and available to everyone (e.g., [RFC 1321, RFC 2437,RFC 2420), even a potential intruder! Clearly, if everyone knows the method for encoding data, then there must be some bit of secret information that prevents an intruder from decrypting the transmitted data. This is where keys come in.

In Figure 2.3 Anita provides a key, KA, - a string of numbers or characters, as input to the encryption algorithm. The encryption algorithm takes the key and the plaintext as input and produces ciphertext as output. Similarly, Bunty will provide a key KB, to the decryption algorithm, that takes the ciphertext and Bunty's key as input and produces the original plaintext as output. In so-called symmetric key systems, Anita and Bunty's keys are identical and are secret. In public key systems, the key that Anita uses is known to all (!), while Bunty's key is secret. In the following two subsections, we consider symmetric key and public key systems in more detail.

2.5.1 Symmetric Key Cryptography

All cryptographic algorithms involve substituting one thing for another, e.g., taking a piece of plaintext and computing the appropriate ciphertext that forms the encrypted message. Before studying a modern key-based cryptographic system, let us first "get our feet wet" by studying a very old simple symmetric key algorithm attributed to Julius Caesar, known as the *Caesar cipher* (a "cipher" is a method for encrypting data).

(1) Key-based Encryption

Keys are the fundamental essential element in generating modern ciphertext. A string of bits used widely in cryptography, allowing people to encrypt and decrypt data; a key can be used to perform other mathematical operations as well. Given a cipher, a key determines the mapping of the plaintext to the ciphertext.

The key to a particular cryptosystem is some value which, when applied to ciphertext, allows the encrypted message to be decrypted and when applied to plaintext encrypts it. It is important to note that in the study of cryptography one talks about the lengths of keys in terms of bits. Messages, too, can be encrypted in 'n-bit blocks'. The longer a key is the more difficult it is to break the encrypted message.

(2) Brute-force Attack

The most common method of breaking ciphers is by a brute-force attack. This sort of attack involves running through possible combinations of keys and applying them to the cryptosystem until the message is decrypted. It is the same as trying to guess a PIN for someone's ATM card by going through all the possible combinations of numbers. It is said that any University computer science major would have enough computer power available to be able to break most 56-bit key cryptosystems in less than one week.

The following table, from B. Schneier. Applied Cryptography, 2e. John Wiley & Sons. 1996, is for symmetric key ciphers. It offers some guidelines on choosing appropriate key lengths.

Nature of Data	**Lifetime Minimum [Symmetric]**	**Key length**
Tactical military information	minutes/hours	56-64 bits
Product announcements, mergers	days/weeks	64 bits
long-term business plans	years	64 bits
Trade secrets	decades	112 bits
H-bomb secrets	>40 years	128 bits
Identities of spies	>50 years	128 bits
Personal affairs	>50 years	128 bits
Diplomatic embarrassments	>65 years	at least 128 bits
U.S. Census data	100 years	at least 128 bits

Also called secret key encryption, symmetric key encryption uses the same key to encrypt and decrypt the data. It provides rapid processing of data and is used in many forms of data encryption for networks and file systems.

In *conventional cryptography*, also called *secret-key* or *symmetric-key encryption*, one key is used both for encryption and decryption. The Data Encryption Standard (DES) is an example of a conventional cryptosystem that is widely employed by the Federal Government of USA. Figure 2.4 is an illustration of the conventional encryption process.

Figure 2.4 Conventional Encryption

Public key encryption has two keys, one public and one private. This technology opens up numerous security strategies and is the basis for several Windows 2000 security features including digital signing, which ensures authenticity, and encryption, which ensures secrecy. These features are dependent on a public key infrastructure (PKI).

Public key encryption is used in a variety of situations. For example, public key encryption is used for Web authentication by the Secure Sockets layer (SSl) protocol.

A substitution cipher is a form of cryptography.In a substitution cipher, a rule is used to change each letter of the message, one at a time. The rule says to replace (or "substitute") each letter with another letter from the alphabet.

An extremely simple example of conventional cryptography is a substitution cipher. A substitution cipher substitutes one piece of information for another.This is most frequently done by offsetting letters of the alphabet.

Caesar Shift Cipher

The Caesar Shift Cipher is simple and very easy to use. Used by Julius Caesar of the Roman Empire, this form of encryption was extremely useful in disguising the messages that he sent. Get a piece of paper and pencil and we'll try out this cipher!

First, write out the alphabet as usual,

A B C ...

Then, write out the alphabet below, but this time start with D. When you reach Z, begin again with A so that each column has 2 letters in it.

A B C D E F G H I J K L M N O P Q R S T U V W X Y Z

D E F G H I J K L M N O P Q R S T U V W X Y Z A B C

What you have written out will be your key for the cipher. Notice that the alphabet in the second row is shifted by three letters. Although folklore claims that Caesar always shifted by three, you could use any number you like.

Now that you have the key, let's put it to use. To encrypt a message, write out what you want to send. We'll use "It is sunny out today" for our message, but you can choose anything you like.

It

Now below the message, substitute for each letter of your message the letter below it in your key:

IT IS SUNNY OUT TODAY

LW LV VXQQB RXW WRGDB

You've now encrypted your message. To decrypt it, use your key to replace each letter in the encrypted message with the corresponding letter in the top row of the key.

The applet below can help you with the Caesar shift cipher. Enter the number of letters to shift by and the message. You can enter either a plaintext message to be encrypted or a ciphertext message to be decrypted. To check the example above, use a shift of 3.

Example 2.1

Original Message : **Talibans are not far away**

By default Caesar's keyword is formed by shifting 3 places, so the keyword shall be:

defghijklmnopqrstuvwxyzabc

and encrypted message shall be:

wdoledqv duh qrw idu dzdb

Now if above encrypted message is decrypted the key is the same ie

defghijklmnopqrstuvwxyzabc

and decrypted message is

talibans are not far away

which is the same as original with one difference that the starting is not in capital.This can be taken as weakness of this method to some extent.

The Caesar Shift Cipher is one example of a Monoalphabetic Cipher. In a monoalphabetic cipher, every letter in the alphabet is represented by exactly one other letter in the key. The monoalphabetic cipher is not restricted to using only letters, but can use symbols and numbers as well. Let's explore another example of a monoalphabetic cipher.

For English text, the Caesar cipher would work by taking each letter in the plaintext message and substituting the letter that is k letters later (allowing wraparound, i.e., having the letter "a" follow the letter "z") in the alphabet. For example if k=4, then the letter "a" in plaintext becomes "d" in ciphertext; "b" in plaintext becomes "e" in ciphertext, and so on. Here, the value of k serves as the key. As an example, the plaintext message "Bunty, I love you. Anita." becomes "yly, f ilsb vlr. xifzb." in ciphertext. While the ciphertext does indeed look like gibberish, it wouldn't take long to break the code if you knew that the Caesar cipher was being used, as there are only 25 possible key values.

Monoalphabetic Cipher

An improvement to the Caesar cipher is the so-called monoalphabetic cipher that also substitutes one letter in the alphabet with another letter in the alphabet. However, rather than substituting according to a regular pattern (e.g., substitution with an offset of k for all letters), any letter can be substituted for any other letter, as long as each letter has a unique substitute letter and vice versa. Many newspaers in the US carry cryptographic puzzles based on this cipher. The substitution rule in Figure 7.2-2 shows one possible rule for encoding plaintext.

plaintext letter	a b c d e f g h i f k l m n o p q r s t u v w x y z
ciphertext letter	m n b v c x z a s d f g h j k l p o i u y t r e w q

Figure 2.5 A monoalphabetic cipher

The plaintext message

`"Bunty, I love you. Anita."`

becomes

`"nkn, s gktc wky. mgsbc"`

Thus, as in the case of the Caesar cipher, this looks like gibberish. A monoalphabetic cipher would also appear to be better than the Caesar cipher in that there are 26! (on the order of 1026) possible pairings of letters rather than 25 possible pairings. A brute force approach of trying all 1026 possible pairings would require far too much work to be a feasible way of breaking the encryption algorithm and decoding the message. However, by statistical analysis of the plaintext language, e.g., knowing that the letters "e" and "t" are the most frequently occurring letters in typical text (accounting for 13% and 9% of letter occurrences), and knowing that particular two- and three-letter occurrences of letters appear quite often together (e.g., "in", "it", "the" "ion", "ing", etc.) make it relatively easy to break this code. If the intruder has some knowledge about the possible contents of the message, then it is even easier to break the code. For example, if Trudy the intruder is Bunty's wife and suspects Bunty of having an affair with Anita, then she might suspect that the names "Bunty" and "Anita" appear in the text." If Trudy knew for certain that those two names appeared in the ciphertext and had a copy of the example ciphertext message above, then she could immediately determine 7 of the 26 letter pairings, since "Anita" is the only five-letter word in the message, and "Bunty" is the only three-letter word that has an identical first and last letter. Thus, Trudy requires 109 fewer possibilities to be checked a by brute force method. Indeed, if Trudy suspected Bunty of having an affair, she might well expect to find some other choice words in the message as well.

When considering how easy it might be for Trudy to break Bunty and Anita's encryption scheme, one can distinguish three different scenarios, depending on what information the intruder has:

(1) Ciphertext only Attack. In some cases, the intruder may only have access to the intercepted ciphertext, with no certain information about the contents of the plaintext message. We have seen how statistical analysis can help in a ciphertext only attack on an encryption scheme.

(2) Known plaintext Attack. We saw above that if Trudy somehow knew for sure that "Bunty" and "Anita" appeared in the ciphertext message then she could have determined the (plaintext, ciphertext) pairings for the letters a, l, i, c, e, b, and o. Trudy might also have been fortunate enough to have recorded all of the ciphertext transmissions and then found Bunty's own decrypted version of one of transmissions scribbled on a piece of paper. When an intruder knows some of the (plaintext, ciphertext) pairings, we refer to this as a known plaintext attack on the encryption scheme.

(3) Chosen plaintext Attack. In a chosen plaintext attack, the intruder is able to choose the plaintext message and obtain its corresponding ciphertext form. For the simple encryption algorithms we've seen so far, if Trudy could get Anita to send the message, "The quick fox jumps over the lazy brown dog," she can completely break the encryption scheme. We'll see shortly that for more sophisticated encryption techniques, a chosen plaintext attack does not necessarily mean that the encryption technique can be broken.

Polyalphabetic Encryption (Vigenere ciphers)

Five hundred years ago, techniques improving on monoalphabetic encryption, known as polyalphabetic encryption were invented. These techniques, incorrectly attributed to Blaise de Vigenere [Kahn 1967] have come to be known as Vigenere ciphers. The idea behind Vigenere ciphers is to use multiple monoalphabetic ciphers, with a specific monoalphabetic cipher to encode a letter in a specific position in the plaintext message. Thus, the same letter, appearing in different positions in the plaintext message might be encoded differently. The Vigenere cipher shown in Figure 7.2-3 has two different Caesar ciphers (with k=6 and k=20), shown as rows in Figure 2.6. One might choose to use these two Caesar ciphers, C1 and C2, in the repeating pattern C1, C2, C2, C1, C2. That is, the first letter of plaintext is to encoded using C1, the second and third using C2, the fourth using C1, and the fifth using C2. The pattern then repeats, with the sixth letter being encoded using C1, the seventh with C2, and so on. The plaintext message "`Bunty, I love you. Anita.`" is thus encrypted "`ghu, n etox dhz.`" Note that the first "b" in the plaintext message is encrypted using C1, while the second "b" is encrypted using C2. In this example, the encryption and decryption "key" is the knowledge of the two Caesar keys (k=4, k=20) and the pattern C1, C2, C1, C2, C2.

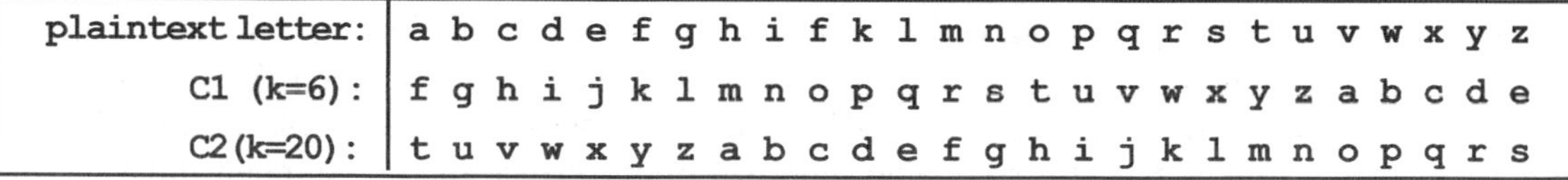

plaintext letter:	a	b	c	d	e	f	g	h	i	f	k	l	m	n	o	p	q	r	s	t	u	v	w	x	y	z
C1 (k=6) :	f	g	h	i	j	k	l	m	n	o	p	q	r	s	t	u	v	w	x	y	z	a	b	c	d	e
C2 (k=20) :	t	u	v	w	x	y	z	a	b	c	d	e	f	g	h	i	j	k	l	m	n	o	p	q	r	s

Figure 2.6 A Vigenere Cipher using Two Caesar Ciphers

2.6.2 Keyphrase Cipher

To construct the key, first select a keyword. We'll use **"Butterfly"**. Now rewrite the codeword but get rid of any duplicate letters. So **"Butterfly"** becomes **"Buterfly"**, leaving the second "t" out. Write out the alphabet as before and underneath write out the new keyword. Write out the rest of the alphabet in order, leaving out any letters in the keyword.

```
A B C D E F G H I J K L M N O P Q R S T U V W X Y Z
B U T E R F L Y A C D G H I J K M N O P Q S V W X Z
```

You have now constructed the key for the cipher. Double check that you don't have any duplicate letters. Encrypting and decrypting works exactly the same for all monoalphabetic ciphers, the only difference is how the key is constructed. Use the applet below to help construct a keyphrase cipher then encrypt and decrypt some messages on word your own.

if you enter keyword as "**heera1951**" then modified key will be "**hera1951**" and key is "**hera195bcdfgijklmnopqstuvwxyz**"

Two examples are Captain Midnight's Secret Decoder Ring, which you may have owned when you were a kid, and Julius Caesar's cipher. In both cases, the algorithm is to offset the alphabet and the key is the number of characters to offset it. For example, if we encode the word "**SECRET**" using Caesar's key value of 3, we offset the alphabet so that the 3rd letter down (D) begins the alphabet.

So starting with

```
A B C D E F G H I J K l M N O P Q R S T U V W X Y Z
```

and sliding everything up by 3, you get

```
A B C D E F G H I J K l M N O P Q R S T U V W X Y Z
D E F G H I J K l M N O P Q R S T U V W X Y Z A B C
```

where **D=A, E=B, F=C**, and so on.

```
S E C R E T
V H F U H W
```

Using this scheme, the plaintext, "SECRET" encrypts as "VHFUHW." To allow someone else to read the ciphertext, you tell them that the key is 3.Obviously, this is exceedingly weak cryptography by today's standards, but in those days it worked for Caesar, and it also illustrates how conventional cryptography works.

For instance, this table gives a rule for a substitution cipher:

```
A B C D E F G H I J K *M N O P Q R S T U V W X Y Z
T H A N K Y O U V E R  M U Z X W S Q B C D F G I J l
```

Using this rule, the sentence **"Twinkle Twinkle little Star"** is changed to **"Bgvurmk Bgvurmk Mvccmk Bctq"**. The Caesar cipher is one example of a substitution cipher.

Substitution ciphers are not safe enough to use for important messages. Substitution ciphers can be broken by an idea called frequency analysis. Some letters are more common than others in English sentences: E is the most common, then T, then A, and so on. A message that has been changed by a substitution cipher will have different common letters, but this gives a hint about the rule. The most common letters in the changed message are likely to be the most common letters in English.

(1) Keyspace

Suppose we have 256 pages of transformations in the notebook; this means there are exactly 256 different keys we can select from. If we write the number 256 in binary we get "100000000"; here the leftmost "1" represents 1 count of 2^8, and we call this an "8 bit" number. Or we can compute the base 2 logarithm by first taking the natural log of 256 (about 5.545) and dividing that by the natural log of 2 (about 0.693); this result is also 8. So we say that having 256 key possibilities is an "8 bit" keyspace. If we choose one of the 256 key values at random, and use that transformation to encipher a message, someone wishing to break our cipher should have to try about 128 decipherings before happening upon the correct one. The effort involved in trying, on average, 128 decipherings (a brute force attack) before finding the right one, is the design strength of the cipher.

If our notebook had 65,536 pages or keys (instead of just 256), we would have a "16 bit" keyspace. Notice that this number of key possibilities is 256 times that of an "8 bit" keyspace, while the key itself has only 8 bits more than the "8 bit" cipher. The strength of the "16 bit" cipher is the effort involved in trying, on average, 32,768 decipherings before finding the right one.

The idea is the same as a modern cipher: We have a machine which can produce a huge number of different transformations between plaintext and ciphertext, and we select one of those transformations with a key value. Since there are many, many possible keys, it is difficult to expose a message, even though the machine itself is not secret. And many people can use the exact same machine for their own secrets, without revealing those secrets to everyone who has such a machine.

(2) Frequency Analysis

Frequency analysis exploits the known patterns of the language used in a cryptographic system. In our case, this will be English, but the same principles could be applied to any language.

Certain letters and combinations of letters are more likely than others to occur in any arbitrary English sentence. For example, the letter "e" is the most common single letter and the digram "th" is the most common two letter combination. This graph shows the percentage of occurrences (ie. frequency) of each letter in the alphabet for English text.

Frequency Ordering

The structure of any language enables cryptanalysts to see patterns that emerge from normal messages. Just by looking at a paragraph of text, one can figure out which letters are most common.

In the English language, vowels and spaces are the most frequent characters. A few constants and a few known bigrams (2 letters combination) are more common than others. By recognizing patterns in ciphers one can often guess what the letters are decipher the message.

These are letters in English, in order of most comon to least common:

E
T
A, O, N, R, I, S
H
D, L, F, C, M, U
G, Y, P, W, B
V, K, X, J, Q, Z

For word games, it is often the frequency of letters in English vocabulary, regardless of word frequency, which is of more interest. Researcher did an analysis of the letters occurring in the words listed in the main entries of the Concise Oxford Dictionary (11th edition revised, 2004) and came up with the following table:

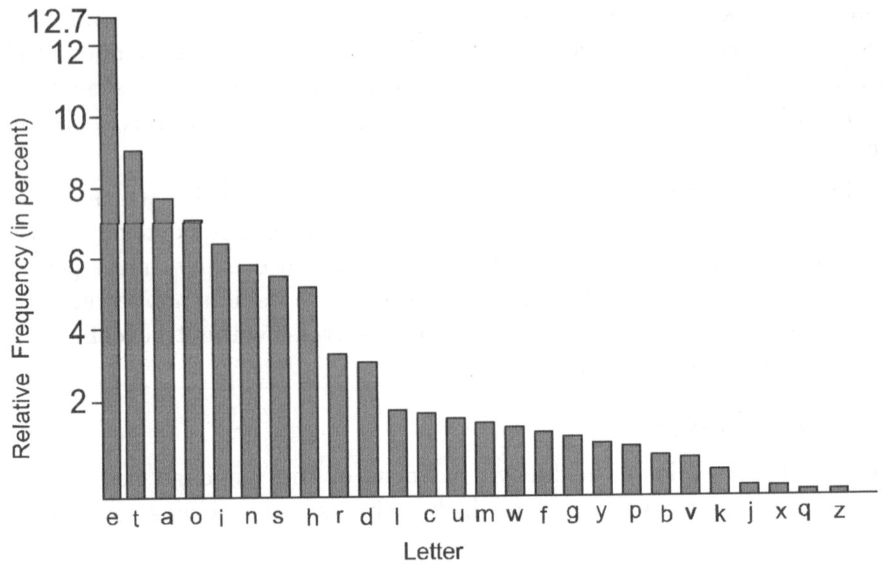

Figure 2.7 Frequency of usage of Letters in English Vocabulary

Cryptographic sources glishsuggest for code-breaking purposes a sequence of 'etaonrish'.The 'top twelve' letters comprise about 80% of the total usage.

Letter	French [1]	German [2]	Spanish [3]	Esperanto [4]	Italian [5]	Turkish [6]	Swedish [7]	Polish [8]	Toki Pona [9]
a	7.636%	6.51%	12.53%	12.12%	11.74%	11.68%	9.3%	8.0%	17.2%
b	0.901%	1.89%	1.42%	0.98%	0.92%	2.95%	1.3%	1.3%	0.0%
c	3.260%	3.06%	4.68%	0.78%	4.5%	0.97%	1.3%	3.8%	0.0%
d	3.669%	5.08%	5.86%	3.04%	3.73%	4.87%	4.5%	3.0%	0.0%
e	14.715%	17.40%	13.68%	8.99%	11.79%	9.01%	9.9%	6.9%	7.4%
f	1.066%	1.66%	0.69%	1.03%	0.95%	0.44%	2.0%	0.1%	0.0%

Besides letter frequency, knowing the frequency of most likely occurring sequence of letters in the particular language may be proven handy as well. In English language, these are sequences in order from most common to least common:

Bigram of Different letters:

TH, HE, AN, RE, ER, IN, ON, AT, ND, ST, ES, EN, OF, TE

Bigram of Same letters:

ll, EE, SS, OO, TT, FF, RR, NN, PP, CC, MM, GG

Trigram (from most common to least common):

THE, ING, CON, ENT, ERE, ERS, EVE, FOR, HER, TED, TER, TIO, VER

Most frequently occurring words have the following characters:

Initial letters:

T, A, O, M, H, W, C, I, P, B, E, S

Second letters

H, O, E, I, A, U, N, R, T

Third letters

E, S, A, R, N, I

Final letters

E, T, S, D, N, R, Y, G

Note : • More than 50% of English words end with "E."

• More than 50% of English words start with T, A, O, S, or W

The method of deciphering encrypted message using this is almost futile against strong cipher used for messages that are encrypted using multi-level encryption using several keys.

This knowledge can be used to attack monoalphabetic ciphers because all occurrences of the same letter in a message will be encrypted the same way.

The Attack

(1) Calculate the frequency of letters in the ciphertext and compare this to the known frequencies in the language.

(2) Then make an intelligent guess of how to decrypt the message.

For example, if we analysed a ciphertext and found that the most commonly occurring letter was H, there is a good chance that all H's would be E's in the plaintext. This is not guaranteed to be the case, of course. The shorter the message, the more likely the frequencies will be unusual. This method is still much faster than trying all possibilities and on longer messages, it will be extremely effective.

Try it Yourself

See if you can decrypt these messages using frequency analysis. Use the frequency graph to help. Try to avoid a systematic search of all possibilities. The first one is easy and the second one is more challenging.

(1) `aqju mudj iqybydw ed jxu muuaudt (hint, solution)`

`Hint`

This message was encrypted with the Caesar cipher. Once you've figured out one letter, you should be able to write out the key and test it on one word to see if it works.

Try working on a short word first if you're stuck and guess what it might be since there are fewer possibilities.

Solution

This message was encrypted with a Caesar Cipher shift of 16. It decrypts to: "kate went sailing on the weekend"

(2) `vejmd krsqbmair ney js fbphbgas`

`Hint`

This message was encrypted with a keyphrase cipher. Try working on a shorter word first if you get stuck.

Solution

This message was encrypted with a Keyphrase cipher using the keyphrase "jumping". The message is: black ostriches fly at midnight

2.7 POLYALPHABETIC CIPHERS

Frequency analysis was a devastating attack on monoalphabetic ciphers and they could no longer be considered secure. The next development in cryptography was Polyalphabetic ciphers. The idea behind the polyalphabetic cipher is that a single letter can be encrypted to several different letters instead of just one.

We will study the Vigenere Cipher, which is a polyalphabetic substitution cipher. The keyspace consists of all ordered permutations of the alphabet and we call it a Vigenere square. You can see there are 25 rows that can be used as keys, each numbered with the amount they are shifted.

There are two ways to use this square to form a polyalphabetic cipher.

(1) Cycle through all 25 rows in turn. This would mean every twenty-fifth letter is encrypted with the same key.

OR

(2) Create a master-key that specifies which order the keys (or rows) are to be used in. This does not have to include all rows. For example we could use k=(5, 2, 16). and then cycle through these three keys. This would mean every third letter is encrypted with the same key.

For each single letter, you are only using 1 key and encryption and decryption works as with monoalphabetic ciphers.

Examples:

Method 1 – `(cycle through all keys in order)`

When doing this it is useful to have a printed version of the Vigenere Square and use a ruler to make sure you're using the correct key. We will be using key 1 to encrypt the d, key 2 to encrypt the r, key 3 to encrypt the a, and so on.

Plaintext: `dragon dream`

Ciphertext: `etdktt kznkx`

Method 2 – using k=(9, 17, 6, 20, 3)

We will use key 9 to encrypt the d, key 17 to encrypt the r, key 6 to encrypt the a, and so on.

Plaintext: `dragon dream`

Ciphertext: `migarw uxydv`

Another way of specifying the key for method 2 is to denote each row by the first letter instead of the number of shifts. Thus, in our example our master-key would be "jrgud". This example is not particularly memorable, but a word could be used as the master-key for method 2. The applet below will let you try out the keyword version of the Vigenere cipher. The numerical master-key is calculated and shown so that you can see the relation between the two notations.

Example

Message	`Talibans are not far away`
Keyword (Master key)	`sapna1978`
Numerical Master key	`k = (18, 0, 15, 13, 0, 0, 0, 0, 0)`
Encrypted Message	`laavbans aje cbt far aoan`

Attacking the Vigenere Cipher

Although the Vigenere Cipher seems to defeat frequency analysis, it was not a perfect solution. If you discover the block length (the length of the key), you can still apply frequency analysis given a long enough message. For example, with a 5-character master-key, you apply frequency analysis on characters four letters apart, since they will have been encrypted with the same key.

The Vigenere cipher is also susceptible to the chosen-plaintext attack. This attack is when the adversary (who is trying to spy on your message) is able to use your cryptographic system to encrypt, but not decrypt. What plaintext would you use to try to crack this cipher? Try out some of your ideas in the applet and see if you can force the ciphertext to give away information.

Hint

Try encrypting the plaintext "aaaaaaaaaaa" and see what conclusions you can draw.

2.8 TRANSPOSITION CIPHERS

Transposition ciphers are rarely encountered nowadays. They differ from both code systems and substitution ciphers; in a transposition cipher the letters of the plaintext are shifted about to form the cryptogram. This can be done in a number of ways and some systems exist where even whole words are transposed, rather than individual letters. To encrypt Chinese, for instance, one can use a transposition cipher operating on the individual signs of written Chinese (using a substitution cipher for a language like Chinese would be awkward if not impossible).

The best known method of transposition, simple columnar transposition, works like this:

Using a key word or phrase, such as CONVENIENCE, assign a number to each letter in the word using this rule: the numbers are assigned starting with 1, and they are assigned first by alphabetical order, and second, where the same letter appears twice, by position in the word.

Then, write in the message under the keyword, writing across - but take out columns, in numerical order, reading down. Thus:

C	O	N	V	E	N	I	E	N	C	E
1	10	7	11	3	8	6	4	9	2	5
H	E	R	E	I	S	A	S	E	C	R
E	T	M	E	S	S	A	G	E	E	N
C	I	P	H	E	R	E	D	B	Y	T
R	A	N	S	P	O	S	I	T	I	O
N										

produces

HECRN CEYI ISEP SGDI RNTO AAES RMPN
SSRO EEBT ETIA EEHS

Of course, it wouldn't be left with the spaces showing the columns that were used.

Decoding is harder - to read a message scrambled this way, you first have to count the letters to determine, in this case, that there are 45 letters, and so the first column will have five letters in it, and the other ones four, so that you know when to stop when filling the letters in vertically to read them out horizontally.

Since the text being transposed is split into nearly regular divisions of almost equal length, even double columnar transposition can be broken without recourse to multiple anagramming: the use of several messages of the same length, enciphered in the same key, to recover the transposition by matching together columns of letters that form reasonable letter pairs.

2.8.1 Single columnar transposition

One of the easiest ways to achieve transposition is the Single Columnar Transposition Cipher. To use it, one needs a keyword or phrase, whose letters are numbered according to their presence in the alphabet. The keyword Ozymandias is numbered in the following way:

O	Z	Y	M	A	N	D	I	A	S
7	10	9	5	1	6	3	4	2	8

That is, the first occurance of the letter A is numbered 1, the second 2. There are no B:s or C:s so the next letter to be numbered are the D followed by I, and so on. Next the plaintext is written in rows under the numbered keyword, one letter under each letter of the keyword. Let's say that the plaintext to be encrypted is Company has reached primary goal. It will look like this:

```
O Z  Y M A N D I A S
7 10 9 5 1 6 3 4 2 8
c o  m p a n y h a s
r e  a c h e d p r i
m a  r y g o a l
```

Now the letters of the plaintext are copied down by reading them off columnwise in the order stated by the enumeration of the keyword. The result is the finished cryptogram, which - of course - are put into groups of five letters, like this:

AHGAR YDAHP LPCYN EOCRM SIMAR OEA

To decrypt a received message enciphered by this method, one first must calculate the number of letters present in the cryptogram. This is done to see how many letters there originally were in the last row. As can be seen above, the two last columns - the ones numbered 2 and 8 - *only contains two letters and this is important.* Now the cryptogram above contains 28 letters and as a legitimate user of the crypto system, one knows that the keyword is ten letters wide. Therefore the last row must consist of eight letters only, the two final positions being empty. Keeping that in mind - or better still, marking the two final position of row three in some way to indicate that they shouldn't be used - one numbers the keyword letters (just as when encrypting) and then start by writing the first three letters of the cryptogram under keyword letter number one, thus:

```
O Z  Y M A N D I A S
7 10 9 5 1 6 3 4 2 8
. .  . . a . . . . .
. .  . . h . . . . .
. .  . . g . . . * *
```

Next comes column number two. Since the last position in column two is marked by a star and shouldn't be used, one only writes the next two letters, instead of three. Continue in the same way by writing the next three letters under keyword letter number three, and so on up to keyword letter eight, it will look like this:

```
O Z  Y M A N D I A S
7 10 9 5 1 6 3 4 2 8
c .  . p a n y h a .
r .  . c h e d p r .
m .  . y g o a l * *
```

Now column eight follows, and there only two letters should be written as stated above (the position marked by a star being left empty). This leaves six letters of the cryptogram, and these - of course - are written in column nine and ten, and then the cleartext can be read in the normal way, row by row.

Usually when employing a transposition cipher like the above, one adds dummy letters to make the final group five letters long if it isn't already full. It is important to do this before transposing the letters, otherwise the receiver can't calculate the columns that haven't a full number of letters if the last row isn't complete. In some cases the last row is always made complete by adding dummy letters, but that reduces the security of the cipher and isn't recommended (now, this cipher is quite easy to break anyway...).

After looking at ciphers which can replace the letters of one's message by completely different letters, a cipher that can't change any letters at all seems weak.

And, if your message might mention, or might not mention, someone with, say, a Q or an X in his name, then a transposition cipher will indeed give that away, although one could solve that by adding some garbage to the end of your message before encrypting it. But transposition ciphers can be secure in themselves, and as well, transposition methods are useful to know, since they can be mixed with substitution methods for a more secure cipher.

2.8.2 Double columnar transposition

Double columnar transposition is similar to single columnar transposition, but the process is repeated twice. One either uses the same keyword both times or, preferably, a different one on the second occasion. Let's encrypt the text Send armoured car to headquarters using the keywords Agamemnon and Mycenae:

```
A G A M E M N O N
1 4 2 5 3 6 7 9 8
s e n d a r m o u
r e d c a r t o h
e a d q u a r t e
r s j
```

(Note dummy letter j added at the end to make the total number of letters a multiple of five)

This first encryption gives: srer-nddj-aau-eeas-dcq-rra-mtr-uhe-oot. These letters are written under the second keyword, thus:

```
M Y C E N A E
5 7 2 3 6 1 4
s r e r n d d
j a a u e e a
s d c q r r a
m t r u h e o
o t
```

And, finally this gives the cryptogram:

DEREE ACRRU QUDAA OSJSM ONERH RADTT

Double columnar transposition is substatially safer against cryptanalysis than single columnar transposition (not impossible, thou).

2.8.3 Varients of Columnar Transposition

Another method of transposition, which appeared in a book by General Luigi Sacco, is a variant of columnar transposition that produces a different cipher:

C	O	N	V	E	N	I	E	N	C	E
1	10	7	11	3	8	6	4	9	2	5
H										
E	R	E	I	S	A	S	E	C	R	
E	T	M	E	S						
S	A	G	E	E	N	C	I			
P	H	E	R	E	D	B	Y	T	R	A
N	S	P	O	S	I	T				
I	O	N								

produces

HEESPNI RR SSEES EIY A SCBT
EMGEPN ANDI CT RTAHSO IEERO

Here, the first row is filled in only up to the column with the key number 1; the second row is filled in only up to the column with the key number 2; and so on. Of course, one still stops when one runs out of plaintext, so the eighth row stops short of the key number 8 in this example. This method has the advantage of dividing the text being transposed in a more irregular fashion than ordinary columnar transposition.

Various methods of modifying ordinary columnar transposition slightly to make it irregular have been used from time to time.

For example, during World War I, the French army used a transposition in which diagonal lines of letters were read off before the rest of the diagram. Also, several countries have used columnar transpositions in which several positions in the grid were blanked out and not used.

The method of transposition used on the digits produced by a straddling checkerboard in the VIC cipher can be illustrated here with the alphabet; first, knowing the number of letters to be encrypted, the area to be filled is laid out, and then the triangular areas on the right to be filled with plaintext last are marked out:

2	4	3	1	5
a	b	c	d	e
f	g	h	i	U
j	k	l	V	W
m	n	X	Y	Z
o	p	q	r	s
t				

here, the alphabet becomes DIVYR AFJMOT CHLXQ BGKNP EUWZS.

2.9 CRYPTANALYSIS

That aspect of cryptology which concerns the strength analysis of a cryptographic system, and the penetration or breaking of a cryptographic system. Also "codebreaking."Because there is no theory which guarantees strength for any conventional cipher, ciphers traditionally have been considered "strong" when they have been used for a long time with "nobody"knowing how to break them easily. Cryptanalysis seeks to improve this process by applying the known attack strategies to new ciphers, and by actively seeking new ones. It is normal to assume that at least known-plaintext is available; often, defined-plaintext is assumed. The result is typically some value for the amount of "work" which will achieve a "break" (even if that value is impractical); this is "the" strength of the cipher.But while cryptanalysis can prove "weakness" for a given level of effort, cryptanalysis cannot prove that there is no simpler attack:lack of proof of weakness is not proof of strength.

Indeed, when ciphers are used for real, The Opponents can hardly be expected to advertise a successful break, but will instead work hard to reassure users that their ciphers are still secure. The fact that apparently "nobody" knows how to break a cipher is somewhat less reassuring from this viewpoint. In this context, using a wide variety of different ciphers can make good sense: This reduces the value of the information protected by any particular cipher, which thus reduces the rewards from even a successful attack. Having a numerous ciphers also requires The Opponents to field far greater resources to identify, analyze, and automate breaking (when possible) of each different cipher.

Many academic attacks are essentially theoretical, involving huge amounts of data and computation. But even when a direct technical attack is practical, that may be the most difficult, expensive and time-consuming way to obtain the desired information. Other methods include making a paper copy, stealing a copy, bribery, coercion, and electromagnetic monitoring. No cipher can keep secret something which has been otherwise revealed. Information security thus involves far more than just cryptography, and even a cryptographic system is more than just a cipher. Even finding that information has been revealed does not mean that a cipher has been broken.

At one time it was reasonable to say: "Any cipher a man can make, another man can break." However, with the advent of serious computer-based cryptography, that statement is no longer valid, provided that every detail is properly handled. This, of course, often turns out to not be the case.

Before proceding further it is necessary to learn certain technical terms as given below:

Cryptanalyst: Someone who attacks ciphers with cryptanalysis. A "codebreaker." Often called the Opponent by cryptographers, in recognition of the (serious) game of thrust and parry between these parties.

Cryptographer: Someone who creates ciphers using cryptography.

Cryptographic Mechanism: A process for enciphering and/or deciphering, or an implementation (for example, hardware, computer software, hybrid, or the like) for performing that process. See also cryptography and mechanism.

Cryptanalysis versus Subversion: Cryptanalysis is hard; it is often tedious, repetitive, and very, very expensive. Success is never assured, and resources are always limited.

Consequently, other approaches for obtaining the hidden information (or the key!) can be more effective.

Approaches other than a direct technical attack on ciphertext include getting the information by cunning, outright theft, bribery, or intimidation. The room or computer could be bugged, secretaries subverteaphyd, files burglarized, etc. Most information can be obtained in some way other than "breaking" ciphertext.When the strength of a cipher greatly exceeds the effort required to obtain the same information in another way, the cipher is probably strong enough. And the mere fact that information has escaped does not necessarily mean that a cipher has been broken.

Secret Ciphers

Although, in some cases, cryptanalysis might succeed even if the ciphering process was unknown, we would certainly expect that this would make The Opponents' job much harder. It thus can be argued that the ciphering process should remain secret. Certainly, military cipher systems are not actually published (although it may be assumed internally that the equipment is known to the other side). But in commercial cryptography we normally assume (see Kerckhoff's Requirements) that The Opponents will know every detail of the cipher (although not the key, of course). There are several reasons for this:

First, it is common for a cipher to have unexpected weaknesses which are not found by its designers. But if the cipher design is kept secret, it cannot be examined by various interested parties, and so the weakness will not be publicly exposed. And this means that the weakness might be exploited in practice, while the cipher continues to be used.

Next, if a cipher itself is a secret, that secret is increasingly compromised by making it available for use: For a cipher to be used, it must be present at various locations, and the more widely it aphy used, the greater the risk the secret will be exposed. So whatever advantage there may be in cipher secrecy cannot be maintained, and The Opponents eventually will have the same advantage they would have had from public disclosure. Only now the cipher designers can comfort themselves with the dangerous delusion that their Opponents do not have an advantage they actually will have.

There is another level of secrecy here, and that is the trade secrecy involved with particular software designs. Very few large companies are willing to release source code for their products without some serious controls, and those companies may have a point. While the crypto routines themselves presumably might be patented, releasing that code alone probably would not support a thorough security evaluation. Source code might reasonably be made available to customers under a nondisclosure agreement, but this will not satisfy everyone. And while it might seem nice to have all source code available free, this will certainly not support an industry of continued cipher design and development. Unfortunately, there appears to be no good solution to this problem.

2.10 IMPROVING SUBSTITUTION

A cipher based on the use of a secret alphabet is not very secure; such ciphers are presented as puzzles in crossword puzzle magazines. To achieve security it is required to do something better.

Today, even to people not acquainted with cryptography, a number of possibilities suggest themselves. Originally, though, the new ideas came one at a time, separated by hundreds or thousands of years.

The basic ways to improve on simple substitution are the following:

Instead of using just 26 substitutes, make the problem harder by using a bigger substitution. This is divided into several cases:

- Use several substitutes for each letter (homophonic substitution)
- Replace every two letters, or every three letters, by something else that stands for that combination of two letters or three letters (polygraphic substitution)
- Replace common combinations of letters, or words, or phrases, by their own substitutes (nomenclators and codes)

Instead of using the same set of substitutes all the time, change from one secret alphabet to another as you encipher a message (polyalphabetic substitution).

Another way of improving on simple substitution is less obvious. Today, text is often converted from the letters, punctuation marks, digits, and other symbols you find on a typewriter to the binary bits of ASCII. Before that, other representations of text were used to substitute for the printed word, such as Morse code. The ancient Greeks used the Polybius square for signalling, by means of which each letter was represented by two groups of from one to five signal fires.

If a letter can be broken up into smaller pieces for purposes of signalling, those smaller pieces can also be used in a cipher. For example, one can take the letters of a message apart into smaller pieces, transpose the smaller pieces, and then put the pieces back together again into letters.

This is called fractionation, and is closely related to polygraphic substitution for two reasons; one is that both deal with different sized units - parts of letters and letters, or letters and pairs of letters - and the other is that fractionation is sometimes used as a method of polygraphic substitution.The following are the other classical methods of improving Substitution:

- Homophones and Nomenclators
- Polygraphic Ciphers and Fractionation
- Playfair and its Relatives
- The Bifid, the Trifid, and the Straddling Checkerboard
- Fractionated Morse, and Other Oddities
- The VIC Cipher
- Two Trigraphic Ciphers, and a Heptagraphic One
- Polyalphabetic Substitution

2.11 CLASSICAL ENCRYPTION TECHNIQUES

The oldest, simplest and the most primitive of all of the methods, the 'translation table', has been used long since, before the first computer was invented. Each 'chunk' of data (usually 1 byte) is used as an offset within a 'translation table', and the resulting 'translated' value from within the table is then written into the output stream. The encryption and decryption programs would each use a table that translates to and from the encrypted data. While this method is very simple and fast, the down side is that once the translation table is known, the code is broken. Further, such a method is relatively straightforward for code breakers to decipher. Still, for general "unreadability" of encoded data, without adverse effects on performance, the 'translation table' method lends itself well.

2.11.1 Classical Cryptanalysis

Normally, cryptanalysis is thought of as the way ciphers are broken. But cryptanalysis is really analysis — the ways we come to understand a cipher in detail. Since most ciphers have weaknesses, a deep understanding can expose the best attacks for a particular cipher.

Most books cover some classical "pen and paper" ciphers, which might be thought to be simpler and easier to understand than modern ciphers. But, lacking even basic tools like hashing, random number generation, and shuffling, the classical forms tend to be very limited, and so are somewhat misleading as introductions to modern cryptanalysis. (Except Decrypted Secrets by Bauer.) For example:

The Caesar Cipher replaces each plaintext letter with the letter n (originally 3) places farther along in the normal alphabet. Classically, the only possible key is the value for n, but in a computer environment, it is easy to be general: We can select n for each position in the message by using a random number generator (this could be a stream cipher), and also key the alphabet by shuffling it into a unique ordering (which is Monoalphabetic Substitution).

Monoalphabetic Substitution replaces each plaintext letter with an associated letter from a (keyed) random alphabet. Classically, it was tough to specify an arbitrary order for the alphabet, so this was often based on understandable keywords (skipping repeated letters), which helped make the cipher easier to crack. But in the modern computer version, it is easy to select among the set of all possible permutations by shuffling the alphabet with a keyed random number generator.

Another problem with monoalphabetic substitution is that the most frequently used letters in the plaintext become the most frequently used letters in the ciphertext, and statistical techniques can be used to help identify which letters are which. Classically, multiple different alphabets (Polyalphabetic Substitution) or multiple ciphertext letters for a single plaintext letter (Homophonic Substitution) were introduced to avoid this. But in a modern computer version, we can continue to permute the single alphabet, as in Dynamic Substitution (see my article). Moreover, if the original "plaintext" is evenly distributed (which can be assured by a previous combining), then statistical techniques are little help.

Polyalphabetic Substitution replaces each plaintext letter with an associated letter from one of multiple "random" alphabets. But, classically, it was tough to produce arbitrary alphabets, so the "multiple alphabets" tended to be different offset values as in Caesar ciphers. Moreover, it was tough even to choose alphabets at random, so they tended to be used in rotating sequence, which gave the cryptanalyst enormous encouragement. On the other hand, a modern improved version of polyalphabetic substitution, with a special keyed Latin square combiner, with each "alphabet" selected character-by-character by a keyed random number generator, can be part of a very serious cipher.

Transposition Ciphers re-arrange the plaintext letters to form ciphertext. But, classically, it was tough to form an arbitrary re-arrangement (or permutation), so the re-ordering tended to occur in particular graphic patterns (along columns instead of rows, across diagonals, etc.). Normally, two messages of the same size would be transposed similarly, leading to a "multiple anagramming" attack: Two equal-size messages were permuted in the same way until they both "made sense." But, in the modern general form, a keyed random number generator can shuffle blocks of arbitrary size in a general way, almost never permute two blocks similarly, and work on a randomized content which may not make sense, making the classical attack useless (see my article).

Thus, it was often the restrictions on the general design — necessary for "pen and paper" practicality — which made these classical ciphers easy to attack. And the attacks which work well on specific classical versions may have very little chance on a modern very-general version of the same cipher.

2.11.2 Classification of Classical Cryptographic Methods

There are generally two broad classification of classical cryptographic methods:

- **Masking**

The use of masking leads to substitution. Often message is masked in such a way that the resulting message that goes out in an open communication channel, seems harmless and inconspicuous.

- **Veiling**

The use of veiling leads to transposition, as veiled messages are usually not masked at all, but simply combined within other items regularly in such a way that resulting message takes form of yet another message, called acrostics.

2.12 ONE-TIME PAD (OTP)

The use of pencil-and-paper one-time pads is limited because of the practical and logistical problems. Intelligence agencies use them to communicate with their agents in the field, where security has absolute priority. With OTP, they don't have to carry compromising crypto systems or computer programs with them. They can carry a large number of OTP keys in very small booklets, on microfilm or even printed on clothing. These are easy to hide and to destroy. One way to send OTP-encrypted messages to agents in the field is via numbers stations.

One-time pads were widely used by foreign service communicators until the 1980's, often in combination with code books. Such a code book contained all kinds of words or entire phrases, which were represented by a three or four figure code. For special non-listed names or expressions the book included codes that represent one letter that allowed the spelling of words. There was a book to encode, sorted by alphabet and/or category, and a book to decode, sorted by numbers. These book were valid for a long period of time and were not only to encode the message - which would be a poor encryption method by itselfe - but especially to reduce its length for transmission over commercial cable or telex. Once the message was converted in numbers, the communicator enciphered these numbers with the one-time pad. Usually there was a set of two different pads, one for incoming and one for outgoing messages. Although a one-time pad normally has only two copies of a key, one for sender and one for receiver, some systems used more than two copies to address mutiple receivers. The pads were like note blocks with random numbers on each small page, but with the edges sealed. One could only read the next pad by tearing off the previous pad. Each pad was used only once and destroyed immediately. This system enabled absolute secure communication.

2.12.1 Definition of One-time Pad

The one-time pad (OTP), also called Vernam-cipher or the perfect cipher, is a crypto algorithm where plaintext is combined with a random key. One-time pad was developed in 1917 by Gilbert Vernam for use on telex machines. Each transmitted 5-bit Baudot code was mixed with a random 5-bit code on a paper tape. Such tapes contained a large number of these random 5-bit codes and were called one-time-tape. The one-time-tape ran synchronously on both the sender's and the receiver's telex. Vernam's invention was the basis for several pencil-and-paper versions. The name one-time pad refers to the small notepads on which the keys are printed. These pads are small booklets or microfilms with groups of five numbers or letters. Today, digital one-time key versions enable the storage of much more random data and the encryption of large data files.

We can only talk about OTP if four important rules are followed. If these rules are applied correctly, the one-time pad can be proven to be unbreakable. However, if only one of these rules is disregarded, the cipher is no longer unbreakable.

- The key is as long as the plaintext.
- The key is truly random (not generated by simple computer Rnd functions or such!)
- There should only be two copies of the key: one for the sender and one for the receiver (some exeptions exist for multiple receivers)
- The keys are used only once, and both sender and receiver must destroy their key after use.

2.12.2 Using the One-time Pad

Although OTP is the perfect cipher it has two major disadvantages. The first problem is the generation of a large quantity of random numbers or letters. For absolutely true randomness we cannot create these keys by simple mechanical devices or computer algorithms like a computer RND function or stream ciphers. The second problem is the key distribution. Since each key can only be used once and has to have the same length as the message, we will need a large number of different keys, physically distributed to both sender and receiver. Of course, it would be useless to send the one-time pads to the receiver by encrypting them with AES, IDEA or another strong algorithm. This would lower the unbreakable security of the pads to the security level of the algorithm, used to encrypt the pads. Therefore, the key distribution creates enormous logistical and security problems if OTP is used on large scale. The costs of secure production, distribution, custody and destruction of OTP-keys can only be supported by government departments such as military, intelligence services and diplomacy.

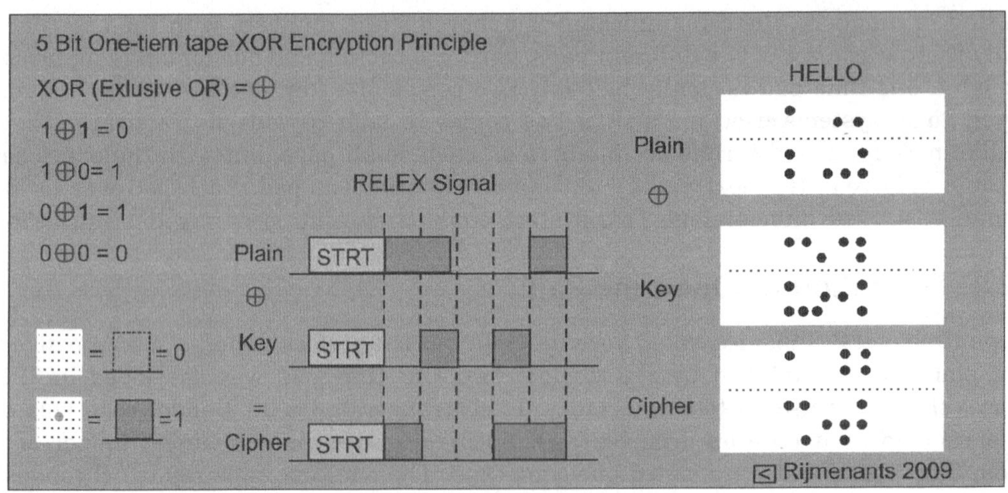

Fig. 2.8 Principle of 5 Bit One-time Tape XOR Principle

The use of pencil-and-paper one-time pads is limited because of the practical and logistical problems. Intelligence agencies use them to communicate with their agents in the field, where security has absolute priority. With OTP, they don't have to carry compromising crypto systems or computer programs with them. They can carry a large number of OTP keys in very small booklets, on microfilm or even printed on clothing. These are easy to hide and to destroy. One way to send OTP-encrypted messages to agents in the field is via numbers stations.

One-time pads were widely used by foreign service communicators until the 1980's, often in combination with code books. Such a code book contained all kinds of words or entire phrases, which were represented by a three or four figure code. For special non-listed names or expressions the book included codes that represent one letter that allowed the spelling of words. There was a book to encode, sorted by alphabet and/or category, and a book to decode, sorted by numbers. These book were valid for a long period of time and were not only to encode the message - which would be a poor encryption method by itselfe - but especially to reduce its length for transmission over commercial cable or telex. Once the message was converted in numbers, the communicator enciphered these numbers with the one-time pad. Usually there was a set of two different pads, one for incoming and one for outgoing messages. Although a one-time pad normally has only two copies of a key, one for sender and one for receiver, some systems used more than two copies to address mutiple receivers. The pads were like note blocks with random numbers on each small page, but with the edges sealed. One could only read the next pad by tearing off the previous pad. Each pad was used only once and destroyed immediately. This system enabled absolute secure communication.

2.12.3 One-Time Pad with Numbers

There are many different ways to apply one-time pads. All of them are absolutely secure if the rules of one-time pad are followed. We can apply OTP with numbers or letters. In our first example we will demonstrate the use of numbers. There are several different ways to convert letters into numbers, mostly based on a table such as a straddling checkerboard (see TAPIR), but for this example we will make use of easiest one. We assign to each letter a numerical value (eg. A=01, B=02 and so on through Z=26). The key consist of random digits from 0 to 9. Each single random key digit is subtracted from the plain text digits without carry (eg. 5 - 9 = 15 - 9 = 6). To decipher the message, we simply add the OTP-key digits to the ciphertext digits, again without carry (eg. 6 + 9 = 5 and not15) and convert the obtained values into letters.

Text:	T	H	I	S	I	S	S	E	C	R	E	T
	20	08	09	19	09	19	19	05	03	18	05	20
OTP-Key:	-52	68	10	27	88	96	23	50	49	67	25	4
Ciphertext:	78	40	99	92	21	23	96	55	64	51	80	89

Ciphertext: 78409 99221 23965 56451 8089

A practical Example

As a little exercise you can open or download the following sound file, a recording of a numbers station. The message is preceded by a call sign melody and "39715", the call sign of the receiver. Each group of five figures is spelled twice to ensure correct reception. Write down the groups - each group once - and add the given OTP key without carry (eg. 6 + 9 = 5 and not15). Then convert the values - in groups of two - into letters (eg. 01=A, 02=B and so on through 26=Z) to obtain the original the message (don't forget to disregard the "39715" call sign!)

This little exercise shows you exactly how secret agents can receive messages in an absolute secure manner, with only one-time pads, a small short-wave receiver and pencil and paper.

Numbers Station Message (1724 Kb)

The one-time pad to decipher this message:

`40626 12159 13103 52724 94956 62062 96654 13713 71963 81646 49584`

Note: Altough the recording is from an original numbers station, the OTP key is fictitious and reverse-calculated in such a way that a readable message is obtained when using this key. In reality there is no way to decipher the original message or to know which key was used. In fact, since a OTP key is truly random, one can calculate any plain text from a cipher text, as long as you use the 'right' wrong key. That's why OTP is unbreakable.

2.12.4 One-Time Pad with Letters

We can also use letters for the OTP-key and the ciphertext. We assign each letter a numerical value (eg. A=0, B=1 C=3 and so on through Z=25). Note that we start with A=0 and not A=1 to use the modulo 26! Text and key values are added together (this time with carry!), with modulo 26 (if a value is more than 25, we subtract 26 from that value). Finally, we convert the result back into letters. To decipher the message, we convert the ciphertext and OTP key into numerical values and subtract OTP-key from ciphertext, again modulo 26 (if a value is less than 0 we add 26 to that value).

Text:	T	H	I	S	I	S	S	E	C	R	E	T
	19	07	08	18	08	18	18	04	02	17	04	19
OTP-Key:	X	V	H	E	U	W	N	O	P	G	D	Z
+	23	21	07	04	20	22	13	14	15	06	03	25
Result:	42	28	15	22	28	40	31	18	17	23	07	44
Mod 26 =	16	02	15	22	02	14	05	18	17	23	07	18
Ciphertext:	Q	C	P	W	C	O	F	S	R	X	H	S

Ciphertext: Q C P W C O F S R X H S

There are two ways to make the calculations easier: the Conversion Table or the Vigenere Square (also called Tabula Recta).

First, we will explain the conversion table. To encrypt by addition we take for example T(19) + X(23). The total is 42, in the conversion table representing the letter Q wich is the encryption result. To decrypt by subtracting we take Q(16) - X(23). If the result would give a negative value (which is in this case) we take the greater equivalent of Q(16), which is (42) in the conversion table. We can now find the deciphered letter with Q(42) - X(23) = T(19)

A	B	C	D	E	F	G	H	I	J	K	L	M	N	O	P	Q	R	S	T	U	V	W	X	Y	Z
00	01	02	03	04	05	06	07	08	09	10	11	12	13	14	15	16	17	18	19	20	21	22	23	24	25
26	27	28	29	30	31	32	33	34	35	36	37	38	39	40	41	42	43	44	45	46	47	48	49	50	—

With a Vigenere Square we can encipher instantly, without the need to first convert into numbers and perform calculations. Note that Vigenere is not used as encryption (which would be very weak) but merely as a methode to easily add the one-time pad to the text. We can consider the horizontal column header of the square as plaintext, the vertical row header as key and the square field as ciphertext. To encrypt with key E the letter H, take the crossing between key-row E and the plain-column H. In our example the resulting ciphertext will be the letter L. To decrypt with key E ciphertext letter L, take key- row E and search for the letter L in that row. The plaintext letter is the column header right above the letter L you just found, in this case the letter H.

There are several practical solution to the Vigenere table.

There are many more variations of one-time pad but they all use the same principle that a random value is added and afterwards subtracted or the other way around.

	A	B	C	D	E	F	G	H	I	J	K	L	M	N	O	P	Q	R	S	T	U	V	W	X	Y	Z
A	A	B	C	D	E	F	G	H	I	J	K	L	M	N	O	P	Q	R	S	T	U	V	W	X	Y	Z
B	B	C	D	E	F	G	H	I	J	K	L	M	N	O	P	Q	R	S	T	U	V	W	X	Y	Z	A
C	C	D	E	F	G	H	I	J	K	L	M	N	O	P	Q	R	S	T	U	V	W	X	Y	Z	A	B
D	D	E	F	G	H	I	J	K	L	M	N	O	P	Q	R	S	T	U	V	W	X	Y	Z	A	B	C
E	E	F	G	H	I	J	K	L	M	N	O	P	Q	R	S	T	U	V	W	X	Y	Z	A	B	C	D
F	F	G	H	I	J	K	L	M	N	O	P	Q	R	S	T	U	V	W	X	Y	Z	A	B	C	D	E
G	G	H	I	J	K	L	M	N	O	P	Q	R	S	T	U	V	W	X	Y	Z	A	B	C	D	E	G
H	H	I	J	K	L	M	N	O	P	Q	R	S	T	U	V	W	X	Y	Z	A	B	C	D	E	G	H
I	I	J	K	L	M	N	O	P	Q	R	S	T	U	V	W	X	Y	Z	A	B	C	D	E	G	H	I
J	J	K	L	M	N	O	P	Q	R	S	T	U	V	W	X	Y	Z	A	B	C	D	E	G	H	I	J
K	K	L	M	N	O	P	Q	R	S	T	U	V	W	X	Y	Z	A	B	C	D	E	G	H	I	J	K
L	L	M	N	O	P	Q	R	S	T	U	V	W	X	Y	Z	A	B	C	D	E	G	H	I	J	K	L
M	M	N	O	P	Q	R	S	T	U	V	W	X	Y	Z	A	B	C	D	E	G	H	I	J	K	L	M
N	N	O	P	Q	R	S	T	U	V	W	X	Y	Z	A	B	C	D	E	G	H	I	J	K	L	M	N
O	O	P	Q	R	S	T	U	V	W	X	Y	Z	A	B	C	D	E	G	H	I	J	K	L	M	N	O
P	P	Q	R	S	T	U	V	W	X	Y	Z	A	B	C	D	E	G	H	I	J	K	L	M	N	O	P
Q	Q	R	S	T	U	V	W	X	Y	Z	A	B	C	D	E	G	H	I	J	K	L	M	N	O	P	Q
R	R	S	T	U	V	W	X	Y	Z	A	B	C	D	E	G	H	I	J	K	L	M	N	O	P	Q	R
S	S	T	U	V	W	X	Y	Z	A	B	C	D	E	G	H	I	J	K	L	M	N	O	P	Q	R	S
T	T	U	V	W	X	Y	Z	A	B	C	D	E	G	H	I	J	K	L	M	N	O	P	Q	R	S	T
U	U	V	W	X	Y	Z	A	B	C	D	E	G	H	I	J	K	L	M	N	O	P	Q	R	S	T	U
V	V	W	X	Y	Z	A	B	C	D	E	G	H	I	J	K	L	M	N	O	P	Q	R	S	T	U	V
W	W	X	Y	Z	A	B	C	D	E	G	H	I	J	K	L	M	N	O	P	Q	R	S	T	U	V	W
X	X	Y	Z	A	B	C	D	E	G	H	I	J	K	L	M	N	O	P	Q	R	S	T	U	V	W	X
Y	Y	Z	A	B	C	D	E	G	H	I	J	K	L	M	N	O	P	Q	R	S	T	U	V	W	X	Y
Z	Z	A	B	C	D	E	G	H	I	J	K	L	M	N	O	P	Q	R	S	T	U	V	W	X	Y	Z

2.13 PLAYFAIR CIPHER

The Playfair cipher is a digraph substitution cipher. It employs a table where one letter of the alphabet is omitted, and the letters are arranged in a 5 x 5 grid. Typically, the J is removed from the alphabet and an I takes its place in the text that is to be encoded. Below is an unkeyed grid.

```
A B C D E
F G H I K
L M N O P
Q R S T U
V W X Y Z
```

To encode a message, one breaks it into two-letter chunks. Repeated letters in the same chunk are usually separated by an X. The message, "HELLO ONE AND ALL" would become "HE LX LO ON EA ND AL LX". Since there was not an even number of letters in the message, it was padded with a spare X. Next, you take your letter pairs and look at their positions in the grid.

"HE" forms two corners of a rectangle. The other letters in the rectangle are C and K. You start with the H and slide over to underneath the E and write down K. Similarly, you take the E and slide over to the H column to get C. So, the first two letters are "KC". "LX" becomes "NV" in the same way.

"LO" are in the same row. In this instance, you just slide the characters one position to the right, resulting in "MP". The same happens for "ON", resulting in "PO". "EA" becomes "AB" in the same way, but the E is at the far edge. By shifting one position right, we scroll around back to the left side and get A.

"ND" are in a rectangle form and beomes "OC". "AL" are both in the same column, so we just move down one spot. "AL" is changed into "FQ". "LX" is another rectangle and is encoded as "NV".

The resulting message is now "KC NV MP PO AB OC FQ NV" or "KCNVMPPOABOCFQNV" if you remove the spaces. This encoder will do all of the lookups for you, but you still need to do a few things yourself.

Manually break apart double letters with X (or any other) characters. Some people break apart all doubles, others break all doubles that happen in the same two-letter chunk. This encoder requires neither in order to be more flexible.

Manually make the message length even by adding an X or whatever letter you want. If you don't, the encoder will automatically add an X for you.

All non-letters are ignored and not encoded. The one letter that you select to share a square in the cipher is translated. Numbers, spaces, and punctuation are also skipped. If you leave two letters together in a two-letter chunk, they will be encoded by moving down and right one square ("LL" becomes "RR") where as traditional Playfair ciphers will automatically insert an X for you.

This particular cipher was used by the future U.S. President, John F. Kennedy, Jr. He sent a message about a boat going down.

Example

Message	Talibans are not far away
Encrypted Message	Qdofcbsx bqc pty lfq bvbzY

2.14 SUBJECT MATTER OF CRYPTOGRAPHY

The general situation: Communication over a problematic channel. The channel may not be secure (any communication may be overheard); the participants in the communication may not be trustworthy. Assurances of various sorts would be valuable.

- **Confidentiality:** assurance that only the participants will know the contents of their communication. Business or government secrets.
- **Integrity:** assurance that the message sent is exactly the message received by the intended participant.
- **Authenticity:** assurance that the message really comes from who it says it comes from
- **Non-repudiation:** assurance that the real sender cannot deny a file was sent.
- **Warrantability:** Alice commits to the truth of some proposition p but does not reveal p. Bob wants some warranty now that commits Alice to p before he commits to some important action. That warranty should be verifiable at a later time.

Generally: verification and securing of communications over channels that are not secure and cannot be assumed to transmit information reliably.

2.15 ENCRYPTION

2.15.1 The solution to several problems: Encryption

Encryption:

1. Plain text message. We call this **M** (for message)
2. Encoding algorithm. We call this **E**.
3. Decoding algorithm (perhaps even more important than 2!) We call this **D**.
4. Key. We call this **K**. In general the longer the key, the more secure the messages sent with it.
5. Cipher text. The result of encoding the message with the key. We call this **C**.

That's all.

Convention: E(M,K) = C.

Convention: D(C,K) = M.

Why **a key**? Why not just two secret algorithm? so that:

E(M) – C

D(C) = M

1. **Short answer:** Secrets always get out. Keys are easier to change than algorithms.
2. **Longer answer:** Kerckoff's Law.

```
A cryptosystem should be secure even if everything about
the system, except the key, is public knowledge.
```

Make the algorithms public. Let the smartest mathematicians in the world amuse themselves by trying to find a weakness. Makes for the strongest possible encryption algorithms.

Encryption solves two of the problems we started with:

1. **Confidentiality:** Only those who know the key can read the message.
2. **Authenticity:** Bob wants to verify that a messsage came from Alice and Alice and Bunty share a secret key known only to them. Bunty challenges Alice to encrypt a random message, say, "2 is fun!" Only Anita can encrypt it correctly.

Integrity, nonrepudiation, and warrantability each call for a little something more, but secret keys can enter into solving these problems as well, as we shall see.

2.15.2The Decryption Key

We can and should distinguish between encryption keys and decryption keys. One important reason is that it gives a more general way of characterizing decryption systems. The key K as a whole can then be viewed as a pair E and D, the E half of which is used for encryption and the D half for decryption.

Another very important reason for spitting K into E and D is that a mathematically nice way to design an encryption system is to use the same function for encoding and decoding. As before:

$$E(M) = C$$

$$D(C) = M$$

But we have keys KE and KD, encryption and decryption keys respectively, and an encryption operation O, such that:

$$E(M) = O(M, K_E) = C$$

$$D(C) = O(C, K_D) = M$$

We saw this setup with several kinds of ciphers.

1. **Shift cipher:** O was modular addition. KE was some number E and KD was E^{-1} mod 26.
2. **Affine cipher:** O was linear combination using the equation:

   $$C = e_1 * M + e_2$$

   K_E was $[e_1, e_2]$ and K_D was $[e_1^{-1} * e_1^{-1}]$.
3. **Hill cipher:** O was matrix multiplication. K_E was the matrix:

$$\begin{bmatrix} e_1 & e_2 \\ e_3 & e_3 \end{bmatrix}$$

K_D was K_E^{-1}.

Mathematically this brings us inview of a kind of mathematical system called a **group**. This is a system with a 2-place operation on a set of elements. In this system there is an identity element and inverses (elements which, combined with the operation give the identity element), In terms of our decryption system, K_E and E and K_D are inverses. Hill and shift encryption systems are very naturally formulated as groups, as are transposition codes, whcih we have not looked at.

We shall see this setup again with RSA public key cryptography where the concept of a group and of inverses will be very important.

2.16 THE PROBLEM WITH KEYS

The problem with keys is exchanging them.

Consider: The internet. Many to many communications among perfect strangers who cannot trust each other (but must in order for the American way to survive). For a community of n users,

meetings are necessary to secure all pairwise communications.

The solution to the problem of key exchange is to make public key exchange possible. The idea is to only exchange K_E publicly, and to keep K_D secret.

Of course this is not possible with shift ciphers and Hill ciphers. Once he knows the encryption key for a shift cipher, any bozo who knows modular arithmetic can figure out the decryption key. Similarly for Hill ciphers and any bozo who knows matrix theory.

This is because there is an easy-to-compute function that takes you from K_E to K_D.

But what if there weren't? What if we could find a system in which getting from K_E to K_D was very difficult? But remember that

$$O(M, K_E) = C$$

What we would also want of course is that, even given C and KE, M is very hard to compute.

This brings us to the topic of one-way functions, functions that are easy to compute in one direction but very hard in the other. Basically we are working our way toward a system in which the encryption function is a one-way function, even when

2.17 ONE-WAY FUNCTIONS

2.17.1 Fair play: A coin-tossing game problem

Anita and **Bunty** (the main characters of our little drama) play a game of heads-ortails.

Version 1: Anita flips coin. Bunty calls it in the air. If Bunty gets it right he wins. If not, Anita wins.

Issues:

- Fair coin

- Bunty calls coin at right time
- Anita and Bunty agree on outcome

Item 3 sounds silly.

But now add: Anita and Bunty are playing over the phone.

How do we do this reliably, assuming Anita and Bunty can't trust each other completely?

2.17.2 A Solution: A one-way function

Wanted: a function f such that:

- For any x, $f(x)$ is pretty easy to compute.
- For any $f(x)$, it is impossible to determine what x is.
- For any x and y, if $x \neq y$, then $f(x) \neq f(y)$

Never mind for now whether such a thing exists. Suppose we had one. Then agree on the following:

- An even x is heads
- An odd x is tails

Then we could play the game as in Table 2.4.

Table 2.1. Head/Tails Game Protocol

Step One	Anita chooses an even/odd x (H or T)
Step Two	She sends $f(x)$ to Bunty
Step Three	Bunty calls H or T (odd or even), essentially guessing what kind of x produced the $f(x)$ he just got.
Step Four	Anita informs Bunty whether he's right by sending him x
Step Five	Bunty computes $f(x)$ and verifies that it agrees with the $f(x)$ Anita sent before.

2.17.3 Verifiable key exchange: A practical almost one-way almostfunction

In reality it just has to be easy to compute the one-way function in one direction and way hard in the other. And in reality it doesnt have to be a function to do much of what we want.

Here is what seems to be the simplest idea, due to Ralph Merkle For the basic idea, see Figure 2.15.

Anita has to do some work to get her key. In fact for a key 20 bits long the task of breaking the code takes about 2^{20} (roughly a million) steps. But our evil eavesdropper Eve has to perform that same task for about 1,000,000 messages, so that's

$$2^{20} * 2^{20} = 2^{40}$$

steps, which is a **lot** more work.

This **might** be good enough. If Anita and Eve can both try 10K keys per second, Anita can do her decoding in about a minute on average, but Eve's decoding takes her about a year on average.

Step One	Bunty sends Anita 1,000,000 messages of the form *This is message number **x**. Use 128-bit key* $\mathbf{K}_x$. So each message gives Anita a different 128-bit key. He encrypts each of these messages using a randomly chosen 20-bit key [easily broken] whose identity doesn't matter.
Step Two	Anita randomly picks one of Bunty's million messages and decrypts it using a brute force method based on the fact that it was encoded using a 20-bit key, She learns $\mathbf{K}_x$ and uses it to encrypt a message m to Bunty, sends the encrypted message, $E(\mathbf{K}_x, m)$, along with the message number **x** (not encrypted).
Step Three	Bunty decrypts the message by looking up $\mathbf{K}_x$ in message x.

Figure 2.15 Merkle Secret Key Protocol

Note that there is no function here, one way or otherwise. What there is is a lot of values (Bunty's 1,000,000 messages) and a random choice among them. The problem is determining what the result of that random choice is. Note that that determination isn't impossible, merely computationally difficult. Note that the amount of security depends on the difficulty of the computation for Eve. If Eve works for the NSA she might have computational resources several orders of magnitude better than Anita's. Then the margin starts to dwindle away quickly.

The hassle: Bunty has to do a lot of computing to generate 1,000,000 appropriate random messages, and he has to tie up a lot of bandwidth to send all of them to Anita. Anita has to do a lot of computing to get her key. Increasing the amount of security can be done by increasing the number of initial messages or increasing the size of the keys Bunty sends (from 20 to, say, 25), thus increasing the amount of hassle.

Moral: A function that is **difficult** to undo would be better and could maybe secure a safer security margin without increasing the hassle.

2.17.4 TwoTrue-to-life One-way Functions

Here are two examples of one-way functions that might give us a better way to accomplish what Merkle's protocol was trying to accomplish in the last section.

1. Multiplication. Multiplication is easy. Factoring is hard. Factoring a number usually is taken to mean finding prime integers that divide it evenly. For very large numbers this is very hard. The idea is roughly this: Pick two primes p, q such that

$$pq = n \approx 10^{200}$$

For example:

$p = 827348899587473894937637660 7$

$q = 152637849009674332455648 11$

$n = 12628475641355305097836036624840660881783606577627 7$

Multiplying p and q together to get n is easy (at least for a computer). Factoring n to find p and q is very hard.

2. Finding logarithms in modular arithmetic (for some large n). Raising a number a to a power x to get result r is easy in modular arithmetic, in fact, easier than in regular arithmetic. Finding what power a has to be raised to to get r is hard. This is called the *discrete logarithm* problem.

Note – That what counts here is not possibility or impossibility but the relative amount of computing.

2.17.5 Verifiable Key Exchange: A One-way Function Protocol

We want Anita and Bunty to construct a key K they can use for their encryption. We want them to construct it by communications on an insecure channel. And of course we want K to be a secret.

Anita and Bunty each contribute half the bits, we'll call Anita's bits A and Bunty's bits B. Then we need some easy-to-compute function *construct-key* which computes K:

construct-key(x, y) = K

As before algorithms aren't assumed to be secret so construct-key is public.

Anita can't send A. That's insecure. So we assume a one-way function f as before.

Anita sends

$f(x)$

Bunty sends

$f(y)$

The exact values of A and B are still secret because f is one-way.

What we now need is for Anita and Bunty to both be able to construct the same key from what each has:

Anita x $f(y)$

Bunty y $f(x)$

So we need a version of construct-key which works even though one of its arguments has gone through f:

alt-construct-key ($f(x)$, y) = alt-construct-key ($f(y)$, x) = construct-key(x, y) = K

Anita x f (y) alt-construct-key $(f\ (y), x)$

Bunty y f (x) alt-construct-key $(f\ (x), y)$

For security we also want a kind of one-wayness for alt-construct-key. It should be impossible to construct K without having either A or B. In particular, the information sent on the insecure channel, f(A) and f(B), shouldn't suffice. So there should be no easy-to-compute function break-key, such that:

$$\text{break-key}\ (f\ (x), f\ (y)) = K$$

In fact, we have already discussed some functions that have the properties we need. These were multiplication in regular arithmetic and raising to a power in modular arithmetic; both have which inverses (factoring and discrete logarithms) which are hard to compute.

The reason these fit the bill is that we don't need to reach the ideal of functions that are impossible to run backwards. We just need a function that, given the complexity of the particular inputs we use, will take an impractical amount of computing time to compute, say 1000 years.

In fact, the protocol we have just described is the Diffie-Hellman protocol for key exchange. The one-way function used there is the discrete power function (inverse: (discrete log function).

2.17.6 Diffie-Hellman Protocol

First, Anita and Bunty publically agree on on a large prime p and a generator g of Z_p^*. The protocol goes like this:

1. Anita chooses a large random number x and sends Bunty:

$$X = g^x \bmod p$$

2. Bunty chooses a large random number y and sends Anita:

$$Y = g^y \bmod p$$

3. Anita computes

$$K = Y^x \bmod p$$

4. Bunty computes

$$K = X^y \bmod p$$

Note that Anita can do her key computation because she knows x, and Bunty can do his because he knows y, but evil eavesdropper Eve doesn't know either of those numbers. Moreoever Anita and Bunty compute the same key because:

$$g^{xy} = g^{yx} = g^{xy}$$

What Eve does know is g, p, X, and Y. But in order to compute the K she has to get back from X to x or from Y to y, and in order to do that she has to find what power g is raised to to give either X or Y . This is what is called the *discrete logarithm problem* and it is, as far as we know, very difficult to compute.

So raising to a power in modular arithmetic is our one way function. Recapping the original idea:

We needed Anita to send

$$f(x)$$

The f here was $g^x \bmod p$ In step 2, Bunty sent

$$f(y) = g^y \bmod p$$

The exact values of A and B are still secret because f is one-way.

What we needed next was for Anita and Bunty to both be able to construct the same key from what each has:

$$\text{Anita } x\ f(y) = Y$$

$$\text{Bunty } y\ f(x) = X$$

So we needed an alternative construct key function which works even though one of its arguments has gone through f:

alt-construct-key (Y, x) = alt-construct-key (X, y) = construct-key(x, y) = K

In the Diffie-Hellman protocol, alt-construct-key is just raising the last received message to a power mod p:

alt-construct-key (X, y) $X^y \bmod p$

alt-construct-key (Y, x) $Y^x \bmod p$

construct-key (x, y) $g^{xy} \bmod p$

And that was all there was to it, given that:

$$X^y = g^{xy} = Y^x = g^{yx} = g^{xy} \bmod p$$

2.17.7 RSA Protocol

The RSA protocol

1. Choose two large random numbers p and q and multiply them together to give n

$$n = p \cdot q$$

2. Randomly choose an encryption kety e such that e and $(p - 1)(q - 1)$ are relatively prime.
3. Use the extended Euclidean Algorithm to compute the inverse of $e \bmod (p - 1)(q - 1)$. Note that e and $(p - 1)(q - 1)$ are also relatively prime. Why?

2.18 HILL CIPHER

This cipher was once implemented in the form of a machine using gears and chains like those used with bicycles. That, and the fact that it is impractical for hand use, while it predates the computer age, has caused me to put it in this section, although the appropriateness of this choice is also doubtful.

Supposing you are given the following problem to solve:

$$2x + y = a$$
$$x - y = b$$

and you want to find out what x and y are in terms of a and b.

The steps you can take to find it are the following:

- You can add or subtract a multiple of one equation from another.
- You can multiply one of the equations by a number.
- You can change the order of the equations.

That last step may seem trivial, but it is included for completeness.

You can make a chart to save you copying the letters x, y, a, and b every time you perform a step:

x y	a b
2 1	1 0
1 -1	0 1

and the rows of this chart can be treated like the equations were. In this case, one might proceed as follows:

x y	a b	
2 1	1 0	2x + y = a
1 -1	0 1	x − y = b
3 0	1 1	3x = a + b
1 -1	0 1	x − y = b
3 0	1 1	3x = a + b
-3 3	0 -3	− 3x + 3y = −3b
3 0	1 1	3x = a + b
0 3	1 -2	3y = a - 2b

Of course, the last step of multiplying each row by 1/3rd (or, equivalently, dividing each row by 3) is still to be taken. I've avoided it here, to omit dealing with fractions.

If one works with numbers in modular arithmetic, particularly if the modulus is not a prime number, the rules change slightly.

If you add or subtract a multiple of one of the equations from another, you can still use any multiple, since a multiple of zero is the same as doing nothing, and so since that does not destroy information, neither will using a number that is not relatively prime to the modulus.

When multiplying a single row by a number, however, you cannot use a number unless it is relatively prime to the modulus. The Hill Cipher deals with modulo-26 arithmetic, and so in addition to zero, 13 and all the even numbers are disallowed for this manipulation.

Enciphering in the Hill Cipher is the same as finding a and b given x and y, where x and y are numbers from 0 to 25 substituted for two letters of a digraph being enciphered, and deciphering is solving for x and y given a and b.

Note that not all systems of linear equations can be solved, and you must choose one that has an inverse. One way to do this is by performing the manipulations allowed for finding an inverse on a square with zeroes everywhere except along the diagonal, since this will always result in a square that can be brought to that form by these same manipulations.

Also, the square formed by the coefficients of this kind of equation is called a matrix. The act of finding a and b for x and y, using the original form of the equations which directly give a and b as functions of x and y, thought of as an operation using the square of numbers we began with in the x and y columns (called a matrix) is called multiplying the vector (x,y) by the matrix to get the vector (a,b). The square representing x, y, and z or a, b, and c on one side of a set of equations, with a 1 at the start of the first row, in the second place in the second row, and so on, with zeroes everywhere else, is called the identity matrix, since if a=x, b=y, c=z, then finding a, b, and c for x, y, and z gives you the same numbers.

The linearity in the Hill cipher is its weak point. So a scrambled alphabet for converting letters to numbers needs to be used, and it is important to remember that that scrambled alphabet is a very important part of the key.

2.19 ROTOR MACHINES

In cryptography, a rotor machine is a electro-mechanical device used for encrypting and decrypting secret messages. Rotor machines were the cryptographic state-of-the-art for a brief but prominent period of history; they were in widespread use in the 1930s– 1950s. The most famous example is the Enigma machine.

The primary component is a set of rotors — rotating disks with an array of electrical contacts on either side. The wiring between the contacts implements a fixed substitution of letters, scrambling them in some complex fashion. On its own, this would offer little security; however, after encrypting each letter, the rotors advance positions, changing the substitution. By this means, a rotor machine produces a complex polyalphabetic substitution cipher.

In classical cryptography, one of the earliest encryption methods was the simple substitution cipher, where letters in a message were systematically replaced using some secret scheme. Monoalphabetic substitution ciphers used only a single replacement scheme — sometimes termed an "alphabet"; this could be easily broken, for example, by using frequency analysis. Somewhat more secure were schemes involving multiple alphabets, polyalphabetic ciphers. Because such schemes were implemented by hand, only a handful of different alphabets could be used; anything more complex would be impractical. However, using only a few alphabets left the ciphers vulnerable to attack. The invention of rotor machines mechanised polyalphabetic encryption, providing a practical way to use a much larger number of alphabets.

The earliest cryptanalytic technique was frequency analysis, in which letter patterns unique to every language could be used to discover information about the substitution alphabet(s) in use in a monoalphabetic substitution cipher. For instance, in English, the plaintext letters E, T, A, O, I, N and S, are usually easy to identify in ciphertext on the basis that since they are very frequent their corresponding ciphertext letters will also be as frequent. In addition, bigram combinations like NG, ST and others are also very frequent, while others are rare indeed (Q followed by anything other than U for instance). The simplest frequency analysis relies on one ciphertext letter always being substituted for a plaintextIn cryptography, plaintext (occasionally, cleartext though there are differences) is information used as input to an encryption algorithm. This could be, for example, a diplomatic message, a bank transaction, an email, a diary — any information that someo letter in the cipher: if this is not the case, deciphering the message is more difficult. For many years, cryptographers attempted to hide the telltale frequencies by using several different substitutions for common letters, but this technique was unable to fully hide patterns in the substitutions for plaintext letters. Such schemes were being widely broken by the 1500s.

In the mid-1400s, a new technique was invented by AlbertiLeone Battista Alberti (February 1404 25th April 1472), Italian painter, poet, linguist, philosopher, cryptographer, musician, architect, and general Renaissance polymath. His life was described in Giorgio Vasari's Vite". In Italy, his first name is usu, now known generally as polyalphabetic ciphers, which recognised the virtue of using more than a single substitution alphabet; he also invented a simple technique for "creating" a multitude of substitution patterns for use in a message. Two parties exchanged a small amount of information (referred to as the key) and used it to create many substitution alphabets, and so many different substitutions for each plaintext letter over the course of a single plaintext. The idea is simple and effective, but proved more difficult to use than might have been expected. Many ciphers were only partial implementations of Alberti's, and so were easier to break than they might have been (e.g. the Vigenère cipherautokey cipher. The Vigenere cipher is a method of encryption invented by Giovan Batista Belaso and described in his 1553 book La cifra del. Giovan Batista Belaso". It was misattributed to Blaise de Vigenere in the 19th century, and given his name.

Not until the 1840s (Babbage) was any technique known which could reliably break any of the polyalphabetic ciphers. His technique also looked for repeating patterns in the ciphertext, which provide clues about the length of the key. Once this is known, the message essentially becomes a series of messages, each as long as the length of the key, to which normal frequency analysis can be applied. Charles BabbageCharles Babbage (December 26 1791 October 18 1871) was an English mathematician, analytical philosopher and (proto-) computer scientist who was the first person to come up with the idea of a programmable computer. Parts of his uncompleted mechanisms are, Friedrich Kasiski, and William F. Friedman are among those who did most to develop these techniques.

Cipher designers tried to get users to use a different substitution for every letter, but this usually meant a very long key, which was a problem in several ways. A long key takes longer to convey (securely) to the parties who need it, and so mistakes are more likely in key distribution. Also, many users do not have the patience to carry out lengthy, letter perfect evolutions, and certainly not under time pressure or battlefield stress. The 'ultimate' cipher of this type would be one in which such a 'long' key could be generated from a simple pattern (ideally automatically), producing a cipher in which there are so many substitution alphabets that frequency counting and statistical attacks would be effectively impossible. Enigma, and the rotor machines generally, were just what was needed since they were seriously polyalphabetic, using a different substitution alphabet for each letter of plaintext, and automatic, requiring no extraordinary abilities from their users. Their messages were, generally, much harder to break than any previous ciphers.

2.20 CRYPTOGRAPHY OF THE EARLY 20TH CENTURY

At the turn of the 20th century (early 1900's), there was a growing need for ciphers to not only be secure, but also fast and easy to use. This was accomplished by designing a machine to encrypt messages instead of doing it by hand. The Germans were the first to use coding machines to their full potential and in the years leading up to and during World War II, the world was to witness the awesome power of the Enigma machine. The Enigma machine is discussed in section 2.20.2.

The 'secret war' to crack the Enigma was one of the most important battles in the war. By cracking the Enigma and having the ability to read enemy messages, allied cryptanalysts saved countless lives. The cryptanalysis of the Enigma machine will be discussed in section 2.20.2.

Perhaps the most successful use of ciphers was the use of the Navajo language. Used primarily by the Americans in the Pacific, Navajo code talkers successfully fooled enemy intelligence for the duration of the Second World War. The use of the Navajo language will be further discussed in section 9.

2.20.1 Digital Electronic Ciphering

One of the consequences of having a digital electronic machine for ciphering, is that it operates very, very fast. This means that someone can try a lot more possibilities than they could with a notebook of paper pages. For example, a "40 bit" keyspace represents about 1012 keys, which sounds like a lot. Unfortunately, special-purpose hardware could try this many decipherings in under 5 seconds,which is not much strength. A "56 bit" keyspace represents about 7 x 1016 different keys, and was recently broken by special brute force hardware in 56 hours; this is also not much strength. The current strength recommendation is 112 to 128 bits, and 256 is not out of the question. 128 bits is just 16 bytes, which is the amount of storage usually consumed by 16 text characters, a very minimal amount. A 128 bit key is "strong enough" to defeat even unimaginably extensive brute force attacks.

2.20.2 The Enigma Machine

The Enigma machine, used by the Germans leading up to and during the Second World War, performed a complex polyalphabetic substitution cipher. The Enigma machine had several components: a keyboard, a light board, a plugboard, and several rotors (or wheels). An operator entering a message would type on the keyboard portion of the machine. The encrypted letter for each plaintext letter would light up on the lightboard. The receiving operator would do the reverse: they would type in the ciphertext letters and the corresponding plaintext letters would light up on the lightboard.

It is important to note that the following description of the wiring and setup of the enigma is the most commonly discussed, but not the only one in use during WWII. Different branches of the German military set up their enigma machines in various ways and modifications were made during the conflict.

Technical Details of the Machine

The main cryptographic functionality of the machine was provided by 3 rotors. There were 5 different rotors from which these 3 could be chosen and placed in any order. This gives a total of $5 \cdot 4 \cdot 3 = 60$ choices for the wheel order. Each wheel is labelled with the letters A-Z so there are 26 possible initial settings for each wheel. This gives a further $26 \cdot 26 \cdot 26 = 17576$ permutations, for a total of $17576 \cdot 60 = 1,054,560$ possibilities.

The rotors connected various electrical circuits in the machine. As they turned, different connections between the keyboard and lightboard would be made and thus, different ciphertext letters would be chosen for the plaintext letters typed. Each wheel had 26 notches associated with the letters and they turned at different rates. The rightmost wheel would turn every time a letter was typed. The middle wheel would turn one notch when the right wheel had done a full revolution, that is, every 26th letter typed. The leftmost wheel would turn a notch when the middle wheel had completed a full revolution, that is, every 676th letter typed.

The plugboard consisted of 26 pairs of plugs, which allowed for pairs of letters to be swapped adding a monoalphabetic substitution cipher component to the cryptographic scheme. This gives $26! = 403,291,461,126,605,635,584,000,000$ possible swapping patterns. Along with the rotor settings, it produced a total number of possible keys of about 159 million million million.

On sending a message, the operator would set up the rotors and plugboard in a pre-arranged fashion, usually changed every day. Then the operator would type a three letter message setting twice (e.g. CTGCTG) which would be encrypted (e.g. FUTGNP) using the daily setting. Then, the operator would set the wheels at this message setting (CTG) for the actual message text. Two security problems arose from this method. Firstly, the operator chose the message setting and consequently, it was not very random. Usually, the three letters would be very close on the keyboard. Secondly, the repetition of the message setting was a valuable clue to cryptanalysts. The Germans must have realised this second problem as the procedure was changed May 1, 1940 to only send the setting once.

2.20.3 Huge Keys

Under the theory that if a little is good, a lot is better, some people suggest using huge keys of 56,000 bits, or 1,000,000 bits, or even more. We can build such devices, and they can operate quickly. We can even afford the storage for big keys. What we do not have is a reason for such keys: a 128 bit key is "strong enough" to defeat even unimaginably extensive brute force attacks. While a designer might use a larger key for convenience, even immense keys cannot provide more strength than "strong enough." And while different attacks may show that the cipher actually has less strength, a huge keyspace is not going to solve those problems.

Some forms of cipher need relatively large key values simply to have a sufficiently large keyspace. Most number-theory based public key ciphers are in this class. Basically, these systems require key values in a very special form, so that most key values are unacceptable and unused. This means that the actual keyspace is much smaller than the size of the key would indicate. For this reason, public key systems need keys in the 1,000 bit range, while delivering strength comparable to 128 bit secret key ciphers.

2.20.4 Naive Ciphers

Suppose we want to hide a name: We might think to innovate a different rule for each letter. We might say: "First we have 'T', but 't' is the 3rd letter in 'bottle' so we write '3.'" We can continue this way, and such a cipher could be very difficult to break. So why is this sort of thing not done? There are several reasons:

First, any cipher construction must be decipherable, and it is all too easy, when choosing rules at random, to make a rule that depends upon plaintext, which will of course not be present until after the ciphertext is deciphered.

(1) The next problem is remembering the rules, since the rules constitute the key. If we choose from among many rules, in no pattern at all, we may have a strong cipher, but be unable to remember the key. And if we write the key down, all someone has to do is read that and properly interpret it (which may be another encryption issue). So we might choose among few rules, in some pattern, which will make a weaker cipher.

(2) Another problem is the question of what we do for longer messages. This sort of scheme seems to want a different key, or perhaps just more key, for a longer message, which is certainly inconvenient. What often happens in practice is that the key is re-used repeatedly, and that will be very, very weak.

(3) Yet another problem is the observation that describing the rule selection may take more information than the message itself. To send the message to someone else, we must somehow transport the key securely to the other end. But if we can transfer this amount of data securely in the first place, we wonder why we cannot securely transfer the smaller message itself.

(4) Modern ciphering is about constructions which attempt to solve these problems. A modern cipher has a large keyspace, which might well be controlled by a hashing computation on a language phrase we can remember. A modern cipher system can handle a wide range of message sizes, with exactly the same key, and normally provides a way to securely re-use keys. And the key can be much, much smaller than a long message.

Moreover, in a modern cipher, we expect the key to not be exposed, even if The Opponent has both the plaintext and the associated ciphertext for many messages (a known-plaintext attack). In fact, we normally assume that The Opponent knows the full construction of the cipher, and has lots of known plaintext, and still cannot find the key. Such designs are not trivial.

Naive Challenges

Sometimes a novice gives us 40 or 50 random-looking characters and says, "Bet you can't break this!" But that is not very realistic.

In actual use, we normally assume that a cipher will be widely distributed, and thus somewhat available. So we assume The Opponent will somehow acquire either the cipher machine or its complete design. We also assume a cipher will be widely used, so a lot of ciphered material will be around somewhere. We assume The Opponent will somehow acquire some amount of plaintext and the associated ciphertext. And even in this situation, we still expect the cipher to hide the key and other messages.

2.20.5 Cryptography without Keys

It is fairly easy to design a complex cipher program to produce a single complex, intermediate form. In this case, the program itself becomes the "key."

But this means that the deciphering program must be kept available to access protected information. So if someone steals your laptop, they probably will also get the deciphering program, which — if it does not use keys — will immediately expose all of your carefully protected data. This is why cryptography generally depends upon at least one remembered key, and why we need ciphers which can produce a multitude of different ciphertexts.

(1) Keyspace

Cryptography deliberately creates the situation of "a needle in a haystack." That is, of all possible keys, only one should recover the correct message, and that one key is hidden among all possible keys. Of course, The Opponent might get lucky, but probably will have to perform about half of the possible decipherings to find the message.

To keep messages secret, it is important that a cipher be able to produce a multitude of different intermediate forms or ciphertexts. Clearly, no cipher can possibly be stronger than requiring the Opponent to check every possible deciphering. If such a brute force search is practical, the cipher is weak. The number of possible ciphertexts is the "design strength" of a cipher.

Each different ciphertext requires a different key. So the number of different ciphertexts which we can produce is limited to the number of different keys we can use. We describe the keyspace by the length in bits of the binary value required to represent the number of possible ciphertexts or keys.

It is not particularly difficult to design ciphers which may have a design strength of hundreds or thousands of bits, and these can operate just as fast as our current ciphers. However, the U.S.

Government generally does not allow the export of data ciphers with a keyspace larger than about 40 bits, which is a very searchable value. Recently, a 56-bit keyspace was searched (with special hardware) and the correct key found in about 56 hours. Note that a 56-bit key represents 216 times as many transformations as a 40-bit key. So, all things being equal, similar equipment might find a 40-bit key in about 3 seconds. But at the same rate, an 80-bit key (which is presumably 224 times as strong as a 56-bit key) would take over 100,000 years.

(2) Strength

Keyspace alone only sets an upper limit to cipher strength; a cipher can be much weaker than it appears. An in-depth understanding or analysis of the design may lead to "shortcuts" in the solution.

Perhaps a few tests can be designed, each of which eliminates vast numbers of keys, thus in the end leaving a searchable keyspace; this is cryptanalysis.

We understand strength as the ability to resist cryptanalysis. But this makes "strength" a negative quality (the lack of any practical attack), which we cannot measure. We can infer the "strength" of a cipher from the best known attack. We can only hope that The Opponent does not know of something much better.

Every user of cryptography should understand that all known ciphers (including the one time pad) are at least potentially vulnerable to some unknown technical attack. And if such a break does occur, there is absolutely no reason that we would find out about it. However, a direct technical attack may be one of the least likely avenues of exposure.

2.20.6 System Design and Strength

Cryptographic design may seem as easy as selecting a cipher from a book of ciphers. But ciphers, per se, are only part of a secure encryption system. It is common for a cipher system to require cryptographic design beyond simply selecting a cipher, and such design is much trickier than it looks.

The use of an unbreakable cipher does not mean that the encryption system will be similarly unbreakable. A prime example of this is the man-in-the-middle attack on public-key ciphers. Public-key ciphers require that one use the correct key for the desired person. The correct key must be known to cryptographic levels of assurance, or this becomes the weak link in the system: Suppose an

Opponent can get us to use his key instead of the right one (perhaps by sending a faked message saying "Here is my new key"). If he can do this to both ends, and also intercept all messages between them (which is conceivable, since Internet routing is not secure), The Opponent can sit "in the middle." He can decipher each message (now in one of his keys), then re-encipher that message in the correct user key, and send it along. So the users communicate, and no cipher has been broken, yet The Opponent is still reading the conversation. Such are the consequences of system design error.

2.20.7 Hardware vs Software Ciphers

Currently, most ciphers are implemented in software; that is, by a program of instructions executed by a general-purpose computer. Normally, software is cheaper, but hardware can run faster, and nobody can change it. Of course, there are levels to hardware, from chips (which thus require significant interface software) to external boxes with communications lines running in and out. But there are several possible problems:

Software, especially in a multi-user system, is almost completely insecure. Anyone with access to the machine could insert modified software which would then be repeatedly used under the false assumption that effective security was still in place. This may not be an issue for home users, and real solution here may depend upon a secure operating system.

(1) Hardware represents a capital expense, and is extremely inflexible. So if problems begin to be suspected in a hardware cipher, the expense of replacement argues against an update. Indeed, a society-wide system might well take years to update anyway.

(2) One logical possibility is the development of ciphering processors — little ciphering computers — in secure packaging. limited control over the processor might allow a public-key authenticated software update, while otherwise looking like hardware. But probably most users will not care until some hidden software system is exposed on some computers.

2.21 STEGNOGRAPHY : HIDING DATA WITHIN DATA

Steganography is the science of hiding information. Whereas the goal of cryptography is to make data unreadable by a third party, the goal of steganography is to hide the data from a third party. According to Dictionary.com, steganography (also known as "steg" or "stego") is "the art of writing in cipher, or in characters, which are not intelligible except to persons who have the key; cryptography". In computer terms, steganography has evolved into the practice of hiding a message within a larger one in such a way that others cannot discern the presence or contents of the hidden message. In contemporary terms, steganography has evolved into a digital strategy of hiding a file in some form of multimedia, such as an image, an audio file (like a .wav or mp3) or even a video file.

There are a large number of steganographic methods that most of us are familiar with (especially if you watch a lot of spy movies!), ranging from invisible ink and microdots to secreting a hidden message in the second letter of each word of a large body of text and spread spectrum radio communication. With computers and networks, there are many other ways of hiding information, such as:

- Covert channels (e.g., Loki and some distributed denial-of-service tools use the Internet Control Message Protocol, or ICMP, as the communications channel between the "bad guy" and a compromised system)
- Hidden text within Web pages
- Hiding files in "plain sight" (e.g., what better place to "hide" a file than with an important sounding name in the c:\winnt\system32 directory?)
- Null ciphers (e.g., using the first letter of each word to form a hidden message in an otherwise innocuous text)

Steganography today, however, is significantly more sophisticated than the examples above suggest, allowing a user to hide large amounts of information within image and audio files. These forms of steganography often are used in conjunction with cryptography so that the information is doubly protected; first it is encrypted and then hidden so that an adversary has to first find the information (an often difficult task in and of itself) and then decrypt it.

There are a number of uses for steganography besides the mere novelty. One of the most widely used applications is for so-called digital watermarking. A watermark, historically, is the replication of an image, logo, or text on paper stock so that the source of the document can be at least partially authenticated. A digital watermark can accomplish the same function; a graphic artist, for example, might post sample images on her Web site complete with an embedded signature so that she can later prove her ownership in case others attempt to portray her work as their own.

Stego can also be used to allow communication within an underground community. There are several reports, for example, of persecuted religious minorities using steganography to embed messages for the group within images that are posted to known Web sites.

While we are discussing it in terms of computer security, steganography is really nothing new, as it has been around since the times of ancient Rome. For example, in ancient Rome and Greece, text was traditionally written on wax that was poured on top of stone tablets. If the sender of the information wanted to obscure the message - for purposes of military intelligence, for instance - they would use steganography: the wax would be scraped off and the message would be inscribed or written directly on the tablet, wax would then be poured on top of the message, thereby obscuring not just its meaning but its very existence.

2.21.1 Steganographic Methods

The following formula provides a very generic description of the pieces of the steganographic process:

cover_medium + hidden_data + stego_key = stego_medium

In this context, the cover_medium is the file in which we will hide the hidden_data, which may also be encrypted using the stego_key. The resultant file is the stego_medium (which will, of course. be the same type of file as the cover_medium). The cover_medium (and, thus, the stego_medium) are typically image or audio files.

Before discussing how information is hidden in an image file, it is worth a fast review of how images are stored in the first place. An image file is merely a binary file containing a binary representation of the color or light intensity of each picture element (pixel) comprising the image.

Images typically use either 8-bit or 24-bit color. When using 8-bit color, there is a definition of up to 256 colors forming a palette for this image, each color denoted by an 8-bit value. A 24-bit color scheme, as the term suggests, uses 24 bits per pixel and provides a much better set of colors. In this case, each pix is represented by three bytes, each byte representing the intensity of the three primary colors red, green, and blue (RGB), respectively. The Hypertext Markup Language (HTML) format for indicating colors in a Web page often uses a 24-bit format employing six hexadecimal digits, each pair representing the amount of red, blue, and green, respectively. The color orange, for example, would be displayed with red set to 100% (decimal 255, hex FF), green set to 50% (decimal 127, hex 7F), and no blue (0), so we would use "#FF7F00" in the HTML code.

The size of an image file, then, is directly related to the number of pixels and the granularity of the color definition. A typical 640 × 480 pix image using a palette of 256 colors would require a file about 307 KB in size (640 • 480 bytes), whereas a 1024 × 768 pix high-resolution 24-bit color image would result in a 2.36 MB file (1024 • 768 • 3 bytes).

To avoid sending files of this enormous size, a number of compression schemes have been developed over time, notably Bitmap (BMP), Graphic Interchange Format (GIF), and

Joint Photographic Experts Group (JPEG) file types. Not all are equally suited to steganography, however.

GIF and 8-bit BMP files employ what is known as lossless compression, a scheme that allows the software to exactly reconstruct the original image. JPEG, on the other hand, uses lossy compression, which means that the expanded image is very nearly the same as the original but not an exact duplicate. While both methods allow computers to save storage space, lossless compression is much better suited to applications where the integrity of the original information must be maintained, such as steganography. While JPEG can be used for stego applications, it is more common to embed data in GIF or BMP files.

The simplest approach to hiding data within an image file is called least significant bit (LSB) insertion. In this method, we can take the binary representation of the hidden_data and overwrite the LSB of each byte within the cover_image. If we are using 24-bit color, the amount of change will be minimal and indiscernible to the human eye. As an example, suppose that we have three adjacent pixels (nine bytes) with the following RGB encoding:

```
10010101   00001101   11001001
10010110   00001111   11001010
10011111   00010000   11001011
```

Now suppose we want to "hide" the following 9 bits of data (the hidden data is usually compressed prior to being hidden): 101101101. If we overlay these 9 bits over the LSB of the 9 bytes above, we get the following (where bits in bold have been changed):

```
10010101   00001100   11001001
10010111   00001110   11001011
10011111   00010000   11001011
```

Note – That we have successfully hidden 9 bits but at a cost of only changing 4, or roughly 50%, of the LSBs.

This description is meant only as a high-level overview. Similar methods can be applied to 8-bit color but the changes, as the reader might imagine, are more dramatic. Gray-scale images, too, are very useful for steganographic purposes. One potential problem with any of these methods is that they can be found by an adversary who is looking. In addition, there are other methods besides LSB insertion with which to insert hidden information.

Without going into any detail, it is worth mentioning steganalysis, the art of detecting and breaking steganography. One form of this analysis is to examine the color palette of a graphical image. In most images, there will be a unique binary encoding of each individual color. If the image contains hidden data, however, many colors in the palette will have duplicate binary encodings since, for all practical purposes, we can't count the LSB. If the analysis of the color palette of a given file yields many duplicates, we might safely conclude that the file has hidden information.

But what files would you analyze? Suppose I decide to post a hidden message by hiding it in an image file that I post at an auction site on the Internet. The item I am auctioning is real so a lot of people may access the site and download the file; only a few people know that the image has special information that only they can read. And we haven't even discussed hidden data inside audio files! Indeed, the quantity of potential cover files makes steganalysis a Herculean task.

2.21.2 Use of Steganography

Like many security tools, steganography can be used for a variety of reasons, some good, some not so good. Legitimate purposes can include things like watermarking images for reasons such as copyright protection. Digital watermarks (also known as fingerprinting, significant especially in copyrighting material) are similar to steganography in that they are overlaid in files, which appear to be part of the original file and are thus not easily detectable by the average person. Steganography can also be used as a way to make a substitute for a one-way hash value (where you take a variable length input and create a static length output string to verify that no changes have been made to the original variable length input). Further, steganography can be used to tag notes to online images (like post-it notes attached to paper files). Finally, steganography can be used to maintain the confidentiality of valuable information, to protect the data from possible sabotage, theft, or unauthorized viewing.

Unfortunately, steganography can also be used for illegitimate reasons. For instance, if someone was trying to steal data, they could conceal it in another file or files and send it out in an innocent looking email or file transfer. Furthermore, a person with a hobby of saving pornography, or worse, to their hard drive, may choose to hide the evidence through the use of steganography. And, as was pointed out in the concern for terroristic purposes, it can be used as a means of covert communication. Of course, this can be both a legitimate and an illegitimate application.

2.21.3 Steganography Tools

There are a vast number of tools that are available for steganography. An important distinction that should be made among the tools available today is the difference between tools that do steganography, and tools that do steganalysis, which is the method of detecting steganography and destroying the original message. Steganalysis focuses on this aspect, as opposed to simply discovering and decrypting the message, because this can be difficult to do unless the encryption keys are known.

2.21.4 Other Forms of Steganography

While much of the steganography employed today is quite high-tech, steganography itself can make use of many low-tech methods. The goal of stego is merely to hide the presence of a message; remember how well the critical missive was hidden in plain sight in Poe's "The Purloined Letter"?

One common, almost obvious, form of steganography is called a null cipher. In this type of stego, the hidden message is formed by taking the first (or other fixed) letter of each word in the cover message. Consider this cablegram that might have been sent by a journalist/spy from the U.S. to Europe during World War I:

```
PRESIDENT'S EMBARGO RULING SHOULD HAVE IMMEDIATE NOTICE. GRAVE
SITUATION AFFECTING INTERNATIONAL LAW. STATEMENT FORESHADOWS RUIN
OF MANY NEUTRALS. YELLOW JOURNALS UNIFYING NATIONAL EXCITEMENT
IMMENSELY.
```

The first letters of each word form the character string: **PERSHINGSAILSFROMNYJUNEI**. A little imagination and some spaces yields the real message: **PERSHING SAILS FROM NY JUNE I**.

Another form of steganography uses a template (e.g., a piece of paper with holes cut in it) or a set of preselected locations on the page to hide a message. In this case, obviously, the sender and receiver must use the same template or rules. Consider this note:

> **THE MOST COMMON WORK ANIMAL IS THE HORSE. THEY CAN BE USED TO FERRY EQUIPMENT TO AND FROM WORKERS OR TO PULL A PLOW. BE CAREFUL, THOUGH, BECAUSE SOME HAVE SANK UP TO THEIR KNEES IN MUD OR SAND, SUCH AS AN INCIDENT AT THE BURLINGTON FACTORY LAST YEAR. BUT HORSES REMAIN A SIGNIFICANT FIND. ON A FARM, AN ALTERNATE WORK ANIMAL MIGHT BE A BURRO BUT THEY ARE NOT AS COMFORTABLE AS A TRANSPORT ANIMAL.**

Applying a template or rule as to which words to read to this message might yield the following:

HORSE	**FERRY**	**SANK**	**IN**
BURLINGTON	**FIND**	**ALTERNATE**	**TRANSPORT**

There are other alternatives to the template method such as:

- Pinpricks in maps to use as an overlay for relevant letters in messages
- Deliberate misspelling to mark words in the message
- Use of small changes in spacing to indicate significant letters or words in a hidden message
- Use of a slightly different font in a typeset message to indicate the hidden letters (e.g., the difference between Courier and Courier New is barely noticeable unless you are looking for it)

Steganography doesn't just apply to written forms of communication. Radio and TV messages, from World War II to today, can be used to hide coded or hidden messages. Some government sources suspect that Osama bin Laden's pre-recorded videos that are re-played on TV stations around the world contain hidden messages.

Some argue that the U.S. Marine Corps Navaho code talkers of WWII represent a form of steganography. The messages themselves weren't encrypted; the plaintext was right there in the open, just in a language that was unknown by the Japanese. Disappearing ink and microdots are other ways in which messages can be hidden from the casual observer.

One of the oldest stego schemes was to shave the head of a messenger and tattoo a message on the messenger's head. After the hair grows back, the messenger can be sent to the intended recipient, where the messenger's head can be shaved and the message recovered. This method is decidingly clever, patient, and very low-tech, and goes right to the heart of steganography's literal meaning of "covered writing."

2.22 MODERN ENCRYPTION

Industrial espionage among highly competitive businesses often requires that extensive security measures be put into place. And, those who wish to exercise their personal freedom, outside of the oppressive nature of governments, may also wish to encrypt certain information to avoid legalities that entailed possession of such.

With respect to the Internet, there are many types of data and messages that people would want to be kept secret. Now that commercial trading on the Net is a reality, one of the main targets of data encryption is credit card numbers. Other information that could otherwise benefit or educate a group or individual can also be used against such groups or individuals.

Many times when data is exchanged electronically the privacy of the data is a requirement. The use of encryption restricts unintended recipients from viewing the data, which are deemed confidential and potentially dangerous if made known to irresponsible parties. Today, encryption is the procedure of transforming plaintext, data that can be read by anyone, to ciphertext, data that can only be read by someone with a secret decryption key. A message before being changed in any way is called plaintext. Plaintext messages are converted to ciphertext via some encryption method. A particular such method is called a cryptosystem.

2.22.1 Why Encryption Matters

Why bother with encryption? Privacy! When you talk over a data network, anybody connected to your network or with access to any of the links your sound data passes through on its way to a distant Internet site can potentially eavesdrop on your conversation. Encryption, based on a key known only to you and person you're talking to, protects against interception by third parties. No encryption scheme can be absolutely guaranteed to be 100% secure and even if it were, you'd still be at risk if somebody gained access to your key. But the encryption offered by Speak Freely, particularly the IDEA algorithm which is also used by PGP to encrypt message bodies, provides a great deal of security, indeed better than any generally available digital cellular telephone.

Recent front page articles in a number of newspapers have discussed the controversy over government control of encryption, in the context both of the Clinton admiminstration's Clipper Chip proposal and the recent controversy over whether Philip Zimmerman is guilty of exporting munitions by making his public domain encryption program available on the Internet. like most public discussions of encryption, these articles understate the importance of the issues at stake. The result is to make the arguments both for and against government control of encryption appear weaker than they really are.

There are two ways of protecting privacy. One is to let people have information about each other but impose legal controls on what they do with it. That is the approach of our current privacy law, embodied in statutes such as the Fair Credit Reporting Act. Anyone who considers that an effective approach can readily test it by offering a reasonably unscrupulous investigator a thousand dollars for a copy of a credit report on a random stranger.

The other way of protecting privacy, the way that works, is to keep other people from getting information about you in the first place. If you are worried about evesdroppers, check under the eves—or hold important conversations in the middle of wide open spaces. Seal your letters and entrust them to reliable messengers. Tell your deepest, darkest secrets to your horse—and nobody else.

Over the past century, technological advance has made that approach more difficult. Many conversations take place over telephone wires—and it is hard to check the entire phone line and every switching station for evesdroppers. Even meetings in the middle of the Mojave desert may not be entirely private in a world of shotgun microphones and spy satellites. A cellular phone conversation can be intercepted by anyone with a suitable receiver. EMail across the Internet is bounced from one machine to another until it finds its destination—and can be read by anyone controlling any one of those machines.

EMail at present makes up only a small part of our communication—less important than ordinary mail and far less important than telephone conversations Only a few tens of millions of people are connected to each other over computer networks and what they send is mostly limited to written text. Both of those constraints are rapidly disappearing. Within a decade or so, most of the people most of us wish to communicate with will be accessible over computer networks—and the bandwidth of those networks, their ability to carry information, will be orders of magnitude greater than it now is. As the rapidly decreasing cost of computer power brings virtual reality out of science fiction and into common use, communicating over a computer network will become an ever closer substitute for being in the same place. The result will be a radical shift in the technology of how we interact with each other and how we keep our interactions private.

Consider following Scenerio:

The year is 2010. From the viewpoint of an observer, I am alone in my office, wearing goggles and earphones. From my viewpoint I am at a table in a conference room, with a dozen other people. The other people are real—seated in offices scattered around the world. The table and the room exist only in the mind of a computer. The scene is being drawn, at a rate of sixty frames a second, on my goggles—a little differently for each eye, to give three dimensional vision. The meeting is virtual, but to my sight and hearing, the two most important senses for communication, it might as well be real. It is sufficiently real for the purposes of a large fraction of human interactions—consulting, teaching, meeting. There is little point to shuttling people around the world when you can achieve the same effect by shuttling electrical signals instead. As wide band networks and sufficiently powerful computers become generally available, a large part of our communication will shift to cyberspace.

This raises an obvious problem for privacy. When communication is on a worldwide network, used simultaneously by tens or hundreds of millions of people, it is hard to know who may be listening. With powerful computers, it is relatively easy for a snoop to sort through millions of intercepted messages to find the interesting ones—already, at least one information utility uses a primitive version of that approach to pre-censor postings for obscenity. The combination of easy interception and computerised searching seems to imply cyberspace as a fishbowl—the end of privacy for a large fraction of our personal and business interactions.

It does no good to intercept a message if you cannot read it. The solution to the problem of privacy in such a world is encryption. The key technology is public key encryption. Every person on the net, using readily available software, creates for himself a pair of keys—each a number of perhaps two hundred digits. The keys function as inverses of each other. Using either key and the appropriate software, I can encrypt a message. To decrypt it requires the other key.

Each person publishes one of his pair of keys—his public key. The public keys of the entire population are available, to anyone who wants them, in the phonebook or some digital equivalent. My private key I keep a closely guarded secret. You wish to send a message to me; today it might be Email, ten years from now it might be the message stream containing your end of our virtual reality conversation. You encrypt it with my public key. Anyone can intercept it—but it can only be decrypted with my private key, which only I have.

I wish to send a message to you and prove that it is from me. I encrypt it with my private key. You decrypt it with my public key. The fact that what comes out of the decryption process is a message and not gibberish means that it was encrypted with my private key. Since only I possess my private key, I must be the source of the message. Thus public key encryption provides not only privacy but verification as well—a digital signature. By encrypting first with my private key and then with your public key, I can send you a message that is both secure and verifiable. Only you can read it, and only I could have sent it.

Related technologies will provide additional elements of privacy. Protocols exist to make communications untracable as well as secure. Others can provide the digital equivalent of cash—transfers of value that cannot be traced, even by someone who intercepts the communications containing the transfers. Combine all of these and we are in a world of strong privacy.

Public discussion of attempts by government to regulate encryption, whether the longstanding policy of discouraging encryption by prohibiting its export or the more recent "Clipper Chip initiative," which attempts to establish a form of encryption good against everyone except the government, focuses mainly on the ability of law enforcement agents to intercept phone calls by drug dealers, international terrorists, and the like. That is a small part of the real issue. Computers and computer networks make possible a level of privacy stronger than we have ever had. In a world of strong privacy, a large part of human activity will be unobservable to anyone save the participants. What cannot be observed cannot be taxed or regulated. The results will be attractive in some ways, unattractive in others, and very different from the world we now live in.

Consider, as one example, income from information services. With high bandwidth networks and strong privacy, I can sell my services as a teacher, lawyer, or business consultant without anyone, even my customers, knowing who I am. My business name and attached reputation are defined by my public key: I can demonstrate that I am the person who does business under that name by my ability to read messages encrypted with that key.. A large and growing part of the economy will no longer be taxable.

The IRS has the alternative of deducing income from expenditure—a traditional approach to dealing with those engaged in illegal professions. But in a world of strong privacy, a substantial part of my expenditure will also be invisible—spent as digital cash to buy information and services over the net. In such a world taxes, whether of production or consumption, will shift away from information goods and services and towards goods that can be physically observed.

Another consequence of strong privacy will be to make certain sorts of legal regulation impractical. In many ways, this will be a good thing—political censorship, for example, will become enormously more difficult. Many professions will no longer be able to use professional licensing or trade barriers to restrict competition. Other consequences are less obviously attractive. In a world of strong privacy, violation of copyright becomes easy. A pirate publisher, operating anonymously, can set up a commercial archive of copyrighted books, music, or programs and sell them over the net just like a legitimate dealer. His customers will be able to communicate with him and he with them, but neither party to the transaction need know the physical location or true identity of the other.

One can imagine the use of privacy for more serious criminal enterprises as well. Buying and selling of trade secrets, purchasing embarassing information for purposes of blackmail, even hiring a contract killer, become easier in a world where businesses can operate, and establish reputations, without revealing their physical location or proprietors. Potential victims will get less protection than they now do from law, but more from the use of privacy in their own defense. It is hard to have a competitor killed, or even to steal his trade secrets, if you have no idea what he looks like or where on the globe he lives.

All of this sounds like, and is, the stuff of science fiction. It is also the world we may be living in twenty or thirty years from now. Without encryption, computers may mean a sharp reduction in individual privacy. With encryption, we may be very private indeed. large parts of our lives will be lived in a world of voluntary association and no government—with both the advantages and disadvantages that such a world implies. That makes the present controversy over encryption, largely ignored by most outside the computer industry, easily the most important privacy issue of the decade, and perhaps the most important policy issue.

2.23 ETHICAL ISSUES CONCERNING PROTECTION OF DATA

Introduction to Existing Situation

The encryption debate has revolved around the permanent conflict when issues of industrial competitiveness and personal privacy, clash with the interests of national security and law enforcement. Often there is mistrust felt by civilians and corporations against state mandate to cryptanalyze several encrypted information.

(1) USA

In view of the American government's firsthand experience of the potential power of encryption in large-scale confrontations such as the World War II, it is thus understood why many governments are keen upon monitoring public dissemination and use of encryption techniques. It was first reflected in the establishment of Computer Security Act of the US Congress of 1987, where a Computer System Security and Privacy The first disparity occurred in 1993, between the US government and citizens who felt that certain human rights of theirs have been violated by imposing Escrowed Encryption Standard (EES) for privately used keys. While this may not seem to be an action that is anything but politically motivated, to some this may pose threat to scientific freedom.

Recently, US Congress has brought two more issues into the policy discussion: scientific freedom to conduct and express cryptographic research, and human rights applications of cryptographic technologies. USA wants to retain 'surveillance capability' over commercial message channel. Potential adversary may build a network of communication under private commercial cover.

(2) Europe

In liberal Europe, private scientific research into encryption, does not seem to be a potential concern to many countries, even though both Britain and France possess a pretty tight policy concerning public cryptography.

'Euro-Encryption' was under discussion by European Union in 1994, to synchronise the interests of the state authorities with the demand for a reasonable degree of scientific freedom to pursue intellectual research into cryptography

(3) Others

Other countries beyond the sphere of North America and Europe have not seem to pay particular concern over the use of encryption. This could perhaps be attributed to the fact that outside the regions mentioned, there have not been any significant localised development of encryption techniques. The level of use of computers may not have reached a stage where governments should start to take action in regulating encryption.

2.24 LEGAL FRAMEWORK REGULATING DATA ENCRYPTION

2.24.1 Escrow Encryption Standard

The USA is one of the countries with specific regulation on the use and the export of cryptographic materials. The two major areas explored here is the newly introduced Escrow Encryption Standard and the US encryption product export law.

Escrow Encryption Standard

Two separate independent escrow agents store two separate chip unique key components. These components are released to authorized government official only when authorized request for electronic surveillance comply with procedures approved by the Attorney-General.

These key components are needed to construct addition modulo 2 key. An 80-bit session key (KS) serves as initialization block for encryption process that could be selected. In law

Enforcement Access Field (lEAF), current session key is stored in encrypted form and by using chip unique key the session key is obtained. In the event that the court orders for government surveillance, a government-controlled decrypt device could extract and decrypt session key from lEAF. At this point, any intercepted message is open to surveillance.

ClIPPER chip used is generally tamper-proof. Though generally EES shows little weakness, however, lEAF is transmitted across open communications and thus still susceptible to unauthorized attempt at decryption.

SKIPJACK algorithm here is used within ClIPPER chip. To restrict its use, it cannot be obtained as software; instead it can only be obtained as a tamper-resistant chip, programmed specifically by Mykotronx (in ClIPPER) under specific configurations. SKIPJACK itself is an algorithm kept private, classified as secret by the government, and most importantly, not releasable to foreign nationals. This last bit corresponds to the US' protectionism policy.

REFERENCES

1. The Codebreakers, by David Kahn (Macmillan, 1967).
2. Decrypted Secrets, by Friedrich Bauer (Springer-Verlag, 1997).
3. Handbook of Applied Cryptography, by Menezes, van Oorschot and Vanstone (CRC Press, 1997).
4. Cryptography and Network Security: Principles and Practice, by William Stallings (2nd ed., Prentice Hall, 1998).
5. Contemporary Cryptology, edited by Gustavus Simmons (IEEE Press, 1992).
6. Spy Catcher, by Peter Wright (Viking Penguin, 1987).
7. The Puzzle Palace, by James Bamford (Houghton Mifflin, 1982).
8. Good books on "The Vietnam War" (and which have nothing to do with cryptography) include.

❑❑❑

3

Model Block Cipher

3.1 BLOCK CIPHER

A *block cipher* is a transformation between plaintext block values and ciphertext block values, and is thus an emulated simple substitution on huge block-wide values. Within a particular block size, both plaintext and ciphertext have the same set of possible values, and when the ciphertext values have the same ordering as the plaintext, ciphering is obviously ineffective. So effective ciphering depends upon re-arranging the ciphertext values from the plaintext ordering, and this is a permutation of the plaintext values. A block cipher is keyed by constructing a particular permutation of ciphertext values.

A block cipher transforms a fixed-length block of plaintext data into a block of ciphertext data of the same length. This transformation takes place under the action of a user-provided secret key. Decryption is performed by applying the reverse transformation to the ciphertext block using the same secret key. The fixed length is called the block size, and for many block ciphers, the block size is 64 bits.

Since different plaintext blocks are mapped to different ciphertext blocks (to allow unique decryption), a block cipher effectively provides a permutation of the set of all possible messages. The permutation effected during any particular encryption is of course secret, since it is a function of the secret key.

It is a cipher which requires the accumulation of data (in a block) before ciphering can complete. Other than simple transposition ciphers, this seems to be the province of ciphers designed to emulate a keyed simple substitution with a table of size far too large to realize. A block cipher operates on a block of data (for example, multiple bytes) in a single ciphering, as opposed to a stream cipher, which operates on bytes or bits as they occur. Block ciphers can be called "codebook-style" ciphers.

3.1.1 Iterated Block Cipher

An iterated block cipher is one that encrypts a plaintext block by a process that has several rounds. In each round, the same transformation or round function is applied to the data using a subkey. The set of subkeys are usually derived from the user-provided secret key by a key schedule.

The number of rounds in an iterated cipher depends on the desired security level and the consequent trade-off with performance. In most cases, an increased number of rounds will improve the security offered by a block cipher, but for some ciphers the number of rounds required to achieve adequate security will be too large for the cipher to be practical or desirable.

3.1.2 Block Cipher Data Diffusion

In an ideal block cipher, changing even a single bit of the input block will change all bits of the ciphertext result, each with independent probability 0.5. This means that about half of the bits in the output will change for any different input block, even for differences of just one bit. This is overall diffusion and is present in a block cipher, but not in a stream cipher. Data diffusion is a simple consequence of the keyed invertible simple substitution nature of the ideal block cipher.

Improper diffusion of data throughout a block cipher can have serious strength implications. One of the functions of data diffusion is to hide the different effects of different internal components. If these effects are not in fact hidden, it may be possible to attack each component separately, and break the whole cipher fairly easily.

3.1.3 Partitioning Messages into Fixed Size Blocks

A large message can be ciphered by partitioning the plaintext into blocks of a size which can be ciphered. This essentially creates a stream meta-cipher which repeatedly uses the same block cipher transformation. Of course, it is also possible to re-key the block cipher for each and every block ciphered, but this is usually expensive in terms of computation and normally unnecessary.

A message of arbitrary size can always be partitioned into some number of whole blocks, with possibly some space remaining in the final block. Since partial blocks cannot be ciphered, some random padding can be introduced to fill out the last block, and this naturally expands the ciphertext. In this case it may also be necessary to introduce some sort of structure which will indicate the number of valid bytes in the last block.

3.1.4 Block Partitioning without Expansion

Proposals for using a block cipher supposedly without data expansion may involve creating a tiny stream cipher for the last block. One scheme is to re-encipher the ciphertext of the preceding block, and use the result as the confusion sequence. Of course, the cipher designer still needs to address the situation of files which are so short that they have no preceding block. Because the one-block version is in fact a stream cipher, we must be very careful to never re-use a confusion sequence. But when we only have one block, there is no prior block to change as a result of the data. In this case, ciphering several very short files could expose those files quickly. Furthermore, it is dangerous to encipher a CRC value in such a block, because exclusive-OR enciphering is transparent to the field of mod 2 polynomials in which the CRC operates. Doing this could allow an Opponent to adjust the message CRC in a known way, thus avoiding authentication exposure.

Another proposal for eliminating data expansion consists of ciphering blocks until the last short block, then re-positioning the ciphering window to end at the last of the data, thus re-ciphering part of the prior block. This is a form of chaining and establishes a sequentiality requirement which requires that the last block be deciphered before the next-to-the-last block. Or we can make enciphering inconvenient and deciphering easy, but one way will be a problem. And this approach cannot handle very short messages: its minimum size is one block. Yet any general-purpose ciphering routine will encounter short messages. Even worse, if we have a short message, we still need to somehow indicate the correct length of the message, and this must expand the message,as we saw before. Thus, overall, this seems a somewhat dubious technique.

On the other hand, it does show a way to chain blocks for authentication in a large-block cipher: We start out by enciphering the data in the first block. Then we position the next ciphering to start inside the ciphertext of the previous block. Of course this would mean that we would have to decipher the message in reverse order, but it would also propagate any ciphertext changes through the end of the message. So if we add an authentication field at the end of the message (a keyed value known on both ends), and that value is recovered upon deciphering (this will be the first block deciphered) we can authenticate the whole message. But we still need to handle the last block padding problem and possibly also the short message problem.

3.1.5 Block Size and Plaintext Randomization

Ciphering raw plaintext data can be dangerous when the cipher has a small block size. Language plaintext has a strong, biased distribution of symbols and ciphering raw plaintext would effectively reduce the number of possible plaintexts blocks. Worse, some plaintexts would be vastly more probable than others, and if some known plaintext were available, the most-frequent blocks might already be known. In this way, small blocks can be vulnerable to classic codebook attacks which build up the ciphertext equivalents for many of the plaintext phrases. This sort of attack confronts a particular block size, and for these attacks Triple-DES is no stronger than simple DES, because they both have the same block size.

The usual way of avoiding these problems is to randomize the plaintext block with an operating mode such as CBC. This can ensure that the plaintext data which is actually ciphered is evenly distributed across all possible block values. However, this also requires an IV which thus expands the ciphertext.

Another approach is to apply data compression to the plaintext before enciphering. If this is to be used instead of plaintext randomization, the designer must be very careful that the data compression does not contain regular features which could be exploited by The Opponents.

An alternate approach is to use blocks of sufficient size for them to be expected to have a substantial amount of uniqueness or "entropy." If we expect plaintext to have about one bit of entropy per byte of text, we might want a block size of at least 64 bytes before we stop worrying about an uneven distribution of plaintext blocks. This is now a practical block size.

3.1.6 Balanced Block Mixer

It is the process or any implementation (for example, hardware, computer software, hybrids, or the like) for performing Balanced Block Mixing.

Balanced Block Mixing

A Balanced Block Mixer is an m-input-port m-output-port mechanism with various properties:

The overall mapping is one-to-one and invertible: Every possible input value (over all ports) to the mixer produces a different output value (including all ports), and every possible output value is produced by a different input value;

- Each output port is a function of every input port;
- Any change to any one of the input ports will produce a change to every output port;
- Stepping any one input port through all possible values (while keeping the other input ports fixed) will step every output port through all possible values.

If we have a two port mixer, with input ports labeled A and B, output ports labeled X and Y, and some irreducible mod 2 polynomial p of degree appropriate to the port size, a Balanced Block

Mixer is formed by the equations:

```
X = 3A + 2B (mod 2)(mod p),
Y = 2A + 3B (mod 2)(mod p).
```

This particular BBM is a self-inverse or involution, and so can be used without change whether enciphering or deciphering. One possible value for p for mixing 8-bit values is 100011011.

Balanced Block Mixing functions probably should be thought of as orthogonal Latin squares. For example, here is a tiny nonlinear "2-bit" BBM:

```
3 1 2 0   0 3 2 1   30 13 22 01
0 2 1 3   2 1 0 3 = 02 21 10 33
1 3 0 2   1 2 3 0   11 32 03 20
2 0 3 1   3 0 1 2   23 00 31 12
```

Suppose we wish to mix (1,3); 1 selects the second row up in both squares, and 3 selects the rightmost column, thus selecting (2,0) as the output. Since there is only one occurrence of (2,0) among all entry pairs, this discrete mixing function is reversible, as well as being balanced on both inputs.

Cryptographic advantages of balanced block mixing include the fact that each output is always balanced with respect to either input, and that no information is lost in the mixing. This allows us to use balanced block mixing as the "butterfly" operations in a fast Walsh-Hadamard transform or the well-known FFT. By using the mixing patterns of these transforms, we can mix 2^n elements such that each input is guaranteed to affect each and every output in a balanced way. And if we use keying to generate the tables, we can have a way to mix huge blocks in small nonlinear mixing tables with overall mixing guarantees.

3.1.7 Balanced Combiner

In the context of cryptography, a combiner mixes two input values into a result value. A balanced combiner must provide a balanced relationship between each input and the result.

In a statically-balanced combiner, any particular result value can be produced by any value on one input, simply by selecting some appropriate value for the other input. In this way, knowledge of only the output value provides no information — not even statistical information — about either input.

The common examples of cryptographic combiner, including byte exclusive-OR (mod 2 polynomial addition), byte addition (integer addition mod 256), or other "additive" combining, are perfectly balanced. Unfortunately, these simple combiners are also very weak, being inherently linear and without internal state.

A Latin square combiner is an example of a statically-balanced reversible nonlinear combiner with massive internal state. A Dynamic Substitution Combiner is an example of a dynamically or statistically-balanced reversible nonlinear combiner with substantial internal state.

Base-64

A public code for converting between 6-bit values 0..63 (or 00..3f hex) and text symbols accepted by most computers:

```
  0 1 2 3 4 5 6 7 8 9 a b c d e f
0 A B C D E F G H I J K L M N O P
1 Q R S T U V W X Y Z a b c d e f
2 g h i j k l m n o p q r s t u v
3 w x y z 0 1 2 3 4 5 6 7 8 9 + /
use "=" for padding
```

IDEA encryption is substantially faster and generally considered to be much more secure than DES encryption. However, IDEA is newer, has not been formally adopted by governments, and is patented, restricting its commercial use. If your CPU is fast enough, you can enable any combination of IDEA, DES, and key file encryption. But since PGP uses IDEA to transmit message bodies, if you rely on PGP to exchange keys with other parties, the fundamental security of your voice link rests upon IDEA alone.

Cipher block chaining is used within each sound packet, but not from packet to packet. If that were done, loss of a single packet would render the entire rest of the conversation unintelligible.

Speak Freely will continue to correctly receive unencrypted sound from a given host even if an IDEA key is specified for the connection.

3.2 SYMMETRIC ENCRYPTION PRINCIPLES

All these systems have evolved from early classical ciphers discussed in the previous lectures. As we have seen, these classical ciphers may operate in the following two ways.

- *Stream cipher*, such as Vigen'ere cipher, encrypts one letter at a time.
- *Block cipher*, such as Hill cipher, treats a n-letter block of plaintext as a whole and produce a ciphertext block of equal length.

3.2.1 Block Cipher Principles

As block cipher have different modes of operation and applies to a broader range of applications than stream cipher, we will focus on its design principles in this section.

A block cipher transform a plaintext block of n letters into an encrypted block. For the alphabet with 26 letters, there are 26^n possible different plaintext blocks. The most general way of encrypting a n-letter block is to take each of the plaintext blocks and map it to a cipher block (arbitrary n-letter substitution cipher). For decryption to be possible, such mapping needs to be one-to-one (*i.e.*, each plaintext block must be mapped to a unique ciphertext block). The number of different one-to-one mappings among n-letter blocks is $(26^n)!$.

The length of block n can not be too short in order to secure the cryptographic scheme. For example, $n = 1$ gives a monoalphabetic cipher. Such schemes, as we have seen, are vulnerable to frequency analysis and brute-force attacks. However, an arbitrary reversible substitution cipher for a large block size n is not practical. Let's consider the problem of specifying a mapping of all possible n-letter blocks. In a cipher, each key specifies such a mapping. Let's assume the key consists of a block of k letters. Then the number of all possible keys is 26^k. Then for a n-letter arbitrary substitution block cipher, the key size needs to satisfy $26^k \geq (26^n)!$, *i.e.*, $k \geq n \times 26^n$!

*So the major challenge to design a symmetric key cryptographic scheme is to provide enough security (*e.g., *using a reasonable large block size) with a reasonable small size key.*

3.3 SHANNON'S THEORY OF CONFUSION AND DIFFUSION

How do we know that a cryptographic system is secure enough? To answer this ,Claude Shannon theoretically deduced the following principles that should be followed to design secure cryptographic systems. These principles aim at thwarting cryptanalysis based on known statistical properties of the plaintext.

- **Confusion:** In Shannon's original definitions, confusion makes the relation between the key and the ciphertext as complex as possible. Ideally, every letter in the key influences every letter of the ciphertext block. Replacing every letter with the one next to it on the typewriter keyboard is a simple example of confusion by substitution. However, good confusion can only be achieved when each character of the ciphertext depends on several parts of the key, and this dependence appears to be random to the observer. Ciphers that do not offer much confusion (such as Vigen'ere cipher) are vulnerable to frequency analysis.

- **Diffusion:** Diffusion refers to the property that the statistics structure of the plaintext is dissipated into long range statistics of the ciphertext. In contrast to confusion, diffusion spreads the influence of a single plaintext letter over many ciphertext letters. In terms of the frequency statistics of letters, digrams, etc in the plaintext, diffusion randomly spreads them across several characters in the ciphertext. This means that much more ciphertexts are needed to do a meaningful statistical attack on the cipher.

In cryptography, confusion and diffusion are two properties of the operation of a secure cipher. Confusion and diffusion were identified by Claude Shannon in his paper, "Communication Theory of Secrecy Systems" published in 1949. In Shannon's original definitions:

Confusion refers to making the relationship between the key and the ciphertext as complex and as involved as possible.Confusion can have the following meanings: Unclarity or puzzlement, e.g. arising from ambiguity. Literally, to mix or join together. The word itself is a confusion of the prefix "con" (a variant on the Latin prefix "com", meaning "with" or "together") and the verb "fuse" (meaning "join").

Diffusion refers to the property that redundancy in the statistics of the plaintext is "dissipated" in the statistics of the ciphertext.Diffusion is associated with the dependency of the output bits on the input bits. In a cipher with good diffusion, flipping an input bit should change each output bit with a probability of one half (this is termed the Strict Avalanche Criterion).

Substitution (a rule for replacing plaintext symbols by another) has been identified as a mechanism for primarily confusion ; on the other hand transposition using P-box (rearranging or swapping the order of symbols) is a technique for diffusion, although other mechanisms are also used in modern practice, such as linear transformations (e.g. in AES). Product ciphers use alternating substitution and transposition phases (rounds) to achieve both confusion and diffusion respectively.

Communication Theory of Secrecy Systems is a paper published by Claude Shannon discussing cryptography from the viewpoint of information theory. It is one of the foundational treatments (arguably the foundational treatment) of modern cryptography.In cryptography, a permutation box (or P-box) is a method of bit-shuffling used to permute or transpose bits (rearrange or swap the order of bits) across S-boxes inputs, maintaining diffusion while transposing.

In block ciphers, the S-boxes and P-Boxes are used to make the relation between the plaintext and the ciphertext difficult to understand

3.3.1 Substitution Box

In cryptography, a substitution box (or S-box) is a basic component of symmetric-key algorithms. In block ciphers, the S-boxes are used to make the relation between the plaintext and the ciphertext difficult to understand — Shannon's property of confusion. The S-boxes are carefully chosen to resist cryptanalysis.

In general, an S-box takes some number of input bits, m, and transforms them into some number of output bits, n: an m×n S-box can be implemented as a lookup table with 2m words of n bits each. Fixed tables are normally used, as in the Data Encryption Standard (DES), but in some ciphers the tables are generated dynamically from the key; e.g. the Blowfish and the Twofish encryption algorithms. Bruce Schneier describes IDEA's modular multiplication step as a key-dependent S-box.One good example is this 6×4-bit S-box from DES (S5):

S_5	Middle (inner) 4 bits of input																
		0000	0001	0010	0011	0100	0101	0110	0111	1000	1001	1010	1011	1100	1101	1110	1111
	00	0010	1100	0100	0001	0111	1010	1011	0110	1000	0101	0011	1111	1101	0000	1110	1001
Outer	01	1110	1011	0010	1100	0100	0111	1101	0001	0101	0000	1111	1010	0011	1001	1000	0110
bits	10	0100	0010	0001	1011	1010	1101	0111	1000	1111	1001	1100	0101	0110	0011	0000	1110
	11	1011	1000	1100	0111	0001	1110	0010	1101	0110	1111	0000	1001	1010	0100	0101	0011

Figure 3.1 A Substitution Box (5-box)

Given a 6-bit input, the 4-bit output is found by selecting the row using the outer two bits, and the column using the inner four bits. For example, an input "011011" has outer bits "01" and inner bits "1101"; the corresponding output would be "1001".

The 8 S-boxes of DES were the subject of intensive studies for many years cause of a concern that a method of bypassing the DES cipher to obtaining access to the plaintext — a vulnerability (susceptibility) known only to its designers — might have been planted (inserted) in the cipher. In 1994, the S-box design criteria were finally published by its designers after the public rediscovery of differential cryptanalysis, showing that they had been carefully tuned the design to increase resistance against differential cryptanalysis attacks. Other research had already indicated that even a very small modifications to one of the 8 S-box used by the DES could weaken it very much.

The design of good S-boxes was the subject for a great amount of researches; now much more is understood about their use in block ciphers than when the DES S-boxes was released.Boolean functions with good cryptographic characteristics are needed for the design of robust pseudo-random generators for stream ciphers and of S-boxes for block ciphers. Very few general constructions of such cryptographic Boolean functions are known. The main ones correspond to concatenating affine or quadratic functions.

3.4 FIESTEL STRUCTURE

A Feistel cipher is a symmetric structure used in the construction of block ciphers, named after the German IBM cryptographer Horst Feistel; it is also commonly known as a Feistel structure or network. A large proportion of block ciphers use the scheme, including the Data Encryption Standard (DES). The Feistel structure has the advantage that encryption and decryption operations are very similar, even identical in some cases, requiring only a reversal of the key schedule. Therefore the size of the code or circuitry required to implement such a cipher is nearly halved.

A Feistel network is an iterated cipher with an internal function called a round function.[2].Feistel networks gained respectability when the US Federal Government adopted the DES (a cipher based on Lucifer, with changes made by the NSA). Like other components of the DES, the iterative nature of the Feistel construction makes implementing the cryptosystem in hardware easier (particularly on the hardware available at the time of DES' design).

Feistel ciphers are a special class of iterated block ciphers (see 55) where the ciphertext is calculated from the plaintext by repeated application of the same transformation or round function. Feistel ciphers are also sometimes called DES-like ciphers (see 64).

In a Feistel cipher, the text being encrypted is split into two halves. The round function f is applied to one half using a subkey and the output of f is exclusive-ored with the other half. The two halves are then swapped. Each round follows the same pattern except for the last round where there is no swap.

A nice feature of a Feistel cipher is that encryption and decryption are structurally identical, though the subkeys used during encryption at each round are taken in reverse order during decryption.

It is possible to design iterative ciphers that are not Feistel ciphers, yet whose encryption and decryption (after a certain re-ordering or re-calculation of variables) are structurally the same. One such example is IDEA .

Product ciphers use the two classical encryption forms: substitution and transposition, alternatively in multiple rounds to achieve both confusion and diffusion respectively. Shannon was the first to investigate the product cryptosystem (so called substitution-permutation network) and show that some sophisticated heuristic ciphers were nothing other than products of some simpler ciphers. Most importantly, Shannon identified the necessary condition of the cipher strength increases as a result of cascading simple ciphers.

One possible way to build a secret key algorithm using substitution-permutation-network is to break the input into manageable-sized chunks, do a substitution on each small chunk, and then take the outputs of all the substitutions and run them through a permuter that is as big as the input, which shuffles the letters around. Then the process is repeated, so that each letter winds up as an input to each of the substitutions.

Since modern cryptosystems are all computer-based, from now on we will assume that both plain and cipher text are strings of bits ({0, 1}), instead of strings of letters ({a, b, c, ..., z}).

The Feistel network shown in Fig. 3.2 is a particular form of the substitution-permutation network.

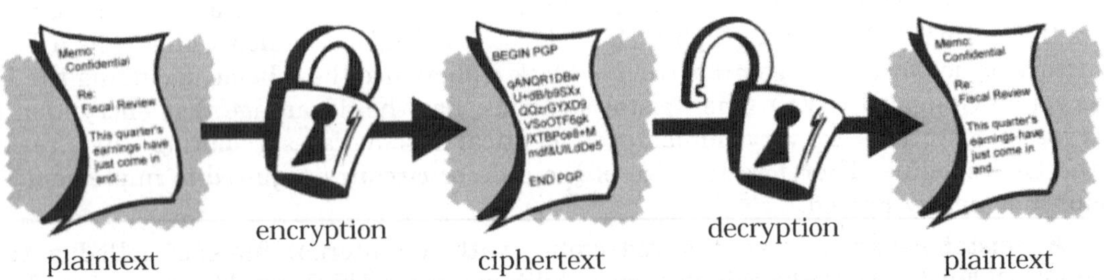

Figure 3.2 Feistel Network

The input to a Feistel network is a plaintext block of n bits, and a key K. The plaintext block is divided into two halves, L0 and R0. The two halves of the data pass through r rounds of processing and then combine to produce the ciphertext block. Each round i has as input Li-1 and Ri-1, derived from the previous round, as well as a subkey Ki, derived from the overall key K. In general, the subkey Ki are different from K and from each other. In this structure, a substitution is performed via the round function F, and permutation is performed that interchanges the two halves of the data.

The exact realization of a Feistel network depends on the choices of the following parameters and design features.

- **Block size:** Larger block size means greater security, but reduces encryption/decryption speed.

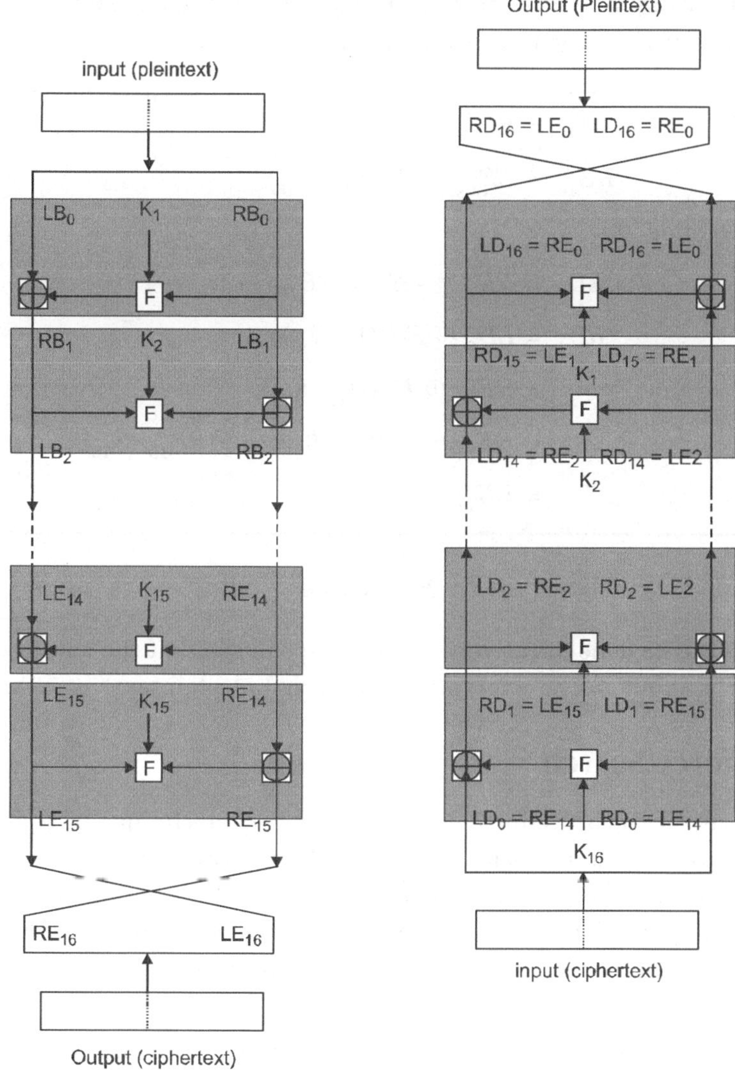

Figure 3.3 The encryption and decryption of Feistel network

- **Key size:** Larger key size means greater security but may decrease encryption/decryption speed.
- **Number of rounds:** Multiple rounds offer increasing security.
- **Subkey generation algorithm:** Greater complexity in subkey generation leads to greater security.
- **Round function:** Greater complexity in round function means greater difficulty of cryptanalysis.

It is worth noting that the process of decryption with a Feistel network is essentially the same as the encryption process by using the ciphertext as input to the network, but using the subkey Ki in reverse order, as shown in Fig 3.4. The reason is explained as follows. Let's consider the last step in encryption, which gives,

$$LE_{16} = RE_{15}$$

$$RE_{16} = LE_{15} \oplus F(RE_{15}, K_{16})$$

On the decryption side,

$$LD_1 = RD_0 = LE_{16} = RE_{15}$$

$$\begin{aligned} RD_1 &= LD_0 \oplus F(RD_0, K_{16}) \\ &= RE_{16} \oplus F(RD_{15}, K_{16}) \\ &= RE_{15} \oplus F(RE_0, K_{16}) \oplus F(RE_{15}, K_{16}) \\ &= LE_{15} \end{aligned}$$

Figure 3.4

The process can be done iteratively. Finally, we will see that the output of the decryption is the same as the input to the encryption (i.e., original plaintext).

3.4.2 Brute-force Search

Exhaustive key search, or brute-force search, is the basic technique of trying every possible key in turn until the correct key is identified. To identify the correct key it may be necessary to possess a plaintext and its corresponding ciphertext, or if the plaintext has some recognizable characteristic, ciphertext alone might suffice. Exhaustive key search can be mounted on any cipher and sometimes a weakness in the key schedule of the cipher can help improve the efficiency of an exhaustive key search attack.

Advances in technology and computing performance will always make exhaustive key search an increasingly practical attack against keys of a fixed length. When DES was designed, it was generally considered secure against exhaustive key search without a vast financial investment in hardware. Over the years, this line of attack will become increasingly attractive to a potential adversary.

While the 56-bit key in DES now only offers a few hours of protection against exhaustive search by a modern dedicated machine, the current rate of increase in computing power is such that Skipjack's 80-bit key can be expected to offer the same level of protection against exhaustive key search in 18 years time as DES does today.

Many modern symmetric block ciphers are based on Feistel networks, and the structure and properties of Feistel ciphers have been extensively explored by cryptographers. Specifically, Michael Luby and Charles Rackoff analyzed the Feistel cipher construction, and proved that if the round function is a cryptographically secure pseudorandom function, with Ki used as the seed, then 3 rounds is sufficient to make the block cipher a pseudorandom permutation, while 4 rounds is sufficient to make it a "strong" pseudorandom permutation (which means that it remains pseudorandom even to an adversary who gets oracle access to its inverse permutation). Because of this very important result of Luby and Rackoff, Feistel ciphers are sometimes called Luby-Rackoff block ciphers. Further theoretical work has generalized the construction somewhat, and given more precise bounds for security.

The most obvious way, perhaps, of taking text and concealing it from the prying eyes of those who don't know your secret is by replacing each letter by something else, like this:

A	B	C	D	E	F	G	H	I	J	K	L	M	N	O	P	Q	R	S	T	U	V	W	X	Y	Z
$	7	+	Q	@	?	)	/	2	X	3	:	!	8	J	9	%	6	*	&	1	5	=	(	;	4

Figure 3.5

which turns "Please send me some money into"

9 : @ $ * @ * @ 8 Q ! @ * J ! @ ! J 8 @ ;

This is called substitution, and ciphers based on this principle date back to ancient times.

For example, the Figure 3.6 illustrates several cipher alphabets used by the ancient Hebrews. Three of them are based on arrangements of the alphabet according to a definite pattern, and these patterns can be illustrated in terms of the 26-letter alphabet used by the English language by showing what the equivalent substitutions are in that alphabet:

Figure 3.6 Cipher Alphabets Used by Ancient Hebrews

Atbash:

A	B	C	D	E	F	G	H	I	J	K	L	M
Z	Y	X	W	V	U	T	S	R	Q	P	O	N

Albam:

A	B	C	D	E	F	G	H	I	J	K	L	M
N	O	P	Q	R	S	T	U	V	W	X	Y	Z

Atbah:

A	B	C	D		J	K	L	M		E		S	T	U	V
I	H	G	F		R	Q	P	O		N		Z	Y	X	W

Note that all three of these are reciprocal, in that if one letter becomes another letter, then that other letter becomes the original letter in turn.

Cryptanalyzing the Simple Substitution Cipher

This page is not complete. It is placed here now to reserve space, to allow other changes to this section to take place.

Here is a short message, enciphered only by replacing each of its letters by a different letter on a consistent basis:

```
MGSVR WWJXS VPTRY SSOEF YYTMQ SVSYM MTPTR XYMGS RVRFJ
NFVGX TYFWF EIFUS AXJJQ SJSNM QPMGS TJOTF IMLSS TYSJO
SLQSL LPLTF OYSHM MRSVO FP
```

How would one go about trying to read it?

The first step that would occur to many people would be to make use of the fact that some letters are more common than others in English. E is the most common letter, and letters like J, Q, X, and Z are quite rare.

And so, we count the letters in our message. This produces the following table of frequencies:

A	E	F	G	H	I	J	L	M	N	O	P	Q	R	S	T	U	V	W	X	Y
1	2	9	4	1	2	7	5	10	2	5	5	4	6	18	9	1	6	3	4	8

In comparison, a frequency count I had my computer perform on a sample of literary text produced these frequencies:

A	443747	8.03	H	331686	6.00	O	420966	7.62	V	54921	0.99
B	88298	1.60	I	382552	6.92	P	102205	1.85	W	114048	2.06
C	152187	2.75	J	7112	0.13	Q	5841	0.11	X	12081	0.22
D	225040	4.07	K	33872	0.61	R	330126	5.97	Y	95514	1.73
E	711756	12.88	L	220858	4.00	S	351389	6.36	Z	3519	0.06
F	139985	2.53	M	141726	2.56	T	514613	9.31			
G	103279	1.87	N	383526	6.94	U	156536	2.83			

Arranged in order of frequency, for clarity, they become:

E	12.88	H	6.00	F	2.53	K	0.61
T	9.31	R	5.97	W	2.06	X	0.22
A	8.03	D	4.07	G	1.87	J	0.13
O	7.62	L	4.00	P	1.85	Q	0.11
N	6.94	U	2.83	Y	1.73	Z	0.06
I	6.92	C	2.75	B	1.60		
S	6.36	M	2.56	V	0.99		

Comparing these frequencies to those of the message:

```
18: S        7: J          3: W
10: M        6: R V        2: E I N
```

```
9: F T    5: L O P    1: A H U
8: Y      4: G Q X
```

it might be tempting to start by aligning like frequencies wherever possible:

```
Cipher: S M Y J W
Plain : e t n i f
```

to begin deciphering the message like this:

```
MGSVR WWJXS VPTRY SSOEF YYTMQ SVSYM MTPTR XYMGS RVRFJ
t e   ffi e n ee  nn t e ent t  nt e  i
NFVGX TYFWF EIFUS AXJJQ SJSNM QPMGS TJOTF IMLSS TYSJO
n f   e     ii    eie t  t e  i   t ee  nei
SLQSL LPLTF OYSHM MRSVO FP
e e   ne t t
```

Here, it looks like we've been luckier than we have a right to expect. With frequencies of 6.94 and 6.92 for N and I respectively, it isn't hard to imagine that I might be more common than N, instead of N being more common than I, in the text of a particular message.

The combination t-e occurs three times from MGS, and once each from MQS and MLS, so it seems reasonable to think that G stands for h. e-ent might be event, and -ffi-e might be office, although it is actually hard to take seriously that W necessarily stands for f.

To make a good start on breaking a simple substitution, however, single-letter frequencies are not enough. They might work for picking out the letters E and T in most cases, but more information is available that can serve as a better guide.

We've seen that N and I have frequencies of 6.94 and 6.92 respectively. This is a very small difference. But one is a consonant, and the other is a vowel. So we might expect them to behave differently. And they do.

3.5 THE DATA ENCRYPTION STANDARD (DES)

Data Encryption Standard (DES) is a widely-used method of data encryption using a private (secret) key that was judged so difficult to break by the U.S. government that it was restricted for exportation to other countries but has subsequently enjoyed widespread use internationally. There are 72,000,000,000,000,000 (72 quadrillion) or more possible encryption keys that can be used. For each given message, the key is chosen at random from among this enormous number of keys. Like other private key cryptographic methods, both the sender and the receiver must know and use the same private key.

The Data Encryption Standard (DES) is a block cipher (a method for encrypting information) that was developed in the 1970s by the National Bureau of Standards with the help of the National Security Agency and was selected by NBS as an official Federal Information Processing Standard (FIPS) for the United States in 1976. Its purpose is to provide a standard method for protecting sensitive commercial and unclassified data. IBM created the first draft of the algorithm, calling it LUCIFER.In 1972, the National Institute of

Standards and Technology (called the National Bureau of Standards at the time) decided that a strong cryptographic algorithm was needed to protect non-classified information. The algorithm was required to be cheap, widely available, and very secure. NIST envisioned something that would be available to the general public and could be used in a wide variety of applications. So they asked for public proposals for such an algorithm. In 1974 IBM submitted the Lucifer algorithm, which appeared to meet most of NIST's design requirements.

NIST enlisted the help of the National Security Agency to evaluate the security of Lucifer. DES officially became a federal standard in November of 1976. It is based on a Symmetric-key algorithm that uses a 56-bit key. The algorithm was initially controversial with classified design elements, a relatively short key length, and suspicions about a National Security Agency (NSA) backdoor. DES consequently came under intense academic scrutiny which motivated the modern understanding of block ciphers and their cryptanalysis.

DES is now considered to be insecure for many applications. This is chiefly due to the 56-bit key size being too small; in January, 1999, distributed.net and the Electronic Frontier Foundation collaborated to publicly break a DES key in 22 hours and 15 minutes. There are also some analytical results which demonstrate theoretical weaknesses in the cipher, although they are unfeasible to mount in practice. The algorithm is believed to be practically secure in the form of Triple DES, although there are theoretical attacks. In recent years, the cipher has been superseded by the Advanced Encryption Standard (AES).

In some documentation, a distinction is made between DES as a standard and DES algorithm which is referred to as the DEA (the Data Encryption Algorithm). When spoken, "DES" is either spelled out (IPA: /di? i? ?s/) as an abbreviation or pronounced as a single syllable (IPA: /d?s/) acronym.

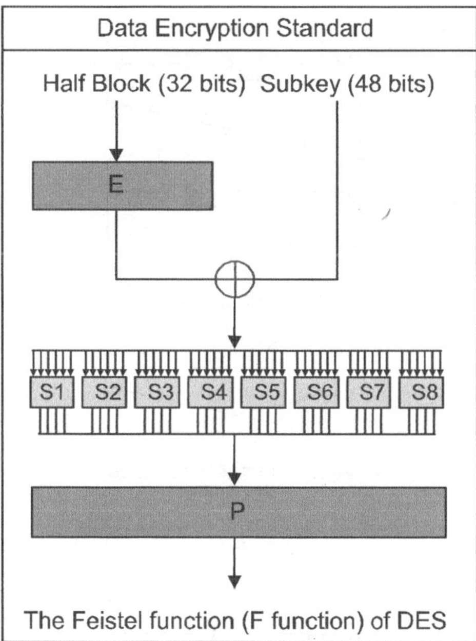

Figure 3.7 Data Encryption Standared

The key ostensibly consists of 64 bits; however, only 56 of these are actually used by the algorithm. Eight bits are used solely for checking parity, and are thereafter discarded. Hence the effective key length is 56 bits.

The algorithm's overall structure is shown in Figure 3.8 there are 16 identical stages of processing, termed rounds. There is also an initial and final permutation, termed IP and FP, which are inverses (IP "undoes" the action of FP, and vice versa). IP and FP have almost no cryptographic significance, but were apparently included in order to facilitate loading blocks in and out of mid-1970s hardware, as well as to make DES run slower in software.

Before the main rounds, the block is divided into two 32-bit halves and processed alternately; this criss-crossing is known as the Feistel scheme. The Feistel structure ensures that decryption and encryption are very similar processes — the only difference is that the subkeys are applied in the reverse order when decrypting. The rest of the algorithm is identical. This greatly simplifies implementation, particularly in hardware, as there is no need for separate encryption and decryption algorithms.

The symbol ⊕ denotes the exclusive-OR (XOR) operation. The F-function scrambles half a block together with some of the key. The output from the F-function is then combined with the other half of the block, and the halves are swapped before the next round. After the final round, the halves are not swapped; this is a feature of the Feistel structure which makes encryption and decryption similar processes

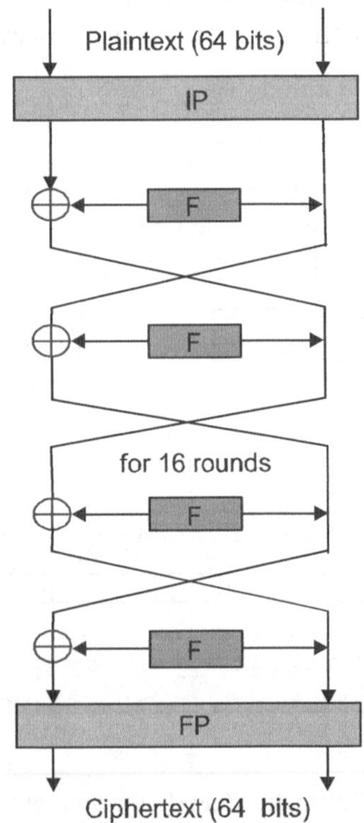

Figure 3.8 Overall Structure of DES Algorithm

Let us now fast forward to modern time and examine the Data Encryption Standard a symmetric key encryption standard published in 1977 and updated most recently in 1993 by the US National Bureau of Standards for commercial and non-classified US government use. DES encodes plaintext in 64 bit chunks using a 64-bit key. Actually, 8 of these 64 bits are odd parity bits (one bit in each of the 8 bytes is an odd partity bit for that byte), so the DES key is effectively 56 bits long. The National Institute of Standards (the successor to the National Bureau of Standards) states the goal of DES as follows: " The goal is to completely scramble the data and key so that every bit of the ciphertext depends on every bit of the data and every bit of the key .... with a good algorithm, there should be no correlation between the ciphertext and either the original data or key." [NIST 1999].

The basic operation of DES is illustrated in Figure 3.9. In our discussion we will overview DES operation, leaving the nitty-gritty bit-level details. The DES consists of two permutation steps (the first and last steps of the algorithm) in which all 64 bits are permuted, and 16 identical "rounds" of operation in between. The operation of each round is identical, taking the output of the previous round as input. During each round, the rightmost 32 bits of the input are moved to the left 32 bits of the output. The entire 64-bit input to the ith round and the 48 bit key for the ith round (derived from the larger DES 56-bit) are taken as input to a function that involves expansion of four-bit input chunks into six-bit chunks, exclusive OR-ing with the expanded six bit chunks of the 48-bit key Ki, a substitution operation and further exclusive OR-ing with the leftmost 32 bits of the input. The resulting 32-bit output of the function is then used as the rightmost 32 bits of the rounds 64-bit output, as shown in Figure 3.9. Decryption works by reversing the algorithm's operations.

How well does DES work? How secure is it? No one can tell for sure, although recent speculation is that one could build a special purpose machine that exhaustively searched through the 56-bit key space for under a million dollars. In 1997, a network security company, RSA Data Security Inc, launched a DES Challenge contest to "crack" (decode) a short phrase it had encrypted using 56-bit DES. The unencoded phrase ("Strong cryptography makes the world a safer place.") was determined only 140 days later by a team that used volunteers throughout the Internet to systematically explore the key space. The team claimed the $10,000 prize after testing only a quarter of the key space - about 18 quadrillion keys [RSA 1997]. The most recent 1999 DES Challenge III was won in a record time of a little over 22 hours, with a network of volunteers and a special purpose computer that was built for less that $250,000 (nick-named "DES Cracker") and is documented on-line.

If 56-bit DES is considered too insecure, one can simply run the 56-bit algorithm multiple times, taking the 64-bit output from one iteration of DES as the input to the next DES iteration, using a different encryption key each time. For example, so-called triple-DES (3DES), is a proposed US government standard [NIST 1999b] and has been proposed as the encryption standard for the Point-to-Point protocol [RFC 2420], PPP, for the data link layer.

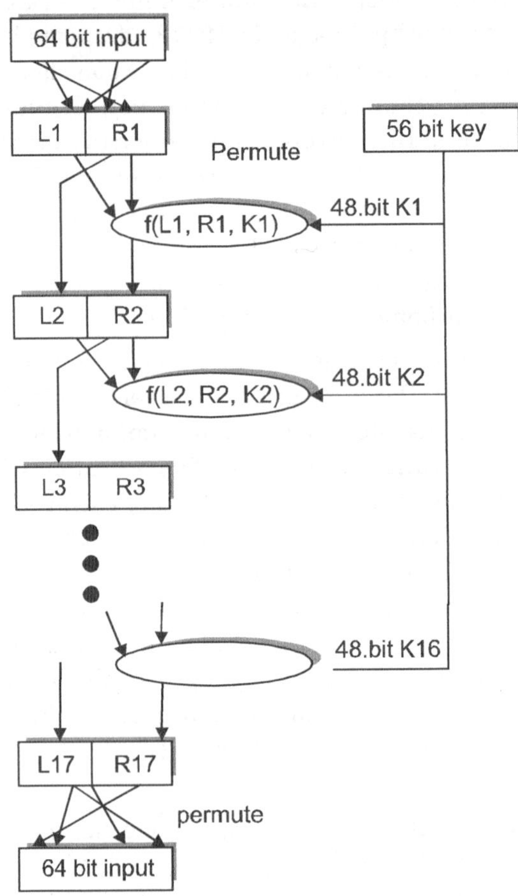

Figure 3.9 Basic operation of the DES

We should also note that our description above has only considered the encryption of a 64-bit quantity. When longer messages are encrypted, which is typically the case, DES is often used with a technique known as cipher-block chaining, in which the encrypted version of the jth 64-bit quantity of data is XOR'ed with the $(j+1)_{st}$ unit of data before the $(j+1)_{st}$ unit of data is encrypted.

Cryptography, the art of concealing the meaning of messages, has been practiced for at least 3000 years. In the past few centuries, it has become an indispensable tool in the military affairs, diplomacy, and commerce of most major nations. During that time there have been many innovations, and cryptography has changed and grown to accommodate the increasingly complex needs of its users. Present techniques are very sophisticated and provide excellent message protection. Current developments in computer technology and information theory, however, are on the verge of revolutionizing cryptography. New kinds of cryptographic systems are emerging that have incredible properties, which appear to eliminate completely some problems that have plagued cryptography users for centuries. One of these new systems is public key cryptography.

The Feistel (F) function

The F-function, depicted in Figure 3.10, operates on half a block (32 bits) at a time and consists of four stages:

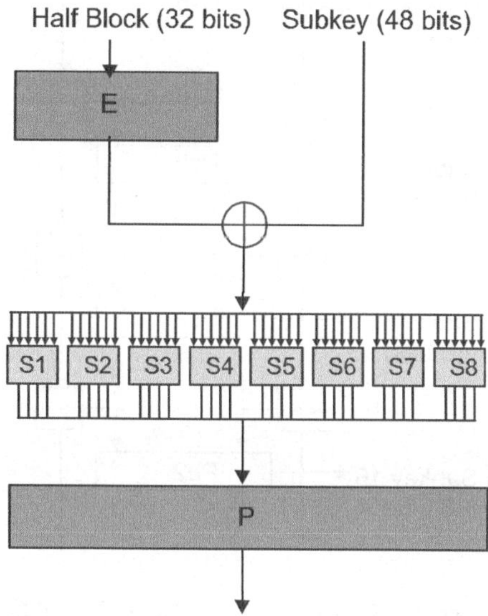

Figure 3.10 Feistel (F) Function of DES Expansion

(1) The 32-bit half-block is expanded to 48 bits using the expansion permutation, denoted E in the diagram, by duplicating some of the bits.

(2) Key mixing — the result is combined with a subkey using an XOR operation. Sixteen 48-bit subkeys — one for each round — are derived from the main key using the key schedule (described below).

(3) Substitution – after mixing in the subkey, the block is divided into eight 6-bit pieces before processing by the S-boxes, or substitution boxes. Each of the eight S-boxes replaces its six input bits with four output bits according to a non-linear transformation, provided in the form of a lookup table. The S-boxes provide the core of the security of DES — without them, the cipher would be linear, and trivially breakable.

(4) Permutation – finally, the 32 outputs from the S-boxes are rearranged according to a fixed permutation, the P-box. The alternation of substitution from the S-boxes, and permutation of bits from the P-box and E-expansion provides so-called "confusion and diffusion" respectively, a concept identified by Claude Shannon in the 1940s as a necessary condition for a secure yet practical cipher.

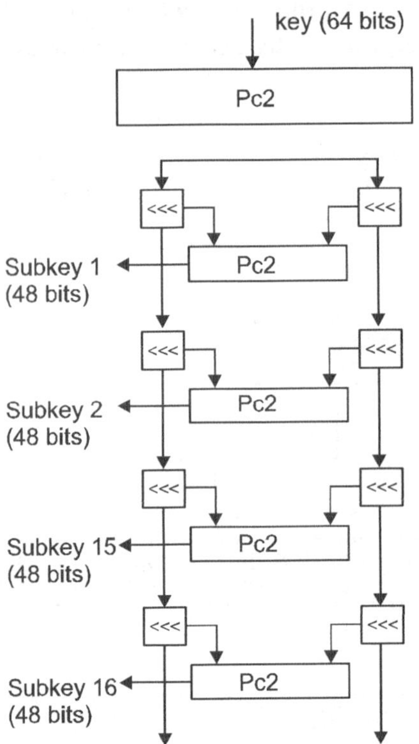

Figure 3.11 The key-schedule of DES

Key Schedule

Figure 3.11 illustrates the key schedule for encryption — the algorithm which generates the subkeys. Initially, 56 bits of the key are selected from the initial 64 by Permuted Choice 1 (PC-1) — the remaining eight bits are either discarded or used as parity check bits. The 56 bits are then divided into two 28-bit halves; each half is thereafter treated separately. In successive rounds, both halves are rotated left by one or two bits (specified for each round), and then 48 subkey bits are selected by Permuted Choice 2 (PC-2) — 24 bits from the left half, and 24 from the right. The rotations (denoted by "<<<" in the diagram) mean that a different set of bits is used in each subkey; each bit is used in approximately 14 out of the 16 subkeys.

The key schedule for decryption is similar — the subkeys are in reverse order compared to encryption. Apart from that change, the process is the same as for encryption.

In general, DES takes as input a 64 bit key, of which only 56 bits are used. From these 56 bits, 16 48 bit subkeys are created. The message is split into 64 bit chunks, and a complex series of steps enciphers the message using each subkey. As Javascript only supports 32 bit integers, all 48 or 64 bit integers are represented by two 32 bit integers in an array.

Creating the Keys - PC1

DES must first create the 16 subkeys. First, the 8 character string representing the key is turned into two integers which are passed to the des_createKeys function. The bits of these two integers are then reorganised according to PC1 (permuted choice 1). The bits end up in the following places:

57	49	41	33	25	17	9	1
58	50	42	34	26	18	10	2
59	51	43	35	27	19	11	3
60	52	44	36	0	0	0	0
63	55	47	39	31	23	15	7
62	54	46	38	30	22	14	6
61	53	45	37	29	21	13	5
28	20	12	4	0	0	0	0

This means that the first 57th bit of the original key becomes the first bit, etc. The permuting is done using a permutation sequence, which is a clever way of rotating and switching bits between 2 integers. For instance, `temp = (left >>> 4) ^ right) & 0x0f0f0f0f; right ^= temp; left ^= (temp << 4)`, rotates 4 x 4 blocks of bits:

33	34	35	36	1	2	3	4
41	42	43	44	9	10	11	12
49	50	51	52	17	18	19	20
57	58	59	60	25	26	27	28
37	38	39	40	5	6	7	8
45	46	47	48	13	14	15	16
53	54	55	56	21	22	23	24
61	62	63	64	29	30	31	32

This permutation function exists in Eric Young's C implementation. He gives credit to John Fletcher for determining the most efficient way to do PC1.

In other DES explanations, the first 28 bits out of PC1 is called C, and the last 28 bits is D. (Note that PC1 only uses 56 of the original 64 bits.) These are then left shifted according to a schedule until 16 subkeys are created. For instance, C1 and D1 are created by left shifting C and D by one place, C2 and D2 by a further one place, etc. Here is what C1 and D1 look like relative to C and D:

2	3	4	5	6	7	8	9
10	11	12	13	14	15	16	17
18	19	20	21	22	23	24	25
26	27	28	1	0	0	0	0
34	35	36	37	38	39	40	41
42	43	44	45	46	47	48	49
50	51	52	53	54	55	56	57
58	59	60	33	0	0	0	0

Creating the Keys - PC2

The 16 subkeys (C1 and D1 through to C16 and D16) are then permuted according to PC2 to create 16 subkeys of 48 bits each. PC2 seems to be a random bit sequence and so the permutation sequence above can't be used. Instead the bits are permuted 4 at a time using the pc2bytes array of arrays. pc2bytes contains 14 subarrays (one for each 4 bits of the 56 bit subkeys). Each subarray contains 16 elements. Every four bits of a subkey are looked up in the corresponding array and the results are all added together. For example, if the first four bits of C1 are 0100 in binary, then the fourth element of pc2bytes[0], 0x00010000 is added to the result. This has the result of moving the 2nd bit of C1 to the 16th bit of the result (some bit shifting is also applied at the end to put everything in the right place). Here is what the resulting K1 though K16 look like relative to C1 and D1 through C16 and D16. Note that this is different from the PC2 given in other DES explanations, the reason for this is explained further down.

0	0	3	28	15	6	21	10
0	0	16	7	27	20	13	2
0	0	34	44	55	49	37	52
0	0	50	46	54	40	33	36
0	0	14	17	11	24	1	5
0	0	23	19	12	4	26	8
0	0	45	56	35	41	51	59
0	0	48	53	43	60	38	57

Encrypting the Message - IP1

With 16 subkeys created, we are now ready to deal with the message. First the whole message is turned into and array of 32 bit integers, then the message is encrypted or decrypted 64 bits at a time. The first step is to perform the permuation IP. This again uses the permutation sequence. Eric Young gives credit to Richard Outerbridge for helping make this more efficient.

58	50	42	34	26	18	10	2
60	52	44	36	28	20	12	4
62	54	46	38	30	22	14	6
64	56	48	40	32	24	16	8
57	49	41	33	25	17	9	1
55	51	43	35	27	19	11	3
61	53	45	37	29	21	13	5
63	55	47	39	31	23	15	7

Encrypting the Message - E

The resulting 64 bits are then encrypted or decrypted using the 16 subkeys. This requires 16 steps, during which the left and right half of the 64 bit message are alternatively operated on. The operation involves taking 32 bits (called R in other explanations), permuting it according to E (which expands are from 32 to 48 bits), XORing with one of the 48 bit subkeys to produce a different 48 bits, then passing it through the S selection functions to get it back down to 32 bits, and finally permuting through P. Note that the E used here (displayed below) is different from other Es, for the reason explained below.

0	0	3	4	5	6	7	8
0	0	11	12	13	14	15	16
0	0	19	20	21	22	23	24
0	0	27	28	29	30	31	32
0	0	31	32	1	2	3	4
0	0	7	8	9	10	11	12
0	0	15	16	17	18	19	20
0	0	23	24	25	26	27	28

Encrypting the Message - S Selection Functions

The step above expands 32 bits into 48 bits, and then XORs them with a subkey. The result is passed through the S selection functions. There are 8 of these functions (labelled S1 through S8 would you believe) which convert 6 bits into 4 bits. (Their randomness is part of the reason why DES is so powerful, because a 1 bit uncertainty in the input yields 4 bits of uncertainty in the output.) The first 6 bits of the output from the E permuation above are passed through S2, the next 6 through S4, then S6, S8, S1, S3, S5 and S7. Using this ordering makes it easier to perform E (as it is essentially done by duplicating the 32 bits), and PC2 was also changed to compensate for this. As with PC2, a series of 8 spfunction arrays of 64 elements are used to perform the S functions. The output of the S functions cannot be shown because it is not about bit movements. The 6 input bits to each S function could produce any one of 16 results. Note that a further efficiency is applied by shifting the input one bit to the left before encrypting, instead of during each encryption step (and the spfunction are also shifted one left to compensate).

Encrypting the Message - P

The 32 bit output from the S functions is permuted again according to P. For efficiency, this permuation is done as part of the S functions array. For example, the first 6 bits out of E are looked up in the second S array, spfunction2. If these 6 bits are all zero, then 0x40084010 is added to the result. If you refer to other DES descriptions, they will tell you exactly what the S functions are, and you would see that the zeroth element of S2 is 15. This means that if you pass binary 000000 into S2, you get 1111 as output. These four bits are then moved around according to P (remembering to shift them left once as well) and the result is 0x80108020. Specifically, the bits are moved to positions 12, 27, 1, and 17.

Encrypting the Message - IP-1

After going through the above steps 16 times, the 64 bits are passed through IP-1 to produce the cipher text. Decryption is performed using exactly the same process but the subkeys are applied in the reverse order.

40	8	48	16	56	24	64	32
39	7	47	15	55	23	63	31
38	6	46	14	54	22	62	30
37	5	45	13	53	21	61	29
36	4	44	12	52	20	60	28
35	3	43	11	51	19	59	27
34	2	42	10	50	18	58	26
33	1	41	9	49	17	57	25

The same algorithm can be used for encryption or decryption. The method described above will encrypt a block of plaintext and return a block of ciphertext. In order to decrypt the ciphertext and get the original plaintext again, the procedure is simply repeated but the subkeys are applied in reverse order, from K[16]-K[1]. That is, stage 2 of the Core Function as outlined above changes from R[I-1] XOR K[I] to R[I-1] XOR K[17-I]. Other than that, decryption is performed exactly the same as encryption.

3.5.1 Basic DES Block Cipher Modes

There are several different modes in which DES can be run. ECB (Electronic Codebook) mode is the simplest mode. In this mode, each 64 bit chunk of the input message is treated independently, thus it is also the least secure. In CBC (Cipher Block Chaining) mode, you supply a 64 bit input vector. The first 64 bits of the message are XORed with this before encrypting. The second 64 bits are then XORed with the cipher text from the first 64 bit before encrypting it, and so on.

In triple DES, every eight bytes are operated on three times (for instance, a triple DES encryption will encrypt, decrypt, and encrypt the data) before being appended to the result. CBC mode uses the result of the first 8 byte triple DES encryption to feed back into the algorithm.

- ECB (Electronic Code Book)
- CBC (Cipher Block Chaining)
- CFB (Cipher Feedback)
- OFB (Output Feedback)

3.5.1.1 ECB (Electronic Code Book)

At the same time that DES was brought to public attention, a number of ways of using DES were recommended.The obvious way of using DES is simply to apply it directly to plaintext, transforming each 64-bit block of plaintext. This is called ECB, or Electronic CodeBook mode.

This is the regular DES algorithm, exactly as described above. Data is divided into 64-bit blocks and each block is encrypted one at a time. Separate encryptions with different blocks are totally independent of each other. This means that if data is transmitted over a network or phone line, transmission errors will only affect the block containing the error. It also means, however, that the blocks can be rearranged, thus scrambling a file beyond recognition, and this action would go undetected. ECB is the weakest of the various modes because no additional security measures are implemented besides the basic DES algorithm. However, ECB is the fastest and easiest to implement, making it the most common mode of DES seen in commercial applications. This is the mode of operation used by Private Encryptor.

There are two reasons this mode might not be found satisfactory. If the same message is sent twice, with the same key, its enciphered form will also be identical. Also, one needs to have eight bytes of plaintext available before performing encipherment. Thus, other ways of using DES were proposed. None of them strengthened the basic cipher, or added to the size of the key.

3.5.1.2 Cipher Block Chaining (CBC)

CBC, for Cipher Block Chaining, is one of the most popular modes. It addresses the first of the two problems with ECB mode. Each plaintext block, before being encrypted normally by DES (as in ECB mode) is XORed with the previous ciphertext block. The first plaintext block is XORed with a random 64-bit block, called the initialization vector, which is transmitted in the clear.

In this mode of operation, each block of ECB encrypted ciphertext is XORed with the next plaintext block to be encrypted, thus making all the blocks dependent on all the previous blocks. This means that in order to find the plaintext of a particular block, you need to know the ciphertext, the key, and the ciphertext for the previous block. The first block to be encrypted has no previous ciphertext, so the plaintext is XORed with a 64-bit number called the Initialization Vector, or IV for short. So if data is transmitted over a network or phone line and there is a transmission error (adding or deleting bits), the error will be carried forward to all subsequent blocks since each block is dependent upon the last. If the bits are just modified in transit (as is the more common case) the error will only affect all of the bits in the changed block, and the corresponding bits in the following block. The error doesn't propagate any further.

This mode of operation is more secure than ECB because the extra XOR step adds one more layer to the encryption process. This mode looks like this:

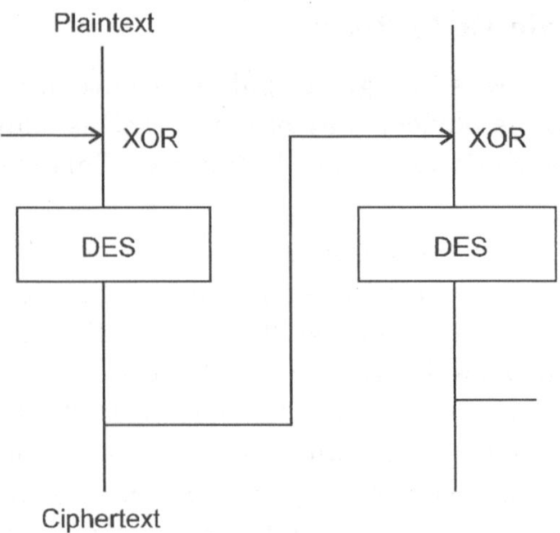

Figure 3.12

The useful properties of CBC mode can be illustrated by means of the following short demonstration:

Let's imagine a block cipher that operates on three-letter groups, and uses Vigenere instead of XOR...

```
Plain:             BIL LNE EDS MON EYX
Previous cipher:   ZQT MNM VTI  UTU LKE
                   --- --- ---  --- --- Vigenere step
                  AYE  XAQ ZWA GHI PIB
                  ===  === === === === Block cipher step
Cipher:       ZQT MNM  VTI UTU LKE MRV
```

Now, if we change the message at the beginning, everything changes all the way through, because information indeed keeps getting propagated:

```
Plain:             MIK ENE EDS MON EYX
Previous cipher:   ZQT RJY QEI RMQ LVI
                   --- --- --- --- --- Vigenere step
                   LYD VWC UHA DAD PTF
                   === === === === === Block cipher step
Cipher:        ZQT RJY QEI RMQ LVI SZR
```

But if, instead, it is the original message that is sent, and a transmission error takes place, so that instead of recieving ZQT MNM VTI UTU LKE MRV the reciever gets ZQT MKM VTI UTU LKE MRV then only two blocks are destroyed. Since each ciphertext block was a function of the plaintext block and the previous ciphertext block, each plaintext block is a function of the ciphertext block and the previous ciphertext block. As long as those two ciphertext blocks are right, the rest of the message is irrelevant.

```
Plain:            ZQI MKM VII UTU LKE MRV
Previous cipher:      === === === === === Inverse Block  cipher step
                      PQK XAQ ZNA GHI PIS (1)
                      ZQT MKM VII UTU LKE (2)
                      --- --- --- --- --- Inverse Vigenere step ((1)-(2))
Cipher:               QAR LFE ED5 MON EYX
```

In this decipherment example, the first plaintext block is totally garbled, because the erroneous ciphertext block is the input into the block cipher; the second plaintext block only has an error which matches that of the plaintext block, because the erroneous block is used in a Vigenere calculation after the block cipher.

Thus, someone could even note that ...EDSMONEY is probably NEEDSMONEY, and work out that LPE should become LNE. That would allow MKM to be corrected to MNM, and the message recovered.

In the binary case, a transmission error in one block will garble that block, and modify the succeeding block by inverting exactly those bits which were in error in the preceding transmitted ciphertext block. Note that since the IV has no corresponding "plaintext", altering bits in the IV can be used by an attacker as a technique for altering corresponding bits of the first plaintext block without causing a garble.

3.5.1.3 Output Feed Back (OFB)

OFB, for Output FeedBack, addresses both the first and second problems noted earlier that exist with ECB mode. An initialization vector is again sent in the clear. It is repeatedly encrypted by DES, and the result of doing so is XORed with the successive blocks of the plaintext.

This is similar to CFB mode, except that the ciphertext output of DES is fed back into the Shift Register, rather than the actual final ciphertext. The Shift Register is set to an arbitrary initial value, and passed through the DES algorithm. The output from DES is passed through the M-box and then fed back into the Shift Register to prepare for the next block. This value is then XORed with the real plaintext (which may be less than 64 bits in length, like CFB mode), and the result is the final ciphertext. Note that unlike CFB and CBC, a transmission error in one block will not affect subsequent blocks because once the recipient has the initial Shift Register value, it will continue to generate new Shift Register plaintext inputs without any further data input. However, this mode of operation is less secure than CFB mode because only the real ciphertext and DES ciphertext output is needed to find the plaintext of the most recent block. Knowledge of the key is not required.

This mode has two problems of its own. The plaintext itself is only subjected to an XOR. This means that if the plaintext is known, another plaintext can be substituted by inverting the same bits of the ciphertext as one would need to invert of the plaintext to do so. This is called a bit-flipping attack. And there is always the possibility, admittedly a slim one, that one might choose a key and an initialization vector such that the successive blocks generated might repeat in a short loop.

3.5.1.4 Cipher Feed Back (CFB)

A mode which seems to avoid most of the problems so far encountered is CFB, for Cipher FeedBack. Here, a plaintext block is enciphered by being XORed to the DES encryption of the previous ciphertext block. For the first plaintext block, an initialization vector again takes the role of the first plaintext block.

In this mode, blocks of plaintext that are less than 64 bits long can be encrypted. Normally, special processing has to be used to handle files whose size is not a perfect multiple of 8 bytes, but this mode removes that necessity (Private Encryptor handles this case by adding several dummy bytes to the end of a file before encrypting it). The plaintext itself is not actually passed through the DES algorithm, but merely XORed with an output block from it, in the following manner: A 64-bit block called the Shift Register is used as the input plaintext to DES. This is initially set to some arbitrary value, and encrypted with the DES algorithm. The ciphertext is then passed through an extra component called the M-box, which simply selects the left-most M bits of the ciphertext, where M is the number of bits in the block we wish to encrypt. This value is XORed with the real plaintext, and the output of that is the final ciphertext. Finally, the ciphertext is fed back into the Shift Register, and used as the plaintext seed for the next block to be encrypted. As with CBC mode, an error in one block affects all subsequent blocks during data transmission. This mode of operation is similar to CBC and is very secure, but it is slower than ECB due to the added complexity.

This mode can be illustrated as follows:

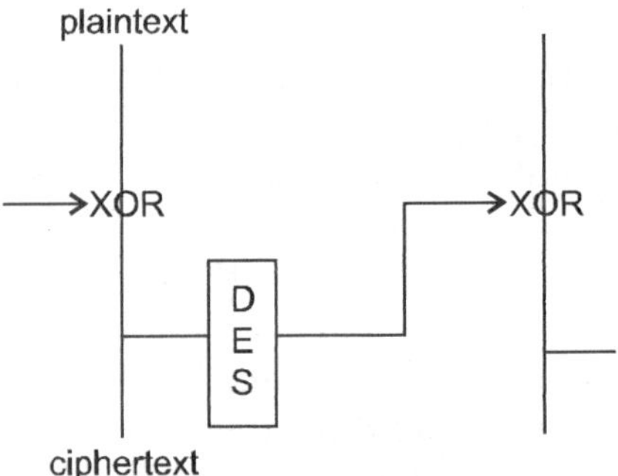

Figure 3.13

A bit-flipping attack will garble subsequent blocks, and so if one takes care that messages have checksums, straddle more than one block, and so on, that is prevented despite the fact that the plaintext is only subjected to an XOR at the time of being enciphered. If no precautions are taken, however, since the last block of the message has no block following it, a bit-flipping attack may be performed against that block.

Since the plaintext modifies what is used to XOR later parts, there is no problem of a generator falling into a short loop.

This mode limits the propagation of transmission errors to the same extent as CBC mode. Once again, this can be illustrated using an alphabetic cipher as an example. To simplify matters, the same block cipher key and the same plaintext are used as in the previous example, and this will show that these two modes are very closely related.

```
Plain:              QXD AYE XAQ ZWA GHI
Previous cipher:    === === === === === Block cipher step
                    ZQI MNX VII UIU LKE
                    BIL LNE EDS MON EYX
                    --- --- --- --- ---  Vigenere step
Cipher:         QXD AYE XAQ ZWA GHI FIS
```

Now, if we change the message at the beginning, everything changes all the way through, because information indeed keeps getting propagated:

```
Plain:              QXD LYD VWC UKA DAD
Previous cipher:    === === === === === Block cipher step
                    ZQI ROY QEI RMQ LVI
                    MIK ENE EDS MON EYX
                    --- --- --- --- --- Vigenere step
Cipher:         QXD LYD VWC UHA DAD PIF
```

But if, instead, it is the original message that is sent, and a transmission error takes place, so that instead of recieving QXD AYE XAQ ZWA GHI PTB the reciever gets QXD AYE XCQ ZWA GHI PTB then only two blocks are destroyed. Since each ciphertext block was a function of the plaintext block and the previous ciphertext block, each plaintext block is a function of the ciphertext block and the previous ciphertext block. As long as those two ciphertext blocks are right, the rest of the message is irrelevant.

```
Previous cipher:                QXD AYE XCQ ZWA GHI
Enciphered Previous cipher: === === === === === Block cipher step
                            ZQI MNM URP UIU LKE (1)
                        QXD AYE XCQ ZWA GHI PIS (2)
                            --- --- --- --- --- Inverse Vigenere ((2)-(1))
Cipher:                     BIL LFE QFL MON EYX
```

In this decipherment example, the first plaintext block only has an error which matches that of the plaintext block, but the second block is totally garbled, because the erroneous ciphertext block went through the block cipher before being applied to the plaintext.

This mode has variants that involve performing DES encryptions more often, such as once for each bit or byte. Some problems have been claimed with these variants, and they require more computation without increasing security.

One other mode among those originally suggested for use with DES was Output Feedback Mode (OFB): this mode encrypted an initial value with DES, and then the result of the encryption was encrypted again repeatedly. The resulting values were used as a keystream to XOR with messages.

This mode was not often used, because of concerns that one might accidentally choose a starting value that led to a short cycle.

This could be avoided with counter mode. This mode was not included among the modes originally recommended for use with DES, but it is included among the basic modes of operation recommended for use with the new AES standard.

Here, a starting value is encrypted in DES to supply the first block of keystream bits, and then the starting value is incremented, and the next block of keystream bits is the encrypted form of it, and so on. This was considered dangerous, because one might accidentally choose a starting value that created a sequence that overlapped with one previously used; starting values would only need to be near each other, not identical, and keeping track of every starting value previously used with a key would excessively complicate the definition of the mode.

To my way of thinking, one could combine both approaches, feeding back the output and XORing the value of a counter to it, thus making it difficult for a short cycle to happen, and making identical sequences much more unlikely. But for some reason this idea has not caught on.

The paper "Guaranteeing the diversity of number generators" by Adi Shamir and Boaz Tsaban discusses a similar mode, but with a second encryption step applied to the XOR of the counter and the first encryption output. For that type of generator, they provide a proof that even if the block ciphers used are bad, it will not make them worse. The example they give of a pathological block cipher for the mode given above, however, is one that is non-bijective; and block ciphers can be easily proved to be bijective, even if it is much more difficult to prove they are secure.

3.5.2 Variations of DES

DES, being the best known of a whole class of ciphers, has inspired many suggestions for variations of it.The initial permutation and inverse initial permutation, and perhaps also permuted choice 1, could be removed, to obtain a cipher of equivalent intrinsic strength, but simpler to perform on a computer.

The sixteen subkeys could be supplied directly as a key, instead of being derived from a short 56-bit key. However, a result reported in Bruce Schneier's book Applied Cryptography shows that the strength of that is only a slight improvement on that of regular DES, essentially equivalent to using a 65-bit key.

If the eight S-boxes are moved, from their regular positions so that the order in which they are applied to the successive six-bit groups of their input is 2, 4, 6, 7, 3, 1, 5, and 8, without altering the permutation P, DES remains highly resistant to differential cryptanalysis, but becomes resistant to linear cryptanalysis as well. (Any re-ordering of the S-boxes in which S-boxes 1, 7, and 4 are consecutive and in that order can make DES very weak against differential cryptanalysis, as noted in Biham and Shamir's original paper on differential cryptanalysis.)

3.5.2.1 Improving the Security of DES

You can improve the security of DES by performing multiple encryptions, known as superencryption. The two most common ways of doing this are with double encryption (Double DES) and with triple encryption (Triple DES).While double DES appears to add significant security, research has found some points of attack, and therefore experts recommend Triple DES for applications where single DES is not adequate.

Double DES

In Double DES, each 64-bit block of data is encrypted twice with the DES algorithm, first with one key, then with another, as follows:

```
Encrypt with (key 1).
Encrypt with (key 2).
Plaintext    (key 1)  (key2)  ciphertext
```

Double DES is not significantly more secure than single DES. In 1981, Ralph Merkle and Martin Hellman published an article in which they outlined a so-called "meet-in-the-middle attack."

The meet-in-the-middle attack is a known plaintext attack which requires that an attacker have both a known piece of plaintext and a block of that same text that has been encrypted. (These pieces are surprisingly easily to get.) The attack requires storing 256 intermediate results when trying to crack a message that has been encrypted with DES (a total of 259 bytes), but it reduces the number of different keys you need to check from 2112 to 257. "This is still considerably more memory storage than one could comfortably comprehend, but it's enough to convince the most paranoid of cryptographers that double encryption is not worth anything," writes Bruce Schneier in his landmark volume, Applied Cryptography.

In other words, because a message encrypted with DES can be forcibly decrypted by an attacker performing an exhaustive key search today, an attacker might also be able to forcibly decrypt a message encrypted with Double DES using a meet-in-the-middle attack at some point in the future.

Triple DES

Triple DES is a block cipher formed from the Data Encryption Standard (DES) cipher by using it three times.For some time it has been common practice to protect and tansport a key for DES encryption with triple-DES. This means that the plaintext is, in effect, encrypted three times. There are, of course. a variety of ways of doing this; we will explore these ways below.

From the time DES was introduced, the 56-bit length of its key was a subject of concern and controversy.A common way to increase the security of DES is to apply DES to a block three times. The reason that it isn't simply applied twice is because of the existence of an attack which reduces the security of double-DES almost to the level of single-DES. This attack, called the meet-in-the-middle attack, requires a very large quantity of memory. The basic principle of this attack is that if one has two or more blocks of ciphertext with known plaintext, instead of having to do a brute-force search over all possible pairs of DES keys, one can simply do a brute-force search over all possible values of the first key, as applied to the plaintext, and over all possible values of the second key, as used to decrypt the ciphertext, and then find which result of the first search is also a result of the second search.

While a random-access memory large enough to hold 2^{58} data items, each at least 128 bits in length, seems preposterous, it is not beyond imagination to put that much information on a medium such as magnetic tape; and, if the values were sorted, they would be useful in that form. Techniques for efficiently sorting files too large to read in to a random-access storage device were intensively studied in the early years of computing, and so they are available.

A number of modes of triple-encryption have been proposed:

- DES-EEE3: Three DES encryptions with three different keys.
- DES-EDE3: Three DES operations in the sequence encrypt-decrypt-encrypt with three different keys.
- DES-EEE2 and DES-EDE2: Same the previrous formats except that the first and third operations use the same key.

Attacks on two-key triple-DES have been proposed by Merkle and Hellman and Van Oorschot and Wiener [VW91], but the data requirements of these attacks make them impractical.

The use of double and triple encryption does not always provide the additional security that might be expected. Preneel provides the following comparisons in the security of various versions of multiple-DES and it can be seen that the most secure form of multiple encryption is triple-DES with three distinct keys.

Usually, Triple-DES is done by encrypting with one key, decrypting with another, and then encrypting again with either the first key or a third one. This way, if all three phases are done with the same key, interoperability with regular single DES is possible. This is called EDE mode, for Encrypt-Decrypt-Encrypt.

If one is going to use DES three times, one can be more elaborate. If one is going to use Triple-DES, one can also increase the effective block size of DES through something called an Outerbridge construction. The Figure 3.13 illustrates a generalization of that construction to quadruple, rather than merely double, the block size, and to increase the effective key size as well. The 64-bit blocks are considered to be divided into four 16-bit parts, which are distributed between DES operations.

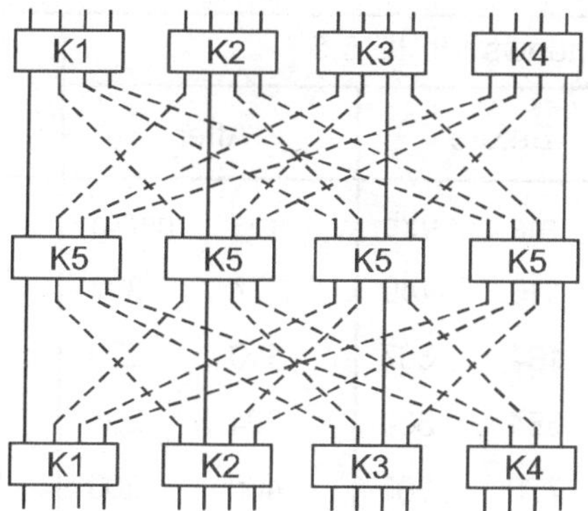

Figure 3.14 The 64-bit blocks

(1) Algorithm

When it was found that a 56-bit key of DES is not enough to guard against brute force attacks, TDES was chosen as a simple way to enlarge the key space without a need to switch to a new algorithm. The use of three steps is essential to prevent meet-in-the-middle attacks that are effective against double DES encryption. Note that DES is not a group; if it were one, the TDES construction would be equivalent to a single DES operation and no more secure. TDES can be operated with variations in two parameters:

- number of keys used and
- order of operations.

(2) Algorithm Speed

The first Javascript DES implemention worked fine for small data sets, but slowed down incredibly on larger blocks. By making a few changes, the speed has been increased dramatically. These changes were: storing the message and result as strings rather than arrays (which take a comparitively long time to look things up); creating the result string in blocks rather than one character at a time (periodically adding 512 characters to a 32000 character string is much faster than adding one character at a time); and bringing all global variables inside the functions (which also meant undoing the previous permute function). Below is a table showing the speed increase on a Pentium 200 with Windows 98 and Internet Explorer 5. I also tested it in the Galleon browser under Redhat Linux 7.2 on the same machine (sadly it was quite a bit slower). This times the single DES algorithm in ECB mode, in milliseconds.

(3) Order of operations

The simplest variant of TDES operates as follows: DES(k3;DES(k2;DES(k1;M))), where M is the message block to be encrypted and k1, k2, and k3 are DES keys. This variant is commonly known as EEE because all three DES operations are encryptions. In order to simplify interoperability between DES and TDES the middle step is usually replaced with decryption (EDE mode): DES(k3;DES-1(k2;DES(k1;M))) and so a single DES encryption with key k can be represented as TDES-EDE with k1 = k2 = k3 = k. The choice of decryption for the middle step does not affect the security of the algorithm.

	Windows 98, IE 5.5				Redhat 7.2 Galleon	
	Before		After			
Bytes	ms	ms/kb	ms	ms/kb	ms	ms/kb
256	110	440	77	307	176	704
512	184	367	110	220	296	591
1024	384	384	204	204	598	598
2048	770	385	400	200	1,138	569
4096	1,647	412	827	207	2,195	549
8192	3,770	472	1,590	199	4,352	544
16384	10,254	641	3,260	204	8,596	638
32768	39,677	1,240	6,517	204	17,490	547

Figure 3.15

(4) Number of keys

Since TDES has three cipher operations it allows for the use of one, two, or three keys. The designation of the number of keys use is appended to the end of the order-of-operation notation (e.g. DES-EEE1, DES-EEE2, DES-EEE3). Using one key is the weakest implementation, especially if using an encrypt-decrypt-encrypt order of operation (DES-EDE1) This would effectively result in only one order of encryption since the first two operatons are cancelled out, being encrypted and decrypted with the same key. Using three distinct keys is the most secure operation and would be designated as DES-EEE3 or DES-EDE3.

(5) Security

In general TDES with three different keys (3-key TDES) has a key length of 168 bits: three 56-bit DES keys (with parity bits 3-key TDES has the total storage length of 192 bits), but due to the meet-in-the-middle attack the effective security it provides is only 112 bits. A variant, called two-key TDES (2-key TDES), uses k1 = k3, thus reducing the key size to 112 bits and the storage length to 128 bits. However, this mode is susceptible to certain chosen-plaintext or known-plaintext attacks and thus it is designated by NIST to have only 80 bits of security.

The best attack known on 3-key TDES requires around 232 known plaintexts, 2113 steps, 290 single DES encryptions, and 288 memory (the paper presents other tradeoffs between time and memory). This is not currently practical and NIST considers 3-key TDES to be appropriate through 2030.If the attacker seeks to discover any one of many cryptographic keys, there is a memory-efficient attack which will discover one of 228 keys, given a handful of chosen plaintexts per key and around 284 encryption operations.

(6) Usage

Electronic payments industry uses TDES and continues to develop and promulgate standards based upon it (e.g. EMV).DES and therefore TDES suffer from slow performance in software; and are better suited to hardware implementations.

(7) Functions Provided

Below are descriptions of each of the functions used in this DES implementation. The first few are the core DES functions. The second set are not required to run DES but were of great help in debugging and creating the pc2bytes and spfunction arrays. The source code of these extra functions is provided below.

des - does DES, takes it's input as strings and calls des_crypt

tripledes - does DES three times

des_crypt - performs DES, but takes it's input as arrays of integers

des_cipher - does the encrypting or decrypting by applying E, the S functions and P

des_createKeys - given the left and right 32 bits of the key, creates an array of 16 subkeys

printHex - prints an integer in hexidecimal

printBinary - prints a number in binary

stringToIntegers - converts a string into an array of 32 bit integers

integerToStrings - converts an array of 32 bit integers into a string

moveBits - this is used to produce an array such as pc2bytes which can move bits around

convertSfunction - converts an S function as found in other DES explanations into the right order

createSfunction - produces the spfunction array given the P bit movements and an S selection function

wherethingsgo - used throughout this page to show what a piece of code does to the bits

timeTrial - used to time how long encryption took for different sized input

3.5.2.2 DESX

RSA Data Security has recommended DESX, which is simply DES strengthened by performing an XOR against additional key bits at the beginning and at the end of encipherment.

One way in which DES might be strengthened by a simple modification that has occurred to me is this: retain the initial and inverse initial permutations, but perform them after rounds 4 and 12 of the cipher respectively. This way, they are contributing something to its strength. Perhaps it would even be possible to use a 112-bit key, as follows: for the first 56 bits, generate the regular key schedule, and use it during rounds 1 through 4 and 13 through 16. For the last 56 bits, use the decrypting key schedule from those bits during rounds 5 through 12. Unlike DESX, though, this kind of modification is only applicable if one is performing DES encryption in software, not when using existing DES hardware.

Another possible way of using a 112-bit key would be by enhancing DES with an idea I use in QUADIBLOC: use 32 subkeys, by applying the f-function twice, first to the right half of the block, then to the first f-function output, before XORing the result to the right half. This propagates changes in the block more quickly. Also, it would seem to me that one could obtain a very strong cipher by alternating pairs of rounds of DES with rounds of SAFER, a block cipher based on very different principles.

A more economical way to realize increased strength would be, perhaps, to take the variation suggested above, with IP after round 4, and IIP after round 12, and apply, before and after each of these permutations a user-supplied substitution, part of the key, acting on the eight bytes of the block. The inverse of this substitution would be used on deciphering. Since differential cryptanalysis depends on substitutions being known, this would seem to improve the strength of the cipher against that kind of attack; and, since a random substitution on the possible byte values from 0 to 255 takes quite a bit more than 56 bits to describe it, key size is also increased. Applying the substitution at the beginning and end of the block cipher would probably be advisable as well; this would increase the amount of this extra key that is actually used, and it would protect all sixteen, rather than just the middle eight, rounds of the block cipher from outside scrutiny.

DES-X (or DESX) is a variant on the DES (Data Encryption Standard) block cipher intended to increase the complexity of a brute force attack using a technique called key whitening. The original DES algorithm was specified in 1976 with a 56-bit key size: 256 possibilities for the key. There was criticism that an exhaustive search might be within the capabilities of large governments, particularly the United States' National Security Agency (NSA). One scheme to increase the key size of DES without substantially altering the algorithm was DES-X, proposed by Ron Rivest in May 1984.

DES-X also increases the strength of DES against differential cryptanalysis and linear cryptanalysis, although the improvement is much smaller than in the case of brute force attacks. It is estimated that differential cryptanalysis would require 261 chosen plaintexts (vs. 247 for DES), while linear cryptanalysis would require 260 known plaintexts (vs. 243 for DES.) Note that with 264 plaintexts (known or chosen being the same in this case), DES (or indeed any other block cipher with a 64 bit block size) is totally broken via the elementary codebook attack.

3.5.3 Strength of DES

Cryptography has long been in use by governments, particularly in the realms of military and diplomatic communication. It is hard to imagine military communication without cryptography; cryptanalysis, or secretly deciphering the opponent's messages, is perhaps of even greater value.

During the early 1970s, it became apparent that the commercial sector also has a legitimate need for cryptography. Corporate secrets must be transmitted between distant sites, without the possibility of eavesdropping by industrial spies. Personal data on databases need to be protected against espionage and alteration.

A familiar example is the communication between an automatic teller machine (ATM) and a central computer.The user inserts a magnetic card and types a few numbers. The ATM sends messages to the computer. The computer checks the account balance and returns a message authorizing the ATM to dispense funds. Obviously, if these messages are unprotected, a thief can tap the wires, find the message authorizing the dispensing of funds, and send multiple copies of that message to the ATM, thereby "cleaning out" the supply of cash from the ATM.

In the early 1970s, a banking customer asked IBM to develop a system for encrypting ATM data. With this problem as a starting point, a team was formed from people at two IBM sites (Kingston and Yorktown Heights, New York). This team, along with several consultants, developed a cryptographic algorithm. This algorithm was then submitted to the National Bureau of Standards (NBS, which later became the National Institute of Standards and Technology, or NIST) and was adopted in 1977 as a national standard: the Data Encryption Standard, or DES. The National Security Agency (NSA) also provided technical advice to IBM.

The entire algorithm was published in the Federal Register [2], but the design considerations were not published at that time. The design took advantage of knowledge of certain cryptanalytic techniques, most prominently the technique of "differential cryptanalysis," which were not known in the published literature. After discussions with NSA, it was decided that disclosure of the design considerations would reveal the technique of differential cryptanalysis, a powerful technique that can be used against many ciphers. This in turn would weaken the competitive advantage the United States enjoyed over other countries in the field of cryptography. disclosure was due to some "trap door" or hidden weakness in the DES.In fact, the reason for not publishing the criteria lay in the hidden strengths of the algorithm, not hidden weaknesses.

Ever since DES was first proposed as a national standard, some people have been suspicious of the algorithm. DES was based on a proprietary encryption algorithm developed by IBM called Lucifer, which IBM had submitted to the National Bureau of Standards (NBS)[16] for consideration as a national cryptographic standard. But whereas Lucifer had a key that was 112 bits long, the DES key was shortened to 56 bits at the request of the National Security Agency. The NSA also requested that certain changes be made in the algorithm's S-boxes. Many people suspected that NSA had intentionally weakened the Lucifer algorithm, so the final standard adopted by NBS would not pose a threat to the NSA's ongoing intelligence collection activities. But nobody had any proof.

Today the DES is more than 20 years old, and the algorithm is definitely showing its age. Recently Michael Weiner, a researcher at Bell Northern Research, published a paper detailing how to build a machine capable of decrypting messages encrypted with the DES by conducting an exhaustive key search. Such a machine could be built for a few million dollars, and could break any DES-encrypted message in about a day. We can reasonably assume that such machines have been built by both governments and private industry.

In June 1994, IBM published a paper describing the design criteria of the DES. The paper claims that the choices of the DES key size, S-boxes, and number of rounds were a direct result of the conflicting goals of making the DES simple enough to fit onto a single chip with 1972 chip-making technology, and the desire to make it resistant to differential cryptanalysis.

These two papers, coupled with many previously published analyses, appear to have finally settled a long-running controversy as to whether or not NSA had intentionally built in weaknesses to the DES. The NSA didn't build a back door into DES that would have allowed it to forcibly decrypt any DES-encrypted transmission: it didn't need to. Messages encrypted with DES can be forcibly decrypted simply by trying every possible key, given the appropriate hardware.

3.5.4 Has DES been Broken?

No easy attack on DES has been discovered, despite the efforts of many researchers over many years. The obvious method of attack is brute-force exhaustive search of the key space; this takes 255 steps on average. Early on it was suggested that a rich and powerful enemy could build a special-purpose computer capable of breaking DES by exhaustive search in a reasonable amount of time. Later, Hellman [Hel80] showed a time-memory trade-off that allows improvement over exhaustive search if memory space is plentiful, after an exhaustive precomputation. These ideas fostered doubts about the security of DES. There were also accusations that the NSA had intentionally weakened DES. Despite these suspicions, no feasible way to break DES faster than exhaustive search was discovered. The cost of a specialized computer to perform exhaustive search (requiring 3.5 hours on average) has been estimated by Wiener at one million dollars.

The first attack on DES that is better than exhaustive search in terms of computational requirements was announced by Biham and Shamir using a new technique known as differential cryptanalysis. This attack requires the encryption of 247 chosen plaintexts, that is, the plaintexts are chosen by the attacker. Although it is a theoretical breakthrough, this attack is not practical because of both the large data requirements and the difficulty of mounting a chosen plaintext attack. Biham and Shamir have stated that they consider DES secure.

More recently Matsui has developed another attack, known as linear cryptanalysis. A DES key can be recovered by the analysis of 243 known plaintexts and the first experimental cryptanalysis of DES was successfully achieved in an attack requiring 50 days on 12 HP 9735 workstations. Clearly however, this attack is still impractical.

The consensus is that DES, when used properly, is still secure and that triple encryption DES is far more secure than DES. Both single and triple encryption DES are used extensively in a wide variety of cryptographic systems.

3.5.5 How Does One Use DES Securely?

When using DES, there are several practical considerations that can affect the security of the encrypted data. One should change DES keys frequently, in order to prevent attacks that require sustained data analysis. In a communications context, one must also find a secure way of communicating the DES key to both sender and receiver. Use of RSA or some other public-key technique for key management solves both these issues: a different DES key is generated for each session, and secure key management is provided by encrypting the DES key with the receiver's RSA public key. RSA, in this circumstance, can be regarded as a tool for improving the security of DES (or any other secret-key cipher).

If one wishes to use DES to encrypt files stored on a hard disk, it is not feasible to frequently change the DES keys, as this would entail decrypting and then re-encrypting all files upon each key change. Instead, one should have a master DES key which encrypts the list of DES keys used to encrypt the files; one can then change the master key frequently without much effort. Alternatively the user may wish to use a dedicated file/disk encryption program like RSA Secure.

Aside from the issues mentioned above, DES can be used for encryption in several officially-defined modes, and these modes have a variety of properties. ECB (electronic codebook) mode simply encrypts each 64-bit block of plaintext one after another under the same 56-bit DES key. In CBC (cipher block chaining) mode, each 64-bit plaintext block is XORed with the previous ciphertext block before being encrypted with the DES key. Thus the encryption of each block depends on previous blocks and the same 64-bit plaintext block can encrypt to different ciphertext depending on its context in the overall message. CBC mode helps protect against certain attacks, but not against exhaustive search or differential cryptanalysis. CFB (cipher feedback) mode allows one to use DES with block lengths less than 64 bits. Detailed descriptions of the various DES modes can be found in.

In practice, CBC is the most widely used mode of DES, and it is specified in several standards. For additional security, one could use triple encryption with CBC .

3.6 DIFFERENTIAL CRYPTANALYSIS

Differential cryptanalysis is a general form of cryptanalysis applicable primarily to block ciphers, but also to stream ciphers and cryptographic hash functions. In the broadest sense, it is the study of how differences in an input can affect the resultant difference at the output. In the case of a block cipher, it refers to a set of techniques for tracing differences through the network of transformations, discovering where the cipher exhibits non-random behaviour, and exploiting such properties to recover the secret key.The discovery of differential cryptanalysis is generally attributed to Eli Biham and Adi Shamir in the late 1980s, who published a number of attacks against various block ciphers and hash functions, including a theoretical weakness in the Data Encryption Standard (DES).

However, if one is fortunate enough to have a large quantity of corresponding plaintext and ciphertext blocks for a particular unknown key, a technique called differential cryptanalysis, developed by Eli Biham and Adi Shamir, is available to obtain clues about some bits of the key, thereby shortening an exhaustive search.

After two rounds of DES, knowing both the input and output, it is trivial to determine the two subkeys used, since the outputs of both f-functions are known. For each S-box, there are four possible inputs to produce the known output. Since each subkey is 48 bits long, but the key is only 56 bits long, finding which of the four possibilities is true for each group of six bits in the subkeys is a bit like solving a crossword puzzle.

Once the number of rounds increases to four, the problem becomes much harder. However, it is still true that the output depends on the input and the key. For a limited number of rounds, it is inevitable, without the need for any flaws in the S-boxes, that there will be some cases where a bit or a combination of bits in the output will have some correlation with a simple combination of some input bits and some key bits. Ideally, that correlation should be absolute with respect to the key bits, since there is only one key to solve for, but it can be probabilistic with respect to the input and output bits, since there need to be many pairs to test.

As the number of rounds increases, though, the simple correlations disappear. Differential cryptanalysis represents an approach to finding more subtle correlations.

Instead of saying "if this bit is 1 in the input, then that bit will be 0 (or 1) in the output", we say "changing this bit in the input changes (or does not change) that bit in the output".

In fact, however, a complete pattern of which bits change and do not change in the input and in the output is the subject of differential cryptanalysis. The basic principle of differential cryptanalysis, in its classic form, is this: the cipher being attacked has a characteristic if there exists a constant X such that given many pairs of plaintexts A, B, such that `B = A xor X`, if a certain statement is true about the key, `E(B,k) = E(A,k) xor Y` for some constant Y will be true with a probability somewhat above that given by random chance.

Differential cryptanalysis is a type of attack that can be mounted on iterative block ciphers. These techniques were first introduced by Murphy in an attack on FEAL-4, but they were later improved and perfected by Biham and Shamir who used them to attack DES. Differential cryptanalysis is basically a chosen plaintext attack (see 63) and relies on an analysis of the evolution of the differences between two related plaintexts as they are encrypted under the same key. By careful analysis of the available data, probabilities can be assigned to each of the possible keys and eventually the most probable key is identified as the correct one.

Differential cryptanalysis has been used against a great many ciphers with varying degrees of success. In attacks against DES, its effectiveness is limited by what was very careful design of the S-boxes during the design of DES in the mid-1970s. Studies on protecting ciphers against differential cryptanalysis have been conducted by Nyberg and Knudsen as well as Lai, Massey and Murphy. Differential cryptanalysis has also been useful in attacking other cryptographic algorithms such as hash functions.

3.6.1 Weak Key for a Block Cipher

Weak keys are secret keys with a certain value for which the block cipher in will exhibit certain regularities in encryption or, in other cases, a poor level of encryption. For instance, with DES there are four keys for which encryption is exactly the same as decryption. This means that if one were to encrypt twice with one of these weak keys, then the original plaintext would be recovered. For IDEA there is a class of keys for which cryptanalysis is greatly facilitated and the key can be recovered. However, in both these cases, the number of weak keys is such a small fraction of all possible keys that the chance of picking one at random is exceptionally slight. In such cases, they pose no significant threat to the security of the block cipher when used for encryption.

Of course for other block ciphers, there might well be a large set of weak keys (perhaps even with the weakness exhibiting itself in a different way) for which the chance of picking a weak key is too large for comfort. In such a case, the presence of weak keys would have an obvious impact on the security of the block cipher.

Algebraic attacks are a class of techniques which rely for their success on some block cipher exhibiting a high degree of mathematical structure.

For instance, it is conceivable that a block cipher might exhibit what is termed a group structure. If this were the case, then encrypting a plaintext under one key and then encrypting the result under another key would always be equivalent to single encryption under some other single key. If so, then the block cipher would be considerably weaker, and the use of multiple encryption would offer no additional security over single encryption. For most block ciphers, the of whether they form a group is still open. For DES, however, it is known that the cipher is not a group.

There are a variety of other concerns with regards to algebraic attacks.

3.6.2 Attack Mechanics

Differential cryptanalysis is usually a chosen plaintext attack, meaning that the attacker must be able to obtain encrypted ciphertexts for some set of plaintexts of his choosing. The scheme can successfully cryptanalyze DES with an effort on the order 247 chosen plaintexts. There are, however, extensions that would allow a known plaintext or even a ciphertext-only attack. The basic method uses pairs of plaintext related by a constant difference; difference can be defined in several ways, but the eXclusive OR (XOR) operation is usual. The attacker then computes the differences of the corresponding ciphertexts, hoping to detect statistical patterns in their distribution. The resulting pair of differences is called a differential. Their statistical properties depend upon the nature of the S-boxes used for encryption, so the attacker analyses differentials (?X,?Y), where eq1.bmp (and xor.bmp denotes exclusive or) for each such S-box S. In the basic attack, one particular ciphertext difference is expected to be especially frequent; in this way, the cipher can be distinguished from random. More sophisticated variations allow the key to be recovered faster than exhaustive search.

In the most basic form of key recovery through differential cryptanalysis, an attacker requests the ciphertexts for a large number of plaintext pairs, then assumes that the differential holds for at least r-1 rounds, where r is the total number of rounds. The attacker then deduces which round keys (for the final round) are possible assuming the difference between the blocks before the final round is fixed. When round keys are short, this can be achieved by simply exhaustively decrypting the ciphertext pairs one round with each possible round key. When one round key has been deemed a potential round key considerably more often than any other key, it is assumed to be the correct round key.

For any particular cipher, the input difference must be carefully selected if the attack is to be successful. An analysis of the algorithm's internals is undertaken; the standard method is to trace a path of highly probable differences through the various stages of encryption, termed a differential characteristic.

Since differential cryptanalysis became public knowledge, it has become a basic concern of cipher designers. New designs are expected to be accompanied by evidence that the algorithm is resistant to this attack, and many, including the Advanced Encryption Standard, have been proven secure against the attack.

3.7 LINEAR CRYPTANALYSIS

Linear cryptanalysis, invented by Mitsuru Matsui, is a different, but related technique. Instead of looking for isolated points at which a block cipher behaves like something simpler, it involves trying to create a simpler approximation to the block cipher as a whole.

Linear cryptanalysis was first devised by Matsui and Yamagishi in an attack on FEAL. It was extended by Matsui to attack DES. Linear cryptanalysis is a known plaintext attack and uses a linear approximation to describe the behavior of the block cipher. Given sufficient pairs of plaintext and corresponding ciphertext, bits of information about the key can be obtained and increased amounts of data will usually give a higher probability of success.

Linear cryptanalysis is a general form of cryptanalysis based on finding affine approximations to the action of a cipher. Attacks have been developed for block ciphers and stream ciphers. Linear cryptanalysis is one of the two most widely used attacks on block ciphers; the other being differential cryptanalysis.There are two parts to linear cryptanalysis. The first is to construct linear equations relating plaintext, ciphertext and key bits that have a high bias; that is, whose probabilities of holding (over the space of all possible values of their variables) are as close as possible to 0 or 1. The second is to use these linear equations in conjunction with known plaintext-ciphertext pairs to derive key bits.

There have been a variety of enhancements and improvements to the basic attack. Langford and Hellman introduced an attack called differential-linear cryptanalysis which combines elements of differential cryptanalysis with those of linear cryptanalysis. Also, Kaliski and Robshaw showed that a linear cryptanalytic attack using multiple approximations might allow for a reduction in the amount of data required for a successful attack.

For a great many plaintext-ciphertext pairs, the key that would produce that pair from the simplified cipher is found, and key bits which tend to be favored are likely to have the value of the corresponding bit of the key for the real cipher. The principle is a bit like the summation of many one-dimensional scans to produce a two-dimensional slice through an object in computer-assisted tomography.

3.7.1 Constructing Linear Equations

For the purposes of linear cryptanalysis, a linear equation expresses the equality of two expressions which consist of binary variables combined with the exclusive-or (XOR) operation. For example, the following equation, from a hypothetical cipher, states the XOR sum of the first and third plaintext bits (as in a block cipher's block) and the first ciphertext bit is equal to the second bit of the key:

$$P_1 \oplus P_3 \oplus C_1 = K_2$$

In an ideal cipher, any linear equation relating plaintext, ciphertext and key bits would hold with probability 1/2. Since the equations dealt with in linear cryptanalysis will vary in probability, they are more accurately referred to as linear approximations.

The procedure for constructing approximations is different for each cipher. In the most basic type of block cipher, a substitution-permutation network, analysis is concentrated primarily on the S-boxes, the only nonlinear part of the cipher (i.e. the operation of an S-box cannot be encoded in a linear equation). For small enough S-boxes, it is possible to enumerate every possible linear equation relating the S-box's input and output bits, calculate their biases and choose the best ones. Linear approximations for S-boxes then must be combined with the cipher's other actions, such as permutation and key mixing, to arrive at linear approximations for the entire cipher. The piling-up lemma is a useful tool for this combination step. There are also techniques for iteratively improving linear approximations.

3.7.2 Deriving key bits

Having obtained a linear approximation of the form:

$$P_{i1} \oplus P_{i2} \oplus \ldots \oplus C_{j1} \oplus C_{j2} \oplus \ldots = K_{k1} \oplus K_{k2} \oplus \ldots$$

We can then apply a straightforward algorithm (Matsui's Algorithm 2), using known plaintext-ciphertext pairs, to guess at the values of the key bits involved in the approximation.

For each set of values of the key bits on the right-hand side (referred to as a partial key), count how many times the approximation holds true over all the known plaintext-ciphertext pairs; call this count T. The partial key whose T has the greatest absolute difference from half the number of plaintext-ciphertext pairs is designated as the most likely set of values for those key bits. This is because it is assumed that the correct partial key will cause the approximation to hold with a high bias. It is important to note that the magnitude of the bias is significant here, as opposed to the magnitude of the probability itself.

This procedure can be repeated with other linear approximations, obtaining guesses at values of key bits, until the number of unknown key bits is low enough that they can be attacked with brute force.

3.8 ADVANCED ENCRYPTION STANDARD (AES) : 128-BIT ERA

Improvements in the speed and power of microprocessor chips have meant that the Data Encryption Standard with its 56-bit key is subject to brute-force attacks that can be carried out by organizations of moderate size.

Although some branches of the Government of the United States, including its Chief Executive, have been pursuing policies such as export restrictions and the "Clipper chip" initiative, based on perceived dangers of the spread of strong encryption, the National Institute of Standards and Technology, another branch of the U. S. Government, has sought public submissions of an improved block cipher which would serve the specific purpose of protecting the unclassified communications of the U. S. Government, but which would also, no doubt, serve the public sector as well.

The block cipher that is accepted will be called the AES, for Advanced Encryption Standard. Since this was written, on October 2, 2000, the cipher that will serve as the Advanced Encryption Standard has been announced, and that cipher is Rijndael, designed by Vincent Rijmen and Joan Daemen.

Because block cipher modes give block ciphers the flexibility of also serving in applications which can make use of stream ciphers, a block cipher was sought. A block length of 128 bits, making dictionary attacks more difficult, is specified, and key lengths of 128, 192, and 256 bits are to be allowed for in the designs submitted.

A larger block length also increases the speed of encipherment, by allowing more text to be enciphered at once. Where a 56-bit key does not provide enough security at present, it is possible to use Triple-DES (enciphering in DES three times over, using either two or three different keys - and with the middle encipherment done in deciphering mode for compatibility reasons) and therefore one of the goals to be met by any submitted cipher is that it be faster than Triple DES.

An idea that might occur upon first hearing about the AES effort: could a simple construction like the following, operating at speeds only slightly slower than those of single DES, provide adequate strength:

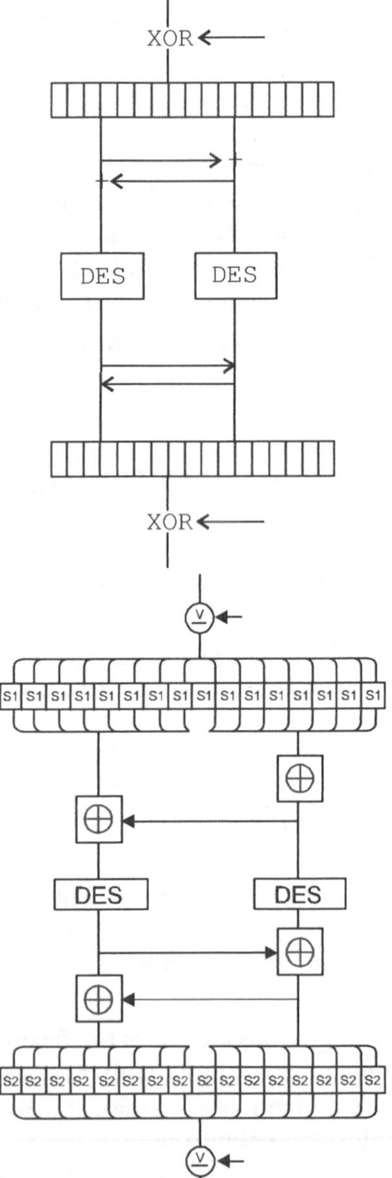

or, in graphical form

Figure 3.16 Simple Graphical Representation of DES

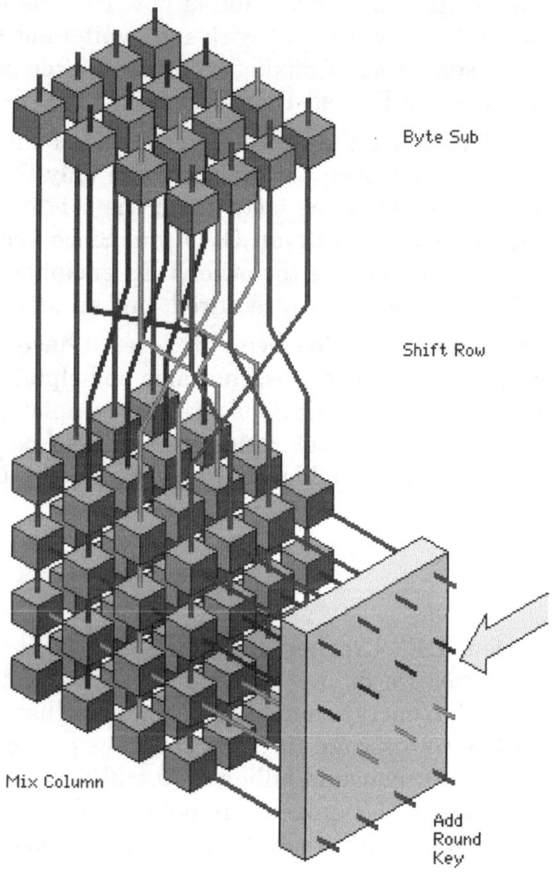

Figure 3.17 Three Dimensional Representation

One might ask. However, while it seems that the series of byte substitutions, followed by a Pseudo-Hadamard Transform, mixes together the two halves of the block well enough, attacks are possible against this type of construction that make it not much stronger than normal DES, at least in theory. If the Pseudo-Hadamard Transform, however, is replaced by something better, such as the mask-driven bit swap used in the cipher ICE, where a mask selects bits to be swapped between a pair of words, and we further enhance it by using a 4 of 8 code to ensure each byte includes both swapped and non-swapped bits, one might have something usable. The additional XOR whitening is applicable, if otherwise all sixteen bytes go through the same byte substitution.

With a better initial mixing step, and a willingness to go to double-DES speeds, though, this approach could lead to something adequate.

As block ciphers like Blowfish demonstrate, it is possible to do better than DES at faster speeds, and DES is designed for hardware implementation, and is unnecessarily slow in software. Thus, something that is designed for fast software encryption, with the required security, will be more optimal if it comes from a fresh design process.

Also, it should be noted that this illustration of how DES could be used as the basis of a 128-bit block cipher is not terribly original with me; whitening has been proposed many times before, and the use of some sort of mixing before and after using DES to increase the block size is part of Terry Ritter's Fenced DES design.

This design is not perfect: since the expression for one of the outputs of a PHT has a factor of two in it, one can, using chosen plaintexts where only the least significant byte of one particular half is varied, uncover some facts about the S-boxes used, for example. This, among other weaknesses, was noted by Bryan G. Olson. Since keeping one block the same still changes the complete output, because the other DES encipherment is different, not 256 chosen plaintexts, but a larger number, are required, but an attack is still possible.

All the AES candidate algorithms have been disclosed. I have written up descriptions of some of them in my own words, with diagrams, that may be helpful to some in understanding the algorithms. In some cases, my descriptions are not complete; for example, in several cases I omit a description of the key schedule. It may also be noted that links to the descriptions of the algorithms are available at the Block Cipher Lounge as well as at the official AES site.

3.9 DES V/S AES KEYS

In the late 1990s, specialized "DES Cracker" machines were built that could recover a DES key after a few hours. In other words, by trying possible key values, the hardware could determine which key was used to encrypt a message.Assuming that one could build a machine that could recover a DES key in a second (i.e., try 255 keys per second), then it would take that machine approximately 149 thousand-billion (149 trillion) years to crack a 128-bit AES key. To put that into perspective, the universe is believed to be less than 20 billion years old.This is approximately a 149 trillion years to 1 second proportion.

3.9.1 Security and Cryptanalysis

Although more information has been published on the cryptanalysis of DES than any other block cipher, the most practical attack to date is still a brute force approach. Various minor cryptanalytic properties are known, and three theoretical attacks are possible which, while having a theoretical complexity less than a brute force attack, require an unrealistic amount of known or chosen plaintext to carry out, and are not a concern in practice.

3.9.2 Brute Force Attack

For any cipher, the most basic method of attack is brute force — trying every possible key in turn. The length of the key determines the number of possible keys, and hence the feasibility of this approach. For DES, s were raised about the adequacy of its key size early on, even before it was adopted as a standard, and it was the small key size, rather than theoretical cryptanalysis, which dictated a need for a replacement algorithm. It is known that the NSA encouraged, if not persuaded, IBM to reduce the key size from 128 to 64 bits, and from there to 56 bits; this is often taken as an indication that the NSA thought it would be able to break keys of this length even in the mid-1970s.

The EFF's US$250,000 DES cracking machine contained 1,856 custom chips and could brute force a DES key in a matter of days.In academia, various proposals for a DES-cracking machine were advanced. In 1977, Diffie and Hellman proposed a machine costing an estimated US$20 million which could find a DES key in a single day. By 1993, Wiener had proposed a key-search machine costing US$1 million which would find a key within 7 hours. However, none of these early proposals were ever implemented—or, at least, no implementations were publicly acknowledged. The vulnerability of DES was practically demonstrated in the late 1990s. In 1997, RSA Security sponsored a series of contests, offering a $10,000 prize to the first team that broke a message encrypted with DES for the contest. That contest was won by the DESCHALL Project, led by Rocke Verser, Matt Curtin, and Justin Dolske, using idle cycles of thousands of computers across the Internet. The feasibility of cracking DES quickly was demonstrated in 1998 when a custom DES-cracker was built by the Electronic Frontier Foundation (EFF), a cyberspace civil rights group, at the cost of approximately US$250,000 (see EFF DES cracker). Their motivation was to show that DES was breakable in practice as well as in theory: "There are many people who will not believe a truth until they can see it with their own eyes. Showing them a physical machine that can crack DES in a few days is the only way to convince some people that they really cannot trust their security to DES." The machine brute-forced a key in a little more than 2 days search.

3.9.3 Attacks faster than Brute-force

There are three attacks known that can break the full sixteen rounds of DES with less complexity than a brute-force search: differential cryptanalysis (DC), linear cryptanalysis (LC), and Davies' attack. However, the attacks are theoretical and are unfeasible to mount in practice; these types of attack are sometimes termed certificational weaknesses.

Differential cryptanalysis was rediscovered in the late 1980s by Eli Biham and Adi Shamir; it was known earlier to both IBM and the NSA and kept secret. To break the full 16 rounds, differential cryptanalysis requires 247 chosen plaintexts. DES was designed to be resistant to DC.

Linear cryptanalysis was discovered by Mitsuru Matsui, and needs 243 known plaintexts (Matsui, 1993); the method was implemented, and was the first experimental cryptanalysis of DES to be reported. There is no evidence that DES was tailored to be resistant to this type of attack. A generalisation of LC — multiple linear cryptanalysis — was suggested in 1994 (Kaliski and Robshaw), and was further refined by Biryukov et al (2004); their analysis suggests that multiple linear approximations could be used to reduce the data requirements of the attack by at least a factor of 4 (i.e. 241 instead of 243). A similar reduction in data complexity can be obtained in a chosen-plaintext variant of linear cryptanalysis (Knudsen and Mathiassen, 2000). Junod (2001) performed several experiments to determine the actual time complexity of linear cryptanalysis, and reported that it was somewhat faster than predicted, requiring time equivalent to 239–241 DES evaluations.

Improved Davies' attack: while linear and differential cryptanalysis are general techniques and can be applied to a number of schemes, Davies' attack is a specialised technique for DES, first suggested by Donald Davies in the eighties, and improved by Biham and Biryukov (1997). The most powerful form of the attack requires 250 known plaintexts, has a computational complexity of 250, and has a 51% success rate.

There have also been attacks proposed against reduced-round versions of the cipher, i.e. versions of DES with fewer than sixteen rounds. Such analysis gives an insight into how many rounds are needed for safety, and how much of a "security margin" the full version retains. Differential-linear cryptanalysis was proposed by Langford and Hellman in 1994, and combines differential and linear cryptanalysis into a single attack. An enhanced version of the attack can break 9-round DES with 215.8 known plaintexts and has a 229.2 time complexity (Biham et al, 2002).

3.10 THE INTERNATIONAL DATA ENCRYPTION ALGORITHM (IDEA) ENCRYPTION ALGORITHM

IDEA, unlike the other block cipher algorithms is patented by the Swiss firm of Ascom. They have, however, been generous in allowing, with permission, free noncommercial use of their algorithm, with the result that IDEA is best known as the block cipher algorithm used within the popular encryption program PGP.

Multiplication by zero always produces zero, and is not invertible. Multiplication modulo n is also not invertible whenever it is by a number which is not relatively prime to n. The way multiplication is used in IDEA, it is necessary that it be always invertible. This is true of multiplication IDEA style.

IDEA is a block cipher which uses a 128-bit length key to encrypt successive 64-bit blocks of plaintext.The 128-bit key is split into eight 16-bit keys which are the first eight subkeys.IDEA uses 52 subkeys, each 16 bits long. Two are used during each round proper, and four are used before every round and after the last round. It has eight rounds.The plaintext block in IDEA is divided into four quarters, each 16 bits long. Three operations are used in IDEA to combine two 16 bit values to produce a 16 bit result, addition, XOR, and multiplication.

Addition is normal addition with carries, modulo 65,536. Multiplication, as used in IDEA, requires some explanation. The digits of the 128-bit key are shifted 25 bits to the left to make a new key which is split into the next eight 16-bit subkeys. The second step is repeated until the fifty two subkeys have been generated. It includes some steps which, at first, make it appear that it might be a non-invertible hash function instead of a block cipher. Also, it is interesting in that it entirely avoids the use of any lookup tables or S-boxes. The procedure is quite complicated using subkeys generated from the key to carry out a series of modular arithmetic and XOR operations on segments of the 64-bit plaintext block. The encryption scheme uses a total of fifty-two 16-bit subkeys. These are generated from the 128-bit subkey as follows:

The number 65,537, which is $2^{16} + 1$, is a prime number. (Incidentally, $2^8 + 1$, or 257, is also prime, and so is $2^4 + 1$, or 17, but $2^{32} + 1$ is not prime, so IDEA cannot be trivially scaled up to a 128-bit block size.) Thus, if one forms a multiplication table for the numbers from 1 through 65,536, each row and column will contain every number once only, forming a Latin square, and providing an invertible operation. The numbers that 16 bits normally represent are from 0 to 65,535 (or, perhaps even more commonly, from -32,768 to 32,767). In IDEA, for purposes of multiplication, a 16 bit word containing all zeroes is considered to represent the number 65,536; other numbers are represented in conventional unsigned notation, and multiplication is modulo the prime number 65,537.

IDEA (International Data Encryption Algorithm) is the second version of a block cipher designed and presented by Lai and Massey [LM91a]. It is a 64-bit iterative block cipher with a 128-bit key and eight rounds. While the cipher is not Feistel, decryption is carried out in the same manner as encryption once the decryption subkeys have been calculated from the encryption subkeys. The cipher structure was designed to be easily implemented in both software and hardware, and the security of IDEA relies on the use of three incompatible types of arithmetic operations on 16-bit words. The speed of IDEA in software is similar to that of DES.

One of the principles during the design of IDEA was to facilitate analysis of its strength against differential cryptanalysis IDEA is considered to be immune from differential cryptanalysis. In addition, no linear cryptanalytic attacks on IDEA have been reported and there is no known algebraic weakness in IDEA. The most significant cryptanalytic result is due to Daemen. He discovered a large class of 251 weak keys for which the use of such a key during encryption could be detected and the key recovered. However, since there are 2128 possible keys, this result has no impact on the practical security of the cipher for encryption. IDEA is generally considered secure and both the cipher development and its theoretical basis have been openly and widely discussed.

3.10.1 Encryption

The encryption involves modular multiplication with a modulus of $((2^{16})+1)$ and addition with a modulus of (2^{16}). The 64-bit plaintext block is split into four 16-bit segment which we'll call p1, p2, p3 and p4. The subkeys are s1, s2, s3, s4 ....s52.

The encryption consists of eight rounds with each round involving the following steps:

```
p1   x    s1   ->  d1
p2   +    s2   ->  d2
p3   +    s3   ->  d3
p4   x    s4   ->  d4
d1   XOR  d3   ->  d5
d2   XOR  d4   ->  d6
d5   x    s5   ->  d7
d6   +    d7   ->  d8
d8   x    s6   ->  d9
d7   +    d9   ->  d10
d1   XOR  d9   ->  d11
d3   XOR  d9   ->  d12
d2   XOR  d10  ->  d13
d4   XOR  d10  ->  d14
```

After this process the output blocks d12, d13 are exchanged so that d11, d13, d12 and d14 are used as input to the next round (in that order) along with the next 6 subkeys, s7 to s12. This procedure is followed for eight rounds in total giving four output blocks which we'll call e1, e2, e3 and e4. Four more steps using the last four subkeys complete the encryption:

```
e1  x  s49 -> c1
e2  +  s50 -> c2
e3  +  s51 -> c3
e4  x  s52 -> c4
```

Note: For the purposes of the algorithm, a key of all zeros is defined as being equal to 2^{16} for modular multiplication steps.

The final four output blocks, c1 to c4, are re-attached to form a 64-bit block of the ciphertext. The whole process is repeated for successive 64-bit blocks of plaintext until all of the plaintext has been encrypted. Decryption uses exactly the same sequence of operations of successive 64-bit blocks of the ciphertext, but with a different set of subkeys. The decryption subkeys are worked out from the encryption subkeys being either multiplicative or additive inverses of them. The decryption subkeys (relative to the encryption subkeys s1 to s52) are shown in the table below:

```
1st round s49* s50# s51# s52* s47 s48
2nd round s43* s45# s44# s46* s41 s42
3rd round s37* s39# s38# s39* s35 s36
4th round s31* s33# s32# s34* s29 s30
5th round s25* s27# s26# s28* s23 s24
6th round s19* s21# s20# s22* s17 s18
7th round s13* s15# s14# s16* s11 s12
8th round s7*  s9#  s8#  s10* s5  s6
```

Final transformation.....s1*   s2#   s3#   s4*

sXX* = multiplicative inverse of sXX modulus $((2^{16})+1)$

sXX# = additive inverse of sXX modulus (2^{16})

[NOTE: A subkey with all bits zero is its own multiplicative inverse in this algorithm]

3.10.2 Description of IDEA

Let the four quarters of the plaintext be called A, B, C, and D, and the 52 subkeys called K(1) through K(52).

(1) Before round 1, or as the first part of it, the following is done:

(2) Multiply A by K(1). Add K(2) to B. Add K(3) to C. Multiply D by K(4).

Round 1 proper consists of the following:

(1) Calculate A xor C (call it E) and B xor D (call it F).

(2) Multiply E by K(5). Add the new value of E to F.

(3) Multiply the new value of F by K(6). Add the result, which is also the new value of F, to E.

(4) Change both A and C by XORing the current value of F with each of them; change both B and D by XORing the current value of E with each of them.

(5) Swap B and C.

Repeat all of this eight times, or seven more times, using K(7) through K(12) the second time, up to K(43) through K(48) the eighth time. Note that the swap of B and C is not performed after round 8. Then multiply A by K(49). Add K(50) to B. Add K(51) to C. Multiply D by K(52).

The intricacies of IDEA encryption may be made somewhat clearer by examining the following diagrams:

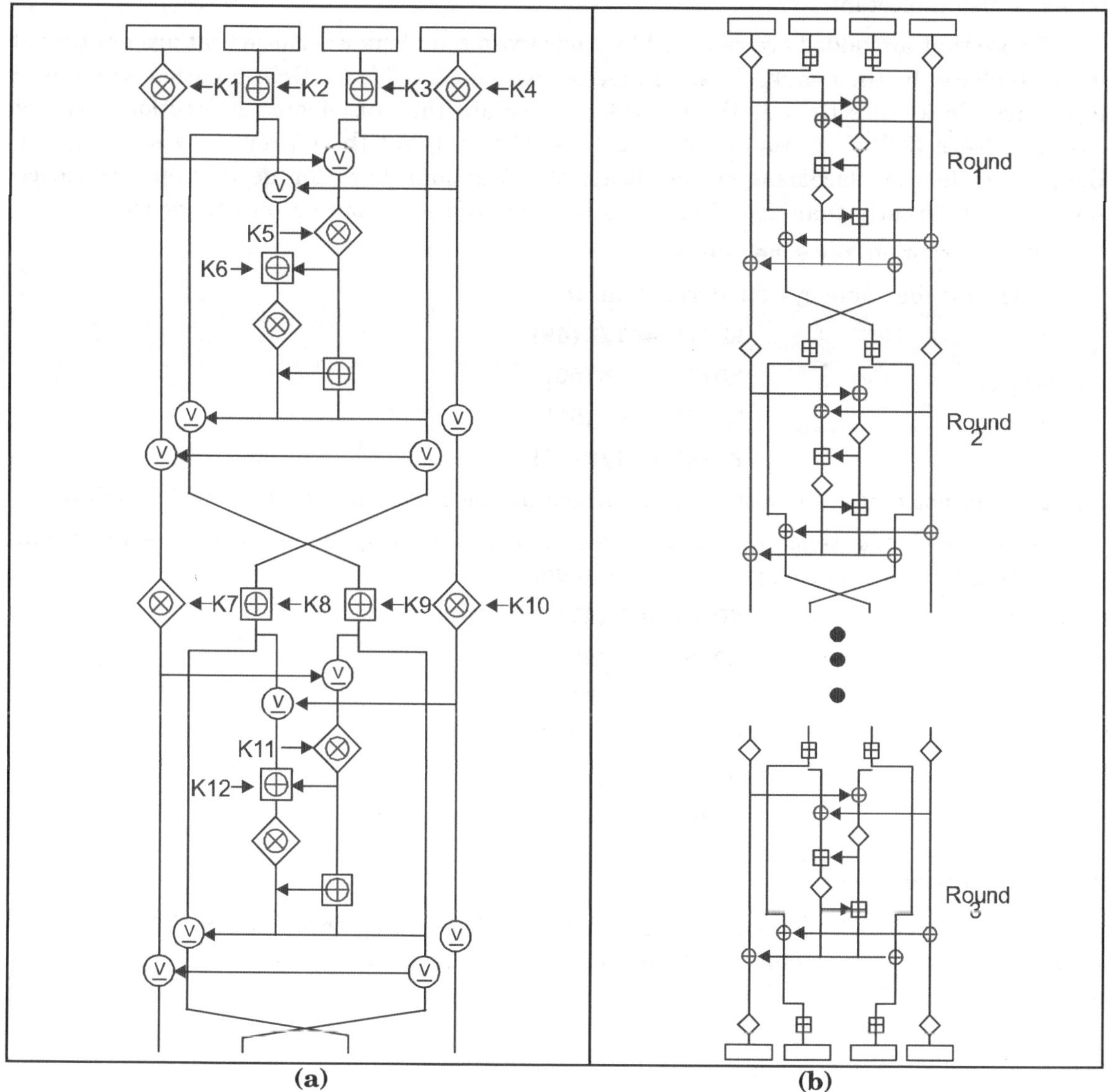

(a) (b)

Figure 3.18

3.10.3 Decryption

How can the round in IDEA be reversed, since all four quarters of the block are changed at the same time, based on a function of all four of their old values? Well, the trick to that is that A xor C isn't changed when both A and C are XORed by the same value, that value cancels out, no matter what that value might be. And the same applies to B xor D. And since the values used are functions of (A xor C) and (B xor D), they are still available.

This cross-footed round, rather than a Feistel round, is the most striking distinguishing factor of IDEA, although its use of multiplication, addition, and XOR to avoid the use of S-boxes is also important.

Those that are added are replaced by their two's complement. Those that are multiplied in are replaced by their multiplicative inverse, modulo 65,537, in IDEA notation when used to change blocks directly, but those used to calculate the cross-footed F-functions are not changed. Keys XORed in would not need to be changed, but there aren't any such keys in IDEA. Due to the placement of the swap, the first four keys for decryption are moved somewhat differently than the other keys used for the same operation between rounds.

The decryption key schedule is:

The first four subkeys for decryption are:

```
KD(1) = 1/K(49)
KD(2) = -K(50)
KD(3) = -K(51)
KD(4) = 1/K(52)
```

and they do not quite follow the same pattern as the remaining subkeys which follow.

The following is repeated eight times, adding 6 to every decryption key's index and subtracting 6 from every encryption key's index:

```
KD(5) = K(47)
KD(6) = K(48)
KD(7) = 1/K(43)
KD(8) = -K(45)
KD(9) = -K(44)
KD(10) = 1/K(46)
```

Subkey Generation

The 128-bit key of IDEA is taken as the first eight subkeys, K(1) through K(8). The next eight subkeys are obtained the same way, after a 25-bit circular left shift, and this is repeated until all encryption subkeys are derived.

This method of subkey generation is regular, and this may be a weakness. However, IDEA is considered to be highly secure, having stood up to all forms of attack so far tried by the academic community.

3.10.4 Strength and weaknesses in IDEA

IDEA is called a block cipher because it operates on 64-bit blocks using a 128-bit key. Part of its operations includes exclusive-ORs, addition modulus and multiplication modulus.IDEA is a symmetric block cipher. The speed of IDEA in software is similar to that of DES. One of the principles during the design of IDEA was to facilitate analysis of its strength against differential cryptanalysis. IDEA is considered to be immune from differential cryptanalysis. In addition, no linear cryptanalytic attacks on IDEA have been reported and there is no known algebraic weakness in IDEA.

The designers analysed IDEA to measure its strength against differential cryptanalysis and concluded that it is immune under certain assumptions. No successful linear or algebraic weaknesses have been reported. Some classes of weak keys have been found — E.g. (Daemen et al, 1994) — but these are of little concern in practice, being so rare as to be unnecessary to avoid explicitly. As of 2007[update], the best attack which applies to all keys can break IDEA reduced to 6 rounds (the full IDEA cipher uses 8.5 rounds)[5].

However over the years it has lost its luster due to:

- IDEA is a rarely used code and thus is prone to security and interoperability problems
- Most implementations either do not support it, do not enable it by default or do not negotiate it when other algorithms are available.
- Development of other faster algorithms,
- Issues with patents and
- Little progress in its cryptanalysis.

3.11 STRENGTH OF CRYPTOGRAPHIC ALGORITHM

In cryptography, key size or key length is the size (usually measured in bits or bytes) of the key used in a cryptographic algorithm (such as a cipher). An algorithm's key length is distinct from its cryptographic security, which is a logarithmic measure of the fastest known computational attack on the algorithm, also measured in bits. The security of an algorithm cannot exceed its key length (since any algorithm can be cracked by brute force), but it can be smaller. For example, Triple DES has a key size of 168 bits but provides at most 112 bits of security, since an attack of complexity 2112 is known. This property of Triple DES is not a weakness provided 112 bits of security is sufficient for an application. Most symmetric-key algorithms in common use are designed to have security equal to their key length. No asymmetric-key algorithms with this property are known; elliptic curve cryptography comes the closest with an effective security of roughly half its key length.

The relative strength of the encryption algorithm is based on key length. Bruce Schneier, creator of the Blowfish encryption algorithm, has calculated that according to what we know of quantum mechanics today, that the entire energy output of the sun is insufficient to break a 197-bit key.

3.11.1 Significance

Keys are used to control the operation of a cipher so that only the correct key can convert encrypted text (ciphertext) to plaintext. Many ciphers are based on publicly known algorithms or are open source, and so it is only the difficulty of obtaining the key that determines security of the system, provided that there is no analytic attack (i.e., a 'structural weakness' in the algorithms or protocols used), and assuming that the key is not otherwise available (such as via theft, extortion, or compromise of computer systems). The widely accepted notion that the security of the system should depend on the key alone has been explicitly formulated by Auguste Kerckhoffs (in the 1880s) and Claude Shannon (in the 1940s); the statements are known as Kerckhoffs' principle and Shannon's Maxim respectively.

A key should therefore be large enough that a brute force attack (possible against any encryption algorithm) is infeasible – i.e, would take too long to execute. Shannon's work on information theory showed that to achieve perfect secrecy, it is necessary for the key length to be at least as large as the message to be transmitted and only used once (this algorithm is called the One-time pad). In light of this, and the practical difficulty of managing such long keys, modern cryptographic practice has discarded the notion of perfect secrecy as a requirement for encryption, and instead focuses on computational security. Under this definition, the computational requirements of breaking an encrypted text must be infeasible for an attacker.

The preferred numbers commonly used as key sizes (in bits) are powers of two, potentially multiplied with a small odd integer.

3.11.2 Key size and encryption system

Encryption systems are often grouped into families. Common families include symmetric systems (e.g. AES) and asymmetric systems (e.g. RSA), or may be grouped according to the central algorithm used (e.g. elliptic curve cryptography).

As each of these is of a different level of cryptographic complexity, it is usual to have different key sizes for the same level of security, depending upon the algorithm used. For example, the security available with a 1024-bit key using asymmetric RSA is considered approximately equal in security to an 80-bit key in a symmetric algorithm (Source: RSA Security).

The actual degree of security achieved over time varies, as more computational power and more powerful mathematical analytic methods become available. For this reason cryptologists tend to look at indicators that an algorithm or key length shows signs of potential vulnerability, to move to longer key sizes or more difficult algorithms. For example as of May 2007[update], a 1039 bit integer was factored, with the special number field sieve using 400 computers over 11 months. The factored number was of a special form; the special number field sieve cannot be used on RSA keys. The computation is roughly equivalent to breaking a 700 bit RSA key. However, this might be an advanced warning that 1024 bit RSA used in secure online commerce should be deprecated, since they may become breakable in the near future. Cryptography professor Arjen Lenstra observed that "Last time, it took nine years for us to generalize from a special to a nonspecial, hard-to-factor number" and when asked whether 1024-bit RSA keys are dead, said: "The answer to that is an unqualified yes."

3.11.3 Brute force attack

Even if a symmetric cipher is currently unbreakable by exploiting structural weaknesses in its algorithm, it is possible to run through the entire space of keys in what is known as a brute force attack. Since longer symmetric keys require exponentially more work to brute force search, a sufficiently long symmetric key will prevent this line of attack.

With a key of length n bits, there are 2n possible keys. This number grows very rapidly as n increases. Moore's law suggests that computing power doubles roughly every 18 to 24 months, but even this doubling effect leaves the larger symmetric key lengths currently considered acceptable well out of reach. The large number of operations (2128) required to try all possible 128-bit keys is widely considered to be out of reach for conventional digital computing techniques for the foreseeable future. However alternative forms of computing technology are anticipated which may have superior processing power than classical computers. If a suitably sized quantum computer capable of running Grover's algorithm reliably becomes available it would reduce a 128-bit key down to 64-bit security, roughly a DES equivalent. This is one of the reasons why AES supports a 256-bit key length. See the discussion on the relationship between key lengths and quantum computing attacks at the bottom of this page for more information.

3.11.4 Symmetric algorithm key lengths

US Government export policy has long restricted the 'strength' of cryptography which can be sent out of the country. For many years the limit was 40 bits. Today, a key length of 40 bits offers little protection against even a casual attacker with a single PC. The restrictions have not been removed (in 2007, it is still illegal to export cryptographic software using key lengths greater than 64-bits without authorization from the U.S. Bureau of Industry and Security), but it became easier to gain authorization to export to certain countries in 1999/2000.

When the Data Encryption Standard cipher was released in 1977, a key length of 56 bits was thought to be sufficient (though there was speculation at the time that the NSA has deliberately reduced the key size from the original value of 112 bits, in IBM's Lucifer cipher, or 64 bits, in one of the versions of what was adopted as DES) so as to limit the 'strength' of encryption available to non-US users. The NSA has major computing resources and a large budget; some thought that 56 bits was NSA-breakable in the late '70s. However, by the late 90s, it became clear that DES could be cracked in a few days' time-frame with custom-built hardware such as could be purchased by a large corporation. The book Cracking DES (O'Reilly and Associates) tells of the successful attempt to break 56-bit DES by a brute force attack mounted by a cyber civil rights group with limited resources; see EFF DES cracker. 56 bits is now considered insufficient length for symmetric algorithm keys, and may have been for some time. More technically and financially capable organizations were surely able to do the same long before the effort described in the book. Distributed.net and its volunteers broke a 64-bit RC5 key in several years, using about seventy thousand (mostly home) computers.

The NSA's Skipjack algorithm used in its Fortezza program employs 80 bit keys. DES has been replaced in many applications by Triple DES, which has 112 bits of security with 168-bit keys.

The Advanced Encryption Standard published in 2001 uses a key size of (at minimum) 128 bits. It also can use keys up to 256 bits (a specification requirement for submissions to the AES contest). 128 bits is currently thought, by many observers, to be sufficient for the foreseeable future for symmetric algorithms of AES's quality. The U.S. Government requires 192 or 256-bit AES keys for highly sensitive data.

In 2003 the U.S. National Institute for Standards and Technology, NIST, proposed that 80-bit keys should be phased out by 2015. As of 2005, 80-bit keys were allowed to be used only until 2010.

3.11.5 Asymmetric Algorithm Key Lengths

The effectiveness of public key cryptosystems depends on the intractability (computational and theoretical) of certain mathematical problems such as integer factorization. These problems are time consuming to solve, but usually faster than trying all possible keys by brute force. Thus, asymmetric algorithm keys must be longer for equivalent resistance to attack than symmetric algorithm keys. As of 2002, a key length of 1024 bits was generally considered the minimum necessary for the RSA encryption algorithm.

As of 2003[update] RSA Security claims that 1024-bit RSA keys are equivalent in strength to 80-bit symmetric keys, 2048-bit RSA keys to 112-bit symmetric keys and 3072-bit RSA keys to 128-bit symmetric keys. RSA claims that 1024-bit keys are likely to become crackable some time between 2006 and 2010 and that 2048-bit keys are sufficient until 2030. An RSA key length of 3072 bits should be used if security is required beyond 2030.[3] NIST key management guidelines further suggest that 15360-bit RSA keys are equivalent in strength to 256-bit symmetric keys.

The Finite Field Diffie-Hellman algorithm has roughly the same key strength as RSA for the same key sizes. The work factor for breaking Diffie-Hellman is based on the discrete logarithm problem, which is related to the integer factorization problem on which RSA's strength is based. Thus, a 3072-bit Diffie-Hellman key has about the same strength as a 3072-bit RSA key.

One of the asymmetric algorithm types, elliptic curve cryptography, or ECC, appears to be secure with shorter keys than those needed by other asymmetric key algorithms. NIST guidelines state that ECC keys should be twice the length of equivalent strength symmetric key algorithms. So, for example, a 224-bit ECC key would have roughly the same strength as a 112-bit symmetric key. These estimates assume no major breakthroughs in solving the underlying mathematical problems that ECC is based on. A message encrypted with an elliptic key algorithm using a 109-bit long key has been broken by brute force.

The NSA specifies that "Elliptic Curve Public Key Cryptography using the 256-bit prime modulus elliptic curve as specified in FIPS-186-2 and SHA-256 are appropriate for protecting classified information up to the SECRET level. Use of the 384-bit prime modulus elliptic curve and SHA-384 are necessary for the protection of TOP SECRET information."

3.11.6 Effect of quantum computing attacks on key strength

The two best known quantum computing attacks are based on Shor's algorithm and Grover's algorithm. Of the two Shor's offers the greatest risk to current security systems.

Derivatives of Shor's algorithm are widely conjectured to be effective against all mainstream public-key algorithms including RSA, Diffie-Hellman and elliptic curve cryptography. According to Professor Gilles Brassard, an expert in quantum computing: "The time needed to factor an RSA integer is the same order as the time needed to use that same integer as modulus for a single RSA encryption. In other words, it takes no more time to break RSA on a quantum computer (up to a multiplicative constant) than to use it legitimately on a classical computer." The general consensus is that these public key algorithms are insecure at any key size if sufficiently large quantum computers capable of running Shor's algorithm become available. The implications of this attack is that all data encrypted using current standards based security systems such as the ubiquitous SSL used to protect e-commerce and Internet banking and SSH used to protect access to sensitive computing systems is at risk. Encrypted data protected using these protocols can be archived and may be broken at a later time.

Mainstream symmetric ciphers (such as AES or Twofish) and collision resistant hash function (such as SHA) are widely conjectured to offer greater security against known quantum computing attacks. They are widely conjectured to be most vulnerable to Grover's algorithm. Bennett, Bernstein, Brassard, and Vazirani proved in 1996 that a brute-force key search on a quantum computer cannot be faster than roughly 2n/2 invocations of the underlying cryptographic algorithm, compared with roughly 2n in the classical case.[6] Thus in the presence of large quantum computers an n-bit key can provide at most n/2 bits of security. Quantum brute force is easily defeated by doubling the key length, which has little extra computational cost in ordinary use. This implies that at least a 160-bit symmetric key is required to achieve 80-bit security rating against a quantum computer.

Here is a more generalized example:

The most common key lengths used by today's web browsers are "40-bit" and "128-bit." As a comparison, a 40-bit key can be "cracked" within a few hours by an average personal computer. However, a 128-bit key would take one BILLION powerful computers, each capable of trying one BILLION keys per second. In other words, it would take MILLIONS of years to try every possible combination of bits in a 128-bit key.

In the preceding example, the 128-bit encryption is not just three times stronger than 40-bit encryption — it is 309,485,009,821,345,068,724,781,056 times stronger. Performing this same analysis on a 448-bit encryption key yields an encryption strength that is 2.1X1096 times stronger than a 128-bit key.

3.11.7 Speed

The speed of the algorithm is also impressive. Some may think a 448 bit key length is excessive. However, when we analyze the effective throughput of the Blowfish algorithm, we see that even large key lengths result in much faster performance than other encryption algorithms.

Speed Comarisons of Block Ciphers				
Algorithm	**Clock cycles per round**	**# of rounds**	**# of clock cycles per byte encrypted**	**Notes**
Blowfish	9	19	18	Free, Not patented
Khufu/Khafre	5	32	20	Patented by Xerox
RCS	12	16	23	Patented by RSA Data Security
DES	18	16	45	56-bit key
IDEA	50	8	50	Patented by Ascom-Systec
Triple-DES	18	48		

3.11.8 Requirements for a Standard Encryption Algorithm

A standard encryption algorithm must be suitable for many different applications:

- Bulk encryption. The algorithm should be efficient in encrypting data files or a continuous data stream.
- Random bit generation. The algorithm should be efficient in producing single random bits.
- Packet encryption. The algorithm should be efficient in encrypting packet-sized data. (An ATM packet has a 48- byte data field.) It should implementable in an application where successive packets may be encrypted or decrypted with different keys.
- Hashing. The algorithm should be efficient in being converted to a one-way hash function.

3.11.9 Platforms

A standard encryption algorithm must be implementable on a variety of different platforms, each with their own requirements. These include:

(1) Special hardware. The algorithm should be efficiently implementable in custom VLSI hardware.

(2) Large processors. While dedicated hardware will always be used for the fastest applications, software implementations are more common. The algorithm should be efficient on 32-bit microprocessors with 4 kbyte program and data caches.

(3) Medium-size processors. The algorithm should run on microcontrollers and other medium-size processors, such as the 68HC11.

(4) Small processors. It should be possible to implement the algorithm on smart cards, even inefficiently.

The requirements for small processors are the most difficult. RAM and ROM limitations are severe for this platform. Also, efficiency is more important on these small machines. Workstations double their capacity almost annually. Small embedded systems are the same year after year, and there is little capacity to spare. If there is a choice, the extra computation burden should be on large processors rather than small processors.

3.11.10 Additional Requirements

These additional requirements should, if possible, be levied on a standard encryption algorithm.

The algorithm should be simple to code. Experiences with DES [19] show that programmers will often make implementation mistakes if the algorithm is complicated. If possible, the algorithm should be robust against these mistakes.

The algorithm should have a flat keyspace, allowing any random bit string of the required length to be a possible key. There should be no weak keys.

The algorithm should facilitate easy key-management for software implementations. Software implementations of DES generally use poor key management techniques. In particular, the password that the user types in becomes the key. This means that although DES has a theoretical keyspace of 256, the actual keyspace is limited to keys constructed with the 95 characters of printable ASCII. Additionally, keys corresponding to words and near words are much more likely.

The algorithm should be easily modifiable for different levels of security, both minimum and maximum requirements. All operations should manipulate data in byte-sized blocks. Where possible, operations should manipulate data in 32-bit blocks.

3.11.11 Design Decisions

Based on the above parameters, we have made these design decisions. The algorithm should:

- Manipulate data in large blocks, preferably 32 bits in size (and not in single bits, such as DES).
- Have either a 64-bit or a 128-bit block size.
- Have a scalable key, from 32 bits to at least 256 bits.
- Use simple operations that are efficient on microprocessors: e.g., exclusive-or, addition, table lookup, modular- multiplication. It should not use variable-length shifts or bit-wise permutations, or conditional jumps.
- Be implementable on an 8-bit processor with a minimum of 24 bytes of RAM (in addition to the RAM required to store the key) and 1 kilobyte of ROM.
- Employ precomputable subkeys. On large-memory systems, these subkeys can be precomputed for faster operation. Not precomputing the subkeys will result in slower operation, but it should still be possible to encrypt data without any precomputations.
- Consist of a variable number of iterations. For applications with a small key size, the trade-off between the complexity of a brute-force attack and a differential attack make a large number of iterations superfluous. Hence, it should be possible to

reduce the number of iterations with no loss of security (beyond that of the reduced key size).

- If possible, have no weak keys. If not possible, the proportion of weak keys should be small enough to make it unlikely to choose one at random. Also, any weak keys should be explicitly known so they can be weeded out during the key generation process.
- Use subkeys that are a one-way hash of the key. This would allow the use of long passphrases for the key without compromising security.
- Have no linear structures (e.g., the complementation property of DES) that reduce the complexity of exhaustive search.
- Use a design that is simple to understand. This will facilitate analysis and increase the confidence in the algorithm. In practice, this means that the algorithm will be a Feistel iterated block cipher.

Most of these design decisions are not new. Almost all block ciphers since Lucifer are Feistel ciphers, and all have a flat keyspace (with the possible exception of a few weak keys). FEAL and Khufu use a variable number of iterations. Khufu has a large number of subkeys that are a one-way function of the key. RC2 has a variable-length key. GOST uses a 32-bit word length and a 64-bit block size. MMB uses a 32-bit word length and a 128-bit block size.

3.11.12 Building Blocks

There are a number of building blocks that have been demonstrated to produce strong ciphers. Many of these can be efficiently implemented on 32-bit microprocessors.

Large S-boxes. Larger S-boxes are more resistant to differential cryptanalysis. An algorithm with a 32-bit word length can use 32-bit S-boxes. Khufu and REDOC III both use a 256-entry, 32-bit wide S-box.

Key-dependent S-boxes. While fixed S-boxes must be designed to be resistant to differential and linear cryptanalysis, key-dependent S-boxes are much more resistant to these attacks. They are used in the Khufu algorithm. Variable S-boxes, which could possibly be key dependent, are used in GOST.

Combining operations from different algebraic groups. The IDEA cipher introduced this concept, combining XOR mod 216, addition mod 216, and multiplication mod 216+1. The MMB cipher uses a 32-bit word, and combines XOR mod 232 with multiplication mod 232-1.

Key-dependent permutations. The fixed initial and final permutations of DES have been long regarded as cryptographically worthless. Khufu XORs the text block with key material at the beginning and the end of the algorithm.

3.12 TRAFFIC FLOW CONFIDENTIALITY (TFC)

Confidentiality has been defined by the International Organization for Standardization (ISO) as "ensuring that information is accessible only to those authorized to have access" and is one of the cornerstones of information security. Confidentiality is one of the design goals for many cryptosystems, made possible in practice by the techniques of modern cryptography.Knowledge about the number and length of messages between nodes may enable an opponent to determine who is taking to whom. This can have obvious implications in a military conflict. Even in commercial applications, traffic analysis may yield information that the traffic generators would like to conceal.

The following are types of information that can be derived from a traffic analysis attack:

- Identities of partners ie Sender, Receiver, and associated parties
- how frequent the partners are communicating,
- message pattern.
- Message length, or quantity of messages that suggest important information is being exchanged, and
- the events that correlate with special conversation between particular partners.

With the use of traffic patterns a covert channel can be established. A covert channel is a means of communication which transfers information unintended by the designers of the communication facility. The channel is used to transfer information in a way that violates a security policy. An employee may wish to communicate information to an outsider through a secured channel evading detection by the management. The two participants could setup a code in which an apparently legitimate message of a less than a certain length represents binary zero, whereas a longer message represents a binary one. Other such schemes are possible.

3.12.1 Traffic Padding

Network layers are encrypted, reducing the opportunity for traffic analysis. It is still possible in those circumstances for an attacker to assess the amount of traffic on a network and to observe the amount of traffic entering and leaving each end system. Countermeasure to this type of attack is traffic padding.

Traffic padding produces cipher text output continuously, even in the absence of plain text. A continuous random data stream is generated. When plain text is available, it is encrypted and transmitted. When input plaintext is not present, random data are encrypted and transmitted. This makes it impossible for an attacker to distinguish between true data flow and padding and therefore impossible to deduce the amount of traffic.

Traffic padding is essentially a link encryption function. If only end-to-end encryption is employed, then the measures available to the defender are more limited. If encryption is implemented at the application layer, then an opponent can determine transport layer, network-layer addresses and traffic patterns which remain accessible.

Null messages can be inserted randomly into the stream. These tactics deny opponent knowledge about the amount of data exchanged between end users and obscure the underlying traffic pattern. Encryption can secure network connections to a larger extent.

3.12.2 Traffic Flow Confidentiality (TFC)

Traffic Flow Confidentiality (TFC) mechanisms are techniques devised tohide/masquerade the traffic pattern to prevent statistical traffic analysis at-tacks.. Their inclusion in widespread security protocols, in conjunction withthe ability for deployers to flexibly control their operation, might boost theiradoption and improve privacy of future networks.

Extensive literature work demonstrates that the traffic pattern generated in a communication carries plenty of information, which can be gathered through specially devised "statistical traffic analysis attacks". These attacks operate irrespective of the deployed encryption means, and allow to extract, from the statistical analysis of the generated packet sizes and of their inter-arrival times, valuable confidential information such as the employed applications, the application layer protocols, the physical devices used, or the web page accessed.

To perform these attacks, a signature for the protocol or the web site to be recognized is typically precomputed as a set of statistical parameters describing packet size and/or packet inter-arrival time distributions. Flow classification can be performed by matching the actual statistics with the pre-stored signatures. Quite interestingly, accurate flow classification may be obtained even by looking only at its very first packets.

Statistical traffic analysis attacks have been also employed for the purpose of breaching security (such as for gathering password transmitted over encrypted sessions [12,13]), and for performing passive or active attacks to anonymization (Mix) networks, aimed at uncovering the identity of the communicating parties.

To duly protect the privacy of the users, "Traffic Flow Confidentiality" (TFC) mechanisms devised to alter or mask the statistical characteristics of the traffic patterns are necessary.

3.12.3 Goals of traffic security system

The goals of traffic security system should be to provide a tool:

- implementing the basic mechanisms to prevent statistical traffic analysis attacks
- Dummy traffic
- Packets padding
- Traffic re-shaping
- Flexible
- Reconfigurable
- Reprogrammable
- Based on common standard
- IPsec
- Providing a underlying layer for the Anonymous Routing Networks
- Supporting different kind of traffic

Use of physical links with greater physical security provides a layer of protection for the confidentiality of the data in the packets as well as traffic analysis protection. If the content of the packets are otherwise protected by end-to-end encryption, using secure links makes it harder for an external adversary to obtain the encrypted data to attack. If the content of the packets is unencrypted plain text, secure links may provide the only protection of data confidentiality.

There are cases where end-to-end encryption can not be used. Examples include paths which incorporate links within nations which restrict encryption, such as France or Australia, and paths which incorporate an amateur radio link, where encryption is prohibited. In these cases, link security is generally the only type of confidentiality available. The proposed TOS will provide a way of requesting the best that the network can do for the security of such unencrypted data.

There are two approaches

(1) Link Encryption Approach

Packet Headers are encrypted

Still possible for Outsiders to assess the amount of traffic entering and leaving each end system. When input plaintext is not present, random data are encrypted, making it possible for an attacker to distinguish true data flow from padding, and thereby deduce the amount of traffic.

(2) End-to-End Encryption Approach

One technique is to pad out data units to a uniform length at either the transport of application level. Additionally, null values can be inserted randomly into the stream. These tactics are designed to deny an Outsider knowledge about the amount of data exchanged between users, and obsure underlying traffic patterns.

3.13 KEY DISTRIBUTION

For encryption to work over a network, the two parties (Sender and Receiver) must exchange and share the same keys, while protecting access to the keys from others.A key could be selected by A and physically delivered to B. A third party could select the key and physically deliver it to A and B. If A and B have previously used a key, one party could transmit the new key to the other, encrypted using the old key. If A and B each have an encrypted connection to a third party C, C could deliver a key on the encrypted links to A and B.

3.13.1 Automatic Key Distribution

(1) Host sends packet requesting connection.

(2) Front end buffers packet; asks KDC for sess key

(3) KDC distributes keys to both front-ends.

(4) Buffer packet transmitted.

- Message Encryption
- Secret key encryption vs. public key encryption

Both encryption algorithms can provide confidentiality.Secret Key Encryption is more efficient and faster

To use secret key encryption

- Communicating peers must share the same key
- The key must be protected from access by others

A secret key becomes insecure when used for a long time, since more ciphertext encrypted using this key is available to the attacker, making it easies to derive the key.

Keys that are used to encrypt the data need to be renewed frequently.

Solution – Key Hierarchy

- Session key – encrypt data, renewed each session
- Master key – distribute session keys, renewed infrequently using non-cryptographic approach

Three approaches

- Via key distribution center (KDC)

  KDC needs to share a secret key with each of the communication parties
- Decentralized

  The communication parties need to share a master key
- Via public key

  – Using public key encryption
- Using Diffie-Hellman key exchange

(1) Via key distribution center (KDC)

Initially A and B both trust KDC

KUA — shared secret key between A and KDC

KUB — shared secret key between B and KDC

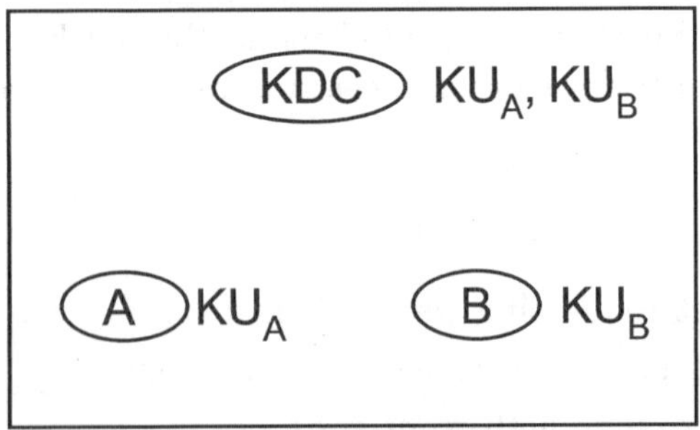

Goal

A and B trust each other

A and B share a secret key KS

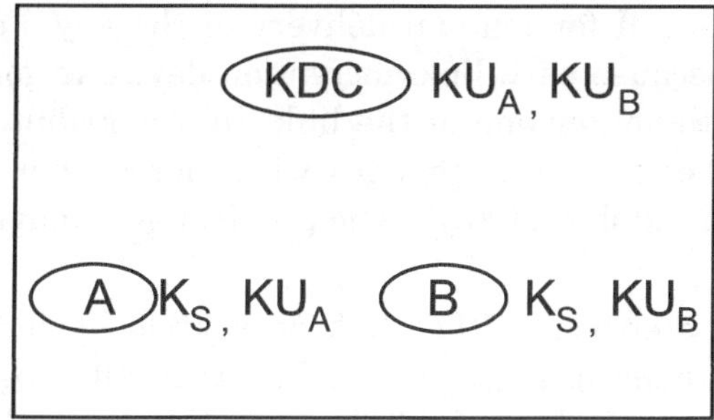

(2) Decentralized Key Distribution

Initially

A and B trust each other

A and B share a master secret key Km

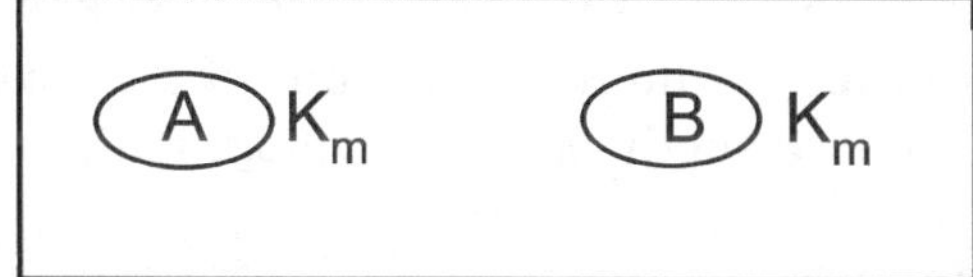

Goal

A and B share a session secret key KS

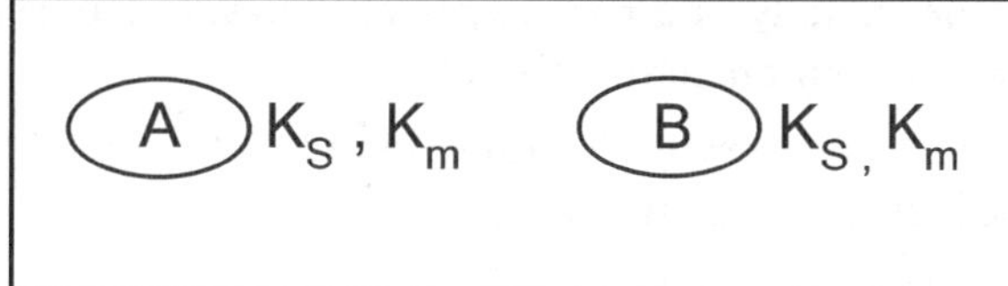

(3) Via Public Key

For conventional encryption to work, the two parties or hosts should have the same key, and that key must be protected from access by others. This key may provide encrypted message. Frequent key changes are usually desirable to limit the amount of data compromised if an attacker learns the key. Therefore, the strength of any cryptographic system results with the key distribution technique, a term that refers to the means of delivering a key to two parties that wish to exchange data without allowing others to see the key.

Key distribution can be achieved in a number of ways. There are various combinations by which a key can be selected for A and B:- A key can be selected by A and physically delivered to B, A third party can select the key and physically deliver the key to A and B, If A and B have previously and recently used a key, one party can transmit to the other the new key, which has been encrypted by using the old key, and If A and B each has an encrypted connection to a third party C, C can deliver a key on the encrypted links to A and B.

The first two options call for manual delivery of the key. For link encryption, this is reasonable requirement because each link encryption device is going to be exchanging data with only its partner on the other end of the link. In a distributed system, any given host or terminal may need to engage in exchanges with many other hosts and terminals over time. Each device needs a number of keys. The problem gets magnified when this system is used for WAN.

Third possibility is to encrypt either link encryption or end to end encryption. If an attacker ever succeeds in gaining access to one key, then all subsequent keys are revealed. Even if frequent changes are made to the link encryption keys, the changes should be done manually. To provide keys for end to end encryption requires encryption of the key along with the data.

Link encryption can be ignored, but it can be added or not as per requirement. When two end systems (hosts, terminals,) wish to communicate, they establish a logical connection, all user data are encrypted with a one time session key.

For symmetric encryption to work, the two parties must share the same key. Frequent key changes are usually desirable to limit the amount of data compromised if an attacker learns the key. Therefore, the strength of any cryptographic system rests with the key *distribution technique.*

Key distribution ways (Options)

(1) A can select a key and physically deliver it to B.

(2) A third party can select the key and physically deliver it to A and B.

(3) If A and B have previously and recently used a key, one party can transmit the new key to the other encrypted using the old key.

(4) If A and B each has an encrypted connection to a third party C, C can deliver a key on the encrypted links to A and B.

1 and 2. Key distribution options 1 and 2.

Manual Delivery

(1) For link encryptions: OK

Each node exchanges data with only its neighboring nodes.

(2) For end-to-end encryptions: Awkward

- Network or IP-level encryption (#N host)
- A distributed system with N nodes : N(N-1)/2 keys are needed.

(3) Application level encryption

- A key is needed for every pair of users or processes that require communication.

3. Key distribution option 3

If A and B have previously and recently used a key, one party can transmit the new key to the other, encrypted using the old key. It can be appropriate for link and end-to-end encryption.

BUT if an attacker ever succeeds in gaining access to one key, then all subsequent keys will be revealed.

Furthermore, the initial distribution of N(N – 1)/2 keys is awkward.

4. Key distribution option 4

If A and B each has an encrypted connection to a third party C, C can deliver a key on the encrypted links to A and B.

For end-to-end encryption, some variation on it has been widely adopted.

Each user must share a unique key with the Key distribution center (KDC) for purposes of key distribution. (N keys in total.)

Session key

Temporary key

Used for the duration of a logical connection between A and B.

Generated by the key distribution center.

[N(N – 1)] / 2 keys are needed at any one time.

Master key

Session keys are encrypted using a master key.

N master keys are required.

Physically delivered.

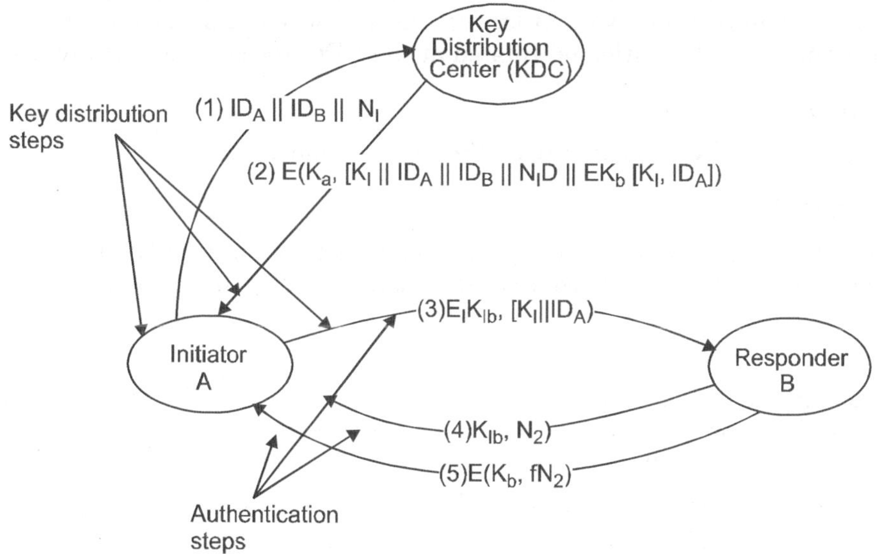

Figure 3.19 Key Distribution Scenario

User A wishes to establish a logical connection with B.

A and B share a master key Ka and Kb with the KDC, respectively.

A Key Distribution Scenario

(1) IDA | | IDB | | N1

A issues a request to the KDC for a session key to connect to B. The message includes

- The identity of A and B
- A unique identifier N1,(nonce) for this transaction.

The nonce may be a timestamp, a counter, or a random number. It must differ with other request's nonce. It should be difficult for an opponent to guess the nonce to prevent masquerade.

Thus, a random number is a good choice for a nonce.

(2) E(Ka,[Ks| |IDA| |IDB| |N1]) | | E(Kb, [Ks| |IDA])

The KDC responds with a message encrypted using Ka. A is the only one who can receive the message and A know that it originated at the KDC. The message includes two items for A.

- The one-time session key Ks
- The original request message IDA| |IDB| |N1
- The message includes two items for B.
- The one-time session key Ks
- An identifier of A, IDA

(3) E (Kb, [Ks,IDA])

A stores the session key and forward E (Kb, [Ks,IDA]) to B. It is encrypted by Kb so it is protected from eavesdropping. Now, B knows the session key Ks, knows the other party is A, and knows that the information originated at the KDC. (because it is encrypted using Kb)

(4) E (Ks, N2)

B sends a nonce N2 to A encrypted with the new session key Ks.

(5) E (Ks, f(N2))

A responds with f(N2). f(N2) an arbitrary function that transforming N2 .For example, f(N2) = N2 + 1. Steps (4) and (5) are to confirm that both A and B have the correct session key.

3.13.2 Hierarchical Key Control

Instead of using one KDC, several KDCs can be used in a hierarchy. A local KDC is responsible for a local domain, such as a single LAN or a single building. For communication among entities within a local domain, the local KDC is responsible for key distribution.

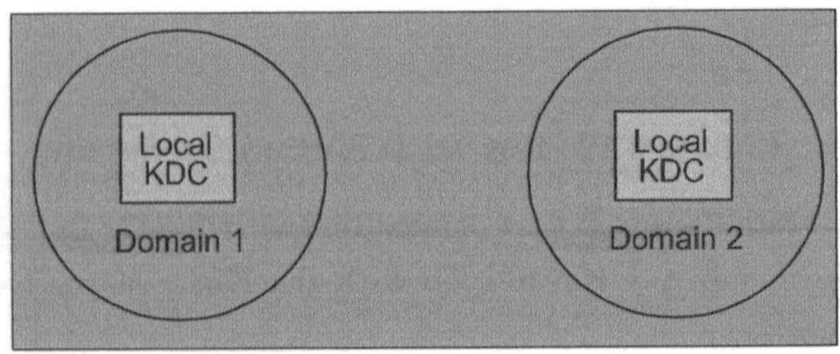

If two entities in different domains desire a shared key, then corresponding local KDCs can communicate through a global KDC. In this case, any one of the three KDCs can select the key.

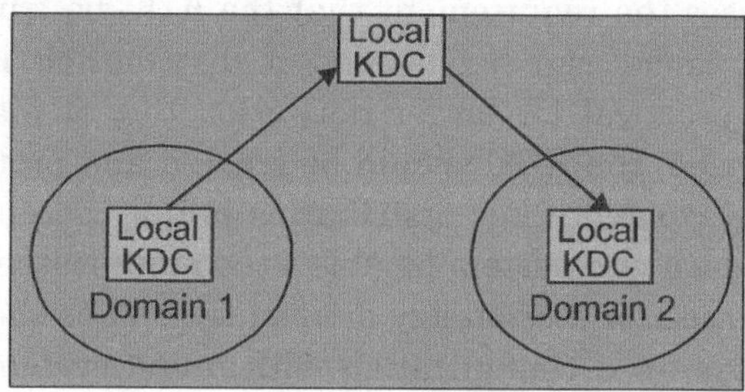

A hierarchical scheme minimizes the effort involved in master key distribution because most master keys are those shared by a local KDC with its local entities. Furthermore, such a scheme limits the damage of a faulty or subverted KDC to its local area only.

Session key lifetime: How often session keys are changed.

The more often the keys are changed, the more secure they are. Because the opponent has less ciphertext for any given session key. The less often the keys are changed, the more efficient they are. Because the key distribution delays data transmission. A security manager have to balance these competing considerations in determining the session key lifetime.

- Connection-oriented protocol

Normally, a session key per connection. However, the session is too long, periodically changing the session key is recommendable.

- Connectionless protocol
- A session key for a fixed period.

Session security module (SSM)

On behalf of the host or terminal, the SSM obtains session keys and performs end-to-end encryption.

A Transparent Key Control Scheme

The approach assumes that communication makes use of a connection-oriented end-to-end protocol. The SSM does the security-related work and is transparent to the hosts.

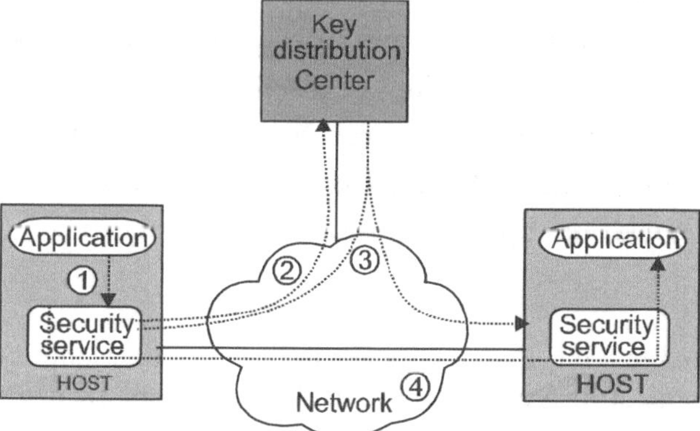

Figure 3.20 Automatic Key Distribution for Connection Oriented Control

3.13.3 Decentralized key Control

The use of a KDC imposes the requirement that the KDC be trusted and be protected from subversion. This requirement can be avoided if distribution is fully decentralized. Full decentralization is not practical for larger networks. But, it may be useful within a local context. When KDC is used, the KDC should be trusted and protected from subversion. But this requirement can be avoided if key distribution is fully decentralization. A decentralized approach requires that each end system be able to communicate in a secure manner with all potential partner for purpose of session key distribution. Thus there may need to be as many as $n(n - 1)/2$ master keys for a configuration with n end systems.

Each node must maintain (n-1) master keys.

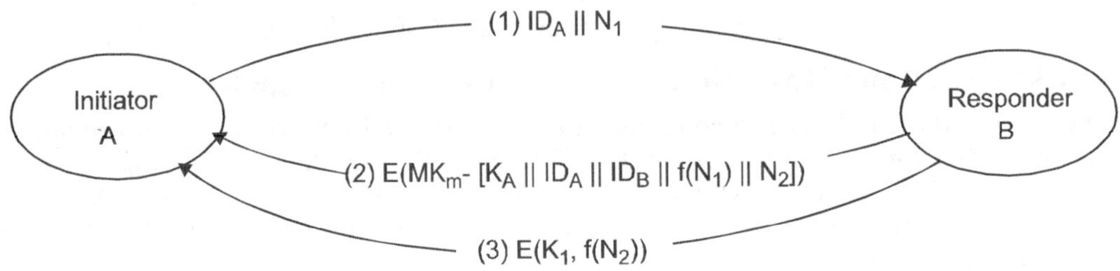

Figure 3.21

3.13.4 Controlling Key Usage

The different types of session keys

- Data-encrypting key
- PIN-encrypting key
- File-encrypting key

Key Usage

- Associate a tag with each key.
- Makes use of the extra 8 parity bits in each 64-bit DES key.
- One bit indicates whether the key is a session key or a master key.
- One bit indicates whether the key can be used for encryption.
- One bit indicates whether the key can be used for decryption.
- The remaining bits are spares for future use.

Drawback

The tag length is limited to 8 bit, limiting its flexibility and functionality. The tag information is used only at the point of decryption because the tag is not transmitted in clear form.

Control vector (for a key)

It consists of a number of fields that specify the uses and restrictions for a session key. The length of the control vector may vary. The control vector is cryptographically coupled with the key at the time of key generation at the KDC.

The control vector is delivered in a clear form.

Ciphertext input

Controlling Key Usage

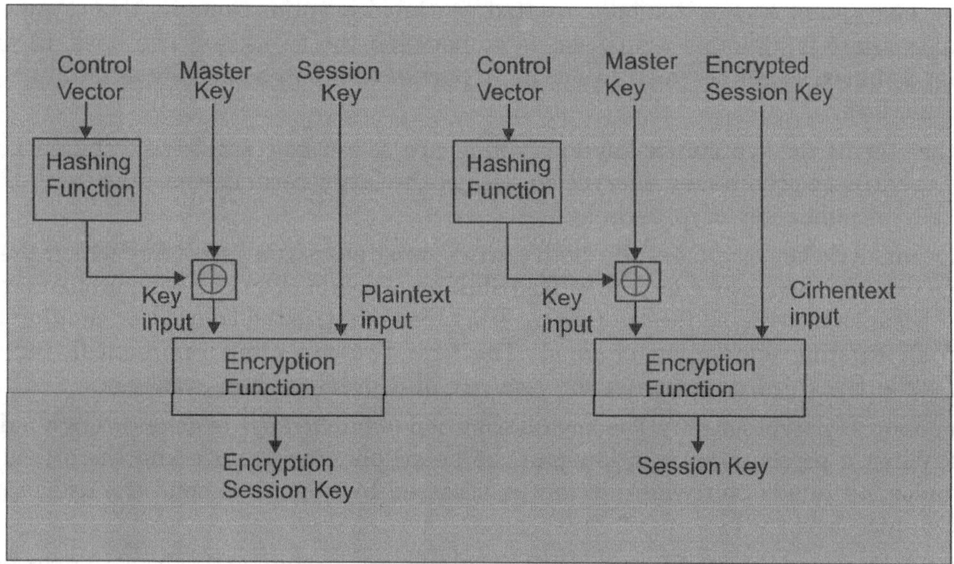

Figure 3.22

Two advantages of using the control vector

- No restriction on length of the control vector
- The control vector is available at all stages of operation

3.13.5 Types of Symmetric-key Algorithms

Symmetric-key algorithms can be divided into stream ciphers and block ciphers. Stream ciphers encrypt the bits of the message one at a time, and block ciphers take a number of bits and encrypt them as a single unit. Blocks of 64 bits have been commonly used; the Advanced Encryption Standard algorithm approved by NIST in December 2001 uses 128-bit blocks.Some examples of popular and well-respected symmetric algorithms include Twofish, Serpent, AES (Rijndael), Blowfish, CAST5, RC4, TDES, and IDEA.

Symmetric vs. Asymmetric Algorithms

Unlike symmetric algorithms, asymmetric key algorithms use a different key for encryption than for decryption. I.e., a user knowing the encryption key of an asymmetric algorithm can encrypt messages, but cannot derive the decryption key and cannot decrypt messages encrypted with that key. A short comparison of these two types of algorithms is given below:

Speed

Symmetric-key algorithms are generally much less computationally intensive than asymmetric key algorithms. In practice, asymmetric key algorithms are typically hundreds to thousands times slower than symmetric key algorithms.Symmetric-key algorithms are a class of algorithms for cryptography that use trivially related, often identical, cryptographic keys for both decryption and encryption.

The encryption key is trivially related to the decryption key, in that they may be identical or there is a simple transform to go between the two keys. The keys, in practice, represent a shared secret between two or more parties that can be used to maintain a private information link.

Other terms for symmetric-key encryption are secret-key, single-key, shared-key, one-key and eventually private-key encryption. Use of the latter term does conflict with the term private key in public-key cryptography.

In symmetric key cryptography, both parties must possess a secret key which they must exchange prior to using any encryption. Distribution of secret keys has been problematic until recently, because it involved face-to-face meeting, use of a trusted courier, or sending the key through an existing encryption channel. The first two are often impractical and always unsafe, while the third depends on the security of a previous key exchange.

In public key cryptography, the key distribution of public keys is done through public key servers. When a person creates a key-pair, he keeps one key private and the other, public-key, is uploaded to a server where it can be accessed by anyone to send the user a private, encrypted, message.

Secure Sockets Layer (SSL) uses Diffie-Hellman key exchange if the client does not have a public-private key pair and a published certificate in the Public Key Infrastructure, and Public Key Cryptography if the user does have both the keys and the credential.

In secret sharing a secret (password, key, trade secret,...) is used as a seed to generate a number of distinct secrets, and the pieces are distributed so that some subset of the recipients can jointly authenticate themselves and use the secret information without learning what it is. Secret sharing is also called secret splitting, key splitting, and split knowledge.

Suppose we want to share N secrets among M people so that any M < N of them (M of N) can regenerate the original information, but no smaller group up to M - 1 can do so. There are mathematical problems of this type, such as the number of points needed to identify a polynomial of a certain degree (used in Shamir's scheme), or the number of intersecting hyperplanes needed to specify a point (used in Blakley's scheme). We can hand out data specifying any number of points on the curve, or hyperplanes through the point, without altering the number needed to solve the problem and, in our application, access the protected resource.

Key distribution is an important issue in wireless sensor network (WSN) design. There are many key distribution schemes in the literature that are designed to maintain an easy and at the same time secure communication among sensor nodes. The most accepted method of key distribution is WSNs is key predistribution, where secret keys are placed in sensor nodes before deployment. When the nodes are deployed over the target area, the secret keys are used to create the network. For more info see: key distribution in wireless sensor networks.

The drawback of symmetric key cryptography was the need for the two communicating parties to have agreed upon their secret key ahead of time. With public key cryptography, this a priori agreement on a secret value is not needed. However, as we saw in our discussion of authentication protocol ap5.0 in Section 6.5, public key encryption has its own difficulties, in particular the problem of obtaining someone's true public key. Both of these problems - determining a shared key for symmetric key cryptography, and securely obtaining the public key for public key cryptography - can be solved using a trusted intermediary. For symmetric key cryptograghy , the trusted intermediary is called a Key Distribution Center (KDC), which is a single, trusted network entity with whom one has established a shared secret key. We will see that one can use the KDC to obtain the shared keys needed to communicate securely with all other network entities. For public key cryptography, the trusted intermediary is called a Certification Authority (CA). A certification authority certifies that a public key belongs to a particular entity (a person or a network entity). For a certified public key, if one can safely trust the CA that the certified the key, then one can be sure about to whom the public key belongs. Once a public key is certified, then it can be distributed from just about anywhere, including a public key server, a personal Web page or a diskette.

3.13.6 The Key Distribution Center (KDC)

Suppose once again that Bunty and Anita want to communicate using symmetric key cryptography. They have never met (perhaps they just met in an on-line chat room) and thus have not established a shared secret key in advance. How can they now agree on a secret key, given that they can only communicate with each other over the network? A solution often adopted in practice is to use a trusted Key Distribution Center (KDC). The KDC is a server that shares a different secret symmetric key with each registered user. This key might be manually installed at the server when a user first registers. The KDC knows the secret key of each user and each user can communicate securely with the KDC using this key. Let's see how knowledge of this one key allows a user to securely obtain a key for communicating with any other registered user. Suppose that Anita and Bunty are users of the KDC; they only know their individual key, KA-KDC and KB-KDC, respective for communicating securely with the KDC. Anita takes the first step, and they proceed as illustrated in Figure 3.45.

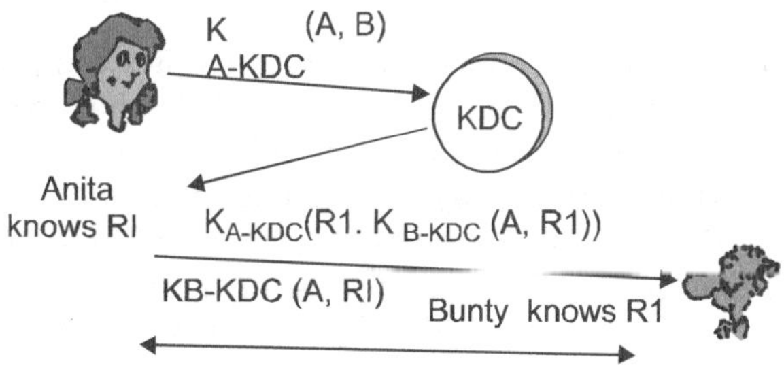

Figure 3.23 Setting up a One-time Session Key using a Key Distribution Center

Using KA-KDC to encrypt her communication with the KDC, Anita sends a message to the KDC saying she (A) wants to communicate with Bunty (B). We denote this message, KA-KDC (A,B). As part of this exchange, Anita should authenticate the KDC (see homework problems), e.g., using an authentication protocol (e.g., our protocol ap4.0) and the shared key KA-KDC .

The KDC, knowing KA-KDC , decrypts KA-KDC (A,B). The KDC then authenticates Anita. The KDC then generates a random number, R1. This is the shared key value that Anita and Bunty will use to perform symmetric encryption when they communicate with each other. This key is referred to as a one-time session key, as Anita and Bunty will use this key for only this one session that they are currently setting up. The KDC now needs to inform Anita and Bunty of the value of R1. The KDC thus sends back an encrypted message to Anita containing the following:

R1, the one-time session key that Anita and Bunty will use to communicate; a pair of values: A, and R1, encrypted by the KDC using Bunty's key, KB-KDC . We denote this KB-KDC(A,R1). It is important to note that KDC is sending Anita not only the value of R1 for her own use, but also an encrypted version of R1 and Anita's name encrypted using Bunty's key. Anita can't decrypt this pair of values in the message (she doesn't know Bunty's encryption key), but then she doesn't really need to. We'll see shortly that Anita will simply forward this encrypted pair of values to Bunty (who can decrypt them).

These items are put into a message and encrypted using Anita's shared key. The message from the KDC to Anita is thus KA-KDC(R1,KB-KDC(R1)). Anita receives the message from the KDC, verifies the nonce, extracts R1 from the message and saves it. Anita now knows the one-time session key, R1. Anita also extracts KB-KDC(A,R1) and forwards this to Bunty.

Bunty decrypts the received message, KB-KDC(A,R1), using KB-KDC and extracts A and R1. Bunty now knows the one-time session key, R1, and the person with whom he is sharing this key, A. Of course, he takes care to authenticate Anita using R1 before proceeding any further.

3.14 RANDOM NUMBER GENERATION (RNG)

A random number generator (often abbreviated as RNG) is a computational or physical device designed to generate a sequence of numbers or symbols that lack any pattern, i.e. appear random. Hardware-based systems for random number generation are widely used, but often fall short of this goal, though they may meet some of the statistical tests for randomness intended to ensure that they do not have any easily discernible patterns. Methods for generating random results have existed since ancient times, including dice, coin flipping, the shuffling of playing cards, the use of yarrow stalks (by divination) in the I Ching, and many other techniques.

The many applications of randomness have led to many different methods for generating random data. These methods may vary as to how unpredictable or statistically random they are, and how quickly they can generate random numbers.

Before the advent of computational random number generators, generating large amounts of sufficiently random numbers (important in statistics) required a lot of work. Results would sometimes be collected and distributed as random number tables. A growing number of government-run lotteries, and lottery games, are using RNGs instead of more traditional drawing methods, such as using ping-pong or rubber balls.

3.14.1 Physical Methods

The earliest methods for generating random numbers — dice, coin flipping, roulette wheels — are still used today, mainly in games and gambling as they tend to be too slow for applications in statistics and cryptography.

Some physical phenomena, such as thermal noise in Zener diodes appear to be truly random and can be used as the basis for hardware random number generators. However, many mechanical phenomena feature asymmetries and systematic biases that make their outcomes not truly random. The many successful attempts to exploit such phenomena by gamblers, especially in roulette and blackjack are testimony to these effects.

There are several imaginative sources of random numbers online. A common technique is to run a hash function against a frame of a video stream from an unpredictable source. This technique was used by Lavarand which used images of a number of lava lamps. Lithium Technologies uses a camera pointed at the sky on a windy and cloudy day. Random.org has a more obvious approach of listening to atmospheric noise. Details about how they turn their input into random numbers can be found on their respective sites.

Completely randomized design falls within the category of true random number generation. The generation of true random numbers outside the computer environment is based on the theory of entropy. Sources of entropy include nuclear decay and atmospheric conditions. HotBits uses radioactive decay, while Random.org uses radio noise to generate randomness.

Another common entropy source is the behavior of human users of the system, if such users exist. While humans are not considered good randomness generators upon request, they generate random behavior quite well in the context of playing mixed strategy games. The utilization of Human gameplay entropy for Randomness Generation was studied by Ran Halprin and Moni Naor.

3.14.2 Computational Methods

Pseudo-random number generators (PRNGs) are algorithms that can automatically create long runs (for example, millions of numbers long) with good random properties but eventually the sequence repeats exactly (or the memory usage grows without bound). One of the most common PRNG is the linear congruential generator, which uses the recurrence random.png to generate numbers. The maximum number of numbers the formula can produce is the modulus, m.

To avoid certain non-random properties of a single linear congruential generator, several such random number generators with slightly different values of the multiplier coeffient a are typically used in parallel, with a "master" random number generator that selects from among the several different generators.A simple pen-and-paper method for generating random numbers is the so-called middle square method suggested by John Von Neumann. While simple to implement, its output is of poor quality.

Most computer programming languages include functions or library routines that purport to be random number generators. They are often designed to provide a random byte or word, or a floating point number uniformly distributed between 0 and 1.

Such library functions often have poor statistical properties and some will repeat patterns after only tens of thousands of trials. They are often initialized using a computer's real time clock as the seed. These functions may provide enough randomness for certain tasks (for example video games) but are unsuitable where high-quality randomness is required, such as in cryptographic applications, statistics or numerical analysis. Much higher quality random number sources are available on most operating systems; for example /dev/random on various BSD flavors, Linux, Mac OS X, IRIX, and Solaris, or CryptGenRandom for Microsoft Windows.

3.14.3 Practical Applications and Uses of Random Numbers

Random number generators have applications in gambling, statistical sampling, computer simulation, cryptography, and other areas where a random number is useful in producing an unpredictable result.Note that, in general, where unpredictability is paramount—such as in security applications— hardware generators are generally preferred, where feasible, over pseudo-random algorithms.Random number generators are very useful in developing Monte Carlo method simulations as debugging is facilitated by the ability to run the same sequence of random numbers again by starting from the same random seed. They are also used in cryptography so long as the seed is secret. Sender and receiver can generate the same set of numbers automatically to use as keys.

The generation of pseudo-random numbers is an important and common task in computer programming. While cryptography and certain numerical algorithms require a very high degree of apparent randomness, many other operations only need a modest amount of unpredictability. Some simple examples might be presenting a user with a "Random Quote of the Day", or determining which way a computer-controlled adversary might move in a computer game. Weaker forms of randomness are also closely associated with hash algorithms and in creating amortized searching and sorting algorithms.

Some applications which appear at first sight to be suitable for randomization are in fact not quite so simple. For instance, a system that 'randomly' selects music tracks for a background music system must only appear to be random; a true random system would have no restriction on the same item appearing two or three times in succession.

The best means of obtaining unpredictable random numbers is by measuring physical phenomena such as radioactive decay, thermal noise in semiconductors, sound samples taken in a noisy environment, and even digitised images of a lava lamp. However few computers (or users) have access to the kind of specialised hardware required for these sources, and must rely on other means of obtaining random data.

The term "practically strong randomness" is used here to represent randomness which isn't cryptographically strong by the usual definitions but which is as close to it as is practically possible.

A good general overview of what constitutes randomness, what sort of sources are useful (and not useful), and how to process the data from them, is given in RFC 1750. Further discussion on the nature of randomness, pseudorandom number generators (PRNG's), and cryptographic randomness is available from a number of sources. Unfortunately the advice presented by various authors is all too often ignored, resulting in insecure random number generators which produce encryption keys which are much, much easier to attack than the underlying cryptosystems they are used with. A particularly popular source of bad random numbers is the current time and process ID. This type of flawed generator, of which an example is shown in Figure 3.23, first gained widespread publicity in late 1995 when it was found that the encryption in Netscape browsers could be broken in around a minute due to the limited range of values provided by this source, leading to some spectacular headlines in the popular press. Because the values used to generate session keys could be established without too much difficulty, even non-crippled browsers with 128-bit session keys carried (at best) only 47 bits of entropy in their session keys.

```
a = mixbits(time.tv_usec);
b = mixbits(getpid() + time.tv_sec + (getppid() << 12);
seed = MD5(a, b);
nonce = MD5(seed++);
key = MD5(seed++);
```

Figure 3.24 The Netscape Generator

Shortly afterwards it was found that Kerberos V4, whose generator is shown in Figure 3.47, suffered from a similar weakness (in fact it was even worse than Netscape since it used random() instead of MD5 as its mixing function). At about the same time, it was announced that the MIT-MAGIC-COOKIE-1 key generation, which created a 56-bit value, effectively only had 256 seed values due to its use of rand(), as shown below:

```
key = rand() % 256: key = rand();
```

This flaw had in fact been discovered in January of that year but the announcement was delayed to allow vendors to fix the problem.

```
srandom( time.tv_usec ^ time.tv_sec ^ getpid() ^ \
gethostid() ^ counter++ );
key = random();
```

Figure 3.25 The Kerberos V4 generator

A variant of this generator was used in Sesame (which just used the output of rand() directly), the glibc resolver (which uses 16 bits of output), and no doubt in many other programs which require a quick source of "random" values. FireWall-1 doesn't even use rand() but instead uses a direct call to time() to generate the secret value for its S/Key authentication and regenerates it after 99 uses, making it a relatively simple task to recover the authentication secret and compromise the firewall. In some cases the use of a linear congruential generator (LCRNG, which is the type usually used in programming language libraries) can interact with the cryptosystem it is used with, for example using an LCRNG or truncated LCRNG with DSA makes it possible to recover the signer's secret key after seeing only three signatures.

3.14.4 Requirements and Limitations of the Generator

There are several special requirements and limitations which affect the design of a practically strong random number generator. The main requirement (and also limitation) imposed upon the generator is that it can't rely on only one source, or on a small number of sources, for its random data. For example even if it were possible to assume that a system has some sort of sound input device, the signal obtained from it is often not random at all, but heavily influenced by crosstalk with other system components or predictable in nature (one test with a cheap 8-bit sound card in a PC produced only a single changing bit which toggled in a fairly predictable manner).

Other traps abound. In the absence of a facility for timing keystrokes, mouse activity is often used as a source of randomness. However some Windows mouse drivers have a "snap to" capability which positions the mouse pointer over the default button in a dialog box or window. Networked applications may transmit the client's mouse events to a server, revealing information about mouse movements and clicks. Some operating systems will collapse multiple mouse events into a single meta-event to cut down on network traffic or handling overhead, reducing the input from wiggle-the-mouse randomness gathering to a single mouse move event. In addition if the process is running on an unattended server, there may be no keyboard or mouse activity at all.

In order to avoid this dependency on a particular piece of hardware or operating system (or correct implementation of the data-gathering code), the generator should rely on as many inputs as possible. This is expanded on in "Polling for Randomness" below.

The generator should also have several other properties:

- It should be resistant to analysis of its input data. An attacker who recovers or is aware of a portion of the input to the generator should be unable to use this information to recover the generator's state.
- As an extension of the above, it should also be resistant to manipulation of the input data, so that an attacker able to feed chosen input to the generator should be unable to influence its state in any predictable manner. An example of a generator which lacked this property was the one used in early versions of the BSAFE library, which could end up containing a very low amount of entropy if fed many small data blocks such as user keystroke information.
- It should be resistant to analysis of its output data. If an attacker recovers a portion of the generator's output, they should be unable to recover any other generator state information from this. For example recovering generator output such as a session key or PKCS #1 padding for RSA keys should not allow any of the generator

state to be recovered.

- It should take steps to protect its internal state to ensure that it can't be recovered through techniques such as scanning the system swap file for a large block of random data.
- The implementation of the generator should make explicit any actions such as mixing the pool or extracting data in order to allow the conformance of the code to the generator design to be easily checked. This is particularly problematic in the code used to implement the PGP 2.x random number pool, which (for example) relies on the fact that a pool index value is initially set to point past the end of the pool so that on the first attempt to read data from it the available byte count will evaluate to zero bytes, resulting in no data being copied out and the code dropping through to the pool mixing function.
- All possible steps should be taken to ensure that the generator state information never leaks to the outside world. Any leakage of internal state which would allow an attacker to predict further generator output should be regarded as a catastrophic failure of the generator. An example of a generator which fails to meet this requirement is the Netscape one presented earlier, which reveals the hash of its internal state when it is used to generate the nonce used during the SSL handshake. It then increments the state value (typically changing a single bit of data) and hashes it again to produce the premaster secret from which all cryptovariables are generated. Although there are (currently) no known attacks on this, it's a rather unsound practice to reveal generator state information to the world in this manner. Since an attack capable of producing MD5 preimages would allow the premaster secret (and by extension all cryptovariables) to be recovered for the SSL handshake, the generator may also be vulnerable to a related-key attack. This flaw is found in the code surrounding several other generators as well, with further details given in the text which covers the individual generators.

3.14.5 Existing Generator Designs and Problems

A typical generator described here consists of two parts, a randomness pool and associated mixing function (the generator itself), and a polling mechanism to gather randomness from the system and add it to the pool (the randomness accumulator). These two parts represent two very distinct components of the overall generator, with the accumulator being used to continually inject random data into the generator, and the generator being used to "stretch" this random data via some form of PRNG as shown in Figure 3.48.

However the PRNG functionality is only needed in some cases. Consider a typical case in which the generator is required to produce a single quantum of random data, for example to encrypt a piece of outgoing email or to establish an SSL shared secret. Even if the transformation function being used in the generator is a completely reversible one such as a (hypothetical) perfect compressor, there is no loss of security because everything nonrandom and predictable is discarded and only the unpredictable material remains as the generator output. Only when large amounts of data are drawn from the system does the "accumulator" functionality give way to the "generator" functionality, at which point a transformation with certain special cryptographic qualities is required (although, in the absence of a perfect compressor, it doesn't hurt to have these present anyway).

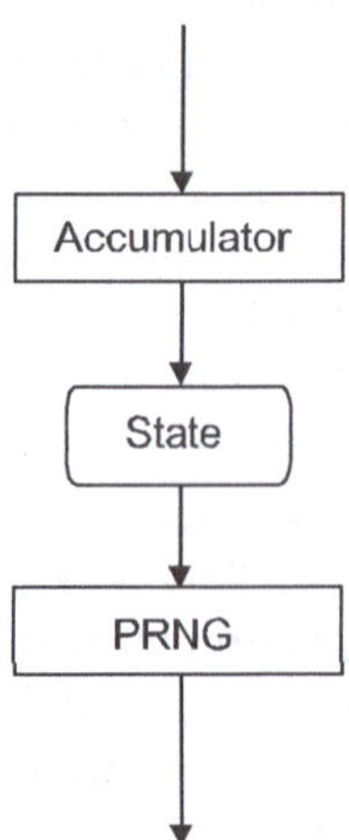

Figure 3.26 Generalised entropy accumulator and PRNG model

Mixing function have to be carefully designed to meet the requirements given in the previous section.

Before discussing the mixing function used by the generator, it might be useful to examine the types of functions which are used by other generators. The following descriptions omit some minor implementation details for simplicity, such as the fact that most generators mix in low-value data such as the time and process ID on the assumption that every little bit helps, will opportunistically use sources such as /dev/random where available (typically this is restricted to Linux and some x86 BSD's), and may store some state on disk for later reuse, a feature first popularised in PGP 2.x. In addition most of the generators have changed slightly over time, most commonly by moving from MD5 to SHA-1 or sometimes to an even more conservative function such as RIPEMD-160, the following descriptions use the most generic form of the generator in order to avoid having to devote several pages to each generator's nuances.

(1) The Applied Cryptography Generator

One of the simplest generators, shown in Figure 3.27, is presented in Applied Cryptography, and consists of a hash function such as MD5 combined with a counter value to create a pseudorandom byte stream generator running in counter mode with a 16-byte output. This generator is very similar to the one used by Netscape and the RSAREF generator, and there may have been cross-pollination between the designs (the Netscape generator is practically identical to the RSAREF one, so it may have been inspired by that).

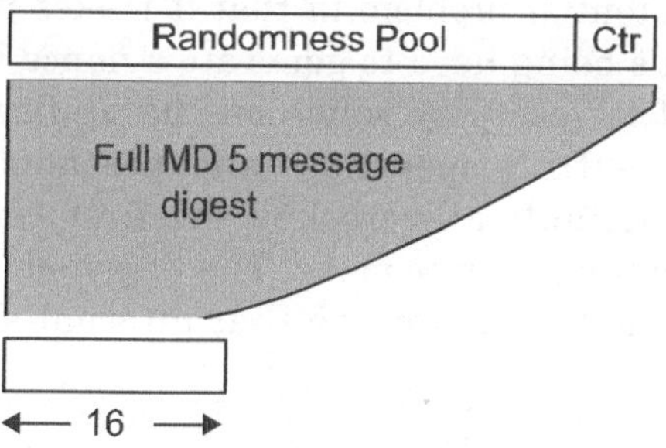

Figure 3.27 The Applied Cryptography generator

This generator uses the full message digest function rather than just the compression function as most other generators do. It therefore relies on the strength of the underlying hash function for security, and would be susceptible to a related-key attack since only one or two bits of input are changed for every block of output produced. A successful attack on this generator would also compromise the Netscape generator, which uses a similar technique and which reveals the generator's previous output to an attacker. In contrast the generator used in newer version of BSAFE avoids this problem by adding a value of the same size as the generator state to ensure that a large portion of the state changes on each iteration (specifically, the update process sets staten+1 = staten + (constant ? n) where the constant value is a fixed bit string initialised at startup).

(2) The ANSI X9.17 Generator

The X9.17 generator [36] in its most common form is a pure PRNG, relying on the triple DES encryption operation for its strength, as shown in Figure 3.28. The encryption step Enc1 ensures that the timestamp is spread over 64 bits and avoids the threat of a chosen-timestamp attack (for example setting it to all-zero or all-one bits), the Enc2 step acts as a one-way function for the generated encryption key, and the Enc3 step acts as a one-way function for the seed value/internal state.

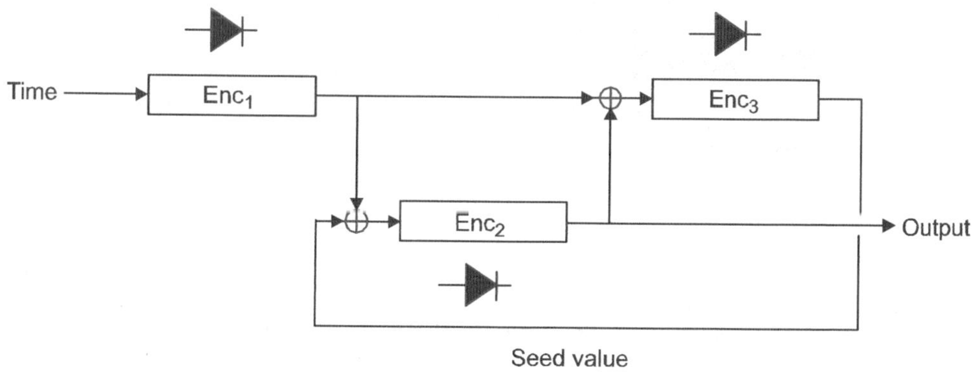

Figure 3.28 The ANSI X9.17 PRNG

This generator has a potential problem in that it makes its internal state available to an attacker (for example if it's being used to generate a nonce which will be communicated in the clear), so that all of its security relies on the ability of the user to protect the value used to key the triple DES operation, and the hope that they'll remember to change it from the factory-default all-zero key the first time they use the device it's contained in. This is a risky assumption to make. The Capstone and cryptlib generatorsinsert an extra mixing step at the output to ensure that internal state will never be visible to an attacker.

(3) The PGP 2.x Generator

PGP 2.x uses a slightly different method which involves "encrypting" the contents of an entropy pool with the MD5 compression function used as a CFB-mode stream cipher in a so-called "message digest cipher" configuration. The key consists of the previous state of the pool, with the data from the start of the pool being used as the 64-byte input to the compression function. The pool itself is 384 bytes long, although other programs such as CryptDisk and Curve Encrypt for the Macintosh, which also use the PGP random pool management code, extend this to 512 bytes.

The data being encrypted is the 16-byte initialisation vector (IV) which is XORd with the data at the current pool position (in fact there is no need to use CFB mode, the generator could just as easily use CBC as there is no need for the "encryption" to be reversible). This process carries 128 bits of state (the IV) from one block to another. The initial IV is taken from the end of the pool, and mixing proceeds until the entire pool has been processed as shown in Figure 3.29. Once the pool contents have been mixed, the first 64 bytes are extracted to form the key for the next round of mixing, and the remainder of the pool is available for use by PGP.

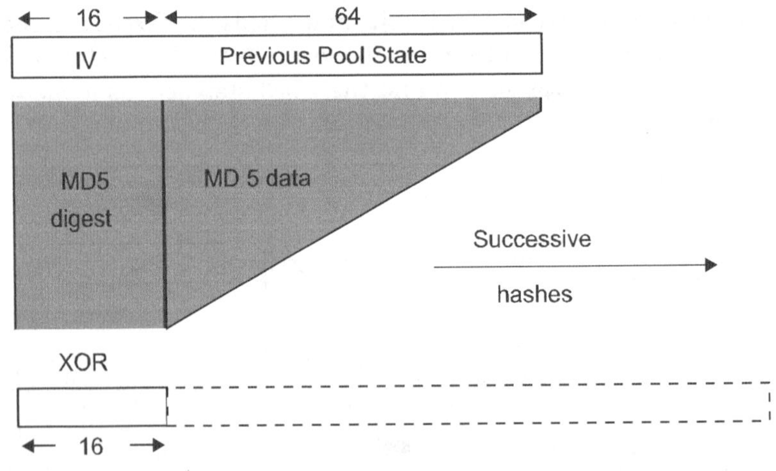

Figure 3.29 The PGP 2.x generator

This generator exhibits something which will be termed the startup problem, in which processed data at the start of the pool (in other words the generator output) depends only on the initial data mixed in. This means that data generated from or at the start of the pool is based on less entropy than data arising from further back in the pool, which will be affected by chaining of data from the start of the pool. This problem also affects a number of other generators, particularly ones such as the SSLeay/OpenSSL one which mix their data in very small, discrete blocks rather than trying to apply as much pool state as possible to each mixed data quantum. Because of this problem, newer versions of PGP and PGP-inspired software perform a second pass over the pool for extra security and to ensure that data from the end of the pool has a chance to affect the start of the pool.

The pool management code allows random data to be read directly out of the pool with no postprocessing, and relies for its security on the fact that the previous pool contents, which are being used as the "key" for the MD5 cipher, cannot be recovered. This problem is further exacerbated by the generator's startup problem. Direct access to the pool in this manner is rather dangerous since the slightest coding error could lead to a catastrophic failure in which the pool data is leaked to outsiders (later versions of the code were changed to fix this problem).

A problem with the implementation itself, which has been mentioned previously, is that the correct functioning of the PGP 2.x random number management code is not immediately obvious, making it difficult to spot problems of this nature (at one point the generator was redesigned and the code simplified because the developers could no longer understand the code they had been working with).

This has lead to problems with the code such as the notorious xorbytes bug in which a two-line function isolated from the rest of the code accidentally used a straight assignment operator in place of an xor-and-assign operator as shown in Figure 3.30. As a result, new data which was added overwrote existing data rather than being mixed into it through the XOR operation, resulting in no real increase in entropy over time, and possibly even a decrease if low-entropy data was added after high-entropy data had been added.

```
while (len—)
*dest++ = *src++;
while (len—)
*dest++ ^= *src++;
```

Figure 3.30 The xorbytes bug (left) and corrected version (right)

PGP also preserves some randomness state between invocations of the program by storing a nonce on disk which is en/decrypted with a user-supplied key and injected into the randomness pool. This is a variation of method used by the ANSI X9.17 generator which utilises a user-supplied key and a timestamp (as opposed to PGP's preserved state).

(4) The PGP 5.x Generator

PGP 5.x uses a slightly different update/mixing function which adds an extra layer of complexity to the basic PGP 2.x system. This retains the basic model used in PGP 2.x (with a key external to the pool being used to mix the pool itself), but changes the hash function from MD5 to SHA-1, the encryption mode from CFB to CBC, and adds feedback between the pool and the SHA-1 key data. The major innovation in this generator is that the added data is mixed in at a much earlier stage than in the PGP 2.x generator, being added directly to the key (where it immediately affects any further SHA-1-based mixing) rather than to the pool. The feedback of data from the pool to the key ensures that any sensitive material (such as a user passphrase) which is added isn't left lying in the key buffer in plaintext form.

In the generator pseudocode shown in Figure 3.53 the arrays are assumed to be arrays of bytes. Where a '32' suffix is added to the name, it indicates that the array is treated as an array of 32-bit words with index values appropriately scaled. In addition the index values wrap back to the start of the arrays when they reach the end. Because of the complexity of the update process, it's not possible to represent it diagrammatically as with the other generators so Figure 3.31 illustrates it as pseudocode.

```
pool[ 640 ], poolPos = 0;
key[ 64 ], keyPos = 0;
addByte( byte )
{
/* Update the key */
key[ keyPos++ ] ^= byte;
if( another 32-bit word accumulated )
key32[ keyPos ] ^= pool32[ poolPos ];
/* Update the pool */
if( about 16 bits added to key )
{
164 Existing Generator Designs and Problems
/* Encrypt and perform IV-style block chaining */
hash( pool[ poolPos ], key );
pool[ next 16 bytes ] ^= pool[ current 16 bytes ];
}
}
```

Figure 3.31 The PGP 5.x Generator

Once enough new data has been added to the key, the resulting key is used to "encrypt" the pool using SHA-1, ensuring that the pool data which was fed back to mask the newly-added keying material is destroyed (the code actually uses a digital differential analyser (DDA) to determine when enough new data has been added to make a pool mixing operation necessary, in the same way that the original DDA was used to determine when to perform an X or Y pixel increment when drawing a line on a graphics device). In this way the entire pool is encrypted with a key which changes slightly for each block rather than a constant key, and the encryption takes place incrementally instead of the using the monolithic update technique preferred by other generators.

A second feature added by PGP 5.x is that the pool contents are not fed directly to the output but are first folded in half (a 20-byte SHA-1 output block has the high and low halves XORd together to produce a 10-byte result) and is then postprocessed by an X9.17 generator (using Cast-128, PGP 5.x's default cipher, instead of triple DES), thus ensuring that an attacker can never obtain information about the internal generator state if they can recover its output data. Since the X9.17 generator provides a 1:1 mapping of input to output, it can never reduce the entropy of its input, and it provides an extra level of security by acting as a one-way filter on the output of the previous generator section. In addition a separate X9.17 generator is used to generate non-cryptographically-strong random data for operations such as generating the public values used in discrete-log public keys, again helping ensure that state information from the real generator isn't leaked to an attacker. In terms of good conservative designs, this generator is probably at the same level as the Capstone generator.

(5) The SSLeay/OpenSSL Generator

The SSLeay/OpenSSL generator uses two completely separate functions, one for mixing in entropy and the other for the PRNG. Unlike most of the other generators, it performs no real polling of entropy sources but relies almost entirely on data supplied by the user, a dangerous assumption.

The first portion of the generator is the entropy mixing function shown in Figure 3.32, which hashes a 20-byte hash value (initially set to all zeros) and successive 20-byte blocks of a 1KB randomness pool and user supplied data to produce 20 bytes of output, which both become the next 20-byte hash value and are XORd back into the pool. Although each block of pool data is only affected by an equivalent-sized block of input data, the use of the hash state value means that some state information is carried across from previous blocks, although it would probably be preferable to hash more than a single 20-byte block to ensure that as much of the input as possible affects each output block. In particular, the generator suffers from an extreme case of the startup problem since the initial pool blocks are only affected by the initial input data blocks. In the case when the generator is first initialised and the pool contains all zero bytes the first 20 bytes of output is simply an SHA-1 hash of the first 20 bytes of user-supplied data.

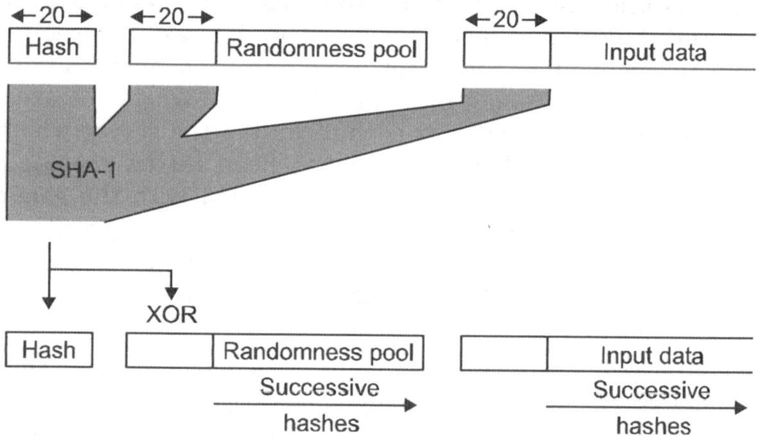

Figure 3.32 The SSLeay/OpenSSL generator's mixing function

The second portion of the generator is the PRNG function shown in Figure 3.33, which both mixes the pool and produces the generator's output. This works by hashing the second 10 bytes of the hash state value (the first 8 bytes remain constant and aren't used) and successive 1...10-byte blocks of the pool (the amount hashed depends on the number of output bytes requested). The first 10 bytes of the hash result are XORd back into the pool, and the remaining 10 bytes are provided as the generator's output and also reused as the new hash state. Again, apart from the 10-byte chaining value, all data blocks are completely independent.

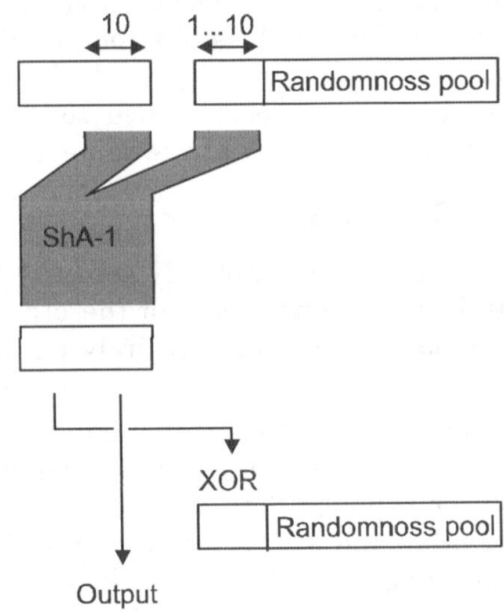

Figure 3.33 The SSLeay/OpenSSL generator's PRNG function

As used in SSLeay/OpenSSL, this generator shares with the ssh generator the flaw that it's possible for an attacker to suck infinite amounts of state information out of it by repeatedly connecting to the server, since it's used to create the 28-byte nonce (the SSL cookie/session ID) which is sent in the server hello.

In addition to this problem, the output also reveals the hash state (but not the pool state). The use on the client side is even more unsound, since it's used to first generate the client cookie which is sent in the client hello and then immediately afterwards to generate the premaster secret from which all other cryptovariables are derived. What makes this practice even more dangerous is that, unlike the server which has probably been running for some time so that the pool has been mixed repeatedly, clients are typically shut down and restarted as required. Combined with the generator's startup problem and (in older versions) the lack of entropy checking and possible lack of seeding described in section 5.1, the first client hello sent by the client will reveal the generator seed data (or lack thereof) and hash state, and the premaster secret follows from this information.

This problem of revealing generator state information also occurs in the Netscape code, the SSLRef code which served as a reference implementation for SSL 3.0 (the cookie/session ID random data is actually initialised twice, the second initialisation overwriting the first one), and no doubt in any a number of other SSL implementations. Part of the blame for this problem lies in the fact that both the original SSL specification and later the TLS specification specify that the cookies should be "generated by a secure random number generator" even though there's no need for this, and it can in fact be dangerously misleading.

Another problem, shared with the PGP generator, is the almost incomprehensible nature of the code which implements it, making it very difficult to analyse. For example the generator contained a design flaw which resulted in it only feeding a small amount of random pool data (one to ten bytes) into the PRNG function, but this wasn't discovered and corrected until July 2001. This problem, combined with the fact that the PRNG hash state is made available as the generator output as described above, would allow an attacker to recover the random pool contents by making repeated 1-byte requests to the generator, which would respond with a hash of the (known) state and successive bytes of the pool.

(6) The CryptoAPI Generator

Like the SSLeay/OpenSSL generator, the CryptoAPI generator uses separate functions for mixing in entropy and for the PRNG. The entropy-mixing stage hashes polled data using SHA-1, and the PRNG stage uses the SHA-1 output to key an RC4 stream cipher, as shown in Figure 3.34. The polled data consists of the traditional time and process ID and a few relatively poor additional sources such as the system's current memory and disk usage, the static data consists of the previous hash output recycled for further use. Unlike PGP, the CryptoAPI preserved state doesn't appear to be protected by a user password.

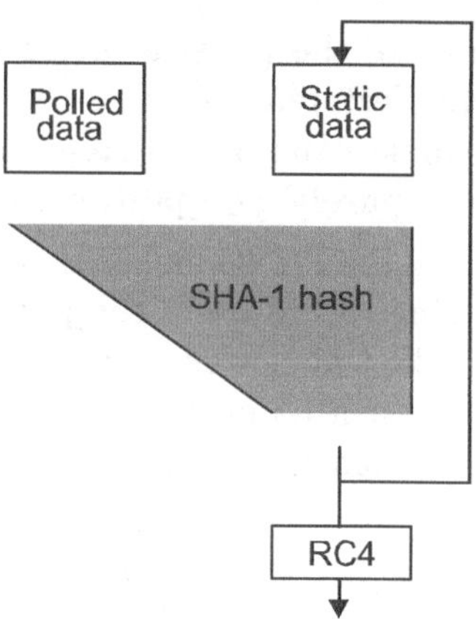

Figure 3.34 The CryptoAPI generator

This generator is, at best, adequate. The static data isn't password-protected like the PGP seed and the polled data doesn't provide much entropy, particularly if the generator is seeded at system startup, which is typically the case as Windows system components make use of CryptoAPI during the boot phase. In addition no steps appear to be taken to mitigate problems such as the fact the RC4 exhibits correlations between its key and the initial bytes of its output as well as having statistical weaknesses, resulting in the generator leaking part of its internal state in the first few bytes of PRNG output or producing some predictable output during its operation.

(7) The Intel Generator

The generator which is available with some chipsets used with the Intel Pentium III CPU samples thermal noise in resistors and, after some internal processing, feeds it into the

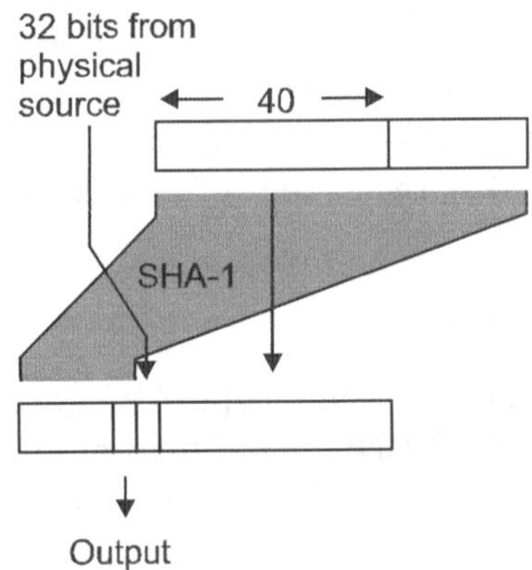

Figure 3.35 The Intel Pentium III generator

PRNG shown in Figure 3.35. Each time the PRNG is stepped, another 32 bits of sampled noise are injected into the PRNG state, ensuring that further entropy is continuously added to the generator as it runs. Details of the physical noise source are given elsewhere. This generator shares with the Capstone/Fortezza generator the use of a physical source and SHA-1-based postprocessor, however it makes the SHA-1 step part of the PRNG rather than using a separate PRNG and using SHA-1 purely as a postprocessing function.

The use of a single source to feed the PRNG makes this generator slightly less conservative than the Capstone/Fortezza one, since a failure of the physical source at some point after it has passed the FIPS 140 tests applied at power-up would result in the generator eternally recycling its internal state (or at least a truncated portion thereof). This might occur if the generator functions correctly when cold (immediately after power-up, when the FIPS 140 tests are applied) but fails in some way once the system warms up.

The existing Pentium III unique serial number capability could be extended to provide a backup source of input to the PRNG by storing with each processor a unique value (which, unlike the processor ID, can't be read externally) which is used to drive some form of generator equivalent to the X9.17-like generator used in the Capstone/Fortezza generator, supplementing the existing physical randomness source. In the simplest case one or more linear feedback shift registers (LFSR's) driven from the secret value would 1 As with literature analysis, it's possible that some of the meaning being read into this would surprise the original authors of the work. Unfortunately the rationale for the Capstone/Fortezza generator design has never been made public.

QUESTIONS

1. General

1. What is a Block Cipher?
2. What is an Iterated Block Cipher?
3. What is a Feistel Cipher?
4. What is Exhaustive Key Search?
5. What is Differential Cryptanalysis?
6. What is Linear Cryptanalysis?
7. What is a Weak Key for a Block Cipher?
8. What are Algebraic Attacks?
9. How Can Data Compression be Used With Encryption?
10. At What Point Does an Attack Become Practical?

2. DES

1. What is DES?
2. Has DES been Broken?
3. How Does One Use DES Securely?
4. Should One Test for Weak Keys in DES?
5. Can DES be Exported from the United States?
6. What are the Alternatives to DES?
7. Is DES a Group?
8. What is DES with Independent Subkeys?
9. What is Triple-DES?
10. How does One Use Triple-DES in CBC Mode?
11. What are G-DES, DESX?

3. Other Block Ciphers

1. What is RC2?
2. What is RC5?
3. What is IDEA?
4. What is SAFER? What
5. What is FEAL?
6. What is Skipjack?
7. What is Blowfish?

REFERENCES

1. C.E. Shannon, Communication theory of secrecy systems, Bell System Tech. J. 28 (1949) 656-715.
2. Handbook of Applied Cryptography by Alfred J. Menezes, Paul C. van Oorschot, Scott A. Vanstone. Fifth Printing (August 2001) page 251.
3. M. Luby and C. Rackoff. "How to Construct Pseudorandom Permutations and Pseudorandom Functions." In SIAM J. Comput., vol. 17, 1988, pp. 373-386.
4. Jacques Patarin, Luby-Rackoff: 7 Rounds Are Enough for Security, Lecture Notes in Computer Science, Volume 2729, Oct 2003, Pages 513 - 529
5. Biham, E. and Dunkelman, O. and Keller, N. "A New Attack on 6-Round IDEA".
6. L. Bernaille, R. Teixeira, and K. Salamatian, "Early Application Identification", Proceedings of The 2nd ADETTI/ISCTE CoNEXT Conference, Portugal, 2006.
7. M. Crotti, F. Gringoli, P. Pelosato, L. Salgarelli, "A statistical approach to IP-level classification of network traffic", IEEE ICC 2006, 11-15 Jun. 2006.
8. T. Kohno, A. Broido, K. C. Claffy. "Remote physical device fingerprinting", in IEEE Symposium on Security and Privacy, pp. 211–225. IEEE Computer Society, 2005.
9. A. Hintz, "Fingerprinting Websites Using Traffic Analysis", Privacy Enhancing Technologies, PET 2002, S. Francisco, USA, April 2002
10. G. D. Bissias, M. Liberatore, D. Jensen, B. N. Levine, "Privacy Vulnerabilities in Encrypted HTTP Streams", PET 2005, Cavtat, Croatia, May 30-June 1, 2005.
11. L. Bernaille, R. Teixeira, "Early Recognition of Encrypted Application" Proc. PAM, April 2007.
12. D. X. Song, D. Wagner, X. Tian, "Timing analysis of keystrokes and timing attacks on SSH", 10th USENIX Security Symposium, 2001.
13. B. Canvel, A. Hiltgen, S.Vaudenay, M. Vuagnoux, "Password Interception in a SSL/TLS Channel", CRYPTO2003, Aug 2003, Santa Barbara, USA
14. Y. Zhu, X. Fu, B. Graham, R. Bettati, W. Zhao "On Flow Correlation Attacks and Countermeasures in Mix Networks", PET 2004, May 2004
15. X.Wang, S. Chen, S. Jajodia, "Tracking anonymous peer-to-peer VoIP calls on the internet", ACM Conf. on Computer and Communications Security, November 2005.
16. G. Danezis, R. Dingledine, N. Mathewson, "Mixminion: Design of a Type III Anonymous Remailer Protocol", 2003 IEEE Symp. on Security and Privacy, May 2003.

Random Number Generator

[1] "Cryptographic Randomness from Air Turbulence in Disk Drives", Don Davis, Ross Ihaka, and Philip Fenstermacher, Proceedings of Crypto '94, Springer-Verlag Lecture Notes in Computer Science, No.839, 1994.

[2] "Truly Random Numbers", Colin Plumb, Dr.Dobbs Journal, November 1994, p.113.

[3] "PGP Source Code and Internals", Philip Zimmermann, MIT Press, 1995.

[4] "Random noise from disk drives", Rich Salz, posting to cypherpunks mailing list, message-ID 9601230431.AA06742@sulphur.osf.org, 22 January 1996.

[5] "A Practical Secure Physical Random Bit Generator", Markus Jacobsson, Elizabeth Shriver, Bruce Hillyer, and Ari Juels, 5th ACM Conference on Computer and Communications Security, 1998,p.103.

[6] "IBM-PC flawless true random number generator", Nico de Vries, posting to sci.crypt newsgroup, message-ID 2670@accucx.cc.ruu.nl, 18 June 1992.

[7] "My favourite random-numbers-in-software package (unix)", Matt Blaze, posting to cypherpunks mailing list, message-ID 199509301946.PAA15565@crypto.com, 30 September 1995.

[8] "Using and Creating Cryptographic-Quality Random Numbers", John Callas, http://www.merrymeet.com/jon/usingrandom.html, 3 June 1996.

[9] "Suggestions for random number generation in software", Tim Matthews, RSA Data Security Engineering Report, 15 December 1995 (reprinted in RSA Laboratories' Bulletin No.1, 22 January 1996).

[10] "Applied Cryptography (Second Edition)", Bruce Schneier, John Wiley and Sons, 1996.

[11] "Cryptographic Random Numbers", IEEE P1363 Working Draft, Appendix G, 6 February 1997.

[12] "Zufallstreffer", Klaus Schmeh and Dr.Hubert Uebelacker, c't, No.14, 1997, p.220. 190 References

[13] "Randomness Recommendations for Security", Donald Eastlake, Stephen Crocker, and Jeffrey Schiller, RFC 1750, December 1994.

[14] "The Art of Computer Programming: Volume 2, Seminumerical Algorithms", Donald Knuth, Addison-Wesley, 1981.

[15] "Handbook of Applied Cryptography", Alfred Menezes, Paul van Oorschot, and Scott Vanstone, CRC Press, 1996.

[16] "Foundations of Cryptography — Fragments of a Book", Oded Goldreich, February 1995, http://theory.lcs.mit.edu/~oded/frag.html.

[17] "Netscape's Internet Software Contains Flaw That Jeopardizes Security of Data", Jared Sandberg, The Wall Street Journal, 18 September 1995.

[18] "Randomness and the Netscape Browser", Ian Goldberg and David Wagner, Dr.Dobbs Journal, January 1996.

[19] "Breakable session keys in Kerberos v4", Nelson Minar, posting to the cypherpunks mailing list, message-ID 199602200828.BAA21074@nelson.santafe.edu, 20 February 1996.

[20] "X Authentication Vulnerability", CERT Vendor-Initiated Bulletin VB-95:08, 2 November 1995.

[21] "glibc resolver weakness", antirez, posting to the bugtraq mailing list, message-ID 20000503034046.A9579@nagash.marmoc.net, 3 May 2000.

[22] "A Stateful Inspection of FireWall-1", Thomas Lopatic, John McDonald, and Dug Song, posting to the bugtraq mailing list, message-ID 20000816140955.5CD7E10865E@naughty.monkey.org, 16 August 2000.

[23] "'Pseudo-random' Number Generation Within Cryptographic Algorithms: The DDS [sic] Case", Mihir Bellare, Shafi Goldwasser, and Daniele Micciancio, Proceedings of Crypto'97, Springer-Verlag Lecture Notes in Computer Science No.1294, August 1997, p.276.

[24] "Murphy's law and computer security", Wietse Venema, Proceedings of the 6th Usenix Security Symposium, July 1996, p.187.

[25] "Internet Gambling Software Flaw Discovered by Reliable Software Technologies Software Security Group", Reliable Software Technologies, 1 September 1999, http://www.rstcorp.com/news/gambling.html.

[26] "A sure bet: Internet gambling is loaded with risks", Ann Kellan, CNN news story, 3 September 1999.

[27] "Re: New standart for encryption software", Albert P.Belle Isle, posting to the sci.crypt newsgroup, message-ID v8e3asks612a3iu8pmr5677uhfes7gupun@4ax.com, 9 February 2000.

[28] "Key Generation Security Flaw in PGP 5.0", Germano Caronni, posting to the coderpunks mailing list, message-ID 20000523141323.A28431@olymp.org, 23 May 2000.

[29] Bodo Möller, private communications, 31 May 2000.

[30] "Yarrow-160: Notes on the Design and Analysis of the Yarrow Cryptographic Pseudorandom Number Generator", John Kelsey, Bruce Schneier, and Niels Ferguson, Proceedings of the Sixth Annual Workshop on Selected Areas in Cryptography (SAC'99), Springer-Verlag (to appear), August 1999.

[31] "Proper Initialisation for the BSAFE Random Number Generator", Robert Baldwin, RSA Laboratories' Bulletin No.3, 25 January 1996.

[32] "Security Requirements for Cryptographic Modules", National Institute of Standards and Technology, 11 January 1994.

[33] "Cryptanalytic Attacks on Pseudorandom Number Generators", John Kelsey, Bruce Schneier, David Wagner, and Chris Hall, Proceedings of the 5th Fast Software Encryption Workshop (FSE 98), Springer-Verlag Lecture Notes in Computer Science No.1372, March 1998, p.168.

[34] "RSAREF Cryptographic Library, Version 1.0", RSA Laboratories, February 1992. Random Number Generation 191.

[35] "Preliminary Analysis of the BSAFE 3.x Pseudorandom Number Generators", Robert Baldwin, RSA Laboratories' Bulletin No.8, 3 September 1998.

[36] "American National Standard for Financial Institution Key Management (Wholesale)", American Bankers Association, 1985.

[37] "SFS — Secure FileSystem", Peter Gutmann, http://www.cs.auckland.ac.nz/- ~pgut001/sfs.html.

[38] Changes.doc, PGP 2.6.1 documentation, 1994.

[39] /dev/random driver source code (random.c), Theodore T'so, 24 April 1996.

[40] "SSH — Secure Login Connections over the Internet", Tatu Ylönen, Proceedings of the 6th Usenix Security Symposium, July 1996, p.37.

[41] "The SSL Protocol", Alan Freier, Philip Karlton, and Paul Kocher, Netscape Communications Corporation, March 1996.

[42] "RFC 2246, The TLS Protocol, Version 1.0", Tim Dierks and Christopher Allen, January 1999.

[43] "OpenSSL Security Advisory: PRNG weakness in versions up to 0.9.6a", Bodo Moeller, posting to the bugtraq mailing list, 10 July 2001, message-ID 20010710130317.A1949@openssl.org.

[44] "Non-biased pseudo random number generator", Matthew Thomlinson, Daniel Simon, and Bennet Yee, US Patent No.5,778, 069, 7 July 1998.

[45] "A Class of Weak Keys in the RC4 Stream Cipher", Andrew Roos, posting to sci.crypt.research newsgroup, 22 September 1995, message-ID 43vf2e$sr8@net.auckland.ac.nz.

[46] "Re: is RC4 weak for the first few K?", Paul Kocher, posting to sci.crypt newsgroup, 30 October 1996, message-ID pckE035up.4y1@netcom.com.

[47] "Disclosures of Weaknesses in RC4 (Re: RC4 Weaknesses?)", Ian Farquhar, posting to sci.crypt newsgroup, 26 November 1996, message-ID 329A242A.41C6@sydney.sgi.com.

[48] "Linear Statistical Weakness of Alleged RC4 Keystream Generator", Jovan Golic, Proceedings of Eurocrypt '97, Springer-Verlag Lecture Notes in Computer Science No.1233, May 1997, p.226.

[49] "Statistical Analysis of the Alleged RC4 Keystream Generator", Scott Fluhrer and David McGrew, Proceedings of the 7th Fast Software Encryption Workshop (FSE 2000), Springer-Verlag Lecture Notes in Computer Science No.1978, April 2000, p.19.

[50] "A Practical Attack on Broadcast RC4", Itsik Mantin and Adi Shamir, Proceedings of the 8th Fast Software Encryption Workshop (FSE 2001., to appear.

[51] "CAPSTONE (MYK-80) Specifications", R21 Informal Technical Report R21-TECH-30-95, National Security Agency, 14 August 1995.

[52] "Intel 82802 Firmware Hub: Random Number Generator Programmer's Reference Manual", Intel Corporation, December 1999.

[53] "The Intel Random Number Generator", Benjamin Jun and Paul Kocher, Cryptography Research Inc white paper, 22 April 1999.

[54] "Formula 1 Technology", Nigel McKnight, Hazelton Publishing, 1998.

[55] "Statistical Testing of Random Number Generators", Juan Soto, Proceedings of the 22nd National Information Systems Security Conference (formerly the National Computer Security Conferengce), October 1999, CDROM distribution.

[56] "Transaction Processing: Concepts and Techniques" Jim Gray and Andreas Reuter, Morgan Kaufmann, 1993.

[57] "Atomic Transactions", Nancy Lynch, Michael Merritt, William Weihl, and Alan Fekete, Morgan Kaufmann, 1994.

[58] "Principles of Transaction Processing", Philip Bernstein and Eric Newcomer, Morgan Kaufman

4

Groups, Ring and Field

4.1 INTRODUCTION TO GROUPS, RING AND FIELD

Everyone is familiar with the basic operations of arithmetic, addition, subtraction, multiplication, and division. In the "new math" introduced during the 1960s in the junior high grades of 7 through 9, students were exposed to some mathematical ideas which formerly were not part of the regular school curriculum. Elementary set theory was one of them. Another was abstract algebra, in which it was illustrated that operations resembling addition and multiplication could exist that had some of their properties.

One of the simplest examples is modular arithmetic.

Here is an addition table, and a multiplication table, for modulo-6 arithmetic:

+	0	1	2	3	4	5
0	0	1	2	3	4	5
1	1	2	3	4	5	0
2	2	3	4	5	0	1
3	3	4	5	0	1	2
4	4	5	0	1	2	3
5	5	0	1	2	3	4

*	0	1	2	3	4	5
0	0	0	0	0	0	0
1	0	1	2	3	4	5
2	0	2	4	0	2	4
3	0	3	0	3	0	3
4	0	4	2	0	4	2
5	0	5	4	3	2	1

and here are the same two tables, but for arithmetic modulo 4.

+	0	1	2	3	4
0	0	1	2	3	4
1	1	2	3	4	0
2	2	3	4	0	1
3	3	4	0	1	2
4	4	0	1	2	3

*	0	1	2	3	4
0	0	0	0	0	0
1	0	1	2	3	4
2	0	2	4	1	3
3	0	3	1	4	2
4	0	4	3	2	1

Because 5 is a prime number, but 6 is not, if you eliminate the row and column containing zero from the multiplication table, for arithmetic modulo 5, but not for arithmetic modulo 6, you get a table where no number is repeated twice in any row or column. This means that if a number is not zero, in modulo 5 arithmetic, one can define the operation of dividing by that number. In both forms of modular arithmetic, one could define subtraction as well as addition.

4.2 Abstract Algebra

Abstract algebra is the subject area of mathematics that studies algebraic structures, such as groups, rings, fields, modules, vector spaces, and algebras. The phrase abstract algebra was coined at the turn of the 20th century to distinguish this area from what was normally referred to as algebra, the study of the rules for manipulating formulas and algebraic expressions involving unknowns and real or complex numbers, often now called elementary algebra.

4.2.1 Groups in Abstract Algebra

A group is an algebraic structure consisting of a set together with an operation that combines any two of its elements to form a third element. To qualify as a group, the set and the operation must satisfy a few conditions called group axioms, namely closure, associativity, identity and invertibility. While these are familiar from many mathematical structures, such as number systems—for example, the integers endowed with the addition operation form a group—the formulation of the axioms is detached from the concrete nature of the group and its operation. This allows one to handle entities of very different mathematical origins in a flexible way, while retaining essential structural aspects of many objects in abstract algebra and beyond. The ubiquity of groups in numerous areas—both within and outside mathematics—makes them a central organizing principle of contemporary mathematics.

Groups share a fundamental kinship with the notion of symmetry. A symmetry group encodes symmetry features of a geometrical object: it consists of the set of transformations that leave the object unchanged, and the operation of combining two such transformations by performing one after the other. Such symmetry groups, particularly the continuous Lie groups, play an important role in many academic disciplines. Matrix groups, for example, can be used to understand fundamental physical laws underlying special relativity and symmetry phenomena in molecular chemistry.

The concept of a group arose from the study of polynomial equations, starting with Évariste Galois in the 1830s. After contributions from other fields such as number theory and geometry, the group notion was generalized and firmly established around 1870. Modern group theory—a very active mathematical discipline—studies groups in their own right.

A *group* is defined as: a set of *elements*, together with an operation performed on pairs of these elements such that:

* The operation, when given two elements of the set as arguments, always returns an element of the set as its result. It is thus fully defined, and closed over the set.
* One element of the set is an identity element. Thus, if we call our operation op, there is some element of the set e such that for any other element of the set x, e op $x = x$ op $e = x$.
* Every element of the set has an inverse element. If we take any element of the set p, there is another element q such that p op $q = q$ op $p = e$.
* The operation is associative. For any three elements of the set, (a op b) op c always equals a op (b op c).

A consequence of the third property is that there are no duplicate elements in any row or column of the operation table for a group. A consequence of the fourth property, together with the others, is that every finite group can be expressed as a set of permutations of n objects for some n, where the operation for the group is applying the second permutation to the elements of the first permutation.

There are many different kinds of finite groups, some with very complex structure. Most groups belong to families of groups with an infinite number of members. Thus, addition modulo 5 yields the cyclic group of order 5, and there are cyclic groups of every integer order starting with 2. However, there are 26 groups that don't belong to these infinite families, called sporadic simple groups.

Definition and Illustration

First example: the integers

One of the most familiar groups is the set of integers Z which consists of the numbers

..., -4, -3, -2, -1, 0, 1, 2, 3, 4, ...

The following properties of integer addition serve as a model for the abstract group axioms given in the definition below.

(1) For any two integers a and b, the sum $a + b$ is also an integer. In other words, the process of adding integers two at a time can never yield a result that is not an integer. This property is known as closure underaddition.

(2) For all integers a, b and c, $(a + b) + c = a + (b + c)$. Expressed in words, adding a to b first, and then adding the result to c gives the same final result as adding a to the sum of b and c, b property known as associativity.

(3) If a is any integer, then $0 + a = a + 0 = a$. Zero is called the identity element of addition because adding it to any integer returns the same integer.

(4) For every integer a, there is an integer b such that $a + b = b + a = 0$. The integer b is called the inverse element of the integer a and is denoted $-a$.

Definition

The integers, together with the operation "+", form a mathematical object belonging to a broad class sharing similar structural aspects. To appropriately understand these structures without dealing with every concrete case separately, the following abstract definition is developed to encompass the above example along with many others, one of which is the symmetry group detailed below.

A group is a set, G, together with an operation "•" that combines any two elements a and b to form another element denoted $a \bullet b$. The symbol "•" is a general placeholder for a concretely given operation, such as the addition above. To qualify as a group, the set and operation, $(G, \bullet)$, must satisfy four requirements known as the group axioms:

(1) Closure

For all a, b in G, the result of the operation $a \bullet b$ is also in $G.b$[›]

(2) Associativity

For all a, b and c in G, the equation $(a \bullet b) \bullet c = a \bullet (b \bullet c)$ holds.

(3) Identity element

There exists an element e in G, such that for all elements a in G, the equation $e \bullet a = a \bullet e = a$ holds.

(4) Inverse element

For each a in G, there exists an element b in G such that $a \bullet b = b \bullet a = e$, where e is the identity element. The order in which the group operation is carried out can be significant. In other words, the result of combining element a with element b need not yield the same result as combining element b with element a; the equation $a \bullet b = b \bullet$ a may not always be true. This equation does always hold in the group of integers under addition, because $a + b = b + a$ for any two integers (commutativity of addition). However, it does not always hold in the symmetry group below. Groups for which the equation $a \bullet b = b \bullet a$ always holds are called abelian (in honour of Niels Abel). Thus, the integer addition group is abelian, but the following symmetry group is not.

4.2.2 Rings in Abstract Algebra

Commonly a ring is defined as a set together with two binary operations (usually called addition and multiplication), where each operation combines two elements to form a third element. To qualify as a ring, the set together with its two operations must satisfy certain conditions; namely the set must be an abelian group under addition, a monoid under multiplication, a[›] such that multiplication distributes over addition. While these operations are familiar from many mathematical structures—such as number systems or the integers, for example—they are also very general in the sense that they take a broad variety of mathematical objects into account. This allows one to handle entities of very different mathematical origins in a flexible way, while retaining essential structural aspects of many objects in abstract algebra and beyond. The ubiquity of rings makes them a central organizing principle of contemporary mathematics. The branch of mathematics that studies rings is known as ring theory.

A ring is a set of elements with two operations, one of which is like addition, the other of which is like multiplication, which we will call add and mul. It has the following properties:

- The elements of the ring, together with the addition operation, form a group.
- Addition is commutative. That is, for any two elements of the set p and q, p add q = q *add* p. (The word Abelian is also used for "commutative", in honour of the mathematician Niels Henrik Abel.)
- The multiplication operation is associative.
- Multiplication distributes over addition: that is, for any three elements of the group a, b, and c, a mul (b add c) = (a mul b) add (a mul c).

Addition and multiplication modulo 5 and modulo 6 both yield rings. Matrix multiplication also leads to rings as well.

The most familiar example of a ring is the set of all integers, Z, consisting of the numbers..., -4, -3, -2, -1, 0, 1, 2, 3, 4, ... [1] together with the usual operations of addition and multiplication.

These operations satisfy the following properties:

(1) The integers form an Abelian group under addition; that is:

- Closure axiom for addition: Given two integers a and b, their sum, $a + b$ is also an integer.
- **Associativity of addition:** For any integers, a, b and c, $(a + b) + c = a + (b + c)$. So, adding b to a, and then adding c to this result, is the same as adding c to b, and then adding this result to a.
- **Existence of additive identity:** For any integer a, $a + 0 = 0 + a = a$. Zero is called the identity element of the integers because adding 0 to any integer (in any order) returns the same integer.
- **Existence of additive inverse:** For any integer a, there exists an integer denoted by $-a$ such that $a + (-a) = (-a) + a = 0$. The element, $-a$, is called the additive inverse of a because adding a to $-a$ (in any order) returns the identity.
- **Commutativity of addition:** For any two integers a and b, $a + b = b + a$. So the order in which you add two integers is irrelevant.

(2) The integers form a multiplicative monoid (a monoid under multiplication); that is:

- Closure axiom for multiplication: Given two integers a and b, their product, $a \cdot b$ is also an integer.
- Associativity of multiplication: Given any integers, a, b and c, $(a \cdot b) \cdot c = a \cdot (b \cdot c)$. So multiplying b with a, and then multiplying c to this result, is the same as multiplying c with b, and then multiplying a to this result.
- Existence of multiplicative identity: For any integer a, $a \cdot 1 = 1 \cdot a = a$. So multiplying any integer with 1 (in any order) gives back that integer. One is therefore called the multiplicative identity.

(3) Multiplication is distributive over addition : These two structures on the integers (addition and multiplication) are compatible in the sense that

- $a \cdot (b + c) = (a \cdot b) + (a \cdot c)$, and
- $(a + b) \cdot c = (a \cdot c) + (b \cdot c)$

for any three integers a, b and c.

An abelian group, also called a commutative group, is a group satisfying the requirement that the product of elements does not depend on their order (the axiom of commutativity). Abelian groups generalize the arithmetic of addition of integers; they are named after Niels Henrik Abel.

The concept of an abelian group is one of the first concepts encountered in undergraduate abstract algebra, with many other basic objects, such as a module and a vector space, being its refinements. The theory of abelian groups is generally simpler than that of their non-abelian counterparts, and finite abelian groups are very well understood.

An important difference between the additive and multiplicative properties enumerated above is that multiplicative inverses are not required to exist. For instance, there is no integer a such that $a \cdot 2 = 1$. This property distinguishes the integers from the rational numbers, which is also a set endowed with operations of addition and multiplication, satisfying all of the above properties but also the existence of a multiplicative inverse for each nonzero element: namely if a and b are nonzero integers the inverse of the rational number a/b is simply b/a. Although in some naive sense the rational numbers are "more complicated" than the integers (e.g. in the sense that a rational number can be viewed as an ordered pair of integers, subject to certain equivalences), in many respects the existence of multiplicative inverses gives the rational numbers a simpler structure. For instance, given a pair of integers a and b we may consider the relation that b is exactly divisible by a, i.e., there exists an integer c such that $a \cdot c = b$, and using this we get a rich theory of prime and composite numbers, factorization, and so forth. In contrast any nonzero rational number divides any other nonzero rational number, a much less interesting relation. This is prototypical of the different and richer structure that an arbitrary ring has in comparison to a field or a division ring.

4.2.3 Fields in Abstract Algebra

A field is a ring in which the elements, other than the identity element for addition, and the multiplication operator, also form a *group*.

A *field is* an algebraic structure with notions of addition, subtraction, multiplication and division, satisfying certain axioms. The most commonly used fields are the field of real numbers, the field of complex numbers, and the field of rational numbers, but there are also finite fields, fields of functions, various algebraic number fields, *p-adic fields*, and so forth.

Any *field* may be used as the scalars for a vector space, which is the standard general context for linear algebra. The theory of field extensions (including Galois theory) involves the roots of polynomials with coefficients in a field; among other results, this theory leads to impossibility proofs for the classical problems of angle trisection and squaring the circle with a compass and straightedge, as well as a proof of the Abel–Ruffini theorem on the insolubility of quintic equations. In modern mathematics, the theory of fields (or field theory) plays an essential role in number theory and algebraic geometry.

As an algebraic structure, every *field* is a *ring*, but not every *ring* is a *field*. The most important difference is that fields allow for division (though not division by zero), while a ring may not possess multiplicative inverses. In addition, the multiplication operation in a field is required to be commutative. A ring in which division is possible but commutativity is not assumed (such as the quaternions) is called a division ring or skew field. (Historically, division rings were sometimes referred to as fields, while fields were called "commutative fields".)

As a ring, a field may be classified as a specific type of integral domain, and can be characterized by the following (not necessarily exhaustive) chain of class inclusions:

There are only two kinds of finite fields. One kind is the field formed by addition and multiplication modulo a prime number. The other kind of finite field has a number of elements that is a power of a prime number. The addition operator consists of multiple independent additions modulo that prime. The elements of the field can be thought of as polynomials whose coefficients are numbers modulo that prime. In that case, multiplication is polynomial multiplication, where not only are the coefficients modulo that prime, but the polynomials are modulo a special kind of polynomial, known as a primitive polynomial. All finite fields, but particularly those of this second kind, are known as Galois fields.

Finite fields whose number of elements is a power of 2 have the bitwise exclusive-OR operation as their addition operation. Such fields were found useful in cryptography.

Definition and illustration

An example of a field is the set Q of rational numbers. In, there are four essential operations: addition together with subtraction, and multiplication with division. Intuitively, a field is a set of numbers which has four such operations. In gaxioms hold:

(1) Closure of F under addition and multiplication : For all a, b in F, both $a + b$ and $a \cdot b$ are in F (or more formally, + and · are binary operations on F).

(2) Associativity of addition and multiplication : For all a, b, and **c** in F, the following equalities hold: $a + (b + c) = (a + b) + c$ and $a \cdot (b \cdot c) = (a \cdot b) \cdot c$.

(3) Commutativity of addition and multiplication: For all a and b in F, the following equalities hold: $a + b = b + a$ and $a \cdot b = b \cdot a$.

(4) Additive and multiplicative identity :There exists an element of F, called the additive identity element and denoted by 0, such that for all a in F, $a + 0 = a$. Likewise, there is an element, called the multiplicative identity element and denoted by 1, such that for all a in F, $a \quad 1 = a$. For technical reasons, the additive identity and the multiplicative identity are required to be distinct.

(5) Additive and multiplicative inverses For every a in F, there exists an element $-a$ in F, such that $a + (-a) = 0$. Similarly, for any a in F other than 0, there exists an element a-1 in F, such that $a \cdot a\text{-}1 = 1$. (The elements $a + (-b)$ and $a \cdot b\text{-}1$ are also denoted $a - b$ and a/b, respectively.) In other words, subtraction and division operations exist.

(6) Distributivity of multiplication over addition For all *a, b* and *c* in *F,* the following equality holds: $a \cdot (b + c) = (a \cdot b) + (a \cdot c)$.

First Example: Rational Numbers

The easiest example for a field are the rational numbers consisting of fractions a/b, where *a* and *b* are integers, and *b* ? 0. The additive inverse of such a fraction is simply *-a/b,* and the multiplicative inverse—provided that *a* ? 0, as well—is *b/a.* To see the latter note that

— • — = — =

The abstractly required field axioms reduce to standard properties of rational numbers, such as the law of distributivity or the law of commutativity and law of associativity.

—(— + —) =

= + / ——

= — + —

= — • + + / —

= — • — + — • —

Second example: a field with four elements + *O I A B*

·	O	I	A	B
O	O	O	O	O
I	O	I	A	B
A	O	A	B	I
B	O	B	I	A

+	O	I	A	B
O	O	I	A	B
I	I	O	B	A
A	A	B	O	I
B	B	A	I	O

In addition to familiar number systems such as the rationals, there are other, less immediate examples of fields. The following example is a field consisting of four elements called *O, I, A* and *B*. The notation is chosen such that *O* plays the role of the additive identity element (denoted *0* in the axioms), and *I* is the multiplicative identity (denoted 1 above). Checking that all field axioms are indeed satisfied is easy, if tedious. For example:

$A \cdot (B + A) = A \cdot I = A$, which equals $A \cdot B + A \cdot A = I + B = A$, as required by the distributivity. The above field is called a finite field with four elements, denoted *F*4. Field theory is concerned with understanding the reasons for the existence of this field, defined in a fairly ad-hoc manner, and with describing its inner structure. For example, from a glance at the multiplication table, it can be seen that any non-zero element, *i.e., I, A,* and B, is a power of *A*. Indeed $A = A1$, $B = A2 = A \cdot A$, and finally $I = A3 = A \cdot A \cdot A$. This is no coincidence, but one of the starting points of a deeper understanding of (finite) fields.

4.2.4 Finite fields

Finite fields (also called Galois fields) are fields with finitely many elements. The above introductory example *F4* is a field with four elements. Highlighted in the multiplication and addition tables above is the field *F2* consisting of two elements *O* and *I*. This is the smallest field, because by definition a field has at least two distinct elements 1 ? 0. Interpreting the addition and multiplication in this latter field as *XOR* and Logical AND operation, this field finds applications in computer science, especially in cryptography and coding theory.

In any finite field, there is necessarily an integer *n* such that 1 + 1 + ... + 1 (n repeated terms) equals 0. It can be shown that the smallest such n must be *a* prime number, called the characteristic of the field. (If 1 + 1 + ... + 1 is never zero, for any number of summands, such as in *Q*, for example, the characteristic is said to be zero.)

The basic class of finite fields are the fields *Fp* with *p* elements (*p a* prime number):

$$Fp = Z/pZ = \{0, 1, ..., p - 1\},$$

where the operations are defined by performing the operation in the set of integers *Z*, dividing by *p* and taking the remainder; see modular arithmetic. Any field of characteristic *p* necessarily contains *Fp,* and thus can be viewed as a vector space over the smaller field, of finite dimension. i.e., any finite field has to have $q = pn$ elements, $n > 0$. By developing more field theory, in particular the notion of the splitting field, which is, in general *a* field containing all roots of *a* given polynomial, and minimal with this property, one can show that any two finite fields with the same number of elements have indeed the same field structure, *i.e.,* multiplication and addition behave the same way. The finite field with q elements is usually denoted *Fq.*

4.3 GROUPS, RINGS, AND FIELDS

Groups, rings, and fields are familiar objects to us, we just haven't used those terms. Roughly, these are all sets of elements with additional structure (that is, various ways of combining elements to produce an element of the set). Studying this finer structure is the key to many deep facts in number theory.

Informal Definitions A GROUP is a set in which you can perform one operation (usually addition or multiplication mod n for us) with some nice properties. A RING is a set equipped with two operations, called addition and multiplication. A RING is a GROUP under addition and satisfies some of the properties of a group for multiplication. A FIELD is a GROUP under both addition and multiplication.

Definition 1. *A GROUP is a set G which is CLOSED under an operation* $*$ *(that is, for any* $x, y \in G$, $x * y \in G$*) and satisfies the following properties:*

(1) *Identity* – There is an element e in G, such that for every $x \in G$, $e * x = x * e = x$.

(2) *Inverse* – For every x in G there is an element $y \in G$ such that $x * y = y * x = e$, where again e is the identity.

(3) *Associativity* – The following identity holds for every $x, y, z \in G$:

$$x * (y * z) = (x * y) * z$$

Examples:

(1) Z/nZ, fancy notation for the integers mod n under addition.

(2) $(Z/nZ)^x$, more fancy notation for the integers mod n under multiplication. REMEMBER, the elements of this set are relatively prime to n so there are $\phi(n)$ elements in this set.

(3) Z, the integers under addition. Groups don't have to be finite. Also note that you can't make the integers into a group under multiplication, since elements like 2 don't have an inverse (1/2). But we really only care about examples of the type above.

A group is said to be "abelian" if $x * y = y * x$ for every $x, y \in \underline{G}$. All of the examples above are abelian groups.

Definition 2. A RING *is a set R which is CLOSED under two operations + and × and satisfying the following properties:*

(1) R is an abelian group under +.

(2) *Associativity of × – For every a, b, c ∈ R,*

$$a \times (b \times c) = (a \times b) \times c$$

(3) *Distributive Properties – For every a, b, c ∈ R the following identities hold:*

$$a \times (b + c) = (a \times b) + (a \times c)$$

and $$(b + c) \times a = b \times a + c \times a.$$

Examples:

(1) All the examples above of groups are also RINGS. Note that we don't require multiplicative inverses.

(2) $Z[x]$, fancy notation for all polynomials with integer coecients. Multiplication and addition is the usual multiplication and addition of polynomials.

Definition 3. A FIELD *is a set F which is closed under two operations + and × such that*

(1) *F is an abelian group under + and*

(2) *F - {0} (the set F without the additive identity 0) is an abelian group under ×.*

Examples:

Z/pZ is a field, since Z/pZ is an additive group and $(Z/pZ) - \{0\} \neq (Z/pZ)^{\times}$ is a group under multiplication. Sometimes when we (or Koblitz) want to emphasize that Z/pZ is a field, we use the notation *Fp*.

Non-Examples: If n is not a prime, then Z/nZ is not a field, since $(Z/nZ) - \{0\} \neq (Z/nZ)^{\times}$. There are, in general, lots of other elements than 0 which are not relatively prime to n and hence have no inverse under multiplication.

The theory of these abstract structures is sometimes simpler than dealing with specific examples because we've pared down and listed all the essential properties that should be used in proofs. Here's a simple result from group theory (though we don't bother with the proof since there's already enough notation so far in this document):

Theorem 1 (Corollary to Lagrange's Theorem). *If* $x \in G$, *a* group of size N, then $x^N = e$.

Notice that when G is Z/nZ, this is Euler's theorem, since the size of G is then $\phi(n)$ and the statement

$$x^N = e$$

translates to (since e, the identity under multiplication, is 1 in this case)

$$x^{\phi(n)} \equiv 1 \pmod{n}.$$

4.3.1 Prime Numbers

This section is all about basic properties of positive whole numbers, especially with regard to multiplication. Most of the time, when we say "number" we mean positive integer. Here is some terminology:

Multiple:

We say one number a is a multiple of another b if there is a positive integer c for which $a = bc$.

EXAMPLE:

35 is a multiple of 7 because.

Divides:

We say one number a divides another b if there is a positive integer c for which $b = ac$. In other words, b is a multiple of a.

EXAMPLE:

7 divides 35 because .

We also say b is divisible by a, and we write $a \mid b$ (pronounced "a divides b"). We can also call a a factor or divisor of b.

Factorization:

A factorization of a number a is a way of writing a as a product of smaller numbers. For instance $6 \times 5 \times 8$, is a factorization of 240.

Prime:

A number p is prime if it is bigger than 1 and its only divisors are 1 and itself.

Composite:

A number is composite if it is bigger than 1 and not prime. That means it has divisors other than itself and 1.

Prime Factorization:

A prime factorization of a number is a way of writing it as a product of prime numbers. For instance, 2 . 3 . 5 . 2 . 2 is a prime factorization of 240.

Greatest Common Divisor:

The greatest common divisor of two numbers a and b is the largest number d that divides both a and b For example, the greatest common divisor of *30* and *42* is *6*. The greatest common divisor is also sometimes called the greatest common factor or highest common factor.

Relatively Prime:

Two numbers a and b are relatively prime if their greatest common divisor is 1.

A proof that there are infinitely many prime numbers appeared in Euclid's Elements more than 2000 years ago.

The Fundamental Theorem of Arithmetic states that every number has a unique prime factorization, subject to rearrangement of the prime factors. For example, the standard way of writing the prime factorization of 240 is

$$240 = 2^4 . 3 . 5$$

4.4 EUCLID'S ALGORITHM

Euclid's algorithm is the most efficient algorithm for finding the greatest common factor of two numbers a and m. If they are relatively prime, which means the greatest common factor is 1, then Euclid's algorithm can also efficiently solve the modular equation

$$ax \equiv 1 \pmod{m}$$

for an integer x, which is the modular inverse of a.

Integer Division

Euclid's algorithm is a sequence of integer divisions. Given two numbers a and b, where b is smaller than a, we may divide

$$a = q.\ b + r$$

where q is an integer called the quotient and r is an integer called the remainder which must satisfy $0 \leq r < b$.

Suppose a = 97 and b = 13. Then 97 = 7 . 13 + 6.9 which means q = 7 and r = 6.

EXAMPLE :

Suppose we want to find x such that $111x \equiv 1 \pmod{257}$

We use Euclid's algorithm as follows:

Dividend	=	Quotient	·	Divisor	+	Remainder	0 1	1 0
257	=	2	·	111	+	35	2	1
111	=	3	·	35	+	6	7	3
35	=	5	·	6	+	5	37	16
6	=	1	·	5	+	1	44	19
5	=	5	·	1	+	0	257	111

In the latter two columns, we multiply the entry above times the current quotient and add it to the entry two floors above.

EXAMPLE:

$$37 = 5 \cdot 7 + 2,\ 19 = 1 \cdot 16 + 3, \text{ etc.}$$

In the step where we finally obtain remainder 1, we always have something like 44 · 11 – 19 · 257 = plus minus 1. It's +1 if it took an even number of steps, and -1 otherwise. In this case 44 · 111 – 19 · 257 = 1. That means 44 · 111 ≡ 1(mod 257). So our solution is $x = 44$.

If the final nonzero remainder is greater than 1, that number is the greatest common factor (or divisor) of the two numbers we started out with.

In the latter two columns, we multiply the entry above times the current quotient and add it to the entry two floors above. Example: 37 = 5· 7 + 2, 19 = 1· 16 + 3, etc. In the step where we finally obtain remainder 1, we always have something like It's + 1 if it took an even number of steps, and -1 otherwise. In this case 9 . 257 = ± 1 That means 44· 111 ≡ 1 9 (mod 257). So our solution is $x = 44$. If the final nonzero remainder is greater than 1, that number is the greatest common factor (or divisor) of the two numbers we started out with.

Formula

Start with positive integers $a < m$. In formulas, Euclid's algorithm looks like the following:

							0	1
Dividend	**=**	**Quotient**	**·**	**Divisor**	**+**	**Remainder**	**1**	**0**
m	=	q_1	·	a	+	r_1	h_1	k_1
a	=	q_2	·	r_1	+	r_2	h_2	k_2
r_1	=	q_3	·	r_2	+	r_3	h_3	k_3
...	=	...	·	...	+	...	...	...
r_{n-2}	=	q_n	·	r_{n-1}	+	r_n	h_n	k_n
r_{n-1}	=	q_{n+1}	·	r_n	+	0	h_{n+1}	k_{n+1}

Subscripts are used to indicate the order in which the numbers appear. For instance, $q_1, q_2, ...,$ is the sequence of quotients.

The remainders form a sequence, too, with r-1 = m, $r0 = a$, $r1$, $r2$, ..., $rn + 1 = 0$. Because the remainder is always less than the divisor, these form a strictly decreasing sequence

$$r - 1 > r_0 > r_1 > r_2 >......> r_n > 0 = r_{0+1}$$

The formula for the h's and k's are as follows:

$$h_1 = q_1\ h_{l-1} + h_{l-2}$$

This is called a two-term recurrence, because to get the next term in the sequence, we have to use the previous two terms.

At every step in Euclid's algorithm we have

$$h_j a - k_j m = (-1)^j rj$$

j is a subscript indicating which step we are at. The power (-1)j is -1 times itself j times; hence, it is +1 if j is even and -1 if j is odd.

Therefore the very last nonzero remainder, which is the smallest, satisfies

$$h_n a - k_n m = (-1)^n r_n$$

That last nonzero remainder rn is the greatest common divisor of a and m. If it turns out to be 1, then our equation says

$$h_n a \equiv (-1)^n \pmod{m}$$

after discarding the multiple of m. That's why the solution to $ax \equiv 1 (\text{mod } m)$ is $x = (-1)^n * hn$, or hn if n is even and $-hn$ if n is odd.

4.5 RELATIVELY PRIME (COPRIME)

The integers a and b are said to be coprime or relatively prime if they have no common factor other than 1 or, equivalently, if their greatest common divisor is 1. The notation $a \perp b$ is sometimes used.

For example, 6 and 35 are coprime, but 6 and 27 are not coprime because they are both divisible by 3. The number 1 is coprime to every integer.

zA fast way to determine whether two numbers are coprime is given by the Euclidean algorithm.

Euler's totient function (or Euler's phi function) of a positive integer n is the number of integers between 1 and n which are coprime to n.

There are a number of conditions which are equivalent to a and b being coprime:

- There exist integers x and y such that $ax + by = 1$.
- The integer b has a multiplicative inverse modulo a: there exists an integer y such that $by = 1$ (mod a). In other words, b is a unit in the ring Z/aZ of integers modulo a. As a consequence, if a and b are coprime and $br = bs$ (mod a), then $r = s$ (mod a) (because we may "divide by b" when working modulo a). Furthermore, if a and $b1$ are coprime, and a and $b2$ are coprime, then a and $b1b2$ are also coprime (because the product of units is a unit).

Another consequence is that if $ba{-}1 = 1$ mod a, then a and $ba{-}1$ are coprime, hence a and b must also be coprime.

If a and b are coprime and a divides the product bc, then a divides c. This can be viewed as a generalisation of Euclid's lemma, which states that if p is prime, and p divides a product bc, then either p divides b or p divides c.

The two integers a and b are coprime if and only if the point with coordinates (a, b) in a Cartesian coordinate system is "visible" from the origin (0, 0), in the sense that there is no point with integer coordinates between the origin and (a, b). (See figure 4.1.)

Properties

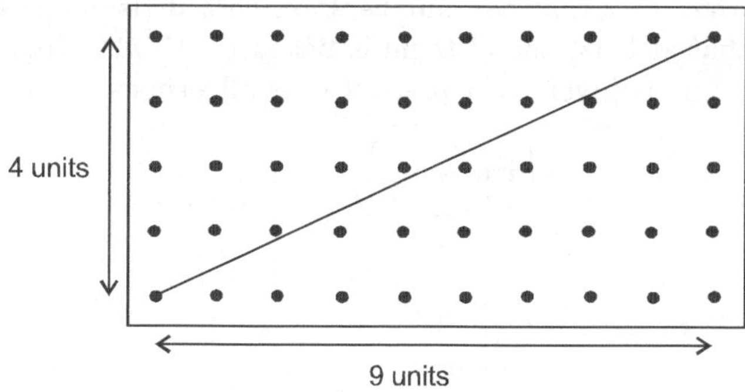

Figure 4.1 The numbers 4 and 9 are coprime because the diagonal does not intersect any other lattice points

The probability that two randomly chosen integers are coprime is 6/*p*2 (see *pi*), which is about 60%.

Two natural numbers *a* and *a* are coprime if and only if the numbers 2*a* . – 1 and 2*b* – 1 are coprime. As a generalization of this, following easily from Euclidean algorithm in base $n > 1$.

– – = –

Cross notation and is an integer, the numbers coprime to *n*, taken modulo *n*, form *a* group with multiplication as operation; it is written as (*Z*/*nZ*) × or *Zn**.

Generalizations

Two ideals *A* and *B* in the commutative ring *R* are called coprime if $A + B = R$. This generalizes Bézout's identity: with this definition, two principal ideals (*a*) and (*b*) in the ring of integers *Z* are coprime if and only if *a* and *b* are coprime.

If the ideals *A* and *B* of *R* are coprime, then *AB* = *AnB*; furthermore, if *C* is a third ideal such that *A* contains *BC*, then *A* contains *C*. The Chinese remainder theorem is an important statement about coprime ideals.

The concept of being relatively prime can also be extended any finite set of integers *S* = {*a*1, *a*2, ... *an*} to mean that the greatest common divisor of the elements of the set is 1. If every pair of integers in the set is relatively prime, then the set is called pairwise relatively prime.

Every pairwise relatively prime set is relatively prime; however, the converse is not truc: {6, 10, 15} is rolativoly primo, but not pairwise relative prime. (In fact, each pair of integers in the set has a non-trivial common factor.)

Probabilities

Given two randomly chosen integers *A* and *B*, it is reasonable to ask how likely it is that *A* and *B* are coprime. In this determination, it is convenient to use the characterization that *A* and *B* are coprime if and only if no prime number divides both of them.

Intuitively, the probability that any number is divisible by a prime (or any integer), *p* is 1 / *p*. Hence the probability that two numbers are both divisible by this prime is 1 / *p*2, and the probability that at least one of them is not is 1 - 1 / *p*2. Thus the probability that two numbers are coprime is given by *a* product over all primes,

$$= \left(\prod^{\infty} \frac{\quad}{-\ -} \right)^{-}$$

$$= \frac{\quad}{\varsigma} = \frac{\quad}{\pi}$$

$$\approx$$

Here ? refers to the Riemann zeta function, the identity relating the product over primes to ?(2) is an example of an Euler product, and the evaluation of ?(2) as *p*2/6 is the Basel problem, solved by Leonhard Euler in 1734. In general, the probability of k randomly chosen integers being coprime is 1 / ?(*k*).

There is often confusion about what *a* "randomly chosen integer" is. One way of understanding this is to assume that the integers are chosen randomly between 1 and an integer *N*. Then for each upper bound *N*, there is a probability *PN* that two randomly chosen numbers are coprime. This will never be exactly 6 / *p*2, but in the limit as $N \to \infty$. $P_N \to 6/\pi^2$ [3]

$$\prod^{\infty} \left(-- \right) \approx$$

4.6 MODULAR ARITHMETIC

In basic cryptology we become very comfortable with arithmetic carried out mod 26, but it rapidly becomes necessary to consider other possible moduli as well. Here we provide the basics of modular arithmetic.

First we have to pick a modulus which is a positive whole number m. We say two numbers *a, b* are equal modulo m (or congruent modulo m; that is the proper term) if m divides *a-b*. In that case, we write $a \equiv b \pmod{m}$ (an equals sign with three bars).

EXAMPLES:

$$a \equiv b \pmod{m}$$

The neat things about modular arithmetic is that all the basic operations, addition, subtraction, multiplication and division, all preserve congruences to the same modulus. Thus, given $26 \equiv 4 \pmod{11}$ and $47 \equiv 3 \pmod{11}$ we can conclude that

$$26 + 47 = \equiv 4 + 3 \pmod{11}$$

$$26 - 47 = \equiv 4 - 3 \pmod{11}$$

$$26 \,.\, 47 = \equiv 4 \,.\, 3 \pmod{11}$$

We have to be a little careful about division, because we do not want to divide by 0, of course, and in modular arithmetic other numbers (such as 11 or 22 in this example) could be equivalent to 0.

Arithmetic modulo 2 is especially simple, because we have a very small addition table.

+	0	1
0	0	1
1	1	0

That's right: we have to define 1 + 1 = 0, since $1 + 1 = 2 \equiv 0 \pmod 2$. This is sometimes called bit arithmetic, because it deals only with 0's and 1's, which are the fundamental building blocks of computer science, or bits.

Here is a more indepth look at modular arithmetic. Suppose we have *a* modulus *m*, and pairs of congruent integers modulo *m*:

$$a \equiv c \pmod m \text{ and } b \equiv b \equiv d \pmod m$$

The properties we were talking about before are

$$a + b \equiv c + d \pmod m$$

$$ab \equiv cd \pmod m$$

Here is why they are always true. The congruences mean that $a - c = km$ and $b - d =$ lm for some integers k and l. Congruence means that the numbers differ by a multiple of m. All right, just add those two equations up, and we have

$$a - c + b - d = km + lm = (k + l)m$$

The right side is still a multiple of m, and the left side is $(a + b) - (c + d)$. That proves the addition formula.

Multiplication is a little harder:

$$\begin{aligned} ab - cd &= ab - cb + cb - cd \\ &= (a - c)b + c(b - d) \\ &= kmb + clm \\ &= (kb + cl)m \end{aligned}$$

The first step is known as "adding-and-subtracting." If you add and subtract the same quantity, you don't change the expression. Theoretically, though, that allows us to see that $ab - cd$ is still a multiple of m. That proves the multiplication property.

These are very powerful properties. For instance, we can use them to compute congruences with extremely large numbers. As an example, suppose we would like to know the last decimal digit of 7100. That number is far too large for our calculator, but all we are asking for is $7^100 \pmod{10}$ (the last decimal digit). Then we might compute a few powers and see that $7^2 = 49 \equiv -1 \pmod{10}$ That means

$$7^2 = 49 \equiv -1 \pmod{10}$$

Thus, the last decimal digit of 7100 is 1. We will be very much concerned with computing powers in modular arithmetic when we discuss some of the state-of-the-art cryptosystems and authentication schemes.

As a final note here, you should be careful of the difference between modular arithmetic and word arithmetic. Words are strings of bits, such as 10111001, which is a word of length 8 bits. We have seen in [Beutelspacher, 1994] the use of arithmetic of words in cipher systems such as the one-time pad and the Data Encryption System. This not quite the same as modular arithmetic. Addition of words is carried out bit by bit. One common notation is

$$11010111 * 01010101 = 10000010$$

where the corresponding bits have been added according to mod 2 arithmetic.

Powers in Modular Arithmetic

Both the Fiat-Shamir Zero-Knowledge Protocol and the RSA public-key cryptosystem involve computing powers in modular arithmetic. We will start out with a simple example, the powers of 3 modulo 19. Instead of entering things like 3^{17} on our calculator, we shall build up slowly, each time multiplying the previous result by 3:

$$a^k \pmod{m} \tag{4.1}$$

We don't really have to go any further, because the remaining sequence of powers will be exactly the negative the sequence we have encountered so far, thanks to $3^9 \equiv -1 \pmod{19}$ That is the full sequence of powers is

$$1, 3, 9, 8, 5, 15, 7, 2, 6, -1, 3, -9, -8, -5, -15, -7, -2, -6$$

or equivalently

$$1, 3, 9, 8, 5, 15, 7, 2, 6, 18, 16, 10, 11. 14, 4, 12, 17. 13$$

using modular equivalence.

Our example, shows a few things that are true in general. First, it is very easy to compute modular powers, since our numbers can always be reduced to less than the modulus m. Secondly, the actual values tend to wander around the numbers from 1 to m-1, but they always eventually repeat. One thing we wish to learn here is how long is before the powers repeat. Since the 0-th power is always 1, that comes down to determining the smallest positive integer k such that the k-th power is congruent to 1. Then the cycle of powers will repeat every k powers.

To be a little more general now, let m be the modulus and let a be the number that we are raising to a power. So we are considering the powers $a^k \pmod{m}$. If then $a^k - 1$ is a multiple of m. Suppose $a^k - 1 = lm$ for some integer l.

That says one very important $a \equiv m \equiv 0 \pmod{d}$ thing about the relation between a and m: they have to be relatively prime. If not, there would an integer $d > 1$ that divides both a and m. That is the same as saying $a^k \equiv 1 (\text{mod } m)$. Then, since $a^k - 1 = \text{lm}$, we conclude

$$1 = lm - s^k \equiv 0 - 0 \pmod{d}$$

That is clearly impossible if $d > 1$. Our conclusion is that a and m must have been relatively prime all along. This situation need a little exploration.

Relatively prime numbers

As an example, suppose the modulus is $m = 12$. The numbers which are not relatively prime to 12 are those that are divisible by 2 or 3, since they make up the factors of 12. If we just consider the numbers from 0 to 11 (since these represent all numbers modulo 12), the ones which avoid 2's and 3's are

$$1, \ 5, \ 7, \ 11$$

There are only four such numbers. Those are the only numbers a for which we have to consider $a^k \equiv 1 \pmod{12}$. Moreover, those are the only numbers that can occur in the cycle of powers of any one of these a's. That alone tells us that the cycle has at most four terms. It's actually less than that: each a has square congruent to 1 modulo 12:

$$1^2 \equiv 5^2 \equiv 7^2 \equiv 11^2 = 1 \pmod{12}$$

Each modulus m has only so many congruence classes of numbers; they correspond to the numbers from 0 to $m - 1$. There is therefore a definite number of these which are relatively prime to m. That number is usually written as $1^2 \equiv 5^2 \equiv 7^2 \equiv 11^2 \equiv 1 \pmod{12}$ and is called Euler's totient function or phi function. (The word totient has something vaguely to do with counting, which is how it came up, but let's face it: it's just another one of those weird math terms.)

We have just seen that

$$\phi(12) = 4$$

Computing the Euler function for *a* prime modulus p is especially simple. Every number from 1 to p – 1 is relatively prime to p; that's what being *a* prime means. So we conclude.

$$\phi(p) = p - 1$$

A prime power $m = p \wedge n$ just a little more complicated. A number ais relatively prime to $p \wedge n$ provide p is not a divisor of a, because p is the only prime divisor of $p \wedge n$. So the numbers that have to be ruled out are $0, p, 2p, 3p, \ldots, (p \wedge (n-1) - 1)\, p$. There are exactly $p \wedge (n - 1)$ of those. That means the number of relatively prime classes is $\phi(p^n) = p^n - p^{n-1}$.

That leads to a general modulus m. In that case, what we do is first factor m into prime powers, and amazingly $1^2 \equiv 5^2 \equiv 7^2 \equiv 11^2 = 1 \pmod{12}$ is the product of the ϕ. function for each one of those prime powers. For example, $12 = 2^2 \,.\, 3^1$. Then $\phi(120 = (2^2 - 2^1)(3^1 - 3^0)$ $(3 - 1) = 4$. This makes it quite easy to compute $1^2 \equiv 5^2 \equiv 7^2 \equiv 11^2 \equiv 1 \pmod{12}$ for larger numbers, provided we know the factorization of m. For example, for $m = 120 = 2^3 \,.\, 3 \,.\, 5$. we have

$$\phi(120) = (2^3 - 2^2)\ (3 - 1)\ (5 - 1) = 32$$

4.7 FERMAT'S AND EULER'S THEOREM

The smallest power congruent to 1: Fermat's theorem

We will begin with *a* prime modulus p. Choose any a from 1 to p-1and consider the multiples

$$1 - a,\ 2 - a,\ 3 - a,\ \text{---},\ (p - 1)a$$

Remembering our experience with multiplicative ciphers, we know that these numbers are all different modulo p. That is, modulo p, these are precisely all the numbers from 1 to $p - 1$.

Here is the trick! Multiply all the numbers together and the result must be the same as multiplying all the numbers from 1 to p-1. Thus,

$$1 - a,\ 2 - a,\ 3 - a,\ ---,\ (p - 1)a$$

The left side also has $(p - 1)!$ in it as well. After some rearrangement

$$(p - 1)!\ a^{p-1} \equiv (p - 1)!\ (\text{mod } p)$$

The prime p does not divide $(p - 1)!$. That means that we can cancel it from both sides of the congruence, and at last obtain. 1 .

Fermat's Theorem: For any number a relatively prime to the prime p, we have

$$a^{p-1} \equiv 1\ (\text{mod } p)$$

By this theorem, we can conclude immediately that a, $2 - a$, $3 - a$, ----, $(p - 1)a$. As a word of caution, it may turn out that a smaller power will produce 1. For example, if $a = 9$, then $9^9 = (3^2)^9 = 3^{18} \equiv 1$ (mod 19). So a smaller power of 9 is congruent to 1 mod 19.

$$9^9 = (3^2)^9 = 3^{18} \equiv 1\ (\text{mod } 19)$$

For some further examples, you can appreciate Fermat's theorem by checking img100.gif, $2^6 = 64 = 9.7 + 1 \equiv 1$ (mod 7) etc. It really is amazing.

$$2^6 = 64 = 9.7 + 1 \equiv 1\ (\text{ mod } 7)$$

$$2^{10} = 1024 \equiv 1\ (\text{mod } 11)$$

It is a little unusual that the smallest power of 3 that is 1 mod 19 is the largest that can be under Fermat's theorem. Such a number is called a primitive root modulo p. That is, a primitive root a has the property that the smallest k for which img102.gif is $p - 1$. A subtle and extremely important fact is that every prime number p has some primitive root g. Then the powers g^0, g^1, g^2, ..., $g^{(p+2)}$, cover every congruence class from 1 to $p - 1$.

Euler discovered the generalization of Fermat's theorem to an arbitrary modulus m. The trick is to consider only numbers a which are relatively prime to m. Then similar reasoning leads to:

Euler's Theorem: For any a relatively prime to m, we have

$$a^{f(m)} \equiv 1\ (\text{mod } m)$$

In the case $m = 12$, that would imply $5^4 \equiv 1$ (mod 12). In fact, we already observed that the square of any such a is 1 mod 12. There is then no primitive root for 12.

$$5^4 \equiv 1\ (\text{mod } 12)$$

Euler's theorem is a nice result that is easy to investigate with simple models from Euclidean geometry, although it is really a topological theorem. One of the advantages of studying it as presented here is that it provides the student many exercises in mental visualization and counting.

4.7.1 The Cube

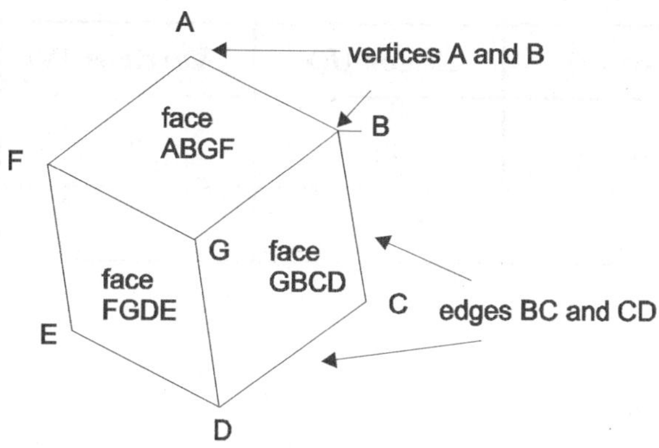

Figure 4.2 Cube

We will begin not with the simplest, but with what is probably the most familiar example of *a* polyhedron for most students: the cube (see Figure 4.4). Here, as well as in most of the examples in this article, we want to count the number of faces, edges, and vertices in the polyhedron. The faces are the flat regions, of which *a* cube has 6. The edges are the line segments between pairs of faces (*a* cube has 12) and the vertices are the "corners" or the points of intersection of the edges, and *a* cube has 8 of those.

Surprisingly, even the cube is complex enough that some people may get these numbers wrong, so it is worthwhile to count the features carefully, and especially to think of counting methods that guarantee a complete and accurate count. As always in counting, it is best if you can count the same things in different ways since this provides *a* check of your answer.

It is useful to have physical models of some of the objects used as examples here, especially at first, when you are getting used to counting the features. It is, however, *a* wonderful visualization exercise to try to make these counts in your head.

To count the faces of *a* cube, orient it so that you are looking at *a* face, and so that two of the faces are parallel to the floor. There are three kinds of faces: top/bottom, left/right, and near/far, making *a* total of 6. To count the vertices, there are two sets: four around the top face and four around the bottom, for *a* total of 8.

Counting edges is the most difficult, and there are a few ways to do it. Notice that there are 4 around the top, 4 around the bottom, and 4 connecting the top and bottom. Alternatively, there are 4 perpendicular to the floor, 4 whose extensions would pass though your body, and 4 that go right and left.

The results for the cube is this: if F, E and V represent the number of faces, edges, and vertices, we have:

$F = 6$, $E = 12$ and $V = 8$. On a separate piece of paper (or off to the side of the blackboard if you're presenting this to *a* class), begin to make *a* table that looks like this with blank space available for *a* few additional entries. Leave space for one additional column on the right:

Object Faces (F) Edges (E) Vertices (V)

Object	**Faces (F)**	**Edges (E)**	**Vertices (V)**	
Cube	6	12	8	

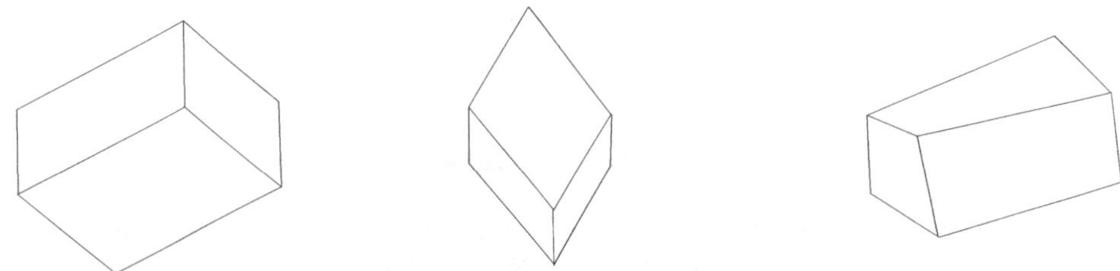

Figure 4.3 Two Parallelepipeds and *a* Distorted Cube

Before continuing, it is useful to make *a* couplemore observations. First, note that there is nothing special for our purposes about the normal cube in Figure 4.2 where all the sides and angles are the same. Figure 4.3 displays three other examples that are simply distortions of the cube, but which contain the same number of faces, edges, and vertices. In fact, in the rightmost example of that figure, the faces are not even flat.

Second, here is another method to count the features. For the cube, this method seems *a* bit clumsy, but for some of the solids we will examine later, this method can vastly simplify the counting.

Suppose we know that the cube has 6 faces. Imagine a model of the cubemade of paper, and with *a* pair of scissors, cut the cube into pieces so that each of the original faces is now a square of paper. After cutting, there are 6 squares, each of which has 4 edges, so there are $6 \times 4 = 24$ edges in all. But notice that each time you cut a single edge on the original cube, it became two edges in the collection of cut squares: one on each of the two squares that were originally joined at that edge. Thus, your count of 24 edges includes each original edge twice, so the original edge count must have been $24/2 = 12$ edges.

Count the vertices similarly. After the cube is cut into 6 squares, each has 4 vertices for *a* total of $6 \times 4 = 24$. In the original cube each vertex before cutting will lie on the corners of three squares. Thus each original vertex appears three times in the cut version, so the original number of vertices was $24/3 = 8$.

4.7.2 The Tetrahedron

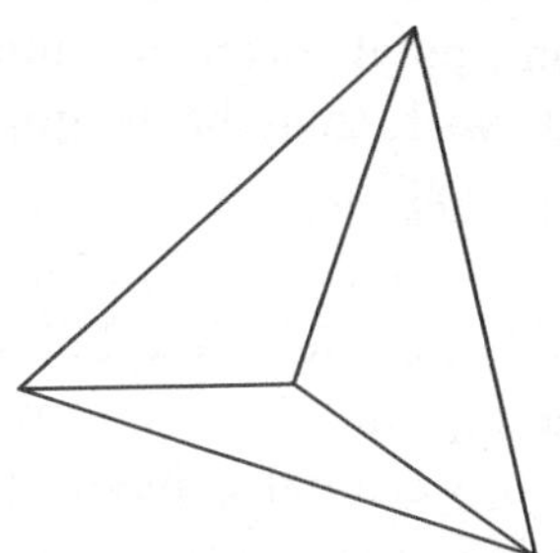

Figure 4.4 Tetrahedron

The simplest polyhedron is the tetrahedron illustrated in Figure 4.4. The only reason we considered the cube first is that the cube is far more familiar to most people. Inspection of the tetrahedron gives $F = 4$, $E = 6$, and $V = 4$, but it is worthwhile to find alternative counting methods. (The name "tetrahedron" itself gives away one of the answers—"tetra" means "four" and "hedron" means "faced".)

With one triangular base parallel to the floor and the tip up, we can count the vertices around the base (3) plus the tip to get $V = 4$. A similar argument counts the faces. There are 3 edges around the base, and 3 connecting the tip to the base for a total of 6.

Or cut the tetrahedron into 4 triangles as you did with the cube: The cut triangles contain $4 \times 3 = 12$ vertices and 12 edges, but each edge is counted twice and each vertex three times, giving $E = 12/2 = 6$ and $V = 12/3 = 4$.

Be sure to add the tetrahedron to your table, which should now look like this:

Object	Faces (F)	Edges (E)	Vertices (V)
Cube	6	12	8
Tetrahedron	4	6	4

An Egyptian Pyramid

Everyone can visualize an Egyptian pyramid. Try to count the edges, faces, and vertices mentally. Here, we are only concerned with closed solids, so be sure to count the square bottom as an additional face.

The Octahedron

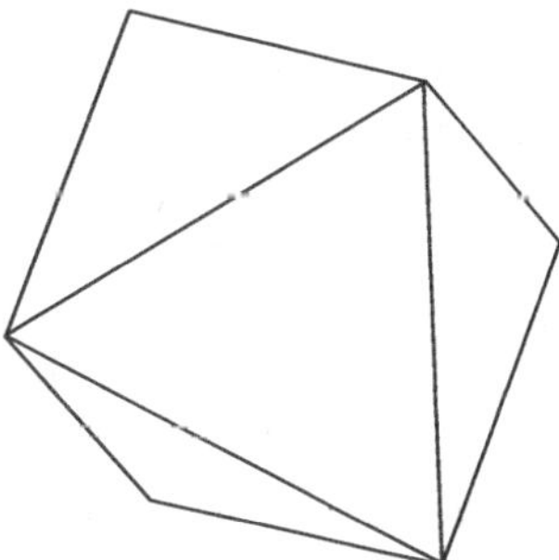

Figure 4.5 Octahedron

The name "octahedron" ("eight-faced") gives away one of the answers immediately. The octahedron is the 8-faced polyhedron ("polyhedron" = "many-faced") illustrated in Figure 4.5. It looks like two Egyptian pyramids with their bases glued together.

To count the features, hold the octahedron with a vertex up. There are obviously 4 triangles in the top half and 4 in the bottom for *a* total of 8. There are 4 vertices around the middle as well as one at the top and bottom for *a* total of 6. Finally, there are 4 edges around the middle plus 4 connecting to the top and 4 more connecting to the bottom for *a* total of 12. Alternatively, cut the figure into 8 triangles having *a* total of 8×3 = 24 edges and 24 vertices. The edges are double counted, and the vertices are counted 4 times each, so there are 24/2 = 12 edges and 24/4 = 6 vertices1.

Our table of values now looks like this:

Object	**Faces (F)**	**Edges (E)**	**Vertices (V)**
Cube	6	12	8
Tetrahedron	4	6	4
Egyptian Pyramid	5	8	5
Octahedron	8	12	6

Or, if you've worked out the numbers for an Egyptian pyramid (F = 5, E = 8 and V = 5), you can double those when you glue two together, but 4 edges, 4 vertices, and 2 faces disappear since the edges and vertices merge and the two faces become interior. This gives: F = 2 × 5 - 2 = 8, E = 2 × 8 - 4 = 12 and V = 2 × 5 - 4 = 6.

4.8 DUALITY

The octahedron is the dual of a cube. The dual of a convex polyhedron is obtained by placing a vertex of the new (dual) polyhedron in the center of each face of the original polyhedron and if two faces of the original polyhedron are joined by an edge, then the vertices in the centers of those faces are joined by an edge in the dual. Visualize *a* point in the center of each of the 6 faces of *a* cube connected as described above, and you can see that the result will be an octahedron.

A property of dual polyhedra is that the dual of the dual is the original polyhedron. The dual of the octahedron is the cube. By the construction of the dual each face in the original corresponds to a vertex in the dual (the vertex placed in the center of the face), and each vertex in the original corresponds to *a* face in the dual. (Why is this?) The number of edges in *a* polyhedron and its dual are always equal, since *a* new edge is constructed for every edge connecting two faces in the original, so the counts for the dual are the same as the counts in the original, but with the number of faces and vertices interchanged.

Visualize the dual of *a* tetrahedron. Did you get *a* tetrahedron? What is the Egyptian pyramid's dual?

4.8.1 The Dodecahedron and Icosahedron

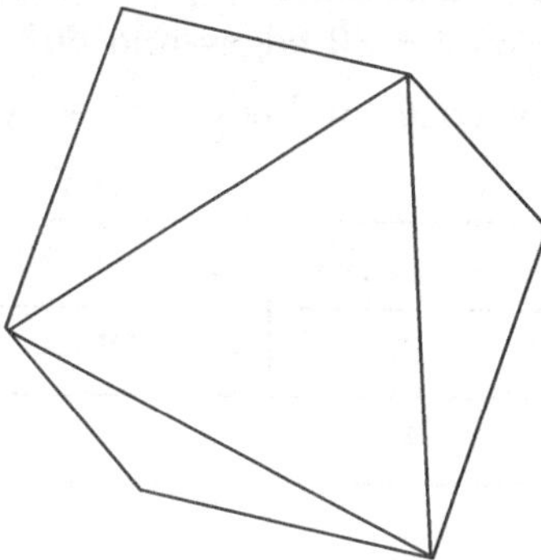

Figure 4.6 Dodecahedron/Icosahedron

Most people know that "tetra" means "four" and "octa" means "eight", but fewer know that "dodeca" means "twelve" and "icosa" means "twenty". If you do, it's easy to guess the number of faces of the dodecahedron and the icosahedron, illustrated in Figure 4.6.

4.9 DODECAHEDRON

Here is the first case where counting the features is *a* bit difficult. Hold the dodecahedron with one face parallel to the floor, and its opposite face will also be parallel to the floor. From the top face, 5 other faces hang down and from the bottom, 5 others "hang" up, making 12 total faces, as the "dodeca" tells us there should be.

Counting vertices and edges can also be done from this configuration. There are 5 vertices around the top and bottom, and 5 each at the bottoms of the edges coming down from the top or up from the bottom for *a* total of 20 vertices.

There are 5 edges around the top and bottom, 5 going down from the top, 5 coming up from the bottom, and the 10 endpoints of those down-going or up-going edges are connected in *a* loop with 10 more edges for *a* total of $5 + 5 + 5 + 5 + 10 = 30$ edges.

The analysis "by scissors" is easier: Cut the figure into 12 pentagons and you will have $12 \times 5 = 60$ edges and 60 vertices. After cutting, the edges in the original are each counted twice and the vertices 3 times, giving $60/2 = 30$ edges and $60/3 = 20$ vertices.

Find other ways to count the faces, edges, and vertices of the dodecahedron.

4.10 ICOSAHEDRON

If you notice that the icosahedron is the dual of the dodecahedron, you get $F = 20$, $E = 30$ and $V = 12$.

(Remember that we simply need to reverse the vertex and face counts in the dual.)

To do the scissors analysis, you first need to count the faces. Orient the icosahedron with one vertex up and its opposite down. There are 5 faces touching the top and bottom vertices, as well as *a* ring of 10 around the middle (or visualize one set of 5 pointed "teeth" going down and another 5 pointing up). Thus there are 20 total faces.

After cutting up the icosahedron with scissors, there are 20 × 3 = 60 vertices and 60 edges in the resulting triangles, where each edge is double counted and each vertex is counted 5 times. Thus there are 60/2 = 30 edges and 60/5 = 12 vertices.

Try to count the number of vertices and edges directly.In any case, if we add this data to our table, we obtain:

Object	**Faces (F)**	**Edges (E)**	**Vertices (V)**
Cube	6	12	8
Tetrahedron	4	6	4
Egyptian Pyramid	5	8	5
Octahedron	8	12	6
Dodecahedron	12	30	20
Octahedron	20	30	12

Before reading on, take a look at all the data in this table and see if you can find any numerical relationships among the numbers in each row.

4.11 EULER'S THEOREM REVISITED

There is enough numerical information in the table at the end of the previous section to find an interesting relationship among the numbers F, E and V. If you have not yet done so, please try to find that relationship yourself. (Hint: it is *a* linear relationship.)

Another hint is this: Because every one of our figures has *a* dual figure, the values of F and V must enter the relationship in the same way. In other words, any equation you obtain connecting the values of F, E and V must remain the same if F and V are interchanged so an equation like $F + 3V - 5E = 11$ cannot hold since interchanging F and V would give $V + 3F - 5E = 11$.

With these hints and a little playing around, you should obtain the equation known as Euler's theorem:

$$F - E + V = 2. \quad (1)$$

Obviously we do not yet have *a* proof (or even *a* complete statement of the theorem—are there any conditions the polyhedron must satisfy to guarantee the truth of the theorem?) We simply have counted the number of faces, edges, and vertices of 6 polyhedra and noticed that the relationship displayed in Equation 1 holds for all of them.

Although the scientific method can never prove anything, it can certainly be applied to mathematics to increase our confidence in the truth of a proposed theorem. Now that we think we have *a* formula relating F, E, and V, let us verify that it holds in at least *a* few other cases.

4.12 CYLINDERS (OR PRISMS)

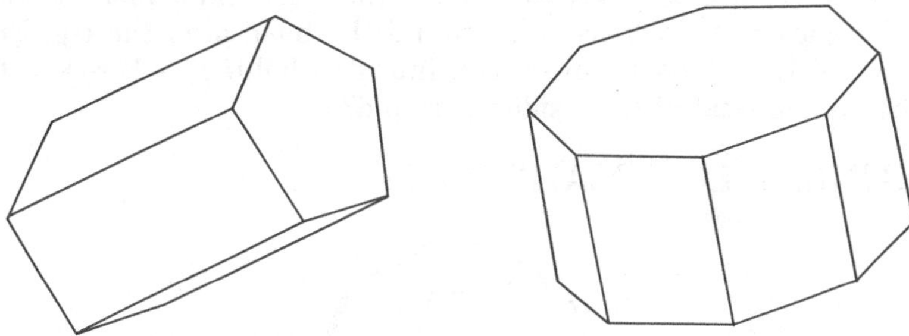

Figure 4.7 Pentagonal and Octagonal Cylinders

Figure 4.7 illustrates both a pentagonal and an octagonal cylinder. They are constructed by "extruding" a base that is either a pentagon or an octagon to make a solid.

The features of both are easy to count. For the pentagonal cylinder, there are 5 faces around the outside and 2 on the top and bottom for a total of 7. There are $5 \times 2 = 10$ edges around the top and bottom and 5 more connecting the top and bottom for a total of 14. Finally, there are 5 vertices on both top and bottom for a total of 10. Thus $F = 7$, $E = 15$ and $V = 10$. $F - E + V = 7 - 15 + 10 = 2$, so our proposed theorem still seems to hold.

Similar reasoning for the octagonal cylinder gives $F = 10$, $E = 24$ and $V = 16$. $F - E + V = 10 - 24 + 16 = 2$, giving one more data point.

Why not add an infinite number of data points? Let's work out the numbers for a cylinder with n sides.

The reasoning is identical: There are $n + 2$ faces, $3n$ edges, and $2n$ vertices. $F - E + V = (n + 2) - 3n + 2n = 3n + 2 - 3n = 2$.

What is the dual of an n-sided cylinder?

4.13 GENERAL PYRAMIDS (OR CONES)

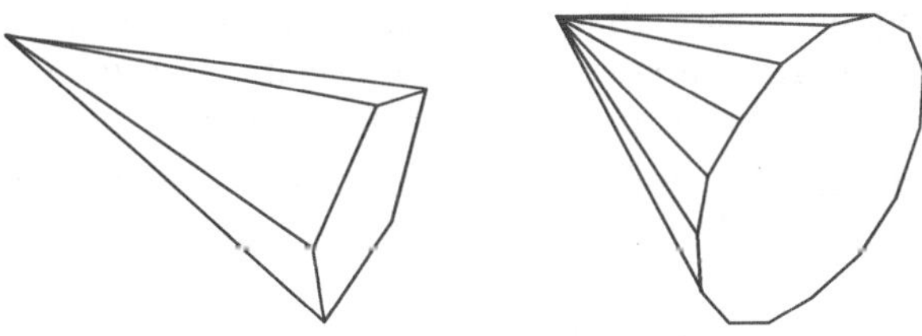

Figure 4.8 Generalized Pyramids

We solved this for an Egyptian pyramid with a square base, but we can construct pyramids with any kind of polygonal base. See Figure 4.8 for examples of pyramids with 5-sided and 15-sided bases.

As above, it is easy to count the features for an infinite number of cases. Consider the situation where our pyramid has an n-sided base. There are $n + 1$ faces (the base plus the n triangular faces), there are $2n$ edges—n around the base and n more connecting the base to the tip, and there are $n + 1$ vertices—n around the base plus the tip. Thus $F = n + 1$, $E = 2n$ and $V = n + 1$. Euler's theorem continues to hold: $F - E + V = (n + 1) - 2n + (n + 1) = 2$. What is the dual of an n-sided pyramid?

4.14 THE TRUNCATED ICOSAHEDRON

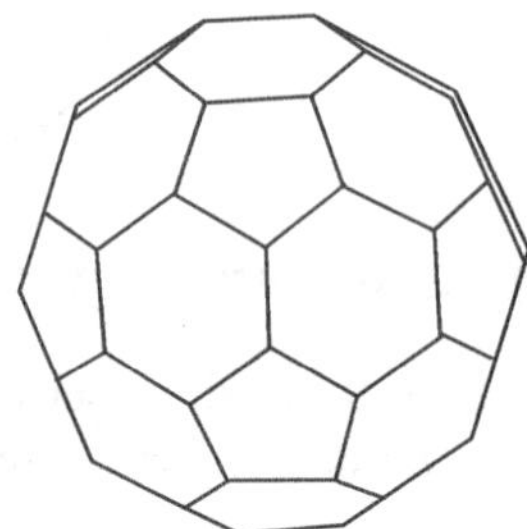

Figure 4.9 Truncated Icosahedron (or Soccer Ball)

We will delay the proof of Euler's theorem for one more section, but if you wish, you can jump ahead.

This example is more difficult, and although it does give one more data point, it is probably most useful as an advanced exercise in counting. The mathematical name of the shape is *a* truncated icosahedron (an icosahedron with the corners cut off), but it looks *a* lot like the patterns on *a* soccer ball. See Figure 4.9.

Even counting the faces is difficult, but (particularly if you are holding a model in your hands) it is not too hard to see that there are 12 pentagonal faces. There is one on top and one on the bottom, and if you follow the points down from the top or up from the bottom, in every case you will arrive at another pentagon. Thus there are 6 pentagons in the top half and another 6 on the bottom.

If you know it is an icosahedron with the vertices chopped off, each vertex chopped gives us a pentagon, and there were none to begin with. An icosahedron has 12 vertices, so there must be 12 pentagonal faces.

To count the hexagons, notice that each edge of each pentagon is shared with exactly one hexagon. But each hexagon touches only 3 pentagons, so the $12 \times 5 = 60$ pentagon edges are used three at *a* time on the hexagons, making $60/3 = 20$ hexagons.

Alternatively, there were originally 20 faces on our icosahedron before we started whacking off the corners, and none were eliminated, so 20 remain afterwards, but the cutting converts triangles to hexagons.

The final count is 12 pentagons plus 20 hexagons for *a* total of $F = 32$.

Now use the scissors. After cutting, there will be 12×5 plus 20×6 or $60 + 120 = 180$ edges and 180 vertices among the cut pieces. Each edge in the original object appears on two pieces so there are $180/2 = 90$ edges. As you can see in Figure 4.9, every vertex marks the intersection of exactly 3 faces, so there are $180/3 = 60$ vertices. So $F = 32$, $E = 90$ and $V = 60$, so again $F - E + V = 32 - 90 + 60 = 2$.

For completeness, here is the final form of our table. If you're presenting it in class, note that *a* final column has been filled to illustrate the sum $F - E + V$:

Object	**Faces (F)**	**Edges (E)**	**Vertices (V)**	**F – E + V**
Cube	6	12	8	2
Tetrahedron	4	6	4	2
EgyptianPyramid	5	8	5	2
Octahedron	8	12	6	2
Dodecahedron	12	30	20	2
n-Cylinder	$n + 2$	$3n$	$2n$	2
n-Pyramid	$n + 1$	$2n$	$n + 1$	2
Truncated Icosahedron	32	90	60	2

4.15 A PROOF OF EULER'S THEOREM

Before we prove the theorem, we had better state exactly what it says:

Theorem 1 (Euler's Theorem) The number of faces, F, edges, E, and vertices, V , of a simple polyhedron are related by the formula $F - E + V = 2$.

The term "simple polyhedron" in the statement of the theorem above means *a* polyhedron that is in one piece without holes. Obviously *a* polyhedron that consisted of two unconnected cubes would satisfy $F - E + V = 4$ since you would just double all the counts, but two unconnected cubes do not constitute a simple polyhedron.

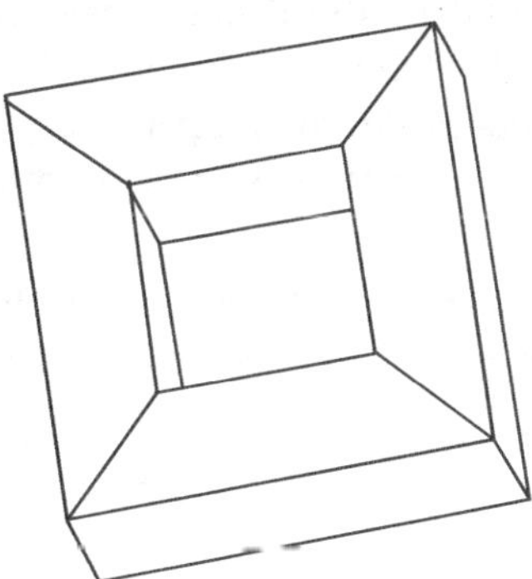

Figure 4.10 Box with Hole (Donut?)

Similarly, the object illustrated in Figure 4.15 is not a simple polyhedron since there is a hole passing through it. In this case it is not hard to determine that $F = 16$, $E = 32$ and $V = 16$, so $F - E + V = 02$.

The proof of Euler's theorem is topological. Imagine that the polyhedra are not made of paper, but of rubber that we can stretch as much as we want.

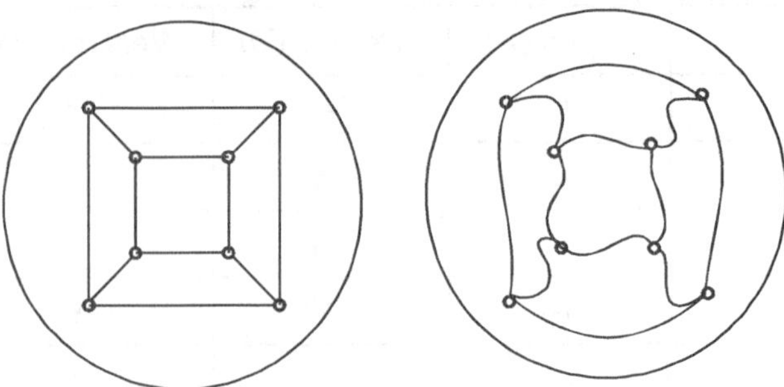

Figure 4.11 Stretched Cube (2 Versions)

Take any polyhedron and punch *a* hole in the middle of one of its faces. Now grab the edges of that hole and pull and pull and pull until the hole is much bigger than the original piece of rubber. Doing this to the cube, for example, will result in *a* figure something like that displayed in Figure 4.11. The vertices of the original cube are displayed as tiny circles, and the large circle surrounding everything represents the enormously stretched hole in one of the faces. For *a* cube, it is easy to draw the stretched version where all the edges remain straight lines as in the example on the left. It makes no difference to our argument, however, if they are curved as illustrated by the example on the right.

The vertices and edges remain vertices and edges. When we count the faces, we have to be sure to include the one on the "outside", since that is the one in which we initially punched *a* hole. In any case, check that in the stretched, flattened cube, there are 6 faces (including the outside one), 8 vertices, and 12 edges.

Draw *a* few more flattened versions of the other polyhedra we have examined earlier in this paper and then count the features and make certain they agree which our previous counts. In fact, *a* better definition of *a* "simple polyhedron" is simply any polyhedron that can be stretched out in this way to make *a* planar diagram. Try to convince yourself that the box with *a* hole in it shown in Figure *9* cannot be stretched out from *a* single hole in any of its faces.

It turns out that an extended form of Euler's theorem holds (that we will not prove here) which states that for a polyhedron with n "holes", the correct formula is $F - E + V = 2 - 2n$.

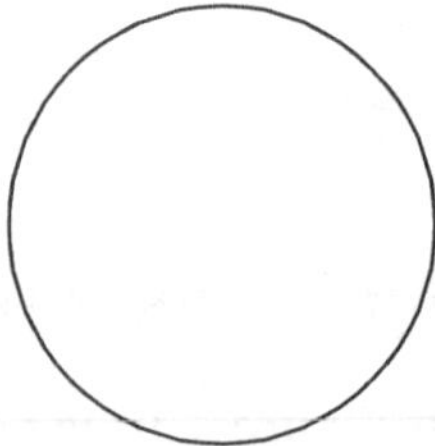

Figure 4.12 Simple "Polyhedron"

The key to the proof is this. For any such figure, we can begin with the very simple diagram in Figure 4.12 and convert it to the figure we desire simply by adding vertices to existing edge segments or by adding edge segments connecting two existing vertices.

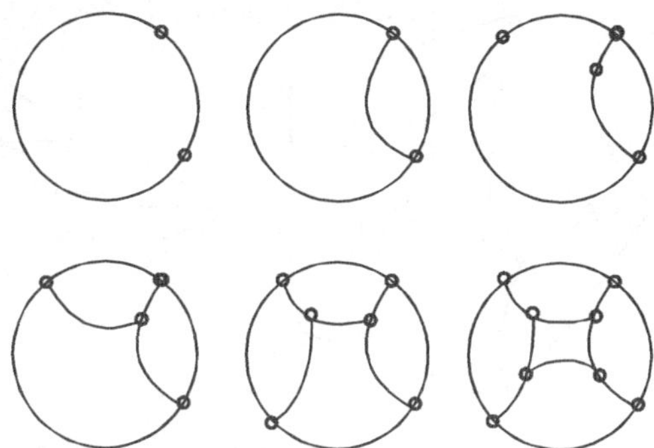

Figure 4.13 Simple "Polyhedron"

The simple polyhedron consists of one vertex and one edge connecting it to itself. We can see that $F = 2$ (remember the outside face), and $V = E = 1$, so $F - E + V = 2$. If we add *a* vertex to an existing edge, both E and V are increased by one so $F - E + V$ remains unchanged. Similarly, adding an edge connecting any two existing vertices adds one edge and divides an existing face into two parts, thus adding one more face. If both F and E are increased by one, again we find that $F - E + V$ remains unchanged.

In Figure 4.15 we will illustrate the first few steps to convert Figure 4.14 to *a* distorted version of Figure 4.13.

In the upper left corner of the figure, *a* single additional point was added to the edge of our simple polyhedron. Next, in the center of the top row, *a* new edge was added that connects the two vertices. On the right side of the top row, two new vertices have been added: one on the newly drawn edge, and one on the original edge.

In the lower left of Figure 4.15, those new vertices are connected with *a* new edge. In the center of the lower line, two new vertices and a new edge were added. Finally, in the lower right, the conversion to Figure 4.13. is completed with the addition of two new vertices and a new edge.

Since every step was one of the two modifications guaranteed to leave the expression $F - E + V$ unchanged, since its initial value was 2, it will remain 2 though the complete transformation to the representation of a flattened cube, or to *a* flattened version of any of the other polyhedr *a* discussed in this article.

This proof seems *a* bit sloppy, but the main idea is there, and it can be modified to *a* rigorous proof of Euler's theorem.

4.16 FLATTENED POLYHEDRA

This section is mostly *a* collection of drawings of some polyhedra that are flattened as described in the previous section. The first two examples are of *a* dodecahedron and an icosahedron and are illustrated in Figure 4.14. Note that the dodecahedron has 11 closed faces, each with 5 sides, and the "outside" is the twelfth face, which also has 5 sides. In the same way, the icosahedron has 19 (instead of 20) closed faces, all triangles, and the outside represents the twentieth face.

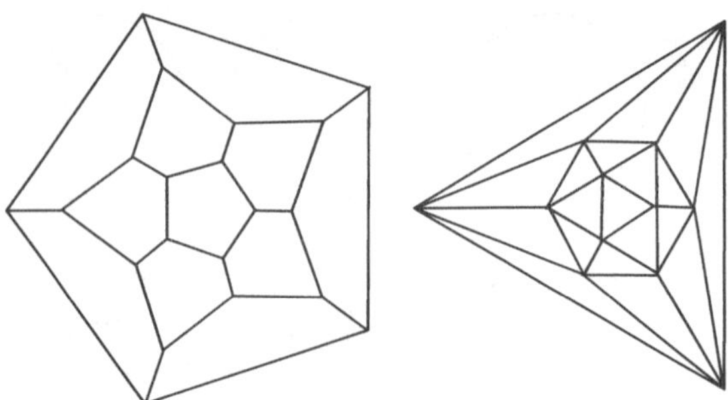

Figure 4.14 Flattened Dodecahedron and Icosahedron

A flattened version of the "soccer ball" appears on the left in Figure 4.15.

We have not examined this possibility yet, but another approach to flattening *a* polyhedron would be to cut *a* tiny hole that includes *a* vertex, and then to do the stretching. If you did this, the point that you removed would behave like *a* "point at infinity" and the lines connecting to it would stretch out forever from the main part of the figure. As an illustration of this, see the drawing on the right in Figure 17. In that figure, notice that there are still 20 "triangles", where 5 of them, on the outside, are infinite. All the arrows at the ends of the lines will meet at the removed point at infinity. Figures such as this also satisfy Euler's theorem, at least if we count the point at infinity as another point. Otherwise it will appear to be off by 1.

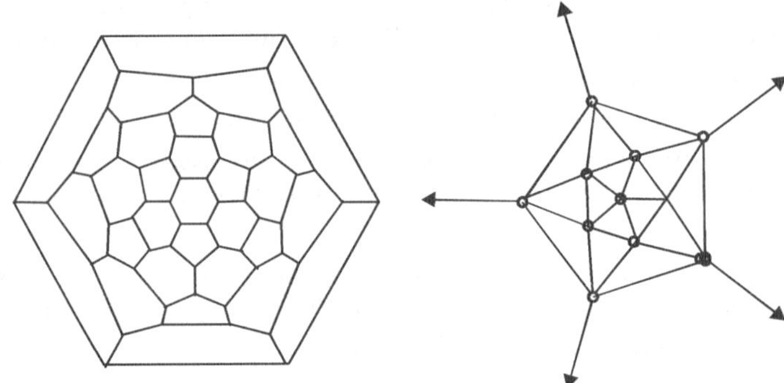

Figure 4.15 A Flattened "Soccer Ball" and Icosahedron with *a* Point at Infinity

Finally, Figure 4.18 illustrates the invariance of Euler's theorem under duality. The figure is basically *a* combination of the drawing on the left side of Figure 4.16 and the drawing on the right in Figure 4.17. One has points indicated by small open circles and the other by filled squares.

There is *a* circle point in the center of every square polygon and vice-versa, assuming, of course, that there is circle at the "point at infinity". One figure is composed of solid line

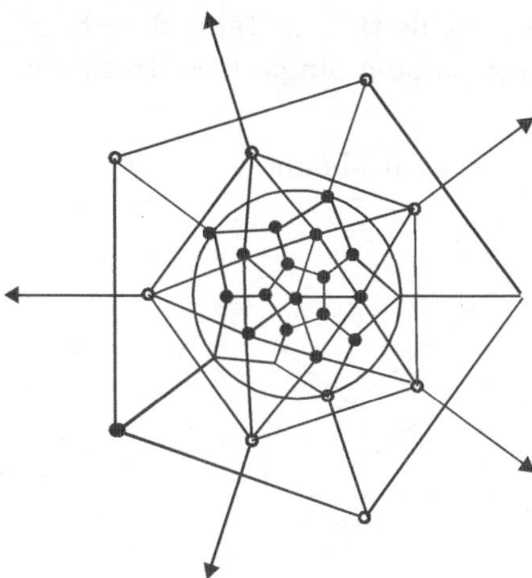

Figure 4.16 Duality of the Dodecahedron and Icosahedron

segments and the other of dashed segments, and every solid segment intersects exactly one dashed segment and vice-versa. Thus the number of edges in both figures is the same. Similarly, every point in one figure corresponds to a face in the other and vice versa.

4.17 ANOTHER PROOF OF EULER'S THEOREM

The following proof is due to Martin Isaacs, and is much more beautiful than the one in the previous section. It is also interesting in that it actually proves *a* more general version of Euler's theorem and the more general form makes the proof easier. It is based on the idea of an invariant that is preserved as you remove edges from *a* figure. Isaacs's proof works on more general figures, which he called "scribbles".

A scribble is any drawing of (possibly curved) lines and points such that:

- Every line segment (edge) has *a* vertex at each end. Note: *a* line segment must have endpoints: *a* circle with no points on it is not *a* valid part of *a* scribble, since it has no endpoints. There is no problem if *a* segment has the same endpoint at both ends, so *a* circle with *a* single vertex on it is *a* valid piece of *a* scribble.

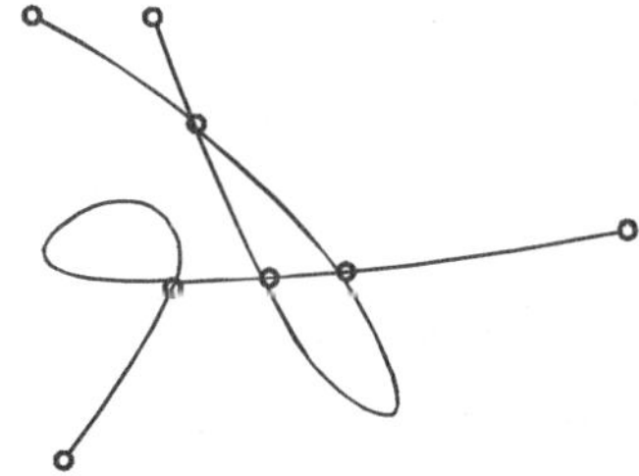

Figure 4.17 A Simple Scribble

- Whenever two or more segments cross, there is *a* vertex at the crossing that separates all the crossing edges into pieces.

Figure 4.19 illustrates *a* scribble that contains 8 vertices, 10 edges, and 4 faces, where the entire exterior is considered to be *a* single face. In this case, $V = 8$, $E = 10$ and $F = 4$, so we have the usual:

$F - E + V = 2$, as it should.

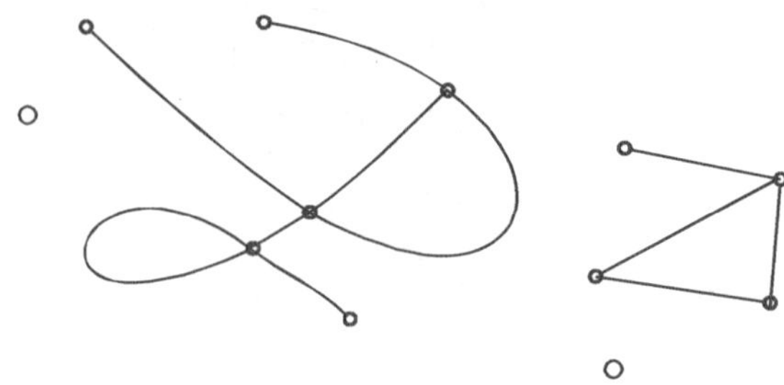

Figure 4.18 A More Complex Scribble

Isaacs, however, added the possibility that a scribble could consist of multiple "components", as illustrated in Figure 4.18. In that figure, there are four components, two of which are single vertices. *A* "component" is *a* set of vertices connected by edges. Two components are different if there is no connection by edges of the vertices of one with the vertices of the other. In the example in Figure 15, we have: $V = 12$, $E = 11$, $F = 4$, and $C = 4$, where "C" is the number of components.

Components are simply disconnected pieces of a scribble. One component could completely surround another, so *a* circle with *a* point on it plus *a* single point inside the circle would be *a* scribble that consists of two components (and two vertices, two faces, and one edge).

If you fool around with some examples (and at this point, it is *a* very good idea to do so), it appears to be the case that:

$$V - E + F - C = 1,$$

which is identical to our original version of Euler's formula in the case where $C = 1$. It has the additional advantage of working for the empty scribble, since in that case $C = V = E = 0$, but $F = 1$.

One other scribble that will turn out to be very interesting is the case where the scribble consists of nothing except for, say, n vertices: $V = n$. In that case, $F = 1$, $E = 0$, $C = V = n$, and we have:

$$V - E + F - C = n - 0 + 1 - n = 1, \text{ as it should.}$$

Isaac's proof works as follows: If we begin with *a* scribble with any degree of complexity (well, assuming there are at most *a* finite number of vertices, edges and faces), then we can show that if any single edge is removed from that scribble, the quantity $Q = V - E + F - C$ is invariant; in other words, the value of Q before and after the removal of the edge remains the same. So for any scribble that we begin with, although originally we don't know the value of Q, we show that successively simpler scribbles have the same value of Q, and when we eventually remove all the edges, we are left with a scribble that consists only of vertices, and we know that all such vertex-only scribbles satisfy $V - E + F - C = 1$.

When we remove *a* single edge from a scribble, there are two cases to consider. First, the removal of the edgemight separate *a* single component into two. This will be the case if there is no other edge connecting the components. If the values for the original scribble are *V, E, F* and *C,* and the values for the new scribble with the edge removed are *V', E', F'* and *C',* it is easy to see that: $V' = V$, $E' = E - 1$, $F' = F$ and $C' = C + 1$. There are no vertices added or removed, one edge is removed, the number of faces is the same, since the removed edge simply "separated" the outside from itself, and there is one more component, since removing the edge split its original component into two. Thus:

$$Q' = V' - E' + F' - C' = V - (E - 1) + F - (C + 1) = V - E + F - C = Q,$$

so *Q* is invariant on removal of such an edge.

The other possibility is that the removal of the edge does not split a component into two pieces, since there is at least one other connection between the parts. In this case, $V' = V$ and $E' = E - 1$ for the same reasons as before. Now $C' = C$ since there is no new component created, and $F' = F - 1$, since the edge that was removed had to separate two different faces. If both sides of it were the "outside", then its removal would split the component. This time, we have:

$$Q' = V' - E' + F' - C' = V - (E - 1) + (F - 1) - C = V - E + F - C = Q,$$

so *Q* is again invariant on removal of this other type of edge and the proof is complete.

4.18 SQUARE ROOTS

The Fiat-Shamir protocol is based on taking squares in modular arithmetic. That is easy to compute. The inverse operation of taking square roots can be much harder. It is fairly easy to compute $5^4 \equiv 1 \pmod{12}$, even by hand, but finding *a* number *x* such that $x^2 \equiv 107 \pmod{257}$ is much more difficult. That is what we mean by taking the square root of 107 modulo 257. Do not even think about computing $\sqrt{\quad}$ on your calculator; it will have nothing to do with computing the modular square root. The number is an endless real number that can't be correlated with an integer mod 257. We must use an entirely different way of thinking for modular square roots.

In the case of *a* prime modulus, there are some methods for computing modular square roots. That is on account of the primitive root g, which we said previously must exist. Every number relatively prime to 257 is a power of *g*. If we would like to compute the square root of *a,* first we find *a* primitive root *g* and then we find the power $a \equiv g^k \pmod{p}$. (This is sometimes called the discrete logarithm; finding an exponent is always something like finding *a* logarithm.) Now if $a = x^2$ and $x \equiv g^l$, then by squaring we see that $g^k = g^{2l}$. The truth is now clear: *a* will have *a* square root only if its exponent *k* is even. Dividing the exponent by 2 gives the exponent of the square root.

$$
\begin{aligned}
3^0 &\equiv 1 && \pmod{19}\\
3^1 &\equiv 3 && \pmod{19}\\
3^2 &\equiv 9 && \pmod{19}\\
3^3 &\equiv 3 \cdot 9 \equiv 27 \equiv 8 && \pmod{19}\\
3^4 &\equiv 3 \cdot 8 \equiv 24 \equiv 5 && \pmod{19}\\
3^5 &\equiv 3 \cdot 5 \equiv 15 && \pmod{19}\\
3^6 &\equiv 3 \cdot 15 \equiv 45 \equiv 7 && \pmod{19}\\
3^7 &\equiv 3 \cdot 7 \equiv 21 \equiv 2 && \pmod{19}\\
3^8 &\equiv 3 \cdot 2 \equiv 6 && \pmod{19}\\
3^9 &\equiv 3 \cdot 6 \equiv 18 \equiv -1 && \pmod{19}
\end{aligned}
$$

As a first example, consider finding the square root of 6 modulo 19. From the table above we see that $6 \equiv 3^8 \pmod{19}$. Then a square root is $3^4 \equiv 5 \pmod{19}$. Sure enough, we may check that $5^2 = 25 \equiv 6 \pmod{19}$. Just as in the process of computing ordinary square roots, there is *a* second square root, too, namely $5^2 = 25 \equiv 6 \pmod{19}$.

There is a very simple way to exploit this to find a square root in the case that the prime p is congruent to 3 modulo 4. These would be primes like 7, 11, 19, 31, 43, etc. In that case $= \frac{+}{}$ is an integer; for example $\frac{+}{} =$. Suppose $a \equiv x^2 \pmod{p}$. Then

$$\frac{+}{} \equiv \quad \frac{+}{} = \quad \frac{-}{} = \quad \frac{}{}$$

This is prompted by Fermat's theorem which says $x^{p-1} \equiv 1 \pmod{p}$. Since p is odd, p-1 is even. Then $\left(\frac{-}{}\right) = \quad \equiv$. the power $\frac{-}{}$ is a square root of 1. Those are easy to compute: 1 and –1. Put these together and you will see that the power of a is bound to be a square root of a (if it has one).

The case p congruent to 1 modulo 4 is more complicated, but there are fast methods for computing square roots in that case as well. The general modulus m is a different matter. However, the congruence $a \equiv x^2 \pmod{m}$ implies the congruence $a \equiv x^2 \pmod{m}$ for any prime power divisor pn of m.

5

Public Key Cryptosystem and RSA

5.1 PRINCIPLES OF CRYPTOGRAPHY

Although cryptography has *a* long history dating back to Julius Caesar (we will look at the so-called Caesar cipher shortly), modern cryptographic techniques, including many of those used in today's Internet, are based on advances made in past twenty years. The books [Kahn 1967, Singh 1999] provide *a* fascinating look at this long history. A detailed (but entertaining and readable) technical discussion of cryptography, particularly from *a* network standpoint, is [Kaufman 1995]. [Diffie 1998] provides *a* compelling and up-to-date examination of the political and social (e.g., privacy) issues that are now inextricably intertwined with cryptography. A complete discussion of cryptography itself requires *a* complete book [Kaufman 1995, Schneier 1996] and so below we only touch on the essential aspects of cryptography, particularly as they are practiced in today's Internet. Two excellent on-line sites are and the *RSA* Labs *FAQ* page [RSA 1999c].

Cryptographic techniques allow *a* sender to disguise data so that an intruder can gain no information from the intercepted data. The receiver, of course must be able to recover the original data from the disguised data.

Suppose now that Anita wants to send *a* message to Bunty. Anita's message in its original form (e.g., "Bunty, I love you. Anita") is known as plaintext, or cleartext. Anita encrypts her plaintext message using an encryption algorithm so that the encrypted message, known as ciphertext, looks unintelligible to any intruder. Interestingly, in many modern cryptographic systems, including those used in the Internet, the encryption technique itself is known -

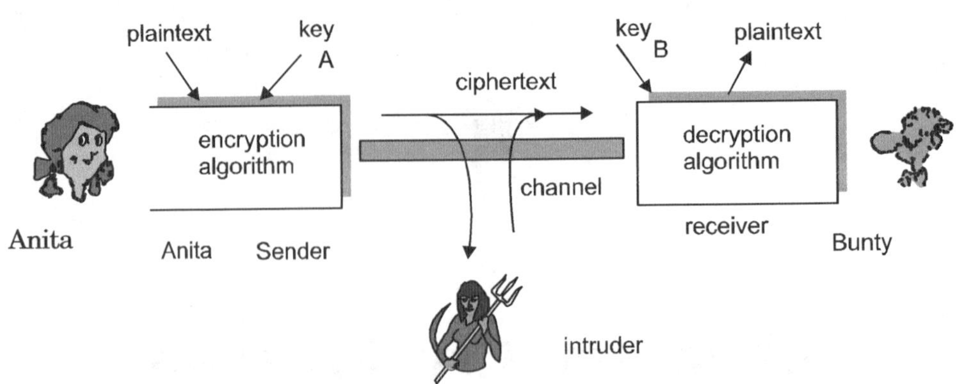

Figure 5.1 Cryptographic components

published, standardized, and available to everyone (e.g., [*RFC* 1321, *RFC* 2437,*RFC* 2420), even *a* potential intruder! Clearly, if everyone knows the method for encoding data, then there must be some bit of secret information that prevents an intruder from decrypting the transmitted data. This is where keys come in.

In Figure 5.1 Anita provides *a* key, *KA*, – *a* string of numbers or characters, as input to the encryption algorithm. The encryption algorithm takes the key and the plaintext as input and produces ciphertext as output. Similarly, Bunty will provide *a* key *KB*, to the decryption algorithm, that takes the ciphertext and Bunty's key as input and produces the original plaintext as output. In so-called symmetric key systems, Anita and Bunty's keys are identical and are secret. In public key systems, the key that Anita uses is known to all (!), while Bunty's key is secret. In the following two subsections, we consider symmetric key and public key systems in more detail.

5.1.1 Symmetric Key Cryptography

All cryptographic algorithms involve substituting one thing for another, e.g., taking *a* piece of plaintext and computing the appropriate ciphertext that forms the encrypted message. Before studying *a* modern key-based cryptographic system, let us first "get our feet wet" by studying a very old simple symmetric key algorithm attributed to Julius Caesar, known as the Caesar cipher (*a* "cipher" is *a* method for encrypting data).

For English text, the Caesar cipher would work by taking each letter in the plaintext message and substituting the letter that is *k* letters later (allowing wraparound, i.e., having the letter "*a*" follow the letter "*z*") in the alphabet. For example if *k* = 4, then the letter "*a*" in plaintext becomes "*d*" in ciphertext; "*b*" in plaintext becomes "*e*" in ciphertext, and so on. Here, the value of *k* serves as the key. As an example, the plaintext message "`Bunty, I love you. Anita.`" becomes "`yly, f  ilsb vlr. xifzb.`" in ciphertext. While the ciphertext does indeed look like gibberish, it wouldn't take long to break the code if you knew that the Caesar cipher was being used, as there are only 25 possible key values.

An improvement to the Caesar cipher is the so-called monoalphabetic cipher that also substitutes one letter in the alphabet with another letter in the alphabet. However, rather than substituting according to a regular pattern (e.g., substitution with an offset of k for all letters), any letter can be substituted for any other letter, as long as each letter has a unique substitute letter and vice versa. Many newspaers in the US carry cryptographic puzzles based on this cipher. The substitution rule in Figure 5.2-2 shows one possible rule for encoding plaintext.

```
plaintext letter:
a b c d e f g h i f k l m n o p q r s t u v w x y z
ciphertext letter:
m n b v c x z a s d f g h j k l p o i u y t r e w q
```

Figure 5.2 A monoalphabetic cipher

The plaintext message "Bunty, I love you. Anita." becomes "nkn, *s* gktc wky. mgsbc" Thus, as in the case of the Caesar cipher, this looks like gibberish. A monoalphabetic cipher would also appear to be better than the Caesar cipher in that there are 26! (on the order of 1026) possible pairings of letters rather than 25 possible pairings. A brute force approach of trying all 1026 possible pairings would require far too much work to be *a* feasible way of breaking the encryption algorithm and decoding the message. However, by statistical analysis of the plaintext language, e.g., knowing that the letters "*e*" and "*t*" are the most frequently occurring letters in typical text (accounting for 13% and 9% of letter occurrences), and knowing that particular two- and three-letter occurrences of letters appear quite often together (e.g., "in", "it", "the" "ion", "ing", etc.) make it relatively easy to break this code. If the intruder has some knowledge about the possible contents of the message, then it is even easier to break the code.

For example, if Trudy the intruder is Bunty's wife and suspects Bunty of having an affair with Anita, then she might suspect that the names "Bunty" and "Anita" appear in the text." If Trudy knew for certain that those two names appeared in the ciphertext and had *a* copy of the example ciphertext message above, then she could immediately determine 7 of the 26 letter pairings, since "Anita" is the only five-letter word in the message, and "Bunty" is the only three-letter word that has an identical first and last letter. Thus, Trudy requires 109 fewer possibilities to be checked a by brute force method. Indeed, if Trudy suspected Bunty of having an affair, she might well expect to find some other choice words in the message as well.

When considering how easy it might be for Trudy to break Bunty and Anita's encryption scheme, one can distinguish three different scenarios, depending on what information the intruder has:

(1) **Ciphertext only attack.** In some cases, the intruder may only have access to the intercepted ciphertext, with no certain information about the contents of the plaintext message. We have seen how statistical analysis can help in a ciphertext only attack on an encryption scheme.

(2) **Known plaintext attack.** We saw above that if Trudy somehow knew for sure that "Bunty" and "Anita" appeared in the ciphertext message then she could have determined the (plaintext, ciphertext) pairings for the letters *a*, l, *i*, *c*, *e*, *b*, and o. Trudy might also have been fortunate enough to have recorded all of the ciphertext transmissions and then found Bunty's own decrypted version of one of transmissions scribbled on *a* piece of paper. When an intruder knows some of the (plaintext, ciphertext) pairings, we refer to this as *a* known plaintext attack on the encryption scheme.

Chosen plaintext attack. In *a* chosen plaintext attack, the intruder is able to choose the plaintext message and obtain its corresponding ciphertext form. For the simple encryption algorithms we've seen so far, if Trudy could get Anita to send the message, "`The quick fox jumps over the lazy brown dog,`" she can completely break the encryption scheme. We'll see shortly that for more sophisticated encryption techniques, *a* chosen plaintext attack does not necessarily mean that the encryption technique can be broken.

Five hundred years ago, techniques improving on monoalphabetic encryption, known as `polyalphabetic encryption` were invented. These techniques, incorrectly attributed to Blaise de Vigenere [Kahn 1967] have come to be known as Vigenere ciphers. The idea behind Vigenere ciphers is to use multiple monoalphabetic ciphers, with *a* specific monoalphabetic cipher to encode *a* letter in *a* specific position in the plaintext message. Thus, the same letter, appearing in different positions in the plaintext message might be encoded differently. The Vigenere cipher shown in Figure 5 . 2 – 3 has two different Caesar ciphers (with $k = 6$ and $k = 20$), shown as rows in Figure 5 – 2 – 3. One might choose to use these two Caesar ciphers, $C1$ and $C2$, in the repeating pattern $C1$, $C2$, $C2$, $C1$, $C2$. That is, the first letter of plaintext is to encoded using $C1$, the second and third using $C2$, the fourth using $C1$, and the fifth using $C2$. The pattern then repeats, with the sixth letter being encoded using $C1$, the seventh with $C2$, and so on. The plaintext message "`Bunty, I love you. Anita.`" is thus encrypted "`ghu, n etox dhz.`" Note that the first "*b*" in the plaintext message is encrypted using $C1$, while the second "*b*" is encrypted using $C2$. In this example, the encryption and decryption "key" is the knowledge of the two Caesar keys ($k = 4$, $k = 20$) and the pattern $C1$, $C2$, $C1$, $C2$, $C2$.

```
plaintext letter:
   a b c d e f g h i f k l m n o p q r s t u v w x y z
C1 (k=6) :
   f g h i j k l m n o p q r s t u v w x y z a b c d e
C2 (k=20) :
   t u v w x y z a b c d e f g h i j k l m n o p q r s
```

Figure 5.3 A Vigenere cipher using two Caesar ciphers

5.1.2 PUBLIC KEY ENCRYPTION

For more than 2000 years (since the time of the Caesar cipher and up to the 1970's), encrypted communication required that the two communicating parties share a common secret-the symmetric key used for encryption and decryption. One difficulty with this approach is that the two parties must somehow agree on the shared key; but to do so requires (presumably secure) communication! Perhaps the parties could first meet and agree on the key in person (e.g., two of Caesar's centurions might meet at the Roman baths) and thereafter communicate with encryption. In a networked world, however, communicating parties may never meet and may never converse except over the network. Is it possible for two parties to communicate with encryption without having a shared secret key that is known in advance? In 1976, Diffie and Hellman demonstrated an algorithm (known now as Diffie-Hellman Key Exchange) to do just that - a radically different and marvelously elegant approach towards secure communication that has led to the development of today's public key cryptography systems. We will see shortly that public key cryptography systems also have several wonderful properties that make them useful not only for encryption, but for authentication and digital signatures as well. The ideas begun with have evolved, with a significant milestone being [RSA 1978], into the public key systems in use today.

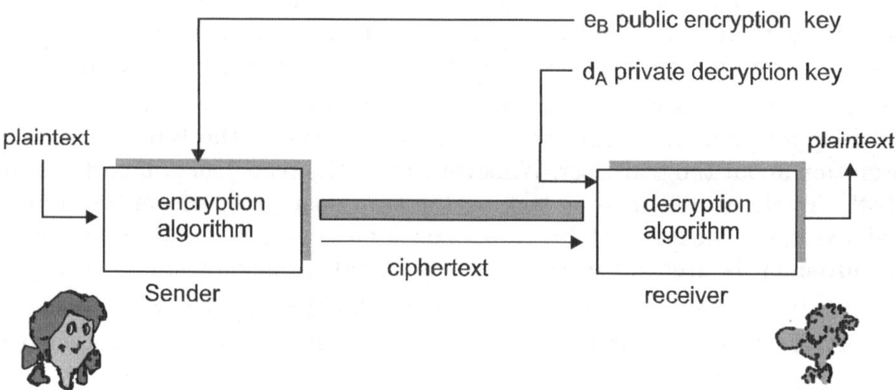

Figure 5.4 Public key cryptography

Traditional cryptography is based on the sender and receiver of a message knowing and using the same secret key: the sender uses the secret key to encrypt the message, and the receiver uses the same secret key to decrypt the message. This method is known as secret-key or symmetric cryptography. The main problem is getting the sender and receiver to agree on the secret key without anyone else finding out. If they are in separate physical locations, they must trust *a* courier, or a phone system, or some other transmission medium to prevent the disclosure of the secret key being communicated. Anyone who overhears or intercepts the key in transit can later read, modify, and forge all messages encrypted or authenticated using that key. The generation, transmission and storage of keys is called key management; all cryptosystems must deal with key management issues. Because all keys in a secret-key cryptosystem must remain secret, secret-key cryptography often has difficulty providing secure key management, especially in open systems with *a* large number of users.

The concept of public-key cryptography was introduced in 1976 by Whitfield Diffie and Martin Hellman in order to solve the key management problem. In their concept, each person gets *a* pair of keys, one called the public key and the other called the private key. Each person's public key is published while the private key is kept secret. The need for the sender and receiver to share secret information is eliminated: all communications involve only public keys, and no private key is ever transmitted or shared. No longer is it necessary to trust some communications channel to be secure against eavesdropping or betrayal. The only requirement is that public keys are associated with their users in a trusted (authenticated) manner (for instance, in a trusted directory). Anyone can send a confidential message by just using public information, but the message can only be decrypted with a private key, which is in the sole possession of the intended recipient. Furthermore, public-key cryptography can be used not only for privacy (encryption), but also for authentication (digital signatures).

Trap Door One-way function

A one-way function is a mathematical function that is significantly easier to perform in one direction (the forward direction) than in the opposite direction (the inverse direction). It might be possible, for example, to compute the function in seconds but to compute its inverse could take months or years. A trap-door one-way function is *a* one-way function where the inverse direction is easy given *a* certain piece of information (the trap door), but difficult otherwise.

Public-key cryptosystems are based on (presumed) trap-door one-way functions. The public key gives information about the particular instance of the function; the private key gives information about the trap door. Whoever knows the trap door can perform the function easily in both directions, but anyone lacking the trap door can perform the function only in the forward direction. The forward direction is used for encryption and signature verification; the inverse direction is used for decryption and signature generation.

In almost all public-key systems, the size of the key corresponds to the size of the inputs to the one-way function; the larger the key, the greater the difference between the efforts necessary to compute the function in the forward and inverse directions (for someone lacking the trap door). For *a* digital signature to be secure for years, for example, it is necessary to use *a* trap-door one-way function with inputs large enough that someone without the trap door would need many years to compute the inverse function.

All practical public-key cryptosystems are based on functions that are believed to be one-way, but no function has been proven to be so. This means that it is theoretically possible that an algorithm will be discovered that can compute the inverse function easily without a trap door; this development would render any cryptosystem based on that one-way function insecure and useless. On the other hand, further research in theoretical computer science may result in concrete lower bounds on the difficulty of inverting certain functions, and this would be a landmark event with significant positive ramifications for cryptography.

5.2 PUBLIC KEY CRYPTOGRAPHY

In public key systems, as in most forms of cryptography, a piece of information called a key is used to transform a message into cryptic form. In conventional cryptography this key must be kept secret, for it can also be used to decrypt the message. In public key cryptography, however, a message remains secure even if its encryption key is publicly revealed. This unique feature gives public key systems great advantages over conventional systems.

Computers are essential for implementing many modern cryptosystems, including the one described here. Several BASIC-language programs (TRS-80) are included to illustrate algorithms used in this system. These can be used to experiment with the encryption, decryption, and derivation of small keys.

Conventional Cryptosystems.

A cryptosystem must have two methods for transforming messages: a method of encryption, which renders messages unintelligible; and a method of decryption, for restoring them to their original forms. For simplicity, normal message text shall be called plaintext, and the encrypted form, ciphertext. Ciphertext messages may also be called cryptograms, or may just be called messages when it is clear that the encrypted form is meant.

To appreciate the significance of a public key system, we need to know some of the methods and problems of conventional cryptosystems. In a conventional system (see figure 5.5), a plaintext message is converted to a cryptogram by an encryptor and sent over a communication channel. While in transit, the cryptogram may be intercepted by someone other than the intended recipient. If it is encrypted well, it will be meaningless to the interceptor. At the receiving end, the cryptogram is converted back into plaintext by a decryptor. The encryptor and decryptor may be procedures executed by people or computers or may be specially constructed devices. In any case, they are both supplied with keys from a key source.

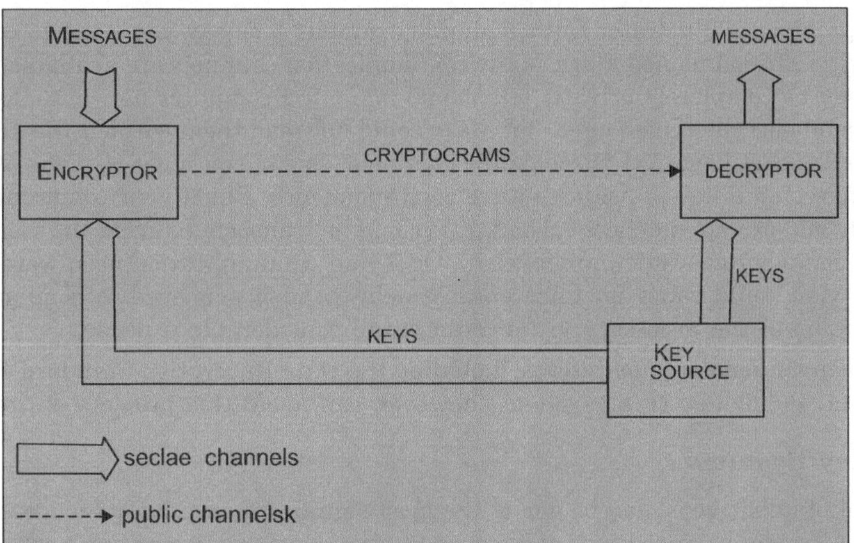

Figure 5.5 A conventional cryptographic system. Encrypted message (cryptograms) are sent over an public communication channel, while the keys needed for encryption and decrypting are sent over secure channels, for example, via courier. The key source may be located at the encryptor or decryptor. in which case one of the secure channels is very short.

Cryptographic keys are analogous to the house and car keys we carry in our daily lives and serve a similar purpose. In many modern systems, each key is a string of digits. For example, keys defined by the Data Encryption Standard of the National Bureau of Standards consist of 64 binary digits, 56 of which are significant. To encrypt a message, a key and the message are somehow inserted into an encryptor, and the cryptogram that emerges is a jumble of characters that depends on both the message and the key. To decrypt the message, the correct key and the cryptogram are inserted into a decryptor, and the plaintext message emerges. In conventional systems, the correct key for decrypting a message is the same one used to encrypt it. Obviously, the keys used must be closely guarded secrets.

In a good system the number of possible keys should be very large, and decryption of any cryptogram should be possible with only very few of the keys, often with only one. These conditions make it impractical to try decrypting a message with one key after another until the one that reveals plaintext is found. The Data Encryption Standard provides more than 7^{16} keys (a 7 followed by 16 zeros), and there is some controversy over whether this number is sufficient!

The keys to be used are obtained from a key source, which selects them, perhaps randomly, from the large set of all usable keys. The key source may be located near the encryptor, near the decryptor, or elsewhere. But each key to be used must be made available to both the encryptor and the decryptor. Therein lies the most serious problem of conventional cryptosystems: some safe method must exist for distributing secret keys to the encryptor and the decryptor.

This problem is illustrated with a simple example: let's say you want to communicate privately with a friend named Mary. Many communication channels are available to you, none of which may be completely private: telephone, mail, and computer networks, for examples. You could send encrypted messages, but Mary could not read them without the keys. And you dare not send secret keys over these public channels. One of you must visit the other, so that you could agree on a key to use for future correspondence. But if your communication need was for only one private message exchange, it could be transacted during the visit, rendering the conventional cryptosystem unnecessary. Or if your communication need were immediate, a personal visit could cause an unacceptable delay. And if you need to communicate with several people, all the necessary visits could entail considerable expense.

Most conventional cryptosystems, including the Data Encryption Standard system, have this problem. Public key cryptosystems, however, can avoid this problem entirely.

Public Key Systems

The concept of public keys may be one of the most significant cryptographic ideas of all time. A public key system has two kinds of keys: encryption keys and decryption keys. It may seem that having two kinds would make the key distribution problem worse, or at least no better. These keys, however, have remarkable, almost magical, properties:

- for each encryption key there is a decryption key, which is not the same as the encryption key
- it is feasible to compute a pair of keys, consisting of an encryption key and a corresponding decryption key

- it is not feasible to compute the decryption key from knowledge of the encryption key

Because of these properties, Mary and you can use a public key system to communicate privately without transmitting any secret keys. To set it up, you generate a pair of keys, and send the encryption key to Mary by any convenient means. It need not be kept secret. It can only encrypt messages—not decrypt them. Revealing it discloses nothing useful about the decryption key. Mary can use it to encrypt messages and send them to you. No one but you, however, can decrypt the messages (not even Mary!), as long as you do not reveal the decryption key. Figure 2 illustrates the flow of information in this situation, with Mary on the left and you on the right. To allow you to send private messages to her, Mary must similarly create a pair of keys, and send her encryption key to you. You can also go a step further. Since your encryption key need not be kept secret, you can make it public, for example, by placing it in a computer network public file. Once you have done so, anyone who wants to send you a private message can look up your public key and use it to encrypt a message. Since you need not transmit the decryption key, and since it cannot be computed from your public key, the message is secure. Only you can decrypt it. Other people can place their encryption keys in the same public file, which would thus become a directory of public keys. Any two people with directory entries could then communicate privately, even if they had no previous contact. It would be necessary, however, to protect the keys in such a file so that no one could change someone else's encryption key, for example, by substituting another encryption key. Fortunately, there is a way to protect the keys themselves with a public key cryptosystem, but that is another topic.

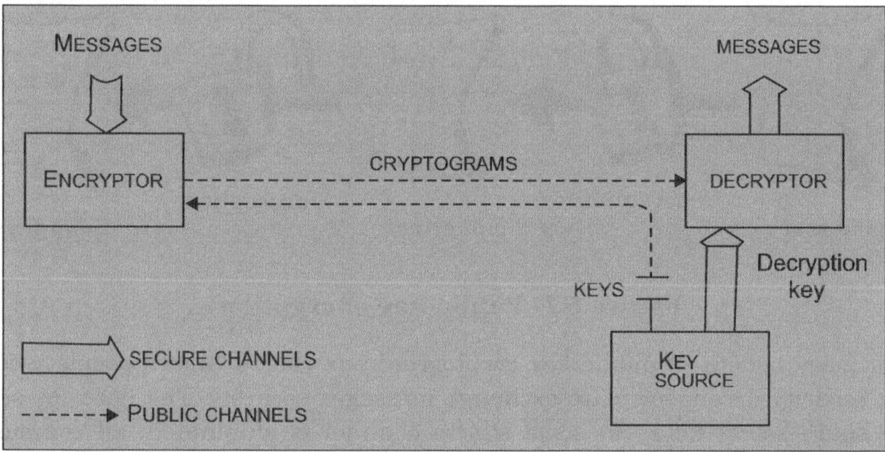

Figure 5.6 A public key cryptographic system. Encryption keys can be safely sent over the ordinary communication channel because the information they contain cannot be used to decrypt messages. Decryption keys are created near the decryptor and are not sent anywhere else. Each person who expects to receive encrypted messages creates a key for encryption and a corresponding key for decryption and sends the encryption key to those who will originate the messages.

5.2.1 Principles of Public key Cryptography

The problems of key distribution are solved by public key cryptography, the concept of which was introduced by Whitfield Diffie and Martin Hellman in 1975. (There is now evidence that the British Secret Service invented it a few years before Diffie and Hellman, but kept it a military secret—and did nothing with it.)

Public key cryptography is an asymmetric scheme that uses a pair of keys for encryption: a public key, which encrypts data, and a corresponding private, or secret key for decryption. You publish your public key to the world while keeping your private key secret. Anyone with a copy of your public key can then encrypt information that only you can read. Even people you have never met.

It is computationally infeasible to deduce the private key from the public key. Anyone who has a public key can encrypt information but cannot decrypt it. Only the person who has the corresponding private key can decrypt the information.

Figure 5.7 Public key encryption

The primary benefit of public key cryptography is that it allows people who have no preexisting security arrangement to exchange messages securely. The need for sender and receiver to share secret keys via some secure channel is eliminated; all communications involve only public keys, and no private key is ever transmitted or shared. Some examples of public-key cryptosystems are Elgamal (named for its inventor, Taher Elgamal), RSA (named for its inventors, Ron Rivest, Adi Shamir, and Leonard Adleman), Diffie-Hellman (named, you guessed it, for its inventors), and DSA, the Digital Signature Algorithm (invented by David Kravitz).

Because conventional cryptography was once the only available means for relaying secret information, the expense of secure channels and key distribution relegated its use only to those who could afford it, such as governments and large banks (or small children with secret decoder rings).

Public key encryption is the technological revolution that provides strong cryptography to the adult masses. Remember the courier with the locked briefcase handcuffed to his wrist? Public-key encryption puts him out of business (probably to his relief).

The use of public key cryptography is quite simple. Suppose Anita wants to communicate with Bunty. As shown in Figure 5.8, rather than Bunty and Anita sharing a single secret key (as in the case of symmetric key systems), Bunty (the recipient of Anita's messages) instead has two keys - a public key that is available to everyone in the world (including Trudy the intruder!) and a private key that is known only to Bunty. In order to communicate with Bunty, Anita first fetches Bunty's public key. Anita then encrypts her message to Bunty using Bunty's public key and a known (e.g., standardized) encryption algorithm. Bunty receives Anita's encrypted message and uses his private key and a known (e.g., standardized) decryption algorithm to decrypt Anita's message. In this manner, Anita can send a secret message to Bunty without either of them having to have to distribute any secret keys!

Using the notation of Figure 5.8, for any message **`m`**, **`dB(eB(m)) = m`**, i.e., applying Bunty's public key then Bunty's private key to the message m gives back m. We will see shortly that we can interchange the public key and private key encryption and get the same result, that is, **`eB(dB(m)) = dB(eB(m)) = m`**.

The use of public key cryptography is thus conceptually simple. But two immediate worries may spring to mind. A first concern is that although an intruder intercepting Anita's encrypted message will only see gibberish, the intruder knows both the key (Bunty's public key, which is available for all the world to see) and the algorithm that Anita used for encryption. Trudy can thus mount a chosen plaintext attack, using the known standardized encryption algorithm and Bunty's publicly available encryption key to encode any message she chooses! Trudy might well try, for example, to encode messages, or parts of messages, that she suspects that Anita might send. Clearly, if public key cryptography is to work, key selection and encryption/decryption must be done in such a way that it is impossible (or at least so hard to be impossible for all practical purposes) for an intruder to either determine Bunty's private key or somehow otherwise decrypt or guess Anita's message to Bunty. A second concern is that since Bunty's encryption key is public, anyone can send an encrypted message to Bunty, including Anita or someone claiming to be Anita. In the case of a single shared secret key, the fact that the sender knows the secret key implicitly identifies the sender to the receiver. In the case of public key cryptography, however, this is no longer the case since anyone can send an encrypted message to Bunty using Bunty's publicly available key. Certificates, which we will study in section 7.5, are needed to bind an entity (such as Bunty) to a specific public key.

5.3 PUBLIC-KEY ENCRYPTION

The development of public-key cryptography is the greatest and perhaps the only true revolution in the entire history of cryptography. From its earliest beginnings, right down to modern times, all cryptographic systems have been based on the eliminator tools of substitution and permutation. Public-key cryptography provides a radical departure from all that has been done before. For one thing, public-key algorithm are based on mathematical functions rather than on substitution or permutation. But more importantly, public-key cryptography is asymmetric, involving the use of two separate keys, in contrast to the symmetric conventional encryption, which uses only one key. The use of two keys has profound consequences in the areas of confidentiality, key distribution, and authentication.

In fact, the security of any encryption scheme depends on the length of the key and the computational work involved in breaking a cipher. There is nothing in principle about either conventional or public-key encryption that makes one superior to another from the point of view of resisting cryptoanalysis.

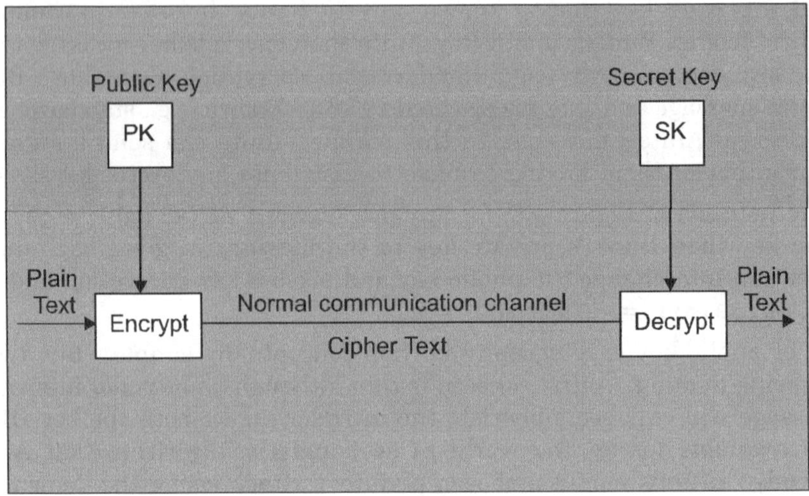

Figure 5.8 Public Key Systems

Public-key encryption is a general-purpose technique that has made conventional encryption obsolete. On the contrary, because of the computational overhead of current public-key encryption schemes, there seems no foreseeable likelihood that conventional encryption will be abandoned. As one of the inventors of public-key encryption has put in: " the restriction of public-key cryptography to key management and signature applications is almost universally accepted".

5.3.1 Public key cryptosystems

For public key systems, the algorithm have characteristics that. It is computationally infeasible to determine the decryption key given only knowledge of the cryptographic algorithm and the encryption key. In addition. some algorithms, such as RSA, also exhibit the characteristic that either of the two related keys can be used for encryption, with the other used for decryption.

5.3.2 Key management

There is a feeling that key distribution is easier when using public-key encryption, compared to the rather cumbersome handshaking involved with keydistribution centres for conventional encryption. The simple essential steps are

(1) Each end system in the network generates a pair of keys to be used for encryption and decryption of messages that it will receive.

(2) Each system publishes its encryption key by placing it in a public register or file. This is the public key. The companion key is kept private.

(3) If A wishes to send a message to B. it encrypts the message using B's public key.

(4) When B receives the message, it decrypt it using B's private key. No other recipient can decrypt the message because only B knows B's private key.

With this approach, all participants have access to public key. Private keys are generated locally by each participant and therefore need never be distributed.

In fact some form of protocols is needed, generally involving a central agent, and the procedures involved are no simpler nor any more efficient than those required for conventional encryption.

5.3.3 Applications of public key cryptosystems

Public key systems are characterised by the use of cryptographic type of algorithm with two keys, one key is held private and the other key is available publicly. Depending on the application, the sender uses either the sender's private key or the receiver's public key, or both to perform some type of cryptographic functions. In broad terms, we can classify the use of public key cryptosystems into three categories:

Encryption/Decryption: The sender encrypts the message with the recipient's public key.

Digital Signature: The sender "signs" a message with his private key. Signing is achieved by a cryptographic algorithm applied to the message or to a small block of data that is bound in some way to the message.

Key Exchange: Two sides cooperate to exchange a session key. Several quite different approaches are possible involving the private key(s) of one or both parties.

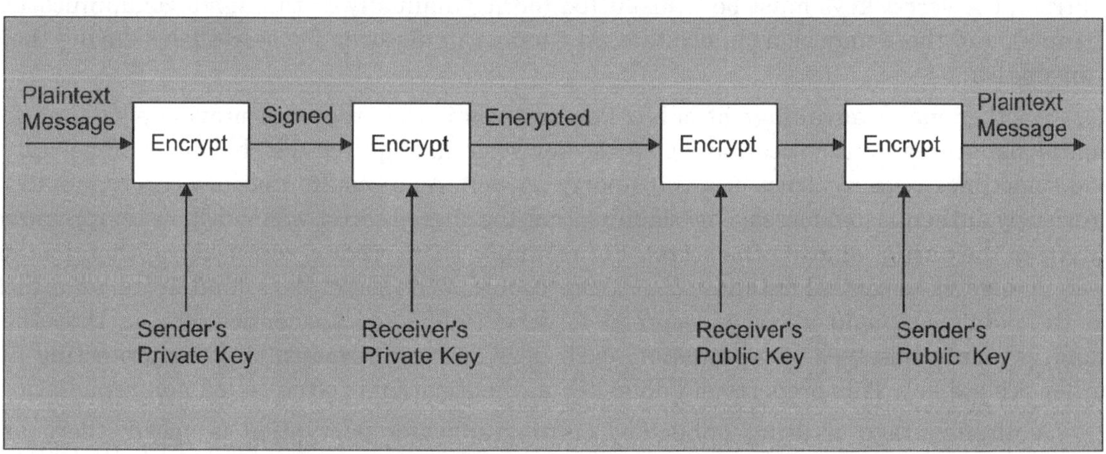

Figure 5.9 Public Key Cryptosystems: Secrecy and Authentication

Some algorithms are suitable for all three applications, whereas others can only be used for one or two of these applications. RSA algorithm, which we select on this project, can be used for the three applications.

5.3.4 Requirements for public Key Cryptography

The public key cryptographic algorithm is based on two related keys. Diffe and Hellman postulated this system without demonstrating that such algorithm exists. The general requirements of public key cryptographic algorithm is:

(1) It is computationally easy for a party B to generate a pair of keys (public key and private key).

(2) It is computationally easy for a sender A, knowing the public key and the message to be encrypted, to generate the corresponding ciphertext.

(3) It is computationally easy for the receiver B. to decrypt the resulting ciphertext using the private key to recover the original message .

(4) It is computationally infeasible for an opponent, knowing the public key and the ciphertext, to recover the original message.

(5) It is computationally infeasible for an opponent, knowing the public key, to determine the private key.

The encryption and decryption functions can be applied in either order. This requirement is not necessary for all public key applications, but it is a useful requirement.

5.3.5 Advantages and Disadvantages of Public-Key Cryptography Compared with Secret-Key Cryptography?

The primary advantage of public-key cryptography is increased security and convenience: private keys never need to transmitted or revealed to anyone. In a secret-key system, by contrast, the secret keys must be transmitted (either manually or through a communication channel), and there may be a chance that an enemy can discover the secret keys during their transmission.

Another major advantage of public-key systems is that they can provide a method for digital signatures. Authentication via secret-key systems requires the sharing of some secret and sometimes requires trust of a third party as well. As a result, a sender can repudiate a previously authenticated message by claiming that the shared secret was somehow compromised by one of the parties sharing the secret. For example, the Kerberos secret-key authentication system involves a central database that keeps copies of the secret keys of all users; an attack on the database would allow widespread forgery. Public-key authentication, on the other hand, prevents this type of repudiation; each user has sole responsibility for protecting his or her private key. This property of public-key authentication is often called non-repudiation.

A disadvantage of using public-key cryptography for encryption is speed: there are popular secret-key encryption methods that are significantly faster than any currently available public-key encryption method. Nevertheless, public-key cryptography can be used with secret-key cryptography to get the best of both worlds. For encryption, the best solution is to combine public- and secret-key systems in order to get both the security advantages of public-key systems and the speed advantages of secret-key systems. The public-key system can be used to encrypt a secret key which is used to encrypt the bulk of a file or message. Such a protocol is called a digital envelope as in the case of RSA.

Public-key cryptography may be vulnerable to impersonation, however, even if users' private keys are not available. A successful attack on a certification authority will allow an adversary to impersonate whomever the adversary chooses to by using a public-key certificate from the compromised authority to bind a key of the adversary's choice to the name of another user.

In some situations, public-key cryptography is not necessary and secret-key cryptography alone is sufficient. This includes environments where secure secret-key agreement can take place, for example by users meeting in private. It also includes environments where a single authority knows and manages all the keys, e.g., a closed banking system. Since the authority knows everyone's keys already, there is not much advantage for some to be "public" and others "private." Also, public-key cryptography is usually not necessary in a single-user environment. For example, if you want to keep your personal files encrypted, you can do so with any secret-key encryption algorithm using, say, your personal password as the secret key. In general, public-key cryptography is best suited for an open multi-user environment.

Public-key cryptography is not meant to replace secret-key cryptography, but rather to supplement it, to make it more secure. The first use of public-key techniques was for secure key exchange in an otherwise secret-key system ; this is still one of its primary functions. Secret-key cryptography remains extremely important and is the subject of much ongoing study and research. Some secret-key cryptosystems are discussed in the sections on block ciphers and stream ciphers.

Possibility of Users of RSA running out of Distinct Primes

There are enough prime numbers that RSA users will never run out of them. The Prime Number Theorem states that the number of primes less than or equal to n is asymptotically n/log n. This means that the number of prime numbers of length 512 bits or less is about 10150, which is a number greater than the number of atoms in the known universe.

How do You Know if a Number is Prime?

It is generally recommended to use probabilistic primality testing, which is much quicker than actually proving that a number is prime. One can use a probabilistic test that determines whether a number is prime with arbitrarily small probability of error, say, less than 2-100.

How is RSA used for Encryption in Practice?

RSA is combined with a secret-key cryptosystem, such as DES (see Question 64), to encrypt a message by means of an RSA digital envelope.

Suppose Anita wishes to send an encrypted message to Bunty. She first encrypts the message with DES, using a randomly chosen DES key. Then she looks up Bunty's public key and uses it to encrypt the DES key. The DES-encrypted message and the RSA-encrypted DES key together form the RSA digital envelope and are sent to Bunty. Upon receiving the digital envelope, Bunty decrypts the DES key with his private key, then uses the DES key to decrypt to message itself. This combines the high speed of DES with the key-management convenience of RSA.

How is RSA Used for Authentication in Practice? What are RSA Digital Signatures?

RSA is usually combined with a hash function to sign a message. Suppose Anita wishes to send a signed message to Bunty. She applies a hash function to the message to create a message digest, which serves as a "digital fingerprint" of the message. She then encrypts the message digest with her RSA private key; this is the digital signature, which she sends to Bunty along with the message itself. Bunty, upon receiving the message and signature, decrypts the signature with Anita's public key to recover the message digest. He then hashes the message with the same hash function Anita used and compares the result to the message digest decrypted from the signature. If they are exactly equal, the signature has been successfully verified and he can be confident that the message did indeed come from Anita. If they are not equal, then the message either originated elsewhere or was altered after it was signed, and he rejects the message. With the method just described, anybody read the message and verify the signature. This may not be applicable to situations where Anita wishes to retain the secrecy of the document. In this case she may wish to sign the document then encrypt it using Bunty's public key. Bunty will then need to decrypt using his private key and verify the signature on the recovered message using Anita's public key. A third party can also verify the signature at this stage.

In practice, the RSA public exponent is usually much smaller than the RSA private exponent; this means that the verification of a signature is faster than the signing. This is desirable because a message will be signed by an individual only once, but the signature may be verified many times.

It must be infeasible for anyone to either find a message that hashes to a given value or to find two messages that hash to the same value. If either were feasible, an intruder could attach a false message onto Anita's signature. Hash functions such as MD5 and SHA have been designed specifically to have the property that finding a match is infeasible, and are therefore considered suitable for use in cryptography.

One or more certificates may accompany a digital signature. A certificate is a signed document that binds the public key to the identity of a party. Its purpose is to prevent someone from impersonating someone else. If a certificate is present, the recipient (or a third party) can check that the public key belongs to a named party, assuming the certifier's public key is itself trusted.

5.3.6 Certification

Certificates are messages that unforgetably associate the contents with the name of an owner. The certificate is usually signed by a trusted certification authority and the contents of the certificate can be verified by any third party who knows the public key of the certification authority. the certification authority is the server that generate and applies a digital signature to the content of the certificate. Thus the certificate is authenticated.

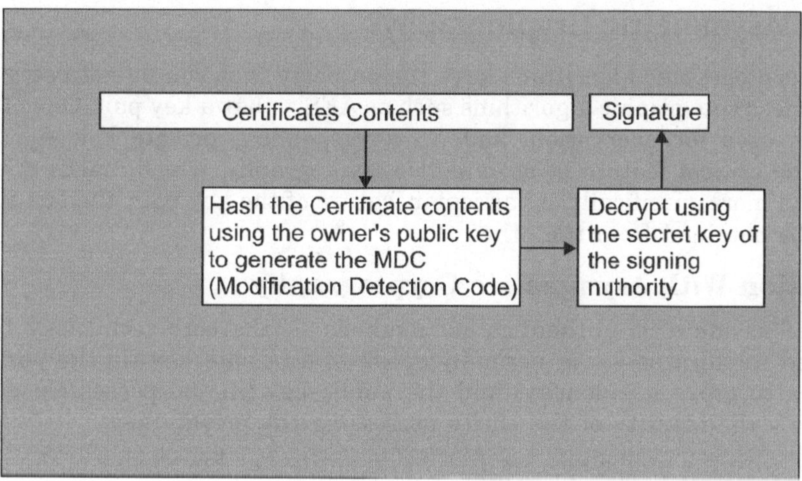

Figure 5.10 Signing a Certificate

All certificates have an expiration time bound to them and therefore after validating the certificate it is necessary to verify that the certificate has not expired. We use the certification authority to sign the certificate, if any entity require a service from any host,

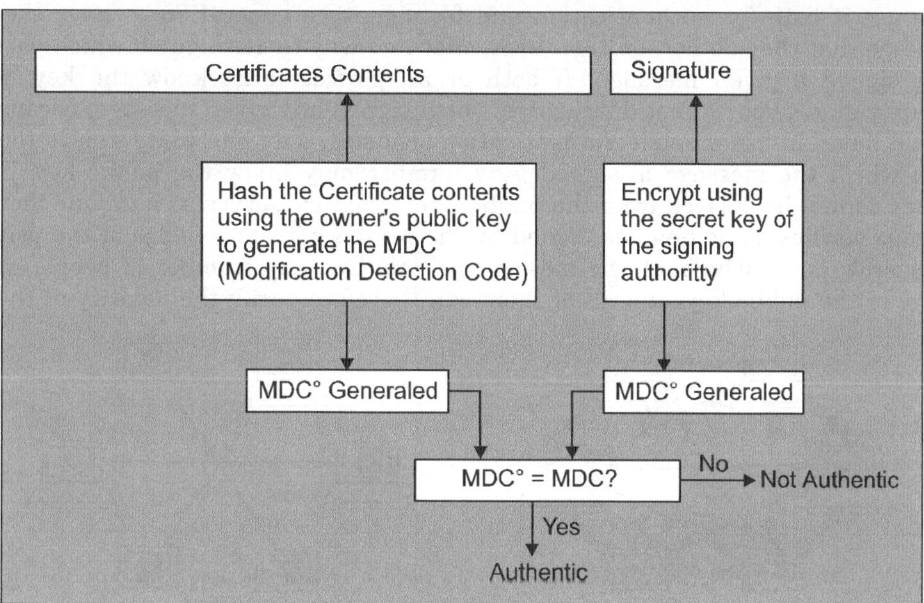

Figure 5.11 Validation of a Certificate

The request is sent with certificate signed by the certification authority. The host validates the certificate and makes sure that the certificate is signed by the central authority, then the host can use this certificate as a trusted information and takes the required action according to the contents of the certificate.

5.3.6 Why Asymmetric Cryptography?

Asymmetric cryptographic algorithms have the property that you do not use a single key — as in symmetric cryptographic algorithms such as AES — but a key pair. One of the keys (the public key) is used for encryption, and its corresponding private key must be used for decryption. The critical feature of asymmetric cryptography, which makes it useful, is this key pair — and more specifically, a particular feature of the key pair: the fact that one of the keys cannot be obtained from the other.

Authentication With Asymmetric Cryptography

In the case of asymmetric authentication methods — the core technology behind digital signatures and certificates — we normally speak of a private key (in the possession of the entity wishing to prove its identity) and the public key (in the possession of anyone who wishes to verify the identity of the entity possessing the private key).

You may, with the public key, verify that an entity has knowledge of the private key — but you cannot derive the private key from the public. This is the critical feature of asymmetric cryptographic schemes that makes them so useful.

This property is useful for a number of things: it greatly simplifies key exchange, as one example, and it solves one critical problem symmetric cryptography cannot solve — the problem of guaranteeing unique authentication and non-repudiation. Symmetric hashing/authentication methods — ones for which there is only one key, and both parties in the exchange use it both for authentication and for signature generation — have the distinct disadvantage that they do not, on their own, offer any way to distinguish which party to the exchange signed a given message. If both or all parties must know the key, based on cryptography alone, you cannot distinguish which signed any given message, because any of them could have. In asymmetric authentication schemes, only one party knows the private key, with which the message is signed. Any number may know the public key. Since the private key cannot be derived from the public, the signature serves as a unique identifier. If the message verifies as having een signed by the person with knowledge of the private key, we can narrow down who sent the message to one. But any number of people may have knowledge of the public key, and all of them can therefore verify the identity of the sender.

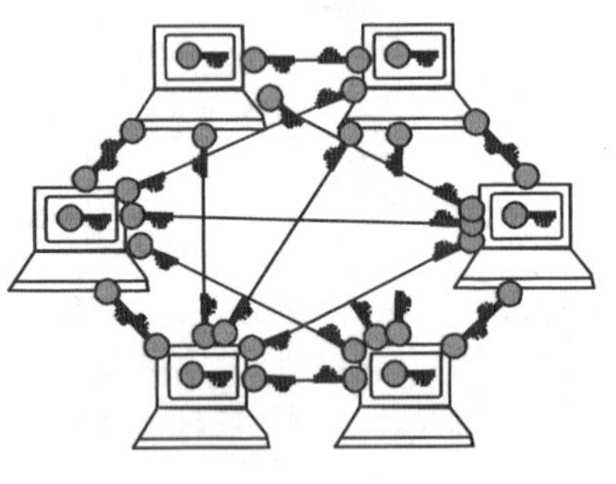

SYMMETRIC

Symmetric cryptography has an equation of $\frac{nxn-1}{2}$ for the number of keys needed. In a situation with 1000 users, that would mean 499,500 keys.

Figure 5.12 Symmetric Cryptography

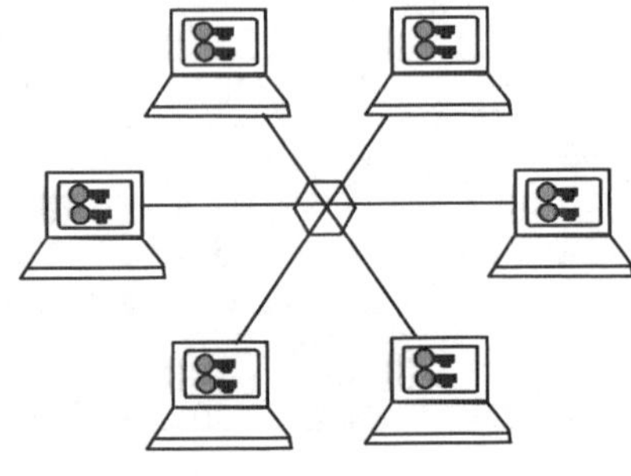

ASYMMETRIC

Asymmetric cryptography, using key pairs for each of its users, has n as the number of key pairs needed. In a situation 1000 users, that would mean 10000 key pairs.

Figure 5.13 Asymmetric Cryptography

5.3.7 How Asymmetric Cryptography is Used in Digital Signatures and Certificates

Digital signatures and certificates are particularly common applications of authentication with asymmetric cryptography.

A digital signature is a `transform` performed on a message using the private key, whose integrity may be verified with the public key.

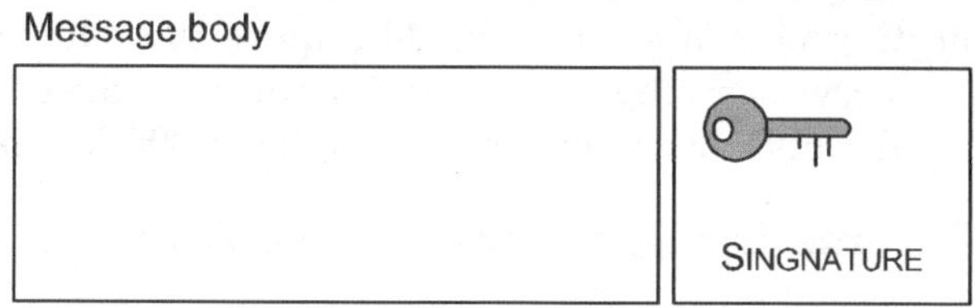

Figure. 5.14 Message digest signed with sender's private key. Verified with public key.

Again, the unique properties of asymmetric cryptography make it particularly useful for generating digital signatures. The correct signature may only be generated with the private key. Knowledge of the public key is only useful for verifying the signature. Any number of people may have knowledge of the public key for verification purposes, without compromising the private key. Since only one entity knows the private key, the private key serves as proof of the sending party's identity, and guarantees the integrity of messages they send.

A digital certificate is a piece of information which is digitally signed by a trusted third party, or certificate authority (CA), and which contains critical identification information, vouching for the identity of an entity. Digital certificates often themselves contain a public key corresponding to the private key the entity itself uses to prove its identity—the well-known web server certificates are examples of this type.

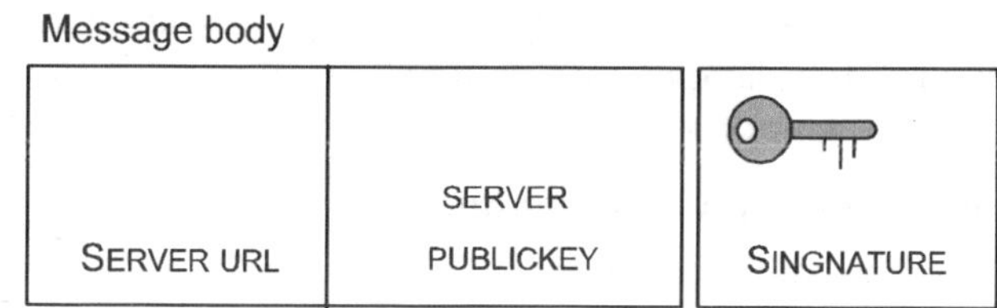

Figure. 515 Message digest signed with sender's private key. Verified with public key.

5.3.8 Encryption Using Asymmetric Cryptography

Asymmetric encryption schemes are used in a variety of applications. Probably the most visible, well-known application is in encrypted email, in peer-to-peer 'keyring' schemes such as Pretty Good Privacy (PGP).

In asymmetric encryption schemes, the public key is used for encrypting messages; these messages, once encrypted, can only be decrypted with the private key. So the recipient publishes or distributes the public key corresponding to a private key of which only they have knowledge. Anyone wishing to communicate securely with the holder of the private key encrypts his or her message using the public key. Only the recipient may decrypt and use the message; other holders of the public key cannot.

This feature of asymmetric cryptosystems greatly simplifies key exchange. In a large network of N communicating entities, if it is fully meshed, maintaining unique symmetric keys for each communicating pair of entities would require the management of $(n \times n\text{-}1) \div 2$ keys. Using asymmetric cryptography, this quantity can be reduced to N key pairs. In a group of 1,000 users, it's the difference between managing 1,000 key pairs or 499,500 keys.

Functions Whose Inverse is Significantly More Difficult

In all asymmetric cryptographic schemes, this property — the property that one key is used for encryption, and another for decryption, and the decryption key cannot be found from the encryption key — is derived from the use of mathematical functions whose inverse is extremely difficult to calculate.

You may understand an asymmetric cryptographic key pair as a pair of numbers which have some relationship associated with a mathematical function which is relatively easy to compute in one direction, but whose inverse is in practical terms intractable. This feature — the function which is tractable in one direction, but intractable in the other, is common to all asymmetric cryptosystems, including ECC.

5.4 RSA ALGORITHM

While there may be many algorithms and keys that have this property, the RSA algorithm (named after its founders, Ron Rivest, Adi Shamir, and Leonard Adleman) has become almost synonymous with public key cryptography. Let's first see how RSA works and then examine why it works. Suppose that Bunty wants to receive encrypted messages, as shown in Figure 5.2-5. The are two inter-related components of RSA:

- choice of the public key and the private key
- the encryption and decryption algorithm

In order to choose the public and private keys, Bunty must do the following:

Choose two large prime numbers, p and q. How large should p and q be? The larger the values, the more difficult it is to break RSA but the longer it takes to perform the encoding and decoding. RSA Laboratories recommends that the product of p and q be on the order of 768 bits for personal use and 1024 bits for corporate use (Which leads one to wonder why corporate use is deemed so much more important than personal use!).

`Compute n = pq and z = (p - 1)(q - 1).`

Choose a number, e, less than n, which has no common factors (other than 1) with z. (In this case, e and z are said to be relatively prime). The letter 'e' is used since this value will be used in encryption.

Find a number, d, such that ed-1 is exactly divisible (i.e., with no remainder) by z. The letter 'd' is used because this value will be used in decryption. Put another way, given e, we choose d such that the integer remainder when ed is divided by z is 1. (The integer remainder when an integer x is divided by the integer n, is denoted x mod n).

The public key that Bunty makes available to the world is the pair of numbers (n, e); his private key is the pair of numbers (n, d).

The encryption by Anita, and the decryption by Bunty is done as follows:

Suppose Anita wants to send Bunty *a* bit pattern, or number, m, such that m < n. To encode, Anita performs the exponentiation, me, and then computes the integer remainder when meis divided by n. Thus, the encrypted value, c, of the plaintext message, m, that Anita sends is:

c = me mod n

To decrypt the received ciphertext message, c, Bunty computes

m = cd mod n

which requires the use of his secret key, (n,d).

As a simple example of RSA, suppose Bunty chooses p=5 and q=7 (admittedly, these values are far too small to be secure). Then n=35 and z=24. Bunty chooses e=5, since 5 and 24 have no common factors. Finally, Bunty chooses d=29, since 5*29 - 1 (i.e., ed -1) is exactly divisible by 24. Bunty makes the two values, n=35 and e=5, public and keeps the value d=29 secret. Observing these two public values, suppose Anita now wants to send the letters 'l' 'o' 'v' and 'e' to Bunty. Interpreting each letter as a number between 1 and 26 (with 'a' being 1, and 'z' being 26), Anita and Bunty perform the encryption and decryption shown in Figures 5.16 and 5.17, respectively:

plaintext letter	m:numeric representation	m^e	ciphertext $c = m^e \bmod n$
l	12	248832	17
o	15	759375	15
v	22	5153632	22
e	5	3125	10

Figure 5.16 Anita's RSA encryption, e=5, n = 35

ciphertext c	c^d	$m = c^d \bmod n$	plaintext letter
17	481968572106750915091411825223072000	248832	17
15	12783403948858939111232757568359400	759375	15
22	8.5164331908653770195619449972111e+38	515632	22
10	100000000000000000000000000000	3125	10

Figure 5.17 Anita's RSA encryption, e=5, n = 35

Given that "toy" example in Figures 5.16 and 5.17 has already produced some extremely large numbers, and given that we know that we saw earlier that p and q should each be several hundred bits long, several practical issues regarding RSA come to mind. How does one choose large prime numbers? How does one then choose e and d? How does one perform exponentiation with large numbers?

We do note here that the exponentiation required by RSA is a rather time consuming process. RSA Data Security [RSA 1999b] says its software toolkit can encrypt/decrypt at a throughput of 21.6 Kbits per second with a 512-bit value for n and 7.4 Kbits per second with a 1024-bit value. DES is at least one hundred times fast in software and between 1000 and 10000 times faster in hardware. As a result, RSA is often used in practice in combination with DES. For example, if Anita wants to send Bunty a large amount of encrypted data at high speed, she could do the following. First Anita chooses a DES key that will be used to encode the data itself; this key is sometimes referred to as a session key, KS. Anita must inform Bunty of the session key, since this is the shared secret key they will use for DES. Anita thus encrypts the session key value using Bunty's public RSA key, i.e., computes c = (KS)e mod n. Bunty receives the RSA-encrypted session key, c, and decrypts to obtain the session key, KS.. Bunty now knows the session key that Anita will use for her DES-encrypted data transfer.

Why does RSA work?

The RSA encryption/decryption above appears rather magical. Why should it be that by applying the encryption algorithm and then the decryption algorithm, one recovers the original message? In order to understand why RSA works, we'll need to perform arithmetic operations using so-called modulo-n arithmetic. In modular arithmetic, one performs the usual operations of addition, multiplication and exponentiation. However, the result of each operation is replaced by the integer remainder that is left when the result is divided by n. We will take $n = pq$, where p and q are the large prime numbers used in the RSA algorithm.

Recall that under RSA encryption, a message (represented by an integer), m, is first exponentiated to the power e using modulo-n arithmetic to encrypt. Decryption is performed by raising this value to the power d, again using modulo n arithmetic. The result of an encryption step, followed by a decryption step is thus (me)d. Let's now see what we can say about this quantity. We have:

(me)d mod n = med mod n

Although we're trying to remove some of the "magic" about why RSA works, we'll need to use a rather magical result from number theory here. Specifically, we'll need the result that says if p and q are prime, and $n = pq$, then xy mod n is the same as x(y mod (p /0 1)(q – 1)) Applying this result, we have

(me)d mod n = m (ed mod (p-1)(q-1)) mod n

But remember that we chose e and d such that ed -1 is exactly divisible (i.e., with no remainder) by (p – 1)(q – 1), or equivalently that ed is divisible by (p – 1)(q – 1) with a reminder of 1, and thus ed mod (p – 1)(q – 1) = 1. This gives us

(me)d mod n = m 1mod n = m

i.e., that

$$(me)d \mod n = m.$$

This is the result we were hoping for! By first exponentiating to the power of e (i.e., encrypting) and then exponentiating to the power of d (i.e., decrypting), we obtain the original value, m. Even more remarkable is the fact that if we first exponentiate to the power of d and then exponentiate to the power of e, i.e., we reverse the order of encryption and decryption, performing the decryption operation first and then applying the encryption operation, we also obtain the original value, m! (The proof for this result follows the exact same reasoning as above). We will see shortly that this wonderful property of the RSA algorithm,

$$(me)d \mod n = m = (md)e \mod n$$

will be of great use.

The security of RSA relies on the fact that there are no known algorithms for quickly factoring a number, in this case the public value n, into the primes p and q. If one knew p and q, then given the public value e, one could then easily compute the secret key, d. On the other hand, it is not know whether or not there exist fast algorithms for factoring a number, and in this sense the security of RSA is not "guaranteed."

RSA Algorithm

The RSA algorithm is named after Ron Rivest, Adi Shamir and Len Adleman, who invented it in 1977 [RIVE78]. The basic technique was first discovered in 1973 by Clifford Cocks [COCK73] of CESG (part of the British GCHQ) but this was a secret until 1997. The patent taken out by RSA Labs has expired.

The RSA algorithm can be used for both public key encryption and digital signatures. Its security is based on the difficulty of factoring large integers.

Key Generation Algorithm

1. Generate two large random primes, p and q, of approximately equal size such that their product n = pq is of the required bit length, e.g. 1024 bits. [See note (1)].
2. Compute n = pq and (ϕ) phi = (p–1)(q–1).
3. Choose an integer e, 1 < e < phi, such that gcd(e, phi) = 1. [See note (2)].
4. Compute the secret exponent d, 1 < d < phi, such that ed = 1 (mod phi). [See note (3)].
5. The public key is (n, e) and the private key is (n, d). Keep all the values d, p, q and phi secret.

(1) n is known as the modulus.

(2) e is known as the public exponent or encryption exponent or just the exponent.

(3) d is known as the secret exponent or decryption exponent.

Encryption

Sender A does the following:

1. Obtains the recipient B's public key (n, e).

2. Represents the plaintext message as a positive integer m [see note].
3. Computes the ciphertext $c = m^e \bmod n$.
4. Sends the ciphertext c to B.

Decryption

Recipient B does the following:-

1. Uses his private key (n, d) to compute $m = c^d \bmod n$.
2. Extracts the plaintext from the message representative m.

Digital signing

Sender A does the following:-

1. Creates a message digest of the information to be sent.
2. Represents this digest as an integer m between 0 and n–1. [See note].
3. Uses her private key (n, d) to compute the signature s = md mod n.
4. Sends this signatures to the recipient, B.

Signature verification

Recipient B does the following:

1. Uses sender A's public key (n, e) to compute integer $v = s^e \bmod n$.
2. Extracts the message digest from this integer.
3. Independently computes the message digest of the information that has been signed.
4. If both message digests are identical, the signature is valid.

Notes on practical applications

1. To generate the primes p and q, generate a random number of bit length b/2 where b is the required bit length of n; set the low bit (this ensures the number is odd) and set the two highest bits (this ensures that the high bit of n is also set); check if prime (use the Rabin-Miller test); if not, increment the number by two and check again until you find a prime. This is p. Repeat for q starting with a random integer of length b-b/2. If p<q, swop p and q (this only matters if you intend using the CRT form of the private key). In the extremely unlikely event that p = q, check your random number generator. Alternatively, instead of incrementing by 2, just generate another random number each time.

   There are stricter rules in ANSI X9.31 to produce strong primes and other restrictions on p and q to minimise the possibility of known techniques being used against the algorithm. There is much argument about this topic. It is probably better just to use a longer key length.
2. In practice, common choices for e are 3, 17 and 65537 ($2^{16} + 1$). These are Fermat primes, sometimes referred to as F0, F2 and F4 respectively (Fx=2^(2^x)+1). They are chosen because they make the modular exponentiation operation faster. Also, having chosen e, it is simpler to test whether gcd(e, p–1)=1 and gcd(e, q–1)=1 while

generating and testing the primes in step 1. Values of p or q that fail this test can be rejected there and then. (Even better: if e is prime and greater than 2 then you can do the less-expensive test (p mod e)!=1 instead of gcd(p–1,e)==1.)

3. To compute the value for d, use the Extended Euclidean Algorithm to calculate $d = e^{-1} \bmod phi$ (this is known as modular inversion).
4. When representing the plaintext octets as the representative integer m, it is usual to add random padding characters to make the size of the integer m large and less susceptible to certain types of attack. If m = 0 or 1 or n-1 there is no security as the ciphertext has the same value. It is important to make sure that m < n otherwise the algorithm will fail. This is usually done by making sure the first octet of m is equal to 0x00.
5. Decryption and signing are identical as far as the mathematics is concerned as both use the private key. Similarly, encryption and verification both use the same mathematical operation with the public key. That is, mathematically, for m < n,

$$m = (m^e \bmod n)^d \bmod n = (m^d \bmod n)^e \bmod n$$

However, note these important differences in implementation:-

- The signature is derived from a message digest of the original information. The recipient will need to follow exactly the same process to derive the message digest, using an identical set of data.
- The recommended methods for deriving the representative integers are different for encryption and signing (encryption involves random padding, but signing uses the same padding each time).

Summary of RSA

- n = pq, where p and q are distinct primes.
- phi, $\phi = (p-1)(q-1)$
- e < n such that gcd(e, phi)=1
- $d = e^{-1} \bmod phi$.
- $c = m^e \bmod n$, $1<m<n$.
- $m = c^d \bmod n$.

Key Length

When we talk about the key length of an RSA key, we are referring to the length of the modulus, n, in bits. The minimum recommended key length for a secure RSA transmission is currently 1024 bits. A key length of 512 bits is now no longer considered secure, although cracking it is still not a trivial task for the likes of you and me. The longer your information is needed to be kept secure, the longer the key you should use.

There is small one area of confusion in defining the key length. One convention is that the key length is the position of the most significant bit in n that has value '1', where the least significant bit is at position 1. Equivalently, key length = ceiling($\log_2$(n+1)). The other convention, sometimes used, is that the key length is the number of bytes needed to store n multiplied by eight, i.e. ceiling($\log_{256}$(n+1)).

The key used in the RSA Example paper [KALI93] is an example. In hex form the modulus is

```
0A 66 79 1D C6 98 81 68 DE 7A B7 74 19 BB 7F B0
C0 01 C6 27 10 27 00 75 14 29 42 E1 9A 8D 8C 51
D0 53 B3 E3 78 2A 1D E5 DC 5A F4 EB E9 94 68 17
01 14 A1 DF E6 7C DC 9A 9A F5 5D 65 56 20 BB AB
```

The most significant byte 0x0A in binary is 00001010'B. The most significant bit is at position 508, so its key length is 508 bits. On the other hand, this value needs 64 bytes to store it, so the key length could also be referred to by some as 64 × 8 = 512 bits. We prefer the former method. You can get into difficulties with the X9.31 method for signatures if you use the latter convention.

Computational Efficiency and the Chinese Remainder Theorem (CRT)

Key generation is only carried out occasionally and so computational efficiency is less of an issue.

The calculation a = be mod n is known as modular exponentiation and one efficient method to carry this out on a computer is the binary left-to-right method. To solve y = x^e mod n let e be represented in base 2 as

$$e = e(k-1)e(k-2)\ldots e_{(1)}e_{(0)}$$

where **e(k-1)** is the most significant non-zero bit and bit e(0) the least.

```
set y = x
for bit j = k - 2 downto 0
begin
  y = y * y mod n   /* square */
  if e(j) == 1 then
    y = y * x mod n  /* multiply */
end
return y
```

The time to carry out modular exponentation increases with the number of bits set to one in the exponent e. For encryption, an appropriate choice of e can reduce the computational effort required to carry out the computation of $c = m^e$ mod n. Popular choices like 3, 17 and 65537 are all primes with only two bits set: 3 = 0011'B, 17 = 0x11, 65537 = 0x10001.

The bits in the decryption exponent d, however, will not be so convenient and so decryption using the standard method of modular exponentiation will take longer than encryption. Don't make the mistake of trying to contrive a small value for d; it is not secure.

An alternative method of representing the private key uses the Chinese Remainder Theorem (CRT). The private key is represented as a quintuple (p, q, dP, dQ, and qInv), where p and q are prime factors of n, dP and dQ are known as the CRT exponents, and qInv is the CRT coefficient. The CRT method of decryption is four times faster overall than calculating m = cd mod n.The extra values for the private key are:-

```
  dP = (1/e) mod (p-1)
  dQ = (1/e) mod (q-1)
qInv = (1/q) mod p where p > q
```

These are pre-computed and saved along with p and q as the private key. To compute the message m given c do the following:-

```
m1 = c^dP mod p
m2 = c^dQ mod q
 h = qInv(m1 - m2) mod p
 m = m2 + hq
```

Even though there are more steps in this procedure, the modular exponentation to be carried out uses much shorter exponents and so it is less expensive overall.

Chris Becke has pointed out that most large integer packages will fail when computing h if m1 < m2. This can be easily fixed by computing

```
h = qInv(m1 + p - m2) mod p
```

or, alternatively, as we do it in our BigDigits implementation of RSA,

```
if (bdCompare(m1, m2) < 0)
   bdAdd(m1, m1, p);
bdSubtract(m1, m1, m2);
/* Let h = qInv ( m_1 - m_2 ) mod p. */
bdModMult(h, qInv, m1, p);
```

A very simple example of RSA encryption

This is an extremely simple example using numbers you can work out on a pocket calculator (those of you over the age of 35 can probably even do it by hand).

1. Select primes p=11, q=3.
2. n = pq = 11.3 = 33

   phi = (p-1)(q-1) = 10.2 = 20
3. Choose e=3

   Check gcd(e, p-1) = gcd(3, 10) = 1 (i.e. 3 and 10 have no common factors except 1),

   and check gcd(e, q-1) = gcd(3, 2) = 1

   therefore gcd(e, phi) = gcd(e, (p-1)(q-1)) = gcd(3, 20) = 1
4. Compute d such that ed = 1 (mod phi)

   i.e. compute d = e-1 mod phi = 3^{-1} mod 20

i.e. find a value for d such that phi divides (ed-1)

i.e. find d such that 20 divides 3d-1.

Simple testing (d = 1, 2, ...) gives d = 7

Check: ed-1 = 3.7 - 1 = 20, which is divisible by phi.

5. Public key = (n, e) = (33, 3)

   Private key = (n, d) = (33, 7).

This is actually the smallest possible value for the modulus n for which the RSA algorithm works.

Now say we want to encrypt the message m = 7,

$$c = m^e \bmod n = 73 \bmod 33 = 343 \bmod 33 = 13.$$

Hence the ciphertext c = 13.

To check decryption we compute

$$m' = cd \bmod n = 13^7 \bmod 33 = 7.$$

Note that we don't have to calculate the full value of 13 to the power 7 here. We can make use of the fact that

$$a = bc \bmod n = (b \bmod n).(c \bmod n) \bmod n$$

so we can break down a potentially large number into its components and combine the results of easier, smaller calculations to calculate the final value.

One way of calculating m' is as follows:-

$$m' = 13^7 \bmod 33 = 13^{(3+3+1)} \bmod 33 = 13^3.13^3.13 \bmod 33$$
$$= (13^3 \bmod 33).(13^3 \bmod 33).(13 \bmod 33) \bmod 33$$
$$= (2197 \bmod 33).(2197 \bmod 33).(13 \bmod 33) \bmod 33$$
$$= 19.19.13 \bmod 33 = 4693 \bmod 33$$
$$= 7.$$

Now if we calculate the ciphertext c for all the possible values of m (0 to 32), we get

m	0	1	2	3	4	5	6	7	8	9	10	11	12	13	14	15	16
c	0	1	8	27	31	26	18	13	17	3	10	11	12	19	5	9	4
m	17	18	19	20	21	22	23	24	25	26	27	28	29	30	31	32	
c	29	24	28	14	21	22	23	30	16	20	15	7	2	6	25	32	

Note that all 33 values of m (0 to 32) map to a unique code c in the same range in a sort of random manner. In this case we have nine values of m that map to the same value of c - these are known as unconcealed messages. m = 0, 1 and n-1 will always do this for any n, no matter how large. But in practice, higher values shouldn't be a problem when we use large values for n in the order of several hundred bits.

If we wanted to use this system to keep secrets, we could let A=2, B=3, ..., Z=27. (We specifically avoid 0 and 1 here for the reason given above). Thus the plaintext message "HELLOWORLD" would be represented by the set of integers m1, m2, ...

(9,6,13,13,16,24,16,19,13,5)

Using our table above, we obtain ciphertext integers c1, c2, ...

`(3,18,19,19,4,30,4,28,19,26)`

Note that this example is no more secure than using a simple Caesar substitution cipher, but it serves to illustrate a simple example of the mechanics of RSA encryption.

Remember that calculating me mod n is easy, but calculating the inverse c-e mod n is very difficult, well, for large n's anyway. However, if we can factor n into its prime factors p and q, the solution becomes easy again, even for large n's. Obviously, if we can get hold of the secret exponent d, the solution is easy, too.

A slightly less simple example of the RSA algorithm

This time, to make life slightly less easy for those who can crack simple Caesar substitution codes, we will group the characters into blocks of three and compute a message representative integer for each block.

ATTACKxATxSEVEN = ATT ACK XAT XSE VEN

In the same way that a decimal number can be represented as the sum of powers of ten, e.g.

$$135 = 1 \times 10^2 + 3 \times 10^1 + 5,$$

we could represent our blocks of three characters in base 26 using A=0, B=1, C=2, ..., Z=25

$$\text{ATT} = 0 \times 26^2 + 19 \times 26^1 + 19 = 513$$

$$\text{ACK} = 0 \times 26^2 + 2 \times 26^1 + 10 = 62$$

$$\text{XAT} = 23 \times 26^2 + 0 \times 26^1 + 19 = 15567$$

$$\text{XSE} = 23 \times 26^2 + 18 \times 26^1 + 4 = 16020$$

$$\text{VEN} = 21 \times 26^2 + 4 \times 26^1 + 13 = 14313$$

For this example, to keep things simple, we'll not worry about numbers and punctuation characters, or what happens with groups AAA or AAB.

In this system of encoding, the maximum value of a group (ZZZ) would be 26^3-1 = 17575, so we require a modulus n greater than this value.

1. We "generate" primes p=137 and q=131 (we cheat by looking for suitable primes around vn)
2. `n = pq = 137.131 = 17947`

   `phi = (p-1)(q-1) = 136.130 = 17680`
3. Select `e = 3`

   check gcd(e, p-1) = gcd(3, 136) = 1, OK and

   check gcd(e, q-1) = gcd(3, 130) = 1, OK.
4. Compute d = e-1 mod phi = 3-1 mod 17680 = 11787.
5. Hence public key, (n, e) = (17947, 3) and private key (n, d) = (17947, 11787).

Question: Why couldn't we use e=17 here?

To encrypt the first integer that represents "ATT", we have

```
c = mᵉ mod n = 5133 mod 17947 = 8363.
```

We can verify that our private key is valid by decrypting

$$m' = cd \bmod n = 8363^{11787} \bmod 17947 = 513.$$

Overall, our plaintext is represented by the set of integers m

```
(513, 62, 15567, 16020, 14313)
```

We compute corresponding ciphertext integers c = me mod n, (which is still possible by using a calculator)

```
(8363, 5017, 11884, 9546, 13366)
```

You are welcome to compute the inverse of these ciphertext integers using $m = c^d \bmod n$ to verify that the RSA algorithm still holds. However, this is now outside the realms of hand calculations unless you are very patient.

To help you carry out these modular arithmetic calculations, download our *free modular arithmetic* command line programs.

Note that this is still a very insecure example. Starting with the knowledge that the modulus 17947 is probably derived from two prime numbers close to its square root, a little testing of suitable candidates from a table of prime numbers would get you the answer pretty quickly. Or just work methodically through the table of prime numbers dividing n by each value until you get no remainder. You could also write a simple computer program to factor n that just divides by every odd number starting from 3 until it reaches a number greater than the square root of n.

A real example

In practice, we don't have a series of small integers to encrypt like we had in the above examples, we just have one big one. We put our message into an octet string, most significant byte first, and then convert to a large integer. Also, rather than trying to represent the plaintext as an integer directly, we generate a random *session key* and use that to encrypt the plaintext with a conventional, much faster symmetrical algorithm like Triple DES or AES-128. We then use the much slower public key encryption algorithm to encrypt just the session key.

The sender A then transmits a message to the recipient B in a format something like this:

```
Session key encrypted with RSA = xxxx
Plaintext encrypted with session key = xxxxxxxxxxxxxxxx
```

The recipient B would extract the encrypted session key and use his private key (n,d) to decrypt it. He would then use this session key with a conventional symmetrical decryption algorithm to decrypt the actual message. Typically the transmission would include in plaintext details of the encryption algorithms used, padding and encoding methods, initialisation vectors and other details required by the recipient. The only secret required to be kept, as always, should be the private key.

If Mallory intercepts the transmission, he can either try and crack the conventionally-encrypted plaintext directly, or he can try and decrypt the encryped session key and then use that in turn. Obviously, this system is as strong as its weakest link.

When signing, it is usual to use RSA to sign the message digest of the message rather than the message itself. A one-way hash function like SHA-1 or SHA-256 is used. The sender A then sends the signed message to B in a format like this

```
Hash algorithm = hh
Message content = xxxxxxxxx...xxx
Signature = digest signed with RSA = xxxx
```

The recipient will decrypt the signature to extract the signed message digest, m; independently compute the message digest, m', of the actual message content; and check that m and m' are equal. Putting the message digest algorithm at the beginning of the message enables the recipient to compute the message digest on the fly while reading the message.

PKCS#1 Schemes

The most common scheme using RSA is PKCS#1 version 1.5 [PKCS1]. This standard describes schemes for both encryption and signing. The encryption scheme PKCS#1v1.5 has some known weaknesses, but these can easily be avoided. See *Weaknesses in RSA* below.

There is an excellent paper by Burt Kalinski of RSA Laboratories written in the early 1990s [KALI93] that describes in great detail everything you need to know about encoding and signing using RSA. There are full examples right down to listing out the bytes. OK, it uses MD2 and a small 508-bit modulus and obviously doesn't deal with refinements built up over the last decade to deal with more subtle security threats, but it's an excellent introduction.

Encryption using PKCS#1v1.5

Algorithm: Encryption using PKCS#1v1.5

INPUT: Recipient's RSA public key, (n, e) of length k = |n| bytes; data D (typically a session key) of length |D| bytes with |D|<=k-11.

OUTPUT: Encrypted data block of length k bytes

1. Form the k-byte encoded message block, EB,
2. `EB = 00 || 02 || PS || 00 || D`

   where || denotes concatenation and PS is a string of `k-|D|-3` non-zero randomly-generated bytes (i.e. at least eight random bytes).
3. Convert the byte string, EB, to an integer, m, most significant byte first,

---

4. `m = StringToInteger(EB, k)`
5. Encrypt with the RSA algorithm
6. `c = m^e mod n`
7. Convert the resulting ciphertext, c, to a k-byte output block, OB
8. `OB = IntegerToString(m, k)`
9. Output OB.

The conversions in steps (2) and (4) from byte string to large integer representative and back again may not be immediately obvious. Large integers and byte (bit) strings are conceptually different even though they may both be stored as arrays of bytes in your computer.

Worked Example

Bunty 1024-bit RSA encryption key in hex format:

```
n=
A9E167983F39D55FF2A093415EA6798985C8355D9A915BFB1D01DA197026170F
BDA522D035856D7A986614415CCFB7B7083B09C991B81969376DF9651E7BD9A9
3324A37F3BBBAF460186363432CB07035952FC858B3104B8CC18081448E64F1C
FB5D60C4E05C1F53D37F53D86901F105F87A70D1BE83C65F38CF1C2CAA6AA7EB
e=010001
d=
67CD484C9A0D8F98C21B65FF22839C6DF0A6061DBCEDA7038894F21C6B0F8B35
DE0E827830CBE7BA6A56AD77C6EB517970790AA0F4FE45E0A9B2F419DA8798D6
308474E4FC596CC1C677DCA991D07C30A0A2C5085E217143FC0D073DF0FA6D14
9E4E63F01758791C4B981C3D3DB01BDFFA253BA3C02C9805F61009D887DB0319
```

A randomly-generated one-off session key for AES-128 might be

```
D=4E636AF98E40F3ADCFCCB698F4E80B9F
```

The encoded message block, EB, after encoding but before encryption, with random padding bytes shown in green,

```
0002257F48FD1F1793B7E5E02306F2D3228F5C95ADF5F31566729F132AA12009
E3FC9B2B475CD6944EF191E3F59545E671E474B555799FE3756099F044964038
B16B2148E9A2F9C6F44BB5C52E3C6C8061CF694145FAFDB24402AD1819EACEDF
4A36C6E4D2CD8FC1D62E5A1268F496004E636AF98E40F3ADCFCCB698F4E80B9F
```

After RSA encryption, the output is

```
3D2AB25B1EB667A40F504CC4D778EC399A899C8790EDECEF062CD739492C9CE5
8B92B9ECF32AF4AAC7A61EAEC346449891F49A722378E008EFF0B0A8DBC6E621
EDC90CEC64CF34C640F5B36C48EE9322808AF8F4A0212B28715C76F3CB99AC7E
```

```
609787ADCE055839829E0142C44B676D218111FFE69F9D41424E177CBA3A435B
```

Note that the output for encryption will be different each time (or should be!) because of the random padding used.

Encrypting a message

For a plaintext message, say,

```
PT="Hello world!"
```

that is, the 12 bytes in hex format,

```
PT=48656C6C6F20776F726C6421
```

Then, using the 128-bit session key from above,

```
KY=4E636AF98E40F3ADCFCCB698F4E80B9F
```

and the uniquely-generated 128-bit initialization vector (IV)

```
IV=5732164B3ABB6C4969ABA381C1CA75BA
```

the ciphertext using AES-128 in CBC mode with PKCS padding is,

```
CT=67290EF00818827C777929A56BC3305B
```

The sender would then send a transmission to the recipient (in this case, Bunty) including the following information in some agreed format

---

```
Recipient: Bunty
Key Encryption Algorithm: rsaEncryption
Encrypted Key:
3D2AB25B1EB667A40F504CC4D778EC399A899C8790EDECEF062CD739492C9CE5
8B92B9ECF32AF4AAC7A61EAEC346449891F49A722378E008EFF0B0A8DBC6E621
EDC90CEC64CF34C640F5B36C48EE9322808AF8F4A0212B28715C76F3CB99AC7E
609787ADCE055839829E0142C44B676D218111FFE69F9D41424E177CBA3A435B
Content Encryption Algorithm: aes128-cbc
IV: 5732164B3ABB6C4969ABA381C1CA75BA
Encrypted Content:
67290EF00818827C777929A56BC3305B
```

The usual formats used for such a message are either a *CMS enveloped-data object* or XML, but the above summary includes all the necessary info (well, perhaps "Bunty" might be defined a bit more accurately). CMS enveloped-data objects (yes, that's *enveloped* not *encrypted*) use ASN.1 and are encoded using either DER- or BER-encoding. Cryptographic Message Syntax (CMS) is a less-ambiguous version of the earlier PKCS#7 standard (also of the same name) and is designed to be used in S/MIME messages. The terminology for CMS and ASN.1 may sound messy, but the end results are well-defined and universally-accepted. On the other hand, the XML cryptographic standards are, to be honest, a complete mess. Pretty Good Privacy (PGP) also has a format for RSA messages, although PGP stopped using RSA because of patent issues back in the 1990s.

Nothing, of course, stops you and your recipient from agreeing on your own format and using that. But be careful, even the experts get these things wrong and accidentally give away more than they realise.

Signing using PKCS#1v1.5

Algorithm: Signing using PKCS#1v1.5

INPUT: Sender's RSA private key, (n, d) of length k = |n| bytes; message, M, to be signed; message digest algorithm, Hash.

OUTPUT: Signed data block of length k bytes

1. Compute the message digest H of the message,
2. `H = Hash(M)`
3. Form the byte string, T, from the message digest, H, according to the message digest algorithm, Hash, as follows

Hash	T
MD5	30 20 30 0c 06 08 2a 86 48 86 f7 0d 02 05 05 00 04 10 || H
SHA-1	30 21 30 09 06 05 2b 0e 03 02 1a 05 00 04 14 || H
SHA-256	30 31 30 0d 06 09 60 86 48 01 65 03 04 02 01 05 00 04 20 || H
SHA-384	30 41 30 0d 06 09 60 86 48 01 65 03 04 02 02 05 00 04 30 || H
SHA-512	30 51 30 0d 06 09 60 86 48 01 65 03 04 02 03 05 00 04 40 || H

4. Where T is an ASN.1 value of type *DigestInfo* encoded using the Distinguished Encoding Rules (DER).
5. Form the k-byte encoded message block, EB,
6. `EB = 00 || 01 || PS || 00 || T`

   where || denotes concatenation and PS is a string of bytes all of value 0xFF of such length so that |EB|=k.
7. Convert the byte string, EB, to an integer m, most significant byte first,
8. `m = StringToInteger(EB, k)`
9. Sign with the RSA algorithm
10. `s = m^d mod n`
11. Convert the resulting signature value, s, to a k-byte output block, OB

12. `OB = IntegerToString(s, k)`
13. Output OB.

Worked Example

Anita's 1024-bit RSA signing key in hex format:

```
n=
E08973398DD8F5F5E88776397F4EB005BB5383DE0FB7ABDC7DC775290D052E6D
12DFA68626D4D26FAA5829FC97ECFA82510F3080BEB1509E4644F12CBBD832CF
C6686F07D9B060ACBEEE34096A13F5F7050593DF5EBA3556D961FF197FC981E6
F86CEA874070EFAC6D2C749F2DFA553AB9997702A648528C4EF357385774575F
e=010001
d=
00A403C327477634346CA686B57949014B2E8AD2C862B2C7D748096A8B91F736
F275D6E8CD1590602731473564 4D95CD6763CEB49F56AC2F376E1CEE0EBF282D
F439906F34D86E085BD5656AD841F313D72D395EFE33CBFF29E4030B3D05A28F
B7F18EA27637B07957D32F2BDE8706227D04665EC91BAF8B1AC3EC9144AB7F21
```

The message to be signed is, of course,

```
M="abc"
```

that is, the 3 bytes in hex format,

```
PT=616263
```

The message digest algorithm is SHA-1, so

```
H = Hash("abc") = A9993E364706816ABA3E25717850C26C9CD0D89D
```

The DigestInfo value for SHA-1 is

```
T=
3021300906052B0E03021A05000414A9993E364706816ABA3E25717850C26C9C
D0D89D
```

The encoded message block, EB, after encoding but before signing is

```
0001FFFFFFFFFFFFFFFFFFFFFFFFFFFFFFFFFFFFFFFFFFFFFFFFFFFFFFFFFFFF
FFFFFFFFFFFFFFFFFFFFFFFFFFFFFFFFFFFFFFFFFFFFFFFFFFFFFFFFFFFFFFFF
FFFFFFFFFFFFFFFFFFFFFFFFFFFFFFFFFFFFFFFFFFFFFFFFFFFFFFFF00302130
0906052B0E03021A05000414A9993E364706816ABA3E25717850C26C9CD0D89D
```

After RSA signing, the output is

```
60AD5A78FB4A4030EC542C8974CD15F55384E836554CEDD9A322D5F4135C6267
A9D20970C54E6651070B0144D43844C899320DD8FA7819F7EBC6A7715287332E
C8675C136183B3F8A1F81EF969418267130A756FDBB2C71D9A667446E34E0EAD
```

9CF31BFB66F816F319D0B7E430A5F2891553986E003720261C7E9022C0D9F11F

Weaknesses in RSA

Small encryption exponent

If you use a small exponent like e=3 and send the same message to different recipients and just use the RSA algorithm without adding random padding to the message, then an eavedropper could recover the plaintext.

Using the same key for encryption and signing

Given that the underlying mathematics is the same for encryption and signing, only in reverse, if an attacker can convince a key holder to sign an unformatted encrypted message using the same key then she gets the original.

Acting as an oracle

There are techniques to recover the plaintext if a user just blindly returns the RSA transformation of the input. So don't do that.

Solutions

1. Don't use the same RSA key for encryption and signing.
2. If using PKCS#v1.5 encoding, use `e=0x10001` for your public exponent.
3. Always format your input before encrypting or signing.
4. Always add fresh random padding - at least 8 bytes - to your message before encrypting.
5. When decrypting, check the format of the decrypted block. If it is not as expected, return an error, not the decrypted string.
6. Similarly, when verifying a signature, if there is any error whatsoever, just respond with "Invalid Signature".

5.4.1 RSA – And The Integer Factorization Problem

The first asymmetric cryptosystem to have seen widespread use is also one of the most accessible illustrations of this principle in action. RSA gets its security from the difficulty of factoring very large numbers. The difficulty of getting the plaintext message back from the ciphertext and the public key is related to the difficulty of factoring a very large product of two prime numbers.

As an illustration of this: imagine you were to take two very large prime numbers — say, 200 digits long, and were then to multiply them together. Now the result you get has two particular properties:

- It is very large (about 400 digits in length),
- It has two, and exactly two factors, both prime numbers — the two primes you just multiplied together

You can easily — given the two prime numbers from which you start — find the product. But finding the primes given only the product is more difficult. So much more, in fact, that once the numbers get adequately large, it is almost impossible to find them. You simply cannot assemble enough computing power to do so.

So the multiplying of two large prime numbers together is the (relatively) easy forward function in this asymmetric algorithm. Its inverse — the factor finding operation — is considerably more difficult, and in practical terms, it's intractable.

The RSA system employs this fact to generate public and private key pairs. The keys are functions of the product and of the primes.

Operations performed using the cryptosystem are arranged so that the operations we wish to be tractable require performing the relatively easy forward function — multiplication.

Conversely, the operations we wish to make difficult — finding the plaintext from the ciphertext using only the public key — require performing the inverse operation — solving the factoring problem.

5.4.2 Significance of Factoring in Cryptography

Factoring is the underlying, presumably hard problem upon which several public-key cryptosystems are based, including RSA. Factoring an RSA modulus would allow an attacker to figure out the private key; thus, anyone who can factor the modulus can decrypt messages and forge signatures. The security of RSA depends on the factoring problem being difficult and the presence of no other types of attack. Unfortunately, it has not been proven that factoring must be difficult, and there remains a possibility that a quick and easy factoring method might be discovered although factoring researchers consider this possibility remote.

Factoring large numbers takes more time than factoring smaller numbers. This is why the size of the modulus in RSA determines how secure an actual use of RSA is; the larger the modulus, the longer it would take an attacker to factor, and thus the more resistant to attack the RSA modulus is.

Factoring has become easier over the last 15 years for two reasons: computer hardware has become more powerful, and better factoring algorithms have been developed.

Hardware improvement will continue inexorably, but it is important to realize that hardware improvements make RSA more secure, not less. This is because a hardware improvement that allows an attacker to factor a number two digits longer than before will at the same time allow a legitimate RSA user to use a key dozens of digits longer than before; a user can choose a new key a dozen digits longer than the old one without any performance slowdown, yet a factoring attack will become much more difficult. Therefore, although the hardware improvement does help the attacker, it helps the legitimate user much more. This general rule may fail in the sense that factoring may take place using fast machines of the future, attacking RSA keys of the past; in this scenario, only the attacker gets the advantage of the hardware improvement. This consideration argues for using a larger key size today than one might otherwise consider warranted. It also argues for replacing one's RSA key with a longer key every few years, in order to take advantage of the extra security offered by hardware improvements. This point holds for other public-key systems as well.

Better factoring algorithms have been more help to the RSA attacker than have hardware improvements. As the RSA system and cryptography in general have attracted much attention, so has the factoring problem, and many researchers have found new factoring methods or improved upon others. This has made factoring easier for numbers of any size, irrespective of the speed of the hardware. However, factoring is still a very difficult problem.

Overall, any recent decrease in security due to algorithm improvement can be offset by increasing the key size. In fact, between general computer hardware improvements and special-purpose RSA hardware improvements, increases in key size (maintaining a constant speed of RSA operations) have kept pace or exceeded increases in algorithm efficiency, resulting in no net loss of security. As long as hardware continues to improve at a faster rate than the rate at which the complexity of factoring algorithms decreases, the security of RSA will increase, assuming RSA users regularly increase their key sizes by appropriate amounts. The open question is how much faster factoring algorithms can get; there could be some intrinsic limit to factoring speed, but this limit remains unknown.

5.4.3 The RSA Cryptosystem

Now that the general concepts of public key cryptography have been examined, the next problem is how to design an actual working system. Indeed, when Whitfield Diffie and Martin Hellman conceived the basic properties of this cryptosystem in 1976, no one knew how to make a system that could employ them. The situation was similar to that of space travel in 1950. It was conceivable, but no one had accomplished it. In 1977, three researchers at the Massachusetts Institute of Technology, Ron Rivest, Adi Shamir, and Len Adleman, published an elegant method for creating and using public keys.

In the Rivest-Shamir-Adleman (or RSA) cryptosystem, the keys are 200-digit numbers. The encryption key is the product of two secret prime numbers, having approximately 100 digits each, selected by the person creating the keys. The corresponding decryption key is computed from the same two prime numbers, using a nonsecret formula.

Anyone who knows the secret prime numbers can compute the decryption key, but the primes are hidden because only their product, the encryption key, is revealed. Of course, the primes may be discovered by factoring the key, but factoring such a number is about as easy as traveling to Alpha Centauri, especially if the person who constructs the number has done it in a way that discourages factoring. Rivest, Shamir, and Adleman estimated that a fast computer would require 3.8 billion years (nearly the estimated age of the earth) to factor a 200-digit key. Estimates of the time required to factor keys of several other lengths are shown in table 5.1.

Table 5.1 The time required to break the RSA public key system by factoring the key, for several different key tengths. these factoring times assume one computer operation per microsecond.

Key Length (digits)	Factoring Time
50	39 hours
100	74 years
150	1.0 million years
200	3.8 billion years
250	5.9 trillion years

Before encryption, a message is converted into a string of numbers. This step is common in cryptosystems, as it is in computers and communication systems. Next, the message is subdivided into blocks, much as computer text files are subdivided into records or sectors. Each block contains the same number of digits, and is treated as one large number during encryption. To encrypt the message, an arithmetic operation involving the encryption key is performed on each block, resulting in a cryptogram containing as many blocks as the original message. The arithmetic operation, described below, is the same for all blocks. To decrypt, the inverse arithmetic operation, which requires the decryption key, is performed on each block of the cryptogram. The result is the original message in its numerical form.

As you can imagine, it would be cumbersome to illustrate these operations with 200-digit numbers, so the detailed descriptions below use small keys and messages; otherwise, the operations shown are the same as those used in a full-size RSA system. Also, the encryption method described here is actually a subset of the original RSA method. This modification, which is due to Donald Knuth uses the basic RSA technique, while lessening somewhat the number of computations involved.

5.4.5 How to Encrypt

While the encryption and decryption operations are normally performed by a computer program, I will describe them as if you were performing them by hand. Normally, the only manual operation required is entering the message to be encrypted.

Suppose you wish to encrypt the message

```
MARY HAD A LITTLE LAMB.
```

Once entered into a computer, the message will be in numerical form, frequently in ASCII (American Standard Code for Information Interchange). In ASCII, this message is

```
77 65 82 89 32 72 65 68 32
65 32 76 73 84 84 76 69 32 76 65 77 66 46
```

This is not yet encrypted, of course. It is merely written as a computer might represent it (all the numbers in this article are decimal). Group the message into blocks with six digits each:

```
776582 893272 656832 653276 738484 766932 766577 664600
```

Each block except the last consists of three consecutive characters from the ASCII representation above. The last block consists of the last two characters plus two zeros added at the right to make the final block as long as the rest. Digits added for this purpose may have any value.

Suppose that the encryption key, usually called n, is 94815109. This is the product of two prime numbers. To encrypt the message, treat each block as a number, and cube it modulo n. For example, to encrypt the first block of the message.

```
(776582 X 776582 X 776582) mod 94815109 = 71611947
```

Performing the cubing operation on all eight blocks produces the cryptogram

```
71611947 48484364 03944704 03741778 61544362 35331577 88278091 50439554
```

Arithmetic modulo n is a fundamental part of the RSA system. It is also used in decryption and creating keys. Most of us have used arithmetic modulo n, although perhaps we didn't call it that. For instance, arithmetic modulo 12 is frequently used in calculations related to keeping time.

Almost any method may be used to convert the text to numbers. It would have worked just as well to use **A = l, B=2, . . . Z = 26,** but the ASCII code is already in wide use, and it includes numbers for spaces and punctuation. The block length should be almost equal to the key length, because making it long minimizes the number of blocks per message. When considered as a number, however, no block should be as large as the key. For the above key, no block should be larger than 94815108. Making the block length slightly less than the key length ensures that this requirement is met. Of course, with full-length keys, there will be about 100 characters per block.

Listing 1 is a BASIC program that uses the above key to encrypt a line of text. Two lines of the program (670 and 680) perform the encryption. The rest deal with input, formatting, and printing. If desired, the encryption key in line 220 may be changed; use a key with seven or eight digits, or reduce the number of characters per block (line 210).

The programs in listings 1 through 4 were written for the TRS-80 BASIC interpreter, which is capable of 16-digit precision. They may be adapted for use with other interpreters, and I have tried to structure and annotate them well enough to make them easy to modify.

Listing 1: A program in BASIC (TRS-80) to demonstrate the encryption process described in the text. Lines 670-680 perform the encryption. When the program prompts you, type the text to be encrypted. The program will then print the text in numerical form, followed by the cryptogram. Use uppercase letters only.

```
100 . ==========================================================
110 . ENCRYPT MESSAGES, USING A MINIATURE VERSION OF THE
120 . RIVEST-SHAMIR-ADLEMAN PUBLIC KEY CRYPTOSYSTEM.
130 .
140 . PROMPT FOR THE MESSAGE TO BE ENCRYPTED, PRINT THE
150 . NUMERIC FORM OF THE MESSAGE, AND PRINT THE CRYPTOGRAM.
160 . ==========================================================
170 . DEFINE PARAMETERS.
180 .
190 DEFDBL C,M,N    '     C, M, AND N HAVE 16 DIGITS
200 DIM M(100)      '     MESSAGE BLOCKS
210 CHRS = 3 '     CHARACTERS PER BLOCK
220 N = 94815109    '     ENCRYPTION KEY, OR MODULUS
230 . ==========================================================
240 . GET THE MESSAGE FROM THE USER.
250 .
260 . PRINT : MS = ""
270 . INPUT "MESSAGE"; MS      '     MESSAGE FOR ENCRYPTION
280 . IF MS = "" THEN END      '     STOP IF NOTHING IS ENTERED
290 . PRINT
300 . ==========================================================
310 . ADD ZEROS TO MESSAGE, IF NECESSARY, TO MAKE ITS LENGTH
320 . A MULTIPLE OF THREE (AN EVEN NUMBER OF BLOCKS).
330 .
340 L = LEN(MS)                  ' LENGTH OF MESSAGE
350 Q = INT(L/CHRS)              ' NUMBER OF COMPLETE BLOCKS
360 R = L - Q* CHRS              ' LENGTH OF PARTIAL BLOCK
370 IF R > 0 THEN MS = MS + CHRS(0) : GOTO 340' ADD A ZERO?
380 . ==========================================================
390 . CONVERT THE MESSAGE TO NUMERIC FORM, AND PRINT IT.
400 .
410 FOR I = 0 TO Q - 1   '     I IS THE BLOCK NUMBER
420 M(I) - 0 '     CONVERT BLOCK I TO NUMBER
450 .    M(I) - M(I)-100 ' SHIFT BLOCK LEFT
460 .    M(I) - M(I)+ A  ' ADD THE CHARACTER
470 . NEXT J
```

```
480  .  PRINT M(I); ' PRINT THE BLOCK
490  NEXT I   ' DO THE NEXT BLOCK
500  PRINT : PRINT
510  .  -----------------------------------------------------
520  .  ENCRYPT THE MESSAGE, AND PRINT THE CRYPTOGRM.
530  .
540  PRINT "CRYPTOGRAM:" ; PRINT
550  FOR I-0 TO Q''1       ' I IS THE BLOCK NUMBER
560  .  M - M(I)
570  .  GOSUB 670    ' ENCRYPT THE BLOCK
580  .  PRINT C;     ' PRINT IT
590  NEXT I   ' DO THE NEXT ONE
600  PRINT
610  .  -----------------------------------------------------
620  GOTO 260 ' RUN THE PROGRAM AGAIN
630  .  -----------------------------------------------------
640  .  SUBROUTINE. ENCRYPT ONE MESSAGE BLOCK.
650  .  COMPUTE C '' (M-3) MOD N.
660  .
670  C = M* M : C = C - INT(C/N) * N  ' (M * M)MOD N
680  C = C * M : C = C - C INT(C/N) * N     ' (M * M) MOD N
690  RETURN
700  .  -----------------------------------------------------
```

5.4.5 How to Decrypt.

Since the RSA system is a public key system, the decryption key, usually called d, differs from the public encryption key. For the above encryption key, *d* is 63196467. Knowing the value of **d**, you can decrypt the message by raising each cryptogram block to the power *d*, modulo n. That is, if a cryptogram block is C, you must compute `(C) mod n`. For example, to decrypt the first block of the above cryptogram:

`(71611947^63196467) mod 94815109 = 776582`

converts this block back to the first three ASCII codes of the original message. Each of the remaining blocks is decrypted in the same way. Fortunately, raising a number to a large power does not require performing a comparable number of multiplications. One efficient algorithm is a variation of the "Russian Peasant Method" of multiplication (see reference 4). It computes M = (C^d) mod n, as follows:

1. Let `M = 1`.
2. If *d* is odd, let `M = (MXC) mod n`.
3. Let `C = (CXC) mod n`.
4. Let `d = integer part of d/2`.
5. If *d* is not zero, repeat from step 2; otherwise, terminate with **M** as the answer.

To raise a number to the power 63196467, this algorithm executes its loop (steps 2 through 5) 26 times. It is employed as a subroutine in the BASIC-language decryption program of listing 2. Line 200 contains the keys, which may be changed, if desired. Lines 340 through 380 execute the algorithm.

Listing 2: A program in BASIC (TRS-80) to demonstrate the decryption process described in the text. Lines 340-390 decrypt one black of a cryptogram by raising it to a power. The program asks for a cryptogram black to be decrypted. Several seconds later. it prints the decrypted characters in ASCII. If you enter 0, the program will terminate.

```
100 . ------------------------------------------------------------
110 . DECRYPT MESSAGES, USING A MINIATURE VERSION OF THE
120 . RIVEST-SHAMIR-ADLEMAN PUBLIC KEY CRYPTOSYSTEM.
130 .
140 . PROMPT FOR THE CRYPTOGRAM BLOCK TO BE DECRYPTED, AND
150 . DECRYPT AND PRINT THE MESSAGE BLOCK, IN NUMERIC FORM.
160 . ------------------------------------------------------------
170 . DEFINE PARAMETERS.
180 .
190 DEFDBL C,D,M,N                    ' DOUBLE PRECISION
200 N = 94815109 : D = 63196467       ' KEYS
210 . ------------------------------------------------------------
220 . MAIN PROGRAM LOOP.
230 .
240 INPUT "CRYPTOGRAM BLOCK"; C       ' USER ENTRY
250 IF C = 0 THEN END                 ' STOP IF NO ENTRY
260 GOSUB 340                         ' DECRYPT BLOCK
270 PRINT M                           ' MESSAGE BLOCK
280 GOTO 240                          ' REPEAT
290 . ------------------------------------------------------------
300 . SUBROUTINE. DECRYPT C, CRYPTOGRAM BLOCK.
310 . COMPUTE M = (C^D) MOD N. USE MODIFIED RUSSIAN PEASANT
320 . ALGORITHM (BYTE, OCTOBER 1981, PAGE 376).
330 .
```

Listing 2 continued:

```
340 DI = D : M = 1
350 IF D1/2 = INT(D1/2) GOTO 370          ' IF D1 IS EVEN, SKIP
360 M = M * C : M = M - INT(M/N) * N      ' M = (M * C) MOD N
370 C = C * C : C = C - INT(C/N) * N      ' C = (C * C) MOD N
380 D1 = INT(D1/2) : IF D1 > 0 GOTO 350
390 RETURN
400 . ------------------------------------------------------------
```

How to Derive Keys.

As learnt earlier, I said that it is feasible to derive a pair of keys, n and d, for encryption and decryption, but not feasible to calculate d from n. That seems incredible, but experts believe it is true when **n** and **d** are constructed in the following way.

The encryption key, n, is the product of two large prime numbers, p and q:

`n = pq (1)` ...(5.1)

The decryption key, d, is calculated from p and q by

`d = [2p-1) (q-1) + 1 ]/3 (2)` ...(5.2)

Although n is made public, p and q remain secret. If n is sufficiently large, say 200 digits, it is practically impossible for anyone to factor it and discover the values of p and q; and without knowing p and q, it is equally difficult to compute d.

For the encryption and decryption examples given earlier, the keys were constructed as follows:

```
prime number, p= 7151 prime numberm, q = 13259 encryption key,
                n= 7151X13259
                 = 94815109 decryption key, d = (2X7150X 13258 + 1) / 3
                 = 63196467
```

Because p and q may have 100 or more digits in an operational RSA system, their selection requires computer assistance. The following three restrictions apply to how they should be chosen. First, neither p – 1 nor q – 1 must be divisily by 3, or the decryption operation will not work correctly. Second, p – 1 and q – 1 should both contain at least oe large prime factor. Third, the ratio p/q should not approximate a simple fraction, e.g., 2/3, 3/4, etc., etc. These last two restrictions help ensure that n will be difficult to factor. Donald nuth, in the second edition of his book (see reference 3), gives a detailed procedure for selecting p and q, which ensures that these restrictions are met. While the procedure described is for constructing 250-digit keys, it is applicable to other key lengths.

Enough keys are available for everyone. The number of 250-digit keys constructible with Knuth's procedure is much greater than 10^80.

To create a different pair of seven-or eight-digit keys, find primes p and q such that neither p – 1 nor q – 1 is divisible by 3, and the product n = pq is a seven-or eight-digit number. Then calculate d form formula (2). Divisibility by 3 is easily checkked by casting out 3s, and the BASIC programs described below are helpful in finding prime numbers.

How to Find Large Prime Numbers.

To find a large prime number, select a random odd number of the required size and determine whether it is prime. If it is not, increase it (or decrease it) by 2 and try again, repeating until finding a prime. It is not necessary, however, to attempt to factor a number to determine whether it is prime.

To test whether a number n is prime, select any number greater than 1 and smaller than n, say x, and calculate

`y = (x^n-1) mod n`

If y is not equal to 1, n is not prime. But if y = 1, n may be prime, and further testing is required. Repeat the test using another value of x. If this test is performed with many different values of x, and if y = 1 for all the test cases, n is probably prime. Listing 3 is a BASIC program that uses 10 values of x to test a number for primality. If the program says the number is not prime, it is not prime. But if the program says the number is probably prime, there is a small chance that it is not.

Listing 3: A program in BASIC (RRS-80) to test whether a numberis prime. This program demonstrates a primality test that does not attempt to factor the number being tested. For very large numbers, it is much faster than factoring.

```
100  . -----------------------------------------------------------
110  . TEST WHETHER A NUMBER IS PRIME.
120  . USE PROBABILISTIC TEST BASED ON FERMAT'S THEOREM.
130  . SEE KNUTH, "SEMINUMERACAL ALGORITIIMS".
140  .
150  . PROMPT FOR NUMBER, TEST IT, AND PRONOUNCE VERDICT.
160  . -----------------------------------------------------------
170  . DEFINE PARAMETERS.
180  .
190  DEFDBL N,P,X,Y                    '  DOUBLE PRECISION
200  K = 10                            '  NUMBER OF TEST CASES
210  . -----------------------------------------------------------
220  . GET A NUMBER TO BE TESTED, CHECK THE SIZE.
230  .
240  PRINT
250  INPUT "NUMBER"; N                 '  GET A NUMBER TO TEST
260  IF N < 3 THEN END
270  IF N > 99999999 THEN PRINT "TOO BIG" : GOTO 240
280  . -----------------------------------------------------------
290  . DETERMINE WHETHER N IS PRIME.
300  .
310  PRINT "TEST NUMBER: ";
320  FOR I = 1 TO K                    '  TEST CASES
330  . X = 2 + INT(N-2)*RND(0))        '  TEST VALUE
340  . PRINT X;
350  . GOSUB 490                       '  PERFORM TEST
360  . IF Y <> 1 GOTO 380              '  NOT PRIME?
370  NEXT I
380  PRINT : PRINT                     '  NOT PRIME IF Y <> 1
390  . -----------------------------------------------------------
400  . PRINT THE VERDICT.
410  .
420  If Y = 1 THEN PRINT N; "IS PROBABLY PRIME."
```

```
430 IF Y <> 1 THEN PRINT N; "IS NOT PRIME."
440 . -----------------------------------------------------
450 GOTO 240                      '  RUN THE PROGRAM AGAIN
460 . -----------------------------------------------------
470 . SUBROUTINE.  COMPUTE Y = [X* (N - 1)] MOD N
480 .
490 Y = 1 : P  = N  1
500 IF P/2 = INT(P.2) GOTO 520     '  IF P IS EVEN, SXIP
510 Y = Y* X ; y = X  INT(Y/N) * N '  (Y * X) MOD N
520 X = X * X ; X = X - INT(X/N) * N '  (X * X)MOD N
530 P = INT(P/2) : IF P * 0 GOTO 500
540 RETURN
550 . -----------------------------------------------------
```

What is the probability that this program will make an error? I don't know, but it illustrates a class of programs, some of which are very good. Knuth (reference 3, page 375) presents one that is slightly more complicated, for which the odds against an error are a million to one when 10 values of x are used for testing, and are a million million to one when 20 values are used. For serious work I would use the more complicated program, but the one presented here illustrates the process of testing without factoring—and it doesn't seem bad. It has not made an error in several hundred trials.

Listing 4 is a BASIC program that searches for a prime number using the same test method as the previous program. The program will begin with the number you enter and search downward until it finds a probable prime, which it will identify. If you enter 99999999, it will find the largest eight-digit prime. This program helps to find primes for constructing small keys like the ones above.

Listing 4: A program in BASIC (TRS-80) that searches for a prime number. It illustrate the search technique and may be used to help construct small keys for the public key cryptosystem described in the text. Enter any number of eight digits or fewer and the program will find a prime number that does not exceed the number entered.

```
100 . -----------------------------------------------------
110 . FIND A PRIME NUMBER NO LARGER THAN THE NUMBER ENTERED.
120 . USE PROBAILISTIC TEST BASED ON FERMAT'S THEOREM.
130 . SEE KNUTH' "SEMINUMERICAL ALGORITHMS".
140 . -----------------------------------------------------
150 . DEFINE PARAMETERS.
160 .
170 DEFDBL N,P,X,Y                '  DOUBLE PRECISION
180 K = 10                        '  NUMBER OF TEST CASES
190 . -----------------------------------------------------
200 . GET A NUMBER TO BE TESTED.   CHECK THE SIZE.
210 .
220 PRINT
```

```
230 INPUT "NUMBER"; N                    '  GET A NUMBER TO TEST
240 IF N < 3 THEN END                    '  STOP IF SMALL NUMBER
250 IF N > 99999999 THEN PRINT "TOO BIG" : GOTO 220
260 . ---------------------------------------------------------------
270 . DETERMINE WHETHER THE NUMBER ENTERED IS EVEN.
280 . IF SO, SUBTRACT ONE.
290 .
300 IF N/2 = INT(N/2) THEN N = N - 1
310 . ---------------------------------------------------------------
320 . PRINT N, THEN DETERMINE WHETHER IT IS PIME.
330 .
340 PRINT N;
350 FOR I = 1 TO K                       '  TEST CASES
360    X = 2 + INT(N-2)^RND(0))          '  TEST VALUE
370    GOSUB 520    ' PERFORM TEST
380    IF Y <> 1 GOTO 400
390 NEXT 1
400 REM
```

5.4.6 One-Way Functions and Trap-Doors.

Public key cryptosystems derive their unusual properties from mathematical functions called trap-door one-way functions, which are useful because they can act as ordinary functions or as one-way functions.

One-way functions are like oneway streets. The ordinary cube function, B = A3, resembles a one-way function in that it is easier to calculate B, given A, than it is to calculate A, given B. The latter calculation, the cube-root function, is called the inverse of the cube function. The inverse of an automobile would convert smog to gasoline. A mathematical function is said to be one-way if it is much more difficult to compute the inverse than to compute the function itself. To qualify as a one-way function, the inverse must be very difficult to compute, even by machine.

A function that could be computed in a few seconds, for which computing an inverse required thousands of years, would fit the definition.

To create a public key cryptosystem, a trap-door one-way function is used. It is easy to compute an inverse of a trap-door one-way function, but it can be very difficult to determine how. Computing an inverse can take millions of years because finding out how to do it can take that long. If the method is known, computing an inverse may take only a few seconds. This is a completely different situation than that created by a one-way function, for which there is no easy way to compute an inverse. When a trap-door one-way function is being constructed, the person constructing it has access to information, called trap-door information, that reveals how to compute inverses. Once the function is constructed, the trap-door information is hidden so well that it can take millions of years to find.

The Knuth modification of the RSA system encryption function, cubing a number modulo n, is a trapdoor one-way function. Its inverse function is the cube root modulo n. In arithmetic modulo n, "cube root" is defined as in ordinary arithmetic: if B is the cube of A, then A is the cube root of B. Notice that this definition does not say how to compute cube roots (in either kind of arithmetic). If you know how to compute cube roots modulo n, you know how to decrypt messages. In modulo n arithmetic, the cube root of B is computed by raising B to some power d, modulo n. But knowing this doesn't help unless you know the value of d. And d can be computed by formula (2) if n has two factors (p and q), and p — 1 and q — 1 are not divisible by 3. If you construct the modulus, n, you know p and q, and can therefore calculate the value of d. Knowing d, you can compute cube roots; in other words, decrypt cryptograms. The values of p and q are hidden from other people by the difficulty of factoring n. They are deprived of the value of d, and therefore cannot compute cube roots. Hence, they cannot decrypt cryptograms created by cubing modulo n. In the RSA system, the value of d is the trap-door information that reveals how to compute inverses (cube roots). You might think of p and q as comprising a trap-door through which the value of d is obtained. Factoring n is analogous to finding the trap-door, but it is very difficult to do.

Other trap-door one-way functions undoubtedly exist, and these could be the foundations for other public key cryptosystems. For each of these systems, the same principles would apply. The creator of the system parameters would have access to certain trap-door information, which would reveal how to compute inverses. For everyone else, the trapdoor would be hidden, and for them the encryption function would be, in effect, a one-way function.

5.4.7 Is the RSA System Unbreakable?.

Successfully analyzing a cryptosystem, and being able to read its cryptograms without authorization, is called breaking the system. Theoretically, the RSA system can be broken by a determined analyst. Factoring the encryption key, or modulus, would do the trick, for then the decryption key could be easily calculated from formula (2), after which any message could easily be decrypted. However, factoring a key of the recommended length and construction does not seem feasible. Knuth gives a procedure for constructing a 250-digit key and considers it inconceivable at this time that such a key could be factored. Experts acknowledge that a breakthrough in the art of factoring large numbers would render the RSA system worthless but consider such a breakthrough extremely unlikely. Apparently, factoring large numbers is not a new problem, but one that expert mathematicians have attacked for centuries, and it is known to be very difficult.

Another way to break the system is to determine the value of d without factoring n. Although you can approach this problem in several ways, experts believe that none of them are likely to be fruitful.

Yet another method of breaking the system is to learn how to compute cube roots modulo n without knowing the value of d. Less seems to be known about the difficulty of doing this than is known about the difficulty of factoring n. At this time, no one knows how to compute such cube roots in a reasonable time without knowing d.

Any new cryptosystem should be viewed with suspicion. The accepted method of demonstrating the adequacy of a new system is to subject it to prolonged, concerted attack by people with experience in breaking other systems. If the new system proves resistant to such an attack, it may tentatively be considered secure. The process of validation is continuing, but a fairly large number of preliminary studies done so far indicate that the system is quite secure.

5.4.8 Possibility of Breaking RSA

There are a few possible interpretations of "breaking RSA." The most damaging would be for an attacker to discover the private key corresponding to a given public key; this would enable the attacker both to read all messages encrypted with the public key and to forge signatures. The obvious way to do this attack is to factor the public modulus, n, into its two prime factors, *p* and *q*. From `p, q,` and `e,` the public exponent, the attacker can easily get `d,` the private exponent. The hard part is factoring n; the security of RSA depends on factoring being difficult. In fact, the task of recovering the private key is equivalent to the task of factoring the modulus: you can use `d` to factor `n,` as well as use the factorization of n to find d. It should be noted that hardware improvements alone will not weaken RSA, as long as appropriate key lengths are used; in fact, hardware improvements should increase the security of RSA

Another way to break RSA is to find a technique to compute e -th roots `mod n.` Since `c = memod n,` the e-th root of `c mod n` is the message `m.` This attack would allow someone to recover encrypted messages and forge signatures even without knowing the private key. This attack is not known to be equivalent to factoring. No general methods are currently known that attempt to break RSA in this way. However, in special cases where multiple related messages are encrypted with the same small exponent, it may be possible to recover the messages.

The attacks just mentioned are the only ways to break RSA in such a way as to be able to recover all messages encrypted under a given key. There are other methods, however, that aim to recover single messages; success would not enable the attacker to recover other messages encrypted with the same key. Some people also studied whether part of the message can be recovered from an encrypted message

The simplest single-message attack is the guessed plaintext attack. An attacker sees a ciphertext, guesses that the message might be "Attack at dawn," and encrypts this guess with the public key of the recipient; by comparison with the actual ciphertext, the attacker knows whether or not the guess was correct. This attack can be thwarted by appending some random bits to the message. Another single-message attack can occur if someone sends the same message m to three others, who each have public exponent e = 3. An attacker who knows this and sees the three messages will be able to recover the message m; this attack and ways to prevent it are discussed by Hastad [Has88]. Fortunately, this attack can also be defeated by padding the message before each encryption with some random bits. There are also some chosen ciphertext attacks (or chosen message attacks for signature forgery, in which the attacker creates some ciphertext and gets to see the corresponding plaintext, perhaps by tricking a legitimate user into decrypting a fake message.

Of course, there are also attacks that aim not at RSA itself but at a given insecure implementation of RSA; these do not count as "breaking RSA" because it is not any weakness in the RSA algorithm that is exploited, but rather a weakness in a specific implementation. For example, if someone stores a private key insecurely, an attacker may discover it. One cannot emphasize strongly enough that to be truly secure RSA requires a secure implementation; mathematical security measures, such as choosing a long key size, are not enough. In practice, most successful attacks will likely be aimed at insecure implementations and at the key management stages of an RSA system.

5.4.9 How Fast is RSA?

An "RSA operation," whether for encrypting or decrypting, signing or verifying, is essentially a modular exponentiation, which can be performed by a series of modular multiplications.

In practical applications, it is common to choose a small public exponent for the public key; in fact, entire groups of users can use the same public exponent, each with a different modulus. (There are some restrictions on the prime factors of the modulus when the public exponent is fixed.) This makes encryption faster than decryption and verification faster than signing. With typical modular exponentiation algorithms, public-key operations take O(k2) steps, private-key operations take O(k3) steps, and key generation takes O(k4) steps, where k is the number of bits in the modulus. (O-notation refers to the upper bound on the asymptotic running time of an algorithm.) "Fast multiplication" techniques, such as FFT-based methods, require asymptotically fewer steps, though in practice they are not as common due to their great software complexity and the fact that they may actually be slower for typical key sizes.

There are many commercially available software and hardware implementations of RSA, and there are frequent announcements of newer and faster chips. On a 90 MHz Pentium, RSA Data Security's cryptographic toolkit BSAFE 3.0 has a throughput for private-key operations of 21.6 Kbits per second with a 512-bit modulus and 7.4 Kbits per second with a 1024-bit modulus. The fastest RSA hardware [SV93] has a throughput greater than 300 Kbits per second with a 512-bit modulus, implying that it performs over 500 RSA private-key operations per second. (There is room in that hardware to execute two RSA 512-bit RSA operations in parallel [Sha95], hence the 600 Kbits/s speed reported in For 970-bit keys, the throughput is 185 Kbits/s.) It is expected that RSA speeds will reach 1 Mbits/second within a year or so.

By comparison, DES is much faster than RSA. In software, DES is generally at least 100 times as fast as RSA. In hardware, DES is between 1,000 and 10,000 times as fast, depending on the implementation. Implementations of RSA will probably narrow the gap a bit in coming years, as there are growing commercial markets, but DES will get faster as well.

Advantages of RSA over other public-key cryptosystems include the fact that it can be used for both encryption and authentication, and that it has been around for many years and has successfully withstood much scrutiny. RSA has received far more attention, study, and actual use than any other public-key cryptosystem, and thus RSA has more empirical evidence of its security than more recent and less scrutinized systems.

5.4.10 Popularity of RSA

The use of RSA is practically ubiquitous today. It is currently used in a wide variety of products, platforms, and industries around the world. It is found in many commercial software products and is planned to be in many more. It is built into current operating systems by Microsoft, Apple, Sun, and Novell. In hardware, RSA can be found in secure telephones, on Ethernet network cards, and on smart cards. In addition, RSA is incorporated into all of the major protocols for secure Internet communications, including SSL , S-HTTP , SEPP, S/MIME, S/WAN, STT and PCT . It is also used internally in many institutions, including branches of the U.S. government, major corporations, national laboratories, and universities.

RSA is part of many official standards worldwide. The ISO (International Standards Organization) 9796 standard lists RSA as a compatible cryptographic algorithm, as does the

ITU-T X.509 security standard . RSA is part of the Society for Worldwide Interbank Financial Telecommunications (SWIFT) standard, the French financial industry's ETEBAC 5 standard, and the ANSI X9.31 draft standard for the U.S. banking industry. The Australian key management standard, AS2805.6.5.3, also specifies RSA.

RSA is found in Internet standards and proposed protocols including PEM (Privacy Enhanced Mail), S/MIME, PEM-MIME, S-HTTP and SSL (see Question 130 through Question 134) as well as the PKCS standard (see Question 166) for the software industry. The OSI Implementors' Workshop (OIW) has issued implementors' agreements referring to PKCS and PEM, each of which includes RSA.

A number of other standards are currently being developed and will be announced over the next couple of years; many are expected to include RSA as either an endorsed or a recommended system for privacy and/or authentication.

5.5 KEY MANAGEMENT AND CONVENTIONAL ENCRYPTION

Conventional encryption has benefits. It is very fast. It is especially useful for encrypting data that is not going anywhere. However, conventional encryption alone as a means for transmitting secure data can be quite expensive simply due to the difficulty of secure key distribution. Recall a character from your favorite spy movie: the person with a locked briefcase handcuffed to his or her wrist. What is in the briefcase, anyway? It's probably not the missile launch code/biotoxin formula/invasion plan itself. It's the key that will decrypt the secret data. For a sender and recipient to communicate securely using conventional encryption, they must agree upon a key and keep it secret between themselves. If they are in different physical locations, they must trust a courier, the Bat Phone, or some other secure communication medium to prevent the disclosure of the secret key during transmission. Anyone who overhears or intercepts the key in transit can later read, modify, and forge all informationm encrypted or authenticated with that key. From DES to Captain Midnight's Secret Decoder Ring, the persistent problem with conventional encryption is key distribution: how do you get the key to the recipient without someone intercepting it?

5.5.1 Keys

A key is a value that works with a cryptographic algorithm to produce a specific ciphertext. Keys are basically really, really, really big numbers. Key size is measured in bits; the number representing a 1024-bit key is darn huge. In public key cryptography, the bigger the key, the more secure the ciphertext.

However, public key size and conventional cryptography's secret key size are totally unrelated. A conventional 80-bit key has the equivalent strength of a 1024-bit public key. A conventional 128-bit key is equivalent to a 3000-bit public key. Again, the bigger the key, the more secure, but the algorithms used for each type of cryptography are very different and thus comparison is like that of apples to oranges.

While the public and private keys are related, it's very difficult to derive the private key given only the public key; however, deriving the private key is always possible given enough time and computing power. This makes it very important to pick keys of the right size; large enough to be secure, but small enough to be applied fairly quickly. Additionally, you need to consider who might be trying to read your files, how determined they are, how much time they have, and what their resources might be.

Larger keys will be cryptographically secure for a longer period of time. If what you want to encrypt needs to be hidden for many years, you might want to use a very large key. Of course, who knows how long it will take to determine your key using tomorrow's faster, more efficient computers? There was a time when a 56-bit symmetric key was considered extremely safe. Keys are stored in encrypted form. PGP stores the keys in two files on your hard disk; one for public keys and one for private keys. These files are called keyrings. As you use PGP, you will typically add the public keys of your recipients to your public keyring. Your private keys are stored on your private keyring. If you lose your private keyring, you will be unable to decrypt any information encrypted to keys on that ring.

5.6 DIFFIE-HELLMAN KEY EXCHANGE

If you've had any experience choosing a cryptographic algorithm, you've probably faced a common dilemma at one time or another: should you use an asymmetric (public key) or symmetric (private key) algorithm?

From a key exchange point-of-view, public key algorithms are much simpler to administer. Users may freely share their public keys over insecure transmission channels without fear of compromising the cryptosystem. In order for pure private key systems to remain truly secure, offline key exchange techniques (such as a floppy diskette) must be used. On the other hand, symmetric algorithms generally operate much faster than their asymmetric counterparts.

Diffie-Hellman key exchange offers the best of both worlds — it uses public key techniques to allow the exchange of a private encryption key! Let's take a look at how the protocol works, from the perspective of Anita and Bunty, two users who wish to establish secure communications. We can assume that Anita and Bunty know nothing about each other but are in contact. Here are the nine steps of the process:

(1) Communicating in the clear, Anita and Bunty agree on two large positive integers, n and g, with the stipulation that n is a prime number and g is a generator of n.

(2) Anita randomly chooses another large positive integer, XA, which is smaller than n. XA will serve as Anita's private key.

(3) Bunty similarly chooses his own private key, `XB`.

(4) Anita computes her public key, `YA`, using the formula `YA = (g^XA) mod n`.

(5) Bunty similarly computes his public key, `YB`, using the formula `YB = (g^XB) mod n`.

(6) Anita and Bunty exchange public keys over the insecure circuit.

(7) Anita computes the shared secret key, `k`, using the formula `k = (YB ^XA)` mod n.

(8) Bunty computes the same shared secret key, `k`, using the formula `k = (YA ^XB)` mod n.

(9) Anita and Bunty communicate using the symmetric algorithm of their choice and the shared secret key, k, which was never transmitted over the insecure circuit.

Diffie-Hellman key exchange is actually nothing new. It's been around since Whitfield Diffie and Martin Hellman published it in their 1976 paper, "New Directions in Cryptography." However, the recent surge of interest in cryptography and secure communications have increased awareness of the protocol. In fact, you've probably unknowingly used the Diffie-Hellman protocol on a daily basis. It's used by popular protocols like SSL and SSH.

The Diffie-Hellman key exchange is vulnerable to a middleperson attack. In this attack, an opponent, Carol, intercepts Anita's public value and sends her own public value to Bunty. When Bunty transmits his public value, Carol substitutes it with her own and sends it to Anita. Carol and Anita thus agree on one shared key and Carol and Bunty agree on another shared key. After this exchange, Carol simply decrypts any messages sent out by Anita or Bunty, and then reads and possibly modifies them before re-encrypting with the appropriate key and transmitting them to the correct party. This vulnerability is due to the fact that Diffie-Hellman key exchange does not authenticate the participants. Possible solutions include the use of digital signatures and other protocol variants

5.6.1 Advantages of Diffie + Hellman Scheme

The Diffie-Hellman algorithm has two distinct advantages, that could be made use of in protocols. The keys could be computed only when needed. This makes sure that there is no necessity for a key to remain secret for a long period of time, thereby overcoming the problem of keeping a secret! The key exchange does not require any key-server and can be easily deployed.

Disadvantages

The original Diffie-Hellman algorithm has a known set of weaknesses.

- There is no identity of the parties involved in the exchange.
- It is easily susceptible to man-in-the-middle attacks. A third party C, can exchange keys with both A and B, and can listen to the communication between A and B.
- The algorithm is computationally intensive. Each multiplication varies as the square of n, which must be very large. The number of multiplications required by the exponentiation increases with increasing values of the exponent, x or y in this case.
- The computational nature of the algorithm could be used in a denial-of-service attack very easily.

5.6.2 Diffie-Hellman key exchange

Diffie-Hellman key exchange (D-H) is a cryptographic protocol that allows two parties that have no prior knowledge of each other to jointly establish a shared secret key over an insecure communications channel. This key can then be used to encrypt subsequent communications using a symmetric key cipher. U.S. Patent 4,200,770 , now expired, describes the algorithm and credits Hellman, Diffie, and Merkle as inventors.

Description

Anita		**Bunty**
a, g, p		b
$A = g^a \bmod p$	$\longleftarrow$ g, p, A $\longrightarrow$	$B = g^b \bmod p$
$K = B^a \bmod p$	$\longleftarrow$ B $\longrightarrow$	$K = A^b \bmod p$

$$K = A^b \bmod p = (g^a \bmod p)^b \bmod p = g^{ab} \bmod p = (g^b \bmod p)^a \bmod p = B^a \bmod p$$

The simplest, and original, implementation of the protocol uses the Multiplicative group of integers modulo *p*, where *p* is prime and *g* is primitive root mod *p*. Here is an example of the protocol:

Anita		**Bunty**	1. Anita and Bunty agree to use *a* prime number $p = 23$ and base $g = 5$.
Sec		Calc	2. Anita chooses a secret integer $a = 6$, then sends Bunty ($g^a \bmod p$) 0 $5^6 \bmod 23 = 8$.
	→		3. Bunty chooses a secret integer $b = 15$, then
Calc	←	Sec	sends Anita ($g^b \bmod p$)
	=		0 $5^{15} \bmod 23 = 19$.
			4. Anita computes ($g^b \bmod p)^a \bmod p$
p, g		p, g	0 $19^6 \bmod 23 = 2$.
			5. Bunty computes ($g^a \bmod p)^b \bmod p$
			0 $8^{15} \bmod 23 = 2$.
a			
		b	
		...	
$g^a \bmod p$			
		$g^b \bmod p$	
...			
$(g^b \bmod p)^a \bmod p$		$(g^a \bmod p)^b \bmod p$	

Both Anita and Bunty have arrived at the same value, because g^{ab} and g^{ba} are equal mod *p*. Note that only *a*, *b* and $g^{ab} = g^{ba} \bmod p$ are kept secret. All the other values -- *p*, *g*, g^a *mod p*, and g^b *mod p* -- are sent in the clear. Once Anita and Bunty compute the shared secret they can use it as an encryption key, known only to them, for sending messages across the same open communications channel. Of course, much larger values of *a*, *b*, and p would be needed to make this example secure, since it is easy to try all the possible values of gab mod 23 (there will be, at most, 22 such values, even if *a* and *b* are large). If *p* were a prime of at least 300 digits, and *a* and *b* were at least 100 digits long, then even the best algorithms known today could not find *a* given only *g*, *p*, and ga mod *p*, even using all of mankind's computing power. The problem is known as the discrete logarithm problem. Note that g need not be large at all, and in practice is usually either 2 or 5.

Here's a more general description of the protocol:

1. Anita and Bunty agree on a finite cyclic group *G* and a generating element *g* in *G*. (This is usually done long before the rest of the protocol; *g* is assumed to be known by all attackers.) We will write the group *G* multiplicatively.

2. Anita picks *a* random natural number *a* and sends g^a to Bunty.
3. Bunty picks *a* random natural number *b* and sends g^b to Anita.
4. Anita computes $(g^b)^a$.
5. Bunty computes $(g^a)^b$.

Both Anita and Bunty are now in possession of the group element gab, which can serve as the shared secret key. The values of (g^b)a and $(g^a)^b$ are the same because groups are power associative.

Chart

Here is a chart to help simplify who knows what. (Eve is an eavesdropper-she watches what is sent between Anita and Bunty, but she does not alter the contents of their communications.)

Let s = shared secret key. $s = 2$

Let a = Anita's private key. $a = 6$

Let b = Bunty's private key. $b = 15$

Let g = public base. $g = 5$

Let p = public (prime) number. $p = 23$

Anita knows doesn't know	**Bunty** knows doesn't know	**Eve** knows doesn't know
$p = 23$ $b = 15$ base $g = 5$ $a = 6$	$p = 23$ $a = 6$ base $g = 5$ $b = 15$	$p = 23$ $a = 6$ base $g = 5$ $b = 15$ $s = 2$
$5^6 \bmod 23 = 8$ $5^b \bmod 23 = 19$ $19^6 \bmod 23 = 2$ $8^b \bmod 23 = 2$ $19^6 \bmod 23 = 8^b \bmod 23$	$5^6 \bmod 23 = 8$ $5^b \bmod 23 = 19$ $8^{15} \bmod 23 = 2$ $19^a \bmod 23 = 2$ $8^{15} \bmod 23 = 19^a \bmod 23$	$5^6 \bmod 23 = 8$ $5^b \bmod 23 = 19$ $19^a \bmod 23 = s$ $8^b \bmod 23 = s$ $19^a \bmod 23 = 8^b \bmod 23$
$s = 2$	$s = 2$	

Note: It should be difficult for Anita to solve for Bunty's private key or for Bunty to solve for Anita's private key. If it isn't difficult for Anita to solve for Bunty's private key (or vice versa), Eve may simply substitute her own private / public key pair, plug Bunty's public key into her private key, produce a fake shared secret key, and solve for Bunty's private key (and use that to solve for the shared secret key. Eve may attempt to choose a public / private key pair that will make it easy for her to solve for Bunty's private key).

5.6.3 Security

The protocol is considered secure against eavesdroppers if G and g are chosen properly. The eavesdropper ("Eve") must solve the Diffie-Hellman problem to obtain gab. This is currently considered difficult. An efficient algorithm to solve the discrete logarithm problem would make it easy to compute a or b and solve the Diffie-Hellman problem, making this and many other public key cryptosystems insecure.

The order of G should be prime or have a large prime factor to prevent use of the Pohlig-Hellman algorithm to obtain a or b. For this reason, a Sophie Germain prime q is sometimes used to calculate $p = 2q + 1$, called a safe prime, since the order of G is then only divisible by 2 and q. g is then sometimes chosen to generate the order q subgroup of G, rather than G, so that the Legendre symbol of g^a never reveals the low order bit of a.

If Anita and Bunty use random number generators whose outputs are not completely random and can be predicted to some extent, then Eve's task is much easier.

The secret integers a and b are discarded at the end of the session. Therefore, Diffie-Hellman key exchange by itself trivially achieves perfect forward secrecy because no long-term private keying material exists to be disclosed.

5.6.4 Authentication

In the original description, the Diffie-Hellman exchange by itself does not provide authentication of the communicating parties and is thus vulnerable to a man-in-the-middle attack. A person in the middle may establish two distinct Diffie-Hellman key exchanges, one with Anita and the other with Bunty, effectively masquerading as Anita to Bunty, and vice versa, allowing the attacker to decrypt (and read or store) then re-encrypt the messages passed between them. A method to authenticate the communicating parties to each other is generally needed to prevent this type of attack.

A variety of cryptographic authentication solutions incorporate a Diffie-Hellman exchange. When Anita and Bunty have a public key infrastructure, they may digitally sign the agreed key, or g^a and g^b, as in MQV, STS and the IKE component of the IPsec protocol suite for securing Internet Protocol communications. When Anita and Bunty share a password, they may use a password-authenticated key agreement form of Diffie-Hellman.

5.6.5 The Diffie Hellman/DSA Cryptosystems and the Discrete Logarithm Problem

Diffie Hellman — along with the Digital Signature Algorithm (DSA) based on it — is another of the asymmetric cryptosystems in general use.

ECC, in a sense, is an evolved form of Diffie Hellman. So to understand how ECC works, it helps to understand how Diffie Hellman works first.

Diffie Hellman uses a problem known as the discrete logarithm problem as its central, asymmetric operation. The discrete log problem concerns finding a logarithm of a number within a finite field arithmetic system.

Prime fields are fields whose sets are prime – that is, they have a prime number of members. These are of particular interest in asymmetric cryptography because, over a prime field, exponentiation turns out to be a relatively easy operation, while the inverse — computing the logarithm – is very difficult.

To generate a key pair in the discrete logarithm (DL) system, therefore, you calculate:

y= (gx) mod p

where p is a large prime — the field size. x and g are smaller than p. y is the public key. x is used as the private key. In Diffie Hellman, again, the operations we wish to make 'easy', or tractable, we harness to the operation in the field which is (relatively) easy — exponentiation. So encryption using the public key is an exponentiation operation. Decryption using the private key is as well. Decryption using the public key, however, would require performing the difficult inverse operation — solving the discrete logarithm problem.

The discrete logarithm problem, using the values in the equation above, is simply finding x given only y, g and p.

Expanding that thought slightly: someone has multiplied g by itself x times, and reduced the result into the field (performed the modulo operation) as often as necessary to keep the result smaller than p. Now, knowing y, g and p, you're trying to find out what value of x they used.

It turns out that for large enough values of p, where p is prime, this is extraordinarily difficult to do — much more difficult than just finding y from g, x and p.

If you grasp what's going on in the operations above, you're now in a position to grasp the basic math behind the DSA and discrete logarithm systems.

And, by extension, you also understand some of the principles behind ECC. ECC — as we'll discuss in greater detail a little later — also uses a discrete log problem in a finite group. The difference is that ECC defines its group differently. And it is, in fact, the difference in how the group is defined — and particularly how the mathematical operations within the group are defined — that give ECC its greater security for a given key size.

Before we discuss this, however, we should first briefly discuss why greater security at the same key size is something you might want.

5.6.6 Asymmetric Cryptography as a Fine Balance

As noted above, in all of the asymmetric cryptosystems, the fact that the system works at all relies upon the comparative difficulty of doing two types of operations — a 'forward' operation which must be tractable, and an 'inverse' operation which must be in practical terms intractable. In fact, in all cases, the degree of difference between the difficulties of these operations actually depends in a quite precise way on the size of the key pairs that are being generated. Both operations get more difficult as the key is made longer. The inverse operation, however, gets much more difficult, much more rapidly.

In all asymmetric cryptosystems, as mentioned above, the key length is the parameter that determines how difficult are both the forward and inverse algorithms.

As described in the preceding sections, the common characteristic of all asymmetric cryptosystems is a function whose inverse is significantly harder. We are now in a position to expand upon this: in all cases, the hardness of the forward and inverse operations is actually defined as two functions on the key length — two functions describing an 'order of growth' of the difficulty of the forward and inverse algorithms.

So, to make more precise our previous description: asymmetric cryptosystems work because the inverse operation rapidly gets more difficult as key length increases than does the forward operation.

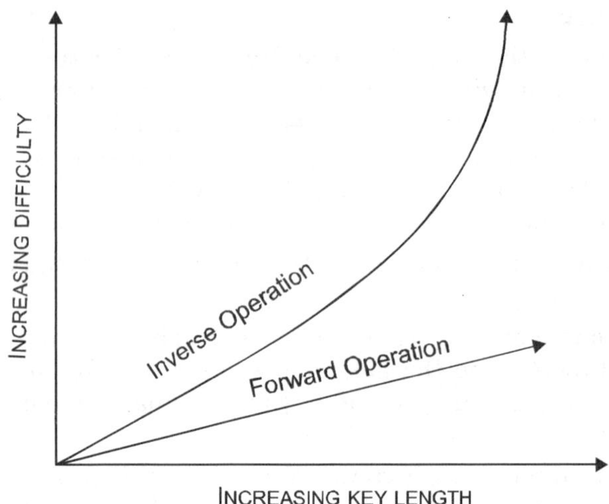

What this means in practical terms is: asymmetric cryptography is always a fine balance. Somewhere, for any given application, and any given cryptosystem, there is a key length x which is long enough that the users of the system can say the inverse operation is as hard as they need it to be to offer the level of security they desire — and yet key length x is not so long that the forward operations become unnecessarily unwieldy.

5.6.7 A Race Between Guns and Armour

This key length x isn't even a constant for a given cryptosystem and application. Rather, as microprocessors become faster and cheaper, a key length which seemed quite adequate a few years ago may no longer offer adequate security, as more and more processing power can be assembled to calculate the inverse function.

As a quick illustration of the speed of progress in the development of faster microprocessors, consider the following bit of history: Intel's 8086 processor, the heart of IBM's XT system, operating at a clock speed of 5 Mhz, could perform approximately .33 Millions of Instructions Per Second (MIPS).

By the year 2000, you could purchase the Pentium 4. It operated at 1.5 GHz, and could do approximately 1500 MIPS. As a rough measure, in terms of operations per second, the processor power you can buy has increased by 1.6 every year for the past 10 years. This is commonly referred to as Moore's Law.

Moore's Law means each year chipmakers cram more gates into less and less space. Besides this, each year, clock speeds increase. And chipmakers and system builders come up with new approaches to old problems — pipelining, parallel processors, etc. Those MIPS counts keep climbing. And so key lengths in asymmetric cryptography — just as in symmetric cryptosystems — creep ever upward as a direct consequence of this progress.

Consider again the difference in the MIPS available in a cheap, readily available processor in the late 80s (.33) and in the year 2000 (1500). The processor available 20 years later can perform 4500 times as many calculations in the same amount of time.

As a rough measure, considering brute force methods of attack against a basic symmetric cryptosystem, that corresponds approximately to a key length 12 bits longer over twenty years to get equivalent security.

It's the race between guns and armour, and it's reasonable to predict it may never end. In the realm of symmetric cryptography, DES' 56 bit key is now history; it does not offer adequate security given the resources available to do brute force attacks — attacks which check every possible key. It is for this reason that the standard, which once defined DES as the appropriate symmetric encryption algorithms to use for the encryption of sensitive information within the US government, has been declared obsolete. The new standard specifies the recently developed AES algorithm, whose keys can offer 128, 192 or 256 bits of security.

5.6.8 ECC as the Answer for High Security and for the Future

Consider these three facets of the problem, now:

First, the fact that the security and practicality of a given asymmetric cryptosystems relies upon the difference in difficulty between doing a given operation and its inverse.

Second, the fact that the difference in difficulty between the forward and the inverse operation in a given system is a function of the key length in use, due to the fact that the difficulty of the forward and the inverse operations increase as very different functions of the key length; the inverse operations get harder faster.

Third, the fact that as you are forced to use longer key lengths to adjust to the greater processing power now available to attack the cryptosystem, even the 'legitimate' forward operations get harder, and require greater resources (chip space and/or processor time), though by a lesser degree than do the inverse operations.

If you understand these three things, you are now in a position to grasp the advantages ECC offers over other asymmetric cryptosystems.

ECC's advantage is this: its inverse operation gets harder, faster, against increasing key length than do the inverse operations in Diffie Hellman and RSA.

What this means is: as security requirements become more stringent, and as processing power gets cheaper and more available, ECC becomes the more practical system for use. And as security requirements become more demanding, and processors become more powerful, considerably more modest increases in key length are necessary, if you're using the ECC cryptosystem — to address the threat.

This keeps ECC implementations smaller and more efficient than other implementations. ECC can use a considerably shorter key and offer the same level of security as other asymmetric algorithms using much larger ones. Moreover, the gulf between ECC and its competitors in terms of key size required for a given level of security becomes dramatically more pronounced, at higher levels of security.

NIST guidelines for public key sizes for AES			
ECC KEY SIZE	RSA KEY SIZE	KEY SIZE	AES KEY SIZE
(Bits)	(Bits)	(Bits)	(Bits)
163	1024	1 : 6	
256	3072	1 : 12	128
384	7680	1 : 20	192
512	15360	1 : 30	256

Figure 5.20: Equivalent key sizes for ECC and RSA

In the next section, we will describe what ECC is, and explore why its security increases more rapidly as key length increases.

5.7 ELLIPTIC CURVE CRYPTOGRAPHY

Over the past 30 years, public key cryptography has become a mainstay for secure communications over the Internet and throughout many other forms of communications. It provides the foundation for both key management and digital signatures. In key management, public key cryptography is used to distribute the secret keys used in other cryptographic algorithms (e.g. DES). For digital signatures, public key cryptography is used to authenticate the origin of data and protect the integrity of that data. For the past 20 years, Internet communications have been secured by the first generation of public key cryptographic algorithms developed in the mid-1970's. Notably, they form the basis for key management and authentication for IP encryption (IKE/IPSEC), web traffic (SSL/TLS) and secure electronic mail.

In their day these public key techniques revolutionized cryptography. Over the last twenty years however, new techniques have been developed which offer both better performance and higher security than these first generation public key techniques. The best assured group of new public key techniques is built on the arithmetic of elliptic curves. This paper will outline a case for moving to elliptic curves as a foundation for future Internet security. This case will be based on both the relative security offered by elliptic curves and first generation public key systems and the relative performance of these algorithms. While at current security levels elliptic curves do not offer significant benefits over existing public key algorithms, as one scales security upwards over time to meet the evolving threat posed by eavesdroppers and hackers with access to greater computing resources, elliptic curves begin to offer dramatic savings over the old, first generation techniques.

5.7.1 First Generation Public Key Algorithms

The two noteworthy first generation public key algorithms used to secure the Internet today are known as

- RSA and
- Diffie-Hellman (DH).

The security of the first is based on the difficulty of factoring the product of two large primes. The second is related to a problem known as the discrete logarithm problem for finite groups. Both are based on the use of elementary number theory. Interestingly, the security of the two schemes, though formulated differently, is closely related.

Both algorithms have been subject to intense scrutiny since their invention around 1975. In the years immediately following their invention, there were a number of attacks based on a variety of degenerate ways to generate the prime numbers and such that define the system. Such parameters were quickly excluded from specifications. In the public domain, more general theoretic attacks on the fundamental problems of factoring and discrete logs made steady progress until the early 1990's. Since that time, no dramatic improvements in these attack algorithms have been published. However, there have been several efforts aimed at designing theoretical special purpose computers that would implement the existing attack algorithms far faster than general computing resources.

Since their use in cryptography was discovered in 1985, elliptic curve cryptography has also been an active area of study in academia. Similar to both RSA and Diffie-Hellman, the first years of analysis yielded some degenerate cases for elliptic curve parameters that one should avoid. However, unlike the RSA and Diffie-Hellman cryptosystems that slowly succumbed to increasingly strong attack algorithms, elliptic curve cryptography has remained at its full strength since it was first presented in 1985.

5.7.2 Elliptic Curve Security and Efficiency:

The majority of public key systems in use today use 1024-bit parameters for RSA and Diffie-Hellman. The US National Institute for Standards and Technology (NIST) has recommended that these 1024-bit systems are sufficient for use until 2010. After that, NIST recommends that they be upgraded to something providing more security. The question is what should these systems be changed to? One option is to simply increase the public key parameter size to a level appropriate for another decade of use. Another option is to take advantage of the past 30 years of public key research and analysis and move from first generation public key algorithms and on to elliptic curves.

One way judgments are made about the correct key size for a public key system is to look at the strength of the conventional (symmetric) encryption algorithms that the public key algorithm will be used to key or authenticate. Examples of these conventional algorithms are the:

- Data Encryption Standard (DES) created in 1975 and the
- Advanced Encryption Standard (AES) now a new standard.

The length of a key, in bits, for a conventional encryption algorithm is a common measure of security. To attack an algorithm with a k-bit key it will generally require roughly **2k-1** operations. Hence, to secure a public key system one would generally want to use parameters that require at least **2k-1** operations to attack. The table 5.2 gives the key sizes recommended by the National Institute of Standards and Technology to protect keys used in conventional encryption algorithms like the (DES) and (AES) together with the key sizes for RSA, Diffie-Hellman and elliptic curves that are needed to provide equivalent security.

Table 5.2: NIST Recommended Key Sizes

Symmetric Key Size (bits)	RSA and Diffie-Hellman Key Size (bits)	Elliptic Curve Key Size (bits)
80	1024	160
112	2048	224
128	3072	256
192	7680	384
256	15360	521

1. These estimates are based on the theoretic costing of an n-bit multiply modulo a large prime as costing roughly **n2** operations. It is also based on an estimate that computing an inverse modulo a large prime is roughly 8 multiplies. Actual implementations could be radically different based on computer architecture.
2. In the elliptic curve case, there is actually one additional bit that needs to be transmitted in each direction which allows the recovery of both the x and y coordinates of an elliptic curve point.

To use RSA or Diffie-Hellman to protect 128-bit AES keys one should use 3072-bit parameters: three times the size in use throughout the Internet today. The equivalent key size for elliptic curves is only 256 bits. One can see that as symmetric key sizes increase the required key sizes for RSA and Diffie-Hellman increase at a much faster rate than the required key sizes for elliptic curve cryptosystems. Hence, elliptic curve systems offer more security per bit increase in key size than either RSA or Diffie-Hellman public key systems.

Security is not the only attractive feature of elliptic curve cryptography. Elliptic curve cryptosystems also are more computationally efficient than the first generation public key systems, RSA and Diffie-Hellman. Although elliptic curve arithmetic is slightly more complex per bit than either RSA or DH arithmetic, the added strength per bit more than makes up for any extra compute time. The table 5.3 shows the ratio of DH computation versus EC computation for each of the key sizes listed in Table 5.2.

Table 5.3: Relative Computation Costs of Diffie-Hellman and Elliptic Curves(1)

Security Level (bits)	Ratio of DH Cost : EC Cost
80	3:1
112	6:1
128	10:1
192	32:1
256	64:1

Closely related to the key size of different public key systems is the channel overhead required to perform key exchanges and digital signatures on a communications link. The key sizes for public key in Table 5.2 is also roughly the number of bits that need to be transmitted each way over a communications channel for a key exchange2. In channel-constrained environments, elliptic curves offer a much better solution than first generation public key systems like Diffie-Hellman.

In choosing an elliptic curve as the foundation of a public key system there are a variety of different choices. The National Institute of Standards and Technology (NIST) has standardized on a list of 15 elliptic curves of varying sizes. Ten of these curves are for what are known as binary fields and 5 are for prime fields. Those curves listed provide cryptography equivalent to symmetric encryption algorithms (e.g. AES, DES or SKIPJACK) with keys of length 80, 112, 128, 192, and 256 bits and beyond.

For protecting both classified and unclassified National Security information, the National Security Agency has decided to move to elliptic curve based public key cryptography. Where appropriate, NSA plans to use the elliptic curves over finite fields with large prime moduli (256, 384, and 521 bits) published by NIST.

The United States, the UK, Canada and certain other NATO nations have all adopted some form of elliptic curve cryptography for future systems to protect classified information throughout and between their governments. The Cryptographic Modernization Initiative in the US Department of Defense aims at replacing almost 1.3 million existing equipments over the next 10 years. In addition, the Department's Global Information Grid will require a vast expansion of the number of security devices in use throughout the US Military. This will necessitate change and rollover of equipment with all major US allies. Most of these needs will be satisfied with a new generation of cryptographic equipment that uses elliptic curve cryptography for key management and digital signatures.

5.7.3 Elliptic curve cryptography (ECC) Method

Elliptic curve cryptography (ECC) was proposed by Victor Miller and Neal Koblitz in the mid 1980s. Elliptic curve cryptography (ECC) is an approach to public-key cryptography based on the algebraic structure of elliptic curves over finite fields.

An elliptic curve is the set of solutions (x,y) to an equation of the form $y^2 = x^3 + Ax + B$, together with an extra point O which is called the point at infinity. For applications to cryptography we consider finite fields of q elements, which I will write as F_q or GF(q). When q is a prime one can think of F q as the integers modulo q.

We usually write E for the equation $y^2 = x^3 + Ax + B$ and use the notation E(F_q) for the set of points (x,y) with coordinates in the field F_q together with the point O (which is defined over every field).

The set of points on an elliptic curve forms a group under a certain addition rule, which we write using the notation +. The point O is the identity element of the group. When we work over a finite field then this group is necessarily finite (as there are only finitely many points). The set of points on such a curve — all solutions of the above equation together with a point at infinity — form an Abelian group, with the point at infinity as identity element. If the coordinates x and y are chosen from a finite field, the solutions form a finite abelian group. If the finite field is large, the discrete logarithm problem on such elliptic curve groups is believed to be more difficult than the corresponding problem in the underlying finite field's multiplicative group. Thus keys in elliptic curve cryptography can be chosen to be much shorter for a comparable level of security compared to integer-based methods.

Given a point P=(x, y) and a positive integer n we define [n]P = P + P + ... + P (n times). The order of a point P=(x, y) is the smallest positive integer n such that [n]P = O.

We denote by < P > the group generated by P. In other words < P > = {O, P, P+P, P+P+P, . . .}.

As for other popular public key cryptosystems, no mathematical proof of difficulty has been published for ECC as of 2006[update]. However, the U.S. National Security Agency has endorsed ECC technology by including it in its Suite B set of recommended algorithms and allows their use for protecting information classified up to top secret with 384-bit keys.[4] Although the RSA patent has expired, there are patents in force covering some aspects of ECC.

Elliptic curve cryptosystems are analogs of public-key cryptosystems such as RSA and ElGamal in which modular multiplication is replaced by the elliptic curve addition operation.

The curves used in elliptic curve analogs of discrete logarithm cryptosystems are normally of the form

$y^2 = x^3 + ax + b \pmod{p}$,

where p is prime. The problem tapped by the discrete logarithm analogs in elliptic curves is the elliptic curve logarithm problem, defined as follows: given a point G on an elliptic curve with order r (number of points on the curve) and another point Y on the curve, find a unique x (0 x r - 1) such that Y = xG, i.e., Y is the xth multiple of G.

Until recently, the best attacks on elliptic curve logarithm problems were the general methods applicable to any group. The methods have a running time of about a constant times the square root of r on average, which is much slower than specialized attacks on certain types of groups. The lack of specialized attacks means that shorter key sizes for elliptic cryptosystems give the same security as larger keys in cryptosystems that are based on discrete logarithm problem . However, for certain elliptic curves, Menezes, Okamoto, and Vanstone have been able to reduce the elliptic logarithm problem to a discrete logarithm problem. It is possible that algorithm development in this area will change the security of elliptic curve discrete logarithm cryptosystems to be equivalent to that of general discrete logarithm cryptosystems; this is an open research problem.

Elliptic curve analogs of RSA have been proposed, and they are based on the difficulty of factoring, just as RSA is. The elliptic curve analogs do not seem to offer any significant advantage over RSA, as the underlying problem is the same and the key sizes are similar for equivalent levels of security. Two of their purported advantages resistance to "low-exponent" attacks and to signature forgery against a chosen message attack have recently been shown not to hold.

5.7.4 Merits of Using Elliptic Curve Cryptography (ECC)

In case of asymmetric cryptography, the following are the advantages of using elliptic curve cryptography (ECC) over other methods:

- ECC offers considerably greater security for a given key size — something we'll explain at greater length later in this paper.
- The smaller key size also makes possible much more compact implementations for a given level of security, which means faster cryptographic operations, running on smaller chips or more compact software. This means less heat production and less power consumption — all of which is of particular advantage in constrained devices, but of some advantage anywhere.
- There are extremely efficient, compact hardware implementations available for ECC exponentiation operations, offering potential reductions in implementation footprint even beyond those due to the smaller key length alone.

5.7.5 Limitation of Using Elliptic Curve Cryptosystems

Despite the many advantages of elliptic curves and despite the adoption of elliptic curves by many users, many vendors and academics view the intellectual property environment surrounding elliptic curves as a major roadblock to their implementation and use. Various aspects of elliptic curve cryptography have been patented by a variety of people and companies around the world. Notably the Canadian company, Certicom Inc. holds over 130 patents related to elliptic curves and public key cryptography in general.

As a way of clearing the way for the implementation of elliptic curves to protect US and allied government information, the National Security Agency purchased from Certicom a license that covers all of their intellectual property in a restricted field of use. The license would be limited to implementations that were for national security uses and certified under FIPS 140-2 or were approved by NSA. Further, the license would be limited to only prime field curves where the prime was greater than 2255. On the NIST list of curves 3 out of the 15 fit this field of use: the prime field curves with primes of 256 bits, 384 bits and 521 bits. Certicom identified 26 patents that covered this field of use. NSA's license includes a right to sublicense these 26 patents to vendors building products within the restricted field of use. Certicom also retained a right to license vendors both within the field of use and under other terms that they may negotiate with vendors.

Commercial vendors may receive a license from NSA provided their products fit within the field of use of NSA's license. Alternatively, commercial vendors may contact Certicom for a license for the same 26 patents. Certicom is planning on developing and selling software toolkits that implement elliptic curve cryptography in the field of use. With the toolkit a vendor will also receive a license from Certicom to sell the technology licensed by NSA in the general commercial marketplace. Vendors wishing to implement elliptic curves outside the scope of the NSA license will need to work with Certicom if they wish to be licensed.

The security of elliptic curve cryptography relies on the following problem:

Elliptic Curve Discrete Logarithm Problem (ECDLP): Let E be an elliptic curve over a finite field F_q. Suppose P is some point of $E(F_q)$ and let Q be a point in $\langle P \rangle$. Find an integer t such that $Q = [t]P$.

It is widely believed that the elliptic curve discrete logarithm problem is hard to computationally solve when the point P has large prime order. The known methods for solving the ECDLP are:

(1) The Pohlig-Hellman algorithm (which reduces the problem to subgroups of prime order).

(2) Shanks' baby-step-giant-step method.

(3) Pollard's methods, the rho method and the kangaroo method, both of which have parallel versions due to van Oorschot and Wiener.

(4) The Menezes-Okamoto-Vanstone (MOV) attack using the Weil pairing.

(5) The Frey-Rueck attack using the Tate pairing.

The attacks on anomalous elliptic curves (i.e., elliptic curves over F_p which have p points) due to Semaev, Satoh-Araki and Smart.

Weil descent (for some special finite fields).

Of the above methods, only the anomalous curves attack runs in polynomial time. The MOV, Frey-Rueck and Weil descent methods are (at their fastest) subexponential in complexity.

Due to the Pohlig-Hellman algorithm we always restrict to the case where the point P has large prime order. Then the only algorithms which are applicable for all elliptic curves are the methods of Shanks and Pollard, and these methods have exponential complexity.

The public key cryptosystems available for ECC are analogues of the cryptosystems available for other discrete logarithm based systems (such as the multiplicative group of a finite field). These include Diffie-Hellman key exchange, El Gamal public key encryption, and ECDSA (an analogue of the US government's digital signature standard).

In fact, the security of cryptosystems based on elliptic curves usually relies on related problems like the (computational) Diffie-Hellman problem (CDH) or the Decision Diffie-Hellman problem (DDH).

What ECC Is

Elliptic Curve Cryptography, as described above, is a relative of discrete logarithm cryptography.

The DL system, as described above, relies upon the difficulty of the discrete logarithm problem — a logarithm problem calculated within the multiplicative group of a finite field — to frustrate attempts to use the public key to compromise the private one.

ECC uses groups and a logarithm problem too.

What ECC also offers, however, is a difference in the method by which the group is defined — how the elements of the group are defined, and how the fundamental operations on them are defined.

It's the difference in the way the group is defined—both the numbers in the set and the definitions of the arithmetic operations used to manipulate them—that give ECC its more rapid increase in security as key length increases.

To clarify this point, we'll describe briefly how elliptic curves are defined.

Elliptic Curves

The way that the elliptic curve operations are defined is what gives ECC its higher security at smaller key sizes.

An elliptic curve is defined in a standard, two dimensional x,y Cartesian coordinate system by an equation of the form:

$$y^2 = x^3 + ax + b$$

The graphs turns out to be gently looping lines of various forms.

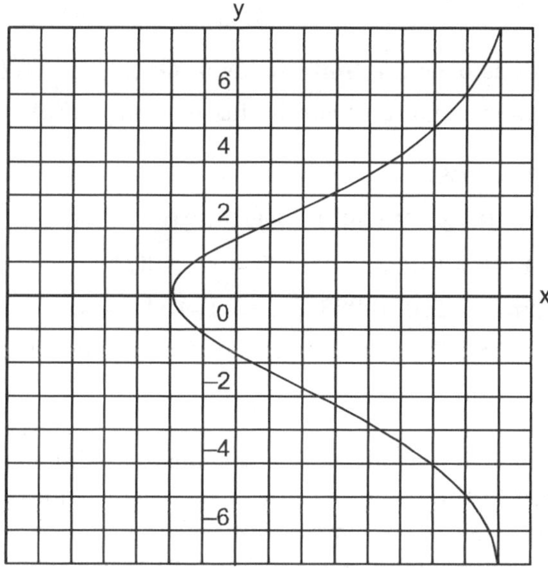

Figure 5.21 an elliptic curve

In elliptic curve cryptosystems, the elliptic curve is used to define the members of the set over which the group is calculated, as well as the operations between them which define how math works in the group.

It's done as follows: imagine a graph labeled along both axes with the numbers of a large prime field. That is to say: a square graph, p x p in size, where p is a very large prime number. Fp is the field of integers modulo p, and consists of all the integers from 0 to p-1.

Now the prime numbers actually employed in practical ECC implementations are quite large, so it's difficult to visualize this graph if you use the real kinds of numbers used. But as an exercise, you can imagine a more comprehensible prime — such as 17. So you'd be looking at a graph 17x17 units in size.

Now if you define an elliptic curve — an equation of the form given above — so that there are points (x, y) on the curve that satisfy the condition that both x and y are members of the prime field, you have implicitly created a group from the set of integer points on the curve; it is a subset of all the points in the p by p matrix created when you drew the graph — specifically the ones the curve passes directly through.

Note that unlike the groups used in Diffie Hellman, the elements of the set aren't integers, but points. But the system that will result is still going to be, in most senses, the same, familiar arithmetic system as those discussed above. It contains a set of elements (points, in this case), and when you add one point to another, or subtract one from another, there are rules that say what point in the set you wind up at when you do so — just as for the integers in the groups used in Diffie Hellman. And these rules still follow many of the familiar rules for the arithmetic you already know.

Industry use

- Elliptic curve groups over the finite fields of GF(p) and GF(2m)
- Koblitz EC groups over GF(2m) can be faster than GF(p)

NIST recommended curves:

- Over GF(p): P-192, P-224, P-256, P-384, P-521
- Koblitz GF(2m): K-163, K-233, K-283, K-409, K-571
- Non-Koblitz GF(2m): B-163, B-233, B-283, B-409, B-571

For more information on Elliptic Curve Group Operations see Appendix B.

Point Multiplication

The dominant operation in ECC cryptographic schemes is point multiplication. This is the operation which is the key to the use of elliptic curves for asymmetric cryptography — the critical operation which is itself fairly simple, but whose inverse (the elliptic curve discrete logarithm problem — defined below) is very difficult. ECC arranges itself so that when you wish to perform an operation the cryptosystem should make easy — encrypting a message with the public key, decrypting it with the private key — the operation you are performing is point multiplication.

Point multiplication is simply calculating kP, where k is an integer and P is a point on the elliptic curve defined in the prime field.

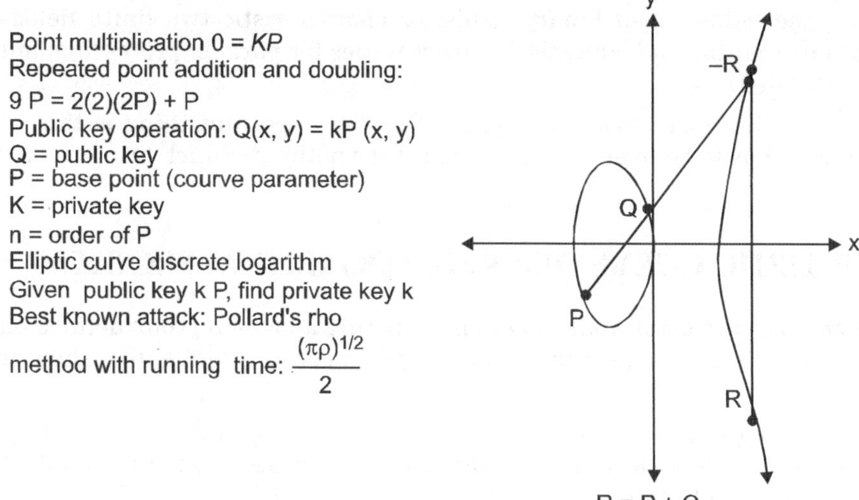

Figure 5.22 Eliptical curve cryptography

In terms of the addition operation we defined above, and the corresponding diagram, you can see how the following would look: take a point, add it to itself (doubling). Then take the result, and the original point, and add them together again, using the chord and tangent rule. Then take that result, and the original point again, and use the chord and tangent rule yet again. And so on — doing one doubling, and k-2 chord and tangent additions, until you've added P to itself k-1 times, giving kP.

Now if the only way of doing this were in fact to repeat those precise operations — finding the points P, 2P, 3P, and so on up to kP — elliptic curves would be useless for cryptography, since the operation which searches for k given only P and kP (see the elliptic curve discrete logarithm problem, below) would be no harder than doing this. You could thus search for k from kP as quickly as you could calculate kP directly given p and k.

However, there are shortcuts for point multiplication. Given the known shape of the curve, there are in fact several algorithms available which run in considerably less time than would such a stepwise operation. Which of them you choose to use depends on a number of factors — including which calculations you might be able to do ahead of time (which is practical for some cryptographic protocol purposes, in which P is known ahead of time), how much RAM you can set aside for lookup tables, and that sort of thing.

None of the operations is exactly what you'd call trivial. But all of them are vastly easier than doing it by stepwise addition — easier by many orders of magnitude. And they also run in nearconstant time for a given field size, regardless of what k and P you feed them as input. Some of the fastest working are in the NIST P192 curve, defined using the prime 2192-264+1. Here, you are able to get kP in the equivalent of 38 addition and 192 doubling operations, when counting only those which are usable even when P isn't known ahead of time.

You can do better still, in fact, in hardware implementations, in fields of order 2m. In these fields— the fields called binary fields, or characteristic two finite fields—hardware implementations that take advantages of opportunities for parallel processing, multiplication has been accelerated.

Now these still aren't trivial operations. But the important thing is this: compared to what the attacker has to do to get k back from kP, it's nothing. Which brings us to the inverse operation.

5.8 THE ELLIPTIC CURVE DISCRETE LOGARITHM PROBLEM

The inverse operation to point multiplication — finding a log in a group defined on an elliptic curve over a prime field — is defined as follows: given points `Q` and `P`, find the integer `k` such that `Q = kP`.

This is the elliptic curve discrete logarithm problem — and this is the inverse operation in the cryptosystem — the one you effectively have to perform to get the plaintext back from the ciphertext, given only the public key.

Now naively the obvious, certain way of finding k would be to perform repeated addition — operations — stepping through P, 2P, 3P, and so on, until you find kP. You'd start by doubling P, then adding P to 2P finding 3P, then 3P to P finding 4P and so on. This is the brute force method. The trouble with this is if you use a large enough prime field, the number of possible values for k becomes inconveniently large. So inconveniently large that it's quite practical to create a sufficiently large prime field that searching through the possible values of k would take all the processor time currently available on the planet thousands of years.

In the case of the NIST-defined P192 curve used as an example above, you'd have to do (on average) a doubling followed by on the order of 3x1057 additions. In the worst case, you'd have to do twice as many additions.

It is probably unnecessary at this point to point out that 3x1057 is really a very, very large number. And a lot larger than the few hundreds of operations we needed to do the multiplication in the first place.

This may sound unfair. And it is. It's so grossly unfair, in fact, that you can, conveniently, do those multiplication operations in the rather limited processor of a tiny little handheld Blackberry unit or cellular phone operating on a 2.5 V battery in the course of routine communications, in a handshake at the beginning of a secure exchange, in considerably less than a second. And you can then quite safely send kP through the air where anyone can hear it. Indeed, you can publish kP and ask other people to use it as a component of the public key via which they communicate with you. And then that someone can take kP and go looking for k — the value you've kept to yourself for use as your private key. And even if that someone isn't restricted to a portable phone and less than a second — even if that someone has a cave full of the latest massively parallel supercomputers and several years — even then, they're still not getting k back.

That's basically because 3x1057 divided by a few hundred adds up to an awfully large number. Though there is a bit more to the story we have to get to now, to distinguish between how difficult it is to break ECC versus how difficult it is to break Diffie Hellman and RSA.

5.9 POLLARD'S RHO ATTACK VERSUS INDEX CALCULUS

As we noted earlier in this paper, there is a profound difference in the difficulty of the forward and inverse operations at the centre of all popular asymmetric schemes — that is the soul of their usefulness. In RSA, it's integer multiplication (forward) and factorization (inverse) that make the system work. In Diffie Hellman it's discrete exponentiation (forward) and log (inverse). In ECC it's point multiplication (forward) and the elliptic curve discrete logarithm problem (inverse).

In all of these cases, it's easy to see that the difficulty of the brute force approach to the inverse operation increases exponentially with the size of the key. Simply look at the number of values that must be tried; it doubles with each bit added to the key length.

Now it turns out that for all of these cryptosystems, the brute force method isn't quite the best you can do. You can, in fact, for Diffie Hellman and for RSA, try to retrieve the private key from the public (or the plaintext from the public key and the ciphertext) via the index calculus method. It's difficulty grows subexpotentially with the key length.

There are, in other words, shortcuts for doing the inverse operations, just as there was a shortcut for doing point multiplication.

The difference is, the shortcuts for doing the inverse operations aren't good shortcuts. A typical number field sieve variant of the index calculus method — the best you can do for Diffie Hellman — gets subexponentially more difficult as the field size increases —technically at a rate of `e1.9(lnn)1/3(lnlnn)2/3` where `n` is the field size which is itself, remember, exponential to the key length. It's not as steep an increase as 2k, where k is the key length — but a graph of the number of steps you must perform (on average) to find a key via the index calculus method versus the key size is still pretty steep.

And that's the point. That curve of number of steps versus key size — and the index calculus attack it describes — are what you have to keep in mind when you choose your key length in doing asymmetric cryptography. And that's the calculation you're actually doing when you choose the size of your RSA and your Diffie Hellman keys. How big do I have to make this so the best attack available — index calculus, in this case — is still too much trouble, for now and for some decades, assuming hardware continues to get faster at roughly the rate it has in the past? And that's the estimate you're counting on when you chose that 2048 bit key, and assume it's good enough for the useful life of your product—a figure taken as being 20 years and up, usually. And that's where ECC really starts to shine.

Index calculus attacks are demanding enough that asymmetric cryptography is feasible despite them, provided the key is kept large enough. But ECC can do better, and with smaller keys. And that's because ECC cryptosystems aren't vulnerable to index calculus attacks. Index calculus attacks rely on certain group properties not present in groups defined using elliptic curves. The best you can do for ECC is another attack — a more general-purpose attack called Pollard's rho attack.

Pollard's rho attack is a class of what are known as 'collision search' attacks. They also do better than brute force. But they also get a lot harder a lot faster than do the index calculus attacks, as the field size increases.

Pollard's rho attack gets more difficult as ÷(pn)/2, where n is the group size (again, remember, itself exponential to the key size). The resulting curve — a plot of the number of operations against key length — is considerably steeper than is the curve for the index calculus attack described above.

1 Astute readers will note that the prime p, using P192, is around 6.2x1057. And though there are actually therefore (6.2x1057)2 points in the graph you draw, it turns out the curve usually intersects around p points, giving a final field size not far from the size of the prime itself.

2 Note—there are subexponential running time attacks against certain, specific ECC groups, defined on certain curves; but these curves are easily avoided.

5.10 NECESSITY OF STRONG PRIMES IN RSA

In the literature pertaining to RSA, it has often been suggested that in choosing a key pair, one should use so-called "strong" primes p and q to generate the modulus n. Strong primes are those with certain properties that make the product n hard to factor by specific factoring methods; such properties have included, for example, the existence of a large prime factor of p-1 and a large prime factor of p+1. The reason for these concerns is that some factoring methods are especially suited to primes p such that p -1 or p+1 has only small factors; strong primes are resistant to these attacks.

However, advances in factoring over the last ten years appear to have obviated the advantage of strong primes; the elliptic curve factoring algorithm is one such advance. The new factoring methods have as good a chance of success on strong primes as on "weak" primes. Therefore, choosing traditional "strong" primes alone does not significantly increase security. Choosing large enough primes is what matters. However, there is no danger in using strong, large primes, though it may take slightly longer to generate a strong prime than an arbitrary prime.

It is possible that new factoring algorithms may be developed in the future which once again target primes with certain properties; if so, choosing strong primes may once again help to increase security.

5.11 SIZE OF RSA KEY

The best size for an RSA modulus depends on one's security needs. The larger the modulus, the greater the security, but also the slower the RSA operations. One should choose a modulus length upon consideration, first, of one's security needs, such as the value of the protected data and how long it needs to be protected, and, second, of how powerful one's potential enemies are.

Odlyzko's paper considers the security of RSA key sizes based on factoring techniques available in 1995 and the ability to tap large computational resources via computer networks. A specific assessment of the security of 512-bit RSA keys shows that one may be factored for less than $1,000,000 in cost and eight months of effort in 1997. It is believed that 512-bit keys no longer provide sufficient security with the advent of new factoring algorithms and distributed computing. Such keys should not be used after 1997 or 1998. Recommended key sizes are now

768 bits for personal use, 1024 bits for corporate use, and 2048 bits for extremely valuable keys like the key pair of a certifying authority. A 768-bit key is expected to be secure until at least the year 2004.

The key of an individual user may expire after a certain time, say, two years. This gives an opportunity to change keys regularly and thus maintain a given level of security. Upon expiration, the user should generate a new key which is at least a few digits longer than the old key to reflect the speed increases of computers and factoring algorithms over the two years. Recommended key length schedules are published by RSA Laboratories on a regular basis.

Users should keep in mind that the estimated times to break RSA are averages only. A large factoring effort, attacking many thousands of RSA moduli, may succeed in factoring at least one in a reasonable time. Although the security of any individual key is still strong, with some factoring methods there is always a small chance that the attacker may get lucky and factor some key quickly.

As for the slowdown caused by increasing the key size , doubling the modulus length will, on average, increase the time required for public-key operations (encryption and signature verification) by a factor of four, and increase the time taken by private-key operations (decryption and signing) by a factor of eight. The reason that public-key operations are affected less than private-key operations is that the public exponent can remain fixed when the modulus is increased, whereas the private exponent increases proportionally. Key generation time would increase by a factor of 16 upon doubling the modulus, but this is a relatively infrequent operation for most users. (The impact of key size increases other than doubling can be calculated similarly.)

5.12 ELGAMAL ENCRYPTION/DECRYPTION ALGORITHM

ElGamal encryption/decryption algorithm is based on the difficulty of discrete logarithm problem where it is strait forward to raise numbers to large powers but it is much harder to do the inverse computation of the discrete logarithm. The ElGamal algorithm depends on certain parameters which are affecting the performance, speed and security of the algorithm. Here, the importance of these parameters and the role it takes in the security and complexity of the system are analyzed, particularly the effect of changing the length of the modulo number and the private key number are investigated.

The ElGamal encryption system is an asymmetric key encryption algorithm for public-key cryptography which is based on the Diffie-Hellman key agreement. It was described by Taher Elgamal in 1984. ElGamal encryption is used in the free GNU Privacy Guard software, recent versions of PGP, and other cryptosystems. The Digital Signature Algorithm is a variant of the ElGamal signature scheme, which should not be confused with ElGamal encryption.

5.12.1 The algorithm

ElGamal encryption consists of three components: the key generator, the encryption algorithm, and the decryption algorithm.

The key generator works as follows:

- Anita generates an efficient description of a multiplicative cyclic group of order with generator g. See below for a discussion on the required properties of this group.
- Anita chooses a random x from $\{0,..., q - 1\}$.
- Anita computes $h = g^x$.
- Anita publishes h, along with the description of ^{G}, q, g, as her **public key**. Anita retains as her private key which must be kept secret.

The encryption algorithm works as follows: to encrypt a message to Anita under her public key, (G, q, g, h),

- Bunty converts into an element of G.
- Bunty chooses a random y from $\{0,..., q - 1\}$, then calculates $c_1 = g^y$ and $c_2 = m.\ h^y$.
- Bunty sends the ciphertext (c_1, c_2) to Anita.

The decryption algorithm works as follows: to decrypt a ciphertext (c_1, c_2) with her private key x,

- Anita computes — as the plaintext message.

The decryption algorithm produces the intended message, since

$$= \qquad \frac{\cdot}{} = \frac{\cdot}{} =$$

If the space of possible messages is larger than the size of G , then the message can be split into several pieces and each piece can be encrypted independently. Alternately, ElGamal may be used in a hybrid cryptosystem to improve efficiency on long messages.

5.12.2 Security

The security of the ElGamal scheme depends on the properties of the underlying group G as well as any padding scheme used on the messages.

If the computational Diffie-Hellman assumption holds in the underlying cyclic group G, then the encryption function is one-way[2].

If the decisional Diffie-Hellman assumption (DDH) holds in G, then ElGamal achieves semantic security.[2] Semantic security is not implied by the computational Diffie-Hellman assumption alone[3]. See decisional Diffie-Hellman assumption for a discussion of groups where the assumption is believed to hold.

ElGamal encryption is unconditionally malleable, and therefore is not secure under chosen ciphertext attack. For example, given an encryption (c_1,c_2) of some (possibly unknown) message m, one can easily construct a valid encryption $(c_1, 2c_2)$ of the message 2m.

To achieve chosen-ciphertext security, the scheme must be further modified, or an appropriate padding scheme must be used. Depending on the modification, the DDH assumption may or may not be necessary.

Other schemes related to ElGamal which achieve security against chosen ciphertext attacks have also been proposed. The Cramer-Shoup system is secure under chosen ciphertext attack assuming DDH holds for G. Its proof does not use the random oracle model. Another proposed scheme is DHAES[3], whose proof requires an assumption that is weaker than the DDH assumption.

5.12.3 Efficiency

ElGamal encryption is probabilistic, meaning that a single plaintext can be encrypted to many possible ciphertexts, with the consequence that a general ElGamal encryption produces a 2:1 expansion in size from plaintext to ciphertext.

Encryption under ElGamal requires two exponentiations; however, these exponentiations are independent of the message and can be computed ahead of time if need be. Decryption only requires one exponentiation (instead of division, exponentiate c_1 to $q - x$). Unlike in the RSA and Rabin systems, ElGamal decryption *cannot* be sped up via the Chinese remainder theorem.

The ElGamal system was, in part, the basis for several later signature methods, including one by Schnorr , which in turn was the basis for DSS, the Digital Signature Standard.The ElGamal system has been used successfully in applications; it is slower for encryption and verification than RSA and its signatures are larger than RSA signatures.

The ElGamal system is a public-key cryptosystem based on the discrete logarithm problem. It consists of both encryption and signature algorithms. The encryption algorithm is similar in nature to the Diffie-Hellman key agreement protocol

The system parameters consist of a prime p and an integer g, whose powers modulo p generate a large number of elements, as in Diffie-Hellman. Anita has a private key a and a public key y, where $y = g^a \pmod p$. Suppose Bunty wishes to send a message m to Anita. Bunty first generates a random number k less than p. He then computes

$$y_1 = g^k \bmod p \text{ and } y_2 = y^k\, m \bmod p$$

where xor denotes the bit-wise exclusive-or. Bunty sends (y1 ,y2) to Anita. Upon receiving the ciphertext, Anita computes

$$m = (y_1^a \bmod p) \text{ xor } y_2$$

The ElGamal signature algorithm is similar to the encryption algorithm in that the public key and private key have the same form; however, encryption is not the same as signature verification, nor is decryption the same as signature creation as in RSA DSA (see Question 26) is based in part on the ElGamal signature algorithm.

Analysis based on the best available algorithms for both factoring and discrete logarithms shows that RSA and ElGamal have similar security for equivalent key lengths. The main disadvantage of ElGamal is the need for randomness, and its slower speed (especially for signing). Another potential disadvantage of the ElGamal system is that message expansion by a factor of two takes place during encryption. However, such message expansion is negligible if the cryptosystem is used only for exchange of secret keys.

5.13 WHAT IS QUANTUM CRYPTOGRAPHY?

Quantum cryptography is a method for secure key exchange over an insecure channel based on the nature of photons. Photons have a polarization, which can be measured in any basis, where a basis consists of two directions orthogonal to each other. If a photon's polarization is read in the same basis twice, the polarization will be read correctly and will remain unchanged. If it is read in two different bases, a random answer will be obtained in the second basis, and the polarization in the initial basis will be changed randomly.

The following protocol can be used by Anita and Bunty to exchange secret keys.

(1) Anita sends Bunty a stream of photons, each with a random polarization, in a random basis. She records the polarizations.

(2) Bunty measures each photon in a randomly chosen basis and records the results.

(3) Bunty announces, over an authenticated but not necessarily private channel (e.g., by telephone), which basis he used for each photon.

(4) Anita tells him which choices of bases are correct.

(5) The shared secret key consists of the polarization readings in the correctly chosen bases.

Quantum cryptography has a special defense against eavesdropping: If an enemy measures the photons during transmission, he will use the wrong basis half the time, and thus will change some of the polarizations. That will result in Anita and Bunty having different values for their secret keys. As a check, they can exchange some random bits of their key using an authenticated channel. They will therefore detect the presence of eavesdropping, and can start the protocol over.

REFERENCES

1. D. Denning (Editor), P. Denning (Preface), Internet Besieged : Countering Cyberspace Scofflaws, Addison-Wesley Pub Co, (Reading MA, 1997).
2. G.C. Kessler, An Overview of Cryptography, May 1998, Hill Associates, http://www.hill.com/TechLibrary/index.htm
3. Introduction to Public-Key Cryptography, Netscape Communications Corporation, 1998, http://developer.netscape.com/docs/manuals/security/pkin/contents.htm
4. P. Gutman, Security Resource Link Farm, http://www.cs.auckland.ac.nz/~pgut001/links.html
5. P.Gutmann, Godzilla Crypto Tutorial, http://www.cs.auckland.ac.nz/~pgut001/tutorial/index.html
6. R. Braden, D. Clark, S. Crocker, C. Huitema, "Report of IAB Workshop on Security in the Internet Architecture," RFC 1636, Nov. 1994.
7. RSA's Cryptography FAQ, http://www.rsa.com/rsalabs/faq/
8. Cypherpunks Web Page, ftp://ftp.csua.berkeley.edu/pub/cypherpunks/Home.html

9. Dieter Gollmann (2006). Computer Security Second Edition West Sussex, England: John Wiley & Sons, Ltd.
10. Non-Secret Encryption Using a Finite Field MJ Williamson, January 21, 1974.
11. Thoughts on Cheaper Non-Secret Encryption MJ Williamson, August 10, 1976.
12. New Directions in Cryptography W. Diffie and M. E. Hellman, IEEE Transactions on Information Theory, vol. IT-22, Nov. 1976, pp: 644-654.
13. Cryptographic apparatus and method Martin E. Hellman, Bailey W. Diffie, and Ralph C. Merkle, U.S. Patent #4,200,770, 29 April 1980
14. The History of Non-Secret Encryption JH Ellis 1987 (28K PDF file) (HTML version)
15. The First Ten Years of Public-Key Cryptography Whitfield Diffie, Proceedings of the IEEE, vol. 76, no. 5, May 1988, pp: 560-577 (1.9MB PDF file)
16. Menezes, Alfred; van Oorschot, Paul; Vanstone, Scott (1997). Handbook of Applied Cryptography Boca Raton, Florida: CRC Press. ISBN 0-8493-8523-7. (Available online)
17. Singh, Simon (1999) The Code Book: the evolution of secrecy from Mary Queen of Scots to quantum cryptography New York: Doubleday ISBN 0-385-49531-5
18. An Overview of Public Key Cryptography Martin E. Hellman, IEEE Communications Magazine, May algamal algorithm
19. [KAL 193] Burton Kalinski. Some examples of the PKCS Standards, RSA Laboratories, 1999

6

Authentication

6.1 AUTHENTICATION

Authentication is the process of proving one's identity to someone else. As humans, we authenticate each other in many ways: we recognize each others' faces when we meet; we recognize each others' voices on the telephone; we are authenticated by the customs official who checks us against the picture on our passport.

In this section we consider how one party can authenticate another party when the two are communicating over a network. We focus here on authenticating a "live" party, at the point in time when communication is actually occurring. We will see that this is a subtly different problem from proving that a message received at some point in the past (e.g., that may have been archived) did indeed come from that claimed sender. This latter problem is referred to as the *digital signature* problem, which we explore in chapter 7.

When performing authentication over the network, the communicating parties can not rely on biometric information, such as a visual appearance or a voiceprint. Indeed, we will see in our later case studies that it is often network elements such as routers and client/server processes that must authenticate each other. Here, authentication must be done solely on the basis of messages and data exchanged as part of an authentication protocol. Typically, an authentication protocol would run before the two communicating parties run some other protocol (e.g., a reliable data transfer protocol, a routing table exchange protocol, or an email protocol). The authentication protocol first establishes the identities of the parties to each others' satisfaction; only after authentication do the parties get down to the work at hand.

Authentication is the act of establishing identity via the presentation of information that allows the verifier to know the presenter is who or what it claims. This identity could be any number of things, including:

- People
- Systems
- Applications
- Messages

Why would one want to verify an identity in the first place? Hopefully, most people reading this recognize that as sarcastic humor. If not, here are a few common reasons:

- To control access to a system or application
- To bind some sensitive data to an individual, such as for encryption
- To establish trust between multiple parties to form some interaction with them
- To assure that a piece of information is genuine

Within an application, one or all of these aspects may apply. This section presents different types of authentication and ways of adding it to your applications.

6.1.1 Types of Authentication

There are many different types of authentication that can be used in an application. The selection of the most appropriate type of authentication will depend on the needs of the application; use this guide to determine which makes the most sense for your application.

- Basic, single-factor authentication
- Multi-factor authentication
- Cryptographic authentication

These authentication types apply to all classes of entity that require authentication: systems, users, messages, and applications.

6.2 BASIC AUTHENTICATION

Basic authentication is a commonly used term that most people probably understand already. It refers to password-based authentication. A password can be any information that is used to verify the identity of a presenter. Common examples that fall into this category are:

- The common password
- Host or system names
- Application names
- Numerical IDs

Authentication entails the validation of a single credential pair—the presenter's identity reference and their password. The authentication process typically takes the password and compares it to that which is stored in the authentication database. This comparison is often done as a plain text comparison where the provided password exactly matches that expected password, or with some permutation function where the password first undergoes an alteration such as hashing or encryption and the resulting data is then compared. The storage of the password is the next piece that is also often in plaintext or some permutation based on the aforementioned cryptographic function. Basic authentication has the following benefits. It is:

- Easy to manage within an application
- Easy to deploy across applications
- Easy for end users to use

There are some important caveats when using basic authentication of which every developer should be aware:

- Passwords are commonly weakly specified
- Identities can be spoofed and impersonated
- Passwords can be susceptible to theft
- Requires considerable effort to provide strong security
- Can be difficult to scale across distributed and large environments

Basic authentication often entails the transmission of a name (username or system name), and the password, which can be easily stolen and compromised if they're transmitted unprotected across the network. Here are some of the ways to increase the strength of Basic authentication:

- Use digest authentication—hash or encrypt the password prior to transmission
- Use pass phrases (longer passwords)* and set minimum password lengths
- Enforce the usage of diverse character sets that include alpha-numeric, special characters, and mixed-case passwords that are not in a dictionary
- Add security to the connection wherein the password is not transmitted in the clear across the network, such as TLS/SSL
- Do not store passwords in plaintext in whatever mechanism is used—database, file system, directory

6.2.1 Authentication Requirements

The basic access authentication is a method designed to allow a web browser, or other client program, to provide credentials – in the form of a user name and password – when making a request.

Before transmission, the user name is appended with a colon and concatenated with the password. The resulting string is encoded with the Base64 algorithm. For example, given the user name Aladdin and password open sesame, the string Aladdin:open sesame is Base64 encoded, resulting in `QWxhZGRpbjpvcGVuIHNlc2FtZQ==`. The Base64-encoded string is transmitted and decoded by the receiver, resulting in the colon-separated user name and password string.

While encoding the user name and password with the Base64 algorithm makes them unreadable, security is not the intent of the encoding step, as the Base64 decoding algorithm is not computationally expensive. Rather, the intent of the encoding is to encode non-HTTP-compatible characters that may be in the user name or password into those that are HTTP-compatible.

This specification outlines the fundamental authentication mechanisms a client can expect. Servers may provide additional authentication mechanisms with more robust qualities of service but must provide at least the capabilities described below.

6.2.2 Specification

The most basic and fundamental requirement is that the service provider MUST support HTTP Basic authentication, described in detail in RFC2617. And, due to the insecure nature of basic authentication (passwords are essentially passed in plaintext) it is expected that a provider will provide access to all services over HTTP/S to provide security.

Additionally service implementors should consider the following additional capabilities:

- The provision of an authentication token, so when basic authentication succeeds a token is returned to the client so that they do not have to deal with the 401 error in subsequent requests. This is handled in many web frameworks using the common browser "Cookie" header.
- Basic authentication is generally supported by most programmatic clients, and browsers, however the Digest authentication mechanism (see Wikipedia again) is more secure and servers may choose to support this. The issue is how a server expresses a preferrence for digest over basic authentication.
- As mentioned above the server could choose to provide access, all or in part, to the repository over HTTP/S as opposed to HTTP for security. The drawback to HTTP/S is that it makes access less able to use general caching infrastructure.

Advantages

One advantage of the basic access authentication is that it is supported by all popular† web browsers. It is rarely used on publicly accessible Internet web sites but may sometimes be used by small, private systems. A later mechanism, digest access authentication, was developed in order to replace the basic access authentication and enable credentials to be passed in a relatively secure manner over an otherwise insecure channel.

Disadvantages

Although the scheme is easily implemented, it relies on the assumption that the connection between the client and server computers is secure and can be trusted. Specifically, the credentials are passed as plaintext and could be intercepted easily. The scheme also provides no protection for the information passed back from the server.

According to RFC 2616, existing browsers retain authentication information indefinitely. HTTP does not provide a method for a server to direct clients to discard these cached credentials. This means that there is no effective way to "log out" without closing the browser. This is a significant defect that requires either further extensions to HTTP, or use of existing alternative techniques such as retrieving the page over SSL/TLS with an unguessable string in the URL.

Example

When a client attempts to access resource without providing an Authorization header, or provides credentials that are not recognized, the server MUST respond with a 401 Unauthorized status code and a WWW-Authenticate response header indicating that authentication credentials are required (this response is known as a "challenge"). Only client requests with an Authorization header providing recognized credentials will receive attention.

The client MUST be prepared to be challenged on any request. Although Basic authentication is currently the only kind of challenge that the server will issue, the client SHOULD be written so that it will be easy to handle other kinds of challenges in the future. For a Basic authentication challenge, the client MUST compute an appropriate Authorization header from the user id and password (as detailed in RFC2617).

A client MAY proactively set the Authentication header if it knows the server's requirements, and thereby avoid the initial challenge in most cases (but not if the credential are no longer valid). Many HTTP client frameworks, such as the Apache HTTP Client, provide simple ways of setting the log in credentials and handling authorization challenges automatically.

Consider the following trace, first a GET request that does not specify any credentials and therefore fails to authenticate, then one where the user authenticates and succeeds.

```
GET - No Credentials
Request
GET /jazz/resources/main/A HTTP/1.1
Host: example.com
Date: [t2000]
Response
HTTP/1.x 401 Unauthorized
Host: example.com
Date: [t2000]
Content-Length: [nnn]
WWW-Authenticate: basic realm="IBM Team Services Emdedded WebContainer"
GET - With Credentials
Request
GET /jazz/resources/main/A HTTP/1.1
Host: example.com
Date: [t2000]
Authorization: Basic [zoe's credential hash]
Response
HTTP/1.1 200 OK
Host: example.com
Date: [t2000]
Content-Length: [nnn]
Content-Type: text/plain
<xml/>
```

The following guidelines have been found to be useful when producing authentication requirements:

Many authentication requirements can be identified and specified in term of the following:

Component of Requirement	Possible Values
External Authenticated	Various Types of Users Various Types of External Systems Various Senders of Messages
State	Normal processing Degraded mode Under attack
Authentication Type	Repeated Sign-on Single Sign-on
Prior to Execution of	User Task Use Case Transaction Interaction
Measurement	Percent of valid identities authenticated Percent of invalid identities not authenticated

(1) Authentication depends on identification. If identity is important enough to specify, then so is authentication.

(2) Authentication requirements are typically insufficient by themselves, but they are necessary prerequisites for authorization requirements.

(3) Do not analyze and specify authentication mechanisms with essential use cases. A very common requirements mistake is to specify the use of user identifiers and associated passwords using design-level logon use cases.

(4) Because of the close relationship between identification and authentication requirements, they are sometimes grouped together in requirements specifications

(5) Authentication requirements should not be specified in terms of the types of security architecture mechanisms that are typically used to implement them.

(6) Note that some of the above authentication security architecture mechanisms can be used to simultaneously implement both identification and authentication requirements.

6.3 MULTI-FACTOR AUTHENTICATION

Multi-factor authentication is the use of a combination of authentication methods to validate identity. The most commonly used description of multi-factor authentication is the use of information that is known only by the person, combined with something in his or her possession. These are typically:

- The name and password
- Some form of token

A token is a hardware component that is used during the authentication process; it typically provides another piece of information that cannot be ascertained without physical control of the token. Different types of tokens used in multi-factor authentication are:

- Smart cards
- One-time password/phrases
- Single-use PINs or pseudo-random numbers
- Biometric information

Multi-factor authentication provides the following additional benefits:

- Difficult to spoof and impersonate
- Easy to use

As security components are layered, the complexity also rises. The following potential drawbacks are had with multi-factor authentication—each environment is different; therefore, the influence of these on the decision-making process will vary:

- Deployment can be difficult
- Tokens easily can be stolen
- Management of the tokens can be challenging, especially in the event of lost or stolen tokens

6.4 CRYPTOGRAPHIC AUTHENTICATION

The final form of authentication outlined here is that which utilizes cryptography. This includes the following forms:

- Public Key Authentication
- Digital Signatures
- Message Authentication Code
- Password permutation

(1) Public Key Authentication

Public key authentication occurs when the owner of a key pair (private and public) communicates the public key, in some form, to the authenticating party, at which point it is verified to be true. There are a couple of methods for public key authentication worth discussing:

- The use of the public key itself
- Public key certificates

To verify the identity of the presenter of the public key, a nonce is encrypted using the public key. If the nonce can be decrypted and returned to the sender, that means the owner of the public key also has possession of the corresponding private key.

The use of public-key certificates builds on this relationship between the public and private key. Verification of a public key, alone, may indicate that the identity is as expected, but there is still a bit missing—trust. How does one know whether the party presenting the keys has not stolen them from the legitimate owner? Also, just because a person, system, or application may be truly who or what it says it is, how does the authenticating party know it can or should trust it? A public key certificate adds a trust relationship between a mutually known and trusted third party. The certificate is created when a mutually trusted third-party signs a public key with its own key. The authenticating party then can verify the identity of the presenter's key and also know that it can be trusted because of the shared relationship with the certificate signer. In the event that the keys are stolen, the trusted third party easily can revoke its trust of the keys and notify its trustees that they are no longer trustworthy.

(2) Digital Signatures

Digital signatures are another piece of the cryptographic puzzle. A digital signature is made when the owner of a key pair (an individual or a system) uses its private key to "sign" a message. This signature can be verified only by the corresponding public key.

This is most recognizable with the signed public key certificate—wherein the Certificate Authority, or trusted third party, signs a public key. The party doing the authentication can verify that the presenter of a public key has possession of the private key, and that a mutually trusted party vouches that the holder of the key is true. Digital signatures are also commonly used on messages such as e-mail, so that the recipient can have some trust that the e-mail message was sent by the person they expect.

(3) Message Authentication Codes (MACs)

A message authentication code is created when a secret key is used in combination with the message or information to be proved authentic. The MAC can be generated by using a hashing algorithm or symmetric encryption. MACs can be used to provide integrity verification as well as authenticity to those possessing the secret key.

(4) Password Permutation

Cryptographic methods cannot discusswithout showing the relationship to basic authentication and its differences. As discussed above, in basic authentication, many passwords are typically encrypted or hashed, and then during the process of authentication, the password goes through the same transformation as that which is stored and then compared. This should not be confused as a method of strong authentication simply because of its use of cryptographic functionality (hashing, encryption). Password schemes are still weak because the cryptography used is only for the storage and comparison piece, but has no relationship to the presenter's authenticity. They are easily stolen and impersonated.

6.4.1 Collaboration Between Authenticating Entities

With the widespread creation and deployment of distributed applications, authentication is critical, but also requiring some attention is the concept of Single Sign-On (SSO). Single sign-on is the mechanism that allows a person, system, or application to identify itself and be authenticated once and, through various methods, have that authentication work across all other related components and applications. A simple example is an application that authenticates a person at the Web interface and then uses the provided credentials to transparently authenticate the person at all other applications within the service. Single sign-on can be done in any of the following ways:

- Simple transparent caching and re-use of provided credentials
- Stateful session information such as cookies and tokens
- Complex authentication services such as Kerberos

The goal of single sign-on is to increase ease-of-use while maintaining some higher degree of security. In cases where different applications are used to provide a single service, the lack of single sign-on could require an individual or application to go authenticate several times to receive a desired service. A more easily used service is one that allows an entity to authenticate once at the outset and transparently gain access to all of the applications required to provide the intended service, on demand.

If several different applications are being hooked together to provide a single service, and if each requires some level of authentication, single sign-on may be a valuable component. Common architectures for single sign-on include proxying authentication information and generating stateful session information.

Proxying authentication information means that one or more applications are caching that data. This has the following potential pitfalls:

- Multiple copies of sensitive credential data are in memory, in different locations and subject to compromise.
- Does not easily handle the case where authentication information differs at each juncture in the service.
- Does not reflect a tight integration between related applications and introduces weaknesses at each level, including identity spoofing and theft of credentials.

Caching of data must handle synchronization safely, or be susceptible to cache corruption and stale information.

Stateful session information is information that has the following aspects:

- Is generated as a result of successful, initial authentication
- Can be verified
- Can be trusted
- Maintains sequencing to avoid insertion, replaying and spoofing

This means that an entity authenticates at the start of a session, and as a result some form of information is generated—this could be a cookie or token—which then can be uniquely identified and verified to have been generated by a known trusted component that is part of the service. This token information then can be passed around to all applications as needed and verified.

6.4.2 Authentication and its Benefits

Authentication is the first part of the Windows 2000 security model. Authentication confirms users are who they claim to be. Authentication can be completed in a variety of ways and provide a range of benefits. Windows 2000 authentication enables single sign-on to all network resources. With single sign-on, a user can log on to the client computer once, using a single password or smart card, and authenticate to any computer in the domain. Authentication in Windows 2000 is implemented by using the Kerberos v5 protocol, NTLM authentication, or the Windows NT logon feature for Windows NT 4.0 domains.

Authentication specifically prevents:

- **Masquerade attacks :** Users must prove their identity, so it is more difficult to masquerade as another.
- **Replay attacks :** Because Windows 2000 authentication protocols use timestamps, it is difficult to reuse stolen authentication information.
- **Identity interception :** Because exchanges are encrypted, intercepted identities are useless.

6.5 TWO-FACTOR AUTHENTICATION

Two-factor authentication requires users that present a physical object that encodes their identity plus a password. The most common example of two-factor authentication is the automated teller machine (ATM) that requires an ATM card that encodes the owners identity and a personal identification number (PIN) that serves as a password.

Biometric identification is another form of two-factor authentication. A special device scans the users handprint, thumbprint, iris, retina, or voiceprint in place of an access card. Then the user enters the equivalent of a password. This approach is expensive but it makes identity interception and masquerading very difficult.

For business enterprises, the emerging two-factor technology is the smart card. This card is the same size as an ATM card and is physically carried by the user. It contains a chip that stores a digital certificate and the users private key. The user enters a password or PIN after inserting the card into a card reader at the client computer. Smart cards are not open to network attacks like a password can be. Smart cards use a private key and a PIN that are never on the network, and the private key never leaves the smart card, reducing the opportunities for attack. Windows 2000 directly supports smart card authentication.

Another common form of two-factor authentication is a token card. Token cards provide a token, such as a string of numbers, that changes at regular intervals. Users enter their PIN and the numbers presented on the card and they are authenticated. However, because the numbers the card presents change at a regular interval, intercepted authentication is only valid for a short time, making it minimally useful to attackers.

6.5.1 Single Sign-on

Authentication with Windows 2000 makes it possible for users to have access to a range of resources that might otherwise require repeated authentication. For example, without single sign-on, a user might have to provide separate passwords to log on to the local computer, to access a file or print server, to send e-mail, to use a database, and so on. Different servers can demand a change of password at different intervals, often with no reuse permitted; so a system without single sign-on might require a typical user to remember half a dozen passwords.

This makes authentication an inconvenience for users, and more seriously, puts your security at risk when users begin to write down a list of current passwords.

The single sign-on strategy makes a user authenticate interactively once and then permits authenticated sign-on to other network applications and devices. These subsequent authentication events are transparent to the user.

6.5.2 Code Authentication

Users often download and install software on their computers. In doing so, users might inadvertently compromise your security if they download software that has been written to steal passwords, data, or other confidential information. Code authentication identifies the code publisher and determines whether the code has been modified since publication. You can configure your Web browser to refuse to run unsigned software and decide which software you will trust. Note that code authentication only ensures that the software has not been modified since it was signed, so if malicious components have been included in software before signing, these will not be detected.

Code authentication specifically prevents:

- Macro viruses : Macro viruses added after code signing are detected by code authentication.
- Malicious mobile code : You can prevent unsigned code from being installed or detect code that has inserted itself into code after that codes signing. This is an example of a Trojan horse.

As in the case of our development of a reliable data transfer protocol, rdt, we will find it instructive here to develop various versions of an authentication protocol, which we will call ap ("authentication protocol"), and poke holes (i.e., find security flaws) in each version as we proceed. Let's begin by assuming that Anita needs to authenticate herself to Bunty.

(1) Authentication Protocol ap1.0

Perhaps the simplest authentication protocol we can imagine is one where Anita simply sends a message to Bunty saying she is Anita. This protocol is shown in Figure 6-1. The flaw here is obvious - there is no way for Bunty to actually know that the person sending the message, "I am Anita" is indeed Anita. For example, Trudy (the intruder) could just as well send such a message.

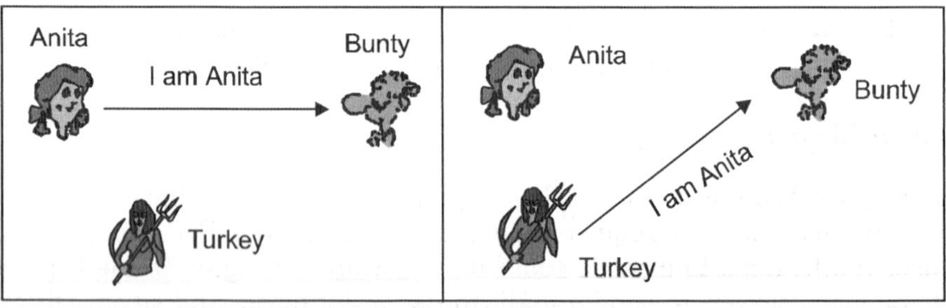

Figure 6.1 Protocol ap1.0 and a failure scenario.

(2) Authentication Protocol ap2.0

In the case that Anita has a well-known network address (e.g., IP address) from which she always communicates, Bunty could attempt to authenticate. Anita by verifying that the source address on the IP datagram carrying the authentication message matches Anita's well-known address. If so, then Anita would be authenticated. This might stop a very network-naive intruder from impersonating Anita. But it wouldn't stop the determined student studying this book, or many others!

Figure 6.2 Protocol ap2.0 and a failure scenario.

Given that we have now studied both the network and data link layers, we know that it is not that hard (e.g., if one had access to the operating system code and could build one's own operating system kernel, as is the case with Linux and several other freely available operating systems) to create an IP datagram, put whatever IP source address we want (e.g., including Anita's well-known IP address) into the IP datagram and send the datagram over the link layer protocol to the first hop router. From then on, the incorrectly-source-addressed datagram would be dutifully forwarded to Bunty. This approach is a form of IP spoofing, a well-known security attack technique. IP spoofing can be avoided if a router is configured to refuse IP datagrams that do not have a given source address. For example, Trudy's first hop router could be configured to only forward datagrams containing Trudy's IP source address. However, this capability is not universally deployed or enforced. Bunty would thus be foolish to assume that Trudy's network manager (who might be Trudy herself!) had configured Trudy's first hop router to only forward appropriately-addressed datagrams.

(3) Authentication Protocol ap3.0

One classical approach to authentication is to use a secret password. We have PIN numbers to identify ourselves to automatic teller machines and login passwords for operating systems. The password is a shared secret between the authenticator and the person being authenticated. HTTP uses a password-based authentication scheme. Telnet and FTP use password authentication as well. In protocol ap3.0, Anita thus sends her secret password to Bunty, as shown in Figure 6.3.

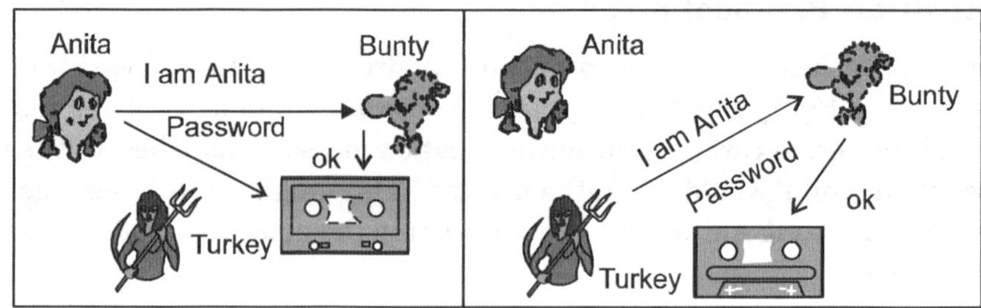

Figure 6.3 Protocol ap3.0 and a failure scenario.

The security flaw here is clear. If Trudy eavesdrops on Anita's communication, then she can learn Anita's password. Lest you think this is unlikely, consider the fact that when one Telnet's to another machine and logs in, the login password is sent unencrypted to the Telnet server. Someone connected to the Telnet client or server's LAN can possibly "sniff" (read and store) all packets transmitted on the LAN and thus steal the login password. In fact, this is a well-known approach for stealing passwords [Jimenez 1997]. Such a threat is obviously very real, so ap3.0 clearly won't do.

(4) Authentication Protocol ap3.1

Having just studied the previous section on cryptography, our next idea for fixing ap3.0 is naturally to use encryption. By encrypting the password, Trudy will not be able to learn Anita's password! If we assume that Anita and Bunty share a symmetric secret key, KA-B, then Anita can encrypt the password, send her identification message, "I am Anita," and her encrypted password to Bunty. Bunty then decrypts the password and, assuming the password is correct, authenticates Anita. Bunty feels comfortable in authenticating Anita since not only does Anita know the password, but she also knows the shared secret key value needed to encrypt the password. Let's call this protocol ap3.1.

While it is true that ap3.1 prevents Trudy from learning Anita's password, the use of cryptography here does not solve the authentication problem! Bunty is again subject to a so-called playback attack: Trudy needs only eavesdrop on Anita's communication, record the encrypted version of the password, and then later play back the encrypted version of the password to Bunty to pretend that she is Anita. The use of an encrypted password doesn't make the situation manifestly different from that in Figure 6-3.

(5) Authentication Protocol ap4.0

The problem with ap3.1 is that the same password is used over and over again. One way to solve this problem would be to use a different password each time. Anita and Bunty could agree on a sequence of passwords (or on an algorithm for generating passwords) and use each password only once, in sequence. This idea is used in the S/KEY system [RFC 1760], adopting an approach due to Lamport for generating a sequence of passwords.

Rather than just stop here with this solution, however, let us consider a more general approach for combating the playback attack. The failure scenario in Figure 6.3 resulted from the fact that Bunty could not distinguish between the original authentication of Anita and the later playback of Anita's original authentication. That is, Bunty could not tell if Anita was "live" (i.e., was currently really on the other end of the connection) or whether the messages he was receiving were a recorded playback of a previous authentication of Anita. The very (very!) observant reader will recall that the 3-way TCP handshake protocol needed to address the same problem - the server side of a TCP connection did not want to accept a connection if the received SYN segment was an old copy (retransmission) of a SYN segment from an earlier connection. How did the TCP server side solve the problem of determining if the client was really "live"? It chose an initial sequence number (which had not been used in a very long time), sent that number to the client, and then waited for the client to respond back with an ACK segment containing that number. We can adopt the same idea here for authentication purposes.

A nonce is a number that a protocol will only ever use once-in-a-lifetime. That is, once a protocol uses a nonce, it will never use that number again. Our ap4.0 protocol uses a nonce as follows:

ap4.0

(1) Anita sends the message, "I am Anita," to Bunty

(2) Bunty chooses a nonce, R, and sends it to Anita

(3) Anita encrypts the nonce using Anita and Bunty's symmetric secret key, KA-B. , and sends the encrypted nonce, KA-B (R) back to Bunty. As in protocol ap3.1, it is the fact that Anita knows KA-B and uses it to encrypt a value that lets Bunty know that the message he receives was generated by Anita. The nonce is used to insure that Anita is "live."

(4) Bunty decrypts the received message. If the decrypted nonce equals the nonce he sent Anita, then Anita is authenticated.

Protocol ap4.0 is illustrated in Figure 6-4. By using the once-in-a-lifetime value, R, and then checking the returned value, KA-B (R), Bunty can be sure that both Anita is who she says she is (since she knows the secret key value needed to encrypt R) and is "live" (since she has encrypted the nonce, R, that Bunty just created).

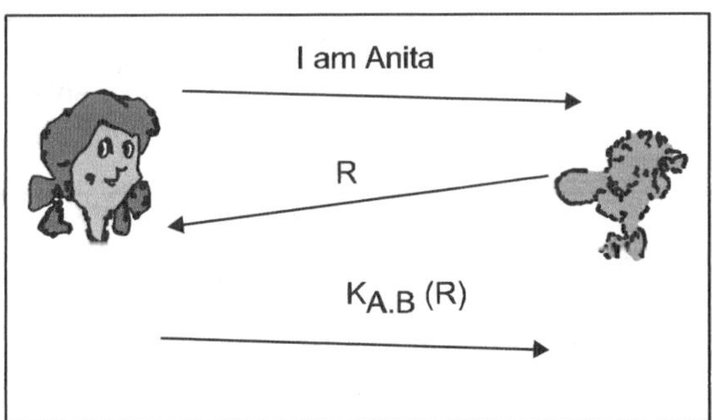

Figure 6.4 Protocol ap 4.0: no failure scenario.

(6) Authentication protocol ap5.0

The use of a nonce and symmetric key cryptography formed the basis of our successful authentication protocol, ap4.0. A natural question is whether we can use a nonce and public key cryptography (rather than symmetric key cryptography) to solve the authentication problem. The use of a public key approach would obviate a difficulty in any shared key system - worrying about how the two parties learn the secret shared key value in the first place. A protocol that uses public key cryptography in a manner analogous to the use of symmetric key cryptography in protocol ap4.0 is protocol ap5.0:

ap5.0

(1) Anita sends the message, "I am Anita," to Bunty

(2) Bunty chooses a nonce, R, and sends it to Anita. Once again, the nonce will be used to insure that Anita is "live."

(3) Anita uses her decryption algorithm with her private key, dA, to the nonce and sends the resulting value dA(R) to Bunty. Since only Anita knows her decryption key, no one except Anita can generate dA(R).

(4) Bunty applies Anita's public encryption algorithm, eA to the received message, i.e., Bunty computes eA(dA(R)). Recall from our discussion of RSA public key cryptography in section 7.2 that eA(dA(R)) = R = dA(eA(R)). Thus Bunty computes R and authenticates Anita.

The operation of protocol ap5.0 is illustrated in Figure 6.5.

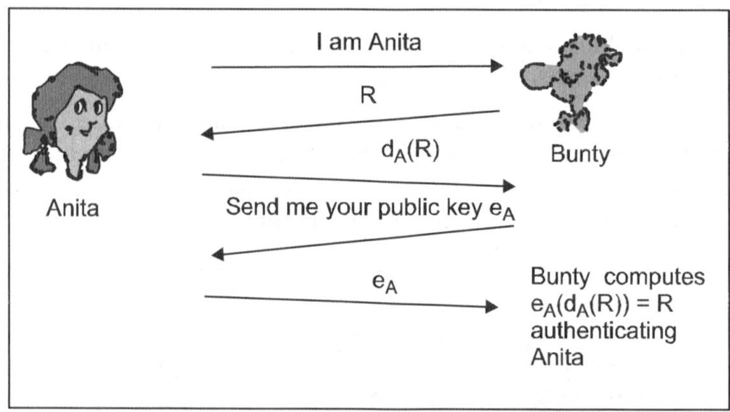

Figure 6.5 Protocol ap 5.0 working correctly.

Is protocol ap5.0 as secure as protocol ap4.0? Both use nonces. Since ap5.0 uses public key techniques, it requires that Bunty retrieve Anita's public key. This leads to an interesting scenario, shown in Figure 6-6, in which Trudy may be able to impersonate Anita to Bunty:

Turkey sends the message, "I am Anita" to Bunty

Chooses a nonce, R, and sends it to Anita, but the message is intercepted by Trudy.

Turkey applies her decryption algorithm with her private key, dT, to the nonce and sends the resulting value, dT(R), to Bunty. To Bunty, dT(R) is just a bunch of bits and he doesn't know whether the bits represent dT(R) or dA(R).

Bunty must now get Anita's public key in order to apply eA to the value he just received. He sends a message to Anita asking her for eA. Turkey intercepts this message as well, and replies back to Bunty with eT, that is Trudy's public key. Bunty computes eT(dT(R)) = R, and thus authenticates Turkey as Anita!

From the above scenario, it is clear that protocol ap5.0 is only as "secure" as is the distribution of public keys. There are secure ways of distributing public keys, a topic we will examine soon in section 7.5.

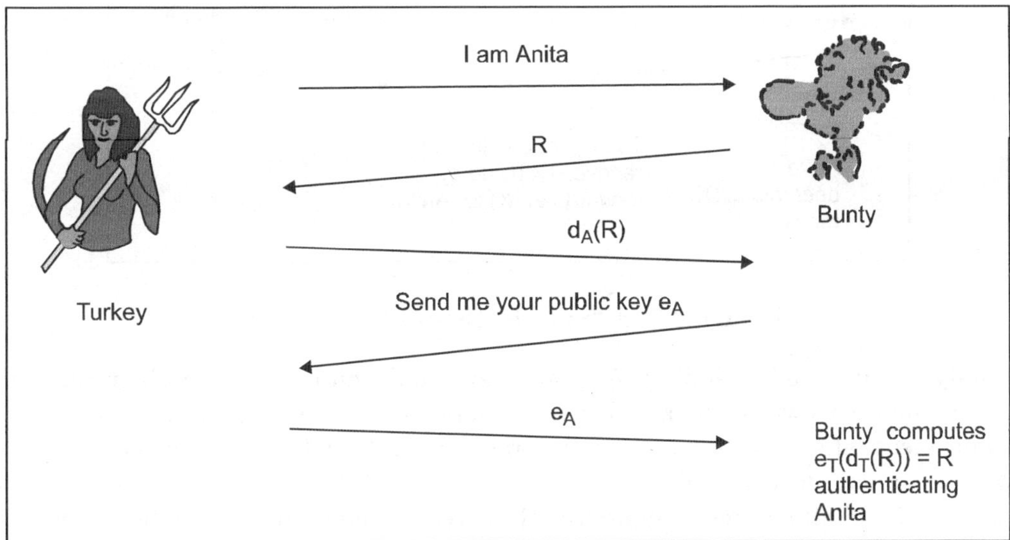

Figure 6.6 A security hole in protocol ap5.0

In the scenario in Figure 6-6, Bunty and Anita might together eventually discover that something is amiss, as Bunty will claim to have interacted with Anita, but Anita knows that she has never interacted with Bunty. There is an even more insidious attack that would avoid this detection. In the scenario in Figure 6-7, both Anita and Bunty are talking to each other, but by exploiting the same hole in the authentication protocol, Turkey is able to transparently interpose herself between Anita and Bunty. In particular, if Bunty begins sending encrypted data to Anita using the encryption key he receives from Turkey, Trudy can recover the plaintext of the communication from Bunty to Anita. At the same time, Turkey can forward Bunty's data to Anita (after re-encrypting data using Anita's real public key).

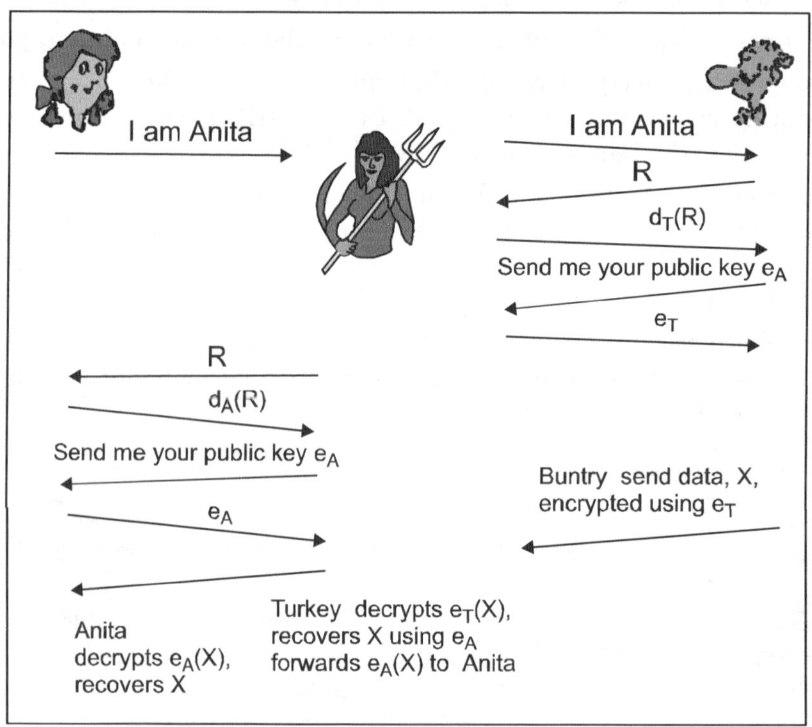

Figure 6.7 A "man-in-the-middle" attack

Bunty is happy to be sending encrypted data, and Anita is happy to be receiving data encrypted using her own public key; both are unaware of Turkeys presence. Should Bunty and Anita meet later and discuss their interaction, Anita will have received exactly what Bunty sent, so nothing will be detected as being amiss. This is one example of the so-called man-in-the-middle attack (more appropriately here, a "woman-in-the-middle" attack). It is also sometimes known as a bucket-brigade attack, since Trudy's passing of data between Anita and Bunty resembles the passing of buckets of water along a chain of people (a so-called "bucket brigade") who are putting out a fire using a remote source of water.

6.5.3 Integrity

Think of the number of the times you've signed your name to a piece of paper during the last week. You sign checks, credit card statements, legal documents, and letters. Your signature attests to the fact that you (as opposed to someone else) have acknowledged and/or agreed with the document's contents. In a digital world, one often want to indicate the owner or creator of a document, or to signify one's agreement with a document's content. A digital signature is a cryptographic technique for achieving these goals in a digital world.

Just as with human signatures, digital signing should be done in such a way that a digital signatures are verifiable, non-forgible, and non-repudiable. That is, it must be possible to "prove" that a document signed by an individual was indeed signed by that individual (the signature must be verifiable) and that only that individual could have signed the document (the signature can not be forged, and a signer can not later repudiate or deny having signed the document). This is easily accomplished with public key cryptography.

6.5.4 Generating Digital Signatures

Suppose that Bunty wants to digitally sign a "document," m. We can think of the document as a file or a message that Bunty is going to sign and send. As shown in Figure 6-8, to sign this document, Bunty simply uses his private decryption key, dB, to compute dB(m). At first, it might seem odd that Bunty is running a decryption algorithm over a document that hasn't been encrypted. But recall that "decryption" is nothing more than a mathematical operation (exponentiation to the power of d in RSA) and recall that Bunty's goal is not to scramble or obscure the contents of the document, but rather to sign the document in a manner that is verifiable, non-forgible, and non-repudiable. Bunty has the document, m, and his digital signature of the document, dB(m).

Figure 6.8 Creating a digital signature for a document.

Does the digital signature, dB(m), meet our requirements of being verifiable, non-forgible, and non-repudiable? Suppose Anita has m and dB(m). She wants to prove in court (being litigious) that Bunty had indeed signed the document and was the only person who could have possibly signed the document. Anita takes Bunty's public key, eB, and applies it to the digital signature, dB(m), associated with the document, m. That is, she computes eB(dB(m)), and voila, with a dramatic flurry, she produces m, which exactly matches the original document! Anita then argues that only Bunty could have signed the document because:

Whoever signed the message must have used the private encryption key, dB in computing the signature dB(m), such that `eB(dB(m)) = m`.

The only person who could known the private key, dB , is Bunty. Recall from our discussion of RSA that knowing the public key eB is of no help in learning the private key dB. Therefore, the only person who could know dB is the person who generated the pair of keys, (eB,dB) in the firstplace, Bunty.

It is also important to note that if the original document, m, is ever modified to some alternate form, `m'`, the signature that Bunty created for `m` will not be valid for `m'`, since `eB(dB(m))` does not equal `m'`.

Thus we see that public key cryptography techniques provide a simple and elegant way to digitally sign documents that is verifiable, non-forgible, and non-repudiable, and that protects against later modification of the document.

6. Hash Functions (also called Message Digests)

A "hash" (also called a "digest", and informally a "checksum") is a kind of "signature" for a stream of data that represents the contents. The closest real-life analog we can think is "a tamper-evident seal on a software package": if you open the box (change the file), it's detected.

A cryptographic hash function is a deterministic procedure that takes an arbitrary block of data and returns a fixed-size bit string, the (cryptographic) hash value, such that an accidental or intentional change to the data will change the hash value. The data to be encoded is often called the "message", and the hash value is sometimes called the message digest or simply digest.

Let's first see some examples of hashes at work.

Many Unix and Linux systems provide the md5sum program, which reads a stream of data and produces a fixed, 128-bit number that summarizes that stream using the popular "MD5" method. Here, the "streams of data" are "files" (two of which we see directly, plus one that's too large to display).

```
$ cat smallfile
This is a very small file with a  few characters
$ cat bigfile
This is a larger file that contains more character.
This demonstrates that no matter how big the input
stream is, the generated hash is the same size (but of course, not the same value).
If two files have a different hash, they surely contain different data.
$ ls - 1 empty-file smallfile bigfile linux-kernel
-rw-rw-r--    1 steve    steve          0    2004-08-20 08:58    empty-file
-rw-rw-r--    1 steve    steve         48    2004-08-20 08:48    smallfile
-rw-rw-r--    1 steve    steve        260    2004-08-20 08:48    bigfile
-rw-r--r--    1 root     root     1122363    2003-02-27 07:12    linux-kernel
$ md 5 sum empty-file smallfile bigfile linux-kernel
d41d8cd98f00b204e9800998ecf8427e    empty-file
75cdbfeb70a06d42210938da88c42991    smallfile
6e0b7a1676ec0279139b3f39bd65e41a    bigfile
c74c812e4d2839fa9acf0aa0c915e022    linux-kernel
```

This shows that all input streams yield hashes of the same length, and to experiment, try changing just one character of a small test file. You'll find that even very small changes to the input yields sweeping changes in the value of the hash, and this is known as the avalanche effect.

The avalanche effect can be best seen by hashing two files with nearly identical content.

We've changed the first character of a file from T to t, and when looking at the binary values for these ASCII characters, we see that they differ by just one bit:

```
T -> 0x54 -> 0 1 0 1  0 1 0 0
t -> 0x74 -> 0 1 1 1  0 1 0 0
```

This single bit of change in the input produces a very large change in the output:

```
$ cat file1
This is a very small file with a few characters
$ cat file2
this is a very small file with a few characters
$ md5sum file?
75cdbfeb70a06d42210938da88c42991  file1
6fbe37f1eea0f802bd792ea885cd03e2  file2
```

Expanding the hex to binary (in 32-bit chunks to avoid really long lines), we can see that our one bit of input change produced 50 different output bits, about 39%:

First 32 bits

```
0111 0101 1100 1101 1011 1111 1110 1011 75cdbfeb file1
0110 1111 1011 1110 0011 0111 1111 0001 6fbe37f1 file2
...X X.X. .XXX ..XX X... X... ...X X.X. 13 bits different
```

Second 32 bits

```
0111 0000 1010 0000 0110 1101 0100 0010 70a06d42 file1
1110 1110 1010 0000 1111 1000 0000 0010 eea0f802 file2
X..X XXX. .... .... X..X .X.X .X.. .... 10 bits different
```

Third 32 bits

```
0010 0001 0000 1001 0011 1000 1101 1010 210938da file1
1011 1101 0111 1001 0010 1110 1010 1000 bd792ea8 file2
X..X XX.. .XXX .... ...X .XX. .XXX ..X. 14 bits different
```

Fourth 32 bits

```
1000 1000 1100 0100 0010 1001 1001 0001 88c42991 file1
1000 0101 1100 1101 0000 0011 1110 0010 85cd03e2 file2
.... XX.X .... X..X ..X. X.X. .XXX ..XX 13 bits different
```

But even though the value of the hash changes, its size does not.

Hashes are "digests", not "encryption"

This is a common confusion, especially because all these words are in the category of "cryptography", but it's important to understand the difference.

Encryption transforms data from a cleartext to ciphertext and back (given the right keys), and the two texts should roughly correspond to each other in size: big cleartext yields big ciphertext, and so on. "Encryption" is a two-way operation.

Fig. 6.9 Encryption - a1 two-way operation

Hashes, on the other hand, compile a stream of data into a small digest (a summarized form: think "Reader's Digest"), and it's strictly a one way operation. All hashes of the same type - this example shows the "MD5" variety - have the same size no matter how big the inputs are:

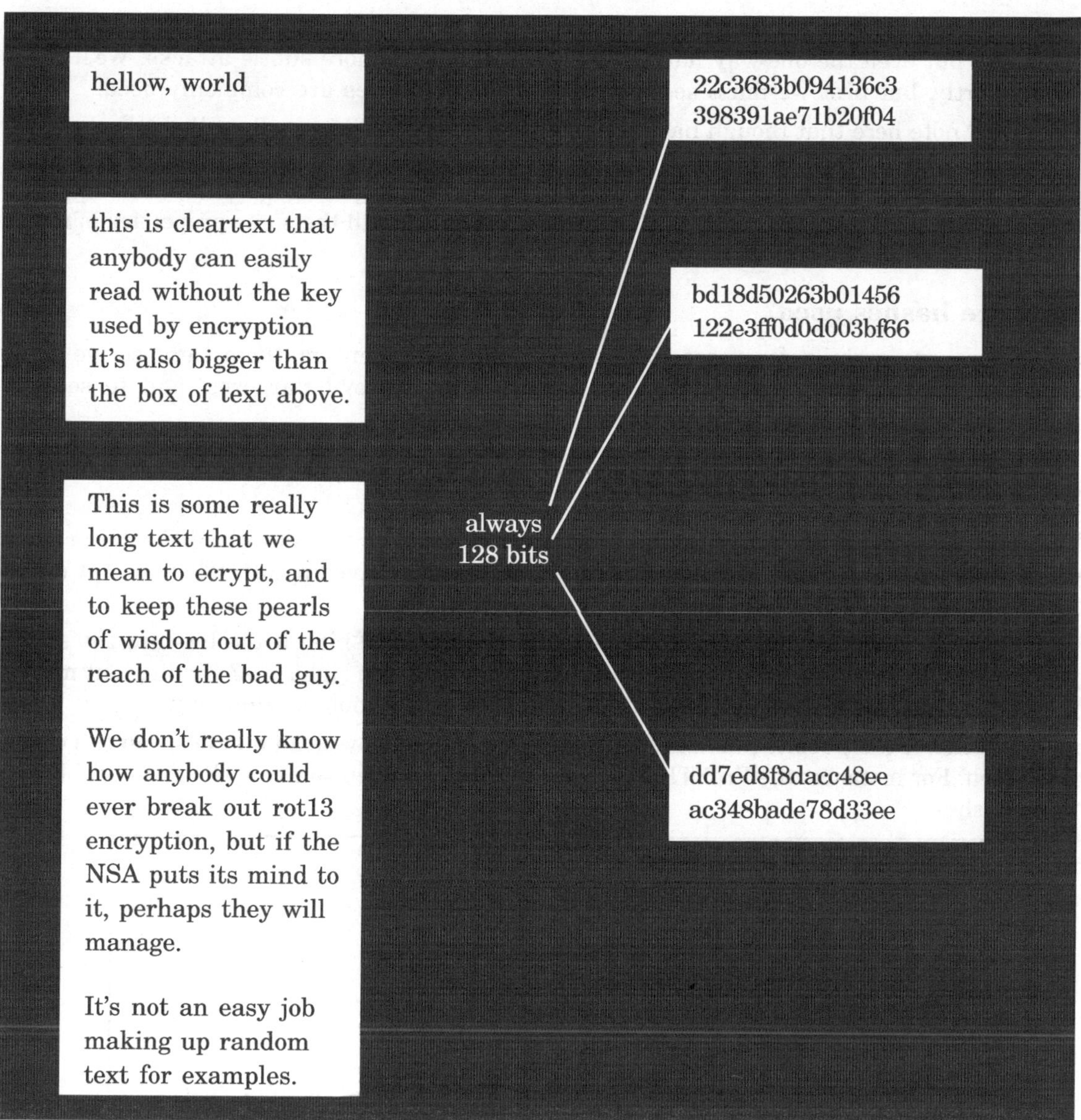

Fig. 6.10 Hashing - a one-way operation

"Encryption" is an obvious target for attack (e.g., "try to read the encrypted text without the key"), but even the one-way nature of hashes admits of more subtle attacks. We'll cover them shortly, but first we must see for what purposes hashes are commonly used.

We'll note here that though hashes and digests are often informally called "checksums", they really aren't. True checksums, such as a Cyclic Redundancy Check are designed to catch data-transmission errors and not deliberate attempts at tampering with data. Aside of the small output space (usually 32 bits), they are not designed with the same properties in mind. We won't mention true checksums again.

"Encryption" is an obvious target for attack (e.g., "try to read the encrypted text without the key"), but even the one-way nature of hashes admits of more subtle attacks. We'll cover them shortly, but first we must see for what purposes hashes are commonly used.

We'll note here that though hashes and digests are often informally called "checksums", they really aren't. True checksums, such as a Cyclic Redundancy Check are designed to catch data-transmission errors and not deliberate attempts at tampering with data. Aside of the small output space (usually 32 bits), they are not designed with the same properties in mind. We won't mention true checksums again.

How are hashes used?

There are quite a few uses for hashes, and we'll mention them here so we have something to build on when we try to subvert them for evil purposes, and to see the ramifications of the recent developments.

6.6 VERIFYING FILE INTEGRITY

The most obvious use is "verifying file integrity". If you have just downloaded a large piece of software from a website, how do you know that you've received it correctly and that it has not been tampered with?

One way is to download the file again and compare the bits: if the bits are the same, you're probably ok, but if they're different, which ones are the right bits? Finding out means yet another download with compare, and this gets very tedious very quickly.

Instead, if the website publishes the hash values of its download bundles, you can check it yourself. For instance, the ProFTPD project (an excellent open source FTP server) publishes their hashes:

ProFTPD

Highly configurable GPL-licensed FTP server software

MD5 sums and PGP signatures of release files

MD5 Digest Hashes

417e41092610816bd203c3766e96f23b	proftpd – 1 . 2 . 8p . tar . bz2
abf8409bbd9150494bc1847ace06857a	proftpd – 1 . 2 . 8p . tar . gz
7c85503b160a36a96594ef75f3180a07	proftpd – 1 . 2 . 9 . tar . bz2
445fbf24e2ec300800a184eb81296bda	proftpd – 1 . 2 . 9 . tar . gz
d834bb822816a2ce48cc2ef1a9533e7	proftpd – 1 . 2 . 10 rc3 . tar . bz2
1e306d2f54ea92895ecff6659498b911	proftpd – 1 . 2 . 10rc3 . tar . gz

Fig. 6.11 MD5 checksums for downloadable software

Now it's just a matter of running the md5sum command on the file you downloaded and comparing it with the published values.

Important!

When considering hash values, close does not count! If the hashes being compared differ in any way, even by just a single bit, the data being digested is not the same! There is no equivalent of "roundoff error" or "almost" in cryptographic hashes.

6.6.1 Hashing passwords

A second example that's very common - but less obvious - is the hashing of access passwords, and we'll reiterate that "hashing is not encryption".

It's a bad idea for computer systems to store passwords in cleartext (in their original form), because if the bad guy can somehow get to where they're stored, he gets all the passwords. Knowing how many people foolishly use one password at multiple sites, getting a stash from one system may give access to others.

A more secure way is to store a hash of the password, rather than the password itself. Since these hashes are not reversible, there is no way to find out for sure "what password produced this hash?" - and the so consequence of a compromise is much lower.

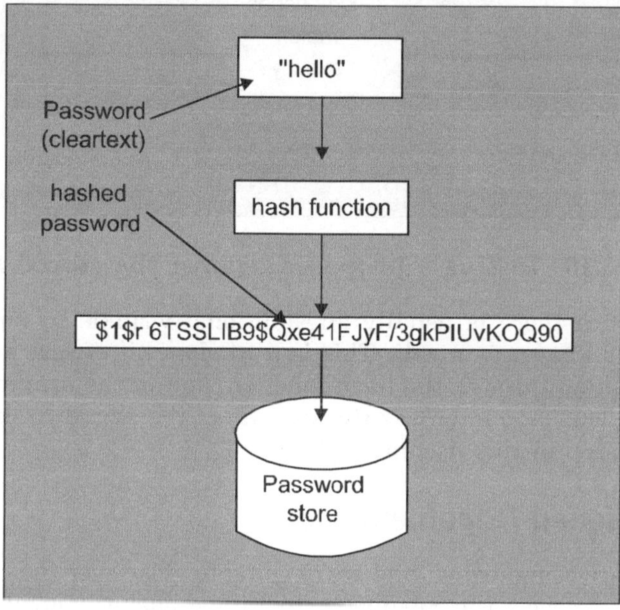

Fig. 6.12 Storting a hash instead of a password

Now we have squirreled away the password into a safe place,but since this is a one-way function, how will we know that some future user at a login prompt gives us the same password?

The answer is simple: we take the proposed password — in cleartext — run it through the same hash function, and see whether this result matches the hash we've saved in the password store. If they match, the user must have known the proper password, so access is granted, but if the hashes are not identical, access is denied.

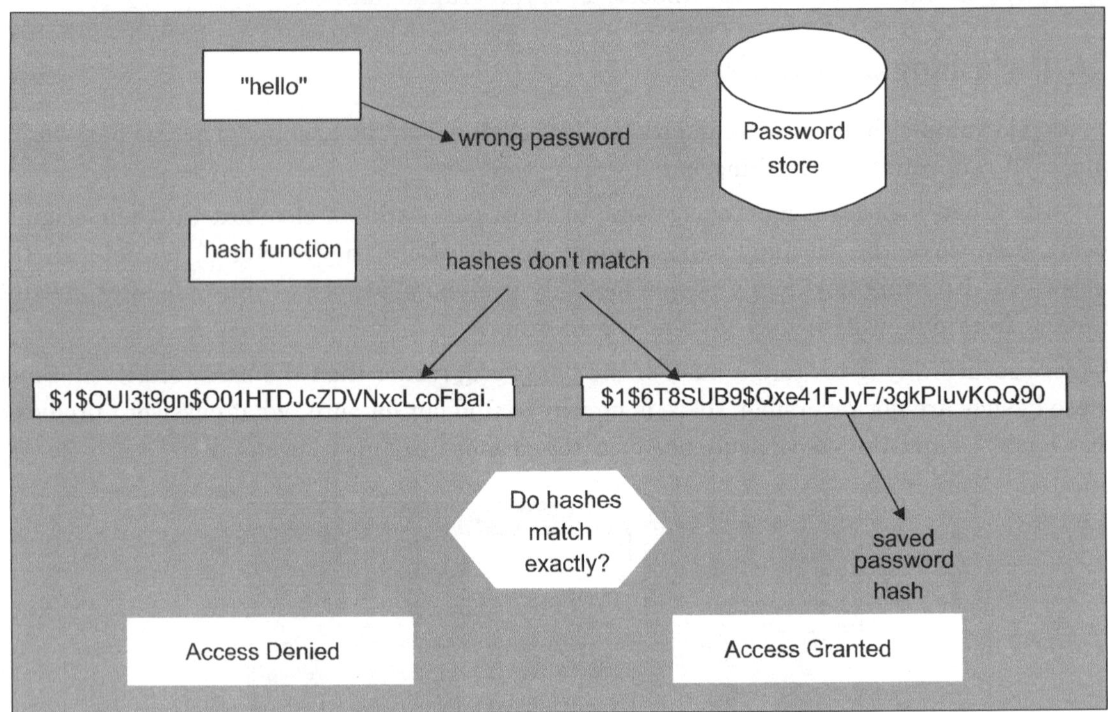

Fig. 6.13 Testing a proposed against the stored hash

Note – in practice there is usually an additional wrinkle to hashed passwords: the introduction of what's known as a salt. This is a random bit of text added to the cleartext passwords before running through the hash function, and in the examples above, the salt is between the $ signs. This step improves the security of the stored hash, but we're not going to elaborate on this step in this document.

6.6.2 Digitally Signed Documents

This is quite a bit more complicated, and we're going to gloss over the details of this subject, covering only enough to show the role of cryptographic hashes. David Youd has written an excellent Introduction to Digital Signatures that covers this in much more detail.

Loosely speaking, "signing" a document electronicall+y is the digital equivalent of placing an autograph on paper, and our discussion revolves around how the signature is represented. How does one know that this digital signature applies to this document?

The answer: one signs (encrypts with one's private key) the hash of the document, the result of which is a digital signature. The process is shown in figure 6.14.

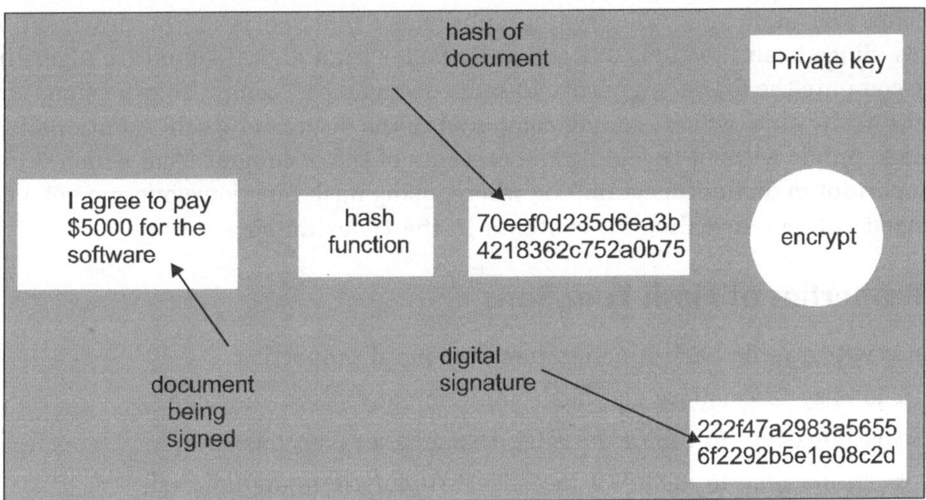

Fig 6.14 Digitally signing a document

At some later date, we can prove that you signed the document by decrypting the signature with your public key, which yields the hash, and showing that the document's hash matches the signed one. We'll see later how a weakness in the hash function could lead to shenanigans.

A hash function H is a transformation that takes a variable-size input m and returns a fixed-size string, which is called the hash value h (that is, `h = H(m)`). Hash functions with just this property have a variety of general computational uses, but when employed in cryptography the hash functions are usually chosen to have some additional properties.

The basic requirements for a cryptographic hash function

- The basic requirements for a cryptographic hash function are:
- The input can be of any length,
- The output has a fixed length,
- H(x) is relatively easy to compute for any given x ,
- H(x) is one-way,
- H(x) is collision-free.

A hash function H is said to be one-way if it is hard to invert, where "hard to invert" means that given a hash value h, it is computationally infeasible to find some input x such that `H(x) = h`.

If, given a message x, it is computationally infeasible to find a message y not equal to x such that `H(x) = H(y)` then H is said to be a weakly collision-free hash function.

A strongly collision-free hash function H is one for which it is computationally infeasible to find any two messages x and y such that H(x) = H(y).

The hash value represents concisely the longer message or document from which it was computed; one can think of a message digest as a "digital fingerprint" of the larger document. Examples of well-known hash functions are MD2 and MD5 and SHA.

Perhaps the main role of a cryptographic hash function is in the provision of digital signatures. Since hash functions are generally faster than digital signature algorithms, it is typical to compute the digital signature to some document by computing the signature on the document's hash value, which is small compared to the document itself. Additionally, a digest can be made public without revealing the contents of the document from which it is derived. This is important in digital timestamping where, using hash functions, one can get a document timestamped without revealing its contents to the timestamping service.

6.6.3 Properties of Hash Functions

The ideal cryptographic hash function has four main properties:

- it is easy to compute the hash value for any given message,
- it is infeasible to find a message that has a given hash,
- it is infeasible to modify a message without changing its hash,
- it is infeasible to find two different messages with the same hash.

Cryptographic hash functions have many information security applications, notably in digital signatures, message authentication codes (MACs), and other forms of authentication. They can also be used as ordinary hash functions, to index data in hash tables; as fingerprints, to detect duplicate data or uniquely identify files; or as checksums to detect accidental data corruption. Indeed, in information security contexts, cryptographic hash values are sometimes called (digital) fingerprints, checksums, or just hash values, even though all these terms stand for functions with rather different properties and purposes.

Most cryptographic hash functions are designed to take a string of any length as input and produce a fixed-length hash value.A cryptographic hash function must be able to withstand all known types of cryptanalytic attack. As a minimum, it must have the following properties:

- Preimage resistance: given h it should be hard to find any m such that **h = hash(m)**. This concept is related to that of one way function. Functions that lack this property are vulnerable to preimage attacks.
- Second preimage resistance: given an input m1, it should be hard to find another input, m_2 (not equal to m1) such that **hash(m_1) = hash(m_2)**. This property is sometimes referred to as weak collision resistance. Functions that lack this property are vulnerable to second preimage attacks.

Collision resistance: it should be hard to find two different messages m1 and m2 such that **hash(m_1) = hash(m_2)**. Such a pair is called a (cryptographic) hash collision, and this property is sometimes referred to as strong collision resistance. It requires a hash value at least twice as long as what is required for preimage-resistance, otherwise collisions may be found by a birthday attack.

These properties imply that not even a malicious adversary can replace or modify the input data without changing its digest. Thus, if two strings have the same digest, one can be very confident that they are identical.

A function meeting these criteria may still have undesirable properties. Currently popular cryptographic hash functions are vulnerable to length-extension attacks: given h(m) and len(m) but not m, by choosing a suitable m' an attacker can calculate `h (m || m')`, where `||` denotes concatenation. This property can be used to break naive authentication schemes based on hash functions. The HMAC construction works around these problems.

Ideally, one may wish for even stronger conditions. It should be impossible for an adversary to find two messages with substantially similar digests; or to infer any useful information about the data, given only its digest. Therefore, a cryptographic hash function should behave as much as possible like a random function while still being deterministic and efficiently computable.

Checksum algorithms, such as CRC32 and other cyclic redundancy checks, are designed to meet much weaker requirements, and are generally unsuitable as cryptographic hash functions. For example, a CRC was used for message integrity in the WEP encryption standard, but an attack was readily discovered which exploited the linearity of the checksum.

6.6.4 Collision

The thoughtful reader may wonder how this could work: if it's possible to uniquely represent every possible stream of data in 128 bits - that's 16 bytes — then why would one ever need a file larger than that? If this isn't the case, then it seems obvious that many input streams are available that can produce any given hash.

When different chunks of data produce the same hash value, this is known as a collision, and it follows from the previous paragraph that they inherently must exist:

A Hypothetical Example

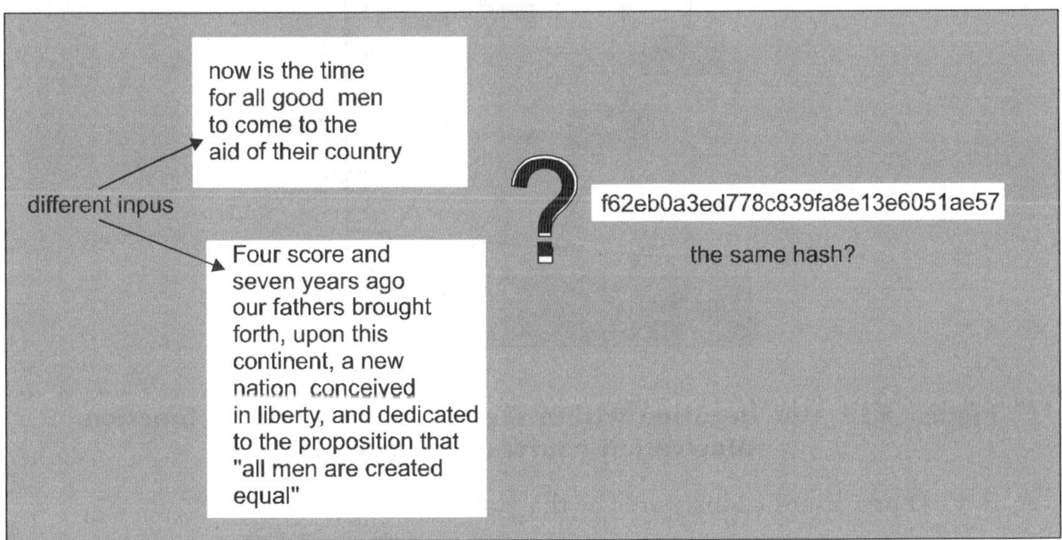

Fig 6.15 What a hash collision might look like (just a hypothetical example)

(just) If so, this seems to undermine the whole premise of cryptographic hashes until one learns that for industrial-strength hashes like MD5, nobody has found a collision yet (well, almost nobody, but we're getting to that) .

This astonishing fact is due to the astonishingly large number of possible hashes available: a 128-bit hash can have 3.4 x 1038 possible values, which is: 340, 282, 366, 920, 938, 463, 463, 374, 607, 431, 768, 211, 456 possible hashes If the hash algorithm is properly designed and distributes the hashes uniformly over the output space, "finding a hash collision" by random guessing is exceedingly unlikely (it's more likely that a million people will correctly guess all the California Lottery numbers every day for a billion trillion years).

Other hashes have even more bits: the SHA-1 algorithm generates 160 bits, whose output space is four billions times larger than that produced by MD5's 128 bits.

6.6.5 What's inside a cryptographic hash?

The first answer is "it depends on the kind of hash", but the second answer usually starts with "a lot of math". A colloquial explanation is that all the bits are poured into a pot and stirred briskly, and this is about as technical we care to delve into here.

There are plenty of resources that show the internal workings of a hash algorithm, almost all of which involve lots of shifting and rotating through multiple "rounds".

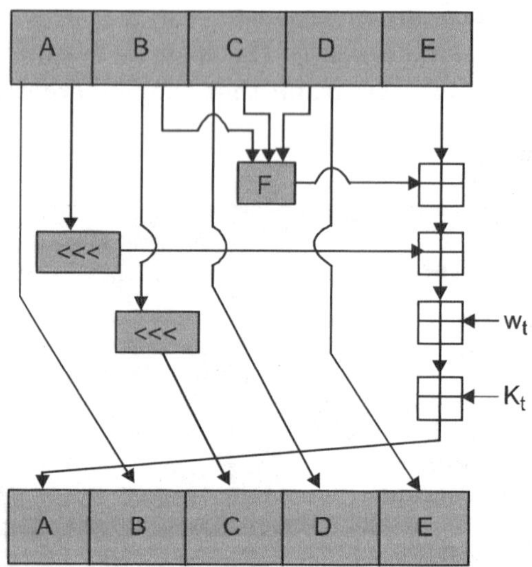

Figure. 6.16 One iteration within the SHA-1 compression function. (Illustration courtesy Wikipedia)

A, B, C, D and E are 32-bit words of the state;

F is a nonlinear function that varies;<<< denotes left circular shift.

Kt is a constant.

Though we're not going to elaborate on the internals, it does seem appropriate to mention some of the popular hash algorithms:

```
MD4 (128 bits, obsolete)
MD5 (128 bits)
RIPEMD-160 (160 bits)
SHA-1 (160 bits)
SHA-256, SHA-384, and SHA-512 (longer versions of SHA-1, with slightly
 different designs)
```

Each has its own advantages in terms of performance, several variations of collision resistance, how well its security has been studied professionally, and so on.

6.6.6 Collision resistance

As we've mentioned several times, "collisions" play a central role in the usefulness of a cryptographic hash, mainly in the sense that the easier it is to find a collision, the less useful the hash is. Some algorithms are better than others at avoiding collisions, and this is measured by three related attributes.

Collision Resistance measures how difficult it is to pick two inputs that produce the same hash value.

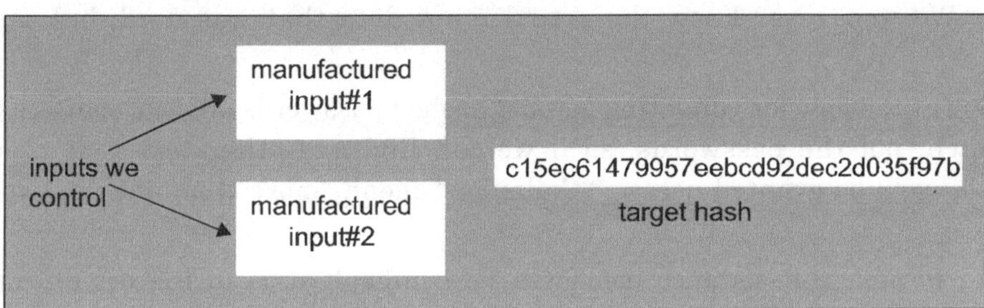

Figure. 6.17 Collision Resistance Depicted

Exploiting weak collision resistance: If we are able to create two inputs that generate the same hash, digital signature become suspect. In our example above, the document signed was "a promise to pay", and being able to substitute one signed document for another would certainly lead to havoc:

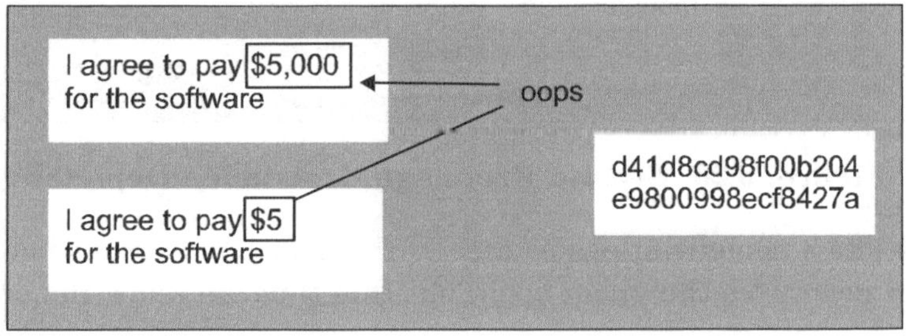

Figure. 6.18 Breaking digital Signatures

As an aside, it's been recommended to always make a cosmetic change to any document you sign: if the person giving you the document secretly has a hash-equivalent pair, your small change - even a byte or two - will render the "other" file useless.

Preimage Resistance measures how difficult it is to concoct an input which hashes to a particular value.

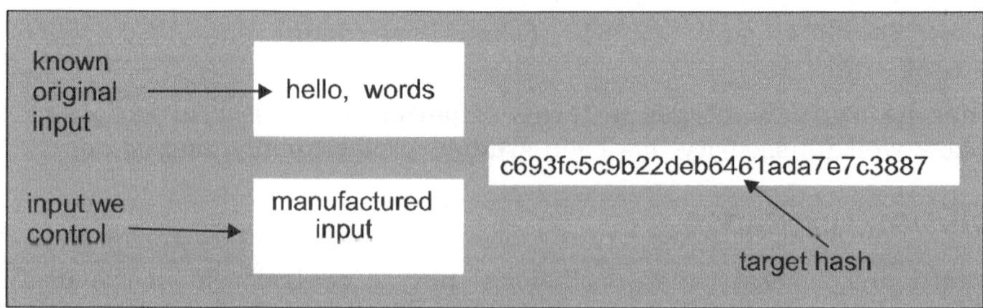

Figure. 6.19 Preimage Resistance Depicted

Exploiting weak preimage resistance: If we are able to "work backwards" from a hash and create some text that produces the same hash, we can use this to beat hashed passwords. We won't ever know the actual input data that was used, but that doesn't matter.

Looking at the flow for validating against hashed passwords, all that matters is that the hashes match, not the passwords, so if we can find any other text that produces the stored hash, we'll be granted access. "Collisions" mean "more than one password will be accepted".

Second Preimage Resistance measures how difficult it is to concoct an input which hashes to the same value that some other given input hashes to.

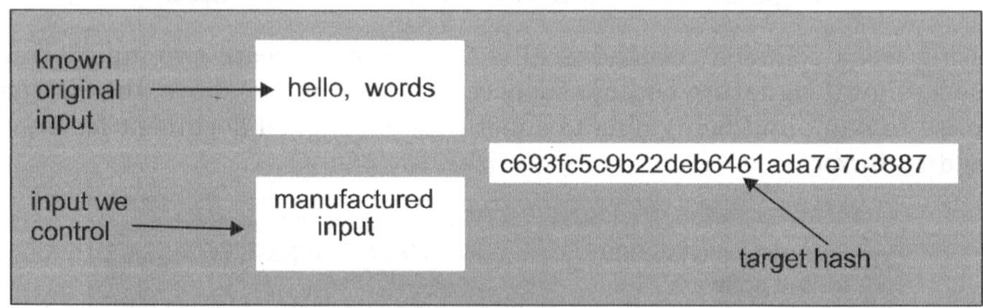

Figure. 6.20 Second Preimage Resistance Depicted

This seems like a somewhat easier case of the previous item: the goal is to produce a new input that generates the given hash, but this time we know the original text that created it.

6.6.7 Exploiting Second Weak Preimage Resistance

As with preimage resistance, we want to fool somebody into authenticating our data as genuine, and we'd most likely use this when trying to introduce a corrupted software distribution.

Earlier we saw that ProFTPD (and many other organizations) publishes software and matching md5 checksums, and if we are able to maliciously modify the source code but nevertheless keep the same checksum, downloaders around the globe will accept our badware as genuine.

Some very bright researchers in China presented a paper, Collisions for Hash Functions MD4, MD5, HAVAL-128 and RIPEMD, at the Crypto 2004 conference in August 2004, and it's shaken up the security world considerably. This was some outstanding cryptography research.

They have found ways to reliably generate collisions in four hash functions much faster than brute-force time, and in one case (MD4, which is admittedly obsolete), with a hand calculation. This has been a stunning development.

These are all of the "we control both inputs" type - the first of our three kinds of collisions - and it holds the most promise in the compromise of digital signatures where the bad guy can create two contradictory documents and pull a switcheroo later.

There are already tools emerging that can reliably generate collision-pairs in "reasonable" amounts of CPU time, and with just a bit of searching found one example for MD5:

Sequence #1

df	31	dd	02	c5	e6	ee	c4	69	3d	9a	06	98	af	f9	5c
2f	ca	b5	**87**	12	46	7e	ab	40	04	58	3e	b8	fb	7f	89
55	ad	34	06	09	f4	b3	02	83	e4	88	83	25	**71**	41	5a
08	51	25	e8	f7	cd	c9	9f	d9	1d	bd	**f2**	80	37	3c	5b
d8	82	3e	31	56	34	8f	5b	ae	6d	ac	d4	36	c9	19	c6
dd	53	e2	**b4**	87	da	03	fd	02	39	63	06	d2	48	cd	a0
e9	9f	33	42	0f	57	7e	e8	ce	54	b6	70	80	**a8**	0d	1e
c6	98	21	bc	b6	a8	83	93	96	f9	65	**2b**	6f	f7	2a	70

Sequence #2

d1	31	dd	02	c5	e6	ee	c4	69	3d	9a	06	98	af	f9	5c
2f	ca	b5	**07**	12	46	7e	ab	40	04	58	3e	b8	fb	7f	89
55	ad	34	06	09	f4	b3	02	83	e4	88	83	25	**f1**	41	5a
08	51	25	e8	f7	cd	c9	9f	d9	1d	bd	**72**	80	37	3c	5b
d8	82	3e	31	56	34	8f	5b	ae	6d	ac	d4	36	c9	19	c6
dd	53	e2	**34**	87	da	03	fd	02	39	63	06	d2	48	cd	a0
e9	9f	33	42	0f	57	7e	e8	ce	54	b6	70	80	**28**	0d	1e
c6	98	21	bc	b6	a8	83	93	96	f9	65	**ab**	6f	f7	2a	70

Both produce MD5 digest 790540255fb1a26e4bc422aef54eb4

Figure. 6.21 A real MD5 collision

This can be checked with this small perl program that was posted on Edward Felton's weblog by Greg Buchholz (origin unknown):

```
#!/usr/bin/perl -w
use strict;
my $v1=<<END_V1;
d1 31 dd 02 c5 e6 ee c4 69 3d 9a 06 98 af f9 5c
2f ca b5 87 12 46 7e ab 40 04 58 3e b8 fb 7f 89
55 ad 34 06 09 f4 b3 02 83 e4 88 83 25 71 41 5a
08 51 25 e8 f7 cd c9 9f d9 1d bd f2 80 37 3c 5b
d8 82 3e 31 56 34 8f 5b ae 6d ac d4 36 c9 19 c6
dd 53 e2 b4 87 da 03 fd 02 39 63 06 d2 48 cd a0
e9 9f 33 42 0f 57 7e e8 ce 54 b6 70 80 a8 0d 1e
c6 98 21 bc b6 a8 83 93 96 f9 65 2b 6f f7 2a 70
END_V1
my $v2=<<END_V2;
d1 31 dd 02 c5 e6 ee c4 69 3d 9a 06 98 af f9 5c
2f ca b5 07 12 46 7e ab 40 04 58 3e b8 fb 7f 89
55 ad 34 06 09 f4 b3 02 83 e4 88 83 25 f1 41 5a
08 51 25 e8 f7 cd c9 9f d9 1d bd 72 80 37 3c 5b
d8 82 3e 31 56 34 8f 5b ae 6d ac d4 36 c9 19 c6
dd 53 e2 34 87 da 03 fd 02 39 63 06 d2 48 cd a0
e9 9f 33 42 0f 57 7e e8 ce 54 b6 70 80 28 0d 1e
c6 98 21 bc b6 a8 83 93 96 f9 65 ab 6f f7 2a 70
END_V2
my $p=join("",map {chr(hex($_))} split /\s+/, $v1);
my $q=join("",map {chr(hex($_))} split /\s+/, $v2);
print `echo -n \'$p\'|md5sum`;
print `echo -n \'$q\'|md5sum`;
```

There is also a buzz about weaknesses in the SHA-0 and SHA-1 algorithms, but this is much more preliminary.

A researcher has managed to find a collision in SHA-0, which is not in such widespread use, and another has found a collision in "reduced SHA-1". A "reduced" algorithm typically eliminates some steps in the hashing process (40 rounds rather than 80), and even though finding a collision in what amounts to 1/2 of SHA-1 doesn't have any immediate impact, it's like a neon sign to the researchers saying "look here".

There is no evidence that preimage resistance or second preimage resistance are at risk in any of the algorithms (e.g., if you have an existing hash, find an input that produces that hash), but many of the cryptorati believe that blood is in the water and the sharks are on their way.

Once a weakness in an algorithm has been identified - even if it's theoretical or only on a reduced version - it's often the start of the whole thing unraveling. What does this mean?

In the short term, this will have only a limited impact on computer security. The bad guys can't suddenly start tampering with software that can fool published checksums, and they can't suddenly start cracking hashed passwords. Previously-signed digital signatures are just as secure as they were before, because one can't retroactively generate new documents to sign with your matched pair of inputs.

What it does mean, though, is that we've got to start migrating to better hash functions. Even though SHA-1 has long been thought to be secure, NIST (the National Institute of Standards and Technology) has a standard for even longer hash functions which are named for the number of bits in their output: SHA-224, SHA-256, SHA-384, and SIIA-512.

Five hundred twelve bits of hash holds 1.34 x 10154 possible values, which is far, far more than the number of hydrogen atoms in the universe. This is likely to be safe from brute-force attacks for quite a while.

6.6.3 Message Digests

We have seen above that public key encryption technology can be used to create a digital signature. One concern with signing data by encryption, however, is that encryption and decryption are computationally expensive. When digitally signing a really important document, say a merger between two large multinational corporations or an agreement with a child to have him/her clean her room weekly, computational cost may not may be important. However, many network devices and processes (e.g., routers exchanging routing table information and email user agents exchanging email) routinely exchange data that may not need to be encrypted. Nonetheless, they do want to ensure that:

- the sender of the data is as claimed, i.e., that the sender has signed the data and this signature can be checked
- the transmitted data has not been changed since the sender created and signed the data.

Given the overheads of encryption and decryption, signing data via complete encryption/decryption can be overkill. A more efficient approach using so-called message digests can accomplish these two goals without full message encryption.

A message digest is in many ways like a checksum. Message digest algorithms take a message, m, of arbitrary length and compute a fixed length "fingerprint" of the data known as a message digest, H(m). The message digest protects the data in the sense that if m is changed to m' (either maliciously or by accident) then H(m), computed for the original data (and transmitted with that data), will not match the H(m) computed over the changed data. While the message digest provides for data integrity, how does it help with signing the message m? The goal here is that rather than having Bunty digitally sign (encrypt) the entire message by computing dB(m), he should be able to sign just the message digest by compting dB(H(m)). That is, having m and dB(H(m)) together (note that m is not typically encrypted) should be "just as good as" having a signed complete message, dB(m); this means that m and dB(H(m)) together should be non-forgible, verifiable, and non-repudiable. Nonforgible will require that the message digest algorithm that computes the message digest have some special properties, as we will see below.

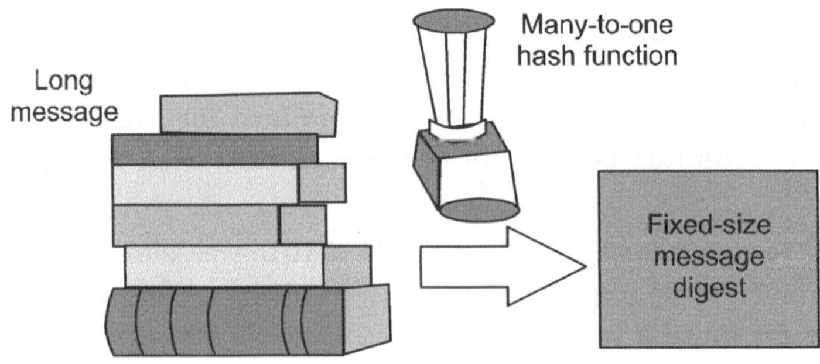

Figure 6.16: Hash functions are used to create message digests.

Our definition of a message digest may seem quite similar to the definition of a checksum or a more powerful error detection code such as a cyclic redundancy check Is it really any different? Checksums, cyclic redundancy checks, and message digests are all examples of so-called hash functions. As shown in Figure 6.16, a hash function takes an input, m, and computes a fixed-size string known as a hash. The Internet checksum, CRC's and message digests all meet this definition. If signing a message digest is going to be "just as good as" signing the entire message, in particular if it is going to satisfy the non-forgibility requirement, then a message digest algorithm must have the following additional properties:

Given a message digest value, x, it is computationally infeasible to find a message, y, such that H(y) = x; It is computationally infeasible to find any two messages x and y such that H(x) = H(y).

Informally, these two properties mean that it is computationally infeasible for an intruder to substitute one message for another message that is protected by a message digest. That is, if (m,H(m)) are the message and message digest pair created by the sender, then an intruder can not forge the contents of another message, y, that has the same message digest value as the original message. When Bunty signs m by computing dB(H(m)), we know that no other message can be substituted for m. Furthermore, Bunty's digital signature of H(m) uniquely identifies Bunty as the verifiable, non-repudiable signer of H(m) (and as a consequence, m as well) as discussed above in section 6.5.2.

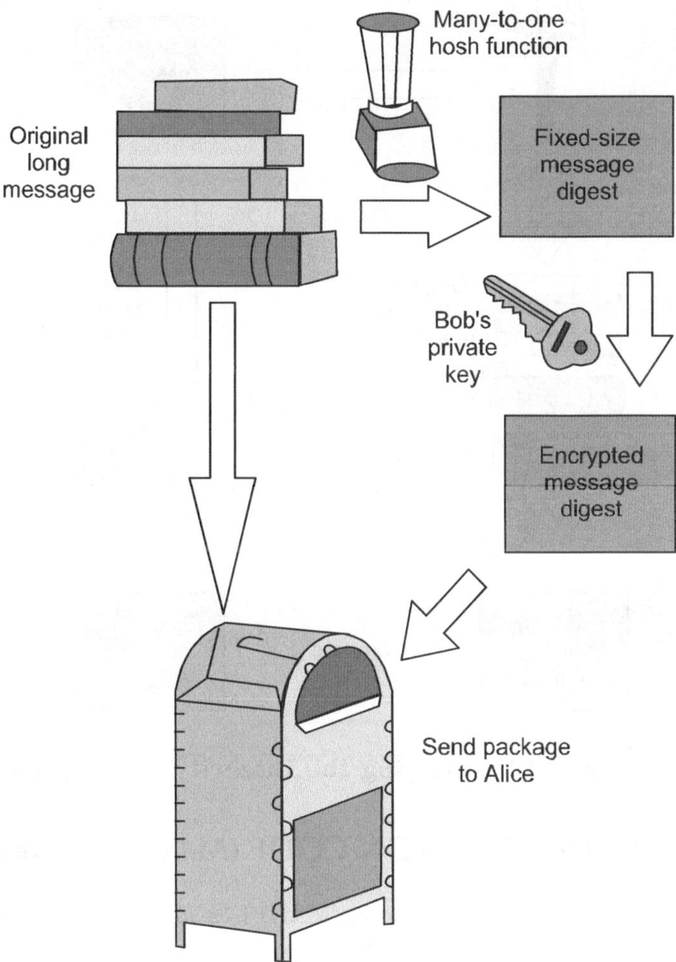

Figure 6.17: Sending a digitally signed message.

In the context of Bunty sending a message to Anita, Figure 6.17 provides a summary of the operational procedure of creating a digital signature. Bunty puts his original long message through a hash function to create a messge digest. He then encrypts the message digest with his own private key. The original message (in clear text) along with the digitally signed message digest (henceforth referred to as the digital signature) is then sent to Anita. Figure 6.18 provides a summary of the operational procedure of verifying message integrity. Anita applies the Bunty's public key to the message to recover the message digest. Anita also applies the hash function to the clear text message to obtain a second message digest. If the two message digests match, then the recipient. Anita can be sure about the integrity of the message, and sure that Bunty sent the message.

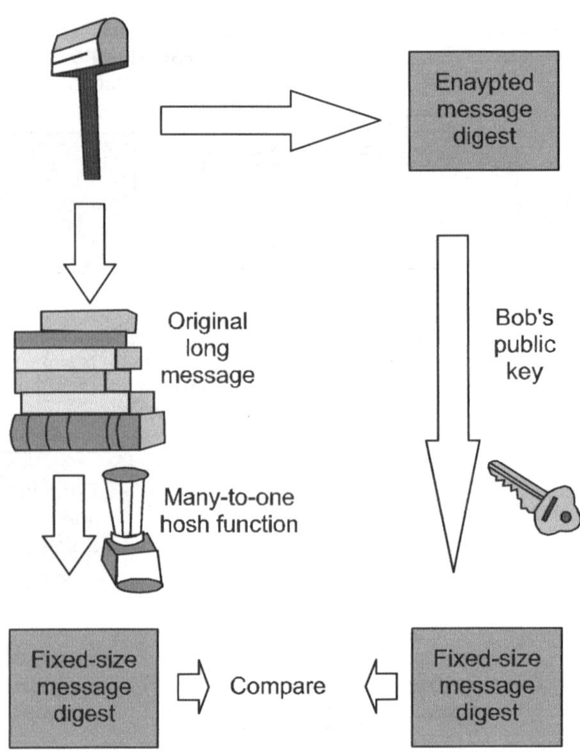

Figure 6.18 Verifying the integrity of a signed message.

6.7 MESSAGE AUTHENTICATION CODE (MAC) ALGORITHM

A cryptographic message authentication code (MAC) is a short piece of information used to authenticate a message.

A MAC algorithm, sometimes called a keyed (cryptographic) hash function, accepts as input a secret key and an arbitrary-length message to be authenticated, and outputs a MAC (sometimes known as a tag). The MAC value protects both a message's data integrity as well as its authenticity, by allowing verifiers (who also possess the secret key) to detect any changes to the message content, and so should be called Message Authentication and Integrity Code (MAIC).

A message integrity code (MIC) is frequently used as a substitute term for the MAC, especially in communications, where MAC acronym is traditionally used for Media Access Control. However, some authors use MIC as a distinctly different term from a MAC in that a secret key is not used in MIC operation, so a MIC should always be encrypted during transmission if it is to be used as a reliable gauge of message integrity. A given message will always produce the same MIC assuming the same algorithm is used to generate both. Conversely, the same message can only generate matching MACs if the same secret key and initialization vector are used with the same algorithms to generate both. MICs do not use secret keys and, when taken on their own, are therefore a much less reliable gauge of message integrity. A MAC that uses a secret key does not necessarily need to be encrypted to provide the same level of assurance.

While MAC functions are similar to cryptographic hash functions, they possess different security requirements. To be considered secure, a MAC function must resist existential forgery under chosen-plaintext attacks. This means that even if an attacker has access to an oracle which possesses the secret key and generates MACs for messages of the attacker's choosing, he can "never" guess the MAC for any message that he has not yet asked the oracle about. (Here "never" means, "not without doing an infeasible amount of computation"). Hash functions can be used to create MAC functions; see for example HMAC.

MACs differ from digital signatures, as MAC values are both generated and verified using the same secret key. This implies that the sender and receiver of a message must agree on keys before initiating communications, as is the case with symmetric encryption. For the same reason, MACs do not provide the property of non-repudiation offered by signatures: any user who can verify a MAC is also capable of generating MACs for other messages. In contrast, a digital signature is generated using the private key of a key pair, which is asymmetric encryption. Since this private key is only accessible to its holder, a digital signature proves that a document was signed by none other than that holder. Thus, digital signatures do offer non-repudiation.

MAC algorithms can be constructed from other cryptographic primitives, such as cryptographic hash functions (as in the case of HMAC) or from block cipher algorithms (OMAC, CBC-MAC and PMAC). However many of the fastest MAC algorithms are constructed based on universal hashing.

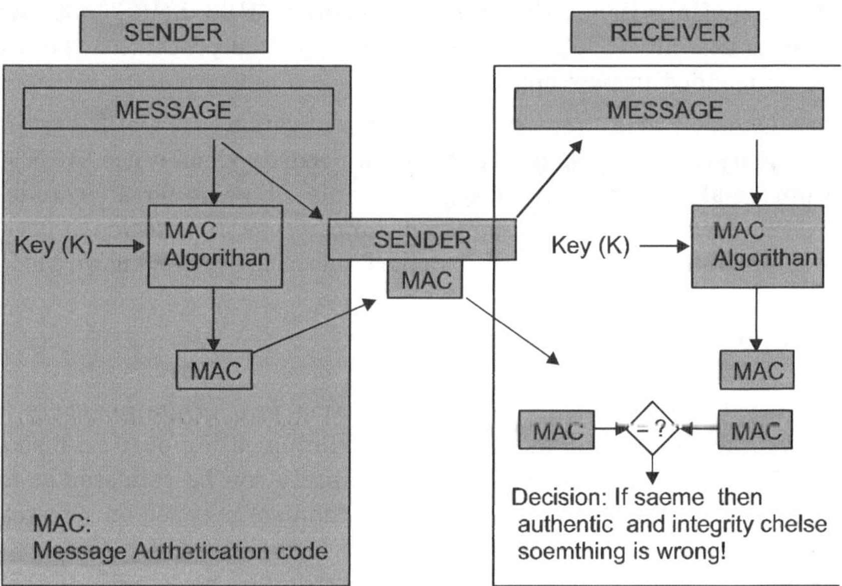

Figure. 6.19 MAC Algorithm

6.8 CRYPTOGRAPHIC HASH FUNCTIONS

Cryptographic hash functions are used in various contexts, for example to compute the message digest when making a digital signature. A hash function compresses the bits of a message to a fixed-size hash value in a way that distributes the possible messages evenly among the possible hash values. A cryptographic hash function does this in a way that makes it extremely difficult to come up with a message that would hash to a particular hash value. Some of the best known and most widely used hash functions are briefly described below.

(1) SHA-1 (Secure Hash Algorithm) (also SHS, Secure Hash Standard): This is a cryptographic hash algorithm published by the United States Government. It produces a 160 bit hash value from an arbitrary length string. SHA-1 is still considered adequately safe for practical applications, but stronger versions, SHA-256, SHA-384, and SHA-512, which produce 256-, 384-, and 512-bit hashes, respectively, are available and will replace SHA-1 as cryptological research on it advances.

(2) RIPEMD-160 is a hash algorithm designed to replace MD4 and MD5. It produces a digest of 20 bytes (160 bits, hence the name) and has been placed in the public domain by its designers.

(3) MD5 (Message Digest Algorithm 5) is a cryptographic hash algorithm developed at RSA Laboratories. It can be used to hash an arbitrary length byte string into a 128-bit value.

(4) MD5's ancestors, MD2 and MD4 have been broken, and there are some concerns about the safety of MD5 as well. In 1996 a collision of the MD5 compression function was found by Hans Dobbertin (Hans Dobbertin, FSE'96, LNCS 1039). Although this result does not directly compromise its security, as a precaution the use of MD5 is not recommended in new applications.

(5) Badger (CryptiCore) is a recent message authentication code which was first presented at the Applied Cryptography and Network Security Conference (ACNS) in 2005. It uses universal hashing as its design principle, allowing for a rigorous proof of its security under randomness assumptions for the keys. In addition, it uses some novel ways of combining the ingredients to make it one of the fastest known MAC algorithms.

6.9 AUTHENTICITY AND MACS

Verifying the integrity and authenticity of information is a prime necessity in computer systems and networks. In particular, two parties communicating over an insecure channel require a method by which information sent by one party can be validated as authentic (or unmodi¯ed) by the other. Most commonly such a mechanism is based on a secret key shared between the parties and takes the form of a Message Authentication Code (MAC). (Other terms used include \Integrity Check Value" or \cryptographic checksum"). In this case, when party A transmits a message to party B, it appends to the message a value called the authentication tag, computed by the MAC algorithm as a function of the transmitted information and the shared secret key. At reception, B recomputes the authentication tag on the received message using the same mechanism (and key) and checks that the value he obtains equals the tag attached to the received message. Only if the values match is the information received considered as not altered on the way from A to B.1 The goal is to prevent forgery, namely, the computation, by the adversary, of a message (not sent by the legitimate parties) and its corresponding valid authentication tag.

6.9.1 MACing with Cryptographic hash functions

MACs have most commonly been constructed out of block ciphers like DES. More recently, however, there has been a surge of interest in the idea of constructing MACs from cryptographic hash functions like MD5 [Ri] and SHA-1. This is particularly visible in the Internet community, where the development of security protocols has led to the need for simple, e±cient, and widely available MAC mechanisms.

It is easy to see why people want to MAC with cryptographic hash functions: the popular hash functions are faster than block ciphers in software implementation; these software implementations are readily and freely available; and the functions are not subject to the export restriction rules of the USA and other countries. The more di±cult question is how best to do it. These hash functions were not originally designed to be used for message authentication. (One of many di±culties is that hash functions are not keyed primitives, ie. do not accommodate naturally the notion of secret key.) So special care must be taken in using them to this end. In particular, although many constructions have been proposed, they lack a sound and realistic security analysis. Thus there is a need for constructions which maintain the e±ciency of the hash functions but are backed by a more rigorous analysis of their security.

6.9.2 Hash Function Algorithms

Let's convince ourselves that a simple checksum, such as the Internet checksum, would make a poor message digest algorithm. Rather than performing 1 complement's arithmetic (as in the Internet checksum), let us compute a checksum by treating each character as a byte and adding the bytes together using 4-byte chunks at a time. Suppose Bunty owes Anita $100.99" and sends an IOU to Anita consisting of the text string "IOU100.99Bunty". The ASCII representation (in hexadecimal notation) for these letters is 49, 4F, 55, 31, 30, 30, 2E, 39, 39, 42, 4F, 42.

Figure 6.20 (top) shows that the 4-byte checksum for this message is B2 C1 D2 AC. A slightly different message (and a much more costly one for Bunty) is shown in the bottom half of Figure 6.20. The message "IOU100.99Bunty" and "IOU900.19Bunty" have the same checksum! Thus, this simple checksum algorithm violates the two required requirements above. Given the original data, it is simple to find another set of data with the same checksum. Clearly, for security purposes. we are going to need a more powerful hash function than a 6.20 checksum.

message	ASCII representation	
I O U 1	49 4F 55 31	
0 0 . 9	30 30 2E 39	
9 B O B	39 42 4F 42	
	B2 C1 D2 AC	checksum

message	ASCII representation	
I O U 9	49 4F 55 39	
0 0 . 1	30 30 2E 31	
9 B O B	39 42 4F 42	
	B2 C1 D2 AC	checksum

Figure 6.20: Initial message and fraudulent message have the same checksum!

The MD5 message digest algorithm by Ron Rivest [RFC 1321] is in wide use today. It computes a 128-bit message digest in a four-step process consisting of a padding step (adding a 1 followed by enough zero's so that the length of the message satisfies certain conditions), an append step (appending a 64-bit representation of the message length before padding), an initialization of an accumulator, and a final looping step in which the message's 16-word blocks are processed (mangled) in four rounds of processing. It is not known whether MD5 actually satisfies the requirements listed above. The author of MD5 claims "It is conjectured that the difficulty of coming up with two messages having the same message digest is on the order of 264 operations, and that the difficulty of coming up with any message having a given message digest is on the order of 2128 operations. "[RFC 1321]. No one has argued with this claim. For a description of MD5 (including a C source code implementation) see [RFC 1321]. Computational aspects of MD5 are discussed in [RFC 1810].

The second major message digest algorithm in use today is SHA-1, the Secure Hash Algorithm. This algorithm is based on principles similar to those used in the design of MD4 [RFC 1320], the predecessor to MD5. The Secure Hash Algorithm (SHA-1), a US federal standard, is required for use whenever a secure message digest algorithm is required for federal applications. It produces a 160-bit message digest

6.10 BIRTHDAY ATTACKS

A birthday attack is a name used to refer to a class of brute-force attacks. It gets its name from the surprising result that the probability that two or more people in a group of 23 share the same birthday is greater than 1/2; such a result is called a birthday paradox.

If some function, when supplied with a random input, returns one of k equally-likely values, then by repeatedly evaluating the function for different inputs, we expect to obtain the same output after about $1.2k^{1/2}$. For the above birthday paradox, replace k with 365.

Birthday attacks are often used to find collisions of hash functions.

Birthday attacks are a class of brute-force techniques used in an attempt to solve a class of cryptographic hash function problems. These methods take advantage of functions which, when supplied with a random input, return one of equally likely values. By repeatedly evaluating the function for different inputs, the same output is expected to be obtained after about $1.2\sqrt{k}$ evaluations.

Consider the probability $Q_1(n, d)$ that no two people out of a group of n will have matching birthdays out of d equally possible birthdays. Start with an arbitrary person's birthday, then note that the probability that the second person's birthday is different is $(d - 1)/d$, that the third person's birthday is different from the first two is $[(d - 1)/d][(d - 2)/d]$, and so on, up through the nth person. Explicitly,

$$Q_1(a, d) = \frac{d-1}{d}\frac{d-2}{d}\cdots\frac{d-(n-1)}{d} \quad \text{...(1)}$$

$$= \frac{(d-1)(d-2)\ldots[d-(n-1)]}{d^{n-1}} \quad \text{...(2)}$$

But this can be written in terms of factorials as

$$Q_1(a, d) = \frac{d!}{(d-n)!\,d^n} \quad \text{...(3)}$$

so the probability $P_2(n, d)$ that two or more people out of a group of n do have the same birthday is therefore

$$P_2(n, d) = 1 - Q_1(n.d) \quad \text{...(4)}$$

$$= 1 - \frac{d!}{(d-n)!\,d^n} \quad \text{...(5)}$$

In general, let $Q_i(n, d)$ denote the probability that a birthday is shared by exactly i (and no more) people out of a group of n people. Then the probability that a birthday is shared by k or more people is given by

$$P_k(n, d) = 1 - \sum_{i=1}^{k-1} Q_i(n.d) \quad \text{...(6)}$$

In general, $Q_k(n, d)$ can be computed using the recurrence relation

$$Q_k(n, d) = \sum_{i=1}^{[n/k]} \left| \frac{n!\,d!}{d^{iK}\,i!(K!)^i(n-ik)!(d-1)!} \sum_{j=1}^{K-1} Qj(n-ik.d-i)\frac{(d-i)^{n-ik}}{d^{n-ik}} \right| \quad \text{...(7)}$$

However, the time to compute this recursive function grows exponentially with k and so rapidly becomes unwieldy.

If 365-day years have been assumed, i.e., the existence of leap days is ignored, and the distribution of birthdays is assumed to be uniform throughout the year (in actuality, there is a more than 6% increase from the average in September in the United States; Peterson 1998), then the number of people needed for there to be at least a 50% chance that at least two share birthdays is the smallest n such that $P_2(n, \geq 365) \geq 1/2$. This is given by n = 23, since

$$P_2(23, 365) = \frac{38093904702297390785243708291051888645406094 7061}{75091883268515350125426207425223147563269805908203125} \quad ...(8)$$

$$= 0.507297 \quad ...(9)$$

The number n of people needed to obtain $P_2(n, d) \geq 1/2$ for $d = 1, 2, ...,$ are 2, 2, 3, 3, 3, 4, 4, 4, 4, 5, ... The minimal number of people to give a 50% probability of having at least n coincident birthdays is 1, 23, 88, 187, 313, 460, 623, 798, 985, 1181, 1385, 1596, 1813, ...

The probability $P_2(n, d)$ can be estimated as

$$P_2(n, d) = 1 - e^{-n(n-1)/2d} \quad ...(10)$$

$$= 1 - \left(1 - \frac{n}{2d}\right)^{n-1} \quad ...(11)$$

where the latter has error

$$\varepsilon < \frac{n^3}{6(d-n+1)^2} \quad ...(12)$$

Q_2 can be computed explicitly as

$$Q_2(n, d) = \frac{n!}{d^n} \sum_{y-1}^{[n/2]} \frac{1}{2^i} \binom{d}{i} \binom{d-i}{n-2i} \quad ...(13)$$

$$= \frac{d!}{d^n (d-n)!} \left[{}_2F_1\left(\frac{1}{2}n, \frac{1}{2}(1-n); d-n+1; 2\right) - 1 \right], \quad ...(14)$$

where $\binom{n}{m}$ is a binomial coefficient and ${}_2F_1(a, b, ; c; z)$ is a hypergeometric function. This gives the explicit formula for $P_3(n, d)$ as

$$P_3(n, d) = 1 - Q_1(n, d) - Q_2(n, d) \quad ...(15)$$

$$= 1 - d^{-n} d!_2 \bar{F}_1\left(\frac{1}{2}n, \frac{1}{2}(1-n); 1+d-n, 2\right), \quad ...(16)$$

where ${}_2\vec{f}_1(a, b, ; c; z)$ is a regularized hypergeometric function.

A good approximation to the number of people n such that $p = P_k(n, d)$ is some given value can be given by solving the equation

$$ne^{-n/(dk)} = \left| d^{k-1} k! \ln\left(\frac{1}{1-p}\right)\left(1 - \frac{n}{d(k+1)}\right)\right|^{1/k} \qquad \text{...(17)}$$

for n and taking $[n]$, where $[n]$ is the ceiling function. For $p = 0.5$ and $k = 1, 2, 3, \ldots$, this formula gives $n = 1, 23, 88, 187, 313, 459, 622, 797, 983, 1179, 1382, 1592, 1809, \ldots$, which differ from the true values by from 0 to 4. A much simpler but also poorer approximation for n such that $p = 0.5$ for $k < 20$ is given by

$$n = 47(k-1.5)3/2 \qquad \text{...(18)}$$

which gives 86, 185, 307, 448, 606, 778, 965, 1164, 1376, 1599, 1832, ... for $k = 3, 4, \ldots$

The "almost" birthday problem, which asks the number of people needed such that two have a birthday within a day of each other, was considered by Abramson and Moser (1970), who showed that 14 people suffice. An approximation for the minimum number of people needed to get a 50-50 chance that two have a match within k days out of d possible is given by

$$n(k, d) = 1.2\sqrt{\frac{d}{2k+1}} \qquad \text{...(19)}$$

How does the length of a hash value affect security?

The essential cryptographic properties of a hash function are that it is both one-way and collision-free. The most basic attack we might mount on a hash function is to choose inputs to the hash function at random until either we find some input that will give us the target output value we are looking for (thereby contradicting the one-way property), or we find two inputs that produce the same output (thereby contradicting the collision-free property).

Suppose the hash function produces an n-bit long output. If we are trying to find some input which will produce some target output value y, then since each output is equally likely we expect to have to try 2^n possible input values.

If we are trying to find a collision, then by the birthday paradox we would expect that after trying $2^{n/2}$ possible input values we would have some collision. Van Oorschot and Wiener showed how such a brute-force attack might be implemented.

With regard to the use of hash functions in the provision of digital signatures, Yuval proposed the following strategy based on the birthday paradox, where n is the length of the message digest.

Adversary selects the target message to be signed and an innocuous message that Alice is likely to want to sign.

The adversary generates 2n/2 variations of the innocuous message (by making, for instance, minor editorial changes), all of which convey the same meaning, and their corresponding message digests. He then generates an equal number of variations of the target message to be substituted.

The probability that one of the variations of the innocuous message will match one of the variations of the target message is greater than 1/2 according to the birthday paradox.

The adversary then obtains Alice's signature on the variation of the innocuous message.

The signature from the innocuous message is removed and attached to the variation of the target message that generates the same message digest. The adversary has successfully forged the message without discovering the enciphering keys.

To avoid an attack that depends on brute-force methods, the output from the hash function must be sufficiently long.

MD2, MD4, and MD5 are message-digest algorithms developed by Rivest. They are meant for digital signature applications where a large message has to be "compressed" in a secure manner before being signed with the private key. All three algorithms take a message of arbitrary length and produce a 128-bit message digest. While the structures of these algorithms are somewhat similar, the design of MD2 is quite different from that of MD4 and MD5 and MD2 was optimized for 8-bit machines, whereas MD4 and MD5 were aimed at 32-bit machines. Description and source code for the three algorithms can be found as Internet RFCs 1319 - 1321.

MD2 was developed by Rivest in 1989. The message is first padded so that its length in bytes is divisible by 16. A 16-byte checksum is then appended to the message, and the hash value is computed on this resulting message. Rogier and Chauvaud have found that collisions for MD2 can be constructed if the calculation of the checksum is omitted [RC95]. This is the only cryptanalytic result known for MD2.

MD4 was developed by Rivest in 1990. The message is padded to ensure that its length in bits plus 448 is divisible 512. A 64-bit binary representation of the original length of the message is then concatenated to the message. The message is processed in 512-bit blocks in the Damgård/Merkle iterative structure, and each block is processed in three distinct rounds. Attacks on versions of MD4 with either the first or the last rounds missing were developed very quickly by Den Boer and Bosselaers [DB92] and others. Dobbertin [Dob95] has shown how collisions for the full version of MD4 can be found in under a minute on a typical PC. Clearly, MD4 should now be considered broken.

MD5 was developed by Rivest in 1991. It is basically MD4 with "safety-belts" and while it is slightly slower than MD4, it is more secure. The algorithm consists of four distinct rounds, which have a slightly different design from that of MD4. Message-digest size, as well as padding requirements, remains the same. Den Boer and Bosselaers have found pseudo-collisions for MD5, but there are no other known cryptanalytic results.

Van Oorschot and Wiener have considered a brute-force search for collisions (see Question 96) in hash functions, and they estimate that a collision search machine designed specifically for MD5 (costing $10 million in 1994) could find a collision for MD5 in 24 days on average. The general techniques can be applied to other hash functions.

The Secure Hash Algorithm (SHA), the algorithm specified in the Secure Hash Standard (SHS), was developed by NIST and published as a federal information processing standard (FIPS PUB 180). SHA-1 was a revision to SHA that was published in 1994. The revision corrected an unpublished flaw in SHA. Its design is very similar to the MD4 family of hash functions developed by Rivest.

The algorithm takes a message of less than 264 bits in length and produces a 160-bit message digest. The algorithm is slightly slower than MD5, but the larger message digest makes it more secure against brute-force collision and inversion attacks.

The best review of hash function techniques is provided by Preneel.

For a brief overview here, we note that hash functions are often divided into three classes according to their design:

- those built around block ciphers,
- those which use modular arithmetic, and
- those which have what is termed a "dedicated" design.

By building a hash function around a block cipher, it is intended that by using a well-trusted block cipher such as DES a secure and well-trusted hash function can be obtained. The so-called Davies-Meyer hash function is an example of a hash function built around the use of DES.

The use of modular arithmetic in the second class of hash functions is intended to save on implementation costs when the hash function is used in conjunction with a digital signature algorithm that also uses modular arithmetic. Unfortunately, the track record of such hash functions is not good from a security perspective and there are no hash functions in this second class that can be recommended today.

The hash functions in the third class, with their so-called "dedicated" design, tend to be fast, giving a considerable advantage over algorithms that are based around the use of a block cipher. Along with MD5 and SHA-1 RIPE-MD and HAVAL are dedicated hash functions that also have a similar design to MD4.

1. What is a Hash Function?
2. What is a birthday attack?
3. How does the length of a hash value affect security?

4. What is a compression function?
5. What are pseudo-collisions?
6. What are MD2, MD4 and MD5?
7. What is the Secure Hash Algorithm (SHA and SHA-1)?
8. What Other Hash Functions Are There?

---

1. Tesler, L. "Not a Coincidence!" http://www.nomodes.com/coincidence.html.
2. Abramson, M. and Moser, W. O. J. "More Birthday Surprises." Amer. Math. Monthly 77, 856-858, 1970.
3. Ball, W. W. R. and Coxeter, H. S. M. Mathematical Recreations and Essays, 13th ed. New York: Dover, pp. 45-46, 1987.
4. Bloom, D. M. "A Birthday Problem." Amer. Math. Monthly 80, 1141-1142, 1973.
5. Bogomolny, A. "Coincidence." http://www.cut-the-knot.org/do_you_know/coincidence.shtml.
6. Clevenson, M. L. and Watkins, W. "Majorization and the Birthday Inequality." Math. Mag. 64, 183-188, 1991.
7. Diaconis, P. and Mosteller, F. "Methods for Studying Coincidences." J. Amer. Statist. Assoc. 84, 853-861, 1989.
8. Feller, W. An Introduction to Probability Theory and Its Applications, Vol. 1, 3rd ed. New York: Wiley, pp. 31-32, 1968.
9. Finch, S. "Puzzle #28 [June 1997]: Coincident Birthdays." http://www.mathcad.com/library/LibraryContent/puzzles/puzzle.asp?num=28.
10. Gehan, E. A. "Note on the 'Birthday Problem.' " Amer. Stat. 22, 28, Apr. 1968.
11. Heuer, G. A. "Estimation in a Certain Probability Problem." Amer. Math. Monthly 66, 704-706, 1959.
12. Hocking, R. L. and Schwertman, N. C. "An Extension of the Birthday Problem to Exactly Matches." College Math. J. 17, 315-321, 1986.
13. Hunter, J. A. H. and Madachy, J. S. Mathematical Diversions. New York: Dover, pp. 102-103, 1975.
14. Klamkin, M. S. and Newman, D. J. "Extensions of the Birthday Surprise." J. Combin. Th. 3, 279-282, 1967.
15. Levin, B. "A Representation for Multinomial Cumulative Distribution Functions." Ann. Statistics 9, 1123-1126, 1981.
16. McKinney, E. H. "Generalized Birthday Problem." Amer. Math. Monthly 73, 385-387, 1966.

17. Mises, R. von. "Über Aufteilungs—und Besetzungs-Wahrscheinlichkeiten." Revue de la Faculté des Sciences de l'Université d'Istanbul, N. S. 4, 145-163, 1939. Reprinted in Selected Papers of Richard von Mises, Vol. 2 (Ed. P. Frank, S. Goldstein, M. Kac, W. Prager, G. Szegö, and G. Birkhoff). Providence, RI: Amer. Math. Soc., pp. 313-334, 1964.
18. Peterson, I. "MathTrek: Birthday Surprises." Nov. 21, 1998. http://www.sciencenews.org/sn_arc98/11_21_98/mathland.htm.
19. Riesel, H. Prime Numbers and Computer Methods for Factorization, 2nd ed. Boston, MA: Birkhäuser, pp. 179-180, 1994.
20. Sayrafiezadeh, M. "The Birthday Problem Revisited." Math. Mag. 67, 220-223, 1994.
21. Sevast'yanov, B. A. "Poisson Limit Law for a Scheme of Sums of Dependent Random Variables." Th. Prob. Appl. 17, 695-699, 1972.
22. Sloane, N. J. A. Sequences A014088, A033810, A050255, and A050256 in "The On-Line Encyclopedia of Integer Sequences."
23. Stewart, I. "What a Coincidence!" Sci. Amer. 278, 95-96, June 1998.

❑❑❑

7

Digital Signatures

7.1 DIGITAL SIGNATURES

A major benefit of public key cryptography is that it provides a method for employing digital signatures. Digital signatures enable the recipient of information to verify the authenticity of the information's origin, and also verify that the information is intact. Thus, public key digital signatures provide authentication and data integrity. A digital signature also provides non-repudiation, which means that it prevents the sender from claiming that he or she did not actually send the information. These features are every bit as fundamental to cryptography as privacy, if not more.

A digital signature serves the same purpose as a handwritten signature. However, a handwritten signature is easy to counterfeit. A digital signature is superior to a handwritten signature in that it is nearly impossible to counterfeit, plus it attests to the contents of the information as well as to the identity of the signer.

Some people tend to use signatures more than they use encryption. For example, you may not care if anyone knows that you just deposited $1000 in your account, but you do want to be darn sure it was the bank teller you were dealing with.

The basic manner in which digital signatures are created is illustrated in Figure 7.1. Instead of encrypting information using someone else's public key, you encrypt it with your private key. If the information can be decrypted with your public key, then it must have originated with you.

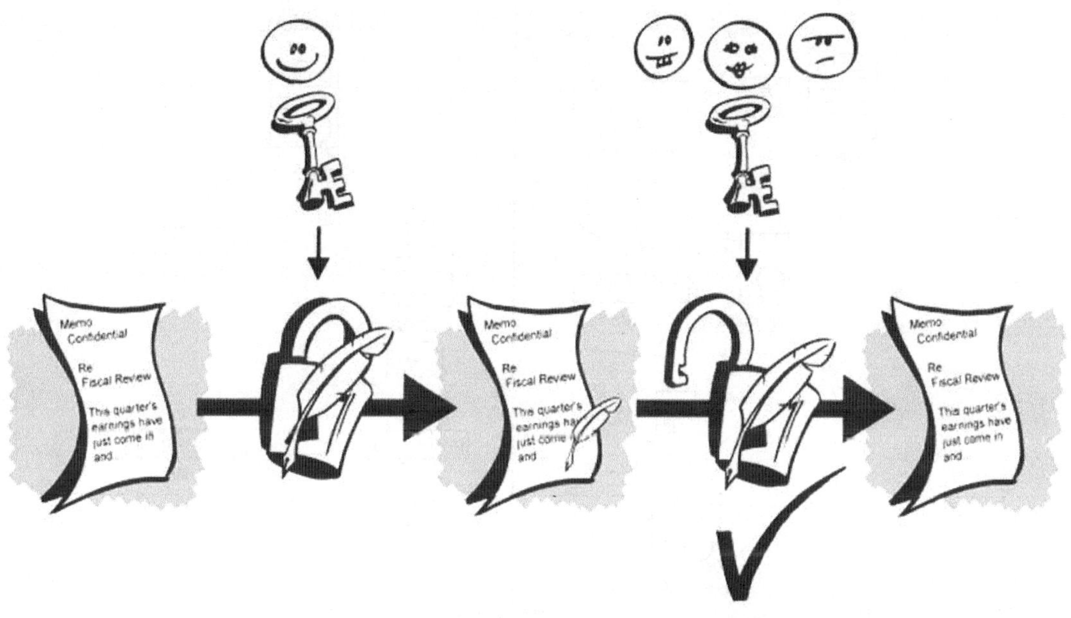

Figure 7.1 Simple Digital Signatures

Digital signature or digital signature scheme is a type of asymmetric cryptography. For messages sent through an insecure channel, a properly implemented digital signature gives the receiver reason to believe the message was sent by the claimed sender. Digital signatures are equivalent to traditional handwritten signatures in many respects; properly implemented digital signatures are more difficult to forge than the handwritten type. Digital signature schemes in the sense used here are cryptographically based, and must be implemented properly to be effective. Digital signatures can also provide non-repudiation, meaning that the signer cannot successfully claim they did not sign a message, while also claiming their private key remains secret; further, some non-repudiation schemes offer a time stamp for the digital signature, so that even if the private key is exposed, the signature is valid nonetheless. Digitally signed messages may be anything representable as a bitstring: examples include electronic mail, contracts, or a message sent via some other cryptographic protocol.

Digital signatures are often used to implement electronic signatures, a broader term that refers to any electronic data that carries the intent of a signature, but not all electronic signatures use digital signatures. In some countries, including the United States, and in the European Union, electronic signatures have legal significance. However, laws concerning electronic signatures do not always make clear whether they are digital cryptographic signatures in the sense used here, leaving the legal definition, and so their importance, somewhat confused.

Definition

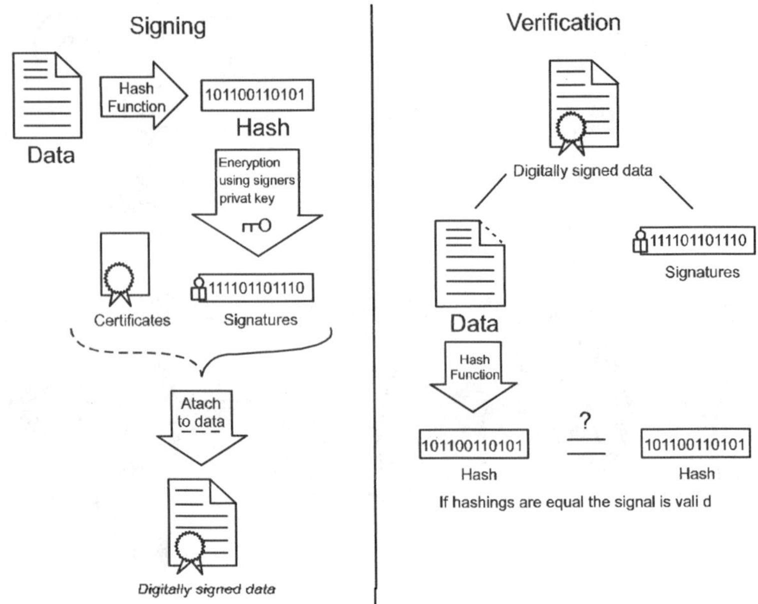

Figure 7.2 Verification for Digital Signature

Figure 7.2 is a diagram showing how an RSA digital signature is applied and then verified. (DSA and NR differ slightly.)

A digital signature scheme typically consists of three algorithms:

- A key generation algorithm that selects a private key uniformly at random from a set of possible private keys. The algorithm outputs the private key and a corresponding public key.
- A signing algorithm which, given a message and a private key, produces a signature.
- A signature verifying algorithm which given a message, public key and a signature, either accepts or rejects.

Two main properties are required. First, a signature generated from a fixed message and fixed private key should verify on that message and the corresponding public key. Secondly, it should be computationally infeasible to generate a valid signature for a party who does not possess the private key.

Digital ID signature or certificate is an installed file resident on a computer validates who you are. Digital signatures are used by programs on the internet and local to the machines to confirm your identity to any third party concerned. Digital signatures have been confused with electronic signatures. Electronic signatures are scanned copies of a physical written signature.

Very closely related to public key cryptography is the concept of digital signatures. One problem with corresponding electronically, such as via a computer network, is that messages can be easily forged—you usually cannot be certain that the sender of a received message is actually the person claimed in the message. A public key cryptosystem, however, can be used to provide positive identification of any sender who has a public key on record. If, for example, Mary has filed a public key in some public access file, she can digitally sign a message to you by decrypting it with her private key before transmitting it. After receiving the message, you (or anyone else) can read the message by encrypting it with Mary's public encryption key. The process is essentially the reverse of the cryptosystem: the message is first decrypted and then encrypted, and anyone can reveal the message, but only Mary with her secret decryption key can create it.

In addition, messages using digital signatures can be subsequently encrypted with another key. After Mary decrypts her message to you with her secret decryption key, she can then encrypt it with your public encryption key. The result is a message that only Mary could have created, and only you can read! Messages with digital signatures have other interesting and useful properties and may be used to advantage with other (non-PKC) cryptosystems. These properties and applications might easily justify an article on digital signatures alone.

7.1.1 Need for Verifying Identity

New ways of verification are being developed daily. Biometrics and other methods keep getting formulated and incorporated into the information technology industry. One interesting biometric authentication mechanism developed by a leading Japanese biometric company has found a way to get your DNA into a pen. You sign a document and it is digitally scanned. This document then can be scanned in the future to verify its authenticity. Identity should be verified when ever there is doubt of the 3rd party being whom they say they are or when there is personal information at risk. Personal information like credit card details and banking information should be kept safe using digital certification as one of the security layers. Some banking institutions require that a user verifies his/her identity by validating identification credentials using a digital certificate. Important e-mail can also use Digital signatures that verify that the e-mail is from the originating sender and that it has not been tampered with. On many occasions users are unsure if they are dealing with reputable suppliers of institutions. Digital certification gives the user a sense of legitimacy and formalizes the process. It ensure that the company that the user is dealing with has a registration with a trusted authority and that the transaction is guaranteed to be done with the intended parties.

7.1.2 Reasons for using Digital Security

1. It insures by means of verification and validation that the user is whom he/she claims to be. This is done by combine the users credential to the digital certificate and in turn this method uses one point of authentication.
2. Digital certificates insure data Integrity giving the user piece of mind that the message or transaction has not been accidentally or maliciously altered. This is done cryptographically.

3. Digital certificates ensure confidentiality and ensure that messages can only be read by authorized intended recipients.
4. Digital certificates also verify date and time so that senders or recipients can not dispute if the message was actually sent or received.
5. The components that a digital signature comprise of.
6. Your public key: This is the part that any one can get a copy of and is part of the verification system.
7. Your name and e-mail address: This is necessary for contact information purposes and to enable the viewer to identify the details.
8. Expiration date of the public key: This part of the signature is used to set a shelf life and to ensure that in the event of prolonged abuse of a signature eventually the signature is reset.
9. Name of the company: This section identifies the company that the signature belongs too.
10. Serial number of the Digital ID: This part is a unique number that is bundled to the signature for tracking ad extra identification reasons.
11. Digital signature of the CA (certification Authority): This is a signature that is issued by the authority that issues the certificates.

7.1.3 The Process of checking the Validity of Digital Signature

User A sends a signed document to User B.

To verify the signature on the document, user B's application first uses the certificate authority's public key to check the signature on user A's certificate.

Successful de-encryption of the certificate proves that the certificate authority created it.

After the certificate is de-encrypted, user B's software can check if user A is in good standing with the certificate authority and that all of the certificate information concerning user A's id1entity has not been altered.

User B's software then takes user A's public key from the certificate and uses it to check user A's signature. If user A's public key de-encrypts the signature successfully, then user B is assured that the signature was created using user A's private key, for the certificate authority has certified the matching public key.

If the signature is found to be valid, then we know that an intruder didn't try to change the signed content.

The importance of private key revocation

At times there may be grounds for believing that a private key may have been compromised. This will then result in the key pair being revoked. When a digital signature is revoked the user that is requesting the revoke needs to be verified. If a key is wrongfully revoked legal action can follow.

Digital signatures deliver assurances in the role that the other party will keep their part of the bargain. Knowing the identity of the other party is one way of gaining that assurance. Keys used for digital signatures are very long series of bits, which can be represented as long series of alphanumeric characters. This makes digital signatures unfeasible for an individual to remember. They must consequently be stored in a method which is suitable, portable and protected. The most likely current technology to support such storage is a chip. Smart cards, bios chips, e-prom ships found in cable modems and other types of descrambles are all examples or primitive forms of digital signatures that act as away of identifying user. No form of identification to this date is used more than digital signature to verify the existence of a user and confirmation of credential over the internet. Digital signatures in some form or other are her to stay.

7.1.4 Validity of Digital Signatures

Normally, a key expires after some period of time, such as one year, and a document signed with an expired key should not be accepted. However, there are many cases where it is necessary for signed documents to be regarded as legally valid for much longer than two years; long-term leases and contracts are examples. By registering the contract with a digital time-stamping service at the time it is signed, the signature can be validated even after the key expires.

If all parties to the contract keep a copy of the time-stamp, each can prove that the contract was signed with valid keys. In fact, the time-stamp can prove the validity of a contract even if one signer's key gets compromised at some point after the contract was signed. Any digitally signed document can be time-stamped, assuring that the validity of the signature can be verified after the key expires.

7.1.5 Legal status of documents signed with Digital Signatures?

If digital signatures are to replace handwritten signatures they must have the same legal status as handwritten signatures, i.e., documents signed with digital signatures must be legally binding.

As per Information Technology Act 2000 Of India notified on 9.06.2000 following provisions have been made. The serial numbers given here are as per this document.

3. Authentication of electronic records

(1) Subject to the provisions of this section any subscriber may authenticate an electronic record by affixing his digital signature.

(2) The authentication of the electronic record shall be effected by the use of asymmetric crypto system and hash function which envelop and transform the initial electronic record into another electronic record.

Explanation.- For the purposes of this sub-section, "hash function" means an algorithm mapping or translation of one sequence of bits into another, generally smaller, set known'as

...Continued

"hash result" such that an electronic record yields the same hash result every time the algorithm is executed with the same electronic record as its input making it computationally infeasible-

(*a*) To derive or reconstruct the original electronic record from the hash result produced by the algorithm;

(*b*) That two electronic records can produce the same hash result using the algorithm.

(3) Any person by the use of a public key of the subscriber can verify the electronic record.

(4) The private key and the public key are unique to the subscriber and constitute a functioning key pair.

(5) Legal recognition of digital signatures. Where any law provides that information or any other matter shall be authenticated by affixing the signature or any document shall be signed or bear the signature of any person (hen, notwithstanding anything contained in such law, such requirement shall be deemed to have been satisfied, if such information or matter is authenticated by means of digital signature affixed in such manner as may be prescribed by the Central Government.

(*c*) ***Explanation***— For the purposes of this section, "signed", with its grammatical variations and cognate expressions, shall, with reference to a person, mean affixing of his hand written signature or any mark on any document and the expression "signature" shall be construed accordingly.

(*d*) (6) Use of electronic records and digital signatures in Government and its agencies.

(1) Where any law provides for–

(*e*) (*a*) the filing of any form. application or any other document with any office, authority, body or agency owned or controlled by the appropriate Government in a particular manner;

(*b*) the issue or grant of any licence, permit, sanction or approval by whatever name called in a particular manner;

(*c*) the receipt or payment of money in a particular manner,

(*f*) then, notwithstanding anything contained in any other law for the time being in force, such requirement shall be deemed to have been satisfied if such filing, issue, grant, receipt or payment, as the case may be, is effected by means of such electronic form as may be prescribed by the appropriate Government.

(*g*) (2) The appropriate Government may, for the purposes of sub-section (1), by rules, prescribe-

(*h*) (*a*) the manner and format in which such electronic records shall be filed, created or issued;

(*b*) the manner or method of payment of any fee or charges for filing, creation or issue any electronic record under clause

...Continued

(i) **7. Retention of electronic records.**

(1) Where any law provides that documents, records or information shall be retained for any specific period, then, that requirement shall be deemed to have been satisfied if such documents, records or information are retained in the electronic form, if-

(j) (*a*) the information contained therein remains accessible so as to be usable for a subsequent reference;

(*b*) the electronic record is retained in the format in which it was originally generated, sent or received or in a format which can be demonstrated to represent accurately the information originally generated, sent or received;

(*c*) the details which will facilitate the identification of the origin, destination, date and time of despatch or receipt of such electronic record are available in the electronic record:

(k) Provided that this clause does not apply to any information which is automatically generated solely for the purpose of enabling an electronic record to be despatched or received.

(l) (2) Nothing in this section shall apply to any law that expressly provides for the retention of documents, records or information in the form of electronic records.

NIST has stated that its proposed Digital Signature Standard should be capable of "proving to a third party that data was actually signed by the generator of the signature. " Furthermore, U.S. federal government purchase orders will be signed by any such standard; this implies that the government will support the legal authority of digital signatures in the courts. Some preliminary legal research has also resulted in the opinion that digital signatures would meet the requirements of legally binding signatures for most purposes, including commercial use as defined in the Uniform Commercial Code (UCC). A GAO (Government Accounting Office) decision requested by NIST also opines that digital signatures will meet the legal standards of handwritten signatures.

However, since the validity of documents with digital signatures has never been challenged in court, their legal status is not yet well-defined. Through such challenges, the courts will issue rulings that collectively define which digital signature methods, key sizes, and security precautions are acceptable for a digital signature to be legally binding.

Digital signatures have the potential to possess greater legal authority than handwritten signatures. If a ten page contract is signed by hand on the tenth page, one cannot be sure that the first nine pages have not been altered. However, if the contract was signed with digital signatures,a third party can verify that not one byte of the contract has been altered.

Currently, if two people want to digitally sign a series of contracts, they might first sign a paper contract in which they agree to be bound in the future by any contracts digitally signed by them with a given signature method and minimum key size. Several efforts are underway to legislate the legality and use of digital signatures. Utah has implemented laws qualifying digital signatures.

7.1.6 Benefits of Digital Signatures

Below are some common reasons for applying a digital signature to communications:

(1) Authentication

Although messages may often include information about the entity sending a message, that information may not be accurate. Digital signatures can be used to authenticate the source of messages. When ownership of a digital signature secret key is bound to a specific user, a valid signature shows that the message was sent by that user. The importance of high confidence in sender authenticity is especially obvious in a financial context. For example, suppose a bank's branch office sends instructions to the central office requesting a change in the balance of an account. If the central office is not convinced that such a message is truly sent from an authorized source, acting on such a request could be a grave mistake.

(2) Integrity

In many scenarios, the sender and receiver of a message may have a need for confidence that the message has not been altered during transmission. Although encryption hides the contents of a message, it may be possible to change an encrypted message without understanding it. (Some encryption algorithms, known as nonmalleable ones, prevent this, but others do not.) However, if a message is digitally signed, any change in the message after signature will invalidate the signature. Furthermore, there is no efficient way to modify a message and its signature to produce a new message with a valid signature, because this is still considered to be computationally infeasible by most cryptographic hash functions (see collision resistance).

7.1.7 Drawbacks of Digital Signatures

Despite their usefulness, digital signatures alone do not solve the following problems:

(1) Association of Digital Signatures and Trusted Time Stamping

Digital signature algorithms and protocols do not inherently provide certainty about the date and time at which the underlying document was signed. The signer might have included a time stamp with the signature, or the document itself might have a date mentioned on it. Regardless of the document's contents, a reader cannot be certain the signer did not, for example, backdate the date or time of the signature. Such misuse can be made impracticable by using trusted time stamping in addition to digital signatures.

(2) Non-repudiation

In a cryptographic context, the word repudiation refers to any act of disclaiming responsibility for a message. A message's recipient may insist the sender attach a signature in order to make later repudiation more difficult, since the recipient can show the signed message to a third party (e.g., a court) to reinforce a claim as to its signatories and integrity. However, loss of control over a user's private key will mean that all digital signatures using that key, and so ostensibly 'from' that user, are suspect. Nonetheless, a user cannot repudiate a signed message without repudiating their signature key. This is aggravated by the fact there is no trusted time stamp, so new documents (after the key compromise) cannot be separated from old ones, further complicating signature key invalidation. A non-repudiation service requires the existence of a public key infrastructure (PKI) which is complex to establish and operate. The Certificate authorities in a PKI usually maintain a public repository of public keys so the associated private key is certified and signatures cannot be repudiated. Expired certificates are normally removed from the repository. It is a matter for the security policy and the responsibility of the authority to keep old certificates for a period of time if non-repudiation of data service is provided.

(3) WYSIWYS

Technically speaking, a digital signature applies to a string of bits, whereas humans and applications "believe" that they sign the semantic interpretation of those bits. In order to be semantically interpreted the bit string must be transformed into a form that is meaningful for humans and applications, and this is done through a combination of hardware and software based processes on a computer system. The problem is that the semantic interpretation of bits can change as a function of the processes used to transform the bits into semantic content. It is relatively easy to change the interpretation of a digital document by implementing changes on the computer system where the document is being processed. From a semantic perspective this creates uncertainty about what exactly has been signed. WYSIWYS (What You See Is What You Sign) means that the semantic interpretation of a signed message can not be changed. In particular this also means that a message can not contain hidden info that the signer is unaware of, and that can be revealed after the signature has been applied. WYSIWYS is a desirable property of digital signatures that is difficult to guarantee because of the increasing complexity of modern computer systems.

7.2 HASH FUNCTIONS

The system described above has some problems. It is slow, and it produces an enormous volume of data—at least double the size of the original information. An improvement on the above scheme is the addition of a one-way hash function in the process. A one-way hash function takes variable-length input—in this case, a message of any length, even thousands or millions of bits—and produces a fixed-length output; say, 160-bits. The hash function ensures that, if the information is changed in any way—even by just one bit—an entirely different output value is produced.

PGP uses a cryptographically strong hash function on the plaintext the user is signing. This generates a fixed-length data item known as a message digest. (Again, any change to the information results in a totally different digest.)

Then PGP uses the digest and the private key to create the "signature." PGP transmits the signature and the plaintext together. Upon receipt of the message, the recipient uses PGP to recompute the digest, thus verifying the signature. PGP can encrypt the plaintext or not; signing plaintext is useful if some of the recipients are not interested in or capable of verifying the signature.

As long as a secure hash function is used, there is no way to take someone's signature from one document and attach it to another, or to alter a signed message in any way. The slightest change in a signed document will cause the digital signature verification process to fail.

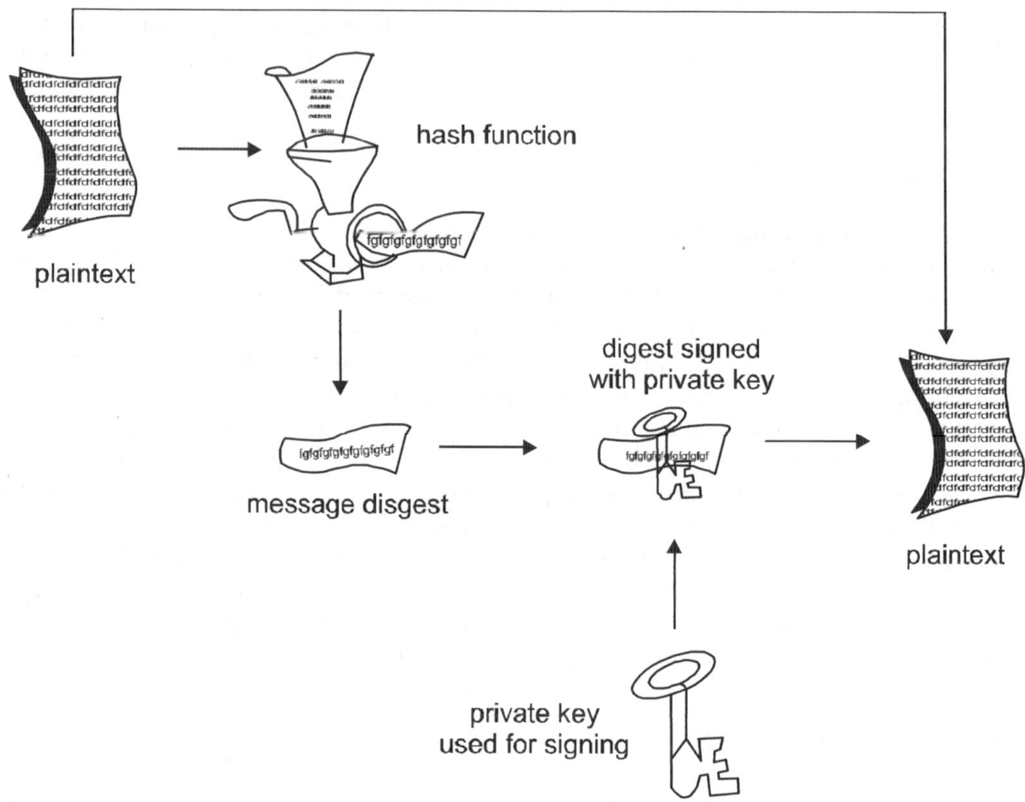

Figure 7.3 PGP Method

7.3 DIGITAL CERTIFICATES

The main Issue with public key cryptosystems is that users must be constantly vigilant to ensure that they are encrypting to the correct person's key. In an environment where it is safe to freely exchange keys via public servers, man-in-the-middle attacks are a potential threat. In this type of attack, someone posts a phony key with the name and user ID of the user's intended recipient.

Data encrypted to— and intercepted by—the true owner of this bogus key is now in the wrong hands.

In a public key environment, it is vital that you are assured that the public key to which you are encrypting data is in fact the public key of the intended recipient and not a forgery. You could simply encrypt only to those keys which have been physically handed to you. But suppose you need to exchange information with people you have never met; how can you tell that you have the correct key?

Digital certificates, or certs, simplify the task of establishing whether a key truly belongs to the purported owner.

Webster's dictionary defines certificate as "a document containing a certified statement, especially as to the truth of something." A certificate is a form of credential. Examples might be your passport, your social security card, or your birth certificate. Each of these has some information on it identifying you and some authorization stating that someone else has confirmed your identity. Some certificates, such as your driver's license, are important enough confirmation of your identity that you would not want to lose them, lest someone use them to impersonate you.

A *digital certificate* is data that functions much like a physical certificate. A digital certificate is information included with a person's public key that helps others verify that a key is genuine or valid. Digital certificates are used to thwart attempts to substitute one person's key for another.

A digital certificate consists of three things:

- A public key.
- Certificate information. ("Identity" information about the user, such as name, user ID, and so on.)
- One or more digital signatures.

The purpose of the digital signature on a certificate is to state that the certificate information has been attested to by some other person or entity. The digital signature does not attest to the authenticity of the certificate as a whole; it vouches only that the signed identity information goes along with, or is bound to, the public key.

While some security experts believe it is not a good practice to mix professional and personal identity information on one key, but rather have separate keys for each, you will come across certificates containing a public key with several associated identities (for example, the user's name and corporate email account, the user's nickname and home email account, the user's maiden name and college email account—all in one certificate). The list of signatures of each of those identities may differ; signatures usually attest to the authenticity of one of the identities, not that all three are authentic.

For example, suppose your coworker, Alice, asks you to sign her certificate.

You look it up on the server and see that Alice has two pieces of identity information associated with the certificate. The first one reads "Alice Petucci, `alice@securecompany.com.`" The second reads "`Cleopatra, cleo@cheops.org.`" Depending on how well you know Alice, you might want to choose to sign only the one that relates to the Alice you know at work.

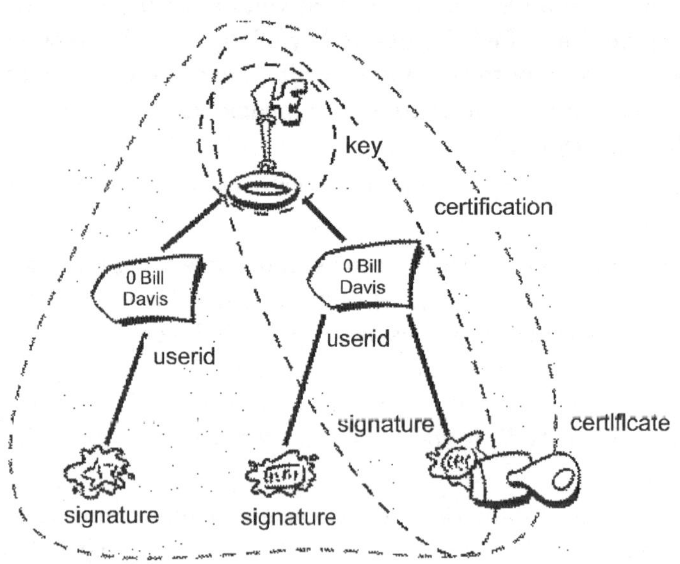

Figure 7.4 Anatomy of a certificate

7.3.1 Digital signature Mechanisms

The term digital signature is used to indicate a particular technique which can be used to provide security services such as non-repudiation and authentication. Digital signature mechanisms require the use of asymmetric cryptographic algorithms. The essential characteristic of the digital signature mechanism is that the signed data unit cannot be created without using the private key. This means that:

(a) the signed data unit cannot be created by any individual except the holder of the private key, and

(b) the recipient cannot create the signed data unit.

Therefore, using publicly available information only, it is possible to identify the signer of a data unit uniquely as the possessor of the private key. In the case of later conflict between participants it is thus possible to prove the identity of the signer of a data unit to a reliable third party, who is called upon to judge the authenticity of the signed data unit. This type of digital signature is called *direct signature scheme* (see Figure 7.5). In other cases, an additional property c) might be needed:

(c) the sender cannot deny sending the signed data unit.

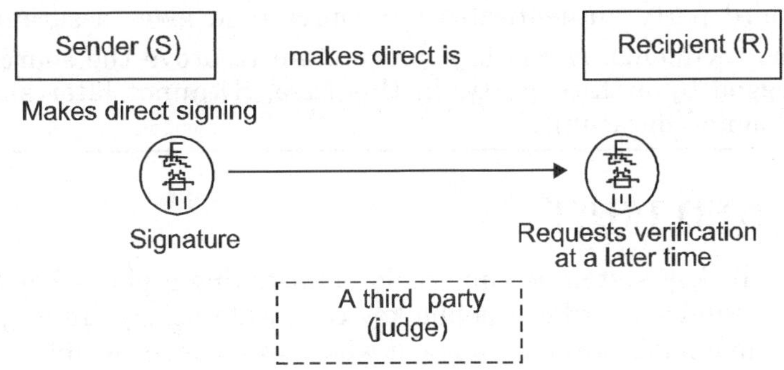

Note — Verifies the sigature when a conflict arises between the participants (S mau be a perjurer or R may be a perjurer)

Figure 7.5 Direct Signature Scheme

A reliable third party (arbitrator) proves to the recipient the source and integrity of the information in this case.

This type of digital signature is sometimes arbitrated signature scheme (see Figure 7.6).

Note - The sender may require that the recipient cannot later deny receiving the signed data unit. This can be accomplished with a non-repudiation service with proof of delivery by means of an appropriate combination of digital signature, data integrity and notarization mechanisms.

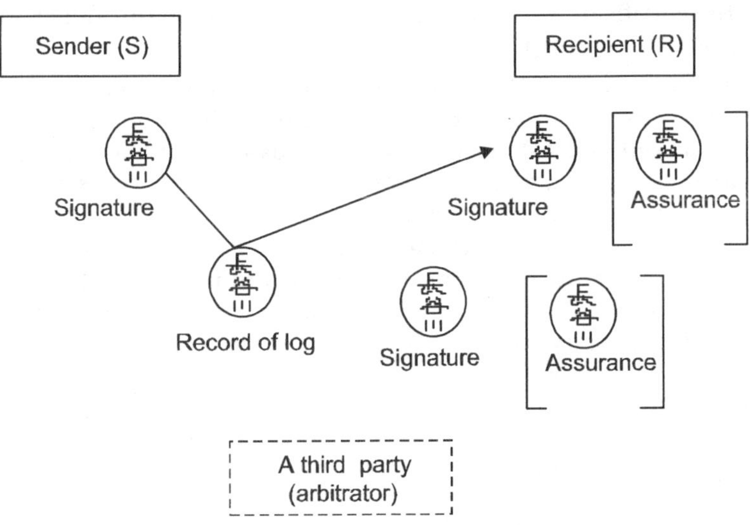

Figure 7.6 Arbitrated Signature Scheme

Note — A third party authenticates the source (and gives assurance (i.e., positive result) for the recipient). Necessary information to prove the source and integrity of data is logged by a third party. In this case, S cannot later successfully deny sending the signed data unit.

7.4 VALIDITY AND TRUST

Every user in a public key system is vulnerable to mistaking a phony key (certificate) for a real one. Validity is confidence that a public key certificate belongs to its purported owner. Validity is essential in a public key environment where you must constantly establish whether or not a particular certificate is authentic.

When you've assured yourself that a certificate belonging to someone else is valid, you can sign the copy on your keyring to attest to the fact that you've checked the certificate and that it's a good one. If you want others to know that you gave the certificate your stamp of approval, you can export the signature to a certificate server so that others can see it.

Some companies designate one or more Certification Authorities (CA), whose job it is to go around and check the validity of all the certificates in the organization and then sign the good ones. The CA is the Grand Pooh-bah of validation in an organization, whom everyone trusts, and in some public key environments, no certificate is considered valid unless it has been attested to by a CA.

7.5 CHECKING VALIDITY

One way to establish validity is to go through some manual process. There are several ways to accomplish this. You could require your intended recipient to physically hand you a copy of his or her public key. But this is often inconvenient and inefficient. Another way is to manually check the certificate's fingerprint. Just as every human's fingerprints are unique, every PGP certificate's fingerprint is unique.

The fingerprint is a hash of the user's certificate and appears as one of the certificate's properties. You can check that a certificate is valid by calling the key's owner (so that you originate the transaction) and asking the owner to read his or her key's fingerprint to you and verifying that fingerprint against the one you believe to be the real one. This works if you know the owner's voice, but, how do you manually verify the identity of someone you don't know? Some people put the fingerprint of their key on their business cards for this very reason. Another way to establish validity of someone's certificate is to trust that a third individual has gone through the process of validating it. A CA, for example, is responsible for ensuring that prior to assigning validity to a certificate, he or she carefully checks it to be sure it belongs to the purported owner. Anyone who trusts the CA will automatically consider any certificates validated by the CA to be valid.

7.6 ESTABLISHING TRUST

You validate keys. You trust people. More specifically, you trust people to validate other people' keys. Typically, unless the owner hands you the certificate, you have to go by someone else's word that it is valid.

7.6.1 Meta and Trusted Introducers

In most situations, people completely trust the CA to establish certificates' validity. This means that everyone else relies upon the CA to go through the whole manual validation process for them. This is fine up to a certain number of users or number of work sites, and then it may not be possible for the CA to maintain the same level of quality validation. In that case, adding other validators to the system is necessary.

A CA can also be a meta-introducer. A meta-introducer bestows not only validity on keys, but bestows the ability to trust keys upon others. Similar to the king who hands his seal to his trusted advisors so they can act on his authority, the meta-introducer enables others to act as trusted introducers. These trusted introducers can validate keys to the same effect as that of the meta-introducer. They cannot, however, create new trusted introducers.

Trust models

In relatively closed systems, such as within a company, it is easy to trace a path of trust back to the root CA. However, in the real world, users must often communicate with people outside of their corporate environment, including some whom they have never met, such as vendors, customers, clients, associates, and so on. Establishing a line of trust to those who have not been explicitly trusted by a CA is difficult.

Companies follow one or another trust model, which dictates how users will go about establishing key validity. There are three different models:

- Direct Trust
- Hierarchical Trust
- A Web of Trust

(1) Direct Trust

Direct trust is the simplest trust model. In this model, a user trusts that a key is valid because he or she knows where it came from. All cryptosystems use this form of trust in some way. For example, in web browsers, the root Certification Authority keys are directly trusted because they were shipped by the manufacturer. If there is any form of hierarchy, it extends from these directly trusted certificates.

In PGP, a user who validates keys herself and never sets another certificate to be a trusted introducer is using direct trust.

(2) Hierarchical Trust

In a hierarchical system, there are a number of "root" certificates from which trust extends. These certificates may certify certificates themselves, or they may certify certificates that certify still other certificates down some chain. Consider it as a big trust "tree." The "leaf" certificate's validity is verified by tracing backward from its certifier, to other certifiers, until a directly trusted root certificate is found.

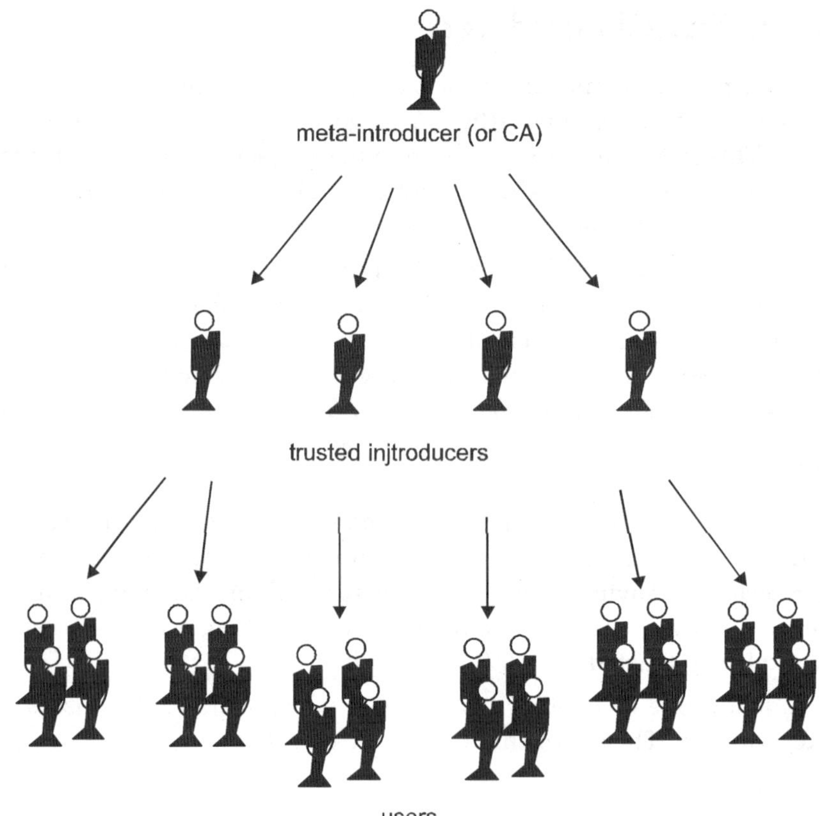

Figure 7.7 Hierarchical Trust

(3) Web of Trust

A web of trust encompasses both of the other models, but also adds the notion that trust is in the eye of the beholder (which is the real-world view) and the idea that more information is better. It is thus a cumulative trust model. A certificate might be trusted directly, or trusted in some chain going back to a directly trusted root certificate (the meta-introducer), or by some group of introducers.

Perhaps you've heard of the term six degrees of separation, which suggests that any person in the world can determine some link to any other person in the world using six or fewer other people as intermediaries. This is a web of introducers.

It is also the PGP view of trust. PGP uses digital signatures as its form of introduction. When any user signs another's key, he or she becomes an introducer of that key. As this process goes on, it establishes a web of trust.

In a PGP environment, any user can act as a certifying authority. Any PGP user can validate another PGP user's public key certificate. However, such a certificate is only valid to another user if the relying party recognizes the validator as a trusted introducer. (That is, you trust my opinion that others' keys are valid only if you consider me to be a trusted introducer. Otherwise, my opinion on other keys' validity is moot.)

Stored on each user's public keyring are indicators of :

- whether or not the user considers a particular key to be valid
- the level of trust the user places on the key that the key's owner can serve as certifier of others' keys

You indicate, on your copy of my key, whether you think my judgement counts. It's really a reputation system: certain people are reputed to give good signatures, and people trust them to attest to other keys' validity.

7.6.2 Levels of Trust in PGP

The highest level of trust in a key, implicit trust, is trust in your own key pair. PGP assumes that if you own the private key, you must trust the actions of its related public key. Any keys signed by your implicitly trusted key are valid.

There are three levels of trust you can assign to someone else's public key:

- Complete trust
- Marginal trust
- No trust (or Untrusted)

To make things confusing, there are also three levels of validity:

- Valid
- Marginally valid
- Invalid

To define another's key as a trusted introducer, you

1. Start with a valid key, one that is either
   - signed by you or
   - signed by another trusted introducer and then
2. Set the level of trust you feel the key's owner is entitled.

For example, suppose your key ring contains Alice's key. You have validated Alice's key and you indicate this by signing it. You know that Alice is a real stickler for validating others' keys. You therefore assign her key with Complete trust. This makes Alice a Certification Authority. If Alice signs another's key, it appears as Valid on your keyring.

PGP requires one Completely trusted signature or two Marginally trusted signatures to establish a key as valid. PGP's method of considering two Marginals equal to one Complete is similar to a merchant asking for two forms of ID. You might consider Alice fairly trustworthy and also consider Bob fairly trustworthy. Either one alone runs the risk of accidentally signing a counterfeit key, so you might not place complete trust in either one. However, the odds that both individuals signed the same phony key are probably small.

Although they facilitate many of the desired attributes of electronic commerce—such as speed of transactions and reduced paper-work—digital signatures are still not a widely-accepted concept in India. Because of the technicalities involved this is very much the norm, except in certain cases where the use of digital signatures has been mandated by law, such as filings with the Ministry of Company Affairs.

Though the concept of digital signatures is a powerful tool, it has been difficult to move the concept from theory to reality because of multiple reasons. Some of the reasons include cultural reticence, unequal access to technology, and the lack of an adequate legal and service infrastructure to support such a major shift. In India, paper-based documents continue to be seen as more trustworthy than electronic ones largely because they are tangible and people are used to them.

7.7 PASSPHRASE

Most people are familiar with restricting access to computer systems via a password, which is a unique string of characters that a user types in as an identification code.

A passphrase is a longer version of a password, and in theory, a more secure one. Typically composed of multiple words, a passphrase is more secure against standard dictionary attacks, wherein the attacker tries all the words in the dictionary in an attempt to determine your password. The best passphrases are relatively long and complex and contain a combination of upper and lowercase letters, numeric and punctuation characters.

PGP uses a passphrase to encrypt your private key on your machine. Your private key is encrypted on your disk using a hash of your passphrase as the secret key. You use the passphrase to decrypt and use your private key. A passphrase should be hard for you to forget and difficult for others to guess. It should be something already firmly embedded in your long-term memory, rather than something you make up from scratch. Why? Because if you forget your passphrase, you are out of luck. Your private key is totally and absolutely useless without your passphrase and nothing can be done about it.

Remember the quote earlier in this chapter? PGP is cryptography that will keep major governments out of your files. It will certainly keep you out of your files, too. Keep that in mind when you decide to change your passphrase to the punchline of that joke you can never quite remember.

7.8 KEY SPLITTING

They say that a secret is not a secret if it is known to more than one person. Sharing a private key pair poses such a problem. While it is not a recommended practice, sharing a private key pair is necessary at times. Corporate Signing Keys, for example, are private keys used by a company to sign—for example—legal documents, sensitive personnel information, or press releases to authenticate their origin. In such a case, it is worthwhile for multiple members of the company to have access to the private key. However, this means that any single individual can act fully on behalf of the company.

In such a case it is wise to split the key among multiple people in such a way that more than one or two people must present a piece of the key in order to reconstitute it to a usable condition. If too few pieces of the key are available, then the key is unusable.

Some examples are to split a key into three pieces and require two of them to reconstitute the key, or split it into two pieces and require both pieces. If a secure network connection is used during the reconstitution process, the key's shareholders need not be physically present in order to rejoin the key.

7.9 HOW DO DIGITAL TIMESTAMPS SUPPORT DIGITAL SIGNATURES?

Consider two questions that may be asked by a computer user as he or she views a digital document or on-line record.

(1) Who is the author of this record - who wrote it, approved it, or consented to it?

(2) When was this record created or last modified?

In both cases, the question is one about exactly this record-exactly this sequence of bits - whether it was first stored on this computer or was created somewhere else and then copied and saved here. An answer to the first question tells who & what: who approved exactly what is in this record? An answer to the second question tells when & what: when exactly did the contents of this record first exist?

Both of the above questions have good solutions. A system for answering the first question is called a digital signature scheme. Such a system was first proposed in and there is a wide variety of accepted designs for an implementation of this kind of system. A system for answering the second question is called a digital timestamping scheme.

Any system allowing users to answer these questions reliably for all their records must include two different sorts of procedures. First, there must be a certification procedure with which

(1) the author of a record can "sign" the record, or

(2) any user can fix a record in time. The result of this procedure is a small certifying file, a certificate if you will, that captures the result of this procedure. Second, there must be a verification procedure by which any user can check a record and its accompanying certificate to make sure it correctly answers

(a) who and what? or

(b) when and what? about the record in question.

The "certificate" returned by the certification procedure of a digital signature system is usually called a signature ; it is a signature for a particular signer (specifying whom) and for a particular record (specifying what). In order to be able to "sign" documents, a user registers with the system by using special software to compute a pair of numbers called keys - a public key and a corresponding private key. The private key should only be available to the user to whom it belongs, and is used (by the certification or "signing" procedure) in order to sign documents; it is by employing the user's private key that the signature and the record are tied to that particular user. The public key may be available to many users of the system, and is used by the verification procedure. That is, the verification procedure takes a particular record, a particular user's public key, and a putative signature for that record and that user, and uses this information to check whether the would-be signature was correctly computed using that record and the corresponding private key.

Special computational methods are employed for signing documents and for verifying documents and signatures; when these methods are carefully implemented, they have the remarkable property that the knowledge of a user's public key does not enable an attacker or hacker to figure out the user's corresponding private key. Of course, if, either through carelessness or deliberate intent, someone else - a hacker, for example - gains access to the user's private key, then this person will be able to "forge" the legitimate user's signatures on documents of the hacker's choice. At that point, even the value of legitimately signed records can be called into question.

The "certificate" returned by the certification procedure of a digital timestamping system is a certificate for a particular record (specifying what) at a particular time (specifying when). The procedure works by mathematically linking the bits of the record to a "summary number" that is widely witnessed by and widely available to members of the public - including, of course, users of the system. The computational methods employed ensure that only the record in question can be linked, according to the "instructions" contained in its timestamp certificate, to this widely witnessed summary number; this is how the particular record is tied to a particular moment in time. The verification procedure takes a particular record and a putative timestamp certificate for that record and a particular time, and uses this information to validate whether that record was indeed certified at the time claimed by checking it against the widely available summary number for that moment.

Two features of a digital timestamping system are particularly helpful in enhancing the integrity of a digital signature system. First, a timestamping system cannot be compromised by the disclosure of a key. This is because digital timestamping systems do not rely on keys, or any other secret information, for that matter. Second, digital timestamp certificates can be renewed so as to remain valid indefinitely.

With these features in mind, consider the following situations.

It sometimes happens that the connection between a person and his or her public signature key must be revoked - for example, if the user's secure access to the private key is accidentally compromised; or when the key belongs to a job or role in an organization that the person no longer holds. Therefore the person-key connection must have time limits, and the signature verification procedure should check that the record was signed at a time when the signer's public key was indeed in effect. And thus when a user signs a record that may be checked some time later - perhaps after the user's key is no longer in effect - the combination of the record and its signature should be certified with a secure digital timestamping service.

There is another situation in which a user's public key may be revoked. Consider the case of the signer of a particularly important document who later wishes to repudiate his signature. By dishonestly reporting the compromise of his private key, so that all his signatures are called into question, the user is able to disavow the signature he regrets. However, if the document in question was digitally timestamped together with its signature (and key-revocation reports are timestamped as well), then the signature cannot be disavowed in this way. This is the recommended procedure, therefore, in order to preserve the non-repudiability desired of digital signatures for important documents.

The statement that private keys cannot be derived from public keys is an over-simplification of a more complicated situation. In fact, this claim depends on the computational difficulty of certain mathematical problems. As the state of the art advances - both the current state of algorithmic knowledge, as well as the computational speed and memory available in currently available computers - the maintainers of a digital signature system will have to make sure that signers use longer and longer keys. But what is to become of documents that were signed using key lengths that are no longer considered secure? If the signed document is digitally timestamped, then its integrity can be maintained even after a particular key length is no longer considered secure.

Of course, digital timestamp certificates also depend for their security on the difficulty of certain computational tasks concerned with one-way hash functions (see Question 94). (All practical digital signature systems depend on these functions as well.) The maintainers of a secure digital timestamping service will have to remain abreast of the state of the art in building and in attacking one-way hash functions. Over time, they will need to upgrade their implementation of these functions, as part of the process of renewal This will allow timestamp certificates to remain valid indefinitely.

7.10 DIGITAL SIGNATURE STANDARD (DSS)

The Digital Signature Algorithm (DSA) was published by the National Institute of Standards and Technology (NIST) in the Digital Signature Standard (DSS), which is a part of the U.S. government's Capstone project DSS was selected by NIST, in cooperation with the NSA , to be the digital authentication standard of the U.S. government. The standard was issued on May 19, 1994.

DSA is based on the discrete logarithm problem and derives from cryptosystems proposed by Schnorr and ElGamal. It is for authentication only.

In DSA, signature generation is faster than signature verification, whereas in RSA, signature verification is faster than signature generation (if the public and private exponents, respectively, are chosen for this property, which is the usual case). NIST claims that it is an advantage of DSA that signing is faster, but many people in cryptography think that it is better for verification to be the faster operation.

DSA has been criticized by the computer industry since its announcement. Criticism has focused on a few main issues: it lacks key exchange capability; the underlying cryptosystem is too recent and has been subject to too little scrutiny for users to be confident of its strength; verification of signatures with DSA is too slow; the existence of a second authentication standard will cause hardship to computer hardware and software vendors, who have already standardized on RSA; and the process by which NIST chose DSA was too secretive and arbitrary, with too much influence wielded by NSA. Other criticisms were addressed by NIST by modifying the original proposal.

DSS was annonced as Federal Information Processing Standards Publications (FIPS PUBS) issued by the National Institute of Standards and Technology (NIST) after approval by the Secretary of Commerce pursuant to Section 5131 of the Information Technology Management Reform Act of 1996 (Public Law 104- 106), and the Computer Security Act of 1987 (Public Law 100-235).

This Standard specifies algorithms appropriate for applications requiring a digital, rather than written, signature. A digital signature is represented in a computer as a string of binary digits. A digital signature is computed using a set of rules and a set of parameters such that the identity of the signatory and integrity of the data can be verified. An algorithm provides the capability to generate and verify signatures. Signature generation makes use of a private key to generate a digital signature. Signature verification makes use of a public key which corresponds to, but is not the same as, the private key. Each user possesses a private and public key pair. Public keys are assumed to be known to the public in general. Private keys are never shared. Anyone can verify the signature of a user by employing that user's public key. Signature generation can be performed only by the possessor of the user's private key.

A hash function is used in the signature generation process to obtain a condensed version of data, called a message digest (see Figure 7.8).

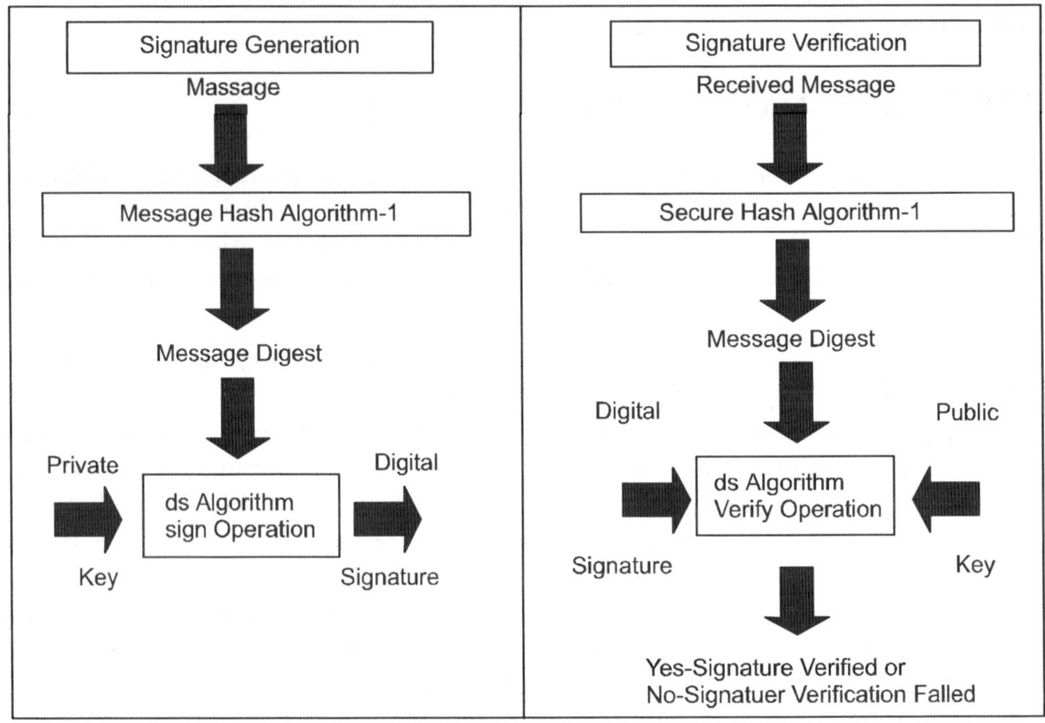

Figure 7.8 Message Digesting

The message digest is then input to the digital signature (ds) algorithm to generate the digital signature. The digital signature is sent to the intended verifier along with the signed data (often called the message). The verifier of the message and signature verifies the signature by using the sender's public key. The same hash function must also be used in the verification process. The hash function is specified in a separate standard, the Secure Hash Standard (SHS), FIPS 180-1. FIPS approved ds algorithms must be implemented with the SHS. Similar procedures may be used to generate and verify signatures for stored as well as transmitted data.This standard shall be used in designing and implementing public-key based signature systems that Federal departments and agencies operate or which are operated for them under contract.

Applications: A digital signature (ds) algorithm authenticates the integrity of the signed data and the identity of the signatory. A ds algorithm may also be used in proving to a third party that data was actually signed by the generator of the signature. A ds algorithm is intended for use in electronic mail, electronic funds transfer, electronic data interchange, software distribution, data storage, and other applications that require data integrity assurance and data origin authentication.A ds algorithm may be implemented in software firmware, hardware or any combination thereof.

When a message is received, the recipient may desire to verify that the message has not been altered in transit. Furthermore, the recipient may wish to be certain of the originator's identity. Both of these services can be provided by a ds algorithm. A digital signature is an electronic analoge of a written signature in that the digital signature can be used in proving to the recipient or a third party that the message was, in fact, signed by the originator. Digital signatures may also be generated for stored data and programs so that the integrity of the data and programs may be verified at any later time.

This publication prescribes two algorithms suitable for digital signature generation and verification.

7.11 DIGITAL SIGNATURE (DS) ALGORITHM

A ds algorithm is used by a signatory to generate a digital signature on data and by a verifier to verify the authenticity of the signature. Each signatory has a public and private key. The private key is used in the signature generation process and the public key is used in the signature verification process. For both signature generation and verification, the data which is referred to as a message,M, is reduced by means of the Secure Hash Algorithm (SHA-1) specified in FIPS 180-1. An adversary, who does not know the private key of the signatory, cannot generate the correct signature of the signatory. In other words, signatures cannot be forged. However, by using the signatory's public key, anyone can verify a correctly signed message. A means of associating public and private key pairs to the corresponding users is required. That is, there must be a binding of a user's identity and the user's public key. This binding may be certified by a mutually trusted party. For example, a certifying authority could sign credentials containing a user's public key and identity to form a certificate. Systems for certifying credentials and distributing certificates are beyond the scope of this standard. NIST intends to publish separate document(s) on certifying credentials and distributing certificates.

7.12 DSA PARAMETERS

The DSA makes use of the following parameters:

1. p = a prime modulus, where $2^\wedge_{L-1} < p < 2^\wedge_L$ for $512 \leq L \leq 1024$ and L a multiple of 64
2. q = a prime divisor of p - 1, where $2^\wedge_{159} < q < 2^\wedge_{160}$

3. $g = h^{(p-1)/q} \bmod p$, where h is any integer with $1 < h < p - 1$ such that $h^{(p-1)/q} \bmod p > 1$ (g has order q mod p)
4. x = a randomly or pseudorandomly generated integer with $0 < x < q$
5. $y = gx \bmod p$
6. k = a randomly or pseudorandomly generated integer with $0 < k < q$

The integers p, q, and g can be public and can be common to a group of users. A user's private and public keys are x and y, respectively. They are normally fixed for a period of time. Parameters x and k are used for signature generation only, and must be kept secret. Parameter k must be regenerated for each signature.

Parameters p and q shall be generated as specified in Appendix 2, or using other FIPS approved security methods. Parameters x and k shall be generated as specified in Appendix 3, or using other FIPS approved security methods.

7.13 DSA SIGNATURE GENERATION

The signature of a message M is the pair of numbers r and s computed according to the equations below:

$$r = (g^{k} \bmod p) \bmod q \text{ and}$$

$$s = (k^{-1} (\text{SHA-1}(M) + xr)) \bmod q.$$

In the above, k^{-1} is the multiplicative inverse of k, mod q; i.e., $(k\text{-}1\ k) \bmod q = 1$ and $0 < k\text{-}1 < q$. The value of SHA-1(M) is a 160-bit string output by the Secure Hash Algorithm specified in FIPS 180-1.

For use in computing s, this string must be converted to an integer.

As an option, one may wish to check if $r = 0$ or $s = 0$. If either $r = 0$ or $s = 0$, a new value of k should be generated and the signature should be recalculated (it is extremely unlikely that $r = 0$ or $s = 0$ if signatures are generated properly).

The signature is transmitted along with the message to the verifier.

7.14 DSA SIGNATURE VERIFICATION

Prior to verifying the signature in a signed message, p, q and g plus the sender's public key and identity are made available to the verifier in an authenticated manner.

Let M′, r′, and s′ be the received versions of M, r, and s, respectively, and let y be the public key of the signatory. To verify the signature, the verifier first checks to see that $0 < r' < q$ and $0 < s' < q$; if either condition is violated the signature shall be rejected. If these two conditions are satisfied, the verifier computes

$$w = (s')^{-1} \bmod q$$

$$u1 = ((\text{SHA-1}(M'))w) \bmod q$$

$$u2 = ((r')w) \bmod q$$

$$v = (((g)^{u1} (y)^{u2}) \bmod p) \bmod q.$$

If v = r′, then the signature is verified and the verifier can have high confidence that the received message was sent by the party holding the secret key x corresponding to y. For a proof that v = r′

when M′ = M, r′ = r, and s′ = s, see Appendix 1.

If v does not equal r′, then the message may have been modified, the message may have been incorrectly signed by the signatory, or the message may have been signed by an impostor. The message should be considered invalid.

7.15 RSA DIGITAL SIGNATURE ALGORITHM

The RSA ds algorithm is a FIPS approved cryptographic algorithm for digital signature generation and verification. This is described in ANSI X9.31.

7.16 ELLIPTIC CURVE DIGITAL SIGNATURE ALGORITHM (ECDSA)

The ECDSA ds algorithm is a FIPS approved cryptographic algorithm for digital signature generation and verification. ECDSA is the elliptic curve analogue of the DSA. ECDSA is described in ANSI X9.62. The recommended elliptic curves for Federal Government use are included in Appendix 6.

APPENDIX 1. A PROOF THAT v = r′ IN THE DSA

This appendix is for informational purposes only and is not required to meet the standard. The purpose of this appendix is to show that in the DSA, if M′ = M, r′ = r and s′ = s in the signature verification then v = r′. We need the following easy result.

LEMMA. Let p and q be primes so that q divides p - 1, h a positive integer less than p, and g = h^$_{(p-1)/q}$ mod p. Then g^q mod p = 1, and if m mod q = n mod q, then g^m mod p = g^n mod p.

Proof: We have

G^q mod p = (h^(p-1)/q mod p)q mod p = h(p-1) mod p = 1 by Fermat's Little Theorem. Now let m mod q = n mod q, i.e., m = n + kq for some integer k. Then

g^m mod p = g^n+kq mod p = (g^n g^kq) mod p

= ((g^n mod p) (g^q mod p)^k) mod p

= g^n mod p

since g^q mod p = 1. n

We are now ready to prove the main result.

THEOREM. If M′ = M, r′ = r, and s′ = s in the signature verification, then v = r′.

Proof: We have

w = (s′)^-1 mod q = s^-1 mod q

u1 = ((SHA-1(M′))w) mod q = ((SHA-1(M))w) mod q

u2 = ((r′)w) mod q = (rw) mod q.

Now y = g^x mod p, so that by the lemma,

v = ((g^u1 y^u2) mod p) mod q
= ((gSHA-1^(M)w y^rw) mod p) mod q
= ((gSHA-1^(M)w g^xrw) mod p) mod q
= ((g(SHA-1^(M)+xr)w) mod p) mod q.

Also

s = (k^-1 (SHA-1(M) + xr)) mod q.

Hence

w = (k(SHA-1(M) + xr)^-1) mod q

(SHA-1(M) + xr)w mod q = k mod q.

Thus by the lemma,

v = (g^ mod p) mod q
= r
= r′

GENERATION OF PRIMES FOR THE DSA

This appendix includes algorithms for generating the primes p and q used in the DSA. These algorithms require a random number generator , and an efficient modular exponentiation algorithm. Generation of p and q shall be performed as specified in this appendix, or using other FIPS approved security methods.

7.17. A PROBABILISTIC PRIMALITY TEST

In order to generate the primes p and q, a primality test is required.

There are several fast probabilistic algorithms available. The following algorithm is a simplified version of a procedure due to M.O. Rabin, based in part on ideas of Gary L. Miller. If this algorithm is iterated n times, it will produce a false prime with probability no greater than ¼^n.

Therefore, $n \geq 50$ will give an acceptable probability of error. To test whether an integer is prime:

Step 1. Set i = 1 and $n \geq 50$.

Step 2. Set w = the integer to be tested, w = 1 + 2^am, where m is odd and 2^a is the largest power of 2 dividing w - 1.

Step 3. Generate a random integer b in the range $1 < b < w$.

Step 4. Set j = 0 and z = b^m mod w.

Step 5. If j = 0 and z = 1, or if z = w - 1, go to step 9.

Step 6. If $j > 0$ and z = 1, go to step 8.

Step 7. j = j + 1. If $j < a$, set z = z^2 mod w and go to step 5.

Step 8. w is not prime. Stop.

Step 9. If $i < n$, set i = i + 1 and go to step 3. Otherwise, w is probably prime.

7.18. GENERATION OF PRIMES

The DSS requires two primes, p and q, satisfying the following three conditions:

a. 2159 < q < 2160

b. 2L-1 < p < 2L for a specified L, where L = 512 + 64j for some 0 < or = to j < or = to 8

c. q divides p - 1.

This prime generation scheme starts by using the SHA and a user supplied SEED to construct a prime, q, in the range 2159 < q < 2160. Once this is accomplished, the same SEED value is used to construct an X in the range 2L-1 < X < 2L. The prime, p, is then formed by rounding X to a number congruent to 1 mod 2q as described below.

An integer x in the range 0 < or = to x < 2g may be converted to a g-long sequence of bits by using its binary expansion as shown below:

x = x1*2g-1 + x2*2g-2 + ... + xg-1*2 + xg -> { x1,...,xg }.

Conversely, a g-long sequence of bits { x1,...,xg } is converted to an integer by the rule

{ x1,...,xg } -> x1*2g-1 + x2*2g-2 + ... + xg-1*2 + xg.

Note that the first bit of a sequence corresponds to the most significant bit of the corresponding integer and the last bit to the least significant bit.

Let L - 1 = n*160 + b, where both b and n are integers and 0 < or = to b < 160.

Step 1. Choose an arbitrary sequence of at least 160 bits and call it SEED. Let g be the length of SEED in bits.

Step 2. Compute

U = SHA[SEED] XOR SHA[(SEED+1) mod 2g].

Step 3. Form q from U by setting the most significant bit (the 2^{159} bit) and the least significant bit to 1. In terms of boolean operations, q = U OR 2159 OR 1. Note that 2^{159} < q < 2160.

Step 4. Use a robust primality testing algorithm to test whether q is prime12(1).

Step 5. If q is not prime, go to step 1.

Step 6. Let counter = 0 and offset = 2.

Step 7. For k = 0,...,n let

Vk = SHA[(SEED + offset + k) mod 2g].

Step 8. Let W be the integer

W = V0/font> + V1*2160 + ... + Vn-1*2(n-1)*160 + (Vn mod 2b) * 2n*160

and let X = W + 2L-1. Note that 0 < or = to W < 2L-1 and hence 2L-1 < or = to X < 2L.

Step 9. Let c = X mod 2q and set p = X - (c - 1). Note that p is congruent to 1 mod 2q.

Step 10. If p < 2L-1, then go to step 13.

Step 11. Perform a robust primality test on p.

Step 12. If p passes the test performed in step 11, go to step 15.

Step 13. Let counter = counter + 1 and offset = offset + n + 1.

Step 14. If counter > or = to 212 = 4096 go to step 1, otherwise (i.e. if counter < 4096) go to step 7.

Step 15. Save the value of SEED and the value of counter for use in certifying the proper generation of p and q.

---

(1) A robust primality test is one where the probability of a non-prime number passing the test is at most $2^{-80.}$

8

Authentication Application

8.1 AUTHENTICATION IN APPLICATIONS

Now that the overview of various authentication methods has been outlined, you can take a look at its use in the applications. The following application-specific areas will be covered for learning Applications and Authentication:

- Identifying what needs authentication
- Choosing the appropriate authentication method(s)
- Guidelines for implementing authentication
- Identifying the Need for Authentication

The following questions help the application designer and developer understand whether there is a need for authentication within their application:

- Are there multiple users or applications that will interact with the application in question?
- If multiple entities are expected, will they all access exactly the same data, configuration, and information, or will each have its own set of information, regardless of how small?
- Is the application running in a completely closed and trusted area, wherein there is no person, system, or application that will access it from untrusted parts—such as the Internet, other networks, or unknown applications?
- Is there a concept of privileged information or functionality and the separation or isolation of this within the application?
- If the answer to any of these questions is "yes," authentication is needed within the application.

8.1.1 Choosing the Appropriate Authentication Methods

Usually, deciding if authentication is necessary is the easy part. Deciding how to perform authentication quite easily can become a difficult path. This section covers an overview of architectural frameworks for providing authentication. The following high-level options for authentication are available:

- Internal or local service-based authentication
- External service-based authentication and integration

8.1.2 Local Authentication

There are several reasons, or combinations of reasons, that may warrant implementation of local, internal authentication within an application:

- Stand-alone application
- No or intermittent communication capabilities
- Limited, small, or embedded applications
- Restricted application resources

If one chooses to have an application utilize its own authentication mechanism, there are several common examples:

- Implement a proprietary authentication scheme, based on standard methodologies
- Rely on the services of the local operating system, if available
- Utilize available libraries for providing authentication functionality

The implementation of one's own proprietary scheme is generally not recommended because there are many potential risks to a home-grown method, unless it has the benefit of expert research and analysis. If a proprietary scheme is absolutely necessary, it should ideally rely on the use of standard security technologies; examples are encryption and one-way functions, protocols, and formats—all of these technologies have been well vetted and are available for everyday use.

Most Operating Systems also have implementations of local authentication services. These include some of the following:

- Pluggable Authentication Modules (PAM)
- Unix/Windows authentication
- File-based authentication

Finally, as hinted above, when implementing authentication features in an application, from-scratch implementation of standard-based technologies should be avoided. There are several encryption libraries available, the most notable of which is OpenSSL (http://www.openssl.org), as well as those provided by the Operating System. More will be explained further in the article.

8.1.3 External Service-based Authentication and Integration

It is often desirable that an application co-exist with other applications and share common information, including authentication information. The selection of internal and/or local authentication can quickly preclude an application from integrating easily with an existing environment. Also, enterprise applications, or those that need to work within an enterprise environment, will likely need to rely on the services present, which include enterprise authentication. Authentication services at the global and enterprise levels often are part of larger directory structures and services. These include:

- LDAP
- Active Directory
- NIS/NIS+
- Kerberos

To work with these services and already installed environments, applications will have to make use of various libraries and interfaces to work with these systems and infrastructure. There are existing libraries for all of these services, in many different programming languages, that allow an application to work directly within the specific framework.8

If an application designer wants to work with standards-based and accepted authentication and other security services, it may be important to avoid a tight integration to one particular service or another. To leverage existing services and maintain flexibility, an application designer can look toward defined standards for general-purpose security services. The GSSAPI—the Generic Security Services API, is an defined set of standards that allows for a common interface to express security services—see RFCs 2743, 1509, and 1964 f8or further information. There exist GSSAPI bindings for the following authentication and security services, among others:

- Kerberos
- Active Directory
- LDAP

Another flexible framework is SASL, Simple Authentication and Security Layer. SASL is defined in RFC 2222. SASL provides a standard way to secure authentication across network channels. SASL works by defining a standard API with support for accessing numerous "mechanisms"—these are the defined series of challenges and responses for authentication, including the following:

- Basic authentication with cleartext passwords
- Hash-based authentication
- One-time passwords and keyed PINs
- Kerberos, via GSSAPI

8.1.4 Custom-defined authentication schemes

These APIs allow application designers to standardize on a common interface for managing security services such as authentication. This allows the application to more easily extend functionality to suppo rt new and different authentication methods, as well as to integrate different security services together in a uniform way as the application and its deployment grows.

8.1.5 Guidelines for Implementation

This section covers some general guidelines that are helpful during implementation of authentication services. The guidelines are organized into the following sections:

- Approaches to sensitive data
- Security strength versus business factors
- Usability
- Approaches to Sensitive Data

Sensitive data refers to any information that is used for authentication or that could be used to the detriment of the application, system, or environment if compromised. The proper handling of sensitive data can quickly increase or decrease the strength of an application. Sensitive data—which may include passwords, keys, or other personal information—can easily be used throughout the internals of an application and become unmanageable. Different internal aspects include:

- In-memory manipulation and storage of data
- Persistent storage
- Message passing—IPC, RPC, network communication

To manipulate data objects, structures, and variables that deal with sensitive information, the rule of thumb is to isolate and limit the use of the data and clear it as soon as operations are done. Isolation is often more difficult to achieve with current memory management, but could be achieved via separate processes and threads, as is commonly seen with privilege separation in applications. Limiting the use of sensitive information means working to keep it around for only as long as necessary. The most common example is the storage of clear-text passwords and credentials in variables. This data is often transformed into some other form such as a hash or ciphertext prior to use. Once the transformation is complete, the memory should be cleared (zeroed) and freed. For those languages that treat strings as immutable objects, care should be taken to use non-immutable buffers and arrays for their storage instead.

Persistent storage presents another challenge when working with sensitive data. One should not consider their local disk or other persistent storage mechanism to be a safe location; this is one of the most common misperceptions—that a local storage device is secure because it's inside of the system. The more correct philosophy to consider is that all local storage devices are easy ways for attackers to get your information. Therefore, if the information is sensitive and needs to be non-volatile, make sure it is done safely. This means encrypting data that needs to be reversed or viewed in plaintext, or hashing things that do not need to be viewed in plaintext. Also, for those bits of information that are encrypted, keys should ideally be stored elsewhere and not on the same storage device. There are also secure hardware devices for storing sensitive information. These include the tokens discussed above, as well as hardened devices meant explicitly for securely storing data.

Message passing with sensitive information should also leverage known-secure protocols. Network communications, especially, can be secured with protocols such as TLS/SSL. Inter-Process Communication (IPC) and Remote Procedure Calls (RPC) can be treated as network protocols, even if they are communicating on the same physical system. Eavesdropping on communications between processes can be done just as easily as that which is done over the network.

8.1.6 Security Strength Versus 77Business Factors

When deciding on an authentication mechanism, the natural pressures of deliverables, schedules, and customers can cause difficult decisions that often leave security out of the picture. The following table provides an easy comparison of the following aspects:

- **Ease of implementation:** This is how simple or complex the implementation can be, taking into consideration the availability of libraries and standards.
- **Ease of management:** The complexity of managing the authentication environment, considering users, addition, and removal of users, updating of credentials.
- **Ease of deployment:** The complexity of deploying the authentication technology across simple and advanced environments, considering hardware and software requirements.
- **Strength:** The overall security strength, considering methods of attack and compromise and inherent weaknesses, scalability over large environments.
- **Risk:** The correlation of other columns to generally categorize the risk the technology poses to an environment or organization. Considers historical weaknesses, availability of tested implementations and libraries, likelihood of attack.

The Internet is an open system, where the identity of the communicating partners is not easy to define. The communication path is non-physical, non-deterministic, and may include any number of eavesdropping and active interference possibilities. Furthermore, in a dialogue between two parties on the Internet, no party can control both sides of the communication channel or even the route between them – neither when sending nor when receiving.

Notwithstanding the presence of a recognized sender's name in a message, the receiver must consider that message as if it were from an unknown sender (i.e., was anonymously sent) until proven otherwise. When sending a message, the sender must always assume until proven otherwise that the message was not received by the intended recipient (i.e., was anonymously received), even if there is a return confirmation message. In addition, both sender and receiver must always assume that anyone (i.e.,anonymously) may have read or changed that message when it was routed from sender to receiver. Thus, Internet communication is much like anonymous postcards that are anonymously routed and answered . However, to be useful, these postcards, open for anyone to read, write, change, or discard, must carry messages between specific endpoints in a secure and private way.

The solution is to use encryption (to assure privacy) and digital certification (to assure that communication is happening between the desired endpoints and that it is tamperproof).

To be secure, Internet communications need both encryption and digital certification – for example, for ecommerce and Internet voting. Three most common digital certification methods in use today, which are based on X.509/PKIX Certificates and Certification Authorities (CAs), PGP and SKIP.

The certification methods are respectively classified as:

- Directory,
- Referral and
- Collaborative based.

For twoparties in a dialogue, the three methods are further classified as extrinsic because they depend on references which are outside the scope of the dialogue. A series of conceptual, legal and implementation flaws –including lack of suitability of purpose – is catalogued for each case, emphasizing X.509 and CAs.

8.1.7 Certification Methods

Public-key cryptography may give the impression that security can be simply achieved. It seems that one only has to distribute the public-key at will, with no need to control it, and anyone can receive secure messages. The same procedure being applied to each side, sender and receiver, both could immediately engage in secure communication.

However, who is at the other side? Is the key really from the sender? Is the key still valid? Questions soon appear and it becomes clear that public-key cryptography has indeed solved the problem of public-key security but not the problems of public-key acquisition, recognition, revocation, distribution, re-distribution, validation and, most importantly, key-binding to an identifier and/or key-attribution to a real-world entity.

In addition, communications can be verified neither for origin authentication (i.e., to verify whether the message was sent by the declared sender) nor for data-integrity authentication (i.e., to verify whether the message was changed after it was sent). Communications can be private but not secure.

Of course, a private communication with a fraudster is not secure just because it is private. Clearly, without binding the key to an identifier such as a person's common name, the key is just a byte string and can be yours as well as anyone else's. But common names or identifiers are oftentimes not enough.

For example, where legal capacities must be defined, one needs to have some assurances that the key can be attributed to one well-defined, real-world entity such as a person or company.

Certificates provide a strong binding between the public-key and some attribute (usually the entity's name and/or the entity's real-world identity). Certificates still entail all the previous questions, such as certificate acquisition, recognition, revocation, distribution, re-distribution, validation and, most importantly, what is the intended meaning of key-binding to an identifier and key-attribution to a real-world entity. And certificates insert new questions, namely the privacy concern for identifiers and real-world entities (e.g., an Internet voter).

However, certificates are very useful and their benefits may far outweigh the difficulties mentioned above. Certificates introduce tamperproof attributes which can be used as convenient references to help someone receiving a message decide whether that message, the key and possibly the sender's name are what they appear to be – without asking the sender.

Absolute certification methods are logically impossible because a certificate cannot certify itself. Even though various methods have been proposed to deal with this situation, for the sake of liability and validity analysis we can recognize three main classes as the author pointed out for the first time in 1997:

- Directory methods: X.509 and CA [X509a,-b], PKIX [PKIX]
- Referral methods: PGP [PGP]
- Collaborative methods: SKIP [SKIP]

Each of the above class presents a different certification paradigm (i.e., deals with certification questions in a different way), as analyzed in the following sections.

However, they have a common ground because for two parties in a dialogue they depend on references which are external to the dialogue between the parties. Hence, these certification methods are also called extrinsic.

8.2 KERBEROS

The Internet is an insecure place. Many of the protocols used in the Internet do not provide any security. Tools to "sniff" passwords off of the network are in common use by malicious hackers. Thus, applications which send an unencrypted password over the network are extremely vulnerable. Worse yet, other client/server applications rely on the client program to be "honest" about the identity of the user who is using it. Other applications rely on the client to restrict its activities to those which it is allowed to do, with no other enforcement by the server.

Kerberos is a computer network authentication protocol, which allows individuals communicating over a non-secure network to prove their identity to one another in a secure manner. It is also a suite of free software published by Massachusetts Institute of Technology (MIT) that implements this protocol. Its designers aimed primarily at a client-server model, and it provides mutual authentication — both the user and the server verify each other's identity. Kerberos protocol messages are protected against eavesdropping and replay attacks.

Kerberos [RFC 1510, Neuman 1994] is an authentication service developed at MIT that uses symmetric key encryption techniques and a Key Distribution Center. Although it is conceptually the same as the generic KDC but its vocabulary is slightly different. Kerberos also contains several nice variations and extensions of the basic KDC mechanisms. Kerberos was designed to authenticate users accessing network servers and was initially targeted for use within a single administrative domain such as a campus or company. Thus, Kerberos is framed in the language of users who want to access network services (servers) using application-level network programs such as Telnet (for remote login) and NFS (for access to remote files), rather than than human-to-human conversants who want to authenticate themselves to each other, as in our examples above. Nonetheless, the key (pun intentded) underlying techniques remains the same.

The Kerberos Authentication Server (AS) plays the role of the KDC. The AS is the repository of not only the secret keys of all users (so that each user can communicate securely with the AS) but also information about which users have access privileges to which services on which network servers.

Authorities in the United States classified Kerberos as a munition and banned its export because it used the DES encryption algorithm (with 56-bit keys). A non-US Kerberos 4 implementation, KTH-KRB developed at the Royal Institute of Technology in Sweden, made the system available outside the US before the US changed its cryptography export regulations (circa 2000). The Swedish implementation was based on a version called eBones. eBones was based on the exported MIT Bones release (stripped of both the encryption functions and the calls to them) based on version Kerberos 4 patch-level 9. This somewhat limited Kerberos was called the eBones release. A Kerberos version 5 implementation, Heimdal, was released by basically the same group of people releasing KTH-KRB.

Kerberos is designed to provide strong authentication for client/server applications by using secret-key cryptography. Kerberos is available in many commercial products as well.

- Windows 2000 and later use Kerberos as their default authentication method. Some Microsoft additions to the Kerberos suite of protocols are documented in RFC 3244 "Microsoft Windows 2000 Kerberos Change Password and Set Password Protocols". RFC 4757 documents Microsoft's use of the RC4 cipher. While Microsoft uses the Kerberos protocol, it does not use the MIT software.
- Apple's Mac OS X also uses Kerberos in both its client and server versions.
- Sun's Solaris also uses Kerberos in both its client and server versions.
- Red Hat Enterprise Linux 4 and later uses Kerberos in both client and server versions.

Some sites attempt to use firewalls to solve their network security problems. Unfortunately, firewalls assume that "the bad guys" are on the outside, which is often a very bad assumption. Most of the really damaging incidents of computer crime are carried out by insiders. Firewalls also have a significant disadvantage in that they restrict how your users can use the Internet. (After all, firewalls are simply a less extreme example of the dictum that there is nothing more secure then a computer which is not connected to the network — and powered off!) In many places, these restrictions are simply unrealistic and unacceptable.

Kerberos was created by MIT as a solution to these network security problems. The Kerberos protocol uses strong cryptography so that a client can prove its identity to a server (and vice versa) across an insecure network connection. After a client and server has used Kerberos to prove their identity, they can also encrypt all of their communications to assure privacy and data integrity as they go about their business.

Kerberos is freely available from MIT, under copyright permissions very similar those used for the BSD operating system and the X Window System. MIT provides Kerberos in source form so that anyone who wishes to use it may look over the code for themselves and assure themselves that the code is trustworthy. In addition, for those who prefer to rely on a professionally supported product, Kerberos is available as a product from many different vendors.Kerberos builds on symmetric key cryptography and requires a trusted third party. Extensions to Kerberos can provide for the use of public-key cryptography during certain phases of authentication.

The Kerberos protocol is used to allow users to log in securely to computers which belong to a network.This protocol assumes a network of computers, with one trusted computer or several verifying the identity of users to the computers to which they wish to log in, and supplying session keys so that the communications between the user and that computer can be encrypted.

When Anita wants to access a service on Bunty (who we now think of as a server), the protocol closely follows our example in Figure 8.1.

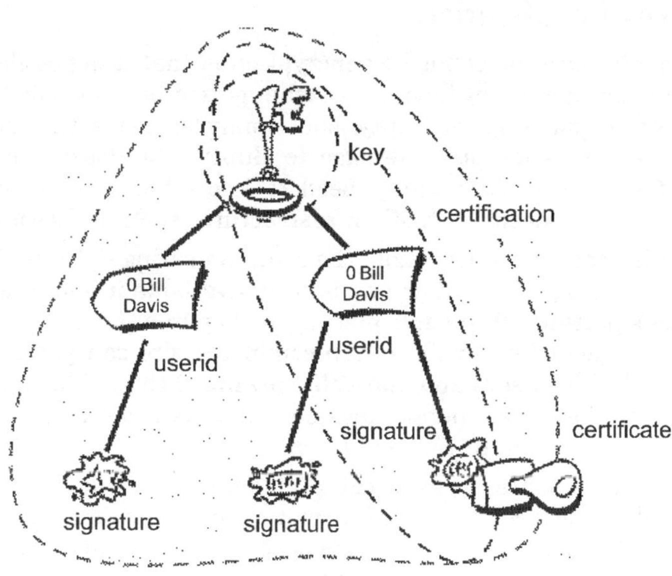

Figure 8.1

Anita contacts the Kerberos AS, indicating that she wants to use Bunty. All communication between Anita and the AS is encrypted using a secret key that is shared between Anita and the AS. In Kerberos, Anita first provides her name and password to her local host. Anita's local host and the AS then determine the one-time secret session key for encrypting communication between Anita and the AS.

The AS authenticates Anita, checks that she has access privileges to Bunty, and generates a one-time symmetric session key, R1, for communication between Anita and Bunty. The Authentication Server (in Kerberos parlance, now referred to as the Ticket Granting Server) sends Anita the value of R1, and also a ticket to Bunty's services. The ticket contains Anita's name, the one-time session key, R1, and an expiration time, all encrypted using Bunty's secret key (known only by Bunty and the AS), as in Figure 8.1. Anita's ticket is valid only until its expiration time, and will be rejected by Bunty is presented after that time. For Kerberos V4, the maximum lifetime of a ticket is about 21 hours. In Kerberos V5, the lifetime must expire before the end of year 9999 - a definite Y10K problem!

Anita then sends her ticket to Bunty. She also sends along an R1-encrypted timestamp that is used as a nonce. Bunty decrypts the ticket using his secret key, obtains the session key, decrypts the timestamp using the just-learned session key. Bunty sends back the timestamp value plus one (in Kerberos V5) or simply the timestamp itself (in Kerberos V5).

The most recent version of Kerberos (V5) provides support for multiple Authentication Servers, delegation of access rights, and renewable tickets.

8.2.1 Public Key Certification

One of the principle features of public key encryption is that it is possible for two entities to exchange secret messages without having to exchange secret keys. For example, when Anita wants to send a secret message to Bunty, she simply encrypts the message with Bunty's public key and sends the encrypted message to Bunty; she doesn't need to know Bunty's secret (i.e., private) key, nor does Bunty need to know her secrect key. Thus, public key cryptography obviates the need for KDC infrastructure, such as Kerberos.

Of course, with public key encryption, the communicating entities still have to exchange public keys. A user can make its public key pubicly available in many ways, e.g., by posting the key on the user's personal Web page, placing the key in a public key server, or by sending the key to a correspondent by e-mail. A Web commerce site can place its public key on its server in a manner that browsers automatically download the public key when connecting to the site. Routers can place their public keys on public key servers, thereby allowing other browsers and network entities to retrieve them.

There is, however, a subtle, yet critical, problem with public key cryptography. To gain insight to this problem, let's consider an Internet commerce example. Suppose that Anita is in the pizza delivery business and she accepts orders over the Internet. Bunty, a pizza lover, sends Anita a plaintext message which includes his home address and the type of pizza he wants. In this message, Bunty also includes a digital signature (e.g.,, an encrypted message digest for the original plaintext message). Anita can obtain Bunty's public key (from his personal Web page, a public key server, or from an e-mail message) and verify the digital signature. In this manner Anita makes sure that Bunty (rather than some adolescent prankster) indeed made the order.

This all sounds fine until clever Trudy comes along. As shown in Figure 8.2, Trudy decides to play a prank. Trudy sends a message to Anita in which she says she is Bunty, gives Bunty's home address, and orders a pizza. She also attaches a digital signature, but she attaches the signature by signing the message digest with her (i.e., Trudy's) private key. Trudy also masquerades as Bunty by sending Anita Trudy's public key but saying that it belongs to Bunty. In this example, also will apply Trudy's public key (thinking that it is Bunty's) to the digital signature and conclude that the plaintext message was indeed created by Bunty. Bunty will be very surprised when the delivery person brings to his home a pizza with everything on it! The man-in-the-middle attack is the room cause of our difficulties.

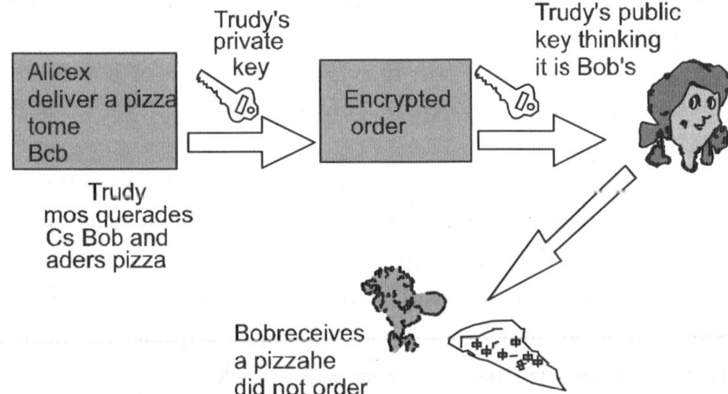

Figure 8.2 Trudy masquerades as Bunty using public key cryptography.

We see from this example that in order for public key cryptography to be useful, entities (users, browsers, routers, etc.) need to know for sure that they have the public key of the entity with which they are communicating. For example, when Anita is communicating with Bunty using public key cryptography, she needs to know for sure that the public key that is supposed to be Bunty's is indeed Bunty's.

Binding a public key to a particular entity is typically done by a certification authority (CA), which validates identities and issue certificates. A CA has the following roles:

• First to verify that entity (a person, a router, etc) is who it says it is. There are no mandated procedures for how certification is done. When dealing with a CA, one must trust the CA to have performed a suitably rigorous identity verification. For example, if Trudy were able to walk into Fly-by-Night Certificate Authority and simply announce "I am Anita" and receive keys associated with the identity of "Anita," then one shouldn't put much faith in public keys offered by the Fly-by-Night Certificate Authority. On the other hand, one might (or might not!) be more willing to trust a CA that is part of a federal- or state-sponsored program One can trust the "identify" associated with a public key only to the extent that one can trust a CA and its identity verification techniques. What a tangled web of trust we spin!

Once the CA verifies the entity of the entity, the CA creates a certificate that binds the public key of the identiy to the identity. The certificate contains the public key and identifying information about the owner of the public key (for example a human name or an IP address). The certificate is digitally signed by the CA. These steps are shown in Figure 8.3.

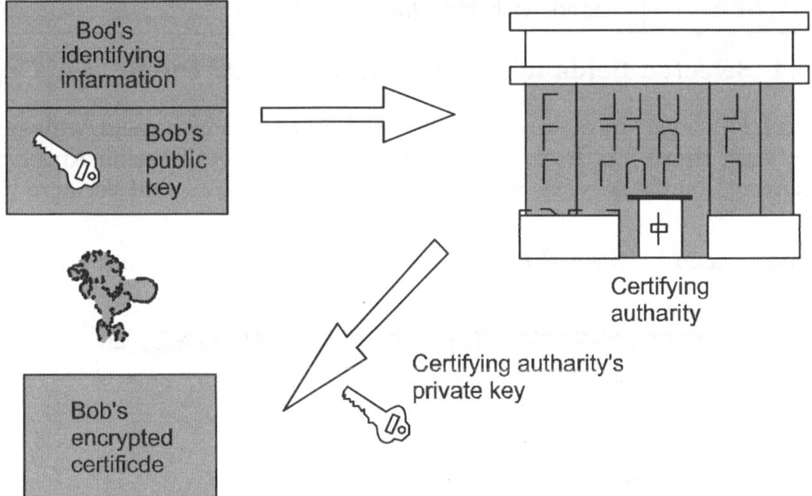

Figure 8.3 Bunty obtains a certificate from the certification authority.

Let us now see how certificates can be used to combat pizza-ordering pranksters, like Trudy, and other undesirables. When Anita recieves Bunty's order, she gets Bunty's certificate, which may be on his Web page, in an e-mail message or in a certificate server. Anita uses the CA's public key to verify that the public key in the certificate is indeed Bunty's. If we assume that the public key of the CA itself is known to all (for example, it could published in a trusted, public, and well-known place, such as The New York Times, so that it is known to all and can not be spoofed), then Anita can be sure that she is indeed dealing with Bunty.

Both the International Telecommunication Union and the IETF have developed standards for Certification Authorities. ITU X.509 [ITU 1993] specifies an authentication service as well as a specific syntax for certificates. RFC 1422 [RFC 1422] describes CA-based key management for use with secure Internet e-mail. It is compatible with X.509 but goes beyond X.509 by establishing procedures and conventions for a key management architecture. Figure 8.4 describes some of the important field in a certificate.

Field name	Description
version	version number of X 509 specificatio
serial number	CA-issued unique identifier for a certificate
signature	specifies the algorithm used by Ca to "sign" this certificate
issuer name	identity of CA issuing this certificate, in so-called Distinguished Name(DN) [RFC 1779] format
validity period	start and end of period of validity for certificate
subject name	identity of entity whose public key is associated with this certificate, in DN format
subject public key	the subject's public key as well as an indication of the public key algorithm (and algorithm parameters) to be used with this key

Figure 8.4 Selected fields in a X.509 and RFC 1422 Public Key Certificate

With the recent boom in electronic commerce and the consequent widespread need for secure transactions, there has been increased interest in Certification Authorities. Among the companies providing CA services are Cybertrust [Cybertrust 1990] Verisign [Verisign 1999] and Netscape

A certificate issued by the US Postal Service, as viewed through a Netscape browser, is shown in Figure 8.5.

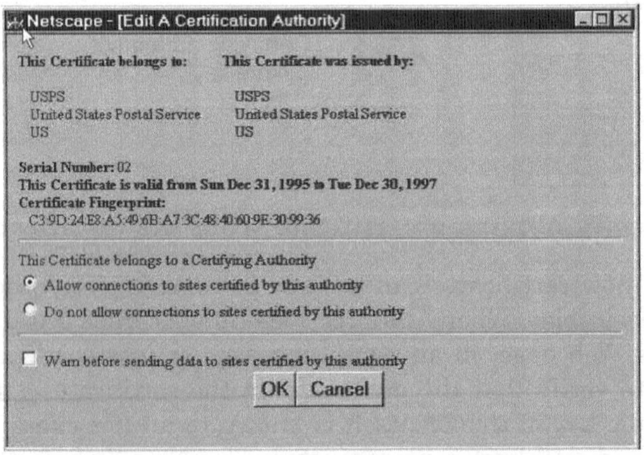

Netscape - [Edit A Certification Authority]

This Certificate belongs to: USPS, United States Postal Service, US

This Certificate was issued by: USPS, United States Postal Service, US

Serial Number: 02

This Certificate is valid from Sun Dec 31, 1995 to Tue Dec 30, 1997

Certificate Fingerprint: C3:9D:24:E8:A5:49:6B:A7:3C:48:40:60:9E:30:99:36

This Certificate belongs to a Certifying Authority

Allow connections to sites certified by this authority

Do not allow connections to sites certified by this authority

Warn before sending data to sites certified by this authority

OK Cancel

Figure 8.5 Example of a Certificate Issued by US Postal Service

8.2.1 One-Time Session Keys

We have seen above that a one-time session key is generated by a KDC for use in symmetric key encryption of a single session between two parties. By using the one-time session keys from the KDC, a user is freed from having to establish a priori its own shared key for each and every network entity with whom it wishes to communicate. Instead, a user need only have one shared secret key for communicating with the KDC, and will receive one-time session keys from the KDC for all of its communication with other network entities. One time session keys are also used in public key cryptography.

A public key encryption technique such as RSA is orders of magnitude more computationally expensive that a symmetric key system such as DES. Thus, public key systems are often used for authentication purposes. Once two parties have authenticated each other, they then use public-key-encrypted communication to agree on a shared one-time symmetric session key. This symmetric session key is then used to encrypt the remainder of the communication using a more efficient symmetric encryption technique, such as DES.

8.2.2 Understanding Kerberos Concepts

Kerberos Version 5 is standard on all versions of Windows 2000 (and according to Mark Walla is senior partner at Enterprise Certified Corp) ensures the highest level of security to network resources. The Kerberos protocol name is based on the three- headed dog figure from Greek mythology known as Kerberos. The three heads of Kerberos comprise the Key Distribution Center (KDC), the client user and the server with the desired service to access. The KDC is installed as part of the domain controller and performs two service functions: the Authentication Service (AS) and the Ticket-Granting Service (TGS). As exemplified in Figure 8.6, three exchanges are involved when the client initially accesses a server resource:

- AS Exchange11111
- TGS Exchange
- Client/Server (CS) Exchange

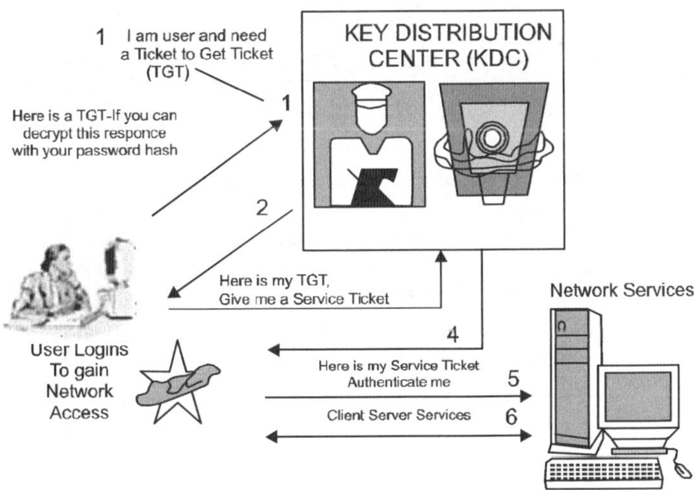

Figure 8.6 Kerbos Ticket Exchange

Let's take a closer look at this exchange process and its component parts.

8.2.3 AS Exchange

When initially logging on to a network, users must negotiate access by providing a log-in name and password in order to be verified by the AS portion of a KDC within their domain. The KDC has access to Active Directory user account information. Once successfully authenticated, the user is granted a Ticket to Get Tickets (TGT) that is valid for the local domain. The TGT has a default lifetime of 10 hours and may be renewed throughout the user's log-on session without requiring the user to re-enter his password. The TGT is cached on the local machine in volatile memory space and used to request sessions with services throughout the network. The following is a discussion of the TGT retrieval process.

Example AS Administration

The AS request identifies the client to the KDC in plain text. If preauthentication is enabled, a time stamp will be encrypted using the user's password hash as an encryption key. If the KDC reads a valid time when using the user's password hash (stored in the Active Directory) to decrypt the time stamp, the KDC knows that request isn't a replay of a previous request. The preauthentication feature may be disabled for specific users in order to support some applications that don't support the security feature. Access the user account from the Active Directory users and the computers will snap-in and select the account tab. From the account options: slide window, check mark the "Do not require Kerberos" preauthentication option (Figure 8.7).

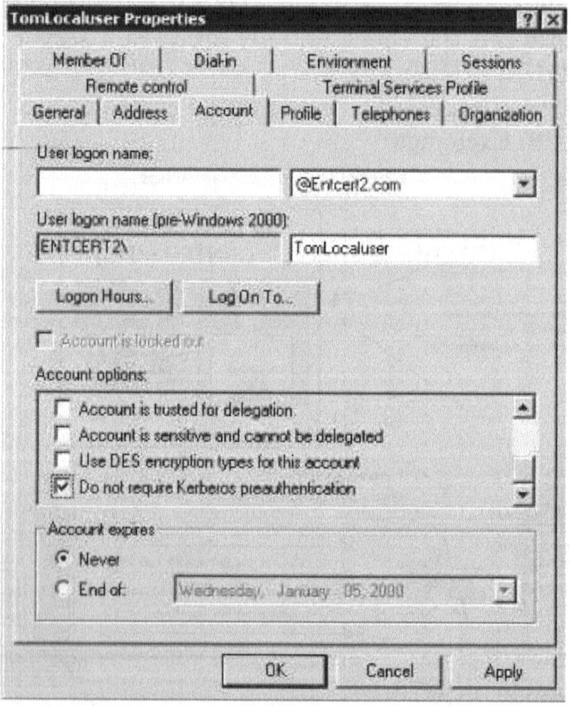

Figure 8.7 Disable Kerberos Preauthentication

If the KDC approves the client's request for a TGT, the reply (referred to as the AS reply) will include two sections: a TGT encrypted with a key that only the KDC (TGS) can decrypt and a session key encrypted with the user's password hash to handle future communications with the KDC. Because the client system cannot read the TGT contents, it must blindly present the ticket to the TGS for service tickets. The TGT includes time to live parameters, authorization data, a session key to use when communicating with the client and the client's name.

8.2.4 TGS Exchange

The user presents the TGT to the TGS portion of the KDC when desiring access to a server service. The TGS on the KDC authenticates the user's TGT and creates a ticket and session key for both the client and the remote server. This information, known as the service ticket, is then cached locally on the client machine.

The TGS receives the client's TGT and reads it using its own key. If the TGS approves of the client's request, a service ticket is generated for both the client and the target server. The client reads its portion using the TGS session key retrieved earlier from the AS reply. The client presents the server portion of the TGS reply to the target server in the client/server exchange coming next.

8.2.5 Client/Server Exchange

Once the client user has the client/server service ticket, he can establish the session with the server service. The server can decrypt the information coming indirectly from the TGS using its own long-term key with the KDC. The service ticket is then used to authenticate the client user and establish a service session between the server and client. After the ticket's lifetime is exceeded, the service ticket must be renewed to use the service.

Client/Server Exchange Detail

The client blindly passes the server portion of the service ticket to the server in the client/server request to establish a client/server session. If mutual authentication is enabled, the target server returns a time stamp encrypted using the service ticket session key. If the time stamp decrypts correctly, not only has the client authenticated himself to the server, but the server also has authenticated itself to the client. The target server never has to directly communicate with the KDC. This reduces downtime and pressure on the KDC.

8.2.6 Further Clarification of the Log-in Process

A TGT and a service ticket are needed to access services on remote computers, but they are also required to successfully log on to a local system. When the log-on window appears, password encryption using a one-way hash algorithm occurs immediately and negotiations commence with the KDC for a valid TGT and service ticket. The process is the same as accessing a remote service. An access token is created for the user containing all security groups to which they belong. This access token is attached to the user's log-on session and is subsequently inherited by any process or application the user starts.

8.2.7 Referral Tickets

The AS and TGS functions are separate within the KDC. This permits the user to use the TGT obtained from an AS in his domain to obtain service tickets from a TGS in other domains. This is accomplished through referral tickets.

Once a trust has been established between two domains, referral tickets can be granted to clients requesting authorization for services in other domains. When there is a trust established between the two domains, an interdomain key based on the trust password becomes available for authenticating KDC functions. This can best be explained by example of a user/client seeking services in another domain. As illustrated in Figure 8.8, a user client in Entcert1.com requests authority for a server in Entcert2.com. He utilizes referral tickets. The numbers in Figure 8.8 correspond to the following numbered explanations:

The client contacts its domain KDC TGS using a TGT. The KDC recognizes a request for a session with a foreign domain server and responds by returning a referral ticket for the KDC in the foreign domain.The client contacts the KDC of the foreign domain with the referral ticket. This ticket is encrypted with the interdomain key. Given that the decryption works, the TGS service for the foreign domain returns a service ticket for the server service in Entcert2.com.

The client performs the client/server exchange with the server and begins the user session with the service.

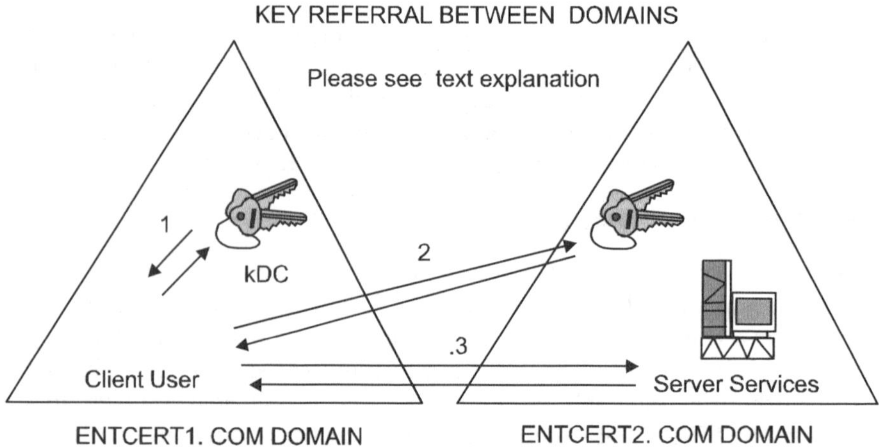

Figure 8.8 Domain Referrals

When more domains are involved, the referral process extends and involves the transitive properties between Windows 2000 domains. Maintaining individual two-way trusts between all domains creates a complex administrative nightmare. The use of Kerberos transitive domains cuts down on interdomain administration. This can best be explained by example of a user/client seeking services in another domain. As illustrated in Figure 8.9, Entcert1.com has a trust relationship with Entcert2.com. Entcert2.com has a trust relationship with Entcert3.com. There is no trust between Entcert1.com and Entcert3.com. A client from

Entcert1.com accessing a service on a server in Entcert3.com would obtain a service ticket through the following steps (the numbers appearing in Figure 8.9 correspond to the following numbered explanations):

(1) Use the TGS service in Entcert1.com to obtain a referral ticket for a KDC in Entcert2.com.

(2) Use the referral ticket with the TGS service on the KDC in Entcert2.com and obtain a referral for Entcert3.com.

(3) Use the second referral ticket with the TGS service on the KDC for Entcert3.com and obtain a service ticket for the server in Entcert3.com.

(4) Use the Client/Server Exchange to open a session with the service in Entcert3.com.

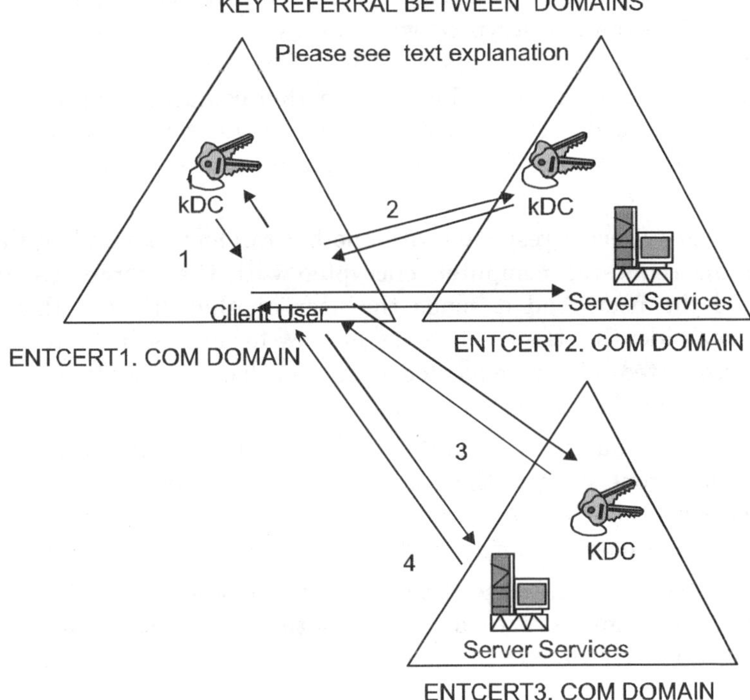

Figure 8.9 Transitive Domain Trusts

8.2.8 Delegation with Forwarding and Proxy

Some server services require access to a second server, such as a back-end database. In order to establish a session with the second server, the primary server must be authenticated on behalf of the client's user account and authority level. This is common in a three-tier client/server model. This activity is commonly accomplished with proxy or forwarding authentication.

Beginning a session with another computer under Kerberos requires the exchange of five messages:

First, a message is sent in the clear to the master security server (also called Kerberos), consisting of the user's login ID and the identity of the security server (called a ticket-granting server) from which the user is requesting authentication to open a session with a computer on the network.

Second, the security server generates a random session key and sends that to the user, encrypted with the user's secret key. (The user's secret key is a hash of the user's password.) It also sends the user, encrypted with its own permanent key, a "ticket", which includes a timestamp, the user's identity, the random session key divulged to the user previously within this message, and the service the user is requesting (of the security server).

Third, the user sends an authenticator to the security server, which consists of the user's name and a timestamp, encrypted with the user's secret key. This authenticator is then encrypted with the session key before sending. The ticket, which identifies the user as authorized to request a ticket for a session with another computer, is sent back as well, and it is intended that the security server may safely rely on reading the ticket to find out what the session key is. Also, the name of the other computer the user wants to communicate with is sent.

Fourth, the security server responds with another random session key, this one intended to be used with the requested computer, encrypted with the current session key for use between itself and the user. And it sends the user another "ticket"; this one includes a timestamp, the user's identity, the random session key for use with the requested computer, and the service requested of the requested computer. This ticket is enciphered with the permanent secret key of the requested computer.

Fifth, the user, now having a "ticket" for use with the requested computer, generates another authenticator, consisting of the user's name and a timestamp, encrypted with the session key for use with that computer, and also sends the "ticket", from which the requested computer can verify the user's identity, and discover what session key is to be used.

It should be noted that while the timestamp on a ticket is intended to prevent replay attacks, it is valid for a somewhat extended period of time; the timestamp on an authenticator is only valid for a very brief amount of time, as authenticators are intended to be only used once.

In Kerberos version 4, when a ticket is sent to a user, it is also encrypted under the key known to the user at that stage: by the user's secret key in the second message, and by the session key for use with the security server in the fourth message. In version 5, this encipherment, not being seen as necessary for security, is omitted to save computer time. In version 4, the PCBC mode of DES is used for encryption; in version 5, CBC mode is used, and there is provision for use of block ciphers other than DES. Incidentally, PCBC mode was used without the transmission of an initialization vector: instead, the DES key, known to both parties, served as the initialization vector without being transmitted.

Also, in Version 5, the user's secret key is derived not only from the user's password, but from "salt", consisting of the user's location on the system and a timestamp added to the first message. This makes dictionary attacks on passwords somewhat more difficult, but they are still possible. For this reason, and because there might be applications where security is desired, but there is no secure initial contact for communicating a password secretly to the user or the server, there are several proposals to improve and extend Kerberos by adding steps involving the use of public-key cryptography to it.

The following diagram may make it clearer what is happening in Kerberos:

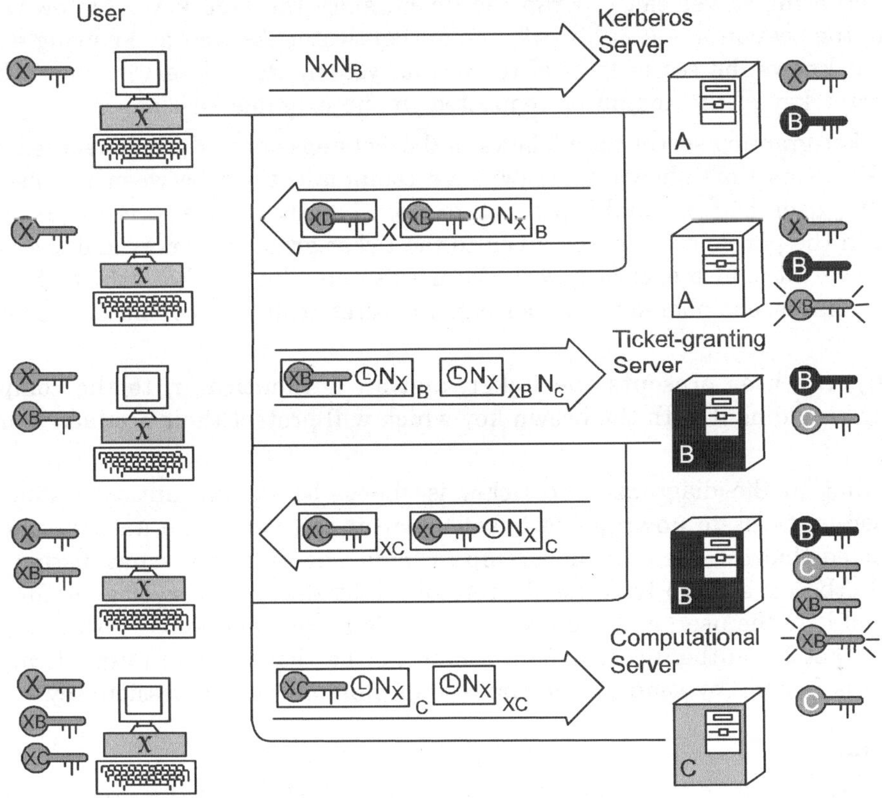

Figure 8.10 Transactions in Kerberos

In the first line, the user machine, colored red, sends a message in the clear identifying itself (a red N) and the ticket-granting server it wants to talk to (its name being a blue N) to the Kerberos server.

The Kerberos server knows the permanent secret keys of all the users, shown by a red key beside it for the current user, and the permanent secret keys of all the ticket-granting servers, shown by a blue key beside it for the ticket-granting server requested.

It responds by providing the user with a session key for communicating with the ticket-granting server, shown as a purple key. This key was generated by the Kerberos server at random, so it knows that key also, shown by a purple key popping out of thin air beside the server. The purple key is in a red box, which means that it is encrypted with the user's secret key. The user also recieves a ticket, which is shown as another purple key, plus a red N, in a blue box: the red/blue session key, and the name of the user, encrypted in the ticket-granting server's key.

The user then presents the ticket to the ticket-granting server, along with an authenticator - a copy of its own name, and a timestamp, encrypted in the session key. As well, it sends a green N to the ticket-granting server, to identify the computer for which it wants a ticket. The ticket-granting server can unwrap the ticket, since the blue key is its own secret key, and finding the session key it can verify the authenticator. As well as knowing a secret key of its own, it knows the secret keys of the ordinary computers it serves, shown by a green key, the secret key of the computer requested in the example session.

The ticket-granting server then follows in the footsteps of the Kerberos server, generating a session key (this time shown as brown) for communications between the user and the computer the user had originally set out to use. This session key is given to the user enciphered in the purple session key given to the ticket-granting server and the user by the Kerberos server; it is also enclosed, with the user's name, in a ticket, which this time is in a green box, that is, enciphered in the permanent secret key of the computer the user wanted to use.

Finally, the user presents the ticket, and an authenticator, to the computational server, thus providing it with the brown key which will protect their productive interactive session.

Note that in the diagrams, the ticket is shown before the authenticator, since the recieving server needs to unwrap the ticket before it can verify the authenticator. Also, it might be noted that the use of a timestamp in the authenticator is what distinguishes and simplifies Kerberos; a more traditional protocol might have the server generate a random number, send it to the user, and the user then sends it back encrypted with the session key inside the ticket for authentication. The server can be requested to authenticate itself; in Kerberos, this is done by sending the timestamp plus one in the session key.

Drawbacks

- *Single point of failure*: It requires continuous availability of a central server. When the Kerberos server is down, no one can log in. This can be mitigated by using multiple Kerberos servers and fallback authentication mechanisms.
- *Kerberos requires the clocks of the involved hosts to be synchronized.* The tickets have a time availability period and if the host clock is not synchronized with the Kerberos server clock, the authentication will fail. The default configuration requires that clock times are no more than 10 minutes apart. In practice Network Time Protocol daemons are usually used to keep the host clocks synchronized.
- The administration protocol is not standardized and differs between server implementations. Password changes are described in RFC 3244.
- Since the secret keys for all users are stored on the central server, a compromise of that server will compromise all users' secret keys. A compromised client will compromise the user's password

8.3 DIRECTORY SERVICE X.509

X.509 is a widely used standard for defining digital certificates. X.509 (Version 1) was first issued in 1988 as a part of the ITU X.500 Directory Services standard. When X.509 was revised in 1993, two more fields were added resulting in the Version 2 format. These two additional fields support directory access control. X.509 Version 3 defines the format for certificate extensions used to store additional information regarding the certificate holder and to define certificate usage. Collectively, the term X.509 refers to the latest published version, unless the version number is stated.

The ITU-T Recommendation X.509 (which has been implemented as a de facto standard) [X509b], describes two levels of authentication: simple authentication, using a password as a verification of claimed identity; and strong authentication, involving credentials formed by using cryptographic techniques. It is this second level that interests us here. It defines a framework for the provision of authentication services under a central control paradigm represented by a "Directory".

The "Directory" is implemented by a Certification Authority (CA), which issues certificates to subscribers (CA clients) in order for such certificates to be verifiable by users (the public in general). There are thus three main entities which can be outwardly recognized in X.509 certification procedures:

8.3.1 Certification Authority (CA)

CA is a general designation for any entity that controls the authentication services and the management of certificates.

The CA is also called the issuer. A CA can be ;

- Public (a bank that issues certificates to allow its clients to access their bank accounts),
- Commercial (a service provider that sellscertificates to other parties, such as Verisign),
- Private (a company that issues certificates to allow its employees to perform job duties), or
- Personal (you, me).

CAs are in general independent, even in the same country. The legal and technical relationships between a CA and its subscribers and users are governed by a Certification Practice Statement (CPS) issued by the CA. The CPS is internally defined by each CA within broad limits and lies outside the scope of X.509, even though X.509 references several items to be defined in the CPS, as discussed in the next items

8.3.2 Subscriber

Subscriber is an entity that supplies to the CA the information that is to be included in the entity's own certificate, signed by the CA. The subscriber is a commercial client to a CA. Usually, as defined in the CA's CPS, the information supplied by the subscriber is "endorsed" by the issuer, where "endorsed" means "copied as received". This corresponds to "endorsement without recourse". For example, in English law one can endorse "without recourse" (or, as it used to be expressed, "sans recours"), which passes on the benefit of a bill of exchange without adding any guarantee. In other words, the CA copies the subscriber's information to the certificate, but neither denotes nor confirms it – there is no warranty.

8.3.3 User

User is any entity which relies upon a certificate issued by a CA in order to obtain information on the subscriber. Also called the verifier. Users may use any CA or any number of CAs, depending on their locat ion and ease of access. The user should be central to the decision process in all steps, since the user is the party who is relying on the information and is thus at risk.

Another entity is the Naming Authority (NA), which is usually not outwardly perceived but which is the actual entity that defines the naming scheme used by a CA. The CA can double as a NA, but they provide two different functions. Semantically, the CA certificate refers to a name; however, it does not denote it. The NA denotes it.

8.4 E-MAIL SECURE

In previous chapters, we have examined fundamental issues in network security, including symmetric key and public key encryption, authentication, key distribution, message integrity and digital signatures. In this section and the following two sections, we'll next examine how these techniques are being used to provide security in the Internet. Being consistent with the general structure of this book, we begin at the top of the protocol stack and discuss application-layer security. Our approach here is use a specific application, namely, e-mail, as a case study for application-layer security. We then move down the protocol stack.

Interestingly, it is possible to provide security services in any of the top four layers of the Internet protocol stack [Molva 1999]. When security is provided for a specific application-layer protocol, then the application using the protocol will enjoy one or more security services, such as secrecy, authentication or integrity. When security is provided for a transport-layer protocol, then all applications that use that protocol enjoy the security services of the transport protocol. When security is provided at the network layer on a host-to-host basis, then all transport layer segments (and hence all application-layer data) enjoy the security services of the network layer. When security is provided on a link basis, then all IP datagrams traveling over the link receive security services of the link.

One might wonder why security functionality is being provided at multiple layers in the Internet? Wouldn't it suffice to simply provide the security functionality at the network layer, and be done with it? There are two answers to this question. First, although security at the network layer can offer "blanket coverage" by encrypting all the data in the datagrams (i.e., all the transport-layer segments) and by authenticating all source IP addresses, it can't provide user-level security. For example, a commerce site can not rely on IP-layer security to authenticate a customer who is purchasing goods at the commerce site. Thus, there is a need for security functionality at higher layers as well as blanket coverage at lower layers. Second, in the Internet it is generally easier to deploy new services, including security services, at the higher-layers of the protocol stack. While waiting for security to be broadly deployed at the network layer (which is arguably still many years in the future) many application developers "just do it" and introduce security functionality into to their favorite applications. A classic example is PGP, which provides for encryption of e-mail (and will be discussed later in this section). Requiring only client and server application code, PGP was one the first security technologies to be broadly used in the Internet. Similarly, transport-layer security with SSL was broadly introduced into the Internet, as it too only required new code in the end systems. However, IP-layer security — so-called IPsec — is taking much longer to broadly deploy, as it requires significant changes in the routers in the network core.

8.4.1 Principle of Secure E-Mail

In this section we use many of the tools introduced in the previous section to create a high-level design of a secure e-mail system. We create this high-level design in an incremental manner, at each step introducing new security services. When designing a secure e-mail system, let us keep in mind the racy example introduced in Section — the illicit love affair between Anita and Bunty. In the context of e-mail, Anita wants to send an e-mail message to Bunty, and Turkey wants to intrude.

Before plowing ahead and designing a secure e-mail system for Anita and Bunty, we should first consider which security features would be most desirable for them. First and foremost is secrecy. As discussed in section 1.8 neither Anita nor Bunty wants Turkey to read Anita's e-mail message. The second feature that Anita and Bunty would most likely want to see in the secure e-mail system is sender authentication. In particular, when Bunty receives the message from Anita, "I don't love you anymore. I never want to see you again. Formerly yours, Anita" , Bunty would naturally want to be sure that the message came from Anita and not from Turkey. Another feature that the two lovers would appreciate is message integrity, i.e., assurance that the message Anita sends is not modified while enroute to Bunty. Finally, the e-mail system should provide receiver authentication, i.e., Anita wants to make sure that she is indeed sending the letter to Bunty and not to someone else (e.g., Turkey) who is impersonating as Bunty.

So let's begin by addressing the foremost concern of Anita and Bunty, namely, secrecy. The most straightforward way to provide secrecy is for Anita to encrypt the message with symmetric key technology (such as DES) and for Bunty to decrypt the message upon message receipt. As discussed in if the symmetric key is long enough, and if only Anita and Bunty have the key, then it is extremely difficult for anyone else (including Turkey) to read the message. Although this approach is straightforward, it has a fundamental problem as we discussed in — it is difficult to distribute a symmetric key so that only Anita and Bunty have copies of the key. So we naturally consider an alternative approach, namely, public key cryptography (using, for example, RSA). In the public-key approach, Bunty makes his public key publicly available (for example, in a public-key server or on his personal Web page), Anita encrypts her message with Bunty's public key, and sends the encrypted message to Bunty's e-mail address. The encrypted message is encapsulated with MIME headers and sent over ordinary SMTP, When Bunty receives the message, he simply decrypts it with his private key. Assuming that Anita knows for sure that the public key is Bunty's public key (and that the key is long enough), then this approach is an excellent means to provide the desired secrecy. One problem, however, is that public-key encryption is relatively inefficient, particularly for long messages. (Long e-mail messages are now commonplace in the Internet, due to increasing use of attachments, images, audio and video.) To overcome the efficiency problem, let's make use of a session key (discussed in Section 7.8). In particular, Anita (1) selects a symmetric key, KS, at random, (2) encrypts her message, m, with the symmetric key, KS,(3) encrypts the symmetric key with Bunty's public key, eB, (4) concatenates the encrypted message and the encrypted symmetric key to form a "package", and (5) sends the package to Bunty's e-mail address. The steps are illustrated in Figure. (In this and the subsequent figures, the "+" represents concatenation and the "-" represents de-concatenation.) When Bunty receives the package, he (1) uses his private key dB to obtain the symmetric key, S, and (2) uses the symmetric key S to decrypt the message m.

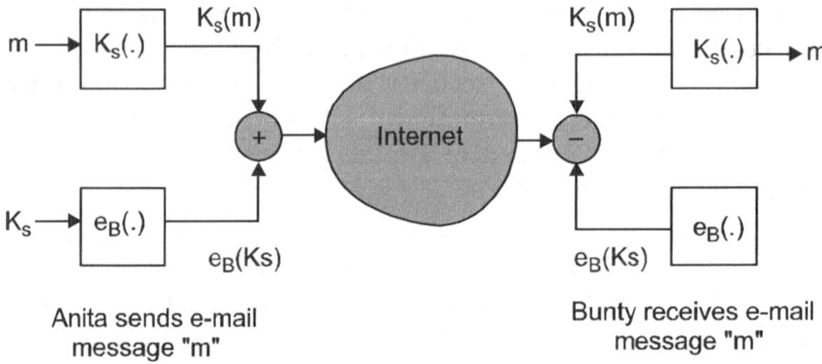

Figure 8.11 Anita uses a symmetric session key, KS, to send a secret e-mail to Bunty.

Having designed a secure e-mail system that provides secrecy, let's now design another system that provides both sender authentication and integrity. We'll suppose, for the moment, that Anita and Bunty are no longer concerned with secrecy (they what to share their feelings with everyone!), and are only concerned about sender authentication and message integrity. To accomplish this task, we use digital signatures and message digests, as described in Section 6.6.3 Specifically, Anita

(1) applies a hash function, H (e.g., MD5), to her message m to obtain a message digest,
(2) encrypts the result of the hash function with her private key, dA, to create a digital signature,
(3) concatenates the original (unencrypted message) with the signature to create a package,
(4) and sends the package to Bunty's e-mail address. When Bunty receives the package, he
(5) he applies Anita's public key, eA, to the electronic signature and

(6) compares the result of this operation to his own hash, H, of the message. The steps are illustrated in Figure 8.7. if the two results are the same, Bunty can be pretty confident that message came from Anita and is unaltered.

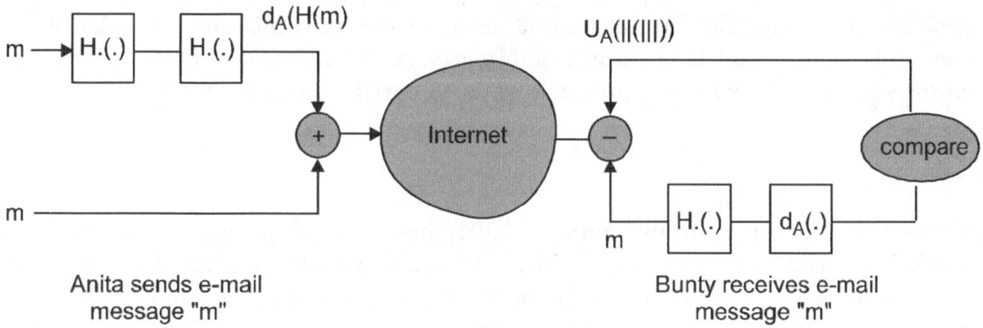

Figure 8.12 Using hash functions and digital signatures to provide sender authentication and message integrity.

Now lets consider designing an e-mail system that provides secrecy, sender authentication and message integrity. This can be done by combining the procedures in Figure 8.7 and 8.8. Anita first creates a preliminary package, exactly as in Figure 8.7, which consists of her original message along with a digitally-signed hash of the message. She then treats this preliminary package as a message in itself, and sends this new message through the sender steps in Figure 8.7, creating a new package that is sent to Bunty. The steps applied by Anita are shown in Figure 8.7. When Bunty receives the package, he first applies his side of Figure 8.8 and then his side of Figure 8.7. It should be clear that this design achieves the goal of providing secrecy, sender authentication and message integrity. Note in this scheme that Anita applies public key encryption twice: once with her own private key and once with Bunty's public key. Similarly, Bunty applies public key encryption twice - once with his private key and once with Anita's public key.

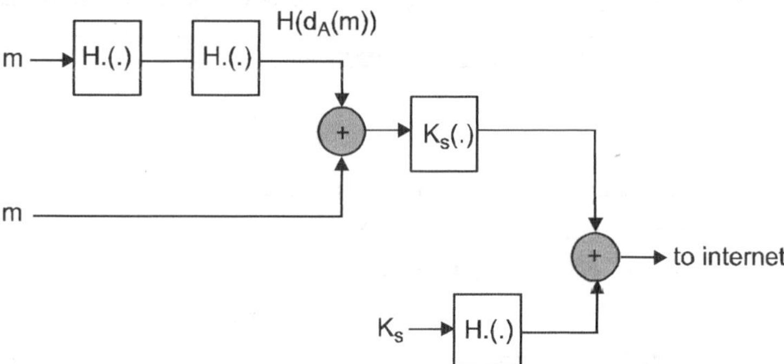

Figure 8.13 Anita uses symmetric-key cryptography, public-key cryptography, a hash function and a digital signature to provide secrecy, sender authentication and message integrity.

The secure e-mail design outlined in Figure 8.8 probably provides satisfactory security for most e-mail users for most occasions. But there is still one important issue that remains to be addressed. The design in Figure 8.8 requires Anita to obtain Bunty's public key, and requires Bunty to obtain Anita's public key. The distribution of these public keys is a non-trivial problem. For example, Turkey might masquerade as Bunty and give Anita her own public key while saying that it is Bunty's public key. As we learned in Section 7.5, a popular approach for securely distributing public keys is to certify the public keys.

8.5 PGP

Originally written by Phil Zimmerman in 1991, pretty good privacy (PGP) is e-mail an encryption scheme that has become a de-facto standard, with thousands of users all over the globe. Versions of PGP are available in the public domain; for example, you can find the PGP software for your favorite platform as well as lots of interesting reading at the International PGP Home Page (A particularly interesting essay by the author of PGP is [Zimmerman 1999]). PGP is also commercially available [Network Associates 1999], and is also available as a plug-in for many e-mail user agents, including Microsoft's Exchange and Outlook, and Qualcomm's Eudora.

The PGP design is, in essence, the same as the design shown in Figure 8.9 Depending on the version, the PGP software uses MD5 or SHA for calculating the message digest; CAST, Triple-DES or IDEA for symmetric key encryption; and RSA for the public key encryption. In addition, PGP provides data compression.

When PGP is installed, the software creates a public key pair for the user. The public key can be posted on the user's Web site or placed in a public key server. The private key is protected by the use of a password. The password has to be entered every time the user accesses the private key. PGP gives the user the option of digitally signing the message, encrypting the message, or both digitally signing and encrypting. Figure 8.9 shows a PGP signed message. This message appears after the MIME header. The encoded data in the message is dA(H(m)), i.e., the digitally signed message digest. As we discussed above, in order for Bunty to verify the integrity of the message, he needs to have access to Anita's public key.

```
—BEGIN PGP SIGNED MESSAGE—
Hash: SHA1
Bunty:
My husband is out of town tonight.
Passionately yours, Anita
—BEGIN PGP SIGNATURE—
Version: PGP for Personal Privacy 5.0
Charset: noconv
yhHJRHhGJGhgg/12EpJ+lo8gE4vB3mqJhFEvZP9t6n7G6m5Gw2
—END PGP SIGNATURE—
```

Figure 8.14 A PGP signed message.

Figure 8.10: shows a PGP secret message. This message also appears after the MIME header. Of course, the plaintext message is not included within the secret e-mail message. When a sender (such as Anita) wants both secrecy and integrity, the PGP would contain a message like that of Figure 8.10 contained within the message of Figure 8.9.

```
—BEGIN PGP MESSAGE—
Version: PGP for Personal Privacy 5.0
u2R4d+/jKmn8Bc5+hgDsqAewsDfrGdszX68liKm5F6Gc4sDfcXyt
RfdSlOjuHgbcfDssWe7/K=lKhnMikLoO+l/BvcX4t==Ujk9PbcD4
Thdf2awQfgHbnmKlok8iy6gThlp
—END PGP MESSAGE
```

Figure 8.15 A secrect PGP message.

PGP also provides a mechanism for public key certification, but the mechanism is quite different from the conventional certification authority tath we examined in section 3.12.6 PGP public keys are certified by a web of trust. Anita can certify any pair of key and user name for which she believes the pair really belongs together. In addition, PGP permits Anita to say that she trusts another user to vouch for the authenticiy of more keys. Some PGP users sign each other's keys is by holding key signing parties. Users physically gather, exchange floppy disks containing public keys, and certify each other's keys by signing them with their private keys. PGP public keys are also distributed by PGP public key servers on the Internet. When a user submits a public key to such a server, the server stores a copy of the key, sends a copy of the key to all the other public-key servers, and serves the key to anyone who requests it. Although key signing parties and PGP public key servers actually exist, by far the most common way for users to distribute their public keys is posting them on their personal Web pages. Of course, keys on personal Web pages are not certified by anyone, but they are easy to access.

8.5.1 How PGP works

PGP combines some of the best features of both conventional and public key cryptography. PGP is a hybrid cryptosystem.

When a user encrypts plaintext with PGP, PGP first compresses the plaintext. Data compression saves modem transmission time and disk space and, more importantly, strengthens cryptographic security. Most cryptanalysis techniques exploit patterns found in the plaintext to crack the cipher.

Compression reduces these patterns in the plaintext, thereby greatly enhancing resistance to cryptanalysis. (Files that are too short to compress or which don't compress well aren't compressed.)

PGP then creates a session key, which is a one-time-only secret key. This key is a random number generated from the random movements of your mouse and the keystrokes you type. This session key works with a very secure, fast conventional encryption algorithm to encrypt the plaintext; the result is ciphertext. Once the data is encrypted, the session key is then encrypted to the recipient's public key. This public key-encrypted session key is transmitted along with the ciphertext to the recipient.

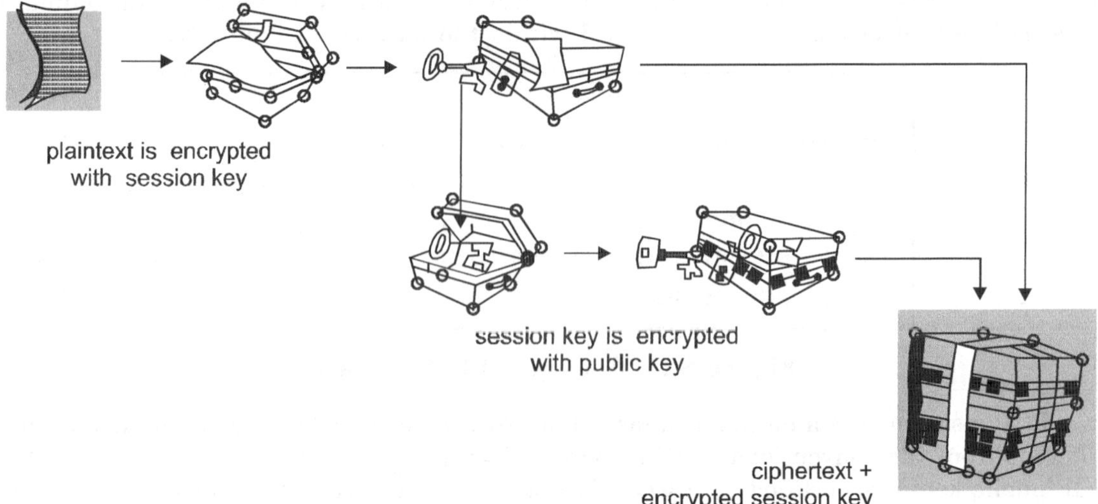

Figure 8.16 How PGP encryption works

Decryption works in the reverse. The recipient's copy of PGP uses his or her private key to recover the temporary session key, which PGP then uses to decrypt the conventionally-encrypted ciphertext.

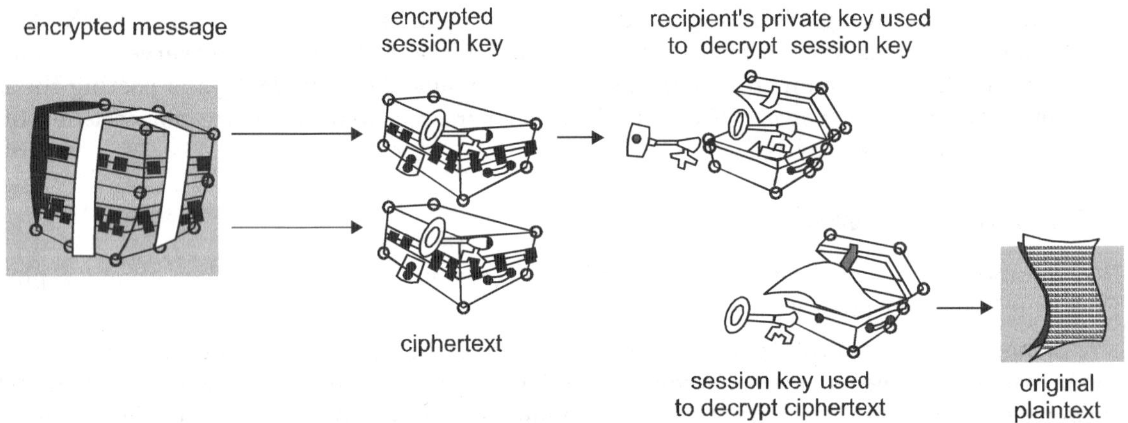

Figure 8.17 How PGP decryption works

The combination of the two encryption methods combines the convenience of public key encryption with the speed of conventional encryption.

Conventional encryption is about 1,000 times faster than public key encryption. Public key encryption in turn provides a solution to key distribution and data transmission issues. Used together, performance and key distribution are improved without any sacrifice in security.

8.5.2 PGP key exchange

If PGP is installed on your computer, Speak Freely will cooperate with it to provide the convenience of public key encryption. To encrypt sound to one or more users on your PGP public keyring, enter enough of their user name(s) to uniquely identify them in the "PGP user name(s)" field of the Option/Connections... dialogue. When you click OK to close the dialogue, Speak Freely generates a 128 bit random session key for subsequent communications, invokes PGP in an MS-DOS window to encrypt it with the public key(s) of the named user(s), and transmits it to the host or multicast group the connection addresses. Sound packets sent subsequently to that connection are IDEA encrypted (the same algorithm PGP uses for message bodies) using the session key. The ability to encrypt a session key with more than one user's public key allows you to transmit securely to multiple subscribers to a multicast.

When a session key is received from a remote host, PGP is invoked to decrypt it using your secret key. If you haven't specified your secret key pass phrase using the PGPPASS environment variable, you'll have to type the pass phrase in the MS-DOS window in which PGP is running.

Speak Freely invokes PGP via the SFPGP.PIF file in Speak Freely's release directory. If you'd like to change the modes used for running PGP (for example, to use full-screen mode instead of an MS-DOS window), edit this file with the PIF editor and select the modes you prefer. If no SFPGP.PIF file is found, Speak Freely attempts to run PGP directly, using whatever default modes you've set for MS-DOS programs launched by Windows applications.

The IDEA encryption algorithm used to encrypt audio following a PGP key exchange is patented and may not be used commercially without a license; see "Patent issues" for further details.

PGP key exchange and its subsequent IDEA encryption are independent of, and can be used in conjunction with, the other secret key encryption options provided by Speak Freely. There's little to be gained in security and everything to be lost in convenience by combining secret and public key encryption, but if you want to for some reason, you can.

8.5.3 The PGP Symmetric Algorithms

PGP offers a selection of different secret key algorithms to encrypt the actual message. By secret key algorithm, we mean a conventional, or symmetric, block cipher that uses the same key to both encrypt and decrypt. The three symmetric block ciphers offered by PGP are CAST, Triple-DES, and IDEA.

They are not "home-grown" algorithms. They were all developed by teams of cryptographers with distinguished reputations. For the cryptographically curious, all three ciphers operate on 64-bit blocks of plaintext and ciphertext. CAST and IDEA have key sizes of 128 bits, while Triple-DES uses a 168-bit key. Like Data Encryption Standard (DES), any of these ciphers can be used in cipher feedback (CFB) and cipher block chaining (CBC) modes. PGP uses them in 64-bit CFB mode.

CAST encryption algorithm wasincluded in PGP because it shows promise as a good block cipher with a 128-bit key size, it's very fast, and it's free. Its name is derived from the initials of its designers, Carlisle Adams and Stafford Tavares of Northern Telecom (Nortel). Nortel has applied for a patent for CAST, but they have made a commitment in writing to make CAST available to anyone on a royalty-free basis. CAST appears to be exceptionally well designed, by people with good reputations in the field.

The design is based on a very formal approach, with a number of formally provable assertions that give good reasons to believe that it probably requires key exhaustion to break its 128-bit key. CAST has no weak or semiweak keys. There are strong arguments that CAST is completely immune to both linear and differential cryptanalysis, the two most powerful forms of cryptanalysis in the published literature, both of which have been effective in cracking DES. CAST is too new to have developed a long track record, but its formal design and the good reputations of its designers will undoubtedly attract the attentions and attempted cryptanalytic attacks of the rest of the academic cryptographic community.

The IDEA (International Data Encryption Algorithm) block cipher is based on the design concept of "mixing operations from different algebraic groups." It was developed at ETH in Zurich by James L. Massey and Xuejia Lai, and published in 1990. Early published papers on the algorithm called it IPES (Improved Proposed Encryption Standard), but they later changed the name to IDEA. So far, IDEA has resisted attack much better than other ciphers such as FEAL, REDOC-II, LOKI, Snefru and Khafre. And IDEA is more resistant than DES to Biham and Shamir's highly successful differential cryptanalysis attack, as well as attacks from linear cryptanalysis. As this cipher continues to attract attack efforts from the most formidable quarters of the cryptanalytic world, confidence in IDEA is growing with the passage of time. Sadly, the biggest obstacle to IDEA's acceptance as a standard has been the fact that Ascom Systec holds a patent on its design, and unlike DES and CAST, IDEA has not been made available to everyone on a royalty-free basis.

As a hedge, PGP includes three-key Triple-DES in its repertoire of available block ciphers. The DES was developed by IBM in the mid-1970s. While it has a good design, its 56-bit key size is too small by today's standards. Triple-DES is very strong, and has been well studied for many years, so it might be a safer bet than the newer ciphers such as CAST and IDEA. Triple-DES is the DES applied three times to the same block of data, using three different keys, except that the second DES operation is run backwards, in decrypt mode. While Triple-DES is much slower than either CAST or IDEA, speed is usually not critical for email applications. Although Triple-DES uses a key size of 168 bits, it appears to have an effective key strength of at least 112 bits against an attacker with impossibly immense data storage capacity to use in the attack.

According to a paper presented by Michael Weiner at Crypto96, any remotely plausible amount of data storage available to the attacker would enable an attack that would require about as much work as breaking a 129-bit key. Triple-DES is not encumbered by any patents.

PGP public keys that were generated by PGP Version 5.0 or later have information embedded in them that tells a sender what block ciphers are understood by the recipient's software, so that the sender's software knows which ciphers can be used to encrypt. Diffie-

Hellman/DSS public keys accept CAST, IDEA, or Triple-DES as the block cipher, with CAST as the default selection. At present, for compatibility reasons, RSA keys do not provide this feature. Only the IDEA cipher is used by PGP to send messages to RSA keys, because older versions of PGP only supported RSA and IDEA.

8.5.4 PGP Data Compression Routines

PGP normally compresses the plaintext before encrypting it, because it's too late to compress the plaintext after it has been encrypted; encrypted data is not compressible. Data compression saves modem transmission time and disk space and, more importantly, strengthens cryptographic security. Most cryptanalysis techniques exploit redundancies found in the plaintext to crack the cipher. Data compression reduces this redundancy in the plaintext, thereby greatly enhancing resistance to cryptanalysis. It takes extra time to compress the plaintext, but from a security point of view it's worth it.

Files that are too short to compress, or that just don't compress well, are not compressed by PGP. In addition, the program recognizes files produced by most popular compression programs, such as PKZIP, and does not try to compress a file that has already been compressed.

For the technically curious, the program uses the freeware ZIP compression routines written by Jean-Loup Gailly, Mark Adler, and Richard B. Wales. This ZIP software uses compression algorithms that are functionally equivalent to those used by PKWare's PKZIP 2.x. This ZIP compression software was selected for PGP mainly because it has a really good compression ratio and because it's fast.

8.5.5 Random Numbers used as Session Keys

PGP uses a cryptographically strong pseudo-random-number generator for creating temporary session keys. If this random seed file does not exist, it is automatically created and seeded with truly random numbers derived from your random events gathered by the PGP program from the timing of your keystroke and mouse movements.

This generator reseeds the seed file each time it is used, by mixing in new material partially derived from the time of day and other truly random sources. It uses the conventional encryption algorithm as an engine for the random number generator. The seed file contains both random seed material and random key material used to key the conventional encryption engine for the random generator.

This random seed file should be protected from disclosure, to reduce the risk of an attacker deriving your next or previous session keys. The attacker would have a very hard time getting anything useful from capturing this random seed file, because the file is cryptographically laundered before and after each use. Nonetheless, it seems prudent to try to keep it from falling into the wrong hands. If possible, make the file readable only by you. If this is not possible, don't let other people indiscriminately copy disks from your computer.

8.5.6 About the message digest

The message digest is a compact (160-bit or 128-bit) "distillate" of your message or file checksum. You can also think of it as a "fingerprint" of the message or file. The message digest "represents" your message, in such a way that if the message were altered in any way, a different message digest would be computed from it. This makes it possible to detect any changes made to the message by a forger. A message digest is computed using a cryptographically strong one-way hash function of the message. It should be computationally infeasible for an attacker to devise a substitute message that would produce an identical message digest. In that respect, a message digest is much better than a checksum, because it is easy to devise a different message that would produce the same checksum. But like a checksum, you can't derive the original message from its message digest.

The message digest algorithm now used in PGP (Version 5.0 and later) is called SHA, which stands for Secure Hash Algorithm, designed by the NSA for the National Institute of Standards and Technology (NIST). SHA is a 160-bit hash algorithm. Some people might regard anything from the NSA with suspicion, because the NSA is in charge of intercepting communications and breaking codes. But keep in mind that the NSA has no interest in forging signatures, and the government would benefit from a good unforgeable digital signature standard that would preclude anyone from repudiating their signatures. That has distinct benefits for law enforcement and intelligence gathering. Also, SHA has been published in the open literature and has been extensively peer-reviewed by most of the best cryptographers in the world who specialize in hash functions, and the unanimous opinion is that SHA is extremely well designed. It has some design innovations that overcome all the observed weaknesses in message digest algorithms previously published by academic cryptographers. All new versions of PGP use SHA as the message digest algorithm for creating signatures with the new DSS keys that comply with the NIST Digital Signature Standard. For compatibility reasons, new versions of PGP still use MD5 for RSA signatures, because older versions of

8.5.7 PGP used MD5 for RSA signatures.

The message digest algorithm used by older versions of PGP is the MD5 Message Digest Algorithm, placed in the public domain by RSA Data Security, Inc. MD5 is a 128-bit hash algorithm. In 1996, MD5 was all but broken by a German cryptographer, Hans Dobbertin. Although MD5 was not completely broken at that time, it was discovered to have such serious weaknesses that no one should keep using it to generate signatures. Further work in this area might completely break it, allowing signatures to be forged. If you don't want to someday find your PGP digital signature on a forged confession, you might be well advised to migrate to the new PGP DSS keys as your preferred method for making digital signatures, because DSS uses SHA as its secure hash algorithm.

8.5.8 How to protect public keys from tampering

In a public key cryptosystem, you don't have to protect public keys from exposure. In fact, it's better if they are widely disseminated. But it's important to protect public keys from tampering, to make sure that a public key really belongs to the person to whom it appears to belong. This may be the most important vulnerability of a public key cryptosystem. Let's first look at a potential disaster, then describe how to safely avoid it with PGP.

Suppose you want to send a private message to Anita. You download Anita's public key certificate from an electronic bulletin board system (BBS). You encrypt your letter to Anita with this public key and send it to her through the BBS's email facility.

Unfortunately, unbeknownst to you or Anita, another user named Charlie has infiltrated the BBS and generated a public key of his own with Anita's user ID attached to it. He covertly substitutes his bogus key in place of Anita's real public key. You unwittingly use this bogus key belonging to Charlie instead of Anita's public key. All looks normal because this bogus key has Anita's user ID.

Now Charlie can decipher the message intended for Anita because he has the matching private key. He may even reencrypt the deciphered message with Anita's real public key and send it on to her so that no one suspects any wrongdoing. Furthermore, he can even make apparently good signatures from Anita with this private key because everyone will use the bogus public key to check Anita's signatures.

The only way to prevent this disaster is to prevent anyone from tampering with public keys. If you got Anita's public key directly from Anita, this is no problem. But that may be difficult if Anita is a thousand miles away or is currently unreachable.

Perhaps you could get Anita's public key from a mutually trusted friend, David, who knows he has a good copy of Anita's public key. David could sign Anita's public key, vouching for the integrity of Anita's public key. David would create this signature with his own private key.

This would create a signed public key certificate, and would show that Anita's key had not been tampered with. This requires that you have a known good copy of David's public key to check his signature. Perhaps David could provide Anita with a signed copy of your public key also. David is thus serving as an "Introducer" between you and Anita.

This signed public key certificate for Anita could be uploaded by David or Anita to the BBS, and you could download it later. You could then check the signature via David's public key and thus be assured that this is really Anita's public key. No impostor can fool you into accepting his own bogus key as Anita's because no one else can forge signatures made by David.

A widely trusted person could even specialize in providing this service of "introducing" users to each other by providing signatures for their public key certificates. This trusted person could be regarded as a "Certifying Authority."

Any public key certificates bearing the Certifying Authority's signature could be trusted as truly belonging to the person to whom they appear to belong to.

All users who wanted to participate would need a known good copy of just the Certifying Authority's public key, so that the Certifying Authority's signatures could be verified. In some cases, the Certifying Authority may also act as a key server, allowing users on a network to look up public keys by asking the key server, but there is no reason why a key server must also certify keys.

A trusted centralized Certifying Authority is especially appropriate for large impersonal centrally-controlled corporate or government institutions. Some institutional environments use hierarchies of Certifying Authorities. For more decentralized environments, allowing all users to act as trusted introducers for their friends would probably work better than a centralized key certification authority.

One of the attractive features of PGP is that it can operate equally well in a centralized environment with a Certifying Authority or in a more decentralized environment where individuals exchange personal keys.

This whole business of protecting public keys from tampering is the single most difficult problem in practical public key applications. It is the "Achilles heel" of public key cryptography, and a lot of software complexity is tied up in solving this one problem.

You should use a public key only after you are sure that it is a good public key that has not been tampered with, and that it actually belongs to the person with whom it purports to be associated. You can be sure of this if you got this public key certificate directly from its owner, or if it bears the signature of someone else that you trust, from whom you already have a good public key. Also, the user ID should have the full name of the key's owner, not just her first name.

No matter how tempted you are, you should never give in to expediency and trust a public key you downloaded from a bulletin board, unless it is signed by someone you trust. That uncertified public key could have been tampered with by anyone, maybe even by the system administrator of the bulletin board.

If you are asked to sign someone else's public key certificate, make certain that it really belongs to the person named in the user ID of that public key certificate. This is because your signature on her public key certificate is a promise by you that this public key really belongs to her. Other people who trust you will accept her public key because it bears your signature. It can be ill-advised to rely on hearsay—don't sign her public key unless you have independent first-hand knowledge that it really belongs to her. Preferably you should sign it only if you got it directly from her.

In order to sign a public key, you must be far more certain of that key's ownership than if you merely want to use that key to encrypt a message. To be convinced of a key's validity enough to use it, certifying signatures from trusted introducers should suffice. But to sign a key yourself, you should require your own independent first-hand knowledge of who owns that key.

Perhaps you could call the key's owner on the phone and read the key fingerprint to her, to confirm that the key you have is really her key—and make sure you really are talking to the right person.

Bear in mind that your signature on a public key certificate does not vouch for the integrity of that person, but only vouches for the integrity (the ownership) of that person's public key. You aren't risking your credibility by signing the public key of a sociopath, if you are completely confident that the key really belongs to him. Other people would accept that key as belonging to him because you signed it (assuming they trust you), but they wouldn't trust that key's owner. Trusting a key is not the same as trusting the key's owner.

It would be a good idea to keep your own public key on hand with a collection of certifying signatures attached from a variety of "introducers," in the hope that most people will trust at least one of the introducers who vouch for the validity of your public key. You could post your key with its attached collection of certifying signatures on various electronic bulletin boards. If you sign someone else's public key, return it to them with your signature so that they can add it to their own collection of credentials for their own public key.

Make sure that no one else can tamper with your own public keyring. Checking a newly signed public key certificate must ultimately depend on the integrity of the trusted public keys that are already on your own public keyring. Maintain physical control of your public keyring, preferably on your own personal computer rather than on a remote time-sharing system, just as you would do for your private key. This is to protect it from tampering, not from disclosure. Keep a trusted backup copy of your public keyring and your private key on write-protected media.

Since your own trusted public key is used as a final authority to directly or indirectly certify all the other keys on your keyring, it is the most important key to protect from tampering. You may want to keep a backup copy on a write-protected floppy disk.

PGP generally assumes that you will maintain physical security over your system and your keyrings, as well as your copy of PGP itself. If an intruder can tamper with your disk, then in theory he can tamper with the program itself, rendering moot the safeguards the program may have to detect tampering with keys.

One somewhat complicated way to protect your own whole public keyring from tampering is to sign the whole ring with your own private key. You could do this by making a detached signature certificate of the public keyring.

How does PGP keep track of which keys are valid?

Before you read this section, you should read the previous section, "How to protect public keys from tampering."

PGP keeps track of which keys on your public keyring are properly certified with signatures from introducers that you trust. All you have to do is tell PGP which people you trust as introducers, and certify their keys yourself with your own ultimately trusted key. PGP can take it from there, automatically validating any other keys that have been signed by your designated introducers. And of course you can directly sign more keys yourself.

There are two entirely separate criteria that PGP uses to judge a public key's usefulness—don't get them confused:

1. Does the key actually belong to the person to whom it appears to belong? In other words, has it been certified with a trusted signature?
2. Does it belong to someone you can trust to certify other keys? PGP can calculate the answer to the first question. To answer the second question, you must tell PGP explicitly. When you supply the answer to question 2, PGP can then calculate the answer to question 1 for other keys signed by the introducer you designated as trusted.

Keys that have been certified by a trusted introducer are deemed valid by PGP.

The keys belonging to trusted introducers must themselves be certified either by you or by other trusted introducers.

PGP also allows for the possibility of your having several shades of trust for people to act as introducers. Your trust for a key's owner to act as an introducer does not just reflect your estimation of th eir personal integrity—it should also reflect how competent you think they are at understanding key management and using good judgment in signing keys. You can designate a person as untrusted, marginally trusted, or completely trusted to certify other public keys. This trust information is stored on your keyring with their key, but when you tell PGP to copy a key off your keyring, PGP does not copy the trust information along with the key, because your private opinions on trust are regarded as confidential.

When PGP is calculating the validity of a public key, it examines the trust level of all the attached certifying signatures. It computes a weighted score of validity—for example, two marginally trusted signatures are deemed to be as credible as one fully trusted signature. The program's skepticism is adjustable—for example, you can tune PGP to require two fully trusted signatures or three marginally trusted signatures to judge a key as valid.

Your own key is "axiomatically" valid to PGP, needing no introducer's signature to prove its validity. PGP knows which public keys are yours by looking for the corresponding private keys on the private key. PGP also assumes that you completely trust yourself to certify other keys.

As time goes on, you will accumulate keys from other people whom you may want to designate as trusted introducers. Everyone else will choose their own trusted introducers. And everyone will gradually accumulate and distribute with their key a collection of certifying signatures from other people, with the expectation that anyone receiving it will trust at least one or two of the signatures. This will cause the emergence of a decentralized fault-tolerant web of confidence for all public keys.

This unique grass-roots approach contrasts sharply with standard public key management schemes developed by government and other monolithic institutions, such as Internet Privacy Enhanced Mail (PEM), which are based on centralized control and mandatory centralized trust. The standard schemes rely on a hierarchy of Certifying Authorities who dictate who you must trust.

The program's decentralized probabilistic method for determining public key legitimacy is the centerpiece of its key management architecture. PGP lets you alone choose who you trust, putting you at the top of your own private certification pyramid. PGP is for people who prefer to pack their own parachutes.

Note that while this decentralized, grass-roots approach is emphasized here, it does not mean that PGP does not perform equally well in the more hierarchical, centralized public key management schemes. Large corporate users, for example, will probably want a central figure or person who signs all the employees' keys. PGP handles that centralized scenario as a special degenerate case of PGP's more generalized trust model.

8.5.9 How to Protect Private Keys from Disclosure

Protect your own private key and your passphrase very carefully. If your private key is ever compromised, you'd better get the word out quickly to all interested parties before someone else uses it to make signatures in your name.

For example, someone could use it to sign bogus public key certificates, which could create problems for many people, especially if your signature is widely trusted. And of course, a compromise of your own private key could expose all messages sent to you.

To protect your private key, you can start by always keeping physical control of it. Keeping it on your personal computer at home is OK, or keep it in your notebook computer that you can carry with you. If you must use an office computer that you don't always have physical control of, then keep your public and private keyrings on a write-protected removable floppy disk, and don't leave it behind when you leave the office. It wouldn't be a good idea to allow your private key to reside on a remote timesharing computer, such as a remote dial-in UNIX system. Someone could eavesdrop on your modem line and capture your passphrase and then obtain your actual private key from the remote system. You should only use your private key on a machine that is under your physical control.

Don't store your passphrase anywhere on the computer that has your private key file. Storing both the private key and the passphrase on the same computer is as dangerous as keeping your PIN in the same wallet as your Automatic Teller Machine bank card. You don't want somebody to get their hands on your disk containing both the passphrase and the private key file. It would be most secure if you just memorize your passphrase and don't store it anywhere but your brain. If you feel you must write down your passphrase, keep it well protected, perhaps even better protected than the private key file.

And keep backup copies of your private key—remember, you have the only copy of your private key, and losing it will render useless all the copies of your public key that you have spread throughout the world.

The decentralized noninstitutional approach that PGP supports for management of public keys has its benefits, but unfortunately it also means that you can't rely on a single centralized list of which keys have been compromised. This makes it a bit harder to contain the damage of a private key compromise. You just have to spread the word and hope that everyone hears about it.

If he worst case happens—your private key and passphrase are both compromised (hopefully you will find this out somehow)—you will have to issue a "key revocation" certificate. This kind of certificate is used to warn other people to stop using your public key. You can use PGP to create such a certificate by using the Revoke command from the PGPkeys menu or by having your Designated Revoker do it for you. Then you must send this to a certificate server so others can find it. Their own PGP software installs this key revocation certificate on their public keyrings and automatically prevents them from accidentally using your public key ever again. You can then generate a new private/public key pair and publish the new public key. You could send out one package containing both your new public key and the key revocation certificate for your old key.

Loosing the private key

But what can you do if you lose your secret key, or if your secret key is destroyed? You can't revoke it yourself, because you must use your own secret key to revoke it, and you don't have it anymore. A future version of PGP will offer a more secure means of revoking keys in these circumstances, allowing trusted introducers to certify that a public key has been revoked. But for now, you will have to get the word out through whatever informal means you can, asking users to disable your public key on their own individual public key rings.

Other users may disable your public key on their own public key rings by using the -kd command. If a user ID is specified that does not correspond to a secret key on the secret key ring, the -kd command will look for that user ID on the public key ring, and mark that public key as disabled. A disabled key may not be used to encrypt any messages, and may not be extracted from the key ring with the -kx command. It can still be used to check signatures, but a warning is displayed. And if the user tries to add the same key again to his key ring, it will not work because the disabled key is already on the key ring. These combined features will help curtail the further spread of a disabled key.

If the specified public key is already disabled, the -kd command will ask if you want the key reenabled.

8.6 SECURE MIME (S/MIME)

S/MIME is the name given to Secure MIME or Secure encryption of attachments when they are added to email messages. S/MIME requires a both a private and public key. The public key is stored and made available to those who wish to send users an encrypted message. So to send a message via S/MIME the sender must look up the public key in a global directory or already have it available. Once the key has been found, the sender must encrypt the message/attachment and forward it to the destination server.

In order for the message to be read, the encrypted message must be decoded by the mail client or by the mail server. There are issues with either of these solutions:

- Decryption by the mail client. At the current time, not many mail clients support S/MIME decryption. Further there is the issue of configuring the mail client with the correct private key so that decryption works OK. Since messages are stored encrypted, if the key becomes compromised at any point in the future and must be changed, there is the risk that the messages will become unavilable in the future.

- Decryption by the mail server. This requires the server to hold both the encryption and decryption key for each user. Clearly there will be additional load on the server as it manages each message and messages are likley to be stored unencrypted on the server itself (there is no point in them being encrypted since the key is available on the server).

There are still several issues to be resolved:

- Global directories To date, there is no global directories where public keys can be obtained. This means that finding the appropriate key can be challenging and may lead to users taking the least resistance and >not encrypting information at all.
- Compatibility There are some issues between different implementations of the S/ MIME protocol.
- Compromised keys Managing and revoking compromised keys without loosing access to information is challenging.

While S/MIME has uses in very specialised areas where control of security options is straight forward, for most people, the additional cost of complexity is prohibitive.

Email Security has become increasingly important because of the possibility of man-in-the-middle attacks or the risk of an unknown third person that may sniff your SMTP traffic within the internet or even your intranet. In addition, in some countries there are laws preventing you from sending insecure email. Therefore Microsoft implemented the S/MIME standard in its Exchange Server architecture. The feature to encrypt or sign your emails became a default feature within all messaging and collaboration systems. Within this article we will look at how S/MIME has to be configured and how it works.

Within earlier versions of Exchange Server, Microsoft enabled S/MIME Security using MAPI clients, but did not recognize that Outlook Web Access became more and more interesting for business use. So with Exchange Server 2003, Microsoft implemented this feature with Outlook Web Access too.

8.7 BASICS OF EMAIL ENCRYPTION AND EMAIL SIGNING

The technique of S/MIME relies on complex algorithms that create the appropriate key pair:

- The public key
- The private key

This key pair needs to be available if any encryption or signing is being used. If one is missing, you won't be able to use the corresponding key anymore.The public key has to be published, the private key can be compared with your identity card or your driving license, it declares your digital identity.

8.7.1 Email Encryption

When you try to secure email to make sure that no one can read the SMTP packages on its way from sender to recipient you will have to encrypt them.

This feature works the following way:

- The messaging platform looks for the public key of the recipient
- It now encrypts the message using this public key
- The message is now being delivered to the target system
- If the recipient tries to open the message his system will have to own his private key to be able to decrypt the message

8.7.2 Email Signature

When you want to use the digital signature you have to make sure that the recipient can recognize that you yourself wrote this email and not anyone else. In addition, you can be sure that the email has not been changed during its way.

Email Signing works the following way :

- The messaging platform looks for the private key of the sender
- It now hashes the message and then encrypts this fingerprint with this private key
- The message is now being delivered to the target system
- If the recipient tries to open the message his system will have to be able to access the recipient's public key
- If now hashes the message again, decrypts the fingerprint using the public key
- If the sender's and recipient's fingerprint are the same you can be sure that the message was originally sent from the sender and has not been changed in between

8.7.3 Configuring Outlook Web Access 2003 for S/MIME Security

With Exchange Server 2003, Microsoft added the S/MIME feature to Outlook Web Access using a control. It relies on the interaction of the Web browser and the Exchange server to provide full functionality. This functionality differs from Outlook Web Access without the S/MIME control because this control provides a fully functional S/MIME email client. It is designed to integrate seamlessly with Microsoft Internet Explorer 6.x or later. The control itself is a Common Object Model (COM) object that also uses dynamic HTML (DHTML) to support the basic message security services. It controls all access to any certificates required for S/MIME security.

To install Outlook Web Access with the S/MIME control using the download, the users must have administrative privileges to install the control itself on his workstation.

These are the steps in details to install the control:

- Use a computer running Windows 2000 or later with Internet Explorer 6 or later and log on to Outlook Web Access.
- In OWA click Options in the navigation pane.
- Under Email-Security click Download
- Install the control on your local machine.

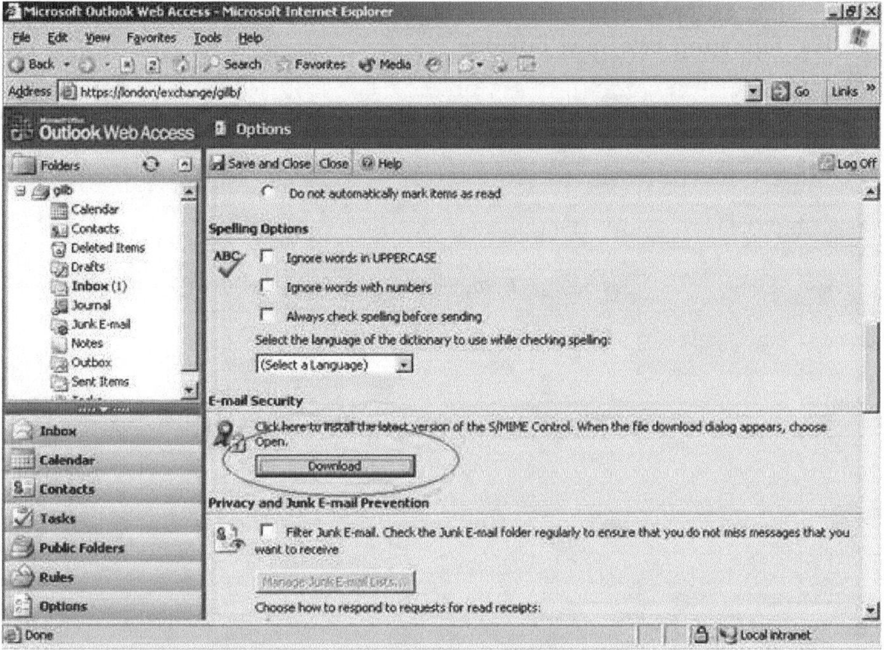

Figure 8.18 Download and install the S/MIME Control

After a successful installation, you can now configure the general options for digital signing and signature.

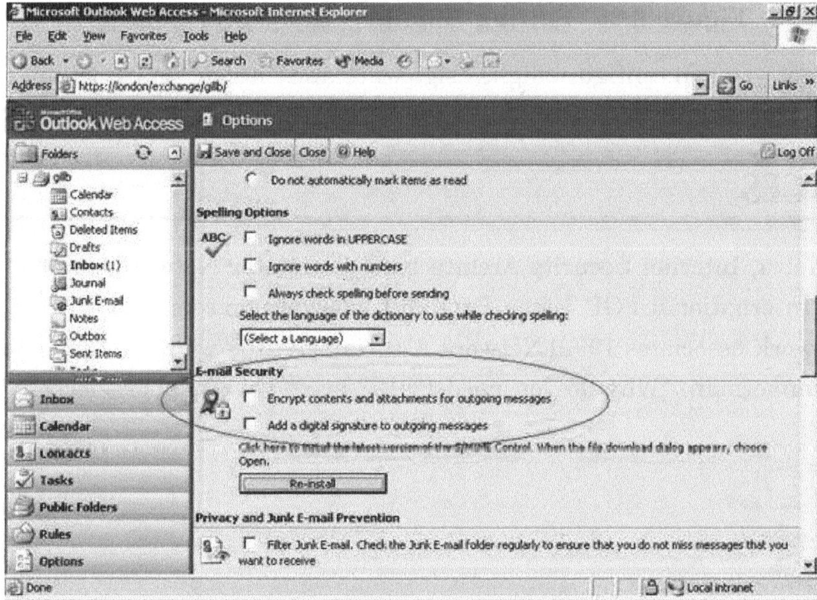

Figure 8.19 General Settings for Encryption and Signature

To digitally sign an or encrypt any messages from now on in Outlook Web Access you will have use the following two new buttons:

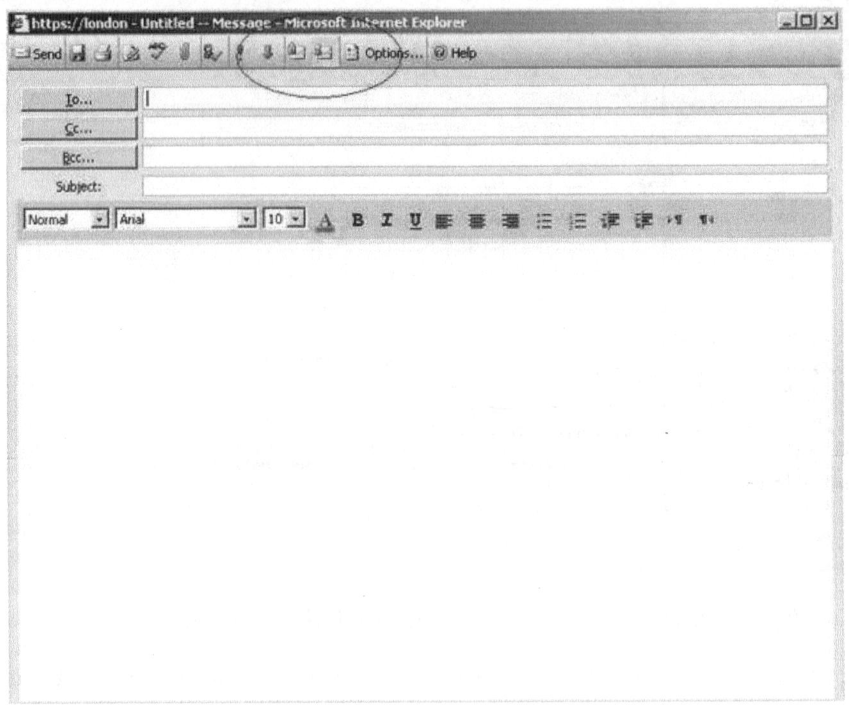

Figure 8.20 Setting Email security individually

If you want you can configure digital signature and encryption by default, you can find these settings on the options page of Outlook Web Access.

REFERENCES

1. R. Molva, Internet Security Architecture, Computer Networks, 1999.
2. The International PGP Home Page, http://www.pgpi.com.
3. [Network Associates 1999] Network Associates, http://www.nai.com/default_pgp.asp.
4. P. Zimmerman, "Why do you need PGP?" http://www.pgpi.org/doc/whypgp/en.

❑❑❑

9

IP Security

9.1 INTRODUCTION TO IP

TCP/IP is the backbone of the internet today. Comprised of two protocols, TCP and IP, the TCP/IP protocol suite is one of the most widely used.In the early 1980's, specifications were finished for the TCP and IP protocols. These two protocols could be considered the most important in the world today - they are the basis of the Internet. Over the past decade, the Internet has grown from a small network connecting a small community of researchers to its present state - a gigantic global network connecting people of all types. The huge success of the Internet has, for the most part, been quite beneficial. The Internet has evolved from a specialized project to a general-purpose tool. However, the growth of the Internet has created problems with security. The TCP and IP protocols were designed when the Internet was small, and users generally trusted each other. The protocols lack many features that are desirable or needed on an insecure network.

9.1.1 Problems with Authentication

The utter lack of authentication with IP packets is a general weakness with TCP/IP. Without authentication, there really is no guarantee that a packet comes from where its source field claims it comes from. This is the foundation of all IP spoofing and consequently, the major issue in IP security. There are many different ways to capitalize on this weakness; we have provided an overview of the problems that come about from the lack of authentication, but our discussion of the myriad ways this may be taken advantage of could never really be complete.

Since a lack of authentication is the broadest, more crippling weakness in TCP/IP, we would really like to clamp down on it as much as possible. Since the conventional IP version

4 does not typically use authentication, it is not possible to completely eradicate the threat in the most ideal way, by providing it at the IP level. However, we cannot simply throw up our hands in defeat; there are several techniques we may employ to blunt this weapon.Due to this IPsec protocol needs to be added for secure transaction.

9.1.2 Internet Protocol

The Internet Protocol (or IP as it generally known), is the network layer of the Internet. IP provides a connection-less service. The job of IP is to route and send a packet to the packet's destination. IP provides no guarantee whatsoever, for the packets it tries to deliver. The IP packets are usually termed datagrams. The datagrams go through a series of routers before they reach the destination. At each node that the datagram passes through, the node determines the next hop for the datagram and routes it to the next hop. Since the network is dynamic, it is possible that two datagrams from the same source take different paths to make it to the destination. Since the network has variable delays, it is not guaranteed that the datagrams will be received in sequence. IP only tries for a best-effort delivery. It does not take care of lost packets; this is left to the higher layer protocols. There is no state maintained between two datagrams; in other words, IP is connection-less.

<table>
<tr><td>Version</td><td>IHL</td><td>Type of Service</td><td colspan="2">Total Length</td></tr>
<tr><td colspan="3">Identification</td><td>Flags</td><td>Fragmentation Offset</td></tr>
<tr><td colspan="2">Time to Live</td><td>Protocol</td><td colspan="2">Header Checksum</td></tr>
<tr><td colspan="5">Source Address</td></tr>
<tr><td colspan="5">Destination Address</td></tr>
<tr><td colspan="4">Options</td><td>Padding</td></tr>
</table>

Figure 9.1 IP Header

The IP Header is shown in Figure 9.1 The Version is currently set to 4. In order to distinguish it from the new version IPv6, IP is also referred to as IPv4. The source address and the destination address are 4-byte Internet addresses. The Options field contains various options such as source based routing, and record route. The source based routing allows the sender to specify the path the datagram should take to reach the destination. Record route allows the sender to record the route the datagram is taking. None of the IP fields are encrypted and there no authentication. It would be extremely easy to set an arbitrary destination address (or the source address), and IP would send the datagram. The destination has no way of ascertaining the fact that the datagram actually originated from an IP address other than the one in the source address field. It is easy to see why any authentication scheme based on IP-addresses would fail.

9.1.3 Transmission Control Protocol

Transmission Control Protocol (TCP) runs on top of IP, and provides a connection oriented service between the sender and the receiver. TCP provides guaranteed delivery, and ensures that the packets are delivered in sequence. The underlying network IP, is highly unreliable and does not provide any guarantee for TCP. In order to provide reliability between the sender and the receiver, TCP uses various mechanisms, such as sequence numbers, acknowledgments, 3-way handshakes and timers.

A TCP connection is identified by the 4-tuple ((destination-ip-address, destination-port), (source-ip-address, source-port)). Ports are the actual end-points of the TCP connection. The working of TCP could be described using a TCP state machine. (see Figure 5). Transitions to different states are based on events received in the form of TCP segments. The TCP states are very closely associated with timers. There are various timers associated with connection establishment (or termination), flow control, and retransmission.

In order to understand the security problems associated with TCP, it is necessary that we look at the state-machine in detail. It is also important to get an overview of TCP implementations, and how they implement the TCP state-machine, the state-transitions and the associated timers.

The TCP layer on either end maintains table entries corresponding to the 4-tuple (remote-ip-address, remote-port, source-ip-address, source-port). This 4-tuple uniquely identifies a connection. For every connection, the end-systems implementing TCP need to keep the TCP state information for the duration of the connection.

9.1.3.1 TCP/IP: The Language of the Internet

TCP/IP (Transport Control Protocol/Internet Protocol) is the "language" of the Internet. Anything that can learn to "speak TCP/IP" can play on the Internet. This is functionality that occurs at the Network (IP) and Transport (TCP) layers in the ISO/OSI Reference Model. Consequently, a host that has TCP/IP functionality (such as Unix, OS/2, MacOS, or Windows NT) can easily support applications (such as Netscape's Navigator) that uses the network.

Open Design

One of the most important features of TCP/IP isn't a technological one: The protocol is an "open" protocol, and anyone who wishes to implement it may do so freely. Engineers and scientists from all over the world participate in the IETF (Internet Engineering Task Force) working groups that design the protocols that make the Internet work. Their time is typically donated by their companies, and the result is work that benefits everyone.

9.1.3.2 IP

As noted, IP is a "network layer" protocol. This is the layer that allows the hosts to actually "talk" to each other. Such things as carrying datagrams, mapping the Internet address (such as 10.2.3.4) to a physical network address (such as 08:00:69:0a:ca:8f), and routing, which takes care of making sure that all of the devices that have Internet connectivity can find the way to each other.

Understanding IP

IP has a number of very important features which make it an extremely robust and flexible protocol. For our purposes, though, we're going to focus on the security of IP, or more specifically, the lack there of.

Attacks Against IP

A number of attacks against IP are possible. Typically, these exploit the fact that IP does not perform a robust mechanism for authentication , which is proving that a packet came from where it claims it did. A packet simply claims to originate from a given address, and there isn't a way to be sure that the host that sent the packet is telling the truth. This isn't necessarily a weakness, per se , but it is an important point, because it means that the facility of host authentication has to be provided at a higher layer on the ISO/OSI Reference Model. Today, applications that require strong host authentication (such as cryptographic applications) do this at the application layer.

IP Spoofing

This is where one host claims to have the IP address of another. Since many systems (such as router access control lists) define which packets may and which packets may not pass based on the sender's IP address, this is a useful technique to an attacker: he can send packets to a host, perhaps causing it to take some sort of action.

Additionally, some applications allow login based on the IP address of the person making the request (such as the Berkeley r-commands). These are both good examples how trusting untrustable layers can provide security that is – at best – weak.

IP Session Hijacking

This is a relatively sophisticated attack, first described by Steve Bellovin. This is very dangerous, however, because there are now toolkits available in the underground community that allow otherwise unskilled bad-guy-wannabes to perpetrate this attack. IP Session Hijacking is an attack whereby a user's session is taken over, being in the control of the attacker. If the user was in the middle of email, the attacker is looking at the email, and then can execute any commands he wishes as the attacked user. The attacked user simply sees his session dropped, and may simply login again, perhaps not even noticing that the attacker is still logged in and doing things.

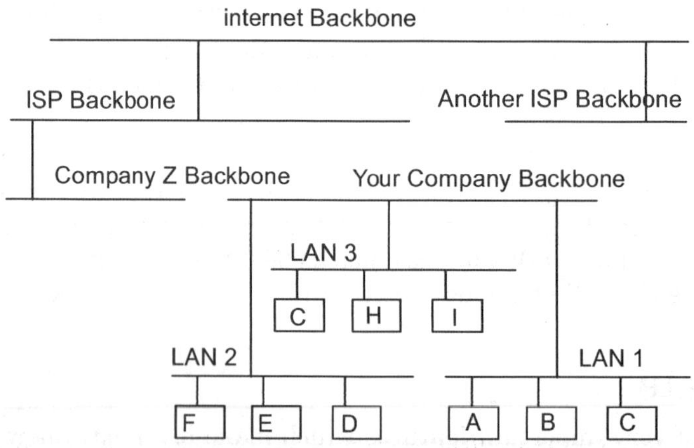

Figure 9.2

For the description of the attack, let's return to our large network of networks in Figure 9.2 In this attack, a user on host A is carrying on a session with host G. Perhaps this is a telnet session, where the user is reading his email, or using a Unix shell account from home. Somewhere in the network between A and G sits host H which is run by a naughty person. The naughty person on host H watches the traffic between A and G, and runs a tool which starts to impersonate A to G, and at the same time tells A to shut up, perhaps trying to convince it that G is no longer on the net (which might happen in the event of a crash, or major network outage). After a few seconds of this, if the attack is successful, naughty person has "hijacked" the session of our user. Anything that the user can do legitimately can now be done by the attacker, illegitimately. As far as G knows, nothing has happened.

This can be solved by replacing standard telnet-type applications with encrypted versions of the same thing. In this case, the attacker can still take over the session, but he'll see only "gibberish" because the session is encrypted. The attacker will not have the needed cryptographic key(s) to decrypt the data stream from G, and will, therefore, be unable to do anything with the session.

9.1.4 TCP

TCP is a transport-layer protocol. It needs to sit on top of a network-layer protocol, and was designed to ride atop IP. (Just as IP was designed to carry, among other things, TCP packets.) Because TCP and IP were designed together and wherever you have one, you typically have the other, the entire suite of Internet protocols are known collectively as "TCP/IP.".

Guaranteed Packet Delivery

Probably the most important is guaranteed packet delivery. Host A sending packets to host B expects to get acknowledgments back for each packet. If B does not send an acknowledgment within a specified amount of time, A will resend the packet.

Applications on host B will expect a data stream from a TCP session to be complete, and in order. As noted, if a packet is missing, it will be resent by A, and if packets arrive out of order, B will arrange them in proper order before passing the data to the requesting application.

This is suited well toward a number of applications, such as a telnet session. A user wants to be sure every keystroke is received by the remote host, and that it gets every packet sent back, even if this means occasional slight delays in responsiveness while a lost packet is resent, or while out-of-order packets are rearranged.

It is not suited well toward other applications, such as streaming audio or video, however. In these, it doesn't really matter if a packet is lost (a lost packet in a stream of 100 won't be distinguishable) but it does matter if they arrive late (i.e., because of a host resending a packet presumed lost), since the data stream will be paused while the lost packet is being resent. Once the lost packet is received, it will be put in the proper slot in the data stream, and then passed up to the application.

9.1.5 UDP

UDP (User Datagram Protocol) is a simple transport-layer protocol. It does not provide the same features as TCP, and is thus considered "unreliable." Again, although this is unsuitable for some applications, it does have much more applicability in other applications than the more reliable and robust TCP.

Lower Overhead than TCP

One of the things that makes UDP nice is its simplicity. Because it doesn't need to keep track of the sequence of packets, whether they ever made it to their destination, etc., it has lower overhead than TCP. This is another reason why it's more suited to streaming-data applications: there's less screwing around that needs to be done with making sure all the packets are there, in the right order, and that sort of thing.

9.1.6 Risk Management: The Game of Security

It's very important to understand that in security, one simply cannot say "what's the best firewall?" There are two extremes: absolute security and absolute access. The closest we can get to an absolutely secure machine is one unplugged from the network, power supply, locked in a safe, and thrown at the bottom of the ocean. Unfortunately, it isn't terribly useful in this state. A machine with absolute access is extremely convenient to use: it's simply there, and will do whatever you tell it, without questions, authorization, passwords, or any other mechanism. Unfortunately, this isn't terribly practical, either: the Internet is a bad neighborhood now, and it isn't long before some bonehead will tell the computer to do something like self-destruct, after which, it isn't terribly useful to you.

This is no different from our daily lives. We constantly make decisions about what risks we're willing to accept. When we get in a car and drive to work, there's a certain risk that we're taking. It's possible that something completely out of control will cause us to become part of an accident on the highway. When we get on an airplane, we're accepting the level of risk involved as the price of convenience. However, most people have a mental picture of what an acceptable risk is, and won't go beyond that in most circumstances. If I happen to be upstairs at home, and want to leave for work, I'm not going to jump out the window. Yes, it would be more convenient, but the risk of injury outweighs the advantage of convenience.

Every organization needs to decide for itself where between the two extremes of total security and total access they need to be. A policy needs to articulate this, and then define how that will be enforced with practices and such. Everything that is done in the name of security, then, must enforce that policy uniformly.

9.1.7 IPSec

Short for IP Security, a set of protocols developed by the IETF to support secure exchange of packets at the IP layer. IPsec has been deployed widely to implement Virtual Private Networks (VPNs). One of the weaknesses of the original Internet Protocol is that it lacks any sort of general purpose mechanism for ensuring the authenticity and privacy of data as it is passed over the internetwork. Since IP datagrams must usually be routed between two devices over unknown networks, any information in them is subject to being intercepted and even possibly changed. With the increased use of the Internet for critical applications, security enhancements were needed for IP. To this end, a set of protocols called IP Security or IPSec was developed.

In general terms, it provides security services at the IP layer for other TCP/IP protocols and applications to use. What this means is that IPSec provides the tools that devices on a TCP/IP network need in order to communicate securely. When two devices (either end user hosts or intermediate devices such as routers or firewalls) want to engage in secure communications, they set up a secure path between themselves that may traverse across many insecure intermediate systems. To accomplish this, they must perform (at least) the following tasks:

- They must agree on a set of security protocols to use, so that each one sends data in a format the other can understand.
- They must decide on a specific encryption algorithm to use in encoding data.
- They must exchange keys that are used to "unlock" data that has been cryptographically encoded.
- Once this background work is completed, each device must use the protocols, methods and keys previously agreed upon to encode data and send it across the network.

As you already know that the data over internet is transfeered in the form of small packets each consisiting of a header followed by data that is called payload.Transport mode encrypts only the data portion (payload) of each packet, but leaves the header untouched. The more secure Tunnel mode encrypts both the header and the payload. On the receiving side, an IPSec-compliant device decrypts each packet. IPSec modes are closely related to the function of the three core protocols:

(1) IPSec Authentication Header (AH),

(2) IPSec Encapsulating Security Payload (ESP) and the

(3) IPSec Internet Key Exchange (IKE).

All the three protocols provide protection by adding to a datagram a header (and possibly other fields) containing security information. The choice of mode does not affect the method by which each generates its header, but rather, changes what specific parts of the IP datagram are protected and how the headers are arranged to accomplish this. In essence, the mode really describes, not prescribes how AH or ESP do their thing. It is used as the basis for defining other constructs, such as security associations (SAs).

For IPsec to work, the sending and receiving devices must share a public key. This is accomplished through a protocol known as Internet Security Association and Key Management Protocol/Oakley (ISAKMP/Oakley), which allows the receiver to obtain a public key and authenticate the sender using digital certificates.

Note: IPSec was initially developed with IPv6 in mind, but has been engineered to provide security for both IPv4 and IPv6 networks, and operation in both versions is similar. There are some differences in the datagram formats used for AH and ESP depending on whether IPSec is used in IPv4 and IPv6, since the two versions have different datagram formats and addressing. These differences will be high lighted where appropriate.

9.2 AUTHENTICATION HEADER

AH is a member of the IPsec protocol suite. AH is intended to guarantee connectionless integrity and data origin authentication of IP packets. Further, it can optionally protect against replay attacks by using the sliding window technique and discarding old packets. AH protects the IP payload and all header fields of an IP datagram except for mutable fields (i.e. those that might be altered in transit).AH protocol provides data origin authentication, data integrity, and replay protection. However, AH does not provide data confidentiality, which means that all of your data is sent in the clear.

AH ensures data integrity with the checksum that a message authentication code, like MD5, generates. To ensure data origin authentication, AH includes a secret shared key in the the algorithm that it uses for authentication. To ensure replay protection, AH uses a sequence number field within the AH header. It is worth noting here, that these three distinct functions are often lumped together and referred to as authentication. In the simplest terms, AH ensures that your data has not been tampered with enroute to its final destination.

Although AH authenticates as much of the IP datagram as possible, the values of certain fields in the IP header cannot be predicted by the receiver. AH does not protect these fields, known as mutable fields. However, AH always protects the payload of the IP packet.

The Internet Engineering Task Force (IETF) formally defines AH in Request for Comment (RFC) 2402, IP Authentication Header. You can view this RFC on the Internet at the following Web site: http://www.rfc-editor.org.

In IPv4, mutable (and therefore unauthenticated) IP header fields include DSCP/TOS, Flags, Fragment Offset, TTL and Header Checksum. AH operates directly on top of IP, using IP protocol number 51.

The following AH packet diagram shows how an AH packet is constructed and interpreted:

<table>
<tr><td>0 - 7 bit</td><td>8 -15 bit</td><td>16 - 23 bit</td><td>24 - 31 bit</td></tr>
<tr><td>Next header</td><td>Payload length</td><td colspan="2">Reserved</td></tr>
<tr><td colspan="4">Security parameters index (SPI)</td></tr>
<tr><td colspan="4">Sequence number</td></tr>
<tr><td colspan="4">Authentication data (veriable)</td></tr>
</table>

Figure 9.3 Authentication Header Packet diagra

Field meanings

1. **Next header :** The Next Header is an 8-bit field that identifies the type of the next payload after the Authentication Header. The value of this field is chosen from the set of IP Protocol Numbers defined in the most recent "Assigned Numbers" RFC from the Internet Assigned Numbers Authority.
2. **Payload length :** Size of AH packet.
3. **RESERVED :** Reserved for future use (all zero until then).

4. **Security parameters index (SPI) :** Identifies the security parameters, which, in combination with the IP address, then identify the security association implemented with this packet.
5. **Sequence number :** A monotonically increasing number, used to prevent replay attacks.
6. **Authentication data :** Contains the integrity check value (ICV) necessary to authenticate the packet; it may contain padding.

The operation of the AH protocol is surprisingly simple—especially for any protocol that has anything to do with network security. It can be considered analogous to the algorithms used to calculate checksums or perform CRC checks for error detection. In those cases, a standard algorithm is used by the sender to compute a checksum or CRC code based on the contents of a message. This computed result is transmitted along with the original data to the destination, which repeats the calculation and discards the message if any discrepancy is found between its calculation and the one done by the source.

This is the same idea behind AH, except that instead of using a simple algorithm known to everyone, we use a special hashing algorithm and a specific key known only to the source and the destination. A security association between two devices is set up that specifies these particulars so that the source and destination know how to perform the computation but nobody else can. On the source device, AH performs the computation and puts the result (called the Integrity Check Value or ICV) into a special header with other fields for transmission. The destination device does the same calculation using the key the two devices share, which enables it to see immediately if any of the fields in the original datagram were modified (either due to error or malice).

It's important that it is pointed out explicitly that just as a checksum doesn't change the original data, neither does the ICV calculation change the original data. The presence of the AH header allows us to verify the integrity of the message, but doesn't encrypt it. Thus, AH provides authentication but not privacy (that's what ESP is for.

9.2.1 Ways of using AH

You can apply AH in two ways: transport mode or tunnel mode. In transport mode, the IP header of the datagram is the outermost IP header, followed by the AH header and then the payload of the datagram. AH authenticates the entire datagram, except the mutable fields. However, the information contained in the datagram is transported in the clear and is, therefore, subject to eavesdropping. Transport mode requires less processing overhead than tunnel mode, but does not provide as much security.

Tunnel mode creates a new IP header and uses it as the outermost IP header of the datagram. The AH header follows the new IP header. The original datagram (both the IP header and the original payload) comes last. AH authenticates the entire datagram, which means that the responding system can detect whether the datagram changed while in transit.

When either end of a security association is a gateway, use tunnel mode. In tunnel mode the source and destination addresses in the outermost IP header do not need to be the same as those in the original IP header. For example, two security gateways may operate an AH tunnel to authenticate all traffic between the networks they connect together. In fact, this is a very typical configuration.

The main advantage to using tunnel mode, is that tunnel mode totally protects the encapsulated IP datagram. In addition, tunnel mode makes it possible to use private addresses.

9.2.2 Neccessity of AH

In many cases, your data only requires authentication. While the Encapsulating Security Payload (ESP) protocol can perform authentication, AH does not affect your system performance as does ESP. Another advantage of using AH, is that AH authenticates the entire datagram. ESP, on the other hand, does not authenticate the leading IP header or any other information that comes before the ESP header.

In addition, ESP requires strong cryptographic algorithms in order to be implemented. Strong cryptography is restricted in some countries, while AH is not regulated and can be used freely around the world.

9.3 ENCAPSULATING SECURITY PAYLOAD (ESP)

The IPSec Authentication Header (AH) provides integrity authentication services to IPSec-capable devices, so they can verify that messages are received intact from other devices. For many applications, however, this is only one piece of the puzzle. We want to not only protect against intermediate devices changing our datagrams, we want to protect against them examining their contents as well. For this level of private communication, AH is not enough; we need to use the Encapsulating Security Payload (ESP) protocol.

ESP is a fundamental element of IPsec that provides integrity, authentication, and confidentiality for IP datagrams. ESP works between hosts, between a host and a security gateway, or between security gateways. The support for security gateways (in Tunnel-mode) permits trustworthy networks behind a security gateway to omit encryption while using security gateways to obtain confidentiality for transmissions over untrustworthy network segments. In Tunnel-mode ESP encapsulates the entire IP datagram within the ESP. (See tunneling.) When there is no intervening security gateway, then the hosts may use the Transport-mode in which only the upper layer protocol data (e.g., TCP or UDP) is encrypted and there is no encrypted IP header. In Transport-mode ESP encapsulates an upper-layer protocol (e.g. UDP or TCP) inside ESP and then adds a cleartext IP header. This cleartext IP header is used to carry the protected data through the intervening networks. Transport-mode can reduce both the bandwidth consumed and the protocol processing costs for users that do not need to keep the entire IP datagram confidential or who encrypt the data in the host application prior to transmission. ESP works with both unicast and multicast

The main job of ESP is to provide the privacy we seek for IP datagrams by encrypting them. An encryption algorithm combines the data in the datagram with a key to transform it into an encrypted form. This is then repackaged using a special format that we will see shortly, and transmitted to the destination, which decrypts it using the same algorithm.

ESP also supports its own authentication scheme like that used in AH, or can be used in conjunction with AH.

The ESP protocol provides data confidentiality, and also optionally provides data origin authentication, data integrity checking, and replay protection. The difference between ESP and the Authentication Header (AH) protocol is that ESP provides encryption, while both protocols provide authentication, integrity checking, and replay protection. With ESP, both communicating systems use a shared key for encrypting and decrypting the data they exchange.

If you decide to use both encryption and authentication, then the responding system first authenticates the packet and then, if the first step succeeds, the system proceeds with decryption. This type of configuration reduces processing overhead, as well as reduces your vulnerability to denial-of-service attacks.

ESP is a member of the IPsec protocol suite. It is the portion of IPsec that provides origin authenticity, integrity, and confidentiality protection of packets. ESP also supports encryption-only and authentication-only configurations, but using encryption without authentication is strongly discouraged because it is insecure. Unlike Authentication Header (AH), ESP does not protect the IP packet header. However, in Tunnel Mode, where the entire original IP packet is encapsulated with a new packet header added, ESP protection is afforded to the whole inner IP packet (including the inner header) while the outer header remains unprotected. ESP operates directly on top of IP, using IP protocol number 50.

9.3.1 Modes of Operation

You can apply ESP in two ways: transport mode or tunnel mode. In transport mode, the ESP header follows the IP header of the original IP datagram. If the datagram already has an IPSec header, then the ESP header goes before it. The ESP trailer and the optional authentication data follow the payload.

Transport mode does not authenticate or encrypt the IP header, which could expose your addressing information to potential attackers while the datagram is in transit. Transport mode requires less processing overhead than tunnel mode, but does not provide as much security. In most cases, hosts use ESP in transport mode.

Tunnel mode creates a new IP header and uses it as the outermost IP header of the datagram, followed by the ESP header and then the original datagram (both the IP header and the original payload). The ESP trailer and the optional authentication data are appended to the payload. When you use both encryption and authentication, ESP completely protects the original datagram because it is now the payload data for the new ESP packet. ESP, however, does not protect the new IP header. Gateways must use ESP in tunnel mode.

ESP uses a symmetric key that both communicating parties use to encrypt and decrypt the data they exchange. The sender and the receiver must agree on the key before secure communication takes place between them. OS/400 VPN uses Data Encryption Standard (DES), triple-DES (3DES), RC5, RC4, or Advanced Encryption Standard (AES) for encryption.

9.3.2 ESP Packet Diagram

The following ESP packet diagram shows how an ESP packet is constructed and interpreted:

0 - 7 bit	8 -15 bit	16 - 23 bit	24 - 31 bit
Security parameters index (SPI)			
Sequence number			
Payload data (veriable)			
	Padding (0-255 bytes)		
		Pad Length	Next Header
Authentication data (veriable)			

Figure 9.4 ESP packet diagram

ESP has several fields that are the same as those used in AH, but packages its fields in a very different way. Instead of having just a header, it divides its fields into three components:

(1) **ESP Header :** This contains two fields, the SPI and Sequence Number, and comes before the encrypted data. Its placement depends on whether ESP is used in transport mode or tunnel mode.

(2) **ESP Trailer :** This section is placed after the encrypted data. It contains padding that is used to align the encrypted data, through a Padding and Pad Length field. Interestingly, it also contains the Next Header field for ESP.

(3) **ESP Authentication Data :** Contains the data used to authenticate the packet.This field contains an Integrity Check Value (ICV), computed in a manner similar to how the AH protocol works, for when ESP's authentication feature is used.

Field meanings

1. **Security parameters index (SPI) :** Identifies the security parameters in combination with IP address.
2. **Sequence number :** A monotonically increasing number, used to prevent replay attacks.
3. **Payload data :** The data to be transferred.
4. **Padding :** Used with some block ciphers to pad the data to the full length of a block.
5. **Pad length :** Size of padding in bytes.

6. **Next header :** Identifies the protocol of the payload data. The value of this field is chosen from the set of IP Protocol Numbers defined in the most recent "Assigned Numbers" RFC from the Internet Assigned Numbers

There are two reasons why these fields are broken into pieces like this. The first is that some encryption algorithms require the data to be encrypted to have a certain block size, and so padding must appear after the data and not before it. That's why padding appears in the ESP Trailer. The second is that the ESP Authentication Data appears separately because it is used to authenticate the rest of the encrypted datagram after encryption. This means it cannot appear in the ESP Header or ESP Trailer.

The IP Authentication Header seeks to provide security by adding authentication information to an IP datagram. This authentication information is calculated using all of the fields in the IP datagram (including not only the IP Header but also other headers and the user data) which do not change in transit. Fields or options which need to change in transit (c.g., hop count, time to live, ident, fragment offset, or routing pointer, such as audio and video. Sources of data can include both live data feeds and stored clips. This protocol is intended to control multiple data delivery sessions, provide a means for choosing delivery channels such as UDP, multicast UDP and TCP, and provide a means for choosing delivery mechanisms bases upon RTP.) are considered to be zero for the calculation of the authentication data. This provides significantly more security than is currently present in IPv4 and might be sufficient for the needs of many users.

When used with IPv6, the Authentication Header normally appears after the IPv6 Hop-by-Hop Header and before the IPv6 Destination Options. When used with IPv4, the Authentication Header normally follows the main IPv4 header.

9.4 IPSEC KEY EXCHANGE (IKE)

IPSec, like many secure networking protocol sets, is based on the concept of a "shared secret". Two devices that want to send information securely encode and decode it using a piece of information that only they know. Anyone who isn't "in" on the secret is able to intercept the information but is prevented either from reading it (if ESP is used to encrypt the payload) or from tampering with it undetected (if AH is used). Before either AH or ESP can be used, however, it is necessary for the two devices to exchange the "secret" that the security protocols themselves will use. The primary support protocol used for this purpose in IPSec is called Internet Key Exchange (IKE).

IKE is defined in RFC 2409, and is one of the more complicated of the IPSec protocols to comprehend. In fact, it is simply impossible to truly understand more than a real simplification of its operation without significant background in cryptography. I don't have a background in cryptography and I must assume that you, my reader, do not either. So rather than fill this topic with baffling acronyms and unexplained concepts, I will just provide a brief outline of IKE and how it is used.

The purpose of IKE is to allow devices to exchange information required for secure communication. As the title suggests, this includes cryptographic keys used for encoding authentication information and performing payload encryption. IKE works by allowing IPSec-capable devices to exchange security associations (SAs), to populate their security association databases (SADs). These are then used for the actual exchange of secured datagrams with the AH and ESP protocols.

IKE is considered a "hybrid" protocol because it combines (and supplements) the functions of three other protocols. The first of these is the Internet Security Association and Key Management Protocol (ISAKMP). This protocol provides a framework for exchanging encryption keys and security association information. It operates by allowing security associations to be negotiated through a series of phases.

- ISAKMP is a generic protocol that supports many different key exchange methods. In IKE, the ISAKMP framework is used as the basis for a specific key exchange method that combines features from two key exchange protocols:
- OAKLEY: Describes a specific mechanism for exchanging keys through the definition of various key exchange "modes". Most of the IKE key exchange process is based on OAKLEY.
- SKEME: Describes a different key exchange mechanism than OAKLEY. IKE uses some features from SKEME, including its method of public key encryption and its fast re-keying feature.

HP-UX IPSec uses the Internet Key Exchange (IKE) protocol to negotiate the protocols, encryption algorithms and encryption keys used. The IKE protocol also provides primary authentication - verifying the identity of the remote system before negotiating the encryption algorithm and keys.

The IKE protocol also allows HP-UX IPSec to dynamically negotiate new keys rather than exposing the same key for long periods. You can configure key lifetimes based on time or number of bytes sent.

The IKE protocol is a hybrid of three other protocols: ISAKMP (Internet Security Association and Key Management Protocol), Oakley and SKEME. ISAKMP provides a framework for authentication and key exchange, but does not define them (neither authentication nor key exchange). The Oakley protocol describes a series of modes for key exchange and the SKEME protocol defines key exchange techniques.

9.5 SECURITY POLICIES, SECURITY ASSOCIATIONS AND ASSOCIATED DATABASES

To manage all of this complexity, IPSec is equipped with a flexible, powerful way of specifying how different types of datagrams should be handled. To understand how this works, we must first define two important logical concepts:

9.5.1 Security Policies

A security policy is a rule that is programmed into the IPSec implementation that tells it how to process different datagrams received by the device. For example, security policies are used to decide if a particular packet needs to be processed by IPSec or not; those that do not bypass AH and ESP entirely. If security is required, the security policy provides general guidelines for how it should be provided, and if necessary, links to more specific detail. Security policies for a device are stored in the device's Security Policy Database (SPD).

9.5.2 Security Associations (SA)

SA is a set of security information that describes a particular kind of secure connection between one device and another. You can consider it a "contract", if you will, that specifies the particular security mechanisms that are used for secure communications between the two.A device's security associations are contained in its Security Association Database (SAD).

It's often hard to distinguish the SPD and the SAD, since they are similar in concept. The main difference between them is that security policies are general while security associations are more specific. To determine what to do with a particular datagram, a device first checks the SPD. The security policies in the SPD may reference a particular security association in the SAD. If so, the device will look up that security association and use it for processing the datagram.

The IP security architecture uses the concept of a security association as the basis for building security functions into IP. A security association is simply the bundle of algorithms and parameters (such as keys) that is being used to encrypt and authenticate a particular flow in one direction. Therefore, in normal bi-directional traffic, the flows are secured by a pair of security associations. The actual choice of encryption and authentication algorithms (from a defined list) is left to the IPsec administrator.

In order to decide what protection is to be provided for an outgoing packet, IPsec uses the Security Parameter Index (SPI), an index to the security association database (SADB), along with the destination address in a packet header, which together uniquely identify a security association for that packet. A similar procedure is performed for an incoming packet, where IPsec gathers decryption and verification keys from the security association database.

For multicast, a security association is provided for the group, and is duplicated across all authorized receivers of the group. There may be more than one security association for a group, using different SPIs, thereby allowing multiple levels and sets of security within a group. Indeed, each sender can have multiple security associations, allowing authentication, since a receiver can only know that someone knowing the keys sent the data. Note that the relevant standard does not describe how the association is chosen and duplicated across the group; it is assumed that a responsible party will have made the choice.

9.5.3 Security Associations and IKE Phases

A secure communication channel and its parameters, such as encryption method, keys and lifetime are sometimes referred to as a Security Association (SA). There are two Security Association negotiation phases within ISAKMP, which are sometimes referred to by the

Oakley modes used to establish the SAs. The general flow of the IKE protocol is as follows:

(1) ISAKMP Phase One (Main Mode)

- Negotiate and establish an ISAKMP Security Association (SA), a secure communication channel for further IKE communication.
- The two systems generate a Diffie-Hellman shared value (described below) that is used as the base for a symmetric (shared) key, and further IKE communication is encrypted using this symmetric key.
- Verify the remote system's identity (primary authentication)

(2) ISAKMP Phase Two (Quick Mode)

Using the ISAKMP/MM SA's secure communication channel, negotiate one or more Security Associations for IPSec AH or ESP encryption.

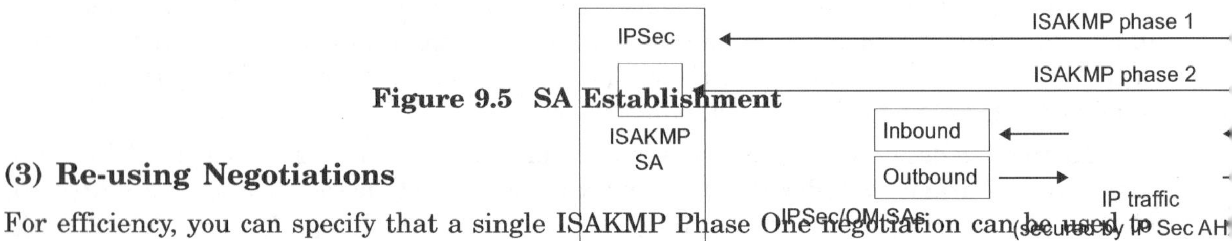

Figure 9.5 SA Establishment

(3) Re-using Negotiations

For efficiency, you can specify that a single ISAKMP Phase One negotiation can be used to negotiate multiple ISAKMP Phase Two negotiations.

Conversely, you can specify that the ISAKMP phase one negotiations cannot be re-used by limiting the maximum number of ISAKMP phase two negotiations to one (The ISAKMP/MM SAs cannot be re-used). This can provide Perfect Forward Secrecy (PFS) of the keys and the identities of both the ISAKMP negotating peers.

9.5.4 Generating Shared Keys: Diffie-Hellman

Security Associations (SAs) use a symmetric key to encrypt communication. This symmetric key is based on a shared value generated using the Diffie-Hellman algorithm.

With Diffie-Hellman key generation, each party generates two numbers, one public and one private. These values are based on a selected, well-known numeric base, or "Diffie-Hellman group." The two parties exchange public values (this exchange may occur via an insecure channel). Each party then uses its private value and the other party's public value to generate a new value. Because of the mathematical properties of the numbers, each party will generate the same value, which can then be used as a symmetric key.

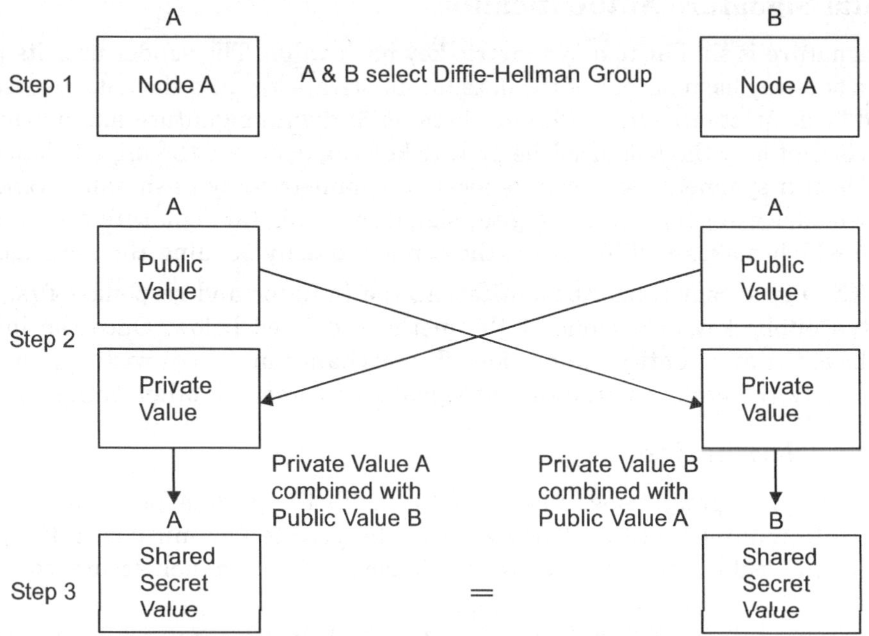

Figure 9.6 Diffie-Hellman Key Exchange

Diffie-Hellman is vulnerable to attacks where a third-party intercepts messages between the sender and receiver and assumes the identity of the other party. Because of this, Diffie-Hellman should be used with some form of authentication to ensure that symmetric keys are established between correct parties.

In summary, if two entities use the same, well-known Diffie-Hellman group, they can publicly exchange values and generate the same shared value that they can use as a symmetric key, or use as a base for a symmetric key. Diffie-Hellman should be used with some form of authentication.

IKE Primary Authentication

IKE must authenticate the identities of the systems using the Diffie-Hellman algorithm. This process is known as primary authentication. HP-UX IPSec IKE can use two primary authentication methods:

Digital Signatures

Preshared keys

Digital signature and public-key encryption are both based on asymmetric key encryption and require a mechanism for distributing public keys. This is usually done using security certificates and a Public Key Infrastructure (PKI).

IKE Digital Signature Authentication

A digital signature is similar to a symmetric-key hash value. The sender uses its private key to encrypt a one-way hash output of the data (or its private key and the data are used as input for a keyed-hash function). One difference between a digital signature and a symmetric-key hash value is that only the holder of the private key can generate the digital signature, while either holder of a symmetric key can generate a symmetric-key hash value. Since only the private key holder can generate the digital signature, a digital signature also provides non-repudiation which makes it difficult for the sender to deny sending the message.

For IKE Digital Signature Authentication, the initiator and responder first obtain the other entity's public key, using one of the methods defined below. Once the initiator and responder have the other entity's public key, they exchange messages with digital signatures. They each verify the other entity's digital signatures using the other entity's public key.

Public Key Distribution

In asymmetric-key cryptosystems, a single entity holds the private key while the public key is distributed to multiple entities. The owner of the private key must keep the private key secret, while the public key can be freely distributed over a non-secure communication channel.

However, there must be some assurance that a particular public key is the actual public key of the entity with which you want to communicate. This is usually done by distributing public keys in the form of security certificates.

Security Certificates

A public key certificate associates (or binds) a public key with a particular person, device, or other entity. The public-key certificate is issued by an entity, in whom users have put their trust, called a certificate authority (CA) that guarantees or confirms the identity of the holder (person, device, or other entity) of the corresponding private key. The CA digitally signs the certificate with the CA's private key, so the certificate can be verified using the CA's public key.

The format for public-key certificates is defined by the International Organization for Standardization (ISO) X.509 standard, Version 3.

Certificates are issued with a specific lifetime, defined by a start date/time and an expiration date/time. However, situations can arise, such as a compromised key value, that necessitate the revocation of the certificate. In this case, the certificate authority can revoke the certificate. This is accomplished by including the certificate's serial number on a Certificate Revocation List (CRL) updated and published on a regular basis by the CA and made available to certificate users.

IKE Public Key Distribution

IKE primary authentication with digital signatures and public/private key encryption both require that the IKE initiator and responder obtain the other entity's public key, typically using security certificates. This may be done as part of the IKE negotiation - the two entities may exchange certificates at the beginning of the IKE negotiation. Alternatively, this may be done independent of the IKE negotiation and each entity may get the other entity's certificate from a CA or certificate directory service. The method used varies according to the CA used and the services provided by the CA.

IKE Public Key Encryption Authentication

For IKE Public key encryption authentication, the initiator and responder first obtain the other entity's public key, using one of the methods defined above.

The initiator sends an authentication "challenge" to the responder: the initiator sends data, including a random number (nonce), encrypted using the responder's public key. To authenticate itself to the sender, the responder decrypts the data using its private key, then sends a hash of the data back, encrypted using the symmetric key negotiated for the ISAKMP/MM SA. The reciprocal process is used by the responder to authenticate the identity of the initiator.

IKE Preshared Key Authentication

With preshared key authentication, the two entities must manually exchange and configure a shared, symmetric key. Note that the preshared key is used only for the primary authentication. The two negotiating entities then generate dynamic shared keys for the IKE SAs and IPSec/QM SAs.

Preshared keys do not require a Certificate Authority or Public Key Infrastructure.

9.5.4 Authentication

Authentication is defined by [KAUF95] as "the process of reliably verifying the identity of someone (or something)".

Authentication can be "One-Way" or "Two-Way." Each of these is described below.

- **One way Authentication :** Involves a single transfer of information from one user (A) intended for another (B), and establishes the following:
- the identity of A and that the authentication token was generated by A;
- the identity of B and that the authentication token was intended to be sent to B;
- the integrity and originality (the property of not having been sent two or three times) of the authentication token being transferred.
- Involves, in addition, a reply from B to A and establishes, in addition, the following:
- that the authentication token generated in the reply was actually generated by B and was intended to be sent to A;
- the integrity and originality of the authentication token sent in the reply;
- (optionally) the mutual secrecy of part of the tokens.

Corroboration of identity is often established by demonstrating the possession of a secret key. Authentication may be accomplished by applying symmetric or asymmetric cryptographic techniques. When using private keys (symmetric) corroboration of identity is often based on a "shared secret."

When using public keys (asymmetric), authentication is accomplished based on digital signatures and digital timestamps. Since the digital signature binds the possessor of the private key with a document and the timestamp can be verified to protect against replays, corroboration of identity can be established by combining digital signature and a timestamp.

9.5.5 Traffic Flow Confidentiality

Cryptographic protocols are designed to resist attacks and also, sometimes, traffic analysis. A specific traffic analysis countermeasure, traffic flow confidentiality, aims to conceal the presence or absence of data and its characteristics. This is important because knowledge of the activity can be as useful to the bad guys as the content of the activity itself.

If cyphertext is relayed, the address must be in the clear at the relays and gateways. If the data are enciphered only on each link, and are deciphered (and are thus made vulnerable) in the relay or gateway, the architecture is said to use link-by-link confidentiality (or encipherment). If only the address (and similar control data) are in the clear in the relay or gateway, the architecture is said to use end-to-end data confidentiality (or encipherment). End-to-end encryption is more desirable from a security point of view, but considerably more complex architecturally.

Furthermore, traffic padding can be used to provide various levels of protection against traffic analysis. This mechanism can be effective only if the traffic is protected by a confidentiality service.

9.5.6 Data Integrity

Data integrity is the property of data which has not been altered or destroyed in an unauthorized manner. It is achieved via a calculated cryptographic checkvalue. The checkvalue may be derived in one or more steps and is a mathematical function of the cryptovariables and the data. These checkvalues are associated with the data to be guarded. If the checkvalue is matched by the value calculated by the data recipient, data integrity is assumed.

Two aspects of data integrity are: the integrity of a single data unit or field, and the integrity of a stream of data units or fields. Determining the integrity of a single data unit involves two processes, one at the sender, and the other at the receiver. The sender appends to the data unit a quantity which is a function of the data itself. This quantity may be supplementary information such as a block code or a cryptographic check value and may itself be enciphered. The receiver generates a corresponding quantity and compares it with the received quantity to determine whether the data has been modified in transit.

Protecting the integrity of a sequence of data units (against misordering, losing, replaying, and inserting or modifying the data) requires additionally some form of explicit ordering such as sequence numbering, time stamping, or cryptographic chaining.

9.5.7 Key Management

Key management encompasses the generation, distribution, and control of cryptographic keys. It is implied by the use of cryptographic algorithms. Important points to be considered are:

(1) The use of a lifetime based on time, use, or other criteria, for each key defined, implicitly, or explicitly. The longer a key's lifetime, the greater the probability that the key will be compromised by the bad guys.

(2) The proper identification of keys according to their functions so that they are used only for their intended function. The greater the key's exposure (to multiple applications) the greater the probability that the key will be compromised.

(3) Physical distribution and archiving of keys. This is both a logistics and security issue, especially in distributed systems such as WANs.

Points to be considered concerning key management for symmetric key algorithms include:

(1) The use of a confidentiality service in the key management protocol.

(2) The use of a key hierarchy ("flat" hierarchies using only data-enciphering keys, multilayer key hierarchies, etc.)

(3) The division of responsibilities so that no one person has a complete copy of an important key.

For asymmetric key management, confidentiality services are used to convey the secret keys. Additionally an integrity service (or a service with proof of origin) is needed to convey the public keys.

10

Web Security

10.1 WEB SECURITY AND INTERNET COMMERCE

Security of data in transit over the Internet becomes increasingly necessary because of steadily growing data volume and importance. Nowadays, every user of a public network sends various types of data, from email to credit card details daily, and he would therefore like them to be protected when in transit over a public network. To this end, a practical SSL protocol has been adopted for protection of data in transit that encompasses all network services that use TCP/IP to support typical application tasks of communication between servers and clients.

We consider Internet commerce to be the purchasing of "goods" over the Internet. Here we'll use the term "goods" in a very broad sense to include books, CDs, hardware, software, airline tickets, stocks and bonds, consulting services, etc. In the 1990s many schemes were designed for Internet commerce, some providing minimal levels of security and others providing a high-level of security along with customer anonymity (similar to the anonymity provided by ordinary person-to-person cash transactions In the late 1990s, however, there was a major shake out, as only a few of these schemes were widely implemented in Web browsers and servers. As of this writing, two schemes have taken hold: SSL, which is currently used by the vast majority of Internet transactions; and SET, which is to expected to fiercely compete with SSL in the upcoming years.

There are three major players in this infrastructure:

- the customer who is purchasing a good,
- the merchant who is selling the good, and

- the merchant's bank, which authorizes the purchase. We shall see below that Internet commerce with SSL provides security for communication between the first two of these three players (i.e., the customer and the merchant), whereas SET provides security for communication among all three players.

10.2 SSL PROTOCOL

The SSL protocol was originally developed by Netscape, to ensure security of data transported and routed through HTTP, LDAP or POP3 application layers. SSL is designed to make use of TCP as a communication layer to provide a reliable end-to-end secure and authenticated connection between two points over a network (for example between the service client and the server). Notwithstanding this SSL can be used for protection of data in transit in situations related to any network service, it is used mostly in HTTP server and client applications. Today, almost each available HTTP server can support an SSL session, whilst IE or Netscape Navigator browsers are provided with SSL-enabled client software.

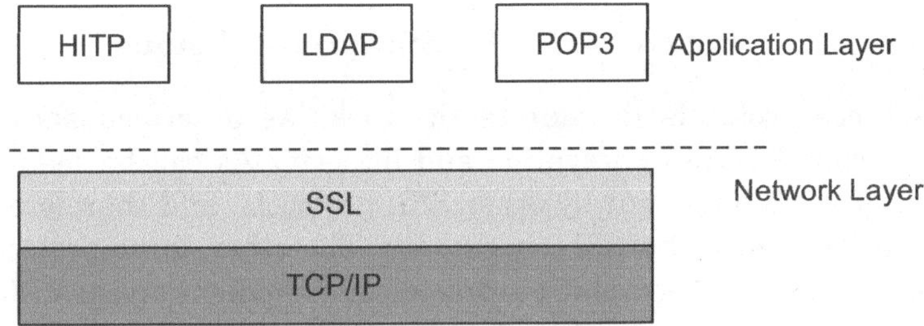

Figure 10.1 SSL between application protocols and TCP/IP

10.2.1 SSL objectives and architecture

The main objectives for SSL are:

- Authenticating the client and server to each other: the SSL protocol supports the use of standard key cryptographic techniques (public key encryption) to authenticate the communicating parties to each other. Though the most frequent application consists in authenticating the service client on the basis of a certificate, SSL may also use the same methods to authenticate the client.
- Ensuring data integrity: during a session, data cannot be either intentionally or unintentionally tampered with.
- Securing data privacy: data in transport between the client and the server must be protected from interception and be readable only by the intended recipient. This prerequisite is necessary for both the data associated with the protocol itself (securing traffic during negotiations) and the application data that is sent during the session

itself. SSL is in fact not a single protocol but rather a set of protocols that can additionally be further divided in two layers:

- the protocol to ensure data security and integrity: this layer is composed of the SSL Record Protocol,
- the protocols that are designed to establish an SSL connection: three protocols are used in this layer: the SSL Handshake Protocol, the SSL ChangeCipher SpecPprotocol and the SSL Alert Protocol.

The SSL protocol stack is illustrated in Figure 10.2.

SSL handshake protocol	SSL cipher change protocol	SSL alert protocol	Application Protocol (e.g. HTTP)
SSL Record Protocol			
TCP			
IP			

Figure 10.2 The SSL protocol stack

SSL uses these protocols to address the tasks as described above. The SSL record protocol is responsible for data encryption and integrity. As can be seen in Figure 10.2 it is also used to encapsulate data sent by other SSL protocols, and therefore, it is also involved in the tasks associated with the SSL check data. The other three protocols cover the areas of session management, cryptographic parameter management and transfer of SSL messages between the client and the server. Prior to going into a more detailed discussion of the role of individual protocols and their functions let us describe two fundamental concepts related to the use of SSL.

10.2.2 SSL session and connection

The concepts as mentioned above are fundamental for a connection between the client and the server, and they also encompass a series of attributes. Let's try to give some more details:

- Connection: this is a logical client/server link, associated with the provision of a suitable type of service. In SSL terms, it must be a peer-to-peer connection with two network nodes.
- Session: this is an association between a client and a server that defines a set of parameters such as algorithms used, session number etc. An SSL session is created by the Handshake Protocol that allows parameters to be shared among the connections made between the server and the client, and sessions are used to avoid negotiation of new parameters for each connection.

This means that a single session is shared among multiple SSL connections between the client and the server. In theory, it may also be possible that multiple sessions are shared by a single connection, but this feature is not used in practice. The concepts of a SSL session and connection involve several parameters that are used for SSL-enabled communication between the client and the server. During the negotiations of the handshake protocol, the encryption methods are established and a series of parameters of the Session State are subsequently used within the session.

A session state is defined by the following parameters:

- Session identifier: this is an identifier generated by the server to identify a session with a chosen client,
- Peer certificate: X.509 certificate of the peer, compression method: a method used to compress data prior to encryption,
- Algorithm specification termed CipherSpec: specifies the bulk data encryption algorithm (for example DES) and the hash algorithm (for example MD5) used during the session,
- Master secret: 48-byte data being a secret shared between the client and server, "is resumable": this is a flag indicating whether the session can be used to initiate new connections.

According to the specification, the SSL connection state is defined by the following parameters:

- Server and client random: random data generated by both the client and server for each connection,
- Server write MAC secret: the secret key used for data written by the server,
- Client write MAC secret: the secret used for data written by the client,
- Server write key: the bulk cipher key for data encrypted by the server and decrypted by the client,
- Client write key: the bulk cipher key for data encrypted by the client and decrypted by the server,
- Sequence number: sequence numbers maintained separately by the server for messages transmitted and received during the data session.

The abbreviation MAC used in the above definitions means Message Authentication Code that is used for transmission of data during the SSL session. The role of MAC will be explained further when discussing the record protocols. A brief description of the terms was necessary to be able to explain the next issues connected with the functioning of the SSL protocol, namely the SSL record protocol.

10.2.3 The SSL Record Protocol

The SSL record protocol involves using SSL in a secure manner and with message integrity ensured. To this end it is used by upper layer SSL protocols. The purpose of the SSL record protocol is to take an application message to be transmitted, fragment the data which needs to be sent, encapsulate it with appropriate headers and create an object just called a record, which is encrypted and can be forwarded for sending under the TCP protocol. The first step in the preparation of transmission of the application data consists in its fragmentation i.e. breaking up the data stream to be transmitted into 16Kb (or smaller) data fragments followed by the process of their conversion in a record. These data fragments may be further compressed, although the SSL 3.0 protocol specification includes no compression protocol, thus at present, no data compression is used.

At this moment, creation of the record is started for each data portion by adding a header to it, possible information to complete the required data size and the MAC. The record header that is added to each data portion contains two elementary pieces of information, namely the length of the record and the length of the data block added to the original data. In the next step, the record data constructed consists of the following elements:

- Primary data,
- Some padding to complete the datagram as required,
- MAC value

MAC is responsible for the verification of integrity of the message included in the transmitted record. It is the result of a hash function that follows a specific hash algorithm, for example MD5 or SHA-1. MAC is determined as a result of a hash function that receives the following data:

MAC = Hash function [secret key, primary data, padding, sequence number].

A secret key in creation of MAC is either a client write MAC secret or a server write MAC secret respectively, it depends on which party prepares the packet. After receiving the packet, the receiving party computes its own value of the MAC and compares it with that received. If the two values match, this means that data has not been modified during the transmission over the network. The length of the MAC obtained in this way depends on the method uses for its computing. Next, the data plus the MAC are encrypted using a preset symmetric encryption algorithm, for example DES or triple DES. Both data and MAC are encrypted. This prepared data is attached with the following header fields:

- *Content type:* identifies what payload is delivered by the packet to determine which higher protocols are to be used for processing of data included in the packet. The possible values are change_cipher_spec, alert, handshake, and application_data that refer to the appropriate protocols.
- *Major version :* establishes the main portion of the protocol version to be used. For SSL 3.0, the value is 3,
- *Minor version :* establishes the additional portion of the used version of the protocol. For SSL 3.0 the value is 0.

With the addition of fields, the process of record preparation is completed. Afterwards, the record is sent to the targeted point. The entire process of preparation of the packet to be sent is illustrated in Figure 10.3.

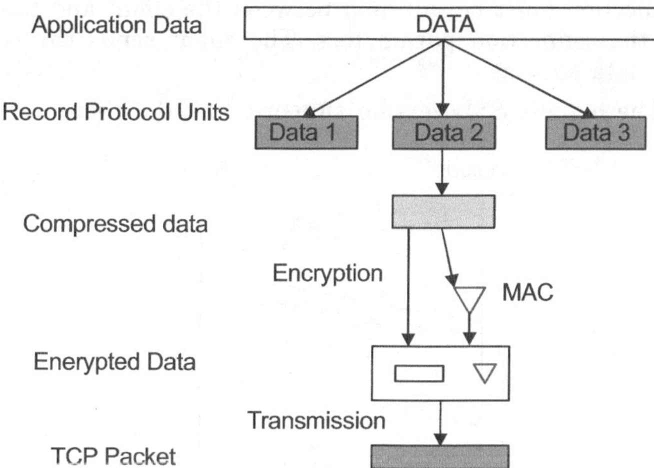

Figure 10.3 The SSL Record Protocol Stack

(1) The SSL Record protocol

The SSL record protocol is used to transfer any data within a session - both messages and other SSL protocols (for example the handshake protocol), as well as for any application data.

(2) The Alert protocol

The Alert Protocol is used by parties to convey session messages associated with data exchange and functioning of the protocol. Each message in the alert protocol consists of two bytes. The first byte always takes a value, "warning" (1) or "fatal" (2) , that determines the severity of the message sent. Sending a message having a „fatal" status by either party will result in an immediate termination of the SSL session. The next byte of the message contains one of the defined error codes, which may occur during an SSL communication session.

(3) The ChangeCipher Spec protocol

This protocol is the simplest SSL protocol. It consists of a single message that carries the value of 1. The sole purpose of this message is to cause the pending session state to be established as a fixed state, which results, for example, in defining the used set of protocols. This type of message must be sent by the client to the server and vice versa. After exchange of messages, the session state is considered agreed. This message and any other SSL messages are transferred using the SSL record protocol.

(4) The handshake protocol

The handshake protocol constitutes the most complex part of the SSL protocol. It is used to initiate a session between the server and the client. Within the message of this protocol, various components such as algorithms and keys used for data encryption are negotiated. Due to this protocol, it is possible to authenticate the parties to each other and negotiate appropriate parameters of the session between them.

The process of negotiations between the client and the server is illustrated in Figure 10.4. It can be divided into 4 phases separated with horizontal broken lines. During the first phase, a logical connection must be initiated between the client and the server followed by the negotiation on the connection parameters. The client sends the server a client_hello message containing data such as:

- **Version:** The highest SSL version supported by the client,

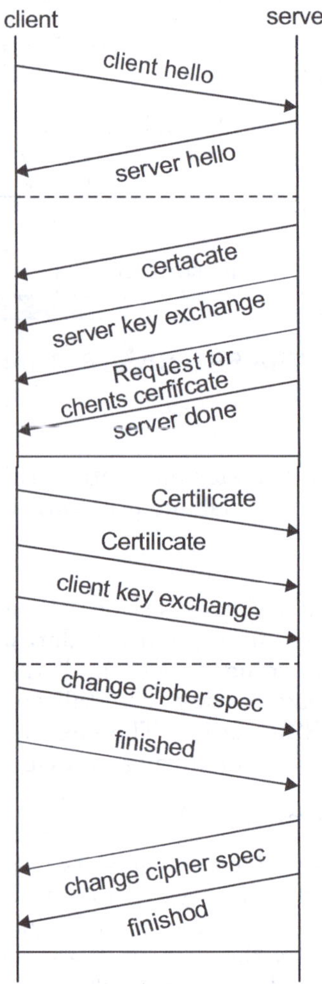

Figure 10.4 The SSL protocol stack

- **Random:** data consisting of a 32-bit timestamp and 28 bytes of randomly generated data. This data is used to protect the key exchange session between the parties of the connection.
- **Session ID:** a number that defines the session identifier. A nonzero value of this field indicates that the client wishes to update the parameters of an existing connection or establish a new connection on this session. A zero value in this field indicates that the client wishes to establish a new connection.

- **CipherSuite:** a list of encryption algorithms and key exchange method supported by the client.

The server, in response to the client_hello message sends a server_hello message, containing the same set of fields as the client message, placing the following data:

- **Version:** the lowest version number of the SSL protocol supported by the server, random data: the same fashion as used by the client, but the data generated is completely independent, session ID: if the client field was nonzero, the same value is sent back; otherwise the server's session ID field contains the value for a new session,
- **CipherSuite:** the server uses this field to send a single set of protocols selected by the server from those proposed by the client. The first element of this field is a chosen method of exchange of cryptographic keys between the client and the server. The next element is the specification of encryption algorithms and hash functions, which will be used within the session being initiated, along with all specific parameters.

The set of encryption algorithms and key exchange method sent in the CipherSuite field establishes three components:

- the method of key exchange between the server and client,
- the encryption algorithm for data encryption purposes,
- a function used for obtaining the MAC value.

The server begins the next phase of negotiations by sending its certificate to the client for authentication. The message sent to the client contains one or a chain of X509 certificates. These are necessary for authentication of both the server and the certification path towards a trusted certification official of the certificating body for the server. This step is not obligatory and may be omitted, if the negotiated method of key exchange does not require sending the certificate (in the case of anonymous Diffie-Hellman method). Depending on the negotiated method of key exchange, the server may send an additional server_key_exchange message, which is however not required in the case when the fixed Diffie-Hellman method or RSA key exchange technique has been negotiated. Moreover, the server can request a certificate from the client. The final step of Phase 2 is the server_done message, which has no parameters and is sent by the server merely to indicate the end of the server messages. After sending this message, the server waits for a client response. Upon receipt of the message, the client should verify the server's certificate, the certificate validation data and path, as well as any other parameters sent by the server in the server_hello message. The client's verification consists of:

Validation date check of the certificate and comparison with the current date, to verify whether the certificate is still valid, checking whether the certifying body is included in the list of trusted Certifying Authorities in possession of the client. If the CA, which has issued the server's certificate is not included in the CAs list, the client attempts to verify the CA signature. If no information about the CA can be obtained, the client terminates the identification procedure by either returning the error signal or signalling the problem for the user to solve it.

Identifying the authenticity of the public key of the CA which has issued the certificate: if the Certifying Authority is included in the client's list of trusted CAs, the client checks the

CA's public key stated in the server's certificate with the public key available from the list. This procedure verifies the authenticity of the certifying body. Checking whether the domain name used in the certificate matches the server name shown in the server's certificate.

Upon successful completion of all steps the server is considered authenticated. If all parameters are matched and the server's certificate correctly verified, the client sends the server one or multiple messages. Next is the client__key_exchange message, which must be sent to deliver the keys. The content of this message depends on the negotiated method of key exchange. Moreover, at the server's request, the client's certificate is sent along with the message enabling verification of the certificate. This procedure ends Phase 3 of negotiations.

Phase 4 is to confirm the messages so far received and to verify whether the pending data is correct. The client sends a change_cipher_spec message (in accordance with the pending SSL ChangeCipher Spec), and then sets up the pending set of algorithm parameters and keys into the current set of the same. Then the client sends the finished message, which is first protected with just negotiated algorithms, keys and secrets. This is to confirm that the negotiated parameters and data are correct. The server in response to the client sends the same message sequence. If the finished message is correctly read by either party this confirms that the transmitted data, negotiated algorithms and the session key are correct. This indicates that the session has been terminated and that it is possible to send the application data between the server and the client, via SSL. At this point the TCP session between the client and the server is closed, however a session state is maintained, allowing it to resume communications within the session using the retained parameters.

It is worth noticing that both Phases 2 and 3 are used by both parties to verify the authenticity of the server's certificate and possibly the client's certificate during the handshake step. If the server cannot be successfully authenticated by the client on the basis of the delivered certificate, the handshake terminates and the client will generate an error message. The same will occur at the server if the client's certificate authenticity cannot be confirmed.

Figure 10.4 Establishing the SSL session between the client and the server (red coloured – messages that are non-mandatory).

At first glance this process seems to be somewhat complicated, however this takes place at each connection with the server of an SSL-enabled service, for example while requesting the address of a site beginning with HTTPS://.

10.2.4 SSL in practice

What is the reason for these complicated things associated with an SSL connection? SSL is used in many services but mostly SSL protects the HTTP communication channel over the Internet and therefore the SSL protocol is seen quite often as associated only with WWW pages. As it has been already mentioned, the SSL protocol can be used to protect the transmission for any TCP/IP service. Apart from the WWW accessing, the second most likely application of this protocol is associated with email sending and receiving.

As for Windows NT/2000/XP applications, SSL is practically used in the system of HTTP and SMTP server services that work in conjunction with IIS. These servers allow an appropriate request to be generated with the user's own certificate (employing the Windows 2000 Server certificate services) or by obtaining the certificate from one of the trusted CAs such as

VeriSign (www.verisgn.com) or Thawte (www.thawte.com). In the same manner as for the WWW server it is possible to obtain and install the certificate on an SMTP server supplied along with IIS or available in Exchange 2000. A possible application of the SSL to support other services depends on the possibility of configuration of such a connection by the server.

Let's walk through a typical Internet commerce scenario. Bunty is surfing the Web and arrives at the Anita Incorporated site which is selling some durable good. The Anita Incorporated site displays a form in which Bunty is supposed to enter the quantity desired, his address and his payment card number. Bunty enters this information, clicks on "submit", and then expects to receive (say, from, ordinary mail) the good; he also expects to receive a charge for the good in his next payment card statement. This all sounds good, but if no security measures are taken – such as encryption or authentication – Bunty could be in for a few surprises:

An intruder could intercept the order and obtain Bunty's payment card information. The intruder could then make purchases at Bunty's expense.

The site could display Anita Incorporated famous logo, but actually be a site maintained by Trudy, who is masquerading as Anita Incorporated. Trudy could take Bunty's money and run. Or Trudy could make her own purchases and have them billed to Bunty's account.

Many other surprises are possible, and we will discuss a few of these in the next subsection. But the two problems listed above are among the most serious. Internet commerce using the SSL protocol can address both these problems.

Secure sockets layer (SSL), originally developed by Netscape, is a protocol designed to provide data encryption and authentication between a Web client and a Web server. The protocol begins with a handshake phase that negotiates an encryption algorithm (e.g., DES or RSA) and keys, and authenticates the server to the client. Optionally, the client can also be authenticated to the server. Once the handshake is complete and the transmission of application data begins, and all data is encrypted using session keys negotiated during the handshake phase. SSL is widely used in Internet commerce, being implemented in almost all popular browsers and Web servers. Furthermore, it is also the basis of the Transport Layer Security (TLS) protocol [RFC 2246].

SSL and TLS are not limited to the Web application; for example, they are also used for authentication and data encryption for IMAP mail access. SSL can be viewed as a layer that sits between the application layer and the transport layer, as shown in Figure 10.5 On the sending side, SSL receives from the application raw application data (such as an HTTP or IMAP message), encrypts the data and directs the encrypted data to a TCP socket.

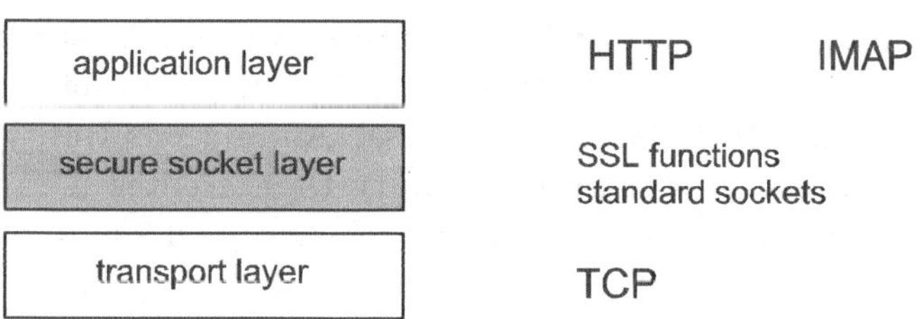

Figure 10.5 Secure socket layer

On the receiving side, SSL reads from the TCP socket, decrypts the data, and directs the data to the application. Although SSL can be used with many Internet applications, we shall discuss it in the context of the Web, where it is principally being used today for Internet commerce.

10.2.5 Features in SSL

SSL server authentication, allowing a user to confirm a server's identity. An SSL-enabled browser maintains a list of trusted certifying authorities (CAs) along with the public keys of the CAs. When the browser wants to do business with an SSL-enabled Web server, the browser obtains from the server a certificate containing the server's public key. The certificate is issued (i.e., digitally signed) by a certificate authority (CA) listed in the client's list of trusted CAs. This feature allows the browser to authenticate the server before the user submits a payment card number. In the context of the earlier example, this server authentication enables Bunty to verify that he is indeed sending his payment card number to Anita Incorporated, and not to someone else who might be masquerading as Anita Incorporated.

An encrypted SSL session, in which all information sent between browser and server is encrypted by sending software (browser or Web server) and decrypted by the receiving software (browser or Web server). This confidentially may be important to both the customer and the merchant. Also, SSL provides a mechanism for detecting tampering of the information by an intruder.

SSL client authentication, allowing a server to confirm a user's identity. Analogous to server authentication, client authentication makes use of client certificates, which have also been issued by CAs. This authentication is important if the server, for example, is a bank sending confidential financial information to a customer and wants to check the recipient's identity. Client authentication, although supported by SSL, is optional. To keep our discussion focused, we will henceforth ignore it.

10.2.6 How SSL Works

A user, say Bunty, surfs the Web and clicks on a link that takes him to a secure page housed by Anita's SSL-enabled server. The protocol part of the URL for this page is "https" rather than the ordinary "http". The browser and server then run the SSL handshake protocol, which (1) authenticates the server and (2) generates a shared symmetric key. Both of these tasks make use of the RSA public-key technology. The main flow of events in the handshake phase is shown in Figure 10.6 During this phase, Anita sends Bunty her certificate, from which Bunty obtains Anita's public key. Bunty then creates a random symmetric key, encrypts it with Anita's public key, and sends the encrypted key to Anita. Bunty and Anita now share a symmetric session key. Once this handshake protocol is complete, all data sent between the browser and server (over TCP connections) is encrypted using the symmetric session key.

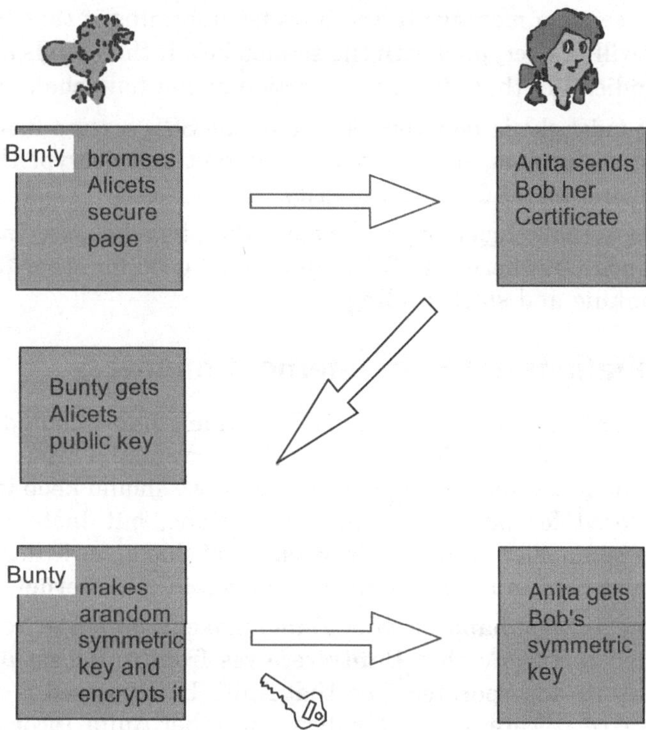

Figure 10.6 High-level overview of the handshake phase of SSL.

Having given a high-level overview of SSL, let's take a closer look at some of more important details. The SSL handshake performs the following steps:

1. The browser sends the server the browser's SSL version number and cryptography preferences. The browser sends its cryptography preferences because the browser and server negotiate which symmetric key algorithm they are going to use.
2. The server sends the browser the server's SSL version number, cryptography preferences and its certificate. Recall that the certificate includes the server's RSA public key and is certified by some CA, that is, the certificate has been encrypted by a CA's private key.
3. The browser has an entrusted list of CAs and a public key for each CA on the list. When the browser receives the certificate from the server, it checks to see if the CA is on the list. If no, the user is warned of the problem and informed that an encrypted and authenticated connection cannot be established. If yes, the browser uses the CA's public key to decrypt the certificate and obtain the server's public key.
4. The browser generates a symmetric session key, encrypts it with the server's public key, and sends the encrypted session key to the server.
5. The browser sends a message to the server informing it that future messages from the client will be encrypted with the session key. It then sends a separate (encrypted) message indicating that the browser portion of the handshake is finished.

6. The server sends a message to the browser informing it that future messages from the server will be encrypted with the session key. It then sends a separate (encrypted) message indicating that the server portion of the handshake is finished.
7. The SSL handshake is now complete, and the SSL session has begun. The browser and the server use the session keys to encrypt and decrypt the data they send to each other and to validate its integrity.

SSL handshake actually has many more steps than listed above. In addition to payment card purchases, we point out here that SSL can (and is) used for other financial transactions including online banking and stock trading.

10.2.7 The Limitations of SSL in Internet Commerce

Due to its simplicity and early development, SSL is widely implemented in browsers, servers and Internet commerce products. These SSL-enabled servers and browsers provide a popular platform for payment card transactions. Nevertheless, we should keep in mind that SSL was not specifically tailored for payment card transactions, but instead for generic secure communication between a client and server. Because of this generic design, SSL lacks many features that payment-card industry would like to see in an Internet commerce protocol.

Consider once again what happens when Bunty makes a purchase from Anita Incorporated over SSL. The signed certificate that Bunty receives from Anita assures Bunty that he is really dealing with Anita Incorporated, and that Anita Incorporated is a bona fide company. However, the generic certificate does not indicate whether Anita Incorporated is authorized to accept payment-card purchases nor if the company is a reliable merchant. This opens the door for merchant fraud. And there is a similar problem for client authorization. Even if SSL client authentication is used, the client certificate does not tie Bunty to a specific authorized payment card; thus, Anita Incorporated has no assurance about whether Bunty is authorized to make a payment-card purchase. This opens the door to all kinds of fraud, including purchases with stolen credit cards and customer repudiation of purchased goods [Abbott 1999].

Of course, this kind of fraud is already rampant in mail order and telephone order (MOTO) purchases. With MOTO transactions, the law dictates that the merchant accepts liability for fraudulent transactions. Thus, if a customer makes a MOTO purchase with a payment card and claims to have never made the purchase, then the merchant is liable, that is, the merchant is legally bound to return the money to the customer (unless the merchant can prove that the customer actually ordered and received the goods). Similarly, if a MOTO purchase is made with a stolen payment card, the merchant is again liable. On the other hand, with physically-present transactions, the merchant's bank accepts the liability; as you might expect, it is more difficult for a customer to repudiate a physcially-present purchase which involves a hand-written signature or a PIN (personal identification number).

SSL purchases are similar to MOTO purchases, and naturally the merchant is liable for a fraudulent SSL purchase. It would be preferable, of course, to use a protocol that provides superior authentication of the customer and of the merchant, something that is as good or better than a physically-present transaction. Authentication involving payment-card authorization would reduce fraud and merchant liability.

10.3 TRANSPORT LAYER SECURITY (TLS)

TLS (Transport Layer Security) is a replacement for Netscape's earlier SSL (Secure Sockets Layer).Transport Layer Security and its predecessor, Secure Sockets Layer (SSL), are cryptographic protocols that provide security and data integrity for communications over TCP/IP networks such as the Internet. TLS and SSL encrypt the segments of network connections at the Transport Layer end-to-end.Several versions of the protocols are in widespread use in applications like

- web browsing,
- electronic mail,
- internet faxing,
- instant messaging and
- voice-over-IP (VoIP).

TLS is an IETF standards track protocol, last updated in RFC 5246, that was based on the earlier SSL specifications developed by Netscape Corporation.Many protocols use TLS (Transport Layer Security) to establish secure connections, including HTTP, IMAP, POP3, and SMTP.

10.3.1 Properties of TLS

The primary goal of the TLS Protocol is to provide privacy and data integrity between two communicating applications. The protocol is composed of two layers: the TLS Record Protocol and the TLS Handshake Protocol. At the lowest level, layered on top of some reliable transport protocol (e.g.,), is the TLS Record Protocol. The TLS Record Protocol provides connection security that two basic properties:

- The connection is private. Symmetric cryptography is used for data encryption (e.g., DES, RC4, etc.) The keys for this symmetric encryption are generated uniquely for each connection and are based on a secret negotiated by another protocol (such as the TLS Handshake Protocol). The Record Protocol can also be used without encryption.
- The connection is reliable. Message transport includes a message integrity check using a keyed MAC. Secure hash functions (e.g., SHA, MD5, etc.) are used for MAC computations. The Record Protocol can operate without a MAC, but is generally only used in this mode while another protocol is using the Record Protocol as a transport for negotiating security parameters.

10.3.2 Goals

The goals of TLS Protocol, in order of their priority, are:

1. **Cryptographic security:** TLS should be used to establish a secure connection between two parties.
2. **Interoperability:** Independent programmers should be able to develop applications utilizing TLS that will then be able to successfully exchange cryptographic parameters without knowledge of one another's code.

3. **Extensibility:** TLS seeks to provide a framework into which new public key and bulk encryption methods can be incorporated as necessary. This will also accomplish wo sub-goals: to prevent the need to create a new protocol (and risking the introduction of possible new weaknesses) and to avoid the need to implement an entire new security library.
4. **Relative efficiency:** Cryptographic operations tend to be highly CPU intensive, particularly public key operations. For this reason, the TLS protocol has incorporated an optional session caching scheme to reduce the number of connections that need to be established from scratch. Additionally, care has been taken to reduce network activity.

10.3.3 TLS Record Protocol

The TLS Record Protocol is used for encapsulation of various higher level protocols. One such encapsulated protocol, the TLS Handshake Protocol, allows the server and client to authenticate each other and to negotiate an encryption algorithm and cryptographic keys before the application protocol transmits or receives its first byte of data. The TLS Handshake Protocol provides connection security that has three basic properties:

- The peer's identity can be authenticated using asymmetric, or public key, cryptography (e.g., RSA [RSA], DSS [DSS], etc.). This authentication can be made optional, but is generally required for at least one of the peers.
- The negotiation of a shared secret is secure: the negotiated secret is unavailable to eavesdroppers, and for any authenticated connection the secret cannot be obtained, even by an attacker who can place himself in the middle of the connection.
- The negotiation is reliable: no attacker can modify thenegotiation communication without being detected by the partiesto the communication.

One advantage of TLS is that it is application protocol independent.

Higher level protocols can layer on top of the TLS Protocol transparently. The TLS standard, however, does not specify how protocols add security with TLS; the decisions on how to initiate TLS handshaking and how to interpret the authentication certificates exchanged are left up to the judgment of the designers and implementors of protocols which run on top of TLS.

10.4 Secure Electronic Transactions (SET)

SET is a protocol specifically designed to secure payment-card transactions over the Internet. It was originally developed by Visa International and MasterCard International in February 1996 with participation from leading technology companies around the world. SET Secure Electronic Transaction LLC (commonly referred to as SETCo) was established in December 1997 as a legal entity to manage and promote the global adoption of SET [SETCo 1999]. Some of the principle characteristics of SET include:

- SET is designed to encrypt specific kinds of payment-related messages; it cannot be used to encrypt arbitrary data (such as text and images) as can SSL.

- The SET protocol involves all three players mentioned at the beginning of this section, namely, the customer, the merchant and the merchant's bank. All sensitiveinformation sent between the three parties is encrypted.
- SET requires all three players to have certificates. The customer's and merchant's certificates are issued by their banks, thereby assuring that these players are permitted to make and receive payment-card. The customer certificate provides merchants with assurance that transactions will not be fraudulently charged back. It is an electronic representation of the customer's payment card. It basically contains information about the account, the issuing financial institution, and other cryptographic information. The merchant certificate assures the consumer that merchant is authorized to accept payment-card purchases. It contains information about the merchant, the merchant's bank, and the financial institution issuing the certificate.
- SET specifies the legal meaning of the certificates held by each party and the apportionment of liabilities connected with a transaction [Abbott 1999].
- In a SET transaction, the customer's payment-card number is passed to the merchant's bank without the merchant ever seeing the number in plain text. This feature prevents fraudulent or careless merchants from stealing or accidentally leaking the payment-card number.

A SET transaction uses three software components:

- Browser wallet: The browser wallet application is integrated with the browser and provides the customer with storage and management of payment cards and certificates while shopping. It responds to SET messages from the merchant, prompting the customer to select a payment card for payment.
- Merchant server: The merchant server is the merchandizing and fulfillment engine for merchants selling on the Web. For payments, it processes cardholder transactions and communicates with the merchant's bank or approval and subsequent payment capture.
- Acquirer gateway: The acquirer gateway is the software component at the merchant's bank. It processes the merchant's payment card transaction for authorization and payment.

In what follows, we give a highly simplified overview of the SET protocol. In reality, the protocol is substantially more complex

Steps in Making a Purchase

Suppose Bunty wants to purchase a good over the Internet from Anita Incorporated.

1. Bunty indicates to Anita that he is interested in making a credit card purchase.
2. Anita sends the customer an invoice and a unique transaction identifier.
3. Anita sends Bunty the merchant's certificate which includes the merchant's public key. Anita also sends the certificate for her bank, which includes the bank's public key. Both of these certificates are encrypted with the private key of a certifying authority.

4. Bunty uses the certifying authority's public key to decrypt the two certificates. Bunty now has Anita's public key and the bank's public key.
5. Bunty generates two packages of information: the order information (OI) package and the purchase instructions (PI) package. The OI, destined for Anita, contains the transaction identifier and brand of card being used; it does not include Bunty's card number. The PI, destined for Anita's bank, contains the transaction identifier, the card number and the purchase amount agreed to Bunty. The OI and PI are dual encrypted: the OI is encrypted with Anita's public key; the PI is encrypted with Anita's bank's public key. (We are bending the truth here in order to see the big picture. In reality, the OI and PI are encrypted with a customer-merchant session key and a customer-bank session key.) Bunty sends the OI and the PI to Anita.
6. Anita generates an authorization request for the card payment request, which includes the transaction identifier.
7. Anita sends to her bank a message encrypted with the bank's public key. (Actually, a session key is used.) This message includes the authorization request, the PI package received from Bunty, and Anita's certificate.
8. Anita's bank receives the message and unravels it. The bank checks for tampering. It also makes sure that the transaction identifier in the authorization request matches the one in Bunty's PI package.
9. Anita's bank then sends a request for payment authorization to Bunty's payment-card bank through traditional bank-card channels — just as Anita's bank would request authorization for any normal payment-card transaction.
10. Once Bunty's bank authorizes the payment, Anita's bank sends a response to the Anita, which is (of course) encrypted. The response includes the transaction identifier.
11. If the transaction is approved, Anita sends its own response message to Bunty. This message serves as a receipt and informs Bunty that the payment was accepted and that the goods will be delivered.

One of the key features of SET is the non-exposure of the credit number to the merchant. This feature is provided in Step 5, in which the customer encrypts the credit card number with the bank's key. Encrypting the number with the bank's key prevents the merchant from seeing the credit card. Note that the SET protocol closely parallels the steps taken in a standard payment-card transaction. To handle all the SET tasks, the customer will have a so-called digital wallet that runs the client-side of the SET protocol and stores customer payment-card information (card number, expiration date, etc.).

REVIEW QUESTIONS

1. What are the differences between message secrecy and message integrity? Can you have one without the other? Justify your answer.
2. What is the difference between an active and a passive intruder?

3. What is an important difference between a symmetric key system and a public key system?
4. Suppose that an intruder has an encrypted message as well as the decrypted version of that message. Can the intruder mount a cipher-text only attack, a known-plaintext or a chosen-plaintext attack?
5. Suppose N people want to communicate with each of the N-1 other people using symmetric key encryption. All communication between any to people, i and j, is visible to all other people, and no other person should be able to decode their communication. How many keys are required in the system as a whole? Now suppose that public key encryption is used. How many keys are required in this case?
6. What is the purpose of a nonce in an authentication protocol?
7. What does it mean to say that a nonce is a once-in-a-lifetime value? In whose lifetime?
8. What is the man-in-the-middle attack? Can this attack occur when symmetric keys are used?
9. What does it mean for a signed document to be verifiable, non-forgible, and non-repudiable?
10. In what way does a message digest provide a better message integrity check than a checksum such as the Internet checksum?
11. In what way does a message digest provide a "better" digital signature than using a public key digital signature?
12. Is the message associated with a message digested encrypted? Since either "yes" or "no" are acceptable answers here, you should explain your answer.
13. What is a key distribution center? What is a certification authority?
14. Summarize the key differences in the services provided by the Authentication Header protocol and the Encapsulation Security Payload (ESP) protocol in IPsec.

DISCUSSION QUESTIONS

1. Suppose that an intruder could both insert and remove DNS messages into the network. Give three scenarios showing the problems that such an intruder could cause.
2. No one has formally "proven" that 3-DES or RSA are "secure." Given this, what evidence do we have they are indeed secure?
3. If IPsec provides security at the network layer, why is it that security mechanisms are still needed at layers above IP?
4. Go to the International PGP homepage (http://www.pgpi.org/). What version of pgp are you legally allowed to download, given the country you are in?

REFERENCES

1. S. Abbott, "The Debate for Secure E-Commerce," Performance Computing, February 1999, http://www.performancecomputing.com/features/9902f1.shtml.
2. L. Loeb, Secure Electronic Transactions : Introduction and Technical Reference," Artech House, New York, 1998.
3. P. Loshin, P. Murphy, "Electronic Commerce : On-Line Ordering and Digital Money", Charles River Media, August 1997.
4. M. Merkow, K. Wheeler, and J. Breithaupt, "Building SET Applications for Secure Transactions," John Wiley and Sons, New York, 1998.
5. SET Secure Electronic Transaction, MasterCard Web site, http://www.mastercard.com/shoponline/set.
6. [NetscapeSecurity 1999] Security Developer Central, Netscape Site, http://developer.netscape.com/tech/security.
7. Quebec Maple Syrup homepage, http://www.jam.ca/syrup.
8. T. Dierks and C. Allen, The TLS Protocol, [RFC 22246], January 1999.
9. SETCo LLC Website, http://www.setco.org.

❑❑❑

11

System Security

11.1 INTRUSION PREVENTION

Intrusion-prevention systems are designed to improve security, enhance network virus protection, and thwart unforeseen attacks. Read about Cisco intrusion prevention systems, network virus protection, and types of network security attacks.As viruses, worms, and hackers continue to plague business-technology systems, companies are turning to new technologies to avert attacks.

Though many companies now use antivirus software, intrusion-detection systems, and firewalls, hackers and worms still infiltrate business-technology systems and cause serious damage. Attacks such as Blaster, MyDoom, and Witty cost businesses more than $10 billion annually.

To combat the growing problem, security professionals are in search of better protection. They need more-intelligent shields that can fend off new attacks as they happen, rather than relying on signatures—tiny snapshots of code used to spot and block attacks—published by security vendors only after attacks are under way.

Intrusion-prevention systems may be the protection companies are looking for. Unlike conventional antivirus, firewall, and intrusion-detection systems, these proactive tools are designed to protect vulnerable computers and thwart unforeseen attack methods. Intrusion-prevention systems have a learning capability, and these engines are more intelligent and better able to identify and stop attacks.

That's important, especially since attacks are getting too fast for reactive security tools. Consider this: When the SQL Slammer worm hit the Internet in January 2003, it attacked a 6-month-old vulnerability in Microsoft SQL Server. But in March of this year, the Witty worm struck a buffer-overflow vulnerability only one day after the flaw was found in various

Internet Security System Inc. products. Security professionals are even more concerned about so-called "zero-day" attacks, those against software vulnerabilities that have no patches or defensive signatures because they haven't yet been publicly disclosed.

There are primarily two types of intrusion-prevention systems:

* Host-based, which protect systems such as servers and PCs, and
* Network-based, which protect traffic from attacks.

Intrusion-prevention systems often use the more traditional attack signatures and also vulnerability signatures, which are chunks of code that protect against potential attacks aimed at known software vulnerabilities. Many intrusion-prevention systems can learn normal application and network behavior so they can block bad activities, such as a file trying to infect the operating system or a worm attempting to wiggle through an application vulnerability and launch a buffer-overflow.

11.1.1 Network Intrusion Detection

Your network should have some network intrusion detection system. With that said, the method of detecting intrusions, how to monitor, and how to interpret the data is a complex subject.

Intrusion Detection Types

These are of two types :

- **Network** - Used to protect the network or a large part of it. It listens to all available network packets and tries to find any intrusion pattern based on the information in the packets. Where this type of IDS is placed on the network is important since it cannot analyze all packets behind routers, bridges, or switches.
- **System** - Used to protect a specific host such as a webserver. This kind of intrusion system can be especially effective when a server is in an area off the firewall such that it is neither on the internet or on the internal network { Known as a Demilitarized zone (DMZ) }. These kinds of intrusion detection systems can usually only protect one service well.

11.1.2 Intrusion Detection Requirements

The intrusion detection requirements mentioned in this section are generally for network intrusion detection systems rather than system intrusion detection systems. The requirements mentioned here are general and will depend on the size of your network, traffic load on your network, and the type of intrusion detection software you install. Read the manufacturers instructions for specific recommendations.

Intrusion detection systems typically consist of two parts which are an engine and a control console. These two parts are usually on separate computers. Obviously the console is used to control and make changes to the behavior of the intrusion detection engine. The engine analyzes the network traffic and takes appropriate action if an intrusion is detected.

Since network intrusion detection systems must process a lot of network data in a short time, these systems require a good deal of processing power. They also require much RAM for high performance, and may require much hard drive space to store log information.

11.1.3 Intrusion Detection Features

- Attack patterns are saved in a database.
- **Data packet reassembly** - Some may or may not re-assemble IP packets the same way a receiving system would reassemble them. Most IDS do not reassemble the packets in this manner. Without reassembling the packets as the receiver, some attacks may go unnoticed.
- **Checksum verification** - A good IDS will verify packet checksums to be sure the packet has not been tampered with.

Intrusion Detection Actions

- Log intrusion information or save raw packets.
- Send an alert to an administrator using email or another method.
- Interfere with the attack. There are several actions that may be taken:

(1) **Session disruption** - The IDS can send ACK-FIN packets to both ends of a connection (by IP spoofing each computer) to close a session. This may be done if a hacker appears to be gaining unauthorized access.

(2) Modify the firewall or router behavior during an attack.

11.2 NETWORK INTRUSION PREVENTION SYSTEM (NIPS)

Intrusion Prevention Systems are the first step in this direction.

11.2.1 Networking

First and foremost, an IPS must exhibit the same throughput, reliability, and latency characteristics of other network infrastructure elements (e.g., switches and routers). Network engineers have carefully architected their networks to deliver traffic from one point to another with specific latency and throughput requirements. Today's business dependence on the network requires that they be highly reliable with near-zero downtime. If an IPS adversely impacts these network characteristics, it will never be given an opportunity to demonstrate its security effectiveness. Furthermore, these performance characteristics should not be dependent on the number of filters (or signatures) that is turned on or the type of traffic that is passing through the network.

Many organizations deploy Intrusion Prevention Systems at the perimeter to augment existing security elements, but most are deploying these systems on internal network segments to protect against attacks from within. When multiple IPS's are deployed internally, they effectively provide "zones of containment" for any attack that may originate from internal sources such as remote office locations, VPNs, or someone plugging in an infected laptop. These internal locations have much more demanding performance and reliability requirements in the range of multi-gigabit per second throughput and sub-millisecond latencies.

11.2.2 Attack Blocking

Security effectiveness is measured in three dimensions: accuracy, coverage, and timeliness. Of these, accuracy is the most important. Accuracy ensures malicious traffic is blocked, and legitimate traffic is not. The performance and accuracy of a software-based product presents a zero-sum game. If a filter is added to the software engine, the CPU must process additional cycles and performance goes down. Conversely, in a hardware product that utilizes massive parallel processing techniques, additional filters do not necessarily impact performance. This relates directly to accuracy as well. For example, it may be determined that five conditions must be met to unequivocally identify an attack, but the 5th condition requires 90% of the CPU cycles for only 10% improvement in accuracy. A software-based solution is forced to choose between ignoring the 5th condition to trade off 10% in accuracy for 90% performance. This situation has plagued many software solutions and resulted in false positives (classifying legitimate traffic as malicious). While this tradeoff is often assumed for a passive Intrusion Detection System, it is unacceptable for an Intrusion Prevention System intended to block only attack traffic.

Coverage refers to the breadth of attacks or attack vectors that an Intrusion Prevention System can protect against. While this is tightly linked to accuracy, it is also dependent on the types of filtering methods that the IPS engine supports. There are four primary filtering methods needed for the broadest protection:

(1) **Signatures** – Basic pattern matching technique used for viruses or known exploits

(2) **Protocol Anomaly** – Normalization technique that can enforce compliance to a protocol specification

(3) **Vulnerability** – Method used to express application-layer rules to identify malicious traffic attempting to exploit an application or design vulnerability. These filters are the most difficult to develop, but the most proactive and comprehensive.

(4) **Traffic Anomaly** – Method used to detect changes in behavioral traffic patterns that deviate from "normal"

These filtering methods are applied to flows not only to individual packets.

Finally, timeliness is the speed with which an IPS can offer protection against a new threat. In some instances, existing filters may actually protect against a zero-day or newly discovered threat. If vulnerability filters are in place, they can protect an organization preemptively before the existence of an exploit or worm. When a new vulnerability is discovered, a new filter or set of filters may be required for protection. Unfortunately, it is not uncommon for 5-10 new critical vulnerabilities to be discovered on a weekly basis. This means that a fundamental component of an IPS is the ability to continuously update the IPS with new filters. As mentioned earlier, these filters should not adversely impact network performance and should be able to be instantiated automatically within seconds on IPS systems globally.

11.2.3 Anatomy of an Intrusion Prevention System (IPS)

In the simplest sense, an Intrusion Prevention System is an inline device that blocks attacks before they can reach their target. In a broader sense, an IPS performs total packet inspection, providing a range of functions due to this depth of analysis and traffic classification. Today, these are predominantly standalone systems that can be placed at key network points for protection. As an inline device, an IPS cannot become a bottleneck, and as an attack blocking device, an IPS must be extremely accurate when classifying traffic.

Access Control

Access control mechanisms are used to enforce a policy of limiting access to a resource to only those users who are authorized. These techniques include the use of access control lists or matrices, passwords, capabilities, and labels, the possession of which may be used to indicate access rights.

11.2.4 Network Layer Security Protocol (NLSP)

NLSP is an international standard that specifies a protocol to be used by end systems and intermediate systems in order to provide security services in the network layer. It is defined by ISO 11577. Much of the material appearing here is from the American National Standards Institute (ANSI) which is the official U.S. representative to ISO.

NLSP specifies a series of services and functional requirements for implementation. The services, as defined in ISO 7498-2 are:

- peer entity authentication.
- data origin authentication.
- access control.
- connection confidentiality.
- connectionless confidentiality.
- traffic flow confidentiality.
- connection integrity without recovery (including data unit integrity, in which individual SDUs on a connection are integrity protected).
- connectionless integrity.

The Procedures of this protocol are defined in terms of:

- requirements on the cryptographic techniques that can be used in an instance on this protocol.
- requirements on the information carried in the security association used in an instance of communication.

Although the degree of protection afforded by some security mechanisms depends on the use of some specific cryptographic techniques, correct operation of this protocol is not dependent on the choice of any particular encipherment of decipherment algorithm that is left as a local matter for the communicating systems.

Furthermore, neither the choice nor the implementation of a specific security policy are within the scope of this international standard. The choice of a specific security policy, and hence the degree of protection that will be achieved, is left as a local matter among the systems that are using a single instance of secure communications. NLSP does not require that multiple instances of secure communications involving a single open system must use the same security protocol.

NLSP supports cryptographic protection either between End Systems (and in this case resembles the Transport Layer Security Protocol - TLSP) or between Intermediate Systems that are located at the borders of security domains. This latter aspect makes NLSP quite appealing to those who would like to provide security services not by securing each and every system in a domain but by forcing all external communications to transit through a small set of secure systems (assuming that communications within the domain need no security services). In this sense, one can see NLSP as supporting (at the domain level) administrative policies (mandatory security) while TLSP is more tuned towards discretionary communication policies.

11.3 VIRUS

Virii (plural of virus) have infected practically each and every computer. They're not as widespread as the news media may lead you to believe,but they are very real nonetheless. Every computer user is susceptible to attacks by computer virii,and using a network increases your vulnerability.

Virii don't just spontaneously appear out of nowhere. virii are computer programs that are created by malicious programmers who've lost a few screws and should be locked up.

What makes a virus is its capability to make copies of itself that can be spread to other computers. These copies,in turn,make still more copies that spread to still more computers,and so on, ad nauseam.

Then, on a certain date or when you type a particular command or press a certain key,the virus strikes,sometimes harmlessly displaying a "gotcha" message,sometimes maliciously wiping out all the data on your hard disk. Ouch.

Virii move from computer to computer mostly by latching themselves onto floppy disks,which are frequently exchanged between computers. But virii also can travel over the network cables that connect the computers in your network. That's why networked computers are especially vulnerable to virus attack.

Keep in mind that the network can't be infected by a virus unless the virus enters the network through some other means, typically through an infected floppy disk. But after one computer on the network has become infected,it's not unlikely that all the computers on the network will soon be infected,as well.

A virus copies itself onto any storage medium with which it comes in contact. If you put a virus-infected floppy disk in your drive, it will copy itself to your hard disk. If you put a virus-infected floppy in a computer attached to a network, the virus will attempt to copy itself to the other computers on the network. If you download a virus-infected program from the Internet, it will infect your hard disk the first time you use it. If you have a floppy disk in the drive, it may be infected too, and if you're connected to a computer network, the other computers on the network may be infected as well.

Viruses almost always infect program files, not data files. Viruses are snippets of code that attach themselves to existing applications—word processors, games, spreadsheets, database management systems, address books, and other programs you use on your computer. If you're using DOS or Windows, this means viruses usually attach themselves to .EXE files.

If you're using UNIX, this means viruses usually attach themselves to .bin files. It is extremely unlikely that a virus will attach itself to a data file on your computer. A data file is a file that is created by a computer program, such as an e-mail message, word processing document, game high score list, or spreadsheet file. Viruses always exhibit some side effect.

The most famous viruses are known for harmful side effects such as erasing your hard disk. Another common harmful effect is destruction of the File Allocation Table (FAT). Your computer won't be able to locate files on a disk if the disk's FAT has been destroyed. Many viruses (probably the majority) have harmless side effects, such as typing "Happy Birthday!" on the screen.

There are several thousand "strains" of virii that computer-virus experts have identified.

Many of them have colorful names,such as the Stoned Virus,the Jerusalem Virus, and the Michelangelo virus.

11.3.1 Classification as to How Virii Infect

Viruses are sometimes also categorized by how they infect. These categorizations often overlap the categories above and may even be included in the description (e.g., polymorphic file virus). These categories include:

- Polymorphic Viruses
- Stealth Viruses
- Fast and Slow Infectors
- Sparse Infectors
- Armored Viruses
- Multipartite Viruses
- Cavity (Spacefiller) Viruses
- Tunneling Viruses
- Camouflage Viruses
- NTFS ADS Viruses

And, in a special category, one might include:

Virus Droppers

Programs that place viruses onto your system but themselves may not be viruses (a special form of Trojan).

11.3.2 Classification of Virii Based on method

Virii can be divided into 4 types depending on their method of infection.

* Boot virii,

* File virii and

* System Area virii.
* Macro Virus

(1) The Boot Virus

This type of virus infects the area referred to as the Boot Sector. The boot sector and the partition table virii, as their name suggests, infect particular areas of a disk. On a hard disk, it can be the boot sector or the partition table and in case of a floppy, it is the boot sector as floppies do not have partition table.

The only way through which this kind of virus gets into the system memory (RAM) is, when the machine is booted using an infected floppy diskette. Once in memory, it first infects the hard disk and then all the diskettes that are used thereafter. The next time you boot the system, it goes into memory as the hard disk is infected and spreads itself to all the diskettes.

All floppies, bootable and non-bootable, have a boot sector. This means all floppies are susceptible to infection by boot sector virii. If by mistake, you boot the system with a non-bootable but infected floppy, the system will still become infected. The infection would have spread by the time the error message "Non system diskette" flashes on the screen.

The same is true with partition table virii. They infect every hard disk even if it does not have a DOS partition. It remains active and spreads under UNIX or any other operating systems. Since this type of virus infects a particular area of the disk, almost all the files on that disk are safe. You can read/write/execute them without fear. Data loss is caused due to deliberate formatting of the hard disk, like March 6, which formats the hard disk on that day. They make the machine slow and some do not let you Format diskettes.

Virus is basically a small program. But the difference between the virus and any other program is that virus manipulates and corrupts information, simultaneously replicating itself. virii are like their organic counterparts. All virii are parasites that invade the body or a machine and attach themselves to a cell or a program. Once they are lodged, they control the activity of the host. This is possible because each strain of virus contains, within itself, all the information required to make perfect copies of itself.

A computer virus is a software code that replicates itself. Most virii work silently making sure that the user is unaware of the infection. If spreads from program to program & disk, manipulating and damaging valuable data. The major cause for concern is the spreading and damaging nature of virii.

To know about them we have to know about the mechanism an operating system uses to store data on the disk. An awareness of the physical and logical layout of a disk, will also help in the fight against virii.

Physically the disk is a flat magnetic surface that stores information on either sides in tracks and sectors. Tracks are concentric circles on the disk. Typically there may be 40,80,613 tracks per side of a diskette/disk. On hard disks that have 4 or more sides, tracks that lie vertically under each other make up a cylinder.

Tracks are further divided into sectors. There may be 9, 15, 17, 18 or /more sectors per track again depending on the size of the diskette/disk. Whenever we want to store data on the disk it is stored in a group of sectors known as an Allocation Unit or Cluster.

The operating system groups 1,2,4,8 or more sectors to form an allocation unit. Number of sectors per allocation units depends on type of diskette or size of the partition on the hard disk. allocation unit is the smallest unit of disk space allocated to a file. The Boot Sector, 2 copies of File Allocation Table (FAT), the Directory Area and the Data Area consisting of files. In case of a hard disk, there is a Partition Tables as well, giving you than one logical drive.

(2) File Virus

A file virus attaches itself to file. For the virus to enter memory, an infected file has to be executed. The executable files have an EXE, COM, SYS, BIN, HEX, OV? extension. Most of the virii limit themselves to infecting COM and EXE files only.

These viruses attach themselves to regular programs, such as COM or EXE files under DOS. Thus, they are invoked each time the infected program is run.

Virii basically do not infect data files because they are never executed. This does not mean that data files are not safe from virii. Far from it they are main targets of destruction. Most of the file virii begin their infection with the COMMAND.COM because this file must be executed while booting. Once this file is infected, virus infects the system memory every time you boot the system. Once in memory the virus waits for you to execute files and infects them when they are executed. These virii spread when you copy executable files from once machine to another.

You have two options either to delete the infected file or to cure the file. Most of the time deleting the file does not help because the memory is normally infected and it infects every file you execute. Curing the file is the only solution.

(3) System Area Virus

These are the virii that use the loophole in the DOS operating systems to infect files. They store their code at a particular place on the disk and misdirect all the files to execute that code before executing their actual code.

As already mentioned above, DOS uses File Allocation Table (FAT) and Directory Area to manage files. The Fat manages the units allocated to each file on the disk in proper sequence. The Directory Area has other information about the file like Name, Extension, Size, Date/Time and Starting Allocation Unit (Cluster) Number. This Starting Cluster number of every executable file is changed by virus like DIR-2 to point to its own code. Thus when DOS loads the file it also loads the Virus code. When this file if executed, the virus is executed too. Thus the virus goes into memory and spreads.

(4) System Infectors

Computer operating systems typically set aside a portion of each disk for code to boot the computer. Under DOS, this section is called a boot sector on floppies or a master boot record (MBR) for hard disks. System infectors store themselves in this area and hence are invoked whenever the disk is used to boot the system. A virus must be executed by someone, perhaps unwittingly, in order to spread. Period. Some ways in which this occurs include:

* Booting from an infected floppy

System infectors are loaded each time an infected disk is used to boot the system. This can happen even if a disk is not equipped with the files needed to truly boot the computer, as is the case with most floppies. With PCs, the initial infection typically occurs when someone boots - or reboots - a computer with an infected floppy accidentally left in drive A. It is always a good habit to check and remove any floppies that might be in the drives before booting your machine.

Running an infected program

As programs infected with a file infector are run, the virus spreads. For this reason, you should regularly scan for viruses any programs you retrieve from a BBS, the net, a colleague, etc. There are even instances of commercial, shrink-wrapped software that have been infected with viruses!

The major data loss by this virus is caused because it manipulates the system area directly, creating cross-linked files. If you correct these errors by CHKDSK, NDD or DRN then the executable files become useless. Curing the disk is the only solution.

Source Code Viruses

Source code found on your system can be infected; usually by adding Trojan code to it. While rare, it is possible to infect actual programming source code found on your computer.

Source code comes in many forms because of the many different types of compilers and languages available. This is one reason why source code viruses are not particularly common. The other is that so few people actually write programs it becomes difficult for a source code-only virus to find victims to infect.

Also, because of programming style and differing designs that individuals use when they write program code it's difficult to write a virus that actually spreads via this mechanism. More typically, a source code virus will not infect via source code but simply add Trojan material to existing source code so that when it is compiled and run it does something different than expected.

Die Hard is one example of a type of source code virus. The virus actually spreads by infecting COM and EXE files (a file virus) but, as part of its payload, in drops Trojan code into any ASM (assembly language) and PAS (Pascal) source files as they are accessed (when the virus is resident in memory).

Source code viruses are not common; but be aware they do exist and have been seen in the wild in the past.

The exploit currently the rage seems to be Visual Basic Script (VBS) worms. What is VBS? Let's see what Microsoft says:

-Microsoft Visual Basic Scripting Edition, a subset of the Microsoft Visual Basic programming language, is a fast, portable, lightweight interpreter for use in World Wide Web browsers and other applications that use Microsoft ActiveX Controls, Automation servers, and Java applets.

Basically, think about VBScript as a super batch language. VBScript is an interpreted language (so scripts are really the source code for whatever needs to be done). Scripts can be embedded into such things as web pages or can be standalone files (with the extension .VBS usually).

If you've got Microsoft's Internet Explorer 5 browser on your system it's likely you also have the Windows Scripting Host (WSH) which is the program used to interpret and run VBS scripts.

Even though VBScript is a scaled down language it is quite capable and can be used to, for example, connect to Microsoft's Outlook mail routines and send files to anyone in your address book. This, of course, makes it possible for VBScript to be a language used by worms to spread themselves.

VBScript can be disabled on your system. We have a page that tells you how to do this if you wish.

Bugs: A bug is an error in a program. It is included here even though it really isn't in the same class as viruses and trojans, because it is similar to a trojan horse in that it causes behavior other than what the user wanted. The difference of course is that with a bug, the aberrant behavior is unintentional! With a trojan horse the author is doing it on purpose.

Droppers: A dropper is a program designed to install or deliver a virus or trojan horse onto a target system. The dropper is specially designed to avoid detection by standard virus detection programs, because the virus is specially encrypted so that the dropper itself doesn't appear to the virus scanners like a regular infected program file would. In some ways, a dropper is like a "virus egg", waiting to be hatched. They are uncommon.

Virus Impostors (Joke Programs): Some oh-so-clever programmers have devised cute programs that mimic the effects of true viruses when they are run. These are not considered viruses themselves, or even trojan horses, because here the user of the file knows that the program is going to do something strange. These are often installed by humor-impaired people on coworkers' PCs to drive them nuts.

(5) Other Virii

Apart from these basic types, there are virii that use more than one method of infection to spread faster. These are known as double-action virii. They infect both the file and the boot sector. The virus gets into memory when either the computer is booted from an infected disk or when an infected file is executed. Once in the memory, it infects the boot sector of the hard disk and all the files that are executed subsequently. Due to their dual action, they spread faster.

Cluster infectors

They modify the file system so that they are run prior to other programs. Note that, unlike file infectors, they do not actually attach themselves to programs.

Macro viruses

Word processing documents can serve as sources of transmission for viruses that take advantage of the auto-execution macro capabilities in products such as Microsoft Word. Simply by opening an infected document, the virus, written in a product's macro language, can spread.

These viruses are collections of macros for MS Word and Excel that can infect documents and document templates under Word as well as spreadsheets and worksheets under Excel (both Windows and Mac platforms). The more common, Concept, is non-destructive, but does attach itself to any Word documents you might create with File, Save As.

* Macro virus publishes private documents

If you do not want to have your confidental Office documents posted on the Internet, watch out for the Polyster macro virus. It posts randomly selected documents in newsgroups like alt.comp.virus or alt.hacker. This polymorphic Word macro virus misuses the newsgroup program Forte Agent for this puspose. The transmitted Word document gets a new name like 'Serial Number List' and is infected by the virus. However, most popular anti virus programs provide protection from the Polyposter.

* Check documents for macros that might contain viruses

A macro virus is a type of computer virus that's stored in the macros within a document or template. When you open such a document, the macro virus is activated, transmitted to your computer, and stored in your Normal template. From that point on, every document you save is automatically "infected" with the macro virus ¾ and if other users open such infected documents, the macro virus is transmitted to their computers as well.

(6) Trojan Horse

The term virus is often used to refer not only to true virus programs (which are able to replicate themselves), but also to any other type of program that's designed to harm your computer.

When the Ancient Greeks used their Trojan horse, little did they know the computer would be programmed to copy their innovative strategy. Computer criminals use the Trojan Horse method to slip in extra commands into programs. Users with legal access unknowingly forced to send off the altered commands, which could include electronic transfer of funds to illegal accounts. In the US, it is said that computer crimes are a very profitable business. In a year, banks and firms lose an estimated $100 million, courtesy of these electronic manipulators. One reason that computers are such good criminals is that they can be programmed to cover their tracks so thoroughly—they simply erase all traces of the altered commands once the crime is done! A far more ingenious invention than the fingerprint protecting glove.

A Trojan horse is a program that appears to have a useful purpose, but really has a secret, harmful purpose. A classic Trojan horse program appeared a few years ago on the Apple Macintosh: A HyperCard stack named "Sexy Ladies." With a name like that, many users (men, mostly) double-clicked its icon to run it, causing a message to appear on the screen: "Stand by to see sexy ladies!" The user eagerly waited in anticipation, unaware that the program was merrily erasing his hard disk.

Another Trojan horse program has been employed by hackers trying to steal people's usernames and passwords on mainframe computer systems. Imagine that you're a legitimate user of such a system. You sit down at the terminal, and on the screen you see USERNAME: You've seen this prompt hundreds of times before—nothing odd here. You type in your account name. Just as you expected, another prompt appears. PASSWORD: You type in the password which you, and only you, know. Okay...you should get access to your account any second now. But today, something strange happens. On the screen, you see sorry, network is not available right now Seems like a normal system message. They must be performing maintenance on the system. You decide to take an unscheduled coffee break and come back later. What you didn't realize is that you weren't experiencing network problems...you were experiencing a program designed to make it look like you were experiencing network problems.

The program saved your username and password and e-mailed this information to your friendly neighborhood hacker.

It rapidly spreads from one computer to another as people pass the warning on to their friends and colleagues.

* Bomb

This term defines specular failure of a program and sabotaging action in a software by deliberately introducing a mistake that will disrupt the entire program.

* Slugs and Leaches

Japan's high-technology companies are turning to leeches, bugs, squids and slugs in a quest to create smarter computers. In nature, caenorhabditis elegans is a free-livingsoil nematode that spends its two-week life eating bacteria and producing several hundred offspring. InNEC's labs, the humble worm becomes an "information-processing system", and its inner workings are "software."

Despite having only 302 nerve cells, the nematode can learn-something today's computers can't do. For example, NEC research shows that if a worm is starved while being kept at a particular temperature, say, 60 degrees, it learns to avoid places of that temperature. It also recognizes patterns, quickly avoids obstacles and adjusts its squirming pace to that of its mate. A robot with any number of chips in its brain can't match those feats.

11.3.4 Virus Behavior

Viruses come in a great many different forms, but they all potentially have two phases to their execution, the infection phase and the attack phase:

11.3.4.1 Infection Phase

Virus writers have to balance how and when their viruses infect against the possibility of being detected. Therefore, the spread of an infection may not be immediate.

When the virus executes it has the potential to infect other programs. What's often not clearly understood is precisely when it will infect the other programs. Some viruses infect other programs each time they are executed; other viruses infect only upon a certain trigger. This trigger could be anything; a day or time, an external event on your PC, a counter within the virus, etc. Virus writers want their programs to spread as far as possible before anyone notices them.

It is a serious mistake to execute a program a few times - find nothing infected and presume there are no viruses in the program. You can never be sure the virus simply hasn't yet triggered its infection phase!

Many viruses go resident in the memory of your PC in the same or similar way as terminate and stay resident (TSR) programs. (For those not old enough to remember TSRs, they were programs that executed under DOS but stayed in memory instead of ending.) This means the virus can wait for some external event before it infects additional programs. The virus may silently lurk in memory waiting for you to access a diskette, copy a file, or execute a program, before it infects anything. This makes viruses more difficult to analyze since it's hard to guess what trigger condition they use for their infection.

On older systems, standard (640K) memory is not the only memory vulnerable to viruses. It is possible to construct a virus which will locate itself in upper memory (the space between 640K and 1M) or in the High Memory Area (the small space between 1024K and 1088K). And, under Windows, a virus can effectively reside in any part of memory.

Resident viruses frequently take over portions of the system software on the PC to hide their existence. This technique is called stealth. Polymorphic techniques also help viruses to infect yet avoid detection.

Note that worms often take the opposite approach and spread as fast as possible. While this makes their detection virtually certain, it also has the effect of bringing down networks and denying access; one of the goals of many worms.

11.3.4.2 Attack Phase

Viruses need time to infect. Not all viruses attack, but all use system resources and often have bugs.

Many viruses do unpleasant things such as deleting files or changing random data on your disk, simulating typos or merely slowing your PC down; some viruses do less harmful things such as playing music or creating messages or animation on your screen. Just as the infection phase can be triggered by some event, the attack phase also has its own trigger.

Does this mean a virus without an attack phase is benign? No. Most viruses have bugs in them and these bugs often cause unintended negative side effects. In addition, even if the virus is perfect, it still steals system resources.

Viruses often delay revealing their presence by launching their attack only after they have had ample opportunity to spread. This means the attack could be delayed for days, weeks, months, or even years after the initial infection.

The attack phase is optional, many viruses simply reproduce and have no trigger for an attack phase. Does this mean that these are "good" viruses? No! Anything that writes itself to your disk without your permission is stealing storage and CPU cycles. (Also see the "good" virus discussion.) This is made worse since viruses that "just infect," with no attack phase, often damage the programs or disks they infect. This is not an intentional act of the virus, but simply a result of the fact that many viruses contain extremely poor quality code.

An an example, one of the most common past viruses, Stoned, is not intentionally harmful. Unfortunately, the author did not anticipate the use of anything other than 360K floppy disks. The original virus tried to hide its own code in an area of 1.2MB diskettes that resulted in corruption of the entire diskette (this bug was fixed in later versions of the virus).

11.4 FIREWALL: VIRUS PROTECTION ON INTERNET

There are number of ways to prevent sites of internal network from being attack by hackers. The most common way is a firewall approach; that is, the connection between the internal network and the Internet is filtered through a firewall device to keep out intruders. By applying a firewall, the focus of security can be concentrated on a limited number of gateway systems rather than spread across every user on every system on the internal network. There are two basic technologies for firewalls: router-based packet filtering and application gateways.

Router- based IP packet filtering is done by using a router designed to filter packets as they pass between the router interfaces. A packet filter usually filters IP address and the destination IP address. There are certain advantages with the router-based packet filtering approach. Besides the relatively low cost of application, it is available from, many suppliers who provides routers, thus the users have more choice. Moreover, the concept of this approach is simple to the users and the policy makers, and is easy to install.

However, this approach retains several disadvantages. First of all, it requires the implementer to have an indepth understanding of protocol and related services. Since the filters are hard to program, it is easy to make a mistake during the configuration process. Second, the packet-filter approach has no log-on facilities to notify the user of attack meaning the routers fail to provide any audit or reporting capability.

This, in turn, makes it impossible to determine. If the filters are even being attacked, let alone determine if the devices are working properly. Users of this approach usually can only find out they have a problem when systems start showing signs of being compromised. Moreover, sometimes it will fail to filter some services.

The architecture of popular TCP/IP application protocols makes it impossible to simply filter out dangerous packets, as potentially harmful packets can look identical to the control packets that are essential to protocol operation.

In order to overcome the weaknesses of router-based packet filtering, some network managers reprogram the host systems to serve as intelligent filters between it and the Internet or other external networks instead of having normal router functions only.

Technically, this configuration is identical to pace filtering using router. The main difference,however, is that now the firewall builder is in control of the source code rather than the router configurer.

A number of computer managers recently surveyed view virii, and particularly Internet-borne viruses, as the greatest threat to information security they face, more worrisome than human error, hackers, and disgruntled employees.

Internet-borne virii are not intercepted by server based antivirus software because the connection to the Internet(i.e. the Internet gateway) typically bypassed the network server (see attached diagram). This allows virii to flow into the internal LAN unchecked.

Connection to the Internet gateway bypasses the network server, because the two use incompatible protocols and different machines. While the network servers typically operate under Netware using the IPX protocol, 80 percent of all Internet gateway operate under Unix using the TCP/IP.

A new approach to internal LAN protection from Internet virii has been developed and implemented in anti-virus software. One of these anti-virus software packages now available from Trend Micro Devices, InterScan 1.5, employs server-based real-time virus scanning at Internet gateways.

Firewalls are used to protect an organization's internal network from those on the outside (internet). It limits and regulates the access from the outside to the internal network and also regulates traffic going out. It is used to keep outsiders from gaining information to secrets or from doing damage to internal computer systems. Firewalls are also used to limit the access of individuals on the internal network to services on the internet along with keeping track of what is done through the firewall.

Firewalls filter traffic based on their protocol, sending or receiving port, sending or receiving IP address, or the value of some status bits in the packet. There are several types of firewalls which include (1) packet filtering, (2) circuit level relay, and (3) application proxy.

If your organization does not have a firewall, get one. At least implement a packet filtering firewall on a Linux based computer, if money is the concern.

The firewall should filter e-mail, FTP file transfers, and web content traffic for potential harmful or hostile code and viruses.

No computer should be directly connected to the internet without going through an IS approved firewall. This means independent modem connections to the internet should be forbidden.

Internet is not a very "safe" place. As a result, network administrators must not only be concerned with keeping the bits flowing smoothly through their network, but also with securing their network infrastructure from outside threats. SNMPv3 provides authentication, encryption and access control in order to secure network management functions. While this is important (certainly, the network administrator does not want others to gain access to network management functionality), it is only a small part of the network administrator's security concerns. In addition to monitoring and controlling the components of one's network, a network administrator also wants to exclude unwanted traffic (i.e., intruders) from the managed network. This is where firewalls come in. A firewall is a combination of hardware and software that isolates an organization's internal network from the Internet at large, allowing specific connections to pass and blocking others. Organizations employ firewalls for one or more of the following reasons:

To prevent intruders from interfering with the daily operation of the internal network. An organization's competitor — or just some Internet prankster looking for a good time — can reek havoc on an unsecured network. In the denial-of-service attack, an intruder monopolizes a critical network resource, bring the internal network (at its network administrator) to its knees. An example of a denial of service attack is so-called SYN flooding, in which a the attacker sends forged TCP connection-establishment segments to a particular host. The host sets aside buffer for each connection, and within minutes there is no TCP buffer space left for "honest" TCP connections.

To prevent intruders from deleting or modifying information stored within the internal network. For example, an attacker can attempt to meddle with an organization's public presence on a Web server — a successful attack may be seen by thousands of people in a matter of minutes. Attackers may also be able to obtain customer purchase card information from Web servers that provide Internet commerce.

* To prevent intruders from obtaining secret information. Most organizations have secret information that is stored on computers. This information includes trade secrets, product development plans, marketing strategies, personal employee records, and financial analysis.

The simplest firewall consists of a packet filter. More sophisticated firewalls consist of combinations of packet filters and application gateways.

11.4.1 Types of firewalls

(1) NAT : Network Address Translation (NAT) places private IP subnetworks behind one or a small pool of public IP addresses, masquerading all requests to one source rather than several.

Advantages

- Can be configured transparently to machines on a LAN
- Protection of many machines and services behind one or more external IP address(es) simplifies administration duties
- Restriction of user access to and from the LAN can be configured by opening and closing ports on the NAT firewall/gateway

Disadvantages

- Cannot prevent malicious activity once users connect to a service outside of the firewall

(2) Packet Filter : A packet filtering firewall reads each data packet that passes within and outside of a LAN. It can read and process packets by header information and filters the packet based on sets of programmable rules implemented by the firewall administrator. The Linux kernel has built-in packet filtering functionality through the Netfilter kernel subsystem.

Advantages

- Customizable through the iptables front-end utility
- Does not require any customization on the client side, as all network activity is filtered at the router level rather than the application level
- Since packets are not transmitted through a proxy, network performance is faster due to direct connection from client to remote host

Disadvantages

- Cannot filter packets for content like proxy firewalls
- Processes packets at the protocol layer, but cannot filter packets at an application layer
- Complex network architectures can make establishing packet filtering rules difficult, especially if coupled with IP masquerading or local subnets and DMZ networks

(3) **Proxy Proxy firewalls** filter all requests of a certain protocol or type from LAN clients to a proxy machine, which then makes those requests to the Internet on behalf of the local client. A proxy machine acts as a buffer between malicious remote users and the internal network client machines.

Advantages

- Gives administrators control over what applications and protocols function outside of the LAN
- Some proxy servers can cache frequently-accessed data locally rather than having to use the Internet connection to request it, which is convenient for cutting down on unnecessary bandwidth consumption
- Proxy services can be logged and monitored closely, allowing tighter control over resource utilization on the network

Disadvantages

- Proxies are often application specific (HTTP, Telnet, etc.) or protocol restricted (most proxies work with TCP connected services only)
- Application services cannot run behind a proxy, so your application servers must use a separate form of network security
- Proxies can become a network bottleneck, as all requests and transmissions are passed through one source rather than directly from a client to a remote service

Application firewalls and Border firewalls offers computer and network security on the internet. Net security is becoming ever more important, as there is an alarming increase in computer network security attacks, as hackers find new ways of breaking into to computer network systems.

Firewalls are made up from a group of related programs that are located at a network gateway server. Once the firewall is installed in the server, it protects the resources of the private network from users from other networks. A firewall, working in conjunction with a router program, filters all incoming network traffic to determine whether it is an internet security risk, before forwarding them toward their destination on the network. If your firewall is correctly installed, at application level or at the network border, nefarious traffic and network security attacks can be monitored by the firewall and stopped before causing major problems to your computer network

11.4.2 Firewall Screening Methods

Research white papers, case studies, product literature and webcasts on Firewall Screening Methods.

A firewall is often installed separately from the rest of the computer network, to increase network security, ensuring that no incoming request can get directly at private network resources. There are a number of firewall screening methods. The basic and most popular firewall screening method is to screen requests to ensure that they come from domain names and / or IP addresses that have been previously identified.

However, there are several routes of access through your firewall (World Wide Web, e-Mail, DNS, FTP, etc), giving hackers more opportunities and more holes in your firewall that they can easily use to attack your network security system. Application firewalls can enhance the security provided by border firewalls, as this type of firewall provides application specific, rather than just protocol specific, protection for your network system.

Border Firewall or Application Firewall

Border firewalls only allow Web traffic (HTTP port 80) to specific, pre-determined hosts on your network, as defined in the set of security conventions that you put in place when setting up your border firewall. This gives you protocol specific protection.

An application firewall also monitors the content of the web traffic, thus protecting the applications that are exposed to the internet, from security issues that are associated with your web server.

Consideration should be given to setting up both a border firewall and an application firewall, if you feel the secure content and applications on your computer network would make you a likely candidate for network security attacks.

Your LAN's own security is a secondary, but important part of your computer network security planning, so it is essential to ensure that both your LAN security protocols and your firewall security are as secure as your budget will allow.

A firewall can help prevent network security attacks, but it is important that is the correct firewall for your system. In the Insights directory, you will find several companies that can give you professional advice on how to prevent network security attacks on your computer or computer network.

11.4.3 Packet Filtering

An organization typically has a router that connects its internal network to its ISP (and hence to the Internet). All traffic leaving and entering the internal network passes through this router. Most router manufacturers provide options for filtering; when these options are turned on, the router becomes a filter in addition to a router. As the name implies, a filter lets some datagrams pass through the router and filters out other datagrams. Filtering decisions are typically based on:

* The IP address the data is (supposedly) coming from.
* IP destination address.
* TCP or UDP source and destination port.
* ICMP message type.
* Connection initialization datagrams using the TCP ACK bit.

As a simple example, a filter can be set to block all UDP segments and all Telnet connections. Such a configuration prevents outsiders from logging onto internal hosts using Telnet, insiders from logging onto external hosts using Telnet, and "weird" UDP traffic from entering or leaving the internal network. The router filters the UDP traffic by blocking all datagrams whose IP protocol field is set to 17 (corresponding to UDP); it filters all Telnet connections by blocking all TCP segments (each encapsulated in a datagram) whose source or destination port number is 23 (corresponding to Telnet). Filtering of UDP traffic is a popular policy for corporations — causing much chagrin to leading audio and video streaming vendors, whose products stream over UDP in the default mode. Filtering Telnet connections is also popular, as it prevents outside intruders from logging onto internal machines.

A filtering policy can also be based on the combination of addresses and port numbers. For example, the router can forward all Telnet packets (port 23) except those going to and coming from a list of specific IP addresses. This policy permits Telnet connections to and from hosts on the list. It is highly recommended to reject all datagrams that have internal source IP addresses — i.e., packets that claim to be coming from internal hosts but are actually coming in from the outside. These packets are part of address spoofing attacks, whereby the attacker is pretending to be coming from an internal machine. Unfortunately, basing the policy on external addresses provides no protection from an external host claiming to be a different external host.

Filtering can also be based on whether or not the TCP ACK bit is set. This trick is quite useful if an organization wants to let its internal clients connect to external servers, but wants to prevent external clients from connecting to internal servers. Recall that the first segment in every TCP connection has the ACK bit set to 0 whereas all the other segments in the connection have the ACK bit set to 1. Thus, if an organization wants to prevent external clients from initiating connections to internal servers, it simply filters all incoming segments with the ACK bit set to 0. This policy kills all TCP connections originating from the outside, but permits connections originating internally.

Packet filtering is a technique whereby routers have ACLs (Access Control Lists) turned on. By default, a router will pass all traffic sent it, and will do so without any sort of restrictions. Employing ACLs is a method for enforcing your security policy with regard to what sorts of access you allow the outside world to have to your internal network, and vice versa.

There is less overhead in packet filtering than with an application gateway, because the feature of access control is performed at a lower ISO/OSI layer (typically, the transport or session layer). Due to the lower overhead and the fact that packet filtering is done with routers, which are specialized computers optimized for tasks related to networking, a packet filtering gateway is often much faster than its application layer cousins. Figure 11.1 shows a packet filtering gateway.

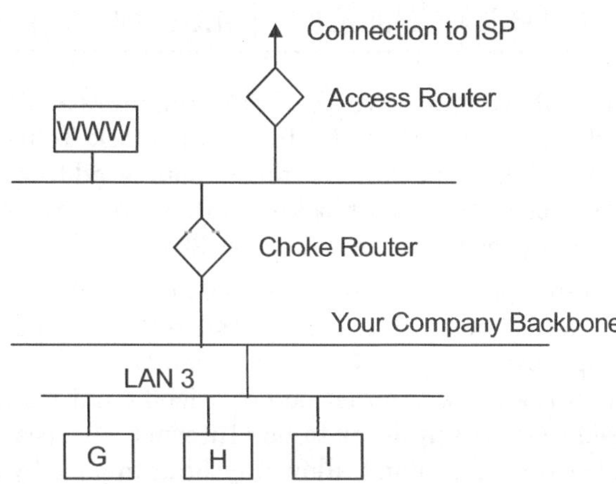

Figure 11.1 A Sample Packet Filtering Gateway

Because we're working at a lower level, supporting new applications either comes automatically, or is a simple matter of allowing a specific packet type to pass through the gateway. (Not that the possibility of something automatically makes it a good idea; opening things up this way might very well compromise your level of security below what your policy allows.)

There are problems with this method, though. Remember, TCP/IP has absolutely no means of guaranteeing that the source address is really what it claims to be. As a result, we have to use layers of packet filters in order to localize the traffic. We can't get all the way down to the actual host, but with two layers of packet filters, we can differentiate between a packet that came from the Internet and one that came from our internal network. We can identify which network the packet came from with certainty, but we can't get more specific than that.

Now suppose an organization doesn't want to block all connections originating from outside; instead it just wants to block only the Telnet connections originating from outside. How can filtering accomplish this task? To see how filters handle this, let's look at how the fields are set for Telnet connections originating internally and Telnet connections originating externally (Table 11.1):

Table 11.1: Header fields for inbound and outbound Telnet connections

Connection Origination	Packet Directaion	Source IP Addrss	Destination IP Address	Source Port	Destination Port
Internal	Outbound	Internal	External	p	23
Internal	Inbound	External	Internal	23	p
External	Inbound	External	Internal	q	23
External	Outbound	Internal	External	23	q

The p and q in the above table are the port numbers (> 1023) assigned to the client machines. From this chart we see that the filter can block Telnet connections originating from outside by blocking inbound packets (external source address and internal destination address) with destination port 23; or by blocking outbound packets (internal source address and external destination address) with source port 23.

The first firewalls were application gateways, and are sometimes known as proxy gateways. These are made up of bastion hosts that run special software to act as a proxy server. This software runs at the Application Layer of our old friend the ISO/OSI Reference Model, hence the name. Clients behind the firewall must be proxitized (that is, must know how to use the proxy, and be configured to do so) in order to use Internet services. Traditionally, these have been the most secure, because they don't allow anything to pass by default, but need to have the programs written and turned on in order to begin passing traffic.

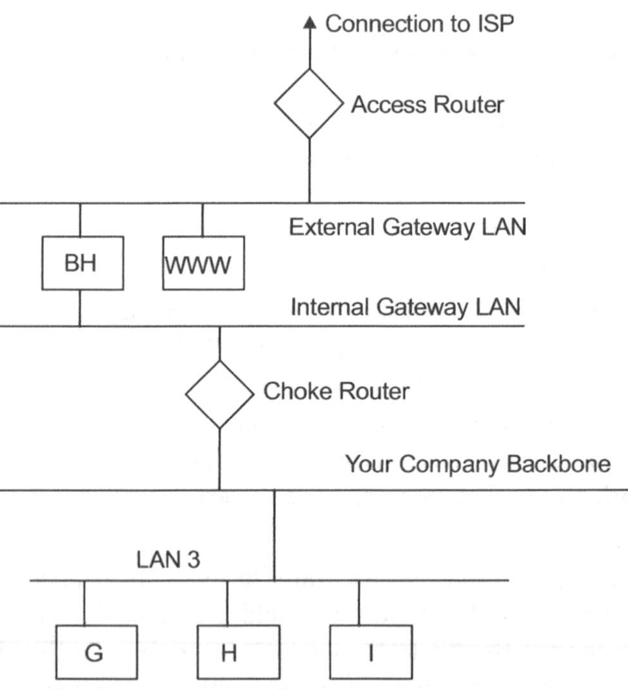

Figure 11.2 A sample Application Gateway

These are also typically the slowest, because more processes need to be started in order to have a request serviced. Figure shows a application gateway.

Filters allow an organization to perform coarse-grain filtering on IP and TCP/UDP headers, including IP addresses, port numbers and acknowledgment bits. For example, filtering based on a combination of IP addresses and port numbers can allow internal clients to Telnet outside while preventing external clients from Telneting inside. But what if an organization wants to provide the Telnet service to a restricted set of internal users? Such a task is beyond the capabilities of a filter. Indeed, information about the identity of the internal users is not included in the IP/TCP/UDP headers, but is instead in the application-layer data.

In order to have a finer level security, firewalls must combine packet filters with application gateways. Application gateways look beyond the IP/TCP/UDP headers and actually make policy decisions based on application data. An application gateway is an application-specific server through which all application data (inbound and outbound) must pass. Multiple application gateways can run on the same host, but each gateway is a separate server with its own processes.

To get some insight into application gateways, let us design a firewall that allows only a restricted set of internal users to Telnet outside and prevents all external clients from Telneting inside. Such a policy can be accomplished by implementing a combination of a packet filter (in a router) and a Telnet application gateway, as shown in Figure 11.3. The filter is configured to block all Telnet connections except those that originate form the IP address of the application gateway. Such a filter configuration forces all outbound Telnet connections to pass through the application gateway. When a internal user wants to Telnet to the the outside world, it first sets up a Telnet session with the gateway. The gateway prompts the user for its user id and password; when the user supplies this information, the gateway checks to see if the user has permission to Telnet to the outside world. If not, the gateway terminates the Telnet session. If the user has permission, then the gateway

(1) prompts the user for the hostname of the external host to which the user wants to connect,

(2) sets up a Telnet session between the gateway and the external host,

(3) relays to the external host all data arriving from the user, and relays to the user all data arriving from the external host. Thus the Telnet application gateway not only performs user authorization but also acts as a Telnet server and a Telnet client. Note that the filter will permit step (2) because the application gateway initiates the Telnet connection.

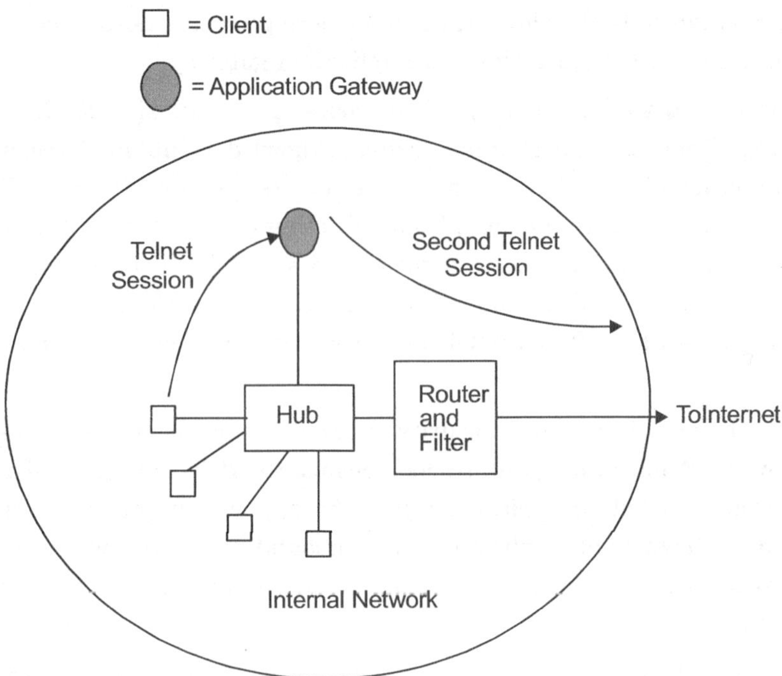

Figure 11.3 Firewall consisting of an application gateway and a filter

Internal networks often have multiple application gateways, for example, gateways for Telnet, HTTP, FTP and e-mail. In fact, an organization's mail server and Web cache are application gateways.

Application gateways do not come without their disadvantages. First, you need a different application gateway for each application, which requires installing and configuring a new server for each application. Second, either:

* The client software must know how to contact the gateway instead of the external server when the user makes a request, and must know how to tell the gateway what external server to connect to;

or

* the user must explicitly connect to the external server through the gateway.

However firewalls are by no means a panacea for all security problems. They introduerce a tradeoff between the degree of communication with the outside world and level of security. Because filters can't stop spoofing of IP addresses and port numbers, filters often use an all or nothing policy (for example, banning all UDP traffic). Gateways can have software bugs, allowing attackers to penetrate them. Also, firewalls or even less effective if the internal users have wireless communication with the external world. For these reasons and others, firewalls remain controversial, with many security experts and network administrators being reluctant to use them.

11.4.4 Application Gateways

The first firewalls were application gateways, and are sometimes known as proxy gateways. These are made up of bastion hosts that run special software to act as a proxy server. This software runs at the Application Layer of our old friend the ISO/OSI Reference Model, hence the name. Clients behind the firewall must be proxitized (that is, must know how to use the proxy, and be configured to do so) in order to use Internet services. Traditionally, these have been the most secure, because they don't allow anything to pass by default, but need to have the programs written and turned on in order to begin passing traffic.

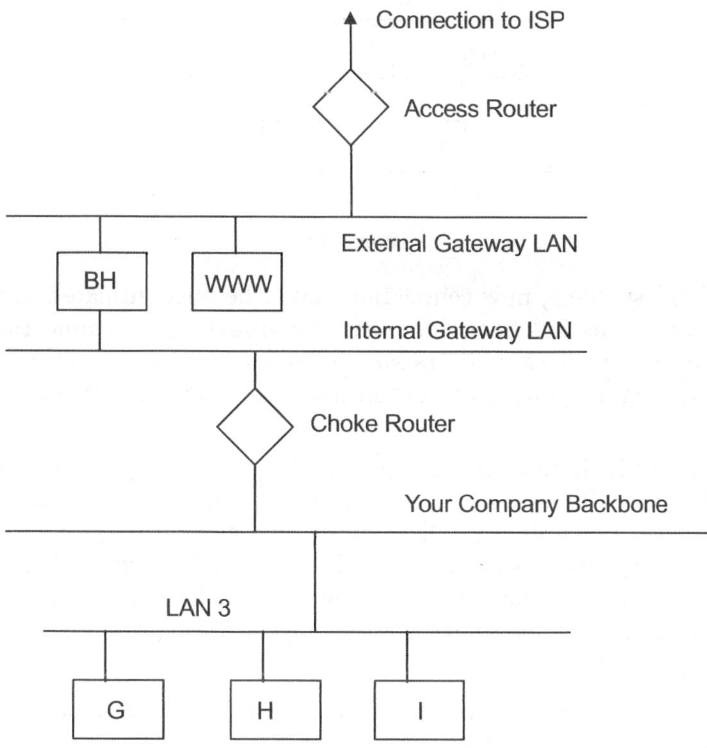

Figure 11.4

These are also typically the slowest, because more processes need to be started in order to have a request serviced. Figure 5 shows a application gateway.

11.4.5 Hybrid Systems

In an attempt to marry the security of the application layer gateways with the flexibility and speed of packet filtering, some vendors have created systems that use the principles of both.

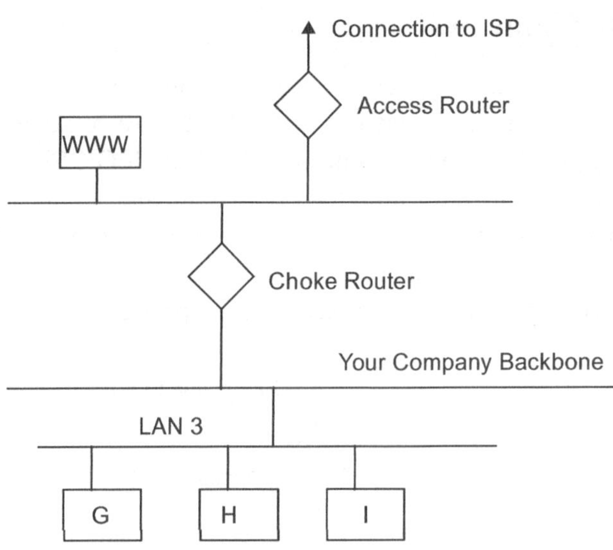

Figure 11.5

In some of these systems, new connections must be authenticated and approved at the application layer. Once this has been done, the remainder of the connection is passed down to the session layer, where packet filters watch the connection to ensure that only packets that are part of an ongoing (already authenticated and approved) conversation are being passed.

Other possibilities include using both packet filtering and application layer proxies. The benefits here include providing a measure of protection against your machines that provide services to the Internet (such as a public web server), as well as provide the security of an application layer gateway to the internal network. Additionally, using this method, an attacker, in order to get to services on the internal network, will have to break through the access router, the bastion host, and the choke router.

So, what's best for me?

Lots of options are available, and it makes sense to spend some time with an expert, either in-house, or an experienced consultant who can take the time to understand your organization's security policy, and can design and build a firewall architecture that best implements that policy. Other issues like services required, convenience, and scalability might factor in to the final design.

Some Words of Caution

The business of building firewalls is in the process of becoming a commodity market. Along with commodity markets come lots of folks who are looking for a way to make a buck without necessarily knowing what they're doing. Additionally, vendors compete with each other to try and claim the greatest security, the easiest to administer, and the least visible to end users. In order to try to quantify the potential security of firewalls, some organizations have taken to firewall certifications. The certification of a firewall means nothing more than the fact that it can be configured in such a way that it can pass a series of tests. Similarly, claims about meeting or exceeding U.S. Department of Defense "Orange Book" standards, C-2, B-1, and such all simply mean that an organization was able to configure a machine to pass a series of tests. This doesn't mean that it was loaded with the vendor's software at the time, or that the machine was even usable. In fact, one vendor has been claiming their operating system is "C-2 Certified" didn't make mention of the fact that their operating system only passed the C-2 tests without being connected to any sort of network devices.

Such gauges as market share, certification, and the like are no guarantees of security or quality. Taking a little bit of time to talk to some knowledgeable folks can go a long way in providing you a comfortable level of security between your private network and the big, bad Internet.

Additionally, it's important to note that many consultants these days have become much less the advocate of their clients, and more of an extension of the vendor. Ask any consultants you talk to about their vendor affiliations, certifications, and whatnot. Ask what difference it makes to them whether you choose one product over another, and vice versa. And then ask yourself if a consultant who is certified in technology XYZ is going to provide you with competing technology ABC, even if ABC best fits your needs.

Single Points of Failure

Many "firewalls" are sold as a single component: a bastion host, or some other black box that you plug your networks into and get a warm-fuzzy, feeling safe and secure. The term "firewall" refers to a number of components that collectively provide the security of the system. Any time there is only one component paying attention to what's going on between the internal and external networks, an attacker has only one thing to break (or fool!) in order to gain complete access to your internal networks.

See the Internet Firewalls FAQ for more details on building and maintaining firewalls.

10 Steps To Securing Firewalls

A properly configured firewall can provide you with a vital line of defense against malevolent Internet invaders. Firewalls filter both inbound and outbound network traffic. They can control access to host applications, and keep track of all attempts to access the network—authorized and unauthorized. Depending on how they're designed and configured, they can do a number of other useful things to keep the crooks out and your proprietary information in. They may even filter out spam and spyware.

However, there are quite a few things that firewalls can't do: They can't stop an employee from writing down her password on a yellow post-it and sticking it on her monitor. Nor can they stop another employee from inadvertently giving away vital access codes to a telephone confidence man. They certainly can't keep your IT people from mis-applying security clearances.

Still, it goes without saying that no network should be without a firewall.

How Do Firewalls Work?

All internet data travels in packets. A traditional network-level firewall (the kind that's probably built-into your router) examines packet headers, and refuses to allow packets to pass through the firewall unless their headers match the rules—as defined by the firewall administrator or designer. Alternatively, a firewall can be configured to allow any packet to pass through as long as it does not match one or more "negative-rules."

Network-level firewalls are not very good at detecting and defusing worms, viruses, and the latest application-specific attacks. Defending the network against this broader set of threats requires deeper inspection of the packet payload itself. The latest application-level firewalls use complex rules to look at the content of a packet, the type of traffic it represents, its source or destination address, the ports involved, the application being called, and many other factors to discover and block packets that contain malicious payloads.

How Much Is This Going To Cost Me?

If you merely want a personal firewall—a piece of software that runs on your own PC and protects it from some-but-not-all attacks—it may not cost much over $100. (In fact, you may already have one, built into Windows or Norton SystemWorks.) However, if you want a firewall that will support multiple users on a large network, with all the latest defensive features (some of which cost extra) you could be looking at $10,000 and up. Way up.

Still, some of those pricey extras are appealing. They include VPN gateways, easy-to-use GUI-based management for multiple workgroup firewalls, monitoring capability, support for applying different security policies to different users, sophisticated authentication mechanisms, and high availability with load balancing and failover.

Ultimately, pricing firewalls is an advanced exercise. Each one boasts a different feature set, plus a unique assortment of add-ons, hardware/software options, and licensing strategies. Our product comparison table provides general price ranges for each product, but in most cases a call to the vendor is the only way to figure out how much you'll really have to pay.

Hardware Vs. Software

Some very powerful firewall software is designed to run on an ordinary computer. Other firewall software is designed to run on proprietary hardware that you have to buy along with the software—turning the bundle into a "security appliance." As a general rule, the appliances are faster, easier to install and operate, and more expensive. But there's no guarantee they'll do a better job than a software-only firewall. A software firewall tends to be more flexible, and it's easier to upgrade the hardware it's running on.

Network-Level Firewalls

The first generation of firewalls worked at the network level by inspecting packet headers, and filtering traffic based on the IP address of the source and the destination, the port, and the service. Some could also filter packets based on protocols, the domain name of the source, and a few other attributes.

Network-level firewalls are fast, and you'll find them built into most network appliances—particularly routers. However, these firewalls don't support sophisticated rule-based models. Nor do they understand languages like HTML and XML, or know how to decode SSL-encrypted packets to examine their content. That means they can't validate user inputs or detect maliciously-modified parameters in a URL request. This leaves your network vulnerable to a number of serious threats.

Circuit-Level Firewalls

These apps monitor TCP handshaking between packets to make sure a session is legitimate. Traffic is filtered based on specified session rules, and may be restricted to recognized computers only. Circuit-level firewalls hide the network itself from the outside, which is useful for denying access to intruders. But they don't filter individual packets.

Application-Level Firewalls

Application-level firewalls (sometimes called proxies) look deeply into the application data going through their filters. By considering the context of client requests and application responses, these firewalls attempt to enforce correct application behavior, block malicious activity, and help organizations ensure the safety of sensitive information and systems. They can log user activity too. Application-level filtering may allow you to stop spam and viruses, as well—and to block undesirable Web sites based on content rather than just their IP address.

Sign you up? Well, not so fast. Literally: Not so fast. The deeper a firewall examines the packets that make up the network data flow, the longer it takes, and the heavier the hit your network performance will sustain.

Stateful Multi-Level Firewalls

SML products deploy the best features of the other three firewall types: They do packet filtering at the network level and they recognize and process application-level data—but since they don't employ proxies they deliver reasonably good performance in spite of the deep packet analysis. On the down side, they are not cheap, and they can be difficult to configure and administer.

Index

A

B

D

E

F

G

H

I

K

L

M

N

O

P

R

S

T

U

V

W

NOTES

NOTES